AMERICAN ECONOMIC HISTORY

Third Edition

Robert C. Puth
University of New Hampshire

D0068941

The Dryden Press
Harcourt Brace Jovanovich College Publishers

Fort Worth   Philadelphia   San Diego   New York   Orlando   Austin   San Antonio
Toronto   Montreal   London   Sydney   Tokyo

Editor in Chief Robert A. Pawlik
Acquisitions Editor Rick Hammonds
Developmental Editor Daryl Fox
Project Editor Amy Schmidt
Production Manager Marilyn Williams
Book Designer Jeanette Barber
Photo/Permissions Editor Sandra Lord

Address for Editorial Correspondence
The Dryden Press, 301 Commerce Street, Suite 3700, Fort Worth, TX
76102

Address for Orders
The Dryden Press, 6277 Sea Harbor Drive, Orlando, FL 32887
1-800-782-4479, or 1-800-433-0001 (in Florida)

ISBN: 0-03-096905-0

Library of Congress Catalogue Number: 92-72940

Printed in the United States of America
3 4 5 6 7 8 9 0 1 2 039 9 8 7 6 5 4 3 2 1

The Dryden Press
Harcourt Brace Jovanovich

The Dryden Press Series in Economics

Asch and Seneca
Government and the Marketplace
Second Edition

Baker
An Introduction to International Economics

Baumol and Blinder
Economics: Principles and Policy
Fifth Edition (Also available in micro and macro paperbacks)

Baumol, Panzar, and Willig
Contestable Markets and the Theory of Industry Structure
Revised Edition

Berch
The Endless Day: The Political Economy of Women and Work

Breit and Elzinga
The Antitrust Casebook: Milestones in Economic Regulation
Second Edition

Campbell, Campbell, and Dolan
Money, Banking, and Monetary Policy

Claudon and Olsen
Eco Talk

Demmert
Economics: Understanding the Market Process

Dolan and Lindsey
Economics
Sixth Edition (Also available in micro and macro paperbacks)

Eckert and Leftwich
The Price System and Resource Allocation
Tenth Edition

Edgmand, Moomaw, and Olson
Economics and Contemporary Issues

Estey
The Unions: Structure, Development, and Management
Third Edition

Friedman
Milton Friedman Speaks (Video)

Gardner
Comparative Economic Systems

Glahe
Microeconomics: Theory and Application
Second Edition

Green
Intermediate Macroeconomics: Analysis and Applications

Gwartney and Stroup
Economics: Private and Public Choice
Sixth Edition (Also available in micro and macro paperbacks)

Gwartney, Stroup, and Clark
Essentials of Economics
Second Edition

Heilbroner and Singer
The Economic Transformation of America: 1600 to the Present
Second Edition

Hirsch and Rufolo
Public Finance and Expenditure in a Federal System

Hirschey and Pappas
Fundamentals of Managerial Economics
Fourth Edition

Hirschey and Pappas
Managerial Economics
Seventh Edition

Hoerneman, Howard, Wilson, and Cole
CAPER: Computer Assisted Program for Economic Review

Hyman
Public Finance: A Contemporary Application of Theory to Policy
Fourth Edition

Johnson and Roberts
Money and Banking: A Market-Oriented Approach
Third Edition

Kaufman
The Economics of Labor Markets
Third Edition

Keating and Wilson
Fundamentals of Managerial Economics

Keating and Wilson
Managerial Economics
Second Edition

Kennett and Lieberman
The Road to Capitalism: The Economic Transformation of Eastern Europe and the Former Soviet Union

Kidwell and Peterson
Financial Institutions, Markets, and Money
Fifth Edition

Kohn
Money, Banking, and Financial Markets
Second Edition

Kreinin
International Economics: A Policy Approach
Sixth Edition

Landsburg
Price Theory and Applications
Second Edition

Link, Miller, and Bergman
EconoGraph II: Interactive Software for Principles of Economics

Lott and Ray
Applied Econometrics with Data Sets

Nicholson
Intermediate Microeconomics and Its Application
Fifth Edition

Nicholson
Microeconomic Theory: Basic Principles and Extensions
Fifth Edition

Ormiston
Intermediate Microeconomics

Oser and Brue
The Evolution of Economic Thought
Fourth Edition

Puth
American Economic History
Third Edition

Ragan and Thomas
Principles of Economics
Second Edition (Also available in micro and macro paperbacks)

Ramanathan
Introductory Econometrics with Applications
Second Edition

Rukstad
Corporate Decision Making in the World Economy: Company Case Studies

Rukstad
Macroeconomic Decision Making in the World Economy: Text and Cases
Third Edition

Samuelson and Marks
Managerial Economics

Scarth
Macroeconomics: An Introduction to Advanced Methods
Second Edition

Smith and Spudeck
Interest Rates: Principles and Applications

Thomas
Economics: Principles and Applications
(also available in micro and macro paperbacks)

Wachtel
Labor and the Economy
Third Edition

Walton and Rockoff
History of the American Economy
Sixth Edition

Welch and Welch
Economics: Theory and Practice
Fourth Edition

Yarbrough and Yarbrough
The World Economy: Trade and Finance
Second Edition

Zimbalist, Sherman, and Brown
Comparing Economic Systems: A Political-Economic Approach
Second Edition

The HBJ College Outline Series

Emery
Intermediate Microeconomics

Emery
Principles of Economics: Macroeconomics

Emery
Principles of Economics: Microeconomics

PREFACE

A half-millenium ago, Europeans made lasting contact with what turned out to be a "new world" in several senses. The recorded history of North America began about a century later, and it was on this continent that humans contrived the changes that most clearly differentiated the New World from the Old. Europe, at the time, had already developed characteristics making it unique. In North America, however, the economy grew far beyond its ancestral foundations, providing a standard of living that has been the envy of the world. The progress was both substantial and rapid; in a few generations, North Americans passed from a state of desperate struggle for survival to a condition where their incomes were as large and their quality of life much better than that of any other nation. If for no other reason than the magnitude of its success, the story of America's economic development is worth recounting.

Because economic growth was so substantial and prolonged in North America, the basis and the ends to which its products were put underwent profound changes. In turn, economic changes stemmed from and created changes in social and political relations and institutions—a process that is still underway. Originally, the United States and its colonial predecessors began as extractive economies, dependent upon the products of forest, soil, and sea, both for subsistence and trading for European goods. During the nineteenth century, however, the United States became the world's greatest industrial power. Despite the fact that over the last five decades economic growth has centered increasingly on the generation, processing, and utilization of information, earlier centers of growth have retained great vitality: In short, the United States remains one of the world's most efficient producers of both agricultural and manufactured products.

The Theme of this Book

Many factors contributed to the growth of the American economy, both in terms of increased output and in terms of the changes in products, methods, and markets, which were its outstanding features. Natural resources shaped the nature of many early ventures. As Americans forged the tools to respond to the opportunities provided by nature, they broadened their range of activities and increased the amounts of resources usable to them. Greater than any other single contribution has been human labor. Here, too, the nature of work has changed. People have moved from farms to urban occupations, from east to west, and north to south. The jobs at which they worked have changed also. Today, few people can realistically expect to spend their working lives in the same occupation in which their careers began.

Change has been a prominent factor in all growing economies. Increases in real per-capita incomes over time have been due to many forces, none of which has been consistently dominant, either in America or elsewhere. Nevertheless, the extraordinary success of the U.S. economy must have distinctive roots. Were there simply more productive resources here, or did Americans enjoy knowledge the rest of the world lacked? Neither scenario seems to be the case. The American success story, to this author, is the result of the superior utilization of human capabilities. From the earliest days of European settlement, Americans have displayed attitudes and developed institutions more responsive to change and better suited to the exercise of individual initiative than have those of any other economic system. Nor did the innovation process end there; once the benefits of change became apparent, Americans devoted even more effort to developing human skills and providing for recognition and reward in both new and existing applications.

Even in the seventeenth and eighteenth centuries, human talent was both recognized and applied to a greater extent in America than in even the most enlightened nations of Europe. Consequently, new ideas were brought into use, and their potential was more fully developed here. From borrowing and utilizing ideas developed elsewhere, it was a short step for Americans to generate them domestically, through education of all types, and in response to high regard for new methods and products by both producers and consumers. Additionally, the process is cumulative, employing the one resource capable of continual development—the human mind. At times, other factors have been influential, even dominant in the growth process, but rational use of human potential contributed to American economic growth as it did in no other economy.

The Intended Audience

This book has been written for students rather than for their instructors. Some of the interpretations or presentations of American economic development may be novel, but the primary purpose of this book is to assist my peers in presenting this topic to students. In so doing, I have tried to explain why the economic history of the United States underlies so much of our social, political, and technical history. What we were, and how we felt about it, has helped to determine what we are today. Thus, I have tried to stress context and consequence over chronology, showing the causes, the nature, and the results (positive or negative) of historical events. The evidence upon which historians' conclusions are based is also illustrated, but in most cases, the technical details of the analyses employed are not. Controversial topics have, I hope, been presented as such. Where I could not overcome my own biases, I have tried to make them explicit.

Organization

The book is divided into five sections presented in chronological order. These sections run from one prominent event, often a war, to another. The purpose is not to suggest that wars necessarily denoted major changes in the economy (generally they did not), but to keep the account of developments within various sectors of the economy manageable.

All economic events are interrelated, directly or indirectly. In a world of scarcity, one use of resources not only precludes their use elsewhere but may also foreclose previously available options or alter their costs. Prior choices affect those that can be made now. To understand developments in any sector of the economy, we must know something of the markets that supply it and of the markets that purchase its products. We must also understand the social, political, legal, and technical contexts determining the rules within which it operates. By presenting these interrelationships in shorter segments, I hope the context of development will be easier for students to grasp.

New Coverage and Content

The basic organization of the book is little changed from earlier editions. However, more information about some topics is now available than was in 1986: the nutrition and health of nineteenth-century Americans; labor-force participation, wages, special burdens upon American women; and the position and capabilities of the United States in the post-1945 world economy are examples. Where recent research has altered or enhanced our knowledge, this informatin has been incorporated. I have tried to stress topics in which economic historians' views run counter to "common knowledge," and to explain why they hold these opinions. In addition, the entire book has been reviewed and often rewritten so that material may be more readily understood.

Acknowledgments

Every author, particularly in history, stands upon the shoulders of others. One of my most pleasant tasks is to recognize contributions that have enhanced my capabilities in general or this book in particular. Over nearly four decades I have accrued debts to many individuals. Like most intellectual debts, they can be acknowledged, but never fully repaid. As an undergraduate at Carleton College, my interest in economics was developed by Ada M. Harrison and Robert Will. At Northwestern University, Harold F. Williamson began my training in economic history. For nearly 30 years, my students have taught me, as I have taught them.

Many people contributed to the previous editions of this book. Terry Anderson, Robert Gallman, William Hutchinson, Paul Koefod, Kenneth Ng, Thomas Ulem, and Mary Yeager all gave me their views on complete drafts. Gavin Wright read both prior editions. Valued comments on specific topics from Louis Cain, Barry Eichengreen, Robert Higgs, Robert Kenney, Pamela Nickless, Tim Sullivan, and Donald Wells saved me from many errors and improved my presentation of specific topics. My colleagues at the University of New Hampshire provided useful insights, often at short notice. The services of Allen Thompson, Dwayne Wrightsman, David Bradford, Fred Kaen, Evangelos Simos, Lee Irwin, William Wetzel, and Karen Smith Conway were particularly helpful.

This edition has been vastly improved by the contributions of Professors Price Fishback (University of Arizona), Robert Margo (Vanderbilt University), and Robert Sexton (Pepperdine University). To all, my thanks and appreciation. Responsibility for errors remains with me and indicates my inability to absorb everything these people had to contribute.

Books are not produced solely by the compilation and comparison of ideas. These must be recognized, organized, and packaged if they are to reach an audience. At The Dryden Press, my special thanks to Daryl Fox, Stacey Fry, Amy Schmidt, and Rick Hammonds, whose many contributions include mixing encouragement and a sense of urgency in the correct proportions. Finally, but in no sense least, I owe a very special debt to my wife. She has borne much more than her share of the burdens of authorship with love, grace, and gentle humor. This book is dedicated to her.

Robert C. Puth
Dover, New Hampshire
January 1993

CONTENTS

INTRODUCTION

THE AMERICAN SUCCESS STORY: ECONOMIC GROWTH AND ITS IMPORTANCE

"Without theory, history becomes undisciplined and disorganized, shaping its material by whim, or purely by rhetoric. Without history, theory loses any grounding in the actual course of human events."
William N. Parker

"Economics is neither social physics nor social engineering: It is more like a peculiar variant of social history. Economics does not merely have a lot to learn from history: History is what it is."
Donald N. McCloskey

*T*hroughout history, humanity has had to deal with a fundamental problem: our desires for goods and services exceed the capacity to satisfy those desires. The available productive resources and the technology with which they are applied are unable to provide us with goods and services sufficient to give each of us all of everything we would like to have. Economists say goods are scarce; a layman might say "there isn't enough to go around." In either case, economic scarcity means that choices are necessary. Because we cannot have all of everything we want, humans must decide which goods are most desirable. They must make these decisions in a context where resources have alternative uses, so that a decision to use sheet steel for dishwashers, for example, means that amount of metal cannot simultaneously be used in refrigerators; thus, the cost of more dishwashers is foregone refrigerators.

The Concept of Scarcity

Economic scarcity does not necessarily refer to the quantities of any commodity available, but rather to the ability to satisfy human desires for a particular one. Commodities are not scarce, whatever their numbers, if nobody wants all that is available. While human ability to want more goods is restricted only by our imaginations, the ability to satisfy those wants is limited by the amounts of natural resources, labor, and capital available and the technological knowledge with which we put them to use. The race between imagination and productive capacity has always been uneven; we have been able to generate new ideas about what we would like to have with greater facility than we have been able to increase our ability to respond. Although our stocks of productive resources and the knowledge of how to employ them have increased spectacularly in the last few centuries, human wants—especially our desire for variety—have risen at least as fast. Consequently, the price of goods and services remains positive. To obtain more of any scarce good, we must pay a price, whether it be money, effort, lifestyle, or something else. Our best responses to scarcity result only in a compromise that fully satisfies no one.

As Table I.1 reveals, per-capita incomes in the United States are very high. But affluence does not mean the end of scarcity. The United States economy provides an income per person that allows choices between a much greater variety of available goods and services than those available to most other people, but choices are still necessary. This table indicates the huge gap between the amounts of goods and services available to the citizens of wealthy economies and those of the world's poor nations. High incomes mean more than a wider range of choices for the average citizen; they mean relative freedom from hunger, epidemic disease, inadequate social services,

Table I.1 *Per-Capita Income Levels and Recent Growth Rates, Selected Countries*

Country	GNP/Capita, 1988*	1965–1988 Average Annual Real Growth (percent)
Switzerland	$27,500	1.5%
Japan	21,020	4.3
Norway	19,990	3.5
United States	19,840	1.6
Sweden	19,300	1.8
Germany (Fed. Rep.)	18,480	2.5
Denmark	18,450	1.8
Canada	16,960	2.7
France	16,090	2.5
United Arab Emirates	15,770	—
Netherlands	14,520	1.9
Italy	13,330	3.0
United Kingdom	12,810	1.8
Australia	12,340	1.7
Hong Kong	9,220	6.3
Singapore	9,070	7.2
Spain	7,740	2.3
Saudi Arabia	6,200	3.8
Libya	5,420	−2.7
Korea (R.O.K.)	3,600	6.8
Venezuela	3,250	−.9
Yugoslavia	2,520	3.4
Argentina	2,520	—
South Africa	2,290	.8
Brazil	2,160	3.6
Mexico	1,760	2.3
Chile	1,510	.1
Turkey	1,280	2.6
Philippines	630	1.6
Indonesia	440	4.3
Pakistan	350	2.5
India	340	1.8
China	330	5.4
Niger	300	−2.3
Nigeria	290	.9
Uganda	280	−3.1
Mali	230	1.6
Bangladesh	170	.4
Ethiopia	120	.1

* At market prices in 1988 U.S. Dollars.
Source: World Bank, *World Development Report, 1990* (Washington, D.C., 1990), 178–179.

and most of those amenities that separate civilized life from mere existence. Only a few centuries ago, however, there was no such contrast; average incomes in all nations were close to the bottom of the range in Table I.1. The economic history of today's wealthy nations is thus a chronicle of a successful struggle against poverty.

The Role of Economic Efficiency

To increase the contrast between rich and poor economies even further, the rich are generally more efficient; they produce more per unit of resources. This is important, because insatiable wants insure that the available resources will always be insufficient to fill humanity's wants. We must use our productive ability to obtain as much as possible of what we want most from our resource endowment, because all we can turn out will never be enough.

The high current standing of American income levels is generally recognized, but many U.S. citizens do not realize that this economy has been among the world's most successful for at least three centuries. Even less do they understand the sources of these high incomes or the reasons for their growth over time. This book is an attempt to illustrate the economic growth of the United States and the colonies from which it sprang. Because the primary focus is on the sources and consequences of economic growth, more emphasis is placed on how and why such growth occurred than on a chronology of the achievement. To accomplish this, the book emphasizes the application of economic theory to historical events.

The Role of Scarcity

All economic decisions involve a weighing of costs against benefits. Economic history adds a time context; it surveys mankind's struggle against scarcity over the course of history.

Economics is not a discipline that stands alone. It has links to other fields of study, both as regards means and the ends toward which they are directed. To the economist, wants are given, meaning that it is accepted that the desire for commodities exists, but the manner in which these desires are generated and studied lies outside the purview of economics. In a wealthy economy like our own, the majority of our wants are not determined by the necessities of physical survival, but through individuals' interactions in society. The desires for goods can be analyzed through sociology, anthropology, psychology, and the other social sciences, as well as through biology. For example, why does eating lobster generally indicate a festive occasion in our society, while eating horsemeat is viewed as a sign of deprivation? The causes are largely determined by our past and present interactions with other people, rather than the nutritional content of either food. The determinants of our ability to produce are likewise not a matter of primary concern to economists. For the answers to questions in this area, we must turn to the physical sciences and their applications in technology as well as to the political and cultural rules we have developed to regulate the use of productive resources. These regulations can be very important; an economy's productive capacity depends not merely on physical resources and knowledge of how to use them, but also on the attitudes and laws that regulate their use. The ages at which people enter and leave the workforce, the number of hours worked during any time period, attitudes toward safety, the preservation of environmental quality, future growth, and the trade-offs between cultural values and productive efficiency that the society accepts are all determined outside economics, but they influence what gets produced, how it is produced, and how this output is distributed among the population. In short, they determine the limits within which economic activity can occur.

Theories of Economic Growth

If we are to attempt to explain the reasons behind America's economic success, some attempt must be made to make sense out of the enormous array of facts revealed to us by history. We need some method of determining which facts are pertinent to our explanation and in what manner. Theories, in economics and elsewhere, are statements of cause and effect. The economic historian seeks to determine which factors caused the growth in incomes we observe in the United States, which were consequences of that growth, and which were not germane to the process. The formulation of an economic theory follows the methodology established in the physical sciences. Preliminary observations of some phenomenon are made, and a hypothesis is advanced about its causes or consequences. Then, to whatever extent possible, the explanation is compared to observed reality. Often this process involves the application of explicit statements of cause and effect (economic models) and employs statistical data and the conclusions drawn from its analysis. If the theory allows accurate predictions of subsequent events, or furnishes better or more accurate explanations of the past than alternatives, the theory is accepted (not proved). If not, it is rejected. Two examples of the use of theory to explain American economic growth will illustrate the point. (The term *American* is used here and throughout the book to connote the United States of America and the colonies from which it was formed, not the entire Western Hemisphere.)

The Resource Endowment Theory
One widely discussed explanation for high U.S. income levels holds that the large and varied natural resources possessed by this country are the chief source of its economic development. The United States is unusually well endowed with fertile soil, fuels, metals, and geographic features that either

encourage their use or impose much lower barriers to such employment than are found elsewhere. For example, the United States has a much greater share of the earth's richest agricultural land than of the planet's total land area, and many other raw materials are also relatively abundant in this country. However, evidence both from America's past and from the experiences of other nations casts grave doubt on the notion that abundant natural resources made U.S. economic growth inevitable.

Table I.1 indicates that there are other countries with large natural resource endowments and high levels of per-capita incomes, such as Canada and Australia. But incomes are at least equally high in Denmark, the Netherlands, and Switzerland. The recent growth of the Japanese economy has produced one of the world's highest income levels. Nevertheless, all these countries are notoriously poor in natural resources. Nor does it appear that mere possession of natural bounty is any guarantee of economic success; Brazil and Indonesia both enjoy enormous and varied natural resources, plus head starts of 100 and 1000 years, respectively, in civilization over the United States. Yet both are still poor. Brazil has only commenced rapid economic growth in the last few decades, and Indonesia remains one of the world's poor countries.

Even more damaging to this theory is the fact that the United States was a high-income economy long before its mineral wealth or even its most fertile soils had been discovered, much less utilized. Colonial Americans enjoyed some of the world's highest per-capita incomes when only the Eastern Seaboard's natural resources were available, and by no means were all of these known, far less exploited. (Americans did have the advantage of a high ratio of resources to population.)[1] It appears that natural resources or their absence can affect the nature of the initial development process, but economic success over time is much more heavily influenced by other factors that provide effective substitutes (or fail to do so) for locally available natural resources.

The Exploitation Theory

A second proposed explanation of American economic development sees the source of high incomes in this country in U.S. ability to exploit other countries or areas, reducing their welfare in order to raise its own. As in the previous example, however, the sequence of observed events does not support this contention. In this discussion, we will employ Robert Zevin's definition of imperialism as "the formal or informal extension of sovereignty beyond the borders within which it was previously exercised."[2] For this explanation to hold water, American power over foreigners must have pre-

---

[1] For a contrary opinion, at least for a later period, see G. Wright, "The Origins of American Industrial Success, 1879–1940," *American Economic Review* (September 1990).
[2] R. Zevin, "An Interpretation of American Imperialism," *Journal of Economic History* (March 1972).

ceded income growth in this country. But America was a wealthy society, probably enjoying higher incomes than its British masters and most of today's world, while it was still a group of colonies.[3] Further, incomes in the United States appear to have grown faster before our most blatantly imperialistic ventures, that is, prior to 1898, than subsequently. The most explicitly imperialistic activity of the United States often occurred in areas where markets, raw materials, or investment outlets were trivial in comparison to those available at home. Before the United States possessed significant international political power, its principal foreign economic and political relations were with nations that it could not hope to control. Even within North America, U.S. territorial expansion did not typically involve the exploitation of the existing populations (which does not excuse attempts to destroy them). The locus of U.S. overseas interests largely remained the same after the United States became a world power; most foreign trade and investment activities linked this country to nations easily able to protect their own interests, and they still do. American imperialism was real enough, but its motives were not economic and its payoff was negative. In no way can the wealth of this country be explained as the proceeds of international exploitation. The impact of such activity was never large enough in aggregate nor crucial enough in detail to have a significant impact on the U.S. economy.[4]

The failure of these two theories to explain American economic growth brings out two important points. First, theories are linked to facts; they are not empty logical exercises. If a theory does not allow accurate predictions to be made, or if it cannot accommodate observed reality that it purports to explain, then the theory is wrong or misapplied. Things are *never* "all right in theory but not in fact." If a theory points to conclusions contrary to observed reality, the facts are not wrong. Second, we need theories to place facts in logical contexts and to draw conclusions from them.

Further Theories of Growth

As later chapters will show, there are many theories that purport to explain at least some elements of the economic growth of this country. Such theories must be evaluated in light of the factual evidence that adds or detracts from their credibility. No single theory explains the entire pattern of American economic growth over the past 375 years, at least in detail, better than all others. On the other hand, a theory need not be universally applicable to be useful.

---

[3] See Chap. 2.
[4] Economic theory indicates that aggregate human welfare cannot be improved by armed conflict. Even should one party gain control of all the loser's goods, the victor can only acquire what his victim lost. Since conflict itself not only requires scarce resources, but generally results in the destruction of labor and capital, overall welfare is reduced, not increased. Particularly in the case of nineteenth-century imperialism, the areas contested were often poorly endowed and the efforts to acquire control over them costly. It is difficult to perceive gains to the economies of any participants in such ventures.

The Value of Growth

As a social science, economics deals with what has or will occur and why; it cannot say what should have or ought to occur. The ideal pace and pattern of economic growth must be drawn from value judgments in which economists have no special expertise. However, it does appear that rising incomes—at least for individuals—raise the recipients' perceptions of their own happiness. Professor Richard Easterlin has found that most people become happier when their incomes rise in relation to those of others in their communities. However, no such increase in well-being occurs when all persons' incomes rise at the same rate. These traits appeared in a wide variety of circumstances: planned as well as market economies, societies with both high and low per-capita incomes, and those with both very rapid and very slow rates of growth.[5]

Does Money Buy Happiness?

In 1991, the average American enjoyed over 12 times the real income of his or her eighteenth-century counterpart,[6] but is more satisfaction derived from this much higher income? We have no convincing measure of comparison (we cannot measure the satisfaction derived by different generations from their life-styles), but we can say with some assurance that late twentieth-century Americans would not be willing to exchange living standards with their ancestors in eighteenth-century Virginia. It also seems obvious that contemporary income levels cannot be significantly reduced except at the cost of emotional trauma. The amounts, quality, and variety of goods made possible by contemporary productive capabilities form our standards of comparison today, and, just as they were in the past, most people appear convinced that "more is better." In Easterlin's terms, individuals and societies are caught on a "hedonic treadmill."

Although more commodities cannot be proved to increase human welfare as time passes, declines in current incomes will reduce well-being. Over time, if an unchanging income level could be achieved, it would probably cause a decrease in human happiness.

ECONOMIC COMPARISONS

The most commonly used comparison of individual well-being between nations is real per-capita income. Recent income trends, which may be good indicators of prospects for the immediate future, are also widely employed. It is generally agreed that the appropriate standard of comparison between

---

[5] R. A. Easterlin, "Does Money Buy Happiness?" *The Public Interest* (Winter 1973).
[6] A. H. Jones, *Wealth of a Nation to Be* (New York: Columbia University Press, 1980) 122–123, 303.

countries is income per person rather than aggregate income. The total income of India, for example, is many times that of Sweden, but the Indian population exceeds the Swedish in far greater proportion. There are so many more Indians who must share their economy's total output than there are claimants against aggregate Swedish production that measured output per person in Sweden is over 50 times that of India.

In concept, per-capita income calculation is simple: The money value of an economy's annual production of final goods and services (gross national product or GNP) is divided by the population. But such figures should be viewed with caution. First, GNP is often compiled under rules that give more weight to convenience of data collection or international status than to accuracy of measurement. Goods and services that are not sold are assigned arbitrary values; the quantity of such production is an approximation. Figures for all countries must be quoted in some common unit to facilitate comparisons. Normally the U.S. dollar is used. But the use of dollars to measure income changes in other countries means that changes in exchange rates may change income figures even in cases where material output remains the same or may mask greater real changes. The relative prices of goods that cannot be traded internationally (such as housing and services) may be quite different in various countries. Finally, per-capita income figures are an arithmetic average of all incomes; they do not indicate the distribution about that average.

Despite these imperfections, large differences in per-capita incomes between nations are reasonably accurate reflections of the direction, if not the exact magnitude, of differences in real income per person. The huge gap between Indian and Swedish incomes indicates what we can readily observe, that is, the average inhabitant of Stockholm has a far higher level of material well-being than does his or her counterpart in Calcutta.

The Need for Economic Growth

Over time, human wants increase rather than decrease, so economic growth appears necessary if economic well-being (the satisfaction gained from income rather than real income itself) is not to decline. The relevance of this point is especially clear if we observe the effects of very low incomes on human life-styles. Higher incomes allow people a wider range of choices, and very low income levels may impose extremely harsh constraints. In the recent past, the Eskimos practiced female infanticide and accepted the idea that in severe winters the elderly might have to die. Such attitudes reflected stark necessity, not cruelty or insensitivity. The Eskimo economy produced so little, at least in bad times, that the population had to be kept within the limits imposed by the available food supply, even if that meant sacrificing lives. Lacking the ability to change their economic environment, the Eskimos had to adapt to it and its limits. If their society was to survive, the Eskimos could only support the unproductive from whatever was surplus to the requirements of working adults. Until they gained knowledge of other societies' economic standards, Eskimos' aspirations were limited by their own experience. In the poorest economies, little effort can be devoted to the provision of anything other than physical necessities. The real difference between rich and poor societies, then, lies in the range of choices open to their citizens.

Higher Incomes and Cultural Expression

If all the resources available to a society must be devoted to survival, there is nothing to devote to the expression of artistic, social, or political values. Before people can begin those activities that distinguish humanity from other life forms, some margin of output above subsistence is necessary. Throughout history, mankind's most noteworthy achievements—Egypt's pyramids and monuments, Indian philosophy, Chinese art and literature, Dutch painting, Elizabethan drama, and today's social and space programs— have come from societies that considered themselves rich. By expanding the range of attainable choices, economic development makes civilization possible. How the choices that growth provides are used—in concern for others, the "good life" of private consumption, artistic expression, further growth, more leisure, or war—is determined by the values of the society and perhaps by its experience during the development process. But enhanced capabilities are essential if choices are to be available.

Costs of Growth

Like any other scarce good, economic growth is not free. Resources devoted to growth cannot simultaneously be used to enhance current consumption, nor can they be left in a natural state. Leisure, foregone consumption, and occasionally some deeply ingrained cultural values may be some of the costs of higher incomes. Moreover, economic growth produces new problems as well as new choices, and these may be as different from any previously encountered as are the new capabilities. Growth may produce income levels beyond the imaginations of previous generations, but it may also worsen the harried conditions of urban life and generate pollution and more threatening forms of warfare. The implications of these developments for human welfare, however, must be assessed in the context of the (usually greater) ability to meet them that is also generated. All of economics is a matter of weighing extra benefits against extra costs; only such cases involve meaningful choice.

The modern world suffers from pollution, but pollution is hardly a new problem. City dwellers in the eighteenth and nineteenth centuries were also subjected to its effects, and their mortality rates indicate that the problem was much more serious then than today. Even if pollution has taken new forms, our abilities to reduce its threat have more than kept pace. Imagine, if possible, the terrifying impact of epidemic disease on societies that lacked all modern responses: medical knowledge to treat it, the biological, chemical, and engineering skills required for its prevention, and even the understanding of its causes that might permit meaningful efforts to avoid it. Is it any wonder that epidemics were considered to be punishments inflicted by God and that the only conceivable response was to endure—if one could? We have not eliminated the ancient scourges, but our capabilities have blunted their effects. Even with modern transportation and communication, local crop failures spell reduced incomes for the affected producers and consumers; two or three centuries ago they meant famine. If we contrast the experiences of Germany and Japan in World War II and its aftermath with those of Central Asia in the wake of Genghis Khan or Germany after the Thirty Years' War, it is not even clear that modern war has (thus far) posed greater threats to civilization. In the past, recurrent energy crises, social upheavals, epidemics, and other phenomena appeared every bit as threatening to those experiencing them as contemporary problems do to us. With our capabilities, we might view the crises of the past as trivial, but those who faced them lacked our means.

SOURCES OF ECONOMIC GROWTH

If economic growth generally creates more benefits than problems, we must understand its sources, both in the United States and elsewhere, if we are to promote it. Is there any reason for the unique economic success of the United States? The theme of this book is that the American record owes a great deal to the superior short-run use of human potential and to institutions developed to promote it. In the long run, both of these encouraged the development of our work force's potential and allocated it and other inputs to their most productive uses. These have long been prominent characteristics of the American economy, and from the earliest days they yielded important economic gains. American economic success stems from making more of the same opportunities available to other nations, not in greater endowments of resources or good fortune.

Other nations made less use of the productive potential of their people. They restricted geographic or occupational mobility, or limited the portion of their population that was allowed to make its fullest contribution, to a greater extent than was the case in America. The result was that ideas or people originating in Europe often made their contributions here rather than in their place of origin.

The American Advantage
American conditions and thinking from the earliest days of European settlement in the New World favored the employment of the available human talent in the areas and uses in which it was most productive. For the entire formative period of the American economy, labor was too valuable to be

wasted in uses that returned less than its maximum possible output. In addition, the prevailing economic circumstances fostered highly pragmatic assessments of change. From both inclination and necessity, Americans were more receptive to new tools, methods, and products, and less tolerant of custom and tradition, than were Old World societies. Not only were Americans inclined to select job candidates, tools, and methods on the basis of productivity, they pushed these concepts considerably farther. They came to accept change as a continuous and largely beneficial element in their lives. Consequently, institutions were developed that accommodated and even encouraged innovation. Americans found it easier to change jobs, work methods, and locations and to introduce what they had learned elsewhere to new situations than did people in other nations. In this climate, innovations were not only adopted rapidly, they were likely to produce a high proportion of their potential because they spread rapidly. Americans prospered not merely because of superior opportunities in the New World, but because they made more of those opportunities.[7]

American superiority in the recognition and utilization of human talent was (and to some extent remains) relative rather than absolute. By no means has every American always been free to make his or her maximum contribution or to develop the abilities to do so. Discrimination against women and blacks is only the most prominent example of the historical waste of talent that occurred in this country. Other nations, however, did much worse. There the evaluation of human potential was more affected by considerations of race, sex, religion, social origin or others of the thousand and one "reasons" men have developed to restrict or disregard the activities of others. In America, a job applicant's responses to "What can you do, and how well?" carried more weight than those to "Who were your parents?"— if the latter were asked at all—than was true in even the most open European societies until the middle of the twentieth century. Once on the job, employees' ideas about methods and tools new to their current situation were likely to attract interest as well as trial. Nor was the supremacy of competence over breeding a widely employed criterion in Europe; many countries were far removed from the standards of Britain or the Netherlands.[8] Not infrequently, European attitudes were a major impetus to the migration of talented and ambitious individuals to this country.

---

[7] D. North, *Structure and Change in Economic History* (New York: Norton, 1981), and M. Olson, *The Rise and Decline of Nations* (New York: Yale University Press, 1982), have made major contributions to the development of this theme. Two recent studies of the effects of mobility are J. Rosenbloom, "Labor Market Integration in the Late Nineteenth-Century United States," *Journal of Economic History* (March 1990); and T. Hatton and J. Williamson, "Integrated and Segmented Labor Markets: Thinking in Two Sectors," *Journal of Economic History* (June 1991).

[8] E. H. Jones, *The European Miracle* (Cambridge, U.K: Cambridge University Press, 1981), Chap. 8–10. See also J. R. Hughes, *Industrialization and Economic History: Theses and Conjectures* (New York: McGraw-Hill, 1970), and D. North and R. Thomas, *The Rise of the Western World* (Cambridge, U.K.: Cambridge University Press, 1973).

The environment of seventeenth-century America provided harsh and conclusive evidence of job eligibility. Attitudes changed rapidly in the new surroundings. The very act of emigration guaranteed that America would obtain an unusually flexible subset of Europe's population, but New World circumstances forced more and continuous revisions in the thinking of the first settlers. Initially, the only clear point about the optimum technology for American conditions was that traditional European methods were not the answer. The needs of physical survival emphasized the urgency of rapid adaptation. Because most efforts were experimental, and initially no one had a monopoly on the right answers, Americans learned to judge adjustments by the results they produced rather than by their authors. In the process, they acquired a lasting appreciation of the potential benefits of change.

The Necessity of Change

It is clear from both theoretical and empirical studies of economic development that change is an essential ingredient in the long-term growth recipe. Productive capabilities must be altered qualitatively if quantitative growth is to continue for very long. Any economy restricted to "more of the same" methods of raising output will soon discover that under such conditions output cannot rise much more than in proportion to the work force in the best of circumstances. Thus, there is a "lid" on per-capita incomes. Even current income levels cannot be maintained indefinitely; growth within these restrictions can continue only as long as additional inputs of equal productivity remain available. With technology fixed, conceivably capital and labor could be increased at constant costs, but natural resources cannot be expected to remain in perfectly elastic supply over large or long-continued increases in production. The result is diminishing returns. Additional increments of variable resources (capital and labor) produce smaller and smaller increases in output. Falling productivity, of course, indicates rising costs; total output rises, but less than in proportion to inputs, and per-capita incomes fall. But if substitutes for scarce resources can be developed, or if new, resource-saving methods are introduced, diminishing returns need not impose a barrier to long-term growth. However, such responses imply change.[9]

Attitudes toward Change

Economic change is seldom an unmixed blessing. New methods and products, however favorable their overall impacts, make life difficult for those with a stake in the old ways. Innovations can change the social status of individuals or produce competitive challenges to established views and

[9] W. Parker, *Europe, America, and the Wider World: Essays in the Economic History of Western Capitalism* (Cambridge, U.K.: Cambridge University Press, 1984), 44–45.

products that are impossible to ignore.[10] Even if change is inevitable over time in any society, its pace and ultimate impact may be heavily influenced by prevailing attitudes and institutions, which also change over time. Is change viewed as a welcome vehicle for general improvement, as something to be tolerated in others but not encouraged, or as a destructive force to be grudgingly accommodated at minimum levels?

When social institutions and the popular opinions that underlie them allow a sizable portion of a society's work force to perform as it wishes in occupations of each individual's choosing and to reap most of the consequences of their decisions, the economic environment encourages a continuous and widespread dispersion of new ideas throughout the system. Such circumstances reach their greatest development within a market economy. By making the authors of change responsible for the results of their innovative activities, the market system encourages changes that raise incomes and discourages those that reduce them, thus producing efficient responses to opportunity. Markets generate continuous feedback on the costs and benefits of economic activity, and they automatically adjust to changes in resources, wants, or institutions. Markets encourage rational thought and the divorce of economic activity from religious or political control, both of which tend toward one-sided views.

Consequences

Over time, the cumulative effects of such a climate are far-reaching indeed. The human mind appears capable of finding substitutes for any input or method, given sufficient time and incentives. This means that diminishing returns may be kept permanently at bay and that there are *no* ultimate restrictions on aggregate economic output. In facilitating these responses, the American economy gained an important advantage, and it did so earlier and more completely than any rival. The market system developed more by default than by any conscious choice as the basic framework for economic activity in America, but this was a most fortuitous accident.

The Role of Institutions and Attitudes

All societies have to work out methods of developing, recognizing, and allocating human talent. Perhaps no other task has more profound long-run implications. How are important jobs assigned to people? Are they assigned on the basis of tradition, nepotism, political favoritism, bribery, social standing, inertia, or ability? No system has ever relied exclusively on a single criterion, but the weights assigned to choice factors have shown great variation. Several historical examples can illustrate this point. In 1588, the king of Spain sought a commander for the Armada. Military experience and

---

[10] S. Kuznets, "Innovations and Adjustments in Economic Growth" in *Poverty, Ecology, and Technological Change* (Durham, N.H., 1973).

ability were important considerations in his selection, but so was social standing. The Duke of Medina-Sidonia was chosen; he was an experienced soldier, but also the scion of one of the oldest noble houses of Spain. The Duke was neither a fool nor a coward, but he wanted to turn down the appointment on grounds of ability (he had no naval experience whatsoever). However, he was trapped by the Spanish value system; he could not refuse such a sign of high royal favor. Elizabethan England, a more flexible society facing a life-or-death situation, used different weights in selecting leaders to oppose the Armada. Perfunctory attention was given to social background, but Elizabeth's captains were seamen first—or even ex-pirates—with other qualities a very distant second.

Over time, the allocation of human talent becomes even more important than it is in response to an immediate crisis. Toward what fields of endeavor does the society urge its "best and brightest"? By what standards are candidates appraised and trained, and what proportion of the population is considered? How are the goals toward which activity is aimed selected? The answers to these questions are critical to any society's long-term success.

Classical China, certain of the superiority of its traditional values, recruited its administrative class through a system of competitive examinations. Important jobs within the imperial government were filled on a merit basis and most of the empire's male population was at least theoretically eligible to take the examinations through which personnel were chosen. However, the subject matter of the tests and the tasks to which the successful candidates were assigned were the maintenance of China's ancient traditions and the exclusion of all things foreign. The system worked only too well. China became extremely resistant to change, particularly to that originating outside its borders. Both internally and externally, the eventual Chinese response to pressures for which tradition allowed no effective answers was a traumatic restructuring that involved both enormous bloodshed and, at least temporarily, the almost total rejection of all aspects of traditional Chinese culture. (The current regime appears scarcely less resistant to change not of its own instigation.) Even in the United States, the stronghold of very different views, the change process has not always run smoothly or peacefully.

In sum, then, if economic development is to be a major social goal, an economic system must alter both its productive capacities and the social institutions that govern their uses and determine their purposes. In the author's view, no other system of economic organization facilitates this process as well as a price or market system. To a much greater degree than any other organization, markets not only foster the introduction of innovation, but provide accurate and automatic assessments of the costs and benefits involved. Because the eventual outcome of really significant departures from established norms can never be fully anticipated, this feedback process is vital for economic efficiency. No claim is made that mistakes are never made within a market system, but the pressures to undo them are generated more quickly and clearly than under any other form of economic organization. Markets also provide a near-ideal mechanism for the diffusion of new ideas throughout the economy. This often produces a greater cumulative impact than the idea's initial introduction.

THE COURSE OF DEVELOPMENT

There is no single universally accepted theory of economic development. This book stresses one viewpoint: Much of America's success stems from its superior utilization of its human potential. But no claim is made that this was the sole source of American growth, or that it was the most important at all times and circumstances. There are many theories stressing other primary causes. Economic development has been claimed to stem from capital accumulation, from entrepreneurs' efforts to introduce innovation, from the success of an export sector, from the incidence of a sudden transformation of the economy's capabilities, from the achievement of secure property rights, and from class strife and the exploitation of labor. This is only a sampling of some of the better-known theories. Various combinations of these and other theories have also been proposed. The more prominent, together with the pertinent historical data, will be presented in later chapters.

The Importance of Continuity

If any single point emerges from studies of the development of modern economies, it is continuity. Much more than in political history, even the most significant events in economic history are best viewed as the consequences of prior events and as the basis for future changes. Even though dates may be assigned to important inventions based on patents or initial demonstrations, these are seldom indicative of the period in which the innovation had its greatest economic impact.[11] So too with the formation of institutions or the appearance of laws. Generally these are the culmination of previous activities, and once instituted, time is required before really different frameworks for economic activity have their full effects. Revolutions in economic capabilities do occur, based both on technology and the rules and attitudes governing the people who apply them. But the pressures that generate them and the culmination of their impacts may require years, decades, or even generations. The full impact of the Industrial Revolution, for example, is not yet apparent even in the countries where that epochal event first appeared. Political manifestations of economic pressures are often

---

[11] Kuznets, "Innovations and Adjustments." See also N. Rosenberg, *Technology and American Economic Growth* (New York: Harper & Row, 1972).

as slow and incomplete as are the economic responses to change in the political environment.

Continuity is prominent in U.S. economic history. The high incomes currently enjoyed by U.S. citizens are the result of a growth process more modest and longer-lived than that of most other countries. In addition, the incomes from which Americans began the process of continued growth were high by contemporary standards. Especially in relation to the rates of economic growth achieved elsewhere since 1950, the American pace has not been outstandingly rapid. In the nineteenth and early twentieth centuries, the U.S. growth rate was among the world's fastest, but even then the pace does not match many of those in Table I.1. Since 1839, U.S. per-capita incomes have risen at an annual average rate of about 1.6 percent. Before that time, the pace was apparently considerably slower and subject to notable variation. It must be remembered, however, that this apparently insignificant rate of increase is compounded; one year's income gains become the base on which the next are based. Thus, a 1.6 percent compound growth rate doubles incomes every 43 years. Over the centuries, the cumulative effect can be enormous.

As the preceding pages have stressed, such growth could not have occurred without major alterations in the American economy. These have taken place and Americans now live and work in different manners and locations than their forebears. With economic development came specialization, which implies growing economic interdependence and exchange between an ever-widening variety of producers, increasingly beyond national borders. Institutions and occupations that foster specialization—trade, transportation, communications, finance, marketing, education, and government—have enrolled a growing portion of the work force. The nature of production has also changed. Not only is the service component of GNP accounting for a larger share than previously, but even within manufacturing and primary production the costs of capital and labor rather than raw materials increasingly determine prices. In some cases the change has been dramatic. Computer prices, for example, are far more heavily affected by the costs of the labor and capital used in making such machines than they are by those of the copper and other raw materials that go into them. The gains from American economic growth have been widespread as well as large. Income distribution has become more equal in the twentieth century than it was in other eras. Even change itself is now different. Increasingly it has become qualitative rather than quantitative—a phenomenon reflected in the emphasis placed on research and education in the modern economy. Finally, as might be expected, not all the dimensions of economic change have been universally acclaimed. We now turn to the background of economic growth in America.

SELECTED REFERENCES

Davis, L., R. Easterlin, W. Parker et al. *American Economic Growth: An Economist's History of the United States.* New York: Harper & Row, 1972.

Hicks, J. *A Theory of Economic History.* New York: Oxford University Press, 1969.

Hughes, J. *Industrialization and Economic History: Theses and Conjectures.* New York: McGraw-Hill, 1970.

Kuznets, S. "Innovation and Adjustments in Economic Growth." In *Poverty, Ecology, and Technological Change: World Problems of Development.* Durham, N.H.: Whittemore School of Business, University of New Hampshire, 1974.

————. "The Meaning and Measurement of Economic Growth." In *The Experience of Economic Growth.* B. Supple, ed. New York: Random House, 1963.

Mokyr, J. *The Lever of Riches: Technological Creativity and Economic Progress.* New York: Oxford University Press, 1990.

North, D. *Growth and Welfare in the American Past.* 3d ed. Englewood Cliffs, N.J.: Prentice-Hall, 1982.

————. *Structure and Change in Economic History.* New York: Norton, 1981.

Olson, M. *The Rise and Decline of Nations.* New Haven, Conn.: Yale University Press, 1982.

Parker, W. *Europe, America, and the Wider World: Essays on the Economic History of Western Capitalism.* Cambridge, U.K.: Cambridge University Press, 1984.

Rosenberg, N. and L. Birdzell. *How the West Grew Rich.* New York: Basic Books, 1986.

Temin, P., ed. *New Economic History.* Baltimore: Penguin, 1973.

World Bank. *World Development Report*, 1990. Washington, D.C., 1990.

European Background and the Colonial Era–1790

Sante Fe 3.
(1610, Spanish)

Dates for all the above taken from: *Timetables of American History*. Laurence Urdang, edition introduction by H.S. Commanger. Simon & Schuster, Inc., 1981.

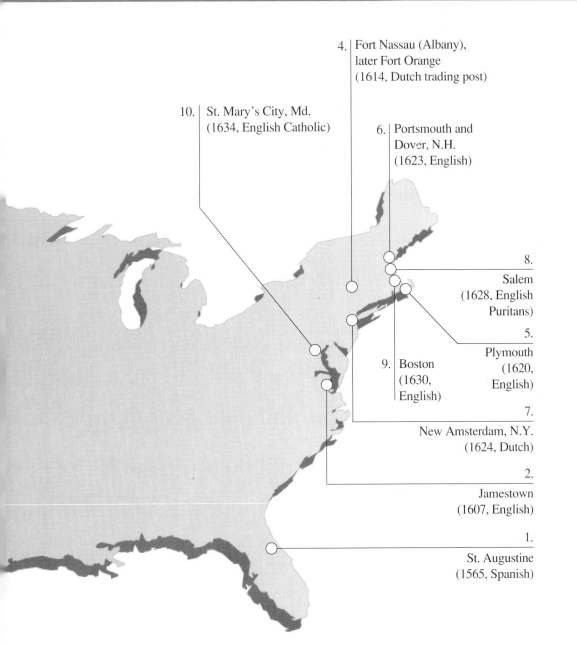

4. Fort Nassau (Albany),
later Fort Orange
(1614, Dutch trading post)

10. St. Mary's City, Md.
(1634, English Catholic)

6. Portsmouth and
Dover, N.H.
(1623, English)

8.
Salem
(1628, English
Puritans)

5.
Plymouth
(1620,
English)

9. Boston
(1630,
English)

7.
New Amsterdam, N.Y.
(1624, Dutch)

2.
Jamestown
(1607, English)

1.
St. Augustine
(1565, Spanish)

INITIAL SETTLEMENTS AND THE EUROPEAN BACKGROUND

THE NORSE

The first European attempt to settle in North America ended in utter failure. Not only were the settlements abandoned, but even the memory of the discovery was almost totally forgotten. Nevertheless, for approximately the first two decades of the eleventh century, the Norse made a series of efforts to establish colonies in what is now Newfoundland. These rugged seafarers had already colonized Iceland, where they displaced the original Irish settlers. Shortly before A.D. 1000, the Icelandic colonists in turn established two settlements in Greenland. In the course of voyages to these colonies, northeastern North America was discovered. The Norse achievements were recounted in sagas, a type of epic poetry, but for a long time the sagas were regarded as mere legends. Only in the twentieth century was it realized that the sagas recounted historical events and that their references to attempts to settle land to the west provided directions to the settlements. By following the sagas' instructions, modern researchers have discovered the remains of a Norse village at the northern tip of Newfoundland.[1]

The physical evidence discovered in Newfoundland strongly supports the sagas. The Norse not only reached North America, at least some of them came to stay. The Newfoundland site's ruins are those of permanent buildings. The group that lived there included women, and at least one saga mentions that the settlers brought cattle to the new land. Yet in only a few years the settlements were abandoned, and the Norse retreated to Greenland.

The Norse Settlements' Failure

Why did the Norse settlements nearly half a millennium before Columbus fail? The immediate cause appears to have been conflict with the indigenous population, either Indian or Eskimo. Their encounters with non-Europeans appear to have shocked the Norse, who at that time had met no other humans in Greenland.[2] The Irish, whom they had driven from Iceland, were familiar; indeed, Celtic monks appear to have been seeking refuge there from Norse attacks on Ireland itself.

The Norse settlements in Newfoundland were very small and peopled by farmers and fishermen. Outnumbered and surprised by the natives, the Norse felt threatened. Yet these settlers were at most a generation or two removed from the Vikings who had raided and conquered along the coasts and rivers of Europe, from Russia and the Black Sea in the east to the British Isles, Normandy, and Sicily in the west. Many of the Icelanders and Greenlanders had been exiled from Norway for excessive violence. The Norse had met and overcome larger, better equipped, and better organized forces than any they would meet in the New World. And the new lands appeared worth a struggle; by the standards of Greenland and Iceland, they were rich. Newfoundland had a milder climate and more varied and plentiful resources—timber, land game, arable land, and fisheries—than did either Iceland or Greenland. The Norse were able to maintain their Greenland colony for at least four centuries, and the Iceland settlement was permanent. Why did the attempt in a more promising area fail?

---

[1] H. Ingstad, *Land Under the Pole Star* (New York: St. Martin's Press, 1966) and *Westward to Vinland* (New York: St. Martin's Press, 1969).

[2] S. Morison, *The European Discovery of America: The Northern Voyages* (New York: Oxford University Press, 1971), 55–57.

Present Costs and Prospective Gains

In the long run the most likely reason for the Norse failure in America was economic, as it was for the demise of the Greenland settlements in the fourteenth or fifteenth century. At the time, the cost of establishing and maintaining a North American colony exceeded the returns. The costs could only have been borne by Europe. Iceland and Greenland were closer to the new area, but they were poor and Greenland in particular had only a tiny population of probably less than 3,000 people. Output per person in both areas was low; what little production margin above direct subsistence existed had to support essential imports from Europe, such as grain and metal. Thus the established colonies could not spare the goods, ships, or people for a settlement effort large enough to promise success, particularly in the face of native opposition.

The Importance of European Support

European support was essential for any colony. Goods and tools that the colonists could not hope to make for themselves were required both to establish a colony and to maintain its living standards at European levels. Over time, these requirements could be obtained only if there was a payoff to the European suppliers. Reports on the initial contacts indicated the new area had few potential exports with good European markets. Furs, fish, and timber were available in Scandinavia itself at low cost. North America appeared to offer no gold, its native population allowed only slight opportunities for trade or plunder, and further exploration would involve high costs with no certainty of better returns. As the long-suffering inhabitants of coastal Europe could testify, the Norse were only too willing to undertake hazardous voyages, but there had to be some prospect of gain to tempt them into sustained efforts. In comparison to North America, eleventh-century Europe appeared to offer opportunities both

more lucrative and more certain. In A.D. 1000, Norway was too poor, thinly populated, and disorganized to generate resources for ventures no more promising than the North American discoveries. The settlements were abandoned and contact with the new discoveries limited to occasional timber voyages from Greenland. These became less frequent and apparently had ceased well before the demise of the Greenland settlements.

THE EUROPEAN SETTING AND ITS DEVELOPMENT

The Europe from which Columbus, very much by accident, rediscovered America was quite different from the continent Lief Eriksson had known. Physical capabilities had increased; there were many more and better ships, and navigational methods were vastly improved. Much more efficient organizations existed and nation-states could draw upon a greater proportion of the resources of larger populations. Perhaps most important of all were the attitudes of the fifteenth century as compared to those of a half-millennium before. In A.D. 1000, European ideas and the institutions that expressed them were strongly opposed to change. New ideas were opposed, not sought. By Columbus' time, there was a growing realization that new knowledge, methods, products, and institutions could enhance the welfare of both individuals and nations. Medieval thought opposing nearly all change slowly shifted to an atmosphere in which new thoughts were given skeptical hearing, then later recognized as possible sources of gain—a concept that had barely existed during the Middle Ages. City-states that had grown wealthy by adjusting ancient practice and custom to meet the demands of customers from other cultures or even religions had appeared in Italy, along the Baltic, and in the Low Countries. The example of Venice, Genoa, and the cities of the Hanseatic League indicated that departures from established rules could be advantageous, rather than a certain route to disaster. By 1450, the beginnings of an organized search for new regions, products, and trade routes were underway. The great voyages of the "Age of Discovery" were not isolated accidents, as the Norse adventures had been. And the response to the opportunities revealed by the discoveries was vigorous and increasingly widespread.

The Structure of the Medieval Economy

Through the period ending in mid-fourteenth century, the dominating economic reality was that output per person was low, especially in agriculture. Because the surplus beyond farmers' immediate subsistence needs was very small, only a tiny nonagricultural population could exist. Medieval cities were small, and trading activity was limited. Much of the limited food surplus was devoted to the support of a military class. Peasants who did the farming were virtually defenseless against raiders. Where production was so unrewarding, attempts to steal other peoples' goods were frequent. At the same time, a professional military class could not produce its own food.

Feudalism

The result was a political-economic structure (the two concepts were interlinked) called feudalism. In return for food and labor services from the local peasants, a lord would provide military protection and political administration. Transportation was incredibly difficult, so effective protection had to be provided locally; the knight and his castle were the peasants' refuge in times of peril. Formally, there was a national political leadership headed by a king to whom all people owed allegiance and

tribute, directly or through their superiors. But the king's ability to enforce his power was limited. It was difficult to raise, supply, or transport a sizable army, given the limited food supplies and the difficulty of transporting men and goods. Control of local affairs was even more difficult for the king under these conditions, so local lords administered the laws in his name. Further, a well-stocked castle was often a secure refuge; its supplies might well outlast those of any besiegers, and its walls be proof against the best efforts of the available military technology. The king was seldom able to obtain resources from his nobles for uses that they opposed. In this period, effective authority was local or at most regional.

The organization of production heavily subordinated the individual to the community. Group activity in agriculture was the rule. Fields were shared among all the families in each peasant village, and planting and harvesting were done in concert. Each village was jointly responsible for the welfare of all its inhabitants, and also for providing the lord with the food and labor services (usually the peasants had to cultivate the lord's fields as well as their own) to which he was entitled. The size of the peasants' contribution to the lord was determined by agricultural productivity, the peasants' mobility (if there were other landlords who desired additional labor, the peasants might be able to play off one against the other by actual or threatened migration), and of course by compulsion. The lord was the chief political authority; he served as judge, jury, and, not infrequently, executioner. Because at the same time the lord was frequently an interested party in disputes over the division of output or the services he owed to the peasants, the system was vulnerable to abuse. The consent of the entire community was generally required before new methods could be adopted. Consequently, productivity-raising changes in agriculture were inhibited. There were improvements in medieval agriculture, but the pace was glacial.

Custom: A Defense and a Curse

One defense open to the peasants was appeals to tradition. Rules concerning the lord's rights and privileges as well as his subjects' obligation were fixed by ancient custom. Because most of the changes people could imagine were changes for the worse—war, famine, epidemics, or other disasters—and because any agreement to change one established rule weakened tradition as a defense against additional demands from the lord, there was great resistance to innovation. Long-established rules bound individuals as well as the community. Nearly all persons were born into the jobs, locations, and social status they would retain for their entire lives. Only a handful of people ever had the opportunity to qualify for a task on the basis of ability alone. This rigidity was nearly universal; men were not merely unable to change their jobs, they were committed to exchange their products for other goods at unchanging ratios, with no regard to relative scarcity or abundance. Exchange was regulated by custom rather than the market.[3]

Religious attitudes strengthened the system. The role of the church was fixed. It too was to be supported by the peasants on terms fixed by ancient practice. Medieval religion stressed the view that life was but a preparation for another world. Current circumstances were to be endured rather than altered. The physical world was also viewed in static terms. The ideas of Aristotle or Ptolemy were cited as final authority in natural science or geography, often with little consideration of whether the ancients' conclusions were in harmony with observed reality. Above all, there was no view of the world as subject to natural laws, the mastery of which might allow human betterment. The overall assumption was that aggregate gains were impossible. Given such attitudes, evidence of personal gain might meet disapproval. Any individual's increase in well-being must have occasioned harm to someone else; the rich man probably had gained his wealth by reducing that of others.

Education was limited and its topics largely the preservation of the status quo. All subjects were open to review by religious and political authorities, who were inclined to view deviations from long-established ideas as threats.

But very gradually the idea that improvements in the conditions of material life were both desirable and possible began to replace the older views. In pursuit of the new goals, people developed more rational and systematic methods of thought based more on observation and less on tradition and faith. The populace began to restrict religious and political control to areas in which their pertinence was clear rather than allowing them to exercise universal influence.

THE END OF THE MEDIEVAL ECONOMY

The economic system outlined here was largely static. Total output could be increased, but only by "more of the same" methods, at least in agriculture. Workers, tools, and land had to be increased in roughly the same proportions because farming methods were essentially fixed. This also implied that the urban population was limited by the size of the agricultural surplus. With its fixed or very slowly changing technology, the Medieval European economy was vulnerable to diminishing returns. If unused land of equal quality to that already utilized was not available as population increased, increases in agricultural production could only be obtained at increasing costs—and costs were already very high. The price of sizable increases might be

---

[3] N. Rosenberg and L. Birdzell, *How the West Grew Rich: The Economic Transformation of the Industrial World* (New York: Basic Books, 1986), 38–39.

insuperable. Population increases were therefore restricted by the supply of natural resources, in particular, unused agricultural land. This description of the Medieval economy and the following discussion are based on the work of Professors North and Thomas.[4]

Extensive and Intensive Growth

North and Thomas hypothesize that from the tenth through the thirteenth centuries, Europe's economic output rose as a growing population was employed on previously unused arable land. Increases in agricultural output allowed growth in the number and size of cities, which in turn facilitated regional specialization and trade. Because the technology of the urban economies was not fixed, productivity growth in the cities initially permitted some growth in per-capita incomes. By 1300, however, diminishing returns in European agriculture were increasingly obvious. Little unused high-quality land remained to be brought into use; as the population grew, each additional laborer added less and less to the food supply. Not only were there more workers per unit of land, but the remaining additions to Europe's arable land were of lower fertility than those previously farmed.

Landlords' bargaining power rose as that of the peasants declined. The supply of labor was rising relative to that of land. In addition, real food prices rose. Landlords responded by increasing rents and labor services required of their tenants in an attempt to capture a larger share of agricultural output. Not coincidentally, Europe began to experience growing social unrest. In the early fourteenth century, the European economy collapsed in a catastrophic series of plagues (the bubonic plague, or "Black Death", outbreak of 1348–1351 may have killed a third of Europe's population), famines, and wars that left no area untouched.

In some regions, the population decreased by as much as one-half over the next century. The sources of decline were viciously reinforcing. Malnutrition made the people more susceptible to epidemics, and epidemics in turn disrupted agriculture. Wars not only had a direct impact, but armies spread disease and disrupted or destroyed normal economic activities.

The Development of New Economic and Social Systems

During the long, painful recovery from these disasters, some areas of Europe developed new economic and social systems. The decrease in population reduced the pressures of diminishing returns. Now the scarce factor of production was labor rather than land, which improved the peasants' bargaining position with the landlords. More significant for the long run were the changes in agricultural patterns and techniques that resulted from the change in factor proportions. These changes were more conducive to increases in agricultural productivity, which in turn allowed a rise in the nonagricultural portion of the population and further productivity gains. In Western Europe, North and Thomas claim, one crucial change was the development of private property rights to land. The old joint cultivation and common effort system was replaced by one in which individuals owned or rented land and were free to determine their own production methods. In Eastern Europe, the landlords' response to the population decline was an increase in physical coercion, which permanently bound the peasants to the soil as serfs. In Western Europe, however, the old constraints on agricultural change were reduced. Individuals could now try new methods without first gaining the consent of the entire community. Land was increasingly oriented toward production for the market instead of local subsistence needs, the

---

[4] D. North and R. Thomas, *The Rise of the Western World* (New York: Cambridge University Press, 1973).

preservation of the status quo, and risk minimization. A growing portion of exchanges were determined by supply and demand rather than by custom. The results were a reduction in the incidence of famine, rising urban populations, enhanced markets for all types of goods, and better use of human talent.

The Unevenly Rising Ceiling

In a few countries where the new agricultural methods could be combined with low-cost water transportation, the food supply rose at a long-term pace first equaling and then exceeding that of population growth. Technological progress also occurred in mining, metallurgy, textiles, printing, and shipbuilding. These developments were most significant in Britain and the Netherlands after 1450; however, in France, and especially in Spain, their influence was less. Italy and Germany, formerly the centers of medieval technology, urbanization, and trade, were least affected, losing ground to the rest of the region, particularly after 1600. By that time, nation-states were combining the city-states' use of human resources with superior military and political power. The result was a further erosion of the old immobilities, but the process had no more than begun when the voyages of discovery commenced.

Changes in Political Structure

Changes in productive capacity were linked to changes in political power. Central governments gained at the expense of the traditional landowning nobility. In the struggle between the old and new power centers, the kings found allies in the towns and the merchants, who found the legal institutions of fragmented agricultural societies unsuited to their needs and slow to change. Economies of scale in the use of force increased; mercenary armies employing new weapons and tactics (massed pikes, longbows, crossbows, and finally muskets) proved superior to the feudal levies of the nobility, and the cannon made their castles vulnerable. Kings now had a source of political power independent of the nobles and greater than that which could be supported from their own lands—if they could finance it. The new armies were expensive and could not be funded from the traditional revenue sources. In exchange for new laws better suited to trade, finance, and manufacturing, the towns' taxes financed the central governments. Urban success in gaining a quid pro quo for taxes was an important influence on further development. In the Netherlands and England, the consent of parliaments was required before taxes could be levied, and this consent was generally forthcoming only as the property rights of individuals were further secured.[5] Gradually, too, it became clear that it was easier to obtain additional taxes if the economy that generated the revenues was growing. The new central governments did not eliminate war between nations, but they greatly reduced the local conflicts between nobles that had plagued the Middle Ages. Nation-states allowed traders to operate in larger areas under uniform laws and with greater security, and the volume of trade and specialization increased.

Trade

Once it became accepted that both parties to a transaction might gain (in contrast to the medieval view that trade was a zero-sum game), attitudes became more secular and rational. Interest in economic matters, especially trade, increased. Exchanges with distant regions whose customs, standards, and often religions were different posed the necessity of responding to customers' wishes. Tradition could not be invoked among peoples whose values differed from those of their would-be trading partners, and trade thus became profoundly subversive of rules based

---

[5] North and Thomas, *Rise of the Western World*, Chaps. 8–10.

on long-established custom. Cities, whose very existence presupposed some trade, had always shown greater response to new ideas than the countryside. This was especially so where cities controlled their own governments. In Italian and German city-states, innovation flourished and opportunities existed for individuals to rise on the basis of talent even during the Middle Ages. The expansion of trade and urban populations in the fifteenth and sixteenth centuries spread these conditions to wider areas of Europe.

The Advent of Empirical Thought

The relaxation of tradition encouraged a view of the natural world as potentially understandable. Moreover, better knowledge might be usable in improving human welfare. Complete and consistent explanations of observed phenomena were now sought, and answers relying on appeals to faith or references to classical authorities no longer found ready acceptance.[6] Means of accurately transmitting the new knowledge improved. Printing reduced the cost of books, literacy became more widespread, and education began to be oriented toward practical subjects. Although these changes did not result in the complete triumph of attitudes comparable to modern scientific thought, it was obvious that horizons had broadened and that inquiry was becoming more efficient.

The new attitudes fostered different means of allocating human resources. Slowly the idea that people should be allowed to do those jobs that they performed most efficiently gained at the expense of the old rules assigning work on the basis of parents' occupations or social group. For the new jobs produced by innovation, this view developed by default;

there were no traditional groups whose members had always done such work. Selection on the basis of ability had obvious advantages, both for talented individuals and for society. These new methods gained particular favor in Britain and the Netherlands. In these countries, institutions such as guilds, which had formalized the old methods of allocation, began to lose ground. These trends were strongest in Dutch and British export industries, where sellers had little choice about matching competitors' efficiency. Elsewhere in Europe, however, guild control over manufacturing probably increased.

Changes in Religious Thought

The profound religious changes of this period also influenced the economic transformation. It is inappropriate to regard the medieval Catholic Church as fundamentally opposed to economic activity or the development of rational thought. Even though the Church is linked with the doctrines of just price, prohibition of interest, and asceticism, by 1400 these views were seldom enforced. Northern Italy, where the Church's religious control was never in doubt, was the cradle of both the Renaissance and the basic institutions of capitalism. Nor, despite the views of their later disciples, were John Calvin and Martin Luther particularly pro-business. It is true that many of the new ideas were developed further or applied more generally either within Protestant countries or by adherents of minority religions within Catholic nations. The Reformation probably contributed to the separation of religious and secular thought, but no religion of this era advocated freedom of thought, all were prone to violent repression of free expression, and all accepted employment discrimination as an expression of moral policy. The loosened grip of religion on all aspects of inquiry encouraged rationality (the resolution of questions by reference to observed reality).

---

[6] D. Landes, *The Unbound Prometheus: Technological Change and Industrial Development in Western Europe from 1750 to the Present* (Cambridge, U.K.: Cambridge University Press, 1969), Chap. 1.

THE EXPANSION OF EUROPEAN VISION

These changes made the Europe of Christopher Columbus more motivated to mount overseas ventures than it had been in Leif Eriksson's time. It was also far more capable of supporting them. Europeans were interested in the wider world for the sake of knowledge, but now it was also realized that foreign lands might produce material gains. If more and better goods were desired than those locally available, trade appeared to be the most efficient vehicle by which they could be obtained. It was not easy to learn foreigners' techniques, and the limited technology then available could not offset disadvantages in climate, raw materials, or skills. Thus, really different foreign products were hard to duplicate.

Europeans also had reason to feel that the risks of seeking information about distant lands were now less than they had been in A.D. 1000. Improved, more seaworthy ships and navigational techniques that allowed a better idea of the relative locations of origin and destination were the primary catalyst. Mariners now could not only find their way to new regions, they could return home, make accurate maps, and repeat the voyage with growing certainty. The possession of cannon and naval tactics that took advantage of both the new capabilities of European ships and the artillery they carried were less important. Still, the improved military potential no doubt bolstered mariners' confidence in surviving voyages into the unknown. In this era, all strangers were assumed hostile until proven otherwise, and, at least at sea, European technology could offset superior numbers. Prior to this period, Europeans had consistently been militarily inferior, both technologically and numerically, to Asian and African foes. On land this was still the case.

Early Trade Patterns

Some trade had always existed both within Europe and between that continent and Africa and Asia. Europe had maintained some cities since the Roman era, and cities cannot exist without trade. Regional specialization and the exchanges it made possible had increased through the twelfth century and again after 1400. The growth of nation-states reduced the risks of trade and sometimes improved transportation. European regions especially suited to the production of wine, wool, salt, timber, fish, grain, and cloth began to exchange these items for commodities that they could not make as well or as cheaply. The specialization process favored urban growth. Cities were collection and distribution centers. They also provided the services, such as finance, primitive forms of insurance, and transportation that supported trade. Eventually some towns became manufacturing sites as well.

Southern Europeans had exchanged their salt, wine, fruit, and manufactures for the fish, timber, metals, and wool of the north in the Middle Ages. The volume of this trade increased, and great market centers developed. Initially these were in northern Italy and southern Germany. Later, as seaborne commerce replaced overland trade, the Low Countries (modern Belgium and the Netherlands) supplanted southern Germany. The region was better situated to handle seaborne trade between north and south than inland German cities. By the fifteenth century, the focus of intra-European trade had begun to shift from the Mediterranean to the North and Baltic Seas, and to the commodities of the north. Concentration on these bulky, high-volume goods had important repercussions on ship design and navigational techniques. It also gave impetus to the development of institutions designed to accommodate continuous exchanges of large amounts of goods through the reduction of transactions costs.

The Social and Political Impact of Trade

In the new trades, regions that facilitated exchange had important advantages. Profits per unit of bulk commodities were low; the key to riches lay in increasing the quantities exchanged. Institutions that provided better information or reduced the risks of transactions attracted more trade, which in turn allowed the development of processing industries and a host of specialized functions. This specialization raised incomes for both the participants in the basic exchanges and through opportunities to utilize economies of scale. Large volumes of trade with many participants made for competitive markets and an appreciation of their benefits. The large numbers of buyers and sellers made it easier to find customers for or sources of almost any good, further reducing transactions costs.

The North Sea coastal area between France and Germany learned these lessons early, and further realized that the advantages could be copied. The key to maintaining trade volume lay in continuous reduction in transport costs. Inconvenient medieval regulations were abandoned, and new laws facilitating exchanges were developed. Merchants from all areas received fair and, above all, predictable treatment, and information on prices and qualities was accurate. Loans were available at the lowest interest rates in Europe. The political rulers came to recognize that tax revenues from low rates on a large and expanding volume of business could far exceed heavier duties on smaller numbers of transactions, and that it paid to take merchants' views into account, both in taxation and in formulating laws.

The Gains from Trade

If exchange is informed and voluntary, both parties benefit. The gains from trade are greatest, however, when the capabilities and values of the trading parties differ widely. Thus, the profits from trade between Europe and distant areas could be very large. Europeans could not produce the fine fabrics, spices, rugs, jewels, and luxury manufactures of the Orient for themselves. Consequently, they were willing to pay high prices to those bringing such items to European markets.

Obtaining Oriental goods was a slow, difficult, and often dangerous process, especially when overland transport was necessary. A round trip even to the eastern Mediterranean required months, and one to China, years, with a good chance the merchant might never return. Such trade also required that merchants obtain knowledge of the markets and customs of different regions, which generally could be gained only through personal experience. Chinese and Indian goods were expensive to transport, often passing through the hands of several sets of middlemen who took advantage of their monopoly positions. Moslems controlled the trade centers of the Levant, and religious as well as political conflicts raised the risks and costs of trade. The merchants of various Italian cities, especially Venice and Genoa, were the first to overcome these obstacles and develop trade with the Orient. Their access to goods that Europe could obtain nowhere else made the Italian trading cities wealthy, and gains also accrued to regional distributors within Europe.

The Italian cities' trade-generated wealth was obvious to other Europeans. So too, if not as great, was that of the towns of the Hanseatic League, which controlled the origins of trade in northern goods from the Baltic. As usual, the evidence of such gains provoked attempts to emulate the traders' success. Cities and states that did not share in these trade monopolies began to search for alternative products, markets, and routes. Because maritime transportation was much cheaper than overland, it seemed obvious that an all-water route to the Orient would provide its discoverer with a major advantage, especially after the Turks gained control of the Moslem world and imposed new restrictions on trade through the eastern Mediterranean. New goods' potential for gain was equally apparent.

The New Competitors

These incentives encouraged British, French, and Portuguese fishermen to search for new fishing grounds to supplement those of the North Sea and the Baltic. Their intent was to break into markets currently controlled by the Hanseatic League and the Dutch. There was a steady demand in southern Europe for dried, salted, or pickled fish, chiefly herring. The northern fishermen used the proceeds to finance imports from the Mediterranean and the Orient. As they developed their maritime skills, the Atlantic nations of Europe probed farther afield. All nations sent ships north and west into the great ocean, and the Portuguese began to send expeditions south along the African coast. Most of these efforts were financed by individuals or groups of merchants, but Portuguese exploration was increasingly systematic. That nation established a school of navigation in the fifteenth century that both compiled much useful information and developed navigational aids and methods to make further use of it, particularly maps on which Portuguese discoveries were accurately portrayed.[7] During these early voyages, some encouraging discoveries were made.

Mercantilism

The increasing European emphasis on secular values was not confined to private citizens. Rulers began to see that a strong economy was an important base for aspirations to political power. Initially, monarchs had developed policies favoring the interests of merchants and towns as the price for tax revenues to support the struggle against the nobility. But soon it appeared that the costs of military power rose even faster than rulers' ambitions, especially when the opposition was another nation-state. It was easier and safer to obtain revenues from a larger tax base than it was to simply raise rates. In pursuit of the goal of political power, efforts were made to expand and enrich the economy through a series of measures called *mercantilism*. To mercantilists, strong economies were a base for political power. The primary mercantilist policies were:

1. *Economic self-sufficiency* Ideally, all domestically consumed goods were to be produced within the country. If some necessary item could not be made or resources for it could not be found at home, it was to be obtained without granting any gains to the nation's rivals, that is, from distant producers or from the mercantilistic nation's colonies. All imports were to be in raw-material form and imported via domestic shipping to obtain the income generated by transporting and processing. To further these aims, nations were to develop import substitutes and obtain colonies where raw materials could be produced.

2. *An export surplus* Mercantilism discouraged imports, especially of manufactured goods. Simultaneously, it encouraged exports, especially of highly processed items and luxuries. Foreigners were to pay the difference between their purchases and their sales to the mercantilistic nation in gold and silver, which could readily be used to obtain the services of mercenary armies at the time. A brimming treasury could easily be converted to military power.

3. *Widespread government direction and control of the economy in pursuit of these goals* Massive state intervention was to be employed both to mobilize the nation's productive resources and to use them for mercantilist purposes. Labor effort was required from all, and coercion might be employed to discourage "idling" or to divert

---

[7] G. Walton and J. Shepherd, *The Economic Rise of Early America* (New York: Cambridge University Press, 1969), Chap. 1.

labor from "unproductive" activities that neither increased exports nor substituted for imports. Luxury consumption was discouraged at home while it was promoted abroad. To increase exports, the state was to regulate their quality. Imports were fended off by tariffs, subsidies to domestic producers, and efforts to steal rivals' trade secrets while safeguarding any the mercantilist nation might have. Preferential treatment was given to products from colonial possessions.

4. *Strong military and naval forces* As both a means and an end of mercantilist policy, military might and arms production had a high priority.

Obviously every nation cannot sell more to foreigners than it buys from them. Perhaps only a little less clearly, mercantilistic policies were intended to injure rivals; one nation's gains were necessarily assumed to be another's losses. No nation interested in mercantilism followed all its prescriptions. But even partial adherence to mercantilist policies and doctrines could and did produce conflict. From the fifteenth through the seventeenth centuries, Europe was already well supplied with motives for war, and mercantilism added to the list. There were direct economic incentives for conflicts at sea. Most long-distance trade was waterborne, and goods' origins and owners might be difficult to establish. There were plenty of buyers willing to take advantage of bargains and nations that regarded anyone damaging rivals' trade as a public benefactor. Piracy flourished in such an atmosphere. Because mercantilism imposed costs upon consumers in order to generate gains for rulers, with little or no consideration of the relative size of either, it is an early example of rent seeking.

The Increase in Trade
Despite the interferences with trade that mercantilism fostered, Europe's internal and external trade increased after 1450. Transportation costs fell as shipping improved,

markets grew larger, and information became more accurate. Even the armed forces developed under mercantilism played a positive role. The navies were used in peacetime to suppress piracy on some of the most heavily traveled routes, particularly in the North and Baltic Seas. After 1550 this allowed ships to carry more cargo, smaller crews, and lighter armament. Ships designed as specialized cargo carriers rather than quasi-warships were more efficient transport vehicles. Because they did not carry cannon, they could be built more lightly, without the heavy timbers necessary to withstand the guns' weight and recoil. Their crews were only large enough to sail the vessel, rather than to deter attack. In an era when transport costs were a large portion (often 20 to 50 percent) of the price of foreign goods, these changes yielded important savings.[8]

Ironically, the very expansion of trade sought by mercantilism undermined its values. Many countries found it expedient to trade with their neighbors, even if they were political rivals, to export precious metals, and to tolerate higher levels of domestic consumption, which produced more effective incentives to increase output than mercantilist compulsion. Expanded foreign trade produced a fundamental lesson: It was easier to sell foreigners what they wanted to buy than to persuade them to take what mercantilist doctrine said ought to be exported to them. To sell in markets where buyers had alternative sources of supply, exporting nations were forced to substitute economic rationality for mercantilist ideology.

The Oriental Trade
One special difficulty arose in trade with the East. A ready market existed throughout Europe for Oriental goods; any surplus over the importer's domestic needs could easily be

---

[8] C. Cipolla, *Before the Industrial Revolution: European Society and Economy 1000–1700* (New York: Norton, 1976), 254–255. See also S. Morison, *The European Discovery of America: The Northern Voyages* (New York: Oxford University Press, 1971).

re-exported. But the Orient was not willing to accept European goods, especially the manufactures European mercantilists wanted to export, on terms favorable to Europe. Woolens were almost the only finished good in which Europe had a comparative advantage, and the market for them in the East was limited. The one commodity always acceptable in exchange for Oriental goods was precious metals. But aside from the opposition of mercantilist thought, Europe produced barely enough gold and silver for its own monetary needs and internal trade. Consequently, searches for both new sources of precious metal and other goods suitable for Oriental markets were intensified as Europeans sought new trade routes to the East.

Portugal

A tiny country on the Atlantic made the first effective responses to these difficulties, finding both trade routes and the commodities—or, rather, services—to supply them. Long before Columbus sailed, Portuguese efforts to improve navigation had been producing useful methods and information. In 1492 Portugal had not yet reached India by sea, but the southern tip of Africa had been rounded in 1488, indicating that the voyage could be made. This knowledge caused Columbus' proposal to the Portuguese Court for an alternate route to the east to be disregarded. In 1498, the first ship returned to Portugal from India with an enormously valuable cargo of spices. Spices were used both to preserve foods, particularly meat, and to disguise the taste of those stored too long.

Portugal's efforts to develop an all-water route to the Orient had generated some direct benefits as well as geographic information. A trade in gold, ivory, low-grade pepper, and slaves had developed along the west coast of Africa. Islands in the Atlantic had been discovered: Madeira (1333), the Canaries (1341), and the Azores (1431). These, Europe's first non-Mediterranean colonies in several centuries, proved to be valuable producers of wine and sugar. In the North Atlantic, the rich fisheries that eventually made codfish a staple of European diets—perhaps even those of the Grand Banks—were being discovered.

These discoveries, rich as they may have seemed, paled in comparison with those of the next 50 years. In that short space of time, Europeans not only reached areas they had never known existed, but they established trade relations and often even political authority in vast regions.

THE NEW EMPIRES

The characteristics of the populations and products of the newly contacted—if not always newly discovered—regions determined the nature of the economic and political relationships that Europeans developed with them. In India, Europeans found themselves dealing with an ancient, highly developed civilization, skilled in the production of the goods so desired in Europe and well able to maintain its political independence. The tiny crews of the first ships to reach India quickly realized that their only option was trade; they could not hope to control the powerful Indian states. Worse, they had little that India would accept in trade.

The Portuguese Conquests

Notwithstanding these handicaps, the Portuguese quickly became a major factor in India's trade with Europe. It was obvious that the key to this trade lay in control of the Indian Ocean. If they could deny their trading rivals access to the sea routes from India to the Middle East and Egypt, the Portuguese could supplant Venice and Genoa by cutting off the supplies of the Arab middlemen from whom the Italians obtained their Oriental goods.

■ Examples of sixteenth-century European ships include the Portuguese caravel (the larger ship), which was used on exploration voyages; and the galley ship, with its many oarsmen, which was used mainly for Mediterranean warfare.
Source: Bibliothèque Nationale, Paris.

In a breathtakingly audacious move, the Portuguese gained naval dominance of the Indian Ocean. There, thousands of miles from home, the Portuguese navy destroyed the Moslem fleet (some of which, they found, had Venetian gunners aboard) in the Battle of Diu (1509). Once victorious, the Portuguese consolidated their position, using sea power to blockade the outlets to the Red Sea and the Persian Gulf. These measures greatly restricted (but did not eliminate) Arab traders' access to the Indian Ocean and cheap sources of Indian goods.

After this, the Portuguese had no need to control India itself because they controlled its best trade routes to the west. Trade along the traditional routes through the Mediterranean did not disappear, but henceforth the growth in trade would be on the new all-water routes around Africa.[9] Attempts to control the production of Oriental goods would have been futile. Europeans had no expertise in these areas, and they lacked the means to achieve the political control on land provided by their ships and cannon at sea.

Portuguese Limitations

Although the Portuguese gained control of trade in an area stretching from the east coast of Africa to Japan, their hold was precarious. The Portuguese "empire" was a string of small forts and trading posts, all dependent on the support of naval forces never more than barely adequate to meet local challenges. It could not withstand competition from any nation possessing modern sea power.

Portuguese domination of Oriental trade lasted less than a century. The population of Portugal was too small to supply the manpower needed to fully exploit her gains. The labor shortage in Portugal was so severe that it was the only country in Europe to use African slaves domestically as well as in its overseas colonies. Other problems were even more serious. Portugal did not market the proceeds of its Oriental trade within Europe; spices were distributed by the Italians and the Dutch after arrival in Lisbon. The country did not develop industries to produce trade goods for the east or for Africa. Portuguese social institutions were not flexible enough to make maximum use of the available human skills. Royal control over trade became ever more extensive and rigid. Portugal itself was annexed by Spain in 1580, and her eastern empire proved unable to withstand pressure from the Netherlands, which by 1600 had become one of Europe's most formidable sea powers.

---

[9] Walton and Shepherd, *The Economic Rise*, 15–16.

The Netherlands

The Dutch role in Oriental trade was more enduring than that of the Portuguese. Although a small country with a limited population and even more limited natural resources than Portugal, the Netherlands was far more successful in offsetting its deficiencies. Until the latter half of the sixteenth century, the Netherlands was ruled by Spain. The Spanish viewed the Netherlands largely as a source of tax revenues to be devoted to causes that were anathema to the Dutch. From this unpromising base, the Netherlands became the wealthiest country in the world and maintained that position for several centuries. The Dutch made the most of what they had: a favorable location for trade and the talents of their people. Dutch institutions used the country's human resources, allowing more scope for competition and innovation than elsewhere. Consequently, the Netherlands was able to counter rivals' quantitative superiority with efficiency and a shrewd grasp of opportunities.

New Institutions

The Low Countries had shaken free of rigid medieval institutions as early as any other area in Europe. Dutch markets were highly developed and open to merchants of all nations. The Netherlands became Europe's market center and the Dutch its delivery service. The Dutch economy produced little from the nation's own resources except fish; manufacturing in the Netherlands involved the processing of imported raw materials, usually for sale in foreign markets. As middlemen, the Dutch enjoyed no markets in which their position could not be challenged. They had no choice but to compete, and the Dutch were formidable competitors indeed. Their situation forced a pervasive economic rationality on the entire economy. Technology that saved on capital, labor, or materials was adopted and adapted. Access to jobs was decided far more on the basis of ability than elsewhere in continental Europe. The Dutch learned to tolerate religious diversity while other Europeans were still at each others' throats over this issue. The country welcomed refugees possessing useful talents; both French Protestants and English Pilgrims found refuge in the Netherlands. The Dutch nation was not completely free of the grasp of tradition, nor was it a democracy by modern standards, but the Netherlands had come far closer to both than any other country in Europe, with the possible exception of England. The Netherlands of this period has been termed "The Last Great City-State," and the description is apt. Political power lay in the hands of the great merchants, and the country was run by and for its trade interests.

The Dutch achieved a great deal more than high incomes. Theirs was the first economy to achieve sustained growth in per-capita incomes rapid enough to be noticeable during the average citizen's lifetime. The Netherlands' economy also supported accomplishments in other fields; Rembrandt, Erasmus, and many other great names in art and science were indications of the high levels of individual freedom that made rational inquiry and expression possible. Although they preferred to trade, the Dutch were a formidable military power as well, especially on the sea. They used military force to prevent the recovery of Antwerp as a rival to Amsterdam and to replace the Portuguese in the Far East.

The Dutch empire was run on frankly mercantilist grounds; spice crops were produced or destroyed with a view to the income of the Netherlands, not the local producers.

The Limits of Dutch Power

In the long run, however, the Dutch were vulnerable. As a trading nation, the Netherlands was injured by other countries' mercantilist policies, particularly those designed to injure their trade at any cost. They had no secrets that others could not learn, and they failed to develop manufacturing to the extent the

English did. Although their decline was relative, not absolute, the Dutch lost ground to the English and the French in the eighteenth century. Like the Portuguese, their trading empire in the Far East was based on the control of seaborne trade, not commodity production. As a result, there were no extensive Dutch settlements, and their position was weakened as other naval powers expanded their activities into Oriental seas.

SPAIN IN THE NEW WORLD

Spain was the first European country to establish colonies in America, and the Spanish colonies differed from European ventures in the Far East almost as much as Spain herself differed from the Netherlands. There could be no greater difference than that between the attitudes of Spain and the Netherlands. The Dutch were pragmatic, flexible traders; Spain was a nation consumed by ideology. Spanish values ranked religion, tradition, and military prowess far above material success, and these goals were pursued both internally and in foreign policy. In foreign endeavors, the Spanish sought "God, gold, and glory"—not necessarily in that order. The Dutch welcomed religious refugees; Spain created them. A crusade might sound ludicrous to the Dutch, but no term better describes the zeal with which Spain tried to push back the Moslems, reestablish Catholicism in Protestant Europe, and further Spain's great-power aspirations. All these efforts were marked by the utter disregard of costs and economic reality that has always characterized fanaticism.

Spanish Government

Spain's government was controlled by the king and the church. The Spanish merchant community had a much smaller voice than in most other European countries. Spain's military ad-

ventures were both far-reaching and never-ending, and internal policy was largely oriented toward the immediate generation of tax revenues to support her armed forces and allies. Consequently, established revenue sources were favored over new industries, especially if the formation of new activity might involve a short-term loss of taxes. Property was not secure in Spain, particularly in the newer forms possessed by merchants and manufacturers. Even older forms were subject to arbitrary taxation or confiscation; there was no effective popular control over the king's claims on his subjects' wealth. Spanish commercial agriculture was retarded in favor of the *Mesta*, the wool producers' association that furnished most of the country's internal revenues. This policy kept Spanish agriculture unproductive and subjected the nation to recurrent famines.

Spain had achieved a precarious sort of political unity only a few years before Columbus' voyage but it was through the marriage of King Ferdinand of Aragon to Isabella, Queen of Castile, and through the new sovereigns' conquest of Granada in 1491, rather than through the development of new institutions. The nation had been willing to pay a high price for a government that could maintain internal order, but in the long run the cost proved to be excessive. The Netherlands, a far greater source of tax revenues than Spain's New World empire, eventually revolted because of the exactions of the Spanish Crown. In the long run, these policies made change very difficult in Spain. The country did have active merchant communities, particularly in Barcelona and Seville, but merchants and their views were scorned by the soldiers and churchmen who constituted Spain's administrative force.[10]

---

[10] North and Thomas, *The Rise of the Western World*, 127–131.

Columbus and Spain

Given these rigidities, it may seem strange that Columbus sailed from Spain rather than from some country where trade was better regarded. In this case, the centralization of authority in the Spanish Crown proved helpful in assembling the resources for the voyage. Although the Crown did not finance Columbus, it did use political pressure to obtain funds, ships, and men from the cities that actually furnished the support.

Within Spain, the initial exhilaration over Columbus' discoveries quickly became disappointment when it was realized that the West Indies were not the gateway to the Orient, but the outliers to a great barrier to that goal. Nor did the islands offer quick payoffs in themselves. There were some opportunities for ranching and mining on Cuba, Jamaica, and Hispaniola, but the Spanish conquest, mistreatment of the Indians, and European diseases soon all but eliminated the native population. Few Spaniards were willing to go to the New World to work for others, and interest in the New World waned.

The Conquest of the Spanish Main

The conquests of the great Aztec (1519–1521) and Inca (1534–1536) empires of the mainland (which were financed from existing settlements in the islands)[11] sparked another abrupt change in Spanish regard for the potential of the New World. Not only was there enormous loot in precious metals (chiefly silver), but the structure of the Indian societies facilitated the Spanish conquest at ridiculously low cost (Pizarro began the attack on Peru with 134 men), and aided the formation of colonial societies highly congenial to Spanish values.

■ The medallion shown depicts Spanish conquistadore, Hernando Cortez, who is known primarily for having vanquished Mexico's Aztec empire. *Source:* Staatliche Museum of Berlin.

The Spanish could overcome large, highly developed, and warlike Indian empires in the first half of the sixteenth century largely because both the Aztecs and the Incas had formed strongly centralized, hierarchical societies. Spanish military superiority was at best marginal. In both conquests, the Spanish gained access to the rulers and killed them or forced them to cooperate, leaving the opposition leaderless. In addition, there were plenty of Indians willing to ally themselves with the Spaniards to settle tribal scores with the Aztecs and Incas. Once the Indian leadership was eliminated, the Spaniards replaced it with their own, leaving many of the society's basic institutions intact. They were thus directing nations with large agricultural labor forces accustomed to devoting much of their output to the needs of the state.

The values of the Spanish conquistadors were feudal, and they found the new circumstances much to their liking. Even better, the

---

[11] G. Walton and J. Shepherd, *The Economic Rise of Early America* (New York: Cambridge University Press, 1979), Chap 2.

payoff to Spain grew; European mining methods made the mines of Mexico and Peru become far more productive than under the Indians. Because labor appeared abundant and its products were valuable, the Spanish used Indian workers harshly. Labor in the mines killed many Indians, and diseases to which they had no resistance proved even more lethal.[12] Under Spanish rule, the economy of the mainland became one of great landed estates that were owned by the conquistadors or their descendants and provided agricultural products to support the labor forces of the mines and ports. In return for "protection," Indians on these estates were obliged to provide agricultural products and labor services to their Spanish overlords. Feudalism was thus reestablished in the New World even as it died out in most of Western Europe. Spain's primary interest in the colonies was in maintaining the flow of treasure to the royal coffers.

The Columbian Exchange

In the long run, the New World produced items far more valuable than precious metals. Food crops developed by the American Indians—maize (corn), white and sweet potatoes, and manioc—are now staples of the human diet in many parts of the world. Some of these crops have enormously enhanced the productivity of agriculture, particularly in tropical areas. Peanuts, beans, squashes, peppers, tomatoes, and cocoa have also contributed to the quality and variety of human diets. Tobacco has had a less benign influence. Several of these crops, particularly maize, spread rapidly through the Old World after importation from South America.[13]

---

[12] A. Crosby, Jr., *The Columbian Exchange: Biological and Cultural Consequences of 1492* (Westport, Conn.: Greenwood Press, 1972), Chap. 2.

[13] Crosby, *The Columbian Exchange*, Chap. 5.

The Results of Spain's Imperial Rule

The new empire, which at first appeared to be a mercantilist dream come true, in the long run did very little to further Spain's economic development. In the colonies, the feudal attitudes that so impeded change in Spain herself were strongly reinforced. There was no mass migration from Spain to America. New Spain's overlords did not encourage the formation of new attitudes and institutions, and the Spanish Colonial Office was even more rigid. The Spanish ruling class was in a position to extract huge incomes for itself with little regard for the effects on the colonies' economy.

Disease, starvation, overwork, and violence decimated the Indian population of Spanish America. In the century after the conquest, the native population of Peru fell by more than one-half; that of Mexico may have decreased as much as 90 percent.[14] Nor did Spanish rule even produce order. Their new status did not incline the conquistadors to humility. The conquest of the Inca empire required only two years; suppressing rebellions among the Spaniards who accomplished that feat required 34 more.

The Economy of New Spain

Economic activity in Spanish America was largely confined to mining, ranching, and agriculture. European domestic stock thrived on the rich pastures of the New World. But aside from new landownership patterns and the introduction of cattle, sheep, horses, and pigs, there were few innovations. Markets were small; the Spanish rulers were few and the Indians both poor and discouraged from acquiring European goods. In particular, there were few innovations in urban life, and almost no independent merchants. Both institutions

---

[14] Walton and Shepherd, *The Economic Rise*, 31–33.

and ruling-class attitudes in New Spain strongly favored the status quo.

Spain had no interest in changing the colonies' economies as long as they continued to produce revenues; if anything, stability made administration easier. Ironically, the flow of New World treasure probably postponed the adaptive responses to changing conditions within Spain itself that were transforming the Dutch and English economies. Spain used the New World treasure to finance a long and ultimately disastrous series of European wars rather than to stimulate its own internal development. The colonies were kept under tight mercantilist control with their trade regulated by monopolies in Spain whose main purpose was to generate more taxes. Spain produced few of the goods shipped to the colonies; American silver was used to buy supplies for the empire and for Spain itself elsewhere in Europe.

The beneficial results of increased demand and a larger money supply were technological change and increases in production, but these occurred in England, France, and the Netherlands, not in Spain. It seems clear that the sixteenth and seventeenth centuries were a period of substantial technological progress, especially in industry. Manufactured goods' real prices fell, even though rising population generated substantial increases in food prices, indicating much smaller productivity gains in agriculture.[15]

So great were Spain's ideological aspirations that treasure flowed out of the country even faster than it could be acquired. Efforts to increase the Crown's share of New World treasure and ever-increasing domestic taxation were preferred to changes that might have allowed the economy to produce more. Much the same policy was followed in the other parts of the Spanish empire. Indeed, it was increasing tax burdens as much as reli-

gion that drove the Netherlands to fight for and win independence.

Spanish Mercantilism

To better control her colonial trade, Spain restricted all trade to one or two great fleets each year. The flotillas brought European goods to the colonies and returned with treasure. To ensure the collection of taxes, all goods—regardless of their ultimate destination within the colonies—had to be shipped via the Caribbean, a clumsy, slow, and expensive system. Both Spanish colonists and the Europeans who were their source of goods found that direct exchanges were more lucrative. Spain made little effort to adjust its regulations to New World conditions and granted local authorities little autonomy. Their requests for change might not be answered for two years, and often the Colonial Office's response would be a request for more information. Even officials selected for their loyalty to the Crown made adjustments contrary to their instructions from Spain. Spanish colonists began to trade directly—and illegally—with other Europeans, an exchange from which both parties received larger benefits than from legal trade.

European Responses

Other European nations were anxious to obtain some of the treasure produced on the "Spanish Main" (the South and Central American portions of the continent). English, French, and Dutch ships combined trade and piracy as advantage dictated. Spain was frequently at war in Europe, and at times military strategy was turned to economic advantage. In 1628 the Dutch navy captured every ship in the annual treasure flotilla, the most successful of many such efforts. Piracy was endemic in the unsettled political climate of the Caribbean, the more so as privateering (legalized piracy) was widely employed in wartime.

---

[15] Walton and Shepherd, *The Economic Rise*, 21–28.

At times the pirate forces grew strong enough to attack not only shipping, but even some of the major ports, such as Panama (1662) and Porto Bello (1670), through which treasure was shipped to Spain.

The Slave Trade

The decline of the Indian population of Spanish America encouraged a new trade in the Caribbean, that in African slaves. The virtual disappearance of the island natives created a demand for labor from Spanish planters, ranchers, and miners. Early in the sixteenth century, Europeans found that they could earn high profits by buying slaves on the West Af-rican coast and selling them in the New World from Brazil to Mexico. Later, North America furnished an additional market. So lucrative was this business that Europeans fought wars over the control of the slave trade.

Other European Settlements in the Caribbean

Traders, pirates, and navies all required bases. After 1600, non-Spanish Europeans began to acquire islands that the Spanish had not settled, and shortly after, to attempt the conquest of some of Spain's more weakly defended

■ In 1585, Britain's Sir Richard Grenville led the expedition to settle Roanoke Island in order to establish it as a base for raiding Spanish ships.
Source: De Bry, *America,* Part I, 1590.

possessions, such as Jamaica (1664). Even earlier, pirates and traders had established less formal settlements. Occupation led to the production of a variety of goods on the islands: fine woods, a few spices (pimento and ginger), tobacco, coffee, indigo, and preserved beef for ships' stores (boucan, meaning "smoked beef," is the origin of the word *buccaneer*—a reflection of the pirates' alternative occupation).

The islands' real value became apparent to Europeans only after sugar cultivation was introduced, chiefly after 1640. Sugar was an ideal mercantilist good; it was in high demand throughout Europe, yet could not be produced there, save in a few Mediterranean islands. Better still, Caribbean production replaced imports from the Spanish empire and Brazil, and any surplus beyond domestic needs could readily be sold to other European nations. Large plantations worked by slave labor had lower production costs than other forms of organization. Many Caribbean islands became highly specialized sugar producers, performing few of the other activities necessary to sustain their populations. Instead, they used their exports of sugar to finance imports of much of their food and nearly all their manufactured goods and to pay for the services of foreign shippers.[16]

Sugar production resulted in another large market for slaves, and not merely because the demand for the product expanded. With slaves readily available at low prices, it was cheaper for planters to work them to death and rely on continuous imports of fresh slaves rather than on natural reproduction to maintain a labor supply. Tropical diseases also reduced slaves' longevity. So valuable were the Sugar Islands to Europe that in 1763 England seriously debated which of its conquests from France to retain after the Seven Years' War— all of Canada or Guadeloupe and a few other tiny islands.

The Atlantic Economy

As succeeding pages will make clear, understanding the economic history of Latin America and especially the Caribbean is essential to comprehension of the economic development of the North American colonies. All European colonies in the Americas were parts of an integrated economic system, and in some cases their relations with each other were fully as important as those with Europe.

NORTH AMERICAN SETTLEMENTS

Europeans colonized the Caribbean and the mainland from Mexico south to Argentina more than a century earlier, and initially in larger numbers, than they did North America. Even after the first settlements on that continent were established in the sixteenth and seventeenth centuries, their growth was very slow and punctuated with disasters. In 1565, the Spanish established St. Augustine in what is now Florida to protect the route of their treasure flotillas. But the town and its hinterland produced nothing that could not be obtained elsewhere, and St. Augustine remained little more than a garrison post.

Farther north, prospects were no better. There were no obvious rewards of the type

---

[16] Several economists, notably Harold Innes and Douglass North, have propounded growth theories in which the development of an economy is based upon the growth of its export commodity, or "staple." They contend that the overall pattern of development depends upon the nature of the export industry and the effects of its expansion upon other sectors, as well as the disposition of the income that it generates. If the staple's production expands rapidly and has substantial linkages with the rest of the economy as a source of markets or supplier of goods and services that aid the development of other sectors, or if a substantial part of the income generated by the staple is plowed back into the economy, the staple's growth will generate overall economic development. See H. Innes, *The Fur Trade in Canada* (Toronto: University of Toronto Press, 1935) and D. North, *The Economic Growth of the United States, 1790–1860* (New York: Norton, 1961).

that beckoned from the Caribbean or the Spanish Main. The Indians had little of immediate value to Europeans except furs, the populations were too small to furnish a labor force if subdued, and conquest of the less developed tribes in both North and South America often proved much more difficult than had that of the great Indian civilizations. Tribes lacking cities to attack, agriculture to tie them to a given area, or rigid leadership patterns proved able to resist European domination for long periods, sometimes centuries.

Early Exploration and Settlements

Shortly after the resumption of European contact with North America, it became clear that if Europeans were to obtain anything from the area, they would have to do so themselves. Rumors of gold, highly developed cities, and easy trade routes to China all proved disappointing. (Hope died hard: In 1634 a French explorer landed in what is now Little Suamico, Wisconsin, in full regalia for the Chinese court; several expeditions from seventeenth-century Virginia hoped to find the Pacific Ocean just beyond the Blue Ridge.) Even though the first voyages to North America followed closely in Columbus' wake (Cabot in 1497), serious attempts at settlement did not occur for half a century, and none succeeded until Jamestown (1607) and Quebec (1608), whose success was anything but clear for years more. Permanent settlements with a high degree of self-sufficiency would be required before the full potential of North America could be assessed. The Caribbean, South America, the Orient, and Europe itself seemed to offer better prospects than did North America.

Early attempts at settlement did nothing to change this opinion. There were at least two Spanish, four French, and several English efforts north of Florida in the sixteenth century. All failed, and several colonies vanished without a single survivor. Europeans

held wildly unrealistic ideas of New World conditions that all but guaranteed disaster. The English, for example, believed that latitude determined climate. To play it safe, they established a colony well south of England, at the latitude of the Riviera. The survivors of a winter at the mouth of Maine's Kennebec River claimed that the theory needed major modification. The French tried to establish a colony on Sable Island, a windswept sandbar in the midst of the North Atlantic's worst weather, from 1598 to 1603. At the end of that time, they rescued 11 insane and probably cannibalistic survivors.[17]

Explorers and settlers alike never seemed to realize that the feasts with which the local Indians greeted them indicated hospitality rather than an unlimited food supply. Attempts to obtain food from the Indians were a frequent source of trouble in the early days of several settlements and may have caused at least one colony's disappearance. Even after Europeans became more realistic about American conditions, other mistakes continued. Many colonies were badly located in terms of harbors, potential food and water sources, defense, and disease. Survivors of these early efforts had grim tales of hunger, deadly new diseases, Indian raids, and extremes of climate. For Europeans, hot American summers were almost as great a surprise as the cold and snow of the new land's winters. If only the most fortunate of the earliest settlers survived to return to Europe, and none improved his welfare, there is little wonder that Europe concentrated its efforts elsewhere. Until early in the seventeenth century, St. Augustine and a few fishermen sun-drying their catches on northeastern shores made up the entire colonial effort in eastern North America.

---

[17] Morison, *The European Discovery: Northern Voyages,* 480–481.

FRENCH AND DUTCH COLONIES

In view of North American conditions and the region's apparent potential, the fur trade appeared to offer the best chance to get quick returns from small investments overseas. Because the French and Dutch intended to trade with the Indians for furs rather than do their own trapping, only a few people would be needed and returns would not be long delayed. Little long-term investment was necessary to establish trading posts. Both nations had gained some experience in fur trading as a sideline to their fishing ventures in the North Atlantic.

The Dutch in America

Given their objectives, the Dutch picked a good location. In 1614, they established a post at Fort Orange (Albany, New York) that gave the easiest access to the interior on the Atlantic coast south of Canada. New Amsterdam, on the present site of New York City, was settled later. Fort Orange possessed the essential element for success in the fur trade—access to a vast hinterland by low-cost water transportation.

Rather surprisingly, in light of their policies at home, the Dutch did not establish colonial institutions particularly conducive to individual effort and initiative. No real effort was made to encourage settlement in New Netherlands, perhaps because the limited Dutch population already had so many other alternatives, both in their homeland with its growing incomes and in other trade locations. Indeed, some policies discouraged mass settlement. It was not easy for the average Dutch citizen to obtain clear title to land that had any real value. Farms had to have access to water transportation so produce could be brought to market. But much of the land along the Hudson River was granted in great estates to landowners called *patroons*, who were more willing to rent land than to sell it. The patroons' rental terms were more favorable to tenants than were those in Europe, but few people were willing to risk the Atlantic voyage and settlement in a new land without the prospect of landownership. Patroons had near-feudal political and social control over their estates, and because their boundaries were ill-defined, title to land abutting their immediate claims was uncertain.[18] Land along the coast was somewhat easier to obtain, but Dutch expansion to the north was soon restricted by Yankees moving down from New England. Movement to the south was contested by Swedes and other English settlers. Although New Netherlands did grow and even managed to annex the Swedish settlements in the Delaware Valley and New Jersey, ambitious Dutch settlers apparently saw better opportunities elsewhere.

Much of the population of New Netherlands was not Dutch; one governor claimed to rule people speaking 18 different languages. The fur trade never had the profit potential of Dutch ventures in other parts of the world, and the colony was always more or less neglected. When the English assaulted it in 1664 (and offered the inhabitants liberal terms of government), neither the Dutch authorities nor the colony's inhabitants offered resistance. But the English did recognize the patroons' land claims, and the colony grew slowly for a long time.

---

[18] S. Kim, *Landlord and Tenant in Colonial New York: Manorial Society 1664–1775* (Chapel Hill, N.C.: University of North Carolina Press, 1978). Since patroons realized they had to attract tenants to derive any revenues from their estates, the costs of obtaining land in New Netherlands differed little from those in nearby colonies. Leases were transferrable by tenants, and rates were low. The main effect was on settlers' choices of location, and the contrast with other areas offering opportunities for full ownership of land.

French North America

It might be argued that even with correct policies, the Dutch simply lacked sufficient resources to establish a successful North American colony. But France was different. In the early seventeenth century, France had the largest population in Western Europe and a government both able and willing to marshall the resources for a colony. But although the French endured for over a century and a half and left an indelible cultural imprint, New France too was eventually taken over by the English.

The Fur Trade

Once again, the root of New France's long-term problem appears to lie in the colony's orientation toward the fur trade. French decisions, given that choice, were excellent, but in the long run the selection of the colony's basic industry was a fatal handicap. The location of their initial settlement in the St. Lawrence River valley gave the French the best route to the interior of North America on the entire East Coast, and they later gained control of the Ohio and Mississippi River valleys as well. But the fur trade had implications for the settlement and conduct of the colony that hindered expansion and eventually made its survival impossible. The pursuit of furs encouraged the French to explore the interior and establish territorial claims, but it also reduced their ability to hold territory devoted to that purpose.

Too great a production of furs from any area wiped out the animal populations on which the trade was based, so the fur trade's volume could be expanded only by increasing the territory in which it was conducted. Territorial expansion was costly; transportation expenses were high, and there was the ever more complicated problem of maintaining good relations with mutually antagonistic tribes. Samuel de Champlain's early intervention in one tribal war (1616) was a serious

mistake; it earned the French the lasting enmity of the Iroquois Federation. This powerful group of tribes menaced New France's communications with the interior and, for many years, the very existence of the colony itself. Most of all, the fur trade depended on the continued existence of the wilderness and of good relations with the Indians, who actually collected the furs. The French were traders, not trappers.

Old Values in a New Land

The fur trade's primacy sharply restricted the type and extent of other economic activity within New France. Above all, European-style agriculture and the population densities it allowed were utterly incompatible with the fur trade.[19] Because New France had to produce its own food, this precluded a large population. Given the difficulties of transatlantic communication, the fact that the St. Lawrence was icebound for at least four months each year, and the memory of New France's forced surrender in 1632 when the English captured that year's supply ships, dependence on outside food supplies was unacceptable. A small population allowed little specialization and thus lower productivity gains and increases in incomes. Limited specialization increased the colony's dependence on France. The French government's attitude toward migration to the colony was consistent with its choice of New France's primary activity. Little was done to encourage French citizens to settle in the New World, except for some efforts to provide New France with a continuous reservoir of military manpower. Some Frenchmen who might have made unusually productive colonists were forbidden to emigrate. Unlike the English, who allowed or even encouraged troublesome religious minorities to form colonies within the

---

[19] For an excellent discussion of the land needs of Indians versus those of agricultural peoples, see S. Lebergott, *The Americans: An Economic Record* (New York: Norton, 1984), Chap. 2.

empire, the French either exiled their Protestants or allowed them to settle in private colonies outside the governmental protection of France. The Huguenots made two such efforts; one colony was abandoned, and the second was wiped out by Spain. When they left France for Britain, the Netherlands, or the British colonies, the Huguenots compiled an unusual record of economic achievement. France forced them to make their contributions to other nations' economies, very much to her own loss.

The Attraction of Landownership

If there was one lure that proved irresistible in attracting seventeenth-century Europeans to North America, it was the prospect of acquiring land. Landownership meant more than mere income to Europeans; it was the major determinant of social status as well. The ownership of land—especially a lot of land—conveyed standing unmatched by any other form of wealth. But immigrants to New France could not normally obtain clear title to land; they found that much of the colony's desirable acreage was in the hands of landlords who imposed conditions of tenancy not much more favorable than those of France itself. New France was also a closely controlled, stratified society. Even within the limits imposed by the small population, there was not much scope for individual initiative in the settled areas.

Despite these limitations, the French had remarkable success. They were proficient traders. Even though their trade goods were higher priced and qualitatively inferior to those of the English, they compensated through lower transportation costs and better relations with the Indians. Until the Hudson's Bay Company was established in 1670, the French alone had access to the area that produced the highest-quality furs. Because they regarded the fur trade as a long-term proposition, the French got along better with the Indians than did the British, for whom the fur trade was generally a prelude to settlement and the Indians a potential nuisance. In the context of the era, French efforts to Christianize the Indians implied an obligation to treat them more nearly as equals. The English policy of mass settlement and agricultural development made the coexistence of English and Indian cultures impossible. The French needed the Indians both as trade partners and as military allies; the English did not.

French Limitations

In the long run, however, concentration on the fur trade made New France unable to resist English and colonial pressure. Not only did it result in population too small to hold New France, but the income it produced was never enough to give France a real incentive to protect its colony. The French were willing to cede all of New France to Britain in order to retain a few Caribbean sugar islands at the close of the Seven Years' (French and Indian) War in 1763. When French authority in North America finally ended, there were about 60,000 persons of French descent in all of New France. Pitted against them were over two million people in British North America.

New France was vast, but the physical presence of French settlers was restricted to a narrow strip of settlement in the St. Lawrence valley, a few locations in the Maritimes, and, in the eighteenth century, New Orleans and its environs. Elsewhere, there were only isolated forts, trading posts, and a few tiny villages. Only geography and British military ineptitude enabled the French to retain control as long as they did.

ENGLISH COLONIES

In terms of wealth, indigenous population, and the generation of institutions suited to the new conditions, the English colonies developed far beyond those of any other nation.

Thus, it might be assumed that the English avoided the mistakes made in the early years of other nations' colonies. Such is not the case; the British made as many or more errors as the French, Dutch, or Spanish. But the English did learn from their mistakes and adapted better to New World conditions than did their rivals.

The first successful colony was established at Jamestown in Virginia (which then connoted the entire Middle Atlantic coast) in 1607. Yet for some years after the initial landings, the colony's survival was in doubt. Many lessons had to be learned by trial and error in circumstances where the stakes were survival. European experience was often a hindrance rather than a help. Ironically, even those nations that had gone farthest in developing flexible institutions seemed determined to reestablish in their colonies the very systems they had discarded at home. It seems particularly ironic that such efforts were made in Virginia by the English; the initial ownership of the colony was vested in a private, profit-seeking corporation. Nor did it appear that subsequent colonies took the hard-won experience of their predecessors to heart; the same recipes for disaster were repeated, and the same lessons learned through suffering and death.

England in the Seventeenth Century

No country except the Netherlands had produced institutions so favorable to economic development as had seventeenth-century England. The country had settled its form of government early and had been wise enough to exploit its island position in trade, limiting its participation in continental wars. England had an able merchant community that was, as new participants in markets generally are, both responsive to new opportunities and engaged in a search for new trade routes and markets.

Like the Netherlands, England had to compete its way into established markets.[20] In the process, she had gone as far as any European nation in freeing her economy from medieval regulations intended to preserve the status quo. As befits interlopers, the English were opposed to monopolies—at least to those that restricted English opportunities.

Royal grants of monopoly at home encountered increasing opposition on both economic and political grounds (they were sold by the sovereign, giving the crown a revenue source outside the control of Parliament). The English foreign trade in both woolen textiles and fish had been developed in the face of foreign monopolies. English labor was as free and mobile between occupations as the Dutch, and a wide spectrum of the population, from nobles to common laborers, took advantage of economic opportunity with less restraint from established custom than elsewhere. Like the Dutch, the English developed markets and the institutions that improved their performance. English law was highly favorable to property rights in ideas as well as physical possessions. Coupled with a receptive attitude toward new technology (England sought new methods, welcomed foreigners possessing them, and rewarded its own inventors), this produced a climate in which new ideas were generated and rapidly adopted.[21] Because they were forced to compete their way into established markets, the English had developed an appreciation of competitive efficiency and the institutions that promoted it.

Other English institutions reflected this attitude. Education, at least outside the ancient universities, was increasingly practical and vocational, which aided the transmission of new

---

[20] W. Parker, *Europe, America, and the Wider World* (New York: Cambridge University Press, 1984), 36, 44–45.

[21] Hughes, *Industrialization and Economic History: Theses and Conjectures*, Chaps. 3–4; Landes, *The Unbound Prometheus*, Chap. 2; North and Thomas, *The Rise of the Western World*, Chap. 12.

information. New types of business organizations had been developed to pool the savings of large numbers of people and reduce individual investors' risks—for example, the joint stock companies. By 1600, England was technically proficient, possessed great maritime capabilities, and had an ambitious merchant class eager to employ these advantages along the lines of economic rationality. Although the influence of tradition, nepotism, and other productivity-inhibiting influences on the use of human talent was still strong, the assessment of human talent was growing more pragmatic. Because the most promising avenue for success open to young men with more ambition than inherited status was "adventures" (anything from piracy or mercenary soldiering to trade and exploration), there was no lack of talent for the merchants' aspirations.

Early English Ventures in the New World

English merchants, particularly those of the West Country (Bristol) who had not yet found secure markets and trade routes, were active in backing exploration, trade, and colonies in the New World. The early ventures were disappointing. Cabot's first voyage (1497) discovered nothing but fish, and he never returned from the second. Several efforts to establish settlements failed. Martin Frobisher's voyages to Baffin Island (1576–1578) generated an initial burst of euphoria when it appeared he had discovered not only gold but the Northwest Passage, but both failed to materialize. Exploration was costly, and there was no guarantee that the information it generated could be retained by those who had financed the voyages; the bulk of the benefits might accrue to others. The English government was interested in discoveries but unwilling to finance them. Colonies might be more lucrative

than exploration, but founding them required even larger sums. In North America, any returns from colonies would probably be long delayed. Even worse, these returns were more likely to accrue to the colonists themselves than to their financial backers in England. The Caribbean and the Orient appeared to offer better prospects, and action followed impression. In 1640, Barbados had a larger British population than the Virginia and Massachusetts Bay colonies combined.[22]

Virginia

One of the new joint-stock companies, the London Company, financed the 1607 investment at Jamestown. In terms of return on investment, the financiers' experience was even more disastrous than the settlers'. A very few of the first arrivals in America survived, but the investors lost every penny. A second colony was attempted in Maine at the same time, and its few survivors returned to England the next spring.

The Initial Struggle
Although the first batch of colonists had strong economic motivation—they had come to America to get rich—they had no idea of the conditions that awaited them. The goals assigned them by the London Company reflected complete innocence of the conditions under which the colonists would live, work, and die. The colonists' instructions were to produce items that England currently had to import including wine, silk, and tropical crops, to search for precious metals and copper, and to find a new trade route to the Orient. At least in England, it was expected that all these goals could be met quickly and easily. Certainly the initial group of settlers was prepared only for easy achievements; very few

---

[22] V. Parry, *The Age of Reconnaissance* (New York: World Publishing, 1963), 276.

■ Comparison with modern maps quickly reveals the inadequacy of these seventeenth-century maps of the Chesapeake region.
Source: Courtesy of Elizabeth Widdicombe.

were accustomed to sustained hard work, and fewer still possessed skills useful in the new surroundings. Jamestown had plenty of soldiers, ex-servants, and "gentlemen," but few carpenters or farmers. The plans for the colony's operation made the worst of these disadvantages. Jamestown was to be operated along military lines; the men marched to work in the fields to the beat of a drum. Whatever was produced was to be shared equally among all the colonists. There were no women in the first group—a strong indication that few if any of the settlers intended to stay in Virginia.

It quickly became apparent that the colony would have to produce its own food. Prior events should have indicated that; Sir Walter Raleigh's Roanoke colony had depended on English supplies. When the relief expedition bringing them arrived three years behind schedule, in 1590, it found no trace of the col-

■ This view of Jamestown in 1607, constructed from available evidence, strikingly reveals the limited size of the colony.
Source: The Bettmann Archive.

ony. Transportation costs were too high to depend on imported provisions, even had communications with England not been slow and uncertain. Jamestown had another reason to produce its own food: For the first few years the colony produced nothing for its English backers but requests for more supplies and people, and even the most optimistic investors were beginning to seek ways of cutting costs. Achieving self-sufficiency in food was not easy. The colony's labor force was unaccustomed to farm work of any sort, and conditions in Virginia were particularly difficult. There were no draft animals, the tools were not suited to American conditions, and clearing virgin forests was brutally hard work under the best conditions. Given the character of the settlers, the conditions under which they la-

bored, the bitter disappointment that grew as hopes for quick fortunes evaporated, and the manner in which output was distributed, the work effort was far below the colony's meager potential. A system better designed to discourage maximum effort from each individual could hardly be imagined. The communal agricultural system not only produced far less food than possible, but it made change and adaptation to Virginia conditions more difficult. Starvation added to the toll already imposed by malaria, Indian raids, and work in a climate much harsher than England's. Over half the original 120 settlers died within the first two years. For the first decade, additional immigrants fared even worse.[23]

---

[23] Walton and Shepherd, *The Economic Rise*, 37–38.

The Necessity for Change

In such conditions the colony could not survive unless changes were made. Work rules were altered to force a contribution from every individual ("He that doth not work, neither shall he eat"). Later a transition was made to greater individual responsibility. The first step was to allow each person a small plot of his own to farm as he wished, with all produce the property of the owner. After 1623, the communal effort was abandoned; each settler was assigned his own land and expected to support himself from the results. Not every colonist proved up to the harsh new system, but it was a decided improvement over its predecessor. Where adaptation to new conditions was so important, it encouraged a variety of methods and rapid innovation of those that appeared successful. Jamestown's margin above starvation was so tiny that anything less than the maximum effort from all concerned or anything that reduced the incentives of the capable was intolerable. Had the colony's founders possessed knowledge of effective methods when settlement occurred, a cooperative effort might have been more successful, but the death rate was grim evidence that such information was lacking. To be successful, planning requires realistic goals, accurate information, and a knowledge of the available resources and techniques. The London Company's directors lacked all three.

Incentives were further strengthened by the arrival of women. This encouraged effort likely to pay off only over time, because now settlers might regard their migration as permanent and attempt to build up estates for their families. Even so, the colony barely survived the first years. On one occasion a relief expedition from England arrived to find the colonists already abandoning Jamestown.

The Need for Exports

Solving Jamestown's food problems did not ensure the survival of the colony. The chief remaining problem was that the colony produced almost nothing with which to finance imports from England. Without English tools and manufactured goods, the colonists could not hope to live much better than the Indians. But with no return on previous investment, the London Company could not be expected to provide for them indefinitely. The company was reorganized to provide additional capital. Nevertheless, it failed in 1623, and the colony's charter reverted to the Crown.

Tobacco

The colony desperately needed a larger population, but potential settlers were reluctant to brave the appalling death rates without the prospect of higher incomes. Even the chance to acquire land meant little if the land could not produce something salable. Tobacco changed this situation. In 1612 the colony began to produce tobacco, and Virginia found its export staple. The Virginia Company (the reorganized, renamed London Company) and even King James abandoned their objections to the "stinking weed" when it appeared that tobacco was an ideal mercantilist commodity. Virginia tobacco not only replaced imports from the Spanish colonies but could be re-exported to Europe in huge quantities. Production required unskilled labor, for the most part, and tobacco was easy to ship. Although it could be grown on farms of any size, there were economies of scale in curing operations and in the maintenance of soil fertility that favored large-scale producers. The prospect of cheap land in Virginia became more alluring with the advent of a profitable cash crop, and migration to the colony was stimulated.

Solving the Labor Problem

The demand for labor in Virginia rose sharply, and the colonists began to offer inducements, chiefly in the form of grants of land, both to emigrants and to those who arranged their passage. The voyage to Virginia cost about as much as the average Englishman earned in a year, so few new arrivals had been able to pay their own way. Typically, the emigrant's pas-

■ Tobacco plantations were the primary source of income for Virginia and Maryland farmers.

sage fees were paid by a ship captain or Virginia planter, who in turn received the rights to three to seven years' labor from the new arrival. This contract could be transferred to other employers, so for its duration, the emigrant was an assured labor source for its owner. In return for labor, the indentured servant received food, clothing, and other maintenance, but no wages. Training was also given—a valuable commodity in the very different environment. When the indenture expired, the now-free individual was entitled to "dues" intended to make him or her self-supporting (and to increase the incentives to fulfill the indenture contract): a plot of land, tools, and sometimes a small cash payment. The risks of such a program were high. The transatlantic passage alone killed an estimated one-fifth of those attempting it in the early years, and the emigrant was exposed to new diseases and hard labor. Such circumstances, when they became known in England, were no spur to recruitment, but as time passed the survival rate in Virginia improved and most indentures were voluntary. Demand for labor in Virginia continued, and awards of land were made to new settlers, their families, and those arranging the migration of others.[24]

Involuntary "Immigrants"

Some indentured servants had little choice but to emigrate. They were prisoners from various sources—common criminals, victims of the civil and political turmoil that beset Britain (especially Ireland and Scotland) in the seventeenth and eighteenth centuries—or victims of kidnappers.[25] Recent research has indicated that only a minority of indentured servants fit this category, but there is evidence that servants furnished a less than ideal work force. Planters not only had to buy the servants' contracts, maintain and train them, and furnish freedom dues on the contracts' expiration, they had to accept the risk that servants might die or run away before the contracts matured. As the colony's population and knowledge of survival skills grew, it became easier for servants to escape. There were no means of identification, such as fingerprints or Social Security numbers, and few persons were well known more than a few miles from home. In Virginia it was not wise to inquire too closely into the backgrounds of "strangers," given the pasts of even some now-respectable settlers. As mortality rates declined, a greater proportion of servants survived their indentures, and freedom dues imposed higher costs on planters. Political problems within the colony also increased with the growing numbers of landless workers and small farmers. (Bacon's Rebellion in 1676 pitted frontiersmen and the

landless against the established planters and the governor.)

Because European labor was expensive and risky, the colonists tried to find other workers. The local Indians were impossible to retain on the plantations, and efforts to force them into such labor led, understandably, to violent conflict. Europeans had long employed Africans as slave labor in the Caribbean, the Atlantic islands, and South America, and, as the seventeenth century wore on, indentured Europeans were increasingly supplemented by blacks. These involuntary immigrants were sold by governments concerned only with the price obtained for them, rather than their long-term prospects in America. Before long they were regarded as "servants for life," and in 1664 slavery was declared to be hereditary.

The Economics of Slavery

The initial price of a slave was higher than that of an indentured European (an indication of the treatment both races received on the Atlantic passage), but the slave's services were obtained for life, and if slaves had children, a permanent source of labor was obtained. Once both types of labor began to survive beyond the usual indenture period, slaves became cheaper labor than indentured servants. In addition, it was much more difficult for blacks to escape successfully. Still, as late as 1700 only 11 percent of the colonial population was black, although by then the slave population was growing faster than the colonial aggregate.

Plymouth and Massachusetts

The Pilgrims and Plymouth

Settlement in New England began shortly after that in Virginia. Plymouth was founded in 1620, New Hampshire in 1623, and Massachusetts Bay in 1629. The Pilgrims repeated most of Jamestown's errors and added a few of their own. They paid in starvation, disease, and death before learning the lessons of sur-

---

[24] E. Perkins, *The Economy of Colonial America* (New York: Columbia University Press, 1980), 69–70.
[25] A. Smith, *Colonists in Bondage* (Chapel Hill, N.C.: University of North Carolina Press, 1947), 3.

vival in the New World. The colony's primary motives were noneconomic. The Pilgrims were apparently as concerned with getting away from Europe for religious reasons as they were with the conditions they would encounter in their new home. The unsurprising result was that the history of Plymouth's early years reads like a list of the things to avoid when founding a colony.

Unlike Jamestown's settlers, the Pilgrims were closely knit by religion and possessed a sense of group unity. At the same time, they may have had even less material and intellectual equipment to face the rigors of settlement. They were largely townspeople, lacking the skills required in the new environment. They seem to have chosen additional people over tools or other equipment. The Pilgrims were not eager to include outsiders who might have skills they lacked. They expected to settle in a mild climate just north of Virginia, but delays, supply shortages, and navigational errors forced them to come ashore nearly 500 miles north of their intended landfall. They arrived in November, with no time to search for a good site. The group was already weakened by sickness when the Plymouth site was chosen.

Plymouth's chief attraction was cleared fields formerly cultivated by an Indian tribe wiped out by disease a few years previously. (To the Pilgrims, the Indians' demise was clear proof of God's blessing.) The Pilgrims by that time did not have the manpower to clear enough land for European-style agriculture.[26] That winter, food supplies were very limited and disease was especially deadly among the cold, half-starved little group. By spring only 39 survivors from the original group of 106 remained. As if the difficulties imposed upon them were not affliction enough, the Pilgrims tried the same form of communal agriculture that had failed in Jamestown. When it was finally abandoned for a system of family-owned and cultivated plots, the work effort greatly increased. Women and children who had not worked in the fields when all crops were shared began to do so when each family became responsible for its own welfare.[27]

The Costs of a Closed Community

In such circumstances, the courage and perseverance that sustained Plymouth were dubious assets. Even after survival was assured, the colony's growth was very slow. The harbor was not well suited to shipping, and the soil was far less fertile than Virginia's. More important was the lack of exports; in addition to their ongoing requirements of tools and manufactured goods, the Pilgrims had borrowed part of the funds to establish their colony. Shipments of what was available—furs and timber—were made, but, even though Plymouth established trading posts along the coast and in the interior, only small amounts of furs could be obtained. Timber was simply too difficult to ship. The company that had financed the Pilgrims soon gave up and allowed them to buy the colony's charter at a fraction of the original sum. The small population did not permit any great degree of specialization, so incomes rose slowly.

The Puritans and the Massachusetts Bay Colony

Later colonies took some of the experience of Jamestown and Plymouth to heart; a few even made efforts to prepare for American conditions. Nine years after the founding of Plymouth, the Puritans established the Massachusetts Bay Colony. They sought information about their destination, sending an advance party to choose a site for the settlement. The results were an excellent harbor at the site of Boston and more than 80 deaths in a group of 180 before the main group of

---

[26] J. Furnas, *The Americans: A Social History of the United States* (New York: Putnam, 1969), 34, 55.

[27] Hughes, *Industrialization*, 112.

settlers arrived. The Puritans made other preparations; they sought advice from Captain John Smith, of Virginia fame, and others. Despite their strong religious feelings, the Puritans admitted, even recruited, "strangers" who possessed skills not found within their ranks. In a world where most religions extended tolerance chiefly to those too strong to be exterminated for any deviation in faith, this was a significant concession. There would be no interference from English financiers; the colony was controlled by its members and brought its charter to Massachusetts. Finally, the Puritans came in large numbers, nearly 20,000 in the first decade. A population of this size allowed a good deal of specialization, which resulted in more and better products at lower cost. Within the first two decades, Massachusetts had established two colonies of its own, Rhode Island and Connecticut, both in part due to religious differences. It had also set up trading posts inland and on the Maine coast.

Early New England Agriculture

New England agriculture never produced much more than enough to feed its own population, and by 1700 not even that. Yankees quickly realized that their fields would not produce the exports they needed, so they turned to the sea and the forest and sent New England's products to areas specializing in other goods. As early as 1635, Massachusetts had begun to "look to the West Indies for a trade," sending fish, leather and wood products, and livestock to the Sugar Islands, and providing shipping services as well. In return, New England received sugar, rum, molasses, and gold, which could be exchanged for European products. Few New England farmers depended on crops alone for income. Some turned out preserved meat and dairy products; others spent the long winters producing tools, shoes, harnesses and other leather goods, barrel staves, and virtually anything else that could be made from wood. Many farmers were

fishermen between spring planting and fall harvests and lumbermen or traders during the winter.

Because of the multitude of small-scale producers, each also a consumer, concentration points for exports were necessary. Towns were important in New England from the beginning of settlement. Urban concentrations were also encouraged by activities such as shipbuilding, which required large labor forces. To New Englanders, shipbuilding furnished a means of transporting their own exports, a device for earning transport charges from other areas, and an export good, ships, which were one of New England's few exports that could be sold in Britain. For the first century of settlement, most New England farmers lived in villages rather than amidst their own fields.

Maryland

It was possible to learn from others' experience in the tobacco colonies also. Founded in 1634, Maryland benefitted by the examples of previous settlements. The colony was intended to serve two purposes: to be a refuge for English Catholics, and to generate income from a large land grant that the Calvert family had received from the king. To meet the latter goal, it was necessary to admit members of other faiths. It was soon obvious that the colony's owners were more tolerant than its settlers. It proved difficult to combine settlers of different faiths, particularly those who provoked animosities among the English Protestants the way Catholicism did. Nevertheless, the colony prospered. Its soil and climate were so similar to Virginia's that there was no groping for an export good. It soon became apparent to the proprietors of the colony that they could obtain income from their land only by attracting settlers to it. This they did by making land available on easy terms, with only nominal quitrents (annual payments to the proprietor) and without the regulations imposed by European landlords. Although they had the legal right to do so, the proprietors of Maryland did not establish a hereditary nobility or impose restrictions on the sale or use of land. The combination of easy access to land and ready markets for its products attracted settlers, and Maryland was the most successful of the early British colonies in North America.

THE FIRST COLONIES

By 1650, Europeans were firmly established on the Atlantic coast of North America. There were perhaps 50,000 Europeans (most of them English) and between 1,000 and 2,000 black Africans scattered from Canada to Florida. Long stretches of coastline without European settlements still remained; even within the colonies, most land was still forested. Nevertheless, further growth now appeared probable. Survival was no longer an issue within most colonies, and positive adjustments to American conditions had been made. Some valuable lessons had been learned.

First, the New World environment required new goals and methods unimaginable from a European point of view. Spectacular wealth might be gained in a short time in other parts of the world, and generally at others' expense, but there were no such opportunities in North America. Increases in income and wealth were possible, but only as the result of sustained hard work. Permanent settlement in large numbers was required if Europeans were to take advantage of North America's potential. This point had profound implications; one had to become an American to profit from this land.

Second, each colony needed an agricultural base; food had to be produced locally, and under very different conditions from those in Europe. There were few guides to optimum measures other than trial and error. Indian crops and farming methods may have saved some colonies from starvation in their formative periods, but Indian agriculture was not intended to support dense populations. In all of North America beyond Mexico, there were no more than two million Indians at the time of European settlement, and it was clear that limited food supplies controlled their numbers. A combination of Indian and European crops and techniques was evolving and being adapted to the new conditions. Corn (maize) could be grown on land that was not fully cleared; wheat was much more difficult to raise under such circumstances. Factor proportions were very different in America; labor was much scarcer than in Europe and land more abundant. Thus, the cost of bringing wilderness land up to the standards of European farmland was very high and that of maintaining soil fertility even greater. New methods of determining the potential fertility of raw land and the appropriate crops to grow on it had to be developed. Allowing each production unit to make its own adjustment to new conditions quickly generated a wide range of useful information. Necessity and the settlers' intense economic motivations helped to ensure rational evaluation of alternatives and rapid adoption of those that worked. They also taught that there were benefits from abandoning less effective methods. Those who refused to learn from others might not last very long in America.

Third, unless the colonists were willing to live solely on what they could produce for themselves, they had to make something that could be exchanged for European goods. This was more than a matter of tastes; tools were needed for the new style of agriculture even more than under English conditions because labor was so scarce. Lacking both capital and skilled labor, the colonists could not hope to produce manufactured goods at costs or qualities comparable to those of Europe. It was far cheaper to make tools indirectly by trading American products for them.

Finally, population in general and labor in particular were in short supply in all colonies, and efforts to increase both paid rich dividends. Large populations were not only more secure from attack and able to generate larger aggregate surpluses, but they had important advantages in land clearance, building, and shipbuilding. The larger the colonial population, the wider the range of specialized occupations it could support and the higher the quality of its goods. Specialization increased the incomes of the community as well as of the specialists themselves.

Even at this early date, colonial responses were apparent. The response to the labor shortage was a high birthrate and a continuing welcome to immigrants. The colonists recognized that even indentured servants required incentives, so they offered what they had—prospects of cheap land and, increasingly, of high standards of material welfare. With slaves, coercion would suffice, but even slaves were expensive labor. It paid for owners to use methods that produced maximum output per worker and maintained slaves over long working lives.

Lessons from the New Environment

The colonists had also learned, often through bitter experience, what not to do. Those settlers most firmly committed to religious or political ideology at the expense of economic rationality often paid a high price. Such thinking might be a barrier to survival, to say nothing of prosperity. The settlers recognized how much their initial ideas had needed to change. Even more, experience in the New World had convinced the colonists that no ideas would be imposed on them by people utterly unfamiliar with colonial circumstances.

If America taught the colonists anything, it was the value of pragmatism. They learned to respect and adopt whatever produced results, be it a method, a tool, or a person. In the next century, the application of this lesson was to garner a rich reward.

SELECTED REFERENCES

Bailyn, B. *The Peopling of British North America: An Introduction.* New York: Knopf, 1986.

Cederberg, H. *An Economic Analysis of English Settlement in North America, 1583–1635.* New York: Arno Press, 1977.

Cipolla, C. *Before the Industrial Revolution: European Society and Economy, 1000–1700.* New York: Norton, 1976.

Clough, S., and R. Rapp. *European Economic History: The Economic Development of Western Civilization.* 3d ed. New York: McGraw-Hill, 1975.

Crosby, A., Jr. *The Columbian Exchange: Biological and Cultural Consequences of 1492.* Westport, Conn.: Greenwood Press, 1972.

Davis, R. *The Rise of the Atlantic Economies.* Ithaca, N.Y.: Cornell University Press, 1973.

Furnas, J. *The Americans: A Social History of the United States.* New York: Putnam, 1969.

Galenson, D. *White Servitude in Colonial America: An Economic Analysis.* Cambridge, U.K.: Cambridge University Press, 1981.

Hughes, J. *Industrialization and Economic History: Theses and Conjectures.* New York: McGraw-Hill, 1970.

Kulikoff, A. *Tobacco and Slaves: The Development of Southern Cultures in the Chesapeake, 1680–1800.* Chapel Hill, N.C.: University of North Carolina Press, 1986.

McCusker, J., and R. Menard. *The Economy of British America, 1607–1789.* Chapel Hill, N.C.: University of North Carolina Press, 1985.

Morison, S. *The European Discovery of America: The Northern Voyages.* New York: Oxford University Press, 1971.

———. *The Southern Voyages.* New York: Oxford University Press, 1974.

North, D., and R. Thomas. *The Rise of the Western World: A New Economic History.* New York: Cambridge University Press, 1973.

Parker, W. *Europe, America, and the Wider World: Vol. I., Europe and the World Economy.* New York: Cambridge University Press, 1984.

Parry, J. *The Age of Reconnaissance.* New York: World Publishing, 1963.

Porter, G., and W. Mulligan, eds. *Economic Change in the Chesapeake Colonies.* Greenville, Del.: Hagley Museum, 1978.

Tawney, R. *Religion and the Rise of Capitalism.* New York: Peter Smith, 1952.

Walton, G., and J. Shepherd. *The Economic Rise of Early America.* New York: Cambridge University Press, 1979.

THE COLONIAL
ECONOMY

B y 1750, the colonies of British North America that would one day comprise the United States had substantially increased their shares of the population and income of the British Empire and the North Atlantic economy. There were now many more colonists than there had been in 1650; nearly 1.2 million as opposed to 50,000, and in another 20 years there would be over 2 million. The details of colonial population growth are outlined in Table 2.1. Population had increased at an annual average rate of 3.4 percent during the colonial era.[1] This rate would be considered high by modern standards; in the eighteenth century it was unprecedented. Surprisingly, the major source of the high population growth rate was natural increase rather than immigration. As early as 1650, a majority of the colonists had been born in America, and the proportion grew with time.

The pace of internal population growth is determined by the difference between birth and death rates. American birth rates were somewhat higher than those in Europe, and death rates were considerably lower. In addition, the average age of first marriage was lower in the colonies than in Europe, and families tended to be larger.

Economics and Population Growth

Children are an economic asset in any unmechanized agricultural society. This was particularly so under colonial conditions. There was a chronic labor shortage and plenty of cheap unused land. Parents thus could have large families and gain the labor services of their children without fear that the family farm might have to be divided into uneconomically small holdings or that satisfactory jobs might not be available for the children who left home. High birthrates were a logical response to colonial circumstances. Hired labor was scarce, expensive, and unreliable; slaves or indentured servants required large cash outlays; and children were the best alternative source of labor. From a very early age, children were expected to "earn their keep" by doing chores and gradually gaining the experience that would allow them to manage their own farms later.

The colonies' lower death rates appear to have been the result of a more abundant and regular food supply, smaller urban populations, and lower incidence of epidemic disease than typified European conditions. These factors were interrelated. Throughout the colonial era most colonists lived close to the sea. Consequently, it was easier to transport food to offset local crop failures than it was where overland transport was required. Frequent local famines in the interior of Europe indicated the difficulty of transporting provisions there. In aggregate, the colonies produced a consistent food surplus above their own consumption requirements, and certain regions, such as the Sugar Islands and New England, were able to depend on food imports from the Middle Atlantic and Southern colonies. Diets were hearty, although inadequate by modern nutritional standards and monotonous to modern tastes. Still, colonial diets were more varied than those of most Europeans, and apparently they furnished greater resistance to epidemic disease than those of less well-fed populations. Only in America were substantial amounts of grain used for animal feed rather than direct consumption, indicating both high levels of food production and more protein consumption than in other countries.[2]

---

[1] U.S. Department of Commerce, Bureau of the Census, *Historical Statistics of the United States: Colonial Times to 1970*, 2 vols. (Washington, D.C.: Government Printing Office, 1975), 1168. See also J. Potter, "The Colonial Period," in *Readings in United States Economic and Business History*, R. Robertson and J. Pate, eds. (Boston: Houghton Mifflin, 1966).

[2] E. Perkins, *The Economy of Colonial America*, 2d ed. (New York: Columbia University Press, 1988), 64, 215.

Table 2.1   Estimated Colonial Population
(Thousands)

Colony	1650	1680	1710	1750	1770
New Hampshire	1.3	2.0	5.7	27.5	62.4
Massachusetts*	16.6	46.2	62.4	188.0	266.3
Rhode Island	.8	3.0	7.6	33.2	58.2
Connecticut	4.1	17.2	39.4	111.3	183.9
New York	4.1	9.8	21.6	76.7	162.9
New Jersey	—	3.4	19.9	71.4	117.4
Pennsylvania	—	.7	24.5	119.7	240.1
Delaware	.2	1.0	3.6	28.7	35.5
Maryland	4.5	17.9	42.7	141.1	202.6
Virginia	18.7	43.6	78.3	231.0	447.0
North Carolina	—	5.4	15.1	73.0	197.2
South Carolina	—	1.2	10.9	64.0	124.2
Georgia	—	—	—	5.2	23.4
Kentucky	—	—	—	—	2.5
Tennessee	—	—	—	—	.2
Total**	50.4	151.5	331.7	1,170.8	2,148.1

* Massachusetts figures include Maine and Plymouth.
** Figures may not add to totals because of rounding.
Source: U.S. Bureau of the Census, *Historical Statistics of the United States: Colonial Times to 1970*, 2 vols. (Washington, D.C.: Government Printing Office, 1975), 1168.

Urban Demography

Today we tend to think of cities as places where better medical care more than offsets a less healthy environment. But, until well into the nineteenth century, European cities had death rates far above their own birthrates, so that even maintenance of urban populations required a continual influx from rural areas. Eighteenth-century London was by no means the worst of these cities, yet an estimated 50 percent of all children born in London died before reaching the age of five.[3] There were virtually no public health measures to counteract the effects of populations crowded into small areas. Because there was no mass transport, the poor had to live within walking distance of their jobs. Tall buildings were impractical with the prevailing construction methods and materials, so crowding was the only way to accommodate urban populations. The means by which diseases spread were unknown. Without metal pipes and modern pumps, water supplies were frequently contaminated. Urban populations ate a poorer and less varied diet than did the countryside, because the only methods of food preservation available reduced the nutritional content of food. In sum, the cities of this period were deathtraps. They were at least as polluted as

---

[3] P. Deane, *The First Industrial Revolution*, 2d ed. (Cambridge, U.K.: Cambridge University Press, 1979), 261. See also M. George, *London Life in the 18th Century* (New York: Capricorn, 1965), 26

modern cities, probably more crime ridden, and subject to recurrent fires. American cities offered no real improvements over their European counterparts except that they were generally smaller; although Philadelphia, with 38,000 inhabitants, contained the second largest urban population in the British Empire on the eve of the Revolution. Still, about 95 percent of all Americans lived in the countryside, and the urban population shrank in proportion to the total after 1700.[4] Americans appear to have been less subject to other catastrophic events, such as war and epidemic disease, than were Europeans.

Despite the favorable comparisons to contemporary Europe, the colonies were no paradise. Life expectancy was short by modern standards—about 40 years—largely due to high rates of infant and maternal mortality.[5] The homes of all but the wealthy were dark, inadequately heated, and frequently vermin infested. Diseases that we now know largely from history, such as malaria and typhus, were deadly menaces to people who understood neither their causes nor their treatment.

Further Immigration

Immigration continued throughout the colonial era and, in later years, differed from the patterns established in the initial settlement period. A smaller number of the arrivals were English. There were more Scots, Irish, Scotch-Irish (Protestants from what is now Northern Ireland), and, especially in the Middle Colonies, southern Germans. These "Pennsylvania Dutch" joined smaller numbers of Huguenots, Swiss, Dutch, and Swedes. A high proportion of the total immigration, perhaps more than half, was indentured. Over time, however, indenture became less prevalent; by 1774 only 2 percent of the total population was indentured. Indenture was never common in New England.

Some indentured servants were fleeing oppression in their native lands; the Irish, Scotch-Irish, and Highland Scots all regarded themselves as victims of British policy toward their homelands. To the Pennsylvania Dutch, government in their native lands had meant taxes, tyranny, and military conscription from which young men often did not return. Other immigrants may have found migration the best way out of difficult personal situations.

Despite the considerable "push" element in migration from Europe, the "pull" of attractive conditions in America was at least as large a motivating force for immigration. It now appears clear that the new arrivals not only had surprisingly accurate information about New World conditions, but they also had a good deal of bargaining power over the terms of their indentures. By no means were all persons who offered their services in return for passage across the Atlantic victims of economic desperation or refugees. Records from the Philadelphia market where many indenture contracts were sold indicate that the servants possessed above-average literacy and a wide variety of job skills. Moreover, the terms of indenture contracts, determined in Europe before the servant took passage, reflected the individual's learning capacity, health, and skills. Often the employer was obligated to provide training in some occupation, and terms invariably specified the length of service required and the "freedom dues" to be paid to the servant by the employer at the end of the indenture period.[6]

The servants' settlement patterns strongly

---

[4] Perkins, *The Economy,* 226.

[5] The high rates of female mortality are disputed. See Perkins, *The Economy,* 7.

[6] D. Galenson, "Immigration and the Colonial Labor System: An Analysis of the Length of Indenture," *Explorations in Economic History* 14 (1977) and R. Heavner, "Indentured Servitude: The Philadelphia Market," *Journal of Economic History* (September 1978).

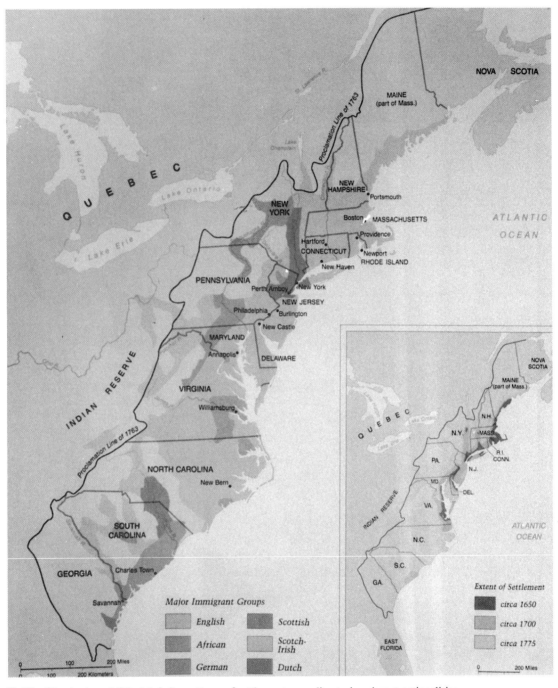

■ The 13 colonies exhibited definite patterns of settlement according to immigrant nationalities.

Source: From *America Past & Present,* Volume 1, by Robert A. Devine and T. H. Breen, front page. Copyright © 1984 by Scott, Foresman and Company. Reprinted by permission of HarperCollins Publishers.

THREE POUNDS REWARD.

RUN AWAY from the Subscriber, living at Warwick furnace, Minehole, on the 23d ult. an Irish servant man, named DENNIS M'CALLIN, about five feet eight inches high, nineteen years of age, has a freckled face, light coloured curly hair. Had on when he went away, an old felt hat, white and yellow striped jacket, a new blue cloth coat, and buckskin breeches ; also, he took with him a bundle of shirts and stockings, and a pocket pistol ; likewise, a box containing gold rings, &c. Whoever takes up said servant and secures him in any goal, so as his master may get him again, shall have the above reward and reasonable charges paid by   JAMES TODD.

N. B. All masters of vessels, and others, are forbid from harbouring or carrying him off, at their peril.

■ Not all indentured servants fulfilled their masters' expectations.
Source: The Historical Society of Pennsylvania.

reinforce this; they tended to choose colonies where land access was easy and the family farm was the standard production unit. Thus, they chose the areas where they could obtain what they had lacked in Europe. New England, with its tightly knit communities, block settlement of new land, limited supply of good arable soil, and grudging tolerance of "strangers," attracted relatively few. Over time, the numbers of servants choosing the plantation colonies also declined. The Middle Colonies, especially Pennsylvania, were more appealing to immigrants. Here, once inden-

tures were over, cheap fertile land was available from a government that granted secure titles and welcomed all Christians.

Redemptioners
Even in Pennsylvania, however, immigrants sometimes encountered less than evenhanded treatment. The Germans settling in limestone-soil valleys just west of the original Quaker colony had little interest in governmental affairs and were offered less. The Scotch-Irish, who located farther west, had even less help from the colony's rulers. Penn-

sylvania regarded them as a buffer against French and Indian raids (which they sometimes provoked). The Scots-Irish so resented the lack of support that on one occasion they marched on Philadelphia. In most colonies, new arrivals and the frontier were underrepresented in colonial legislatures. They often claimed to pay more than their share of colonial taxes, although the major seaports also considered themselves the primary victims of tax discrimination.[7]

Another group of immigrants, the redemptioners, received less favorable terms of indenture. These people boarded ships in Europe without signing an indenture contract or paying their passage. On arrival in the colonies, they had to find someone who would "redeem" them by paying for their passage in return for their labor. To add to their difficulties, redemptioners often came in families (indentured servants were normally single young adults) and sometimes did not speak English. These factors limited their bargaining power and resulted in longer indentures and lower freedom dues paid them on completion of their indentures.

Still, immigrants' letters to the "old country" leave no doubt that most of them considered the colonies in general and Pennsylvania in particular to be "the best poor man's country" in the world.[8] The "America Letters," with their message of easy access to land and a light governmental hand, continued to attract more immigrants.

Slavery

For another large group of immigrants, the conditions under which they came to America and the long-term prospects were less benign. In the eighteenth century, the proportion of blacks in the colonial population nearly doubled; it was about 20 percent in 1770. Although most blacks were slaves in southern agriculture, there were free blacks as well as slaves in all colonies. Slaves were not all unskilled farm laborers; there were noteworthy achievements in craft skills, science, and literature by colonial blacks.

Slaves were an alternative to indentured servants as a labor source. In the late seventeenth and eighteenth centuries, indentured servants' prices increased. Economic conditions in Europe improved, and the life expectancy of indentured servants rose. This meant that not only would colonial employers have to grant more favorable terms of indenture (shorter periods of indenture implied higher long-term training costs), but also that they would have greater and more certain obligations for freedom dues. At the same time, the costs of bringing slaves to America had fallen and increased life expectancy for slaves raised their value to North American purchasers. A longer stream of services could be obtained from each slave, and the prospects for a continuous labor supply through slave reproduction were improved. While this explains the greater influx of slaves after 1700, it does not explain their concentration in plantation agriculture.

The Distribution of Slaves

The most likely cause of the observed geographic distribution of slaves in North America is based on two factors. The crops of the plantation colonies required nearly year-round attention. Those of the North, especially wheat, had very high labor requirements at planting and especially harvest season, but required little labor between sowing and reaping seasons. Such labor requirements were a major influence on the prevalence of slavery, which is best suited to tasks requiring more or less constant effort. Significantly, even slave-worked plantations hired free labor for

[7] E. Perkins, *The Economy of Colonial America*, 2d ed. (New York: Columbia University Press, 1988), 194.
[8] J. Lemon, *The Best Poor Man's Country: A Geographical Study of Early Southeastern Pennsylvania* (Baltimore: Johns Hopkins University Press, 1972).

the wheat harvest when it could be obtained.[9] Slave prices in North American markets were determined by conditions in the Caribbean slave markets. Because slaves were employed in high-productivity uses there (sugar was an extremely valuable crop that generated huge profits), and the cost of transporting them to North America was added to their prices here (which implied their prices would be higher in New England and the Middle Colonies than in the South), they could only be profitably employed if the value of slave output was high. Supervisory costs per slave were reduced as the proportion of slaves held by large plantations increased. By 1700 rice (and later indigo) had become a major plantation crop. Thus, the growth of the slave population reflected changes in the organization and products of plantation agriculture.[10]

American slaves apparently received much better physical treatment than did those in the Caribbean, especially those on the sugar plantations. One authority claims that colonial slaves' "incomes" of food, shelter, and clothing compare quite favorably with those of most inhabitants of contemporary Continental Europe.[11] Better treatment probably owed much less to the colonists' humanitarian principles than it did to economics. In North America, slave prices were high and the costs of adequate maintenance low. Under such circumstances, it was in their masters' best interests to preserve slaves' health. Economics also helped to shape the demographic parameters of the colonies' slave population. Women were unsuited to the grueling work of sugar production, so female slaves were relatively cheaper on the continent. It paid to allow the slaves to form families and have children. There was a greater possibility that

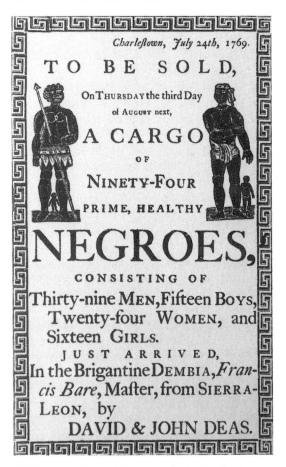

■ This advertisement for slaves, posted in Charlestown in the 1760s, emphasizes their good health and high quality.

these children would eventually add to their owner's work force in North America than was the case in the Caribbean.

In addition to benefiting from treatment that was under owners' control, slaves in North America were much less subject to epidemic diseases than those working in tropical climes. The Caribbean slave population could only be maintained by continuous imports, but North American slaves had a rate of natural increase about equal to that of the aggre-

[9] Perkins, *The Economy,* 103–104, 108.
[10] G. Wright, *The Political Economy of the Cotton South* (New York: Norton, 1978), 11–12.
[11] Perkins, *The Economy,* 104.

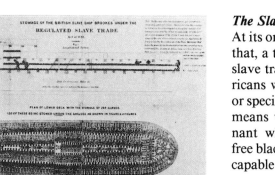

■ In the eighteenth century, regulations to prevent overcrowding aboard slave ships were as much a matter of economics as of humanitarian concern. *Source:* Library of Congress.

The Slave Trade

At its origins in Africa, the slave trade was just that, a trade. European (and a few American) slave traders purchased slaves from other Africans who had captured them in tribal wars or specialized slave-raiding expeditions. By no means was this a matter of militarily dominant whites forcibly kidnapping previously free blacks. The slave-trading tribes were quite capable of defending themselves against Europeans. Because the gathering of slaves was unquestionably increased because of the American demand for them, whites were hardly free of complicity in this inhuman traffic. But they originated neither African slavery nor the methods by which slaves were obtained.[13] As horrifying as the tales of filth, brutality, disease, and death aboard the slaves ships during the "Middle Passage" may be, the voyage to America killed fewer Africans than did the raids and tribal wars in which the victims were obtained.[14]

GEOGRAPHIC EXPANSION

The colonial population did more than just grow; it expanded into new areas. By 1750, the frontier had been pushed well inland for most of the expanse from Maine to Georgia. At several points, settlements were now established in the valleys of the Appalachians, and, by the 1770s, the first tentative efforts at colonization beyond the mountains had begun in Kentucky and Tennessee. New England's expansion to the west and north was still hampered by the French in 1750, but elsewhere existing

gate population. The more rapid overall rate of increase among blacks was due to proportionally higher "immigration." Although only 6 percent of the Africans carried across the Atlantic from 1500 to 1870 (the vast majority had arrived by 1800) were sent to North America, that region had 25 percent of the New World's black population by 1825.[12]

Even for slaves, then, American conditions encouraged rational use of human talent. Survival, of course, is hardly the only measure of the fate of slaves in various regions, but it can hardly be denied that it is an important one.

---

[12] R. Fogel and S. Engerman, *Time on the Cross: The Economics of American Negro Slavery,* 2 vols. (Boston: Little, Brown & Co., 1974), 1:13–20.

---

[13] R. Thomas and R. Bean, "The Fishers of Men," *Journal of Economic History* (December 1974).
[14] R. Fogel, *Without Consent or Contract: The Rise and Fall of American Slavery* (New York: Norton, 1989), 129–131.

colonies had begun to push into regions far from salt water.

North Carolina was settled by people moving overland from Virginia rather than from the coast. For a long time the colony's lack of access to the sea—a low-cost outlet for its cash crops—was a serious handicap to the growth of incomes, if not population. As a result, North Carolina had fewer plantations and more family-farm, subsistence-oriented agriculture than other Southern colonies.

By 1700, South Carolina was established as a highly successful plantation colony specializing initially in tobacco, then in rice. Just before 1750, rice cultivation was supplemented by that of indigo, a blue vegetable dye. All these crops were best suited to production by large-scale plantations, and South Carolina's specialization in that mode was revealed by its population patterns. Blacks constituted a majority of South Carolina's people, as they did in no other mainland colony. As such, its demographic patterns were similar to those of the Sugar Islands.[15] Charlestown, with its excellent harbor, was the only colonial city south of Norfolk.

Georgia was the last colony to be established, in 1733. Once more, altruistic principles clashed with economic reality in the founding of a colony. Georgia had been established by English philanthropists to give people imprisoned for debt a second chance. The colony's charter established rules that proved to be an obstacle to settlement. Initially, the size of land holdings was restricted and slavery was prohibited. But these rules meant that Georgia would have higher production costs in tobacco than other colonies, and rice production was all but out of the question. Without the attraction of competitive cash-crop opportunities, Georgia grew very slowly, and its inhabitants, led by a minister,

petitioned England for permission to allow slavery.[16] In the late 1740s the colony's laws were revised, but Georgia was barely past its formative stage by the Revolution. In 1750, its population was only 5,000, by far the smallest of any seaboard colony.

COLONIAL AGRICULTURE

Although the majority of every colony's population was engaged in agriculture, often in combination with other extractive industries such as fishing, whaling, or lumbering, distinct regional patterns had emerged by 1750. Agricultural products furnished the bulk of colonial exports and enabled the colonists to obtain manufactured goods that could not have been produced as easily, if at all, from domestic resources. Low agricultural productivity also forced the concentration on agriculture. Most colonial farms produced only a small surplus beyond their own consumption requirements, so the proportion of the population that could follow nonagricultural pursuits was limited.

Cheap Land and New Methods
Another feature common to all colonies' agriculture was a great contrast in factor proportions relative to those of Europe. Because colonial populations were small and land relatively abundant, each unit of labor was combined with a great deal more land than normal European practice dictated. It is important to realize that colonial land was never free. Even if it could be obtained without a cash payment, there were sizable costs involved in rendering it suitable for use. Nevertheless, land costs were far lower than they had been in Europe,

---

[15] G. Walton and J. Shepherd, *The Economic Rise of British America* (New York: Cambridge University Press, 1979), 56–57.

[16] R. Gray and B. Wood, "The Transition from Indentured to Involuntary Servitude in Colonial Georgia," *Explorations in Economic History* (Fall 1976).

and social considerations reinforced the strong economic incentives for landownership. Hired labor was relatively expensive while land was cheap, and the colonists' response to their factor cost situation was rational. They used land far more lavishly than did European farmers. It was cheaper for colonists to clear new land when fields lost their fertility than it was to expend the extra labor required to maintain soil quality. This practice made good sense as long as a supply of additional land remained available, but confused European observers, whose values were those of a land with abundant labor and a nearly fixed endowment of arable land. European agriculture maximized output per unit of land, while colonial practice was to seek maximum production per unit of labor. Although European observers accused Americans of "mining" their land, there is little evidence of declining yields per acre over the colonial period.[17] The practice of fallowing (resting) land may have helped to produce this record.

Land Speculation

Low prices for land and the practice of keeping a reserve of untilled land encouraged land speculation in colonial America. Farmers typically held far more land than they currently cultivated as a defense against a reduction of the yields of their current arable land, for woodlots, and as a potential source of capital gains. As populations increased and settlement became more dense, land prices tended to rise. Raw land was initially available at very low prices; under the headright system, payment to those assuming the transportation expenses of indentured servants was often in land. Many colonial governments gave transferrable land warrants to military veterans. Politically influential persons, especially plantation owners, might obtain title to land far beyond the current limits of settlement. Land

could be held at little or no expense, given colonial tax rates and the cost of obtaining it. Because colonial population growth was so rapid, the risks of investment in land were very low; it was all but certain to appreciate in value after its carrying costs were met.

Nonagricultural Activity

Many farming households engaged in nonagricultural activity as well, making furniture, buildings, tools, and land improvements for their own use. Many produced distilled beverages and beer, using almost anything that could be induced to ferment as raw material, including pumpkins. Especially during the first years on a new farm, the output of field crops would be low and expenses heavy, so there was great incentive to produce commodities that could be sold or bartered for goods the household could not make for itself, or even for additional food. Lumber, furs, potash, pearlash, maple sugar, or honey might be exchanged for salt, metal goods, ammunition, grindstones, and the services of specialists, such as blacksmiths, lawyers, and ministers.

Most roads were suitable only for pack animals, and transportation by this method was expensive. Wherever possible, colonial farmers sought access to water transportation, and so bad were the overland alternatives that their assessments of stream navigability appear almost suicidally optimistic today. In addition, crops were processed into less bulky or more easily transported forms. Grain was sent to market as flour, whiskey, or fattened livestock, all of which represented higher value in smaller bulk than unmilled corn, rye, or wheat.

Land clearance was extremely slow and difficult work. Trees were huge, and often the settler had only an axe and a few other hand tools with which to attack the forest. There were also many other demands on his time in the first few years: buildings to be constructed, firewood cut, and numerous other

---

[17] Perkins, *The Economy*, 45.

tasks performed. In addition, unless the family had accumulated a reserve before it made the settlement, something had to be produced to exchange for goods the family could not make for itself. Twenty years might pass before a farm family had cleared as much land as its members could cultivate, and another score might pass before it had erected a full complement of permanent buildings and fences. The timetable depended on the nature of the land, luck, weather, and the number of able-bodied workers available. In a world where draft animals were not always available or suited to the necessary tasks, more hands meant that the basic demands could be met in less time. The response could be direct: One colonial family achieved prosperity because it contained "26 strong, healthy sons."

Farm Income and Investment

Consumption on colonial farms, particularly in the early years, might be modest, but this gave a misleading impression of income. Ground clearing, building construction, building up livestock herds, and other such activities were in fact investment—the production of goods that would add to the family's ability to consume or produce still more in the future.

New England

By 1750, it was apparent that New England had no comparative advantage in agriculture versus the Middle Atlantic or Southern colonies. Not only did those regions have more and better soil per capita, as well as longer growing seasons, their climates allowed the production of crops for export. In contrast, after 1700 New England was a net importer of food. This fact may indicate as much about the growing efficiency of ocean shipping as it does about differences in agricultural capabilities. New England's response in part took the form of a migration of young men seeking better farming opportunities than they could obtain in their native region. In most of New England, landholdings tended to be small and not very productive even by colonial standards. Furthermore, their average size declined over the eighteenth century, although the decline was largely in reserves of unused land.

In its early years, New England's agricultural patterns reflected social and religious influences as well as economic responses to a harsh environment. In most cases, the initial agricultural settlements were made by the members of a church congregation moving into a new area en masse. The congregation would build a village in the midst of the fields cultivated by its members. Each family would have a small garden or orchard plot close to its house, plus a number of strips of land in the town's fields, and the right to graze livestock on the common pasture. The fields were farmed in cooperation with other members of the community; joint action was necessary in planting and harvesting.

Religious and Political Influences

There were some advantages to this type of settlement. In New England, it allowed for better defense against the French and their Indian allies. It provided a larger pool of labor for construction and other activities best accomplished through joint effort, and the members of such a community had access to the group's reserves in case of emergency. Above all, however, such a settlement pattern kept every individual under the watchful eye of the minister and other church officials, ensuring the enforcement of community standards of conduct. Members of the congregation, with varying definitions of "membership," had a voice in community affairs, but the voice of the church spoke very loudly indeed, particularly by modern standards.

As populations grew and the threat of attack receded, this system's clash with more secular values became increasingly apparent. Making everyone live in town certainly promoted religious conformity, but as the town's cleared land and population increased, it also wasted time in commuting to fields distant from the village. The inheritance of land rights also became more complicated as joint cultivation declined; either heirs must receive shrinking allocations within each of a larger number of fields, or some mechanism for determining the relative worth of land parcels in different fields had to be devised. Gradually private ownership of individual parcels of land developed, and families began to live in farmhouses surrounded by their own acres rather than in villages. By 1750 land in New England was largely in the hands of individual owners, as it was in other regions.

The Limits of Yankee Agriculture

But the rise of a private market in land failed to offset New England's other agricultural shortcomings. After a promising start, cultivation of wheat had been halted by plant diseases. The staple crop of New England became corn, which was suited to the region's small fields and short growing season. Other crops, often raised in the cornfields, were beans, pumpkins, squash, and peas. Fruit, particularly apples, was grown, and utilized in many ways: fresh, dried, and as cider and applejack. Livestock was also produced; some areas, such as Rhode Island, exported horses. But most New England farmers found it necessary to supplement their incomes from crops and husbandry by lumbering, fishing, whaling, trading, or the production of shoes, harnesses, wooden items, and other handicraft products.

The nature of New England agriculture, with many small-scale producers, added to the incentives provided by the region's other activities for the formation of towns as concentration centers for exports and for the distribution of imports among its multitude of consuming units. The towns also furnished a growing market for farm produce.

The Middle Atlantic Colonies

The region from New York south to Maryland (and, in later years, even parts of Virginia) developed a more productive agriculture than New England. Possession of fertile soils and development of social institutions that attracted some of the most skillful farmers in America made Pennsylvania a colonial success story. In this region, wheat and meat were produced in large quantities as cash crops. Both products were exported, and the requirements of the export trade gave rise to industries such as milling, which raised wheat's unit value and decreased its bulk, and bakeries, which converted flour into still more portable ships' biscuit or hardtack. The region also produced corn, a portion of which was fed to hogs and cattle, which were eventually exported as pickled or salted meat.

The Middle Atlantic colonies were a stronghold of the family farm; there were no economic advantages for larger units in the production of the region's principal exports. As it had in New England, the presence of many commercially oriented farms encouraged the growth of towns. Philadelphia was a seaport, a market center, and the seat of government. Businesses in the town milled flour, packed meat, and made the barrels and ships in which the products of Pennsylvania, Delaware, and southern New Jersey farms were sent to other colonies, the West Indies, and southern Europe.

New York City performed similar services for its hinterland, the farming areas of Long Island, northern New Jersey, and the Hudson Valley. Later the produce of the Mohawk Valley added to New York's exports. Like Philadelphia, New York transformed its hinterland's output into more portable forms and

■ This painting of a family-operated farm illustrates the good life, eighteenth-century style.
Source: Abby Aldrich Rockefeller Folk Art Center, Williamsburg, Virginia.

provided the transport. The city was a ship-building center and bakeries produced biscuit and hardtack. In these rapidly growing towns the colonists made some of their first efforts at insurance, finance, and small-scale manufacturing. The New England and Middle Atlantic colonies both produced and marketed their products without assistance from the mother country. As such, they were unique among European colonies.

The Pennsylvania Dutch were unique among colonial farmers. Rather than girdling trees and farming among the dead trunks until they could be destroyed by decay or fire, the tireless Pennsylvania Dutch cleared the land of roots and stumps in the first year of cultivation. Their methods allowed the use of animal-drawn plows, which most American farmers did not use. Having made the move to America, the Pennsylvania Dutch appar-

■ Although whale oil was a major Yankee export to England, it still did not eliminate New England's trade deficit with the country. As the drawing indicates, whaling is a good example of the labor-intensive nature of most colonial economic activity.
Source: The Bettmann Archive.

ently became convinced that mobility paid because individuals frequently moved to new or better farms.[18] They maintained the fertility of their land and modified their methods to achieve increased yields per acre over time. Per-acre yields in this region are still among the highest in the United States. This group of farmers originated many of the basic innovations that later generations of American farmers found so useful in the western movement: the barn with hayloft and inclined ramp above and animal stalls below, plow and wagon designs, and the "Kentucky" rifle. Pennsylvania, where the use of advanced agricultural techniques was by no means universal, and South Carolina present the only clear evidence for increases in agricultural pro-

ductivity after the initial period of adjustment to new crops and conditions was over.[19]

Pennsylvania's combination of religious and ethnic tolerance, low-cost land with secure titles, and a light governmental hand owed much to William Penn. Combined with the colony's natural advantages, these institutions produced rapid growth and a prosperous, diversified economy. Pennsylvania was virtually unsettled in 1680, but by 1770 the colony's population was 240,000. Penn's was one of only two proprietary colonies that may have returned a profit to its owners. Maryland, which followed similar policies, was the other.

---

[18] Lemon, *The Best Poor Man's Country*, 109.

[19] G. Walton and D. Ball, "Agricultural Productivity Change in 18th Century Pennsylvania," *Journal of Economic History* (March 1976). See also the comments of R. Menard.

The Southern Colonies

Although both regions furnished markets for English exports, neither New England nor the Middle Atlantic colonies could be termed ideal possessions from a mercantilist standpoint. Neither produced much of use to England, although New England's mast trees had strategic importance. Many New England exports actually competed with those of the mother country. The Middle colonies' exports in large part were sent to other colonies or outside the Empire. The Southern colonies, however, closely approached the mercantilist ideal. They were large-scale exporters of tobacco, rice, and indigo, all products useful within Britain and as re-exports. Their sizable populations, particularly in Virginia and Maryland, furnished good markets for English exports. And the region produced little that competed with British overseas trade.

Although the plantation dominated the region's agriculture, by no means were all the Southern colonies' farms plantations. Parts of the region had been settled too recently for such development, and even in the more established areas most farms were worked by the owner's family, with perhaps one or two servants or slaves. Nor were tobacco, rice, and indigo the only cash crops. Particularly toward the end of the colonial period, the South exported sizable amounts of corn and other foodstuffs (indeed, in some areas of Maryland tobacco production was no longer profitable unless combined with grain and livestock),[20] and it always provided for its own consumption. Nevertheless, the influence of the plantation was pervasive.

Plantations were large-scale production units. Typically a plantation's output would be a sizable portion of a merchant ship's capacity. Plantations tended to trade directly with England, loading their products from their own docks onto the ships that had brought imported goods. With its large labor force, the plantation was also a large-scale import purchaser. Some planters utilized their purchasing advantages and operated stores from which they sold imported goods to the neighboring farmers, thus taking the place of the merchants in other colonies. One result of this was that towns were less necessary than they were in other regions.

Settlement Patterns

Most plantations were located on tidal rivers, and so had direct water transportation links to Europe. Because plantations tended to keep sizable land reserves, and utilized only the most fertile acreage available, plantation-colony populations tended to be scattered rather than concentrated. Many areas without convenient access to navigable water long remained very lightly populated. The initial land grants in many Southern colonies lacked well-defined boundaries, which also discouraged close settlement. The result was that there were few large-scale markets in the Southern colonies accessible from a single point.

Plantations often maintained their own blacksmiths, carpenters, coopers, and other skilled workers. What the plantation could not produce from its own resources would be purchased from the English merchants who bought its crops. Transatlantic shipping costs for English goods tended to be less than those for colonial exports. Southern exports tended to be bulky; thus they required more space than the manufactured goods for which they were exchanged. Ships coming to the colonies were often less than fully loaded and were willing to accept any cargo (including people) that offered to pay more than its handling costs.

The result was another major discouragement to manufacturing and urbanization in the Southern colonies. For a long time, Wil-

---

[20] L. Carr and R. Menard, "Land, Labor, and Economies of Scale in Early Maryland: Some Limits to Growth in the Chesapeake System of Husbandry," *Journal of Economic History* (June 1989).

liamsburg was the only real town in Virginia, and it was a government and social center, active only while the legislature was in session. Charlestown, with its secure harbor on a dangerous coast, was the regional metropolis of the Carolinas as well as a government center, but the South was even more heavily rural than the rest of the colonies.

Tobacco

Tobacco had been responsible for the growth of the plantation colonies. Initially, planters in the Tidewater regions had sent their crops to English merchants who sold the tobacco for them on commission. The merchants would then use the proceeds to pay for the planters' orders of British goods. Because there were many planters in several colonies that had no cooperative policies, there was no way to control the supply of tobacco, which increased

■ Europeans' increasing preference for smoking tobacco, rather than chewing tobacco, led to greater Virginia production of the crop. The painting shown is a detail of what is probably the oldest tobacco wrapping in the world.

very rapidly in the seventeenth century. Prices fluctuated considerably, but the long-run trend was down until about 1720. After that date, low but stable prices prevailed.[21]

Some planters borrowed from English merchants in years of low prices or pressing need for imports, pledging the next year's crop as security. The Tidewater planters were difficult customers. There was no standard grading system initially, and the planters sold each barrel of tobacco individually. They demanded explanations if prices did not vary in accordance with their estimates of quality.[22]

Late in the seventeenth century, tobacco markets began to change. A shift in Europe's preferences from chewing to smoking tobacco increased the demand for Virginia tobacco and reduced that for the Brazilian variety, which was better suited for chewing. This, when coupled with the declining price of Chesapeake tobacco, meant that larger quantities could now be sold, particularly in Continental Europe. England began to export large amounts of American tobacco. This trend accelerated when the French government tobacco monopoly began to buy its supplies in England.

New Trade Patterns and Institutions

The old consignment system of marketing was not suited to large-scale sales, and a few great merchants in Glasgow, London, and Whitehaven controlled the French business. Because these merchants had an assured market for a large portion of the total crop, they were in a better position to extend credit to American producers. Also, they were interested in large amounts of uniform-quality tobacco. The merchants began to open stores in the tobacco colonies. These establishments purchased tobacco, sold English goods, and extended credit

[21] J. Price, "The Economic Growth of the Chesapeake and the European Market, 1697–1775," *Journal of Economic History* (December 1963).

[22] Price, "The Economic Growth."

to farmers. At the same time, it became obvious that the key to profits lay in lower costs of production, not in haggling over prices. Consequently, the Chesapeake colonies developed uniform grading systems and improved packing methods so that larger quantities of tobacco could be shipped in the same amount of space. One result of these changes was that tobacco production began to shift from the large-scale planters to smaller production units and away from its old stronghold in the Tidewater region to the Piedmont. The new producers were less sensitive to price variations because tobacco sales were a smaller portion of their total incomes than they had been for planters.[23] Many Tidewater planters began to produce wheat, corn, and meat as cash crops, facilitating the rise of Baltimore and Norfolk as export centers for these crops. Throughout the colonial period, tobacco was the most important export of the North American colonies, accounting for nearly half the total value of all exports.[24]

Rice, Indigo, and Naval Stores

Another change in export crops occurred in the Carolinas. Originally both colonies had produced tobacco as their major cash crop. In the period of falling tobacco prices after 1650, rice cultivation began along the coast, chiefly in South Carolina. After farmers discovered that rice could be irrigated through a system of dikes and the natural pressure of the tides, which forced fresh water back up the coastal rivers, rice production boomed. Suitable land was limited, however, and the required investment in dikes, sluices, and milling machinery quickly made rice cultivation a rich man's business. But there were growing markets for rice in southern Europe as well as in England, and exports rose from 10,407 pounds in 1698 to an average of 78,485,000 pounds in the 1770–1774 period.[25] Rice planting was very profitable: annual rates of return on planters' investments approached 25 percent.[26]

An additional source of income for rice planters appeared when the British government began offering bounties (subsidies) for the production of indigo, a blue vegetable dye used on textiles. Eliza Lucas, one of America's first female entrepreneurs, showed planters how the crop was grown and processed for export, and by 1750 Carolina indigo had replaced Britain's previous supply from the French West Indies. Indigo was an ideal complement to rice cultivation; it grew on land that was not suitable for rice, and its chief labor requirements occurred while there was little to do in the rice fields. But the British bounty and tariff protection against French production were necessary to make indigo production worthwhile.

The Tarheel Economy

Another English bounty went to Carolina's producers of "naval stores," that is, the pitch, turpentine, and tar so vital for the preservation of wooden ships. Together with masts and spar timbers, naval stores were crucial to the maintenance of Britain's naval supremacy. The Royal Navy's alternate sources were the Baltic, which might be inaccessible in wartime, and Britain's own inadequate production.

COLONIAL MANUFACTURING

In general the colonies had severe handicaps as producers of manufactured goods. Their output had to compete with that from England, even in colonial markets, so colonial

---

[23] Perkins, *The Economy*, 1 ed., 54.
[24] Price, "Economic Growth."

[25] U.S. Department of Commerce, *Historical Statistics*, 2:1192–1193.
[26] Perkins, *The Economy*, 81.

producers had to meet English goods' quality and prices. They succeeded in doing so with only a few items. England had more and cheaper capital than did the colonies, and English labor costs were considerably lower; the typical English worker produced more output for lower wages than his colonial counterpart. Because emigration to the colonies was concentrated among people who hoped to better their situations, the colonies attracted few skilled workmen or other people who were already receiving above-average incomes in Europe. In addition, English manufacturers had better access to a growing pool of new technology. Because British markets were larger, they were better situated to take advantage of any economies of scale. Finally, the British manufacturers enjoyed equal access to markets in all colonies as well as those in Britain itself and the areas outside the empire. Under these circumstances, even the costs of transatlantic shipping (which might raise goods' delivered prices by 20 percent or more over those in England) were not enough to increase imports' prices to levels that covered colonial production costs.

These economic considerations, rather than the regulations of British mercantilism, were the chief barriers to colonial manufacturing. The colonists' productive resources could produce higher incomes in trade and agriculture than in industry. In most types of manufacturing, the colonists could not hope to compete with England until the advantages of the mother country diminished. In most areas of manufacturing, the colonists clearly had a comparative disadvantage in relation to England.

English mercantilists were not very receptive to the idea of colonial manufacturing. Even so, legal restraints on colonial industry were often ineffective. In 1750, Parliament forbade the production of nails in the colonies. Three colonial legislatures subsequently passed laws offering bounties to anyone producing nails within their borders, in open defiance of British law. In most cases, the British government was not totally unresponsive to colonial needs, and laws were sometimes changed or repealed if the products or activities involved were important to the colonists.

Britain's manufacturing advantages, although great, did not hold equally for all products. The colonies were able to compete in the production of some goods, particularly those where shipping costs were a high proportion of final price. Accordingly, the colonies made most of their own beer, furniture, bricks, and similar items.

Iron Production and Shipbuilding

In two items there was a very considerable development of colonial manufacturing activity despite the fact that both products required skilled labor and large amounts of capital. In each case the reason for colonial success lay in the product's raw materials requirements. England in the seventeenth and eighteenth centuries had been experiencing a growing shortage of wood. The problem was more acute in timber than in fuel, because the charcoal used to smelt iron could be made from small trees or brush. Even so, all types of wood were far more expensive in England than in America. Iron making required huge amounts of fuel; a typical iron furnace in the eighteenth century required no less than 10,000 acres of woodland to fuel continuous production. Charcoal could not be transported any distance without deterioration. Because far more fuel than iron ore was required to make a ton of iron, smelting furnaces had to be located at the fuel source rather than at markets or ore sources. This made iron smelting a rural industry.

Development of Colonial Iron Production
Iron was smelted in all the colonies, using local ore deposits, but by 1750 the industry had become concentrated in the Middle colonies. It has been estimated that by that date the

American colonies were producing about one-seventh of the world's iron. Most colonial iron was shipped to Britain for fabrication into finished products. Skilled ironmasters were recruited in England and Europe and brought to America to apply their craft to the abundant resources of the New World.

Shipbuilding

The other manufacturing sector in which it proved efficient to send skilled labor and capital to raw materials was shipbuilding. Timber in the colonies was cheap, and there was plenty of high-quality oak for ship frames and planking and white pine for masts, spars, and decks. England was experiencing increasing shortages of oak, but the really critical problem for British shipbuilders was material for masts and spars. Britain had few trees suitable for this purpose, and contemporary technology produced no satisfactory substitutes. But colonial white pine—tall, straight, and strong—had no equal anywhere in the world. England's sources of ship timber were her own dwindling domestic reserves, plus imports from the Baltic and Scandinavia, source of the only really satisfactory mast timber. The imports were an uncertain resource in wartime, just when assured supplies were crucial. Even in peace timber could be obtained only for gold. Colonial shipbuilding thus satisfied mercantilist ideas better than did most other American industries.

From their founding, most colonies had produced small craft for local use, and the industry quickly expanded to produce a wide variety of vessels. England waived mercantilist regulations restricting the emigration of shipwrights, and between the development of colonial skills and the infusion of new talent, shipbuilding became one of the few areas in which colonial skills matched those of Britain. The colonies produced many high-quality, inexpensive ships for both their own use and for sale to the British merchant marine, and even some warships for the Royal Navy. Perhaps one-third of all the empire's merchant ships were colonial-built just before the Revolution.

Other Manufacturing

Some colonial manufacturing was necessary to support other activities. Barrels, for example, filled the roles of today's oil drums, plastic bags, tin cans, and cardboard boxes, so there was continuous demand for the coopers' output. Goods especially adapted to colonial needs, such as axes and rifles, were also made. Although population growth was relaxing some of the restrictions imposed by small markets in the later eighteenth century, for many items the size of markets still restricted specialization. Paul Revere lived in Boston, one of the largest and wealthiest colonial cities, but he was not able to specialize in silversmithing alone. He made clock faces, branding irons, false teeth, and surgical instruments, and also did copperplate engraving. After the Revolution, he produced an even wider variety of manufactured goods. Like other craftsmen, he was versatile in order to be fully employed. In small towns, the blacksmith-wheelwright-dentist and tanner-harnessmaker-cobbler were typical.

By the close of the colonial period, a few signs of more complete specialization were apparent. In some of the larger cities specialized producers and stores selling only a limited range of items existed. In the Middle colonies there were capital-intensive mills producing flour and gunpowder with the most modern waterpower and machinery techniques in the world. These culminated in Oliver Evans' flour mill, one of the world's first examples of automation. Evans' mill unloaded, weighed, ground, bolted, and barreled as many as three bushels of grain per hour. Ultimately, it used hand labor largely to close flour barrels. The mill did not commence operations until 1785, however, and the techniques it pioneered did not spread beyond milling. Elsewhere in the colonies, factories in the sense of labor forces working as coordinated teams, using powered machinery, and performing specialized inter-dependent operations on a common product were almost unknown even at the end of the eighteenth century.

COLONIAL TRADE

Given their disadvantages in manufacturing, the colonies had little choice but to engage in trade. The tools and luxury goods that they obtained through trade enabled them to main-tain and improve their standards of living.

The North Atlantic Economy

Colonial trade was much more than a simple exchange of the colonies' raw materials for British manufactures. The colonists partici-pated in a network of exchanges involving the entire North Atlantic rather than merely the British possessions. Americans realized that they could not finance the volume of British goods they desired through direct trade with the mother country. By the end of the colonial period, they were buying from one and one-half to three times as much from England as the value of their direct sales to her.

Over time, any country can import more than it exports in trade with any other single nation through three devices. It can borrow to finance its trade deficit; it can provide services ("invisible exports"); or it can pay the differ-ence in cash. In the eighteenth century, cash meant specie, gold or silver. The colonists were willing enough to borrow, but the British were reluctant to lend to them. Aside from limited amounts of short-term credits, partic-ularly to Middle colony merchants, British loans did not finance colonial imports. Eastern North America did not produce precious met-als. The colonists did sell services (and ships)

to the English, and British government spend-ing in the colonies provided another source of funds. Still, a sizable gap remained between the income produced by these efforts and the colonies' purchases from England. It was filled largely through selling more goods and ser-vices to other areas than the value of colonial purchases there. The dimensions of the colo-nies' trade with England just before the Rev-olution are given in Table 2.2.

The colonies sold more goods to southern Europe and Africa (a quantitatively insignifi-cant trading partner) than they purchased from those regions. In addition, they sold far more shipping services to those areas and to the Caribbean than they bought. The total vol-ume of this trade was less than that with En-gland, but it was nevertheless crucial to the maintenance of colonial trade. It provided a means of financing most of the trade imbal-ance that the colonies incurred in their direct trade with Britain. Thus, the extent to which the colonies could fulfill one mercantilistic role—to furnish markets for home-country ex-ports—depended on their violation of an-other—to have no trade with rival nations or their colonies.

French sugar-producing islands provided especially tempting business opportunities for colonial traders. Their sugar was cheaper and at least as good as that of British producers. Moreover, the French merchant marine was inferior to colonial shipping, so there were large profits to be made in both direct trade and in shipping earnings.

Such trade was often illegal and always in violation of mercantilistic ideals. However, economic theory predicts that when there are great opportunities for gain in some activity, laws prohibiting it will be violated unless there is a high probability of detection, conviction, and severe punishment. The British made only sporadic efforts to enforce their trade reg-ulations until the latter half of the eighteenth century. Most of those attempts were made

Table 2.2   Balance of Payments for the Thirteen Colonies,
Yearly Averages, 1768–1772
(In Thousands of 1774 Pounds)

	Debit	Credit
Commodities		
Exports		2,800
Imports	3,920	
Balance of trade	1,120	
Ship sales		140
Invisible earnings		
Shipping earnings		600
Merchant commissions, risk, and insurance		220
Balance on current account from trade	160	
Payments for human beings		
Indentured servants	80	
Slaves	200	
British collections and expenditures in colonies		
Taxes and duties	40	
Salaries of British civil servants		40
Military expenditures		230
Naval expenditures		170
Capital and monetary flows		
Specie and indebtedness		40

Source: G. Walton and J. Shepherd, *The Economic Rise of Early America* (Cambridge, U.K.: Cambridge University Press, 1979), 101.

through colonial courts, whose juries tended to regard smugglers as public benefactors. Under such circumstances, practice followed theory. The colonists were quite willing to trade with the French in addition to the Spanish, Dutch, Danes, Portuguese, and on occasion with pirates. Until the end of the French and Indian War in 1763, British trade regulations could be violated with almost complete impunity. If goods could not be smuggled, corrupt customs officials could be bribed and conscientious ones intimidated. In the unlikely event of prosecution, colonial courts held few terrors for colonists accused of trade violations.

Regional Trade Patterns

The three colonial regions developed differing trade patterns based on their varying capabilities in both commodity production and maritime activity.

The South

This region sent its tobacco, indigo, and naval stores, plus much of its rice, directly to Britain. Most of this trade was carried in English ships. The South also sent substantial amounts of food to the West Indies and southern Europe. Southern colonies' direct exports to England made up as much as 80 percent of the colonial

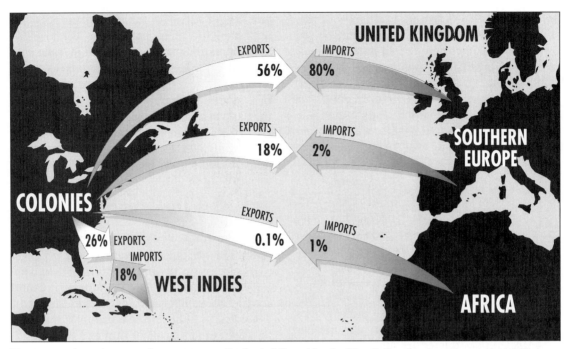

■ The colonies' primary trading partner was England, followed by the West Indies, Southern Europe, and Africa.
Source: J. Sheperd and G. Walton, *Shipping, Maritime Trade, and the Economic Development of North America* (Cambridge, U.K.: Cambridge University Press, 1972), 160–161; *American Economic History,* 3d ed. by Jonathan Hughes. Copyright © 1990, 1987 by Scott, Foresman and Company. Reprinted by permission of HarperCollins Publishers.

total. For most of the colonial period, Southern exports were more than equal to the value of imports from England. Much of the balance was used to finance imports of slaves. After 1750 the plantation colonies began running trade deficits with Africa and the West Indies, largely because of slave imports.

The Middle Colonies
The Middle colonies ran a consistent trade deficit with Britain, buying from two and one-half to seven times the value of their direct exports. The difference was made up by sales of grain, flour, bread, and meat to southern Europe, the West Indies, and other American colonies. In addition, the Middle colonies' merchants were more successful in obtaining British trade credit than were those of other

regions, and they also sold shipping services, ships, and financial services to the British.

New England
From its earliest days, New England ran a large trade deficit with Britain. The major Yankee exports—fish, whale oil, livestock, and shipping services—either competed with English domestic exports or had few markets in Britain. There was a market for lumber in England, but transport costs were very high. Yankees found it more profitable to export wooden products than the wood itself. New England also bought more goods in the West Indies than it sold, but ran a large surplus on shipping services in that region. This, combined with merchandise and service surpluses in Yankee dealings with southern Europe and Africa, financed the New England trade deficit

with Britain. The carrying trade to southern Europe, in which New England transported both its own fish and the Middle colonies' meat and breadstuffs, was especially important. Voyages to this area produced wine, salt, and some fruit and manufactured goods, as well as hard money to apply against the trade deficit with England. Ship sales were another source of British funds for New England.[27]

British Government Spending

The final source of colonial income that could be used to finance overseas trade was British government spending in the colonies. In the latter part of the eighteenth century, Britain spent about 400,000 pounds sterling annually to fulfill its military and governmental obligations in the colonies. Because the colonists paid virtually no direct taxes to the mother country, almost this entire amount could be credited against the trade deficit. A conservative assessment of the colonies' balance of payments over the 1768–1772 period by Professors Walton and Shepherd concluded that no more than 40,000 pounds remained to be paid to England each year by the colonies. Most of this was settled by British extension of trade credit. The total volume of trade at the time was over 4 million pounds annually.[28]

Although the inflow of gold and silver from the West Indies and southern Europe was important to the colonies, the proportion of this specie that was used to finance imports from Britain was no less important to the mother country. Specie was a necessary export component of two vital elements of Britain's foreign trade. It financed imports of timber, iron, naval stores, and hemp from the Baltic, all necessary for the maintenance of Britain's merchant shipping and navy. In addition, that region furnished grain when Britain's own harvest was inadequate for its consumption requirements—a frequent event after 1750. Specie exports were also required in trade with the Orient, where precious metals were exchanged for tea, spices, artwork, and rare fabrics unobtainable elsewhere. Such goods were the basis of a lucrative re-export trade for Britain. Thus, Britain had vital political and economic interests at stake in maintaining the flow of specie from the colonies.

Trade Patterns

Historians once believed that colonial overseas trade was typically conducted in voyages to a succession of foreign ports. These ventures supposedly involved a variety of export goods and exchanges of cargoes at each port visited during the trip. An example might be the carriage of a cargo of rum and trade goods from Newport to West Africa, where it would be exchanged for slaves and perhaps a little gold. The slaves would be carried to the West Indies and exchanged there for sugar, molasses, and hard money, which would be carried to New England. There the sugar would be distilled into more rum, and the voyage repeated. Such multileg voyages were designated triangular trade patterns. New England shippers were thought to be especially partial to such ventures, whose patterns might be triangular, quadrangular, or even more complicated. In each port visited, the ship would sell as much of its cargo as possible, or even the ship itself, reload with whatever item could be obtained on the most favorable terms, and sail off to take advantage of the best opportunities offered by the new cargo. Recent research indicates that such voyages certainly did not typify colonial trading patterns. Although they did occur, the usual colonial trading patterns involved direct exchanges. In particular, less than 3 percent of all New England voyages were made to Africa, and not all of these involved slaving.

---

[27] Walton and Shepherd, *Economic Rise,* 96–101.
[28] Walton and Shepherd, *Economic Rise,* 102–103.

Colonial shippers preferred direct voyages and returns that dealt in as restricted a range of goods as possible for hard business reasons. Multileg voyages depended on either luck or superior access to information (in relation to trade rivals) to be profitable. In the eighteenth century, communications were slow, and information about markets in distant ports was generally at least a month out of date when received. Even if it indicated a chance for high profits, an immediate response to such data was seldom possible; assembling the appropriate cargo and sailing without delay required unusually fortuitous circumstances. Risks were high under the best conditions; prices in most ports could be drastically changed by the sale or purchase of a single ship's cargo. The chances of adverse price movements probably increased at least in proportion to the number of legs in the voyage. Multiple commodities increased risks further. Colonial merchants could not avoid risk, but they certainly did not seek it; wherever possible, they preferred trade ventures involving only one commodity and voyages as short and direct as possible. To obtain current information, many merchants tried to have correspondents in each port where they did business. The correspondents' duties were to send market information and their assessments of any developments that might change it as frequently as communications allowed. Because ships' crews had to be paid and maintained while the ship was in foreign ports but not at home, the costs of multileg voyages were high. If there was competition from other shippers who did not have these handicaps, multileg trade was likely to be unprofitable.

New Englanders were willing enough to engage in the slave trade, but they suffered competitive disadvantages in relation to the English. The African slave sellers demanded manufactured goods as well as rum, and English traders could obtain these more cheaply. Colonial ships were smaller and more lightly crewed than those of England, which increased both carrying costs per slave and the risks of a slave mutiny. In addition, English slave traders had better business connections with the slave "factories" where human cargoes were assembled for shipment. The great majority of slaves imported into North America did not arrive in American ships.

The Importance of Trade

Trade was important to the colonies in several senses. It was one of two methods by which a colonist of ordinary income could hope to become rich. (The other was plantation agriculture, but that required capital beyond the means of most colonists.) Even from a beginning as a common seaman, it was possible for an ambitious young man to progress to ship's officer, and then to ship's captain, while still in his twenties. In addition to their pay, seamen had a minor opportunity to trade on their own account. Officers were entitled to a certain portion of the ship's cargo space for their own use. The proceeds from wise or lucky employment of this opportunity could far exceed even the captain's pay for the voyage. Such gains could finance the purchase of shares in subsequent ventures and a possible progression to shipowner and merchant. This was an uncertain road to wealth; war, pirates, shipwreck, and other catastrophes were frequent, and business risks were high. A dead-end job as a common sailor was another alternative outcome. However, because a New England farm offered no hope at all for high income, there was no lack of seaman recruits throughout the colonial period. Such circumstances forced the development of business skills and responses to opportunity to very high levels.

Rising Trade Productivity
Incomes generated by trade increased over the history of the colonies because the volume of trade increased, the shipping in which it was conveyed became more efficient, and the very

existence of trade allowed a greater degree of specialization within the colonial economy, raising the output that given levels of resources could generate. From 1675 to 1775, the productivity of ocean shipping approximately doubled; a unit of goods could be shipped the same distance at half the 1675 cost by 1775.[29] This gain resulted from two developments, one ashore and the other at sea. As populations grew, the time required to assemble or dispose of a cargo was reduced. Packaging of exports, especially tobacco, became more efficient and growing populations increased the speed of turnover. Consequently, ships could make more voyages and carry a greater value of cargo during a given time period. Port facilities, such as docks, cranes, and warehouses, also improved, further reducing turnaround time. There were minor improvements in ship design and rigging, and possibly in navigation methods as well, which would have increased efficiency, although ship speeds did not rise. The major factor in the increase in shipping efficiency per se was through the reduction in piracy. When the risks of attack by pirates were high, even merchant ships had to carry large crews and cannon for defense. Ship designs had to emphasize naval attributes at the expense of mercantile; cannon and the structural strength to accommodate their recoil cut down on ships' cargo capacity. Some prospective voyages were curtailed because of the risks of pirate activity. But after 1675, the Royal Navy was used to protect merchant shipping in American waters, and the danger from pirates gradually diminished. Consequently, not only could merchant ships carry a much higher proportion of "payload," but they could be redesigned to be more specialized and efficient in their primary function, rather than quasi-warships. Ships plying waters where naval protection was not available or those carrying particularly valuable cargoes still retained their defensive capabilities. Those designed for the East Indian trade, for example, could readily be converted to military purposes, as was John Paul Jones' *Bonhomme Richard.*

Intercolonial Trade

In addition to the colonies' overseas trade, there was an extensive coastal commerce in various North American products. The New England colonies imported foodstuffs, tobacco, and naval stores from the other colonies, in addition to dried fish (for re-export) from the Canadian Maritimes. The Middle colonies imported fish, flax, candles, cheese, and the results of New England's overseas trade, rum and molasses. The South sent corn, wheat, hemp, tobacco, and naval stores to other areas of North America. There was some trade in American manufactured goods, such as soap, beer, furniture, and shoes. The Middle colonies also distributed the results of their southern European trade—wine, salt, and some dried and citrus fruit. This trade was only a fraction of the overseas volume, but it was growing rapidly after 1700.[30]

Not only did external trade account for a considerably higher proportion of the total economic activity of the colonies than it does for the United States today (15 to 20 percent of total output as compared to 12 percent); to a much greater extent than now it produced goods that otherwise would have been unobtainable. In this era, there were no technological means to offset differences in climate or natural resource distribution. Even foreign production techniques often proved difficult to transport.

---

[29] Walton and Shepherd, *Economic Rise,* 117–130.

[30] J. Shepherd and S. Williamson, "The Coastal Trade of the British North American Colonies," *Journal of Economic History* (December 1972). See also G. Walton and J. Shepherd, *Shipping, Maritime Trade, and the Economic Development of Colonial North America* (New York: Cambridge University Press, 1972).

Specialization

It is no accident that productivity gains in foreign trade and related activities were much greater than the average recorded by the colonial economy. Trade promoted specialization. Specialization increased productivity both directly and through "learning by doing," the gains that come from greater experience with any economic activity. Trading activities frequently have economies of scale, particularly where aggregate growth is rapid. Most of the colonies' trading activities were carried out in a highly competitive atmosphere. Colonial exports had to compete their way into world markets in the face of existing substitutes. Moreover, these products were typically produced by large numbers of small-scale (relative to the market) makers operating under the separate political jurisdiction of from two to six colonies. Such conditions further encouraged pragmatic evaluation of methods and efficient allocation of labor. Specialization and exchange increased colonial welfare and that of the entire North Atlantic economy. They produced conditions leading to further gains, and this was well understood at all levels, from the great colonial merchants to the frontier farmer seeking to improve the forest trail that linked him to markets.

THE MONEY SUPPLY

Money is a good traded in all markets, a commodity whose most important economic quality is ready convertibility into anything else. Thus, money increases the efficiency of markets; it fosters trade between two individuals when one of them does not possess a commodity (other than money) desired by the other. Use of money fosters specialization, both directly and through easier exchanges, and specialization increases productivity. Through reducing the time lost in barter trans-

actions and by encouraging specialization, the use of money allows the same real resources to produce more output.

But if a little money is good, more is not necessarily better. Money's value depends on its scarcity; this is true for any commodity used as money, even gold and silver. If, over any considerable period of time, the supply of money increases faster than the supply of goods and services, the purchasing power of a unit of money will decline and inflation will occur. When American gold and silver flowed into Spain in the sixteenth century, the real output of the Spanish economy did not rise in proportion to the influx of precious metals, and prices expressed in money rose even though in every sense of the term "money was as good as gold."

Specie Sources and Substitutes

There were no gold or silver mines in British North America, so specie had to be obtained from other areas by trade or some substitutes for "hard money" developed. Substitutes were used extensively in all colonies—Indian wampum, furs, tobacco and warehouse receipts for it, musket balls, and many other items. All of these had disadvantages as money. They had alternative uses that affected their supply and hence their value in exchange. Some commodities' supplies could not be controlled at all, and units of others were not of uniform quality. Some were not readily transportable or storable, or came in units of inconvenient size or value for most transactions. Monetized commodities might not be acceptable outside the colony that had designated them as such. If they were not acceptable in payment for imports, this was a serious drawback. Consequently, the colonists either had to exchange exports of equivalent value to whatever they imported in each transaction (barter), or obtain some form of money acceptable to trading partners. The first method was highly inconvenient, so the second was used. By selling more to certain areas than the value of their purchases there, the colonists generated a trade balance in their favor that was paid in coins or bullion. The chief sources of this specie inflow were the Caribbean, Latin America, and southern Europe.

Coins at this time were valued by all nations in proportion to their gold or silver content. If a Spanish silver dollar contained 4.5 times as much pure silver as an English shilling, the dollar would exchange for 4.5 shillings. Coins of any nation could thus be used in trade in most markets. The colonies' trade produced a supply of bullion and foreign coins, chiefly Spanish silver dollars (which were sometimes cut into as many as eight "bits," or pieces, to make change). But in the colonies' trade with England, there was a steady outflow of specie to cover the excess of imports over colonial exports.

Trade, Specie Flows, and Colonial Prices

The colonies' trade balance with Britain grew increasingly adverse during the eighteenth century. British manufactured goods were better and cheaper than those of any other nation, and the colonists were not willing to reduce their imports in order to retain specie. The colonists' complaints about the specie drain to England appear exaggerated; while there is no doubt that there was a net specie flow from the colonies to England, colonial prices expressed in specie rose during the eighteenth century, an indication that "hard money" was becoming more rather than less plentiful in relation to goods and services in the colonies.[31] Nevertheless, it was true that the cost of maintaining a large supply of coin and bullion in the colonies was a reduction in imports of British goods and that short-term fluctuations in specie stocks could affect other markets.

Paper Money

As a substitute form of money, paper currency had some obvious advantages. It could be produced at low cost, unlike hard currency: but the same low costs also made it tempting for suppliers of paper money to produce too much and cause inflation. The supply of metallic money was limited by the amount of specie in the world and, for the colonies, by the size of their trade surplus. The surplus in turn depended on the colonists' ability to produce exports and to restrain nonmoney imports. Thus, there were limits on the supply of specie, but these did not hold in the case of paper money. If paper currency was to retain its value, its supply had to be controlled. This could be done either by requiring the issuing authorities to maintain some fixed value between paper currency and other forms of money, or by simply limiting the amount issued.

In the colonial era there were no commercial banks in the modern sense. Today these furnish the bulk of our money supply. There were land banks, institutions that issued notes secured by land or mortgages thereon. These notes circulated and were used as money until the issuing institutions redeemed them or failed. Land banks were forbidden by the English Parliament in 1741. In the colonial period, governments were the primary source of paper money. Nevertheless, in terms of purchasing power rather than nominal value, specie was always the largest component of colonial money supplies.[32] Frequently, colonial governments' paper money issues were interest-bearing notes.

Paper Money and Inflation

Most colonial governments that issued paper money (and all had done so by 1755) did so with caution. In such cases, paper money's exchange ratio with specie and English money

---

[31] Perkins, *The Economy,* 163–165.

[32] Perkins, *The Economy,* 105.

remained fairly constant. Notes issued by Virginia, Maryland, New York, and Pennsylvania depreciated less than 1 percent annually during the eighteenth century. But in Massachusetts, Rhode Island, and the Carolinas, paper money was issued in large amounts and prices expressed in this medium rose. Such currency depreciated relative to specie or more stable forms of paper money.[33]

Legislatures were generally willing to issue paper money to finance military expenditures. Thus, colonial money supplies rose in wartime while real output declined owing to the diversion of resources to wartime uses. Increased demands for goods by the colonial and British military interacted with this reduced supply and produced rapid price increases. After peace returned, the first paper money issues were retired. Currency was accepted in payment of taxes. By limiting government expenditures to less than tax revenues, it could be removed from circulation. But if a surplus was generated too quickly, it might reduce the amount of real output as well as the price level. In any case, taxes have always been less popular than government spending; it was much more politically palatable to place money in circulation than to take it out. Over time, this meant that colonial paper money remained in circulation for longer periods, and new issues were made for a growing variety of reasons in addition to the needs of war.

Real output in the colonies was growing at more than 3 percent annually; this meant that the money supply could grow at the same rate without inducing inflation. In the colonial context, the money supply could rise a little faster. As the volume of economic activity employing money transactions rather than barter increased, more currency would be required. Increasingly, colonists favored issues of paper money as an aid to economic growth. So did most colonial governors, at least after they had gained some experience with the results of a well-managed currency and colonial reluctance to finance governmental activity through taxes.

Problems with Paper Money

The British view of colonial paper money was less favorable. Information about the purchasing power of colonial currency was more out of date the greater the distance from its point of issue. People who knew that Rhode Island currency circulated at much less than its nominal value might take advantage of those lacking this information by using such currency to buy goods at prices that overstated the money's real value. British merchants feared that they would receive colonial money that had depreciated at greater than average rates, and that they would have great difficulty in forcing colonial debtors to pay the full value of their obligations. Paper money was in use within Britain, but there it was issued by privately owned banks, not governments, whose position in their own courts might be very different from private parties.[34] Even so, there is little evidence that British merchants suffered serious losses from this source.

Money and Political Economy

Still, English merchants were represented in Parliament and the colonists were not, and they were increasingly successful in their efforts to restrict colonial paper money issues. As usual, politics and economics made uneasy partners. Although the chief concern of the merchants was to avoid losses caused by inflation, the one situation in which colonial

---

[33] The evidence on the relation between increases in paper currency and inflation in the colonies is mixed. See Perkins, *The Economy,* 179–181.

[34] R. Cameron, *Banking in the Early Stages of Industrialization* (New York: Oxford University Press, 1967), 18–19. See also P. Deane, *The First Industrial Revolution* (Cambridge, U.K.: Cambridge University Press, 1965), 169–171.

currency issues were sure to be permitted was for wartime military expenditures, when they were certain to be inflationary. Moreover, Parliament's initial restrictions generally applied to all colonial uses of paper money rather than just to those involving Britons. The restrictions were very unpopular in the colonies, even among conservatives. After all, most currency issues had not produced the effects that the British feared, and the alternatives to paper money were costly. But in the Currency Act of 1764, Parliament forbade the colonies to authorize private note-issuing banks. In 1751, an act restricting New England currency issues and forbidding them legal tender status even within the issuing colonies had been passed, following the restrictions placed on South Carolina, another chronic offender, in 1731. These laws were enacted with no regard for the state of economic activity within the colonies, and the 1764 legislation worsened a serious business slump. The laws affecting colonial currencies' legal tender status were repealed in 1773, with the proviso that they were not legal tender for private debts, thereby eliminating the risks of British merchants. Further accommodations to colonial needs were made, often after strong colonial protests, but there could be little doubt that Parliament was far more responsive to noncolonial interests, and that its initial consideration of its actions' effects on the colonies was minimal.[35]

Monetary Experiments

In the seventeenth century, Massachusetts attempted to increase its money supply by minting and circulating coins overvalued in terms of their silver content. Colonial legislatures sometimes did the same thing in regard to the Spanish silver dollar, quoting a high legal-tender value. Although these measures attracted specie (sometimes provided by pirates seeking favorable exchange rates for their booty), prices eventually would rise, and coins would flow out to purchase imports at prices determined by their silver content, not the official valuation.

The development of monetary substitutes and means of "stretching" existing money supplies reveals the ingenuity and flexibility that permeated colonial economic activity. The colonists made extensive use of credit, borrowing wherever and whenever they could. Merchants demanded credit from British exporters, frequently on the grounds that they were obliged to extend it to their own customers. Trade credit played a major role in colonial monetary affairs. A wide variety of payments in kind and collateral were employed, and funds were pooled for large endeavors by temporary partnerships, loans from friends or relatives, and by marriage. The corporate form of business, however, was rarely employed and never used in normal production or exchange at this time.

Whatever their failings, and despite the complaints they generated, colonial monetary and financial institutions were successful. Investment was high by contemporary standards, even though most of it was financed quite differently than it might be today. Above all, the source of most colonial capital was individuals' reinvestment of income. The farmer's cleared land, buildings, and livestock increase; the merchant's ships, wharves, and inventories; the increases in plantation labor forces; and increases in individual skills at every level were the result of devoting a portion of current output to uses that expanded future productive capabilities rather than current consumption. A highly developed capital market would have facilitated more efficient applications of savings to the investment projects with the highest rates of return and wasted less effort generating funds, but there is little evidence that promising investment projects were not undertaken because of a lack of sufficient funds.

---

[35] Perkins, *The Economy*, 114–115.

TRENDS IN COLONIAL INCOMES

If we wish to compare the incomes generated by the colonial economy with those we enjoy today, we must combine a strong dose of impressions with any quantitative results we might obtain. Many economists are dissatisfied with modern statistics as indicators of real income. For the entire colonial period, we still have no data of comparable accuracy or scope. Most of the conclusions reached on colonial incomes, trends, and distribution are based on probate records, which indicate the wealth bequeathed at death, on food and fuel consumption (and their relation to total income), and on imports per capita. Evidence from productivity trends and supplies of factors per capita are also useful.[36] We must also remember that comparisons between colonial income levels and those of the modern world cannot really be made in money income figures alone. The colonists lived, and aspired to live, very differently from modern Americans, and many items they consumed differed from their modern counterparts.

Per-capita income figures for even the close of the colonial period vary by as much as 50 percent. Estimates for earlier periods show still greater variation. Estimates of the rate at which incomes grew also show wide variation in both amount and trends over time. Nevertheless, the limits of the debate are

narrower today than previously, and some broad consensus has emerged.

First, aggregate income for the colonies (the total received by all colonists combined) grew at an annual average of something over 3.4 percent. It is known that the colonial population grew at that rate, and the bulk of the evidence supports a view that there was at least some increase in per-capita income. The least optimistic view is that incomes per colonist were static for long periods, but that some growth did occur, particularly in the first few decades of each colony's history. Because colonial population growth was very rapid by eighteenth-century standards, and only a few other economies could have been experiencing per-capita income growth at that time, the colonial economy was the world's fastest-growing.

The Pace of Growth

Second, especially in view of the dismal economic conditions during the formative days of so many colonies, it is probable that the pace of income growth was quite rapid during the first few decades in most colonies settled before 1700. From starvation levels or worse, there was a progression to income levels affording a growing margin above mere subsistence. Evidence on the accumulation of productive assets (wealth) strongly reinforces this conclusion; assets bequeathed per person grew more numerous and varied over the colonial period, indicating more comfortable standards of living.

Third, it is probable that per-capita income growth after the initial adjustment spurt was quite modest, and its pace may well have been slowing. Throughout the colonial period, the vast majority of the colonial population was engaged in agriculture, a sector where technology and productivity changed very little after the first few decades. Thus, at least 80 percent of the population was employed in a sector where output per worker rose only 3 to 6 percent per decade. As the colonial era

---

[36] The primary reference is A. Jones, *Wealth of a Nation to Be* (New York: Columbia University Press, 1980). Other useful works include T. Anderson, "Wealth Estimates for the New England Colonies, 1650–1709," *Explorations in Economic History* (April 1975); M. Egnal, "The Economic Development of the Thirteen Colonies, 1720–1775," *William and Mary Quarterly* (April 1975); A. Jones, "Wealth Estimates for the New England Colonies About 1770," *Journal of Economic History* (March 1972); and R. Gallman, "The Pace and Pattern of American Economic Growth" in *American Economic Growth: An Economist's History of the United States*, L. Davis et al. (New York: Harper & Row, 1972).

progressed, the proportion of the population in new colonies or on the frontier, where increases in agricultural productivity were most likely, was diminishing, and population included more dependents (children and surprising numbers of retired people). There were a few gains in farming efficiency, such as those achieved by the Pennsylvania Dutch and some rice and indigo planters. These, however, affected only a small portion of the agricultural population, and the gains were modest.[37] Agricultural productivity improved mainly from learning by doing, wider use of the best available methods, and improved organization. There were few technological changes. After 1750, the cradle scythe aided wheat farmers, but it was almost the only such innovation. Improvements in the terms of trade raised incomes, but not through higher agricultural productivity.

Fourth, there were sectors of the colonial economy, such as shipping, that achieved gains in productivity. The growth in the size of markets allowed for increased specialization, perhaps lower inventory costs, and gains from the utilization of better and more current information. In a few cases, notably tobacco planting, new institutions increased the efficiency of operations. At the close of the colonial era, manufacturing productivity rose to some extent; there was greater use of water power and more capital per worker. It must be stressed, however, that these gains were achieved by small minorities within the work force.

Finally, colonial imports, for which the data is fairly reliable, increased faster than the population from 1700 to 1770. Because imports were largely tools and luxury goods, this trend indicates that both the standard of living and the ability to produce were increasing.

The portion of slaves to the total colonial population was rising over this era, so rising imports per free colonist almost certainly indicate rising incomes.

Growth in Incomes

In the eighteenth century, per-capita incomes probably rose by something less than 1 percent annually—not a rate that made year-to-year gains obvious to the people generating them. Nor is this a high pace by modern standards. (See Table I.1.) A pace of only 0.5 percent annually, however, would imply that per-capita incomes doubled over the colonial period, and the pace was considerably faster in the early years of most colonies. The "typical" colonist could expect to live considerably better than his or her grandparents had at the same age, and later generations could expect further gains. Elsewhere in the world, continuous growth in incomes was very much the exception.

Not only were colonial incomes growing, they were also very high by world standards. In the eighteenth century, only England and the Netherlands could possibly have had higher levels of income than the colonists. It is at least equally probable that American incomes exceeded those of Europe's wealthiest nations.

Moreover, an equivalent money income provided a higher "quality of life" in America than it did in Europe. It must also be remembered that incomes above subsistence in America went disproportionately to the free population. Britain and the Netherlands contained few slaves, so it is probable that the free population of the colonies enjoyed the highest real incomes in the world in 1750. In 1991 dollars, colonial incomes per capita have been estimated at from $720 to $1,700 per person in 1750, well above those of over 60 percent

---

[37] Walton and Shepherd, *Economic Rise*, 130–133. See also Jones, *Wealth of a Nation to Be*, 304–305.

of the present-day world.[38] It should also be noted that the colonists paid much lower taxes than their British or Dutch counterparts while still receiving most of the services that the British government performed effectively. At the same time, they were able to evade most governmental activity that reduced incomes.

Income Distribution

Arithmetic averages can be deceiving as indicators of the situation of the majority of the population; the distribution of income is also significant. It is obvious that colonial incomes were not evenly distributed, neither over the population nor geographically. Some colonists, especially the great merchants and some plantation owners, received incomes well above the colonial average. The colonial homes that have been preserved are mainly those of these groups, so it is easy to gain an exaggerated idea of real income levels from "museum evidence." Incomes and wealth were higher in the South than in the Middle colonies, and higher still relative to New England, even after deducting slave maintenance from incomes and slave values from wealth. Slaves and indentured servants obviously had below-average incomes (from slightly more than one-third to about 70 percent of the colonial average), respectively.[39] Details of the geographic distribution of colonial incomes in 1774 are given in

Table 2.3. The cities had their poor as well, and the lot of a farmer's or fisherman's widow was not pleasant. Farmers with small or infertile holdings or physical disabilities did not share in the general prosperity.

Several studies have concluded that colonial income disparities were increasing over time, with the merchants and planters, especially those in South Carolina, gaining a larger share of both income and wealth. Because both these groups were experiencing productivity gains (and planters were able to obtain a large share of the income produced by their growing labor forces), this is to be expected. One study of colonial Boston indicated a sharp increase in the share of total wealth held by the wealthy few, but more recent work indicates stability or modest increases in inequality.[40] Boston's circumstances were atypical of the colonies; slowly growing cities would be expected to generate increased income inequalities. Nevertheless, even in the countryside, income distribution was probably becoming less equal, although the disparities were less than those in the cities. Assumptions about the portion of the colonial population in frontier versus settled areas, and the weight assigned to southern populations with many slaves are critical determinants of income distribution. As yet, these are not totally agreed upon.

International Comparisons of Distribution

Even so, it is virtually certain that income distribution was considerably more equal in the colonies than it was in Europe. Despite approximate equality in average incomes

---

[38] Figures are from Walton and Shepherd, *Economic Rise*, 140, 207–208n. Perkins, *Economy of Colonial America*, 145, gives an estimate of $845, somewhat above that of England. Both sets of data are in 1980 dollars, adjusted to 1991 by allowing for 5 percent annual inflation. A. Jones concluded that colonial incomes were slightly less than English. Since her figures are pretax, they support the conclusion that American real income levels exceeded the English (*Wealth of a Nation to Be*). Data on modern income levels from *World Development Report* (Washington, D.C.: World Bank, 1990), 178–179.

[39] Perkins, *The Economy,* 103–104, 212.

[40] J. Henretta, "The Economic and Social Structure of Colonial Boston," *William and Mary Quarterly* (January 1965). See also G. Warden, *Boston, 1689–1776* (Boston: Little, Brown, & Co., 1970), Perkins, *The Economy*, 225, and J. McCusker and R. Menard, *The Economy of British America, 1607–1789* (Chapel Hill, N.C.: University of North Carolina Press, 1985), 270–271.

Table 2.3   Regional Distribution of Income, 1774
(In Pounds Sterling*)

	Population	Per-Capita Income (Mean)	Aggregate Income	Percentage
Southern Colonies				
Free persons	652,585	£26.5	£17,293,000	49.3%
Slaves	433,106	7.0	3,032,000	8.6
Indentured	19,786	9.0	178,000	.5
Subtotal	1,105,477		20,503,000	58.4
Middle Colonies				
Free persons	585,149	13.1	7,665,000	21.8
Slaves	34,172	7.0	239,000	.7
Indentured	21,374	9.0	192,000	.5
Subtotal	640,695		8,096,000	23.0
New England				
Free persons	582,285	10.8	6,289,000	17.9
Slaves	13,654	7.0	96,000	.3
Indentured	11,856	9.0	107,000	.3
Subtotal	607,795		6,492,000	18.5
Total	2,353,967		£35,091,000	

* £1 is calculated to be equal to $65 in 1980 dollars.
Source: E. Perkins, *The Economy of Colonial America* (New York: Columbia University Press, 1980), 154. Data originally from A. Jones, *Wealth of a Nation to Be.* Recent work indicates somewhat greater equality between regional shares of output.

between the colonies and Britain, the richest Americans had far less income and wealth than their counterparts in England, and even slaves received a substantial portion of the income received by the average free colonist. And there was abundant evidence that much of the inequality in colonial incomes was based on economic performance rather than inherited status. The proportion of individuals who could reasonably expect their incomes to rise relative to the average (for example, young adults and indentured servants) was much higher in the colonies than it was in Europe. A large portion of free colonists with below-average incomes were young, owned no land, and often lived with their parents. They could expect incomes and wealth to increase as they became independent and formed their own families. This aspect of colonial demography reinforces the conclusion: Income distribution was more nearly equal than Europe's despite age distribution and social features that should have produced less equality. Because the aged have had more time to accumulate productive assets than the young, they generally hold disproportionate shares of total wealth.

In these relatively open colonial societies, with their acceptance of change, competitive structure, and range of opportunity, individuals had substantially greater opportunities to raise their relative income levels than they did in Europe, or to lose standing by poor performance. This is the essence of income mobility: It is not necessary that the very poorest individuals be able to rise to the highest incomes of the community, or the reverse, but that people can reasonably hope to change their incomes relative to the average. Although by 1750 there were instances of substantial inherited wealth, the colonies were an economic meritocracy by European standards.

COLONIAL GOVERNMENTS

If the initial colonists' material equipment was all too often insufficient, their intellectual baggage was almost equally likely to be excessive. During the seventeenth century, all aspects of human conduct—social, religious, and political, as well as economic—were subject to intensive public regulation. While the colonists might dispute the type of restraints imposed—or, more often, who was to wield such powers—they accepted the idea that most activity was properly the concern of the community and not merely a matter for individual choice. All colonies made attempts to restrict economic and other activities to those acceptable by community standards. But New World conditions forced changes in laws and attitudes just as they had in the tools and production methods brought from Europe.

The colonists had no intellectual commitment to free markets, or for that matter, to free choice in most areas, particularly for "outsiders." Colonial governments were assigned a variety of tasks, and their performance varied widely. But the actual impact of government on the colonists was considerably less than what had been initially intended. Over the colonial era, the influence of governments declined. Some governmental goals were found to be unobtainable or in conflict with other objectives. Over time, governmental activity based on religious or group attitudes held by the early colonists waned. In addition, the colonists were not eager to provide funds for law enforcement.

Property Rights and Public Services

Colonial governments were successful in defining the terms upon which individuals could obtain land. Early in the colonial era, it became apparent that any governmental system that did not allow for the individual ownership of land that could be sold, assigned, or inherited without restraint or subject only to minimal obligations, such as tax payments, was a severe barrier to the immigration desired by all colonies. Europeans simply would not voluntarily migrate to colonies that offered no prospect for at least eventual ownership of land. Defense, too, was largely provided through government (although the burden was shifted from colonial to British government in the eighteenth century). Efforts were made to prevent and punish crimes. Courts were provided to enforce contracts and settle disputes. The destitute (at least those deemed worthy) were grudgingly supported. Conditions of servitude (slavery, indenture, and apprenticeship) were enforced. The degree to which other public facilities were provided varied. New England strongly supported education; the goal was to enable the entire population to read Scripture. To ensure the maintenance of an educated clergy with the proper ideas, colleges were established soon after the founding of some colonies (Harvard was founded in 1636). Particularly in the seventeenth century, there was a great deal of interaction between religion and secular government; in many colonies, the established church received tax support. Most colonies also made some effort to provide roads through taxes paid in labor, goods, or money. Legal-tender laws were established, and colonial success in establishing and controlling monetary systems has already been discussed. In the eighteenth century, the tobacco colonies set up grading and warehousing systems for their primary export.

Other governmental efforts were obvious failures. As with all but the most authoritarian governments since, efforts to control speech, sexual activity, the use of alcohol, and appearance offensive to the established order were unsuccessful. This was not for lack of effort; there were numerous laws against blasphemy, fornication, drunkenness, and inappropriate dress, and efforts to punish violations. Attempts to formally stratify society, as in Maryland and South Carolina, were quickly abandoned.

Government and Economic Controls

Many early attempts to extend governmental authority over economic matters were unsuccessful. Massachusetts attempted to fix wages at English levels in an economy where both factor proportions and prices were very different from the Mother Country. Virginia attempted to reduce the supply of tobacco in order to raise its price without making an agreement with the other tobacco colonies. Both attempts to defy economic reality were short-lived, but apparently long remembered.

Attempts to control the quality and location of work, to limit access to certain jobs, and to set work standards in general probably

had some of the intended effects, but it is difficult to measure their impact on the colonial economy. It is possible to make a few conjectures, however. Regulatory laws were frequently changed, indicating that their effects were not all that had been intended. Compulsory militia training and work on the roads, especially, were often mere drunken frolics. Further, the very low levels of government spending in most colonies indicate a limited effort to enforce most laws.

The Impact of Colonial Government
In effect if not intent, government was a far less pervasive influence on the colonial economy than it was in Britain at that time or in the United States today. It performed fewer functions to a lesser extent than we are accustomed to today. Government did affect noneconomic life to a degree many modern Americans would find offensive. Ideologically, the colonists were seldom opposed to the use of government's coercive powers to achieve their goals. But over time there was a tacit recognition that some early objectives of governmental action either could not be achieved or were not worth their costs; the assessment of government's role became increasingly pragmatic, especially in the case of regulations imposed by distant governments.

There was always concern over tax levels, access to land, and disputes with other colonies. Political ties between most colonies were through their relations with England; outside New England, there were few formal provisions for direct relations between colonies. Most colonists considered themselves citizens first of their colony, then of the British empire, and lastly of America. Their major political interests were in the actions of colonial governments, not the British Parliament. Particularly in the eighteenth century, as migration between colonies became easier, the ability of any single colonial government to impose restrictions not found in other colonies became limited. This plurality of governmental authorities has consistently been a factor that encourages innovation and diversity, from the Greek city-states to the modern world.

The British Legal Heritage

In general, the colonies' legal systems and traditions were based on those of England. Although the ultimate political authority remained the British Parliament, the colonies' internal legal powers were broad. In general, they could pass laws that were not contrary to those of England. By 1700, most colonies were royal colonies, with governors appointed by and directly responsible to the king. Only Maryland, Delaware, and Pennsylvania, which were proprietary colonies, and Connecticut and Rhode Island, which owned their own charters, remained exceptions.

All colonies had legislatures with at least one elected house. Most placed various restrictions on the franchise—restrictions that today would be thought highly discriminatory. Only New England had universal manhood suffrage. There was a strong tradition that "the people" must be consulted before the institution of major political changes in all colonies. The king appointed all high court judges, but most judges and all juries were colonists. Legislatures frequently had the right to deny governors the funds needed to carry out their policies, and were not reluctant to exercise this prerogative. Unpopular governors might find their salaries unpaid for years. While taxes were a source of political controversy, they were very light by the standards of the day, perhaps 1.5 percent of income.[41] Moreover, taxes were devoted entirely to the purposes of colonial rather than British government.

Land Claims

Another recurring political issue was the conflicting claims that many colonies had to territory in the west. Because such land could be acquired very cheaply and held for speculative

---

[41] Perkins, *The Economy*, 125.

purposes, the validity of individual titles to land and the colonial claims through which they were made were major concerns. In addition, land sales were a major revenue source for some colonies, and restricted access to western land might necessitate higher taxes.

Defense

Governmental activity always increases in wartime, but the colonists became increasingly successful in shifting their defense burdens to the British Army and Navy after 1700. In successive wars the colonies' military effort probably declined relative to their population and wealth, perhaps because the bulk of the colonial population was now beyond the effective reach of the French and Indians. Often the British reimbursed colonies for wartime expenditures. In addition, the colonists gouged the British forces to whom they sold supplies and services, and they were not averse to providing the same goods to the French if the prices were right.

THE COLONIAL PEOPLE

By 1750, the colonists' response to the opportunities offered by the New World was an obvious success. They had achieved economic growth beyond that of any other nation, and in doing so had developed some distinctive characteristics. No one would have confused the colonists with their European forebears by this time. Those who had emigrated had not been typical of the European populations from which they came; over 99 percent of all Europeans had stayed at home. Courage and a much greater than normal willingness to face new and different situations than most people possessed were requisites for the transatlantic passage. It must be remembered that theirs was a world in which "strange" meant "dangerous," and minor differences in religion, speech, or customs could provoke hostility even among Europeans. If crossing the Atlantic involved indenture, as it did for so many, there was no return. Even for most others, the costs of a return voyage were beyond reach. Given the risks of the voyage itself, few could have taken emigration lightly. The motivation among those undertaking the journey must have been extremely high. There were a variety of reasons to come to the New World—religion, politics, and in a few cases, an aversion to being hanged—but the primary motive of most emigrants was economic. They wanted to obtain more than had been their lot in the Old World, and this desire appears to have been all but universal among them. The people who would dare such enormous risks were not only more flexible than most of their contemporaries, they were also better informed and educated than the norms for their countries of origin. Most had at least some idea of what would be required of them in America.

Change and Adaptation

Nevertheless, American conditions furthered the emigrants' educations and placed more stress on the ability to adjust than had been anticipated; the initial death rates are grim testimony to that. Many traditional European methods were unsuited to New World conditions; some disastrously so. Many of those that did not have to be abandoned completely required extensive adaptation. The colonists initially tried to build the same type of houses they had known in Europe. But in the New World, labor and tools to shape timbers were far scarcer than in Europe, the only shelter from harsh weather might be a tent, and there was no need to economize on wood. Log cabins were a more effective response to these conditions. The colonists still preferred the European-style house and built modified versions of it after they achieved secure food supplies and met other pressing needs. But it was recognized that this was not the thing to do

in new settlements. By 1750, the cumulative results of many such adaptations had fulfilled many dreams of a better life beyond the sea.

The adjustment process gave all participants an appreciation of the benefits of change. New circumstances placed a premium on rational evaluation of people and opportunities as well as methods, and the competitive structure of colonial economies ensured that this lesson would be stressed long after basic survival needs were met. In the process, ancient prejudices weakened, although they did not disappear. Nevertheless, under American conditions, vital contributions to survival and improvement could and did originate in human sources that Europe would have disregarded had it allowed them to speak at all. Professional soldiers, women, slaves, Indians, even people who were in America "to make Europe better," all added to the new nation's economic knowledge and received recognition for their efforts. Often too, those who had been leaders when the settlements were founded proved least able to adapt and unable to prosper or even survive. The lessons of adjustment were both positive and negative. The basic structure of American institutions owes more to those first desperate years in new colonies than is commonly realized. The lessons were not forgotten, and they served America well.

SELECTED REFERENCES

Bridenbaugh, C. *Cities in the Wilderness: The First Century of Urban Life in America, 1625–1742.* New York: Oxford University Press, 1955.

Bruchey, S., ed. *The Colonial Merchant: Sources and Readings.* New York: Harcourt, Brace, and World, 1966.

Davis, L., R. Easterlin, and W. Parker. *American Economic Growth: An Economist's History of the United States.* New York: Harper & Row, 1972.

Doerflinger, T. *A Vigorous Spirit of Enterprise: Merchants and Economic Development in Revo-*

lutionary Philadelphia. Chapel Hill, N.C.: University of North Carolina Press, 1986.

Furnas, J. *The Americans: A Social History of the United States.* New York: Putnam, 1969.

Galenson, D. *White Servitude in Colonial America: An Economic Analysis.* Cambridge, U.K.: Cambridge University Press, 1981.

Hughes, J. *Social Control in the Colonial Economy.* Charlottesville, Va.: University Press of Virginia, 1976.

Jones, A. *The Wealth of a Nation to Be: The American Colonies on the Eve of the Revolution.* New York: Columbia University Press, 1980.

Kulikoff, A. *Tobacco and Slaves: The Development of the Southern Cultures in the Chesapeake, 1680–1800.* Chapel Hill, N.C.: University of North Carolina Press, 1986.

Lemon, J. *The Best Poor Man's Country: A Geographic Study of Early Southeastern Pennsylvania.* Baltimore: Johns Hopkins University Press, 1972.

Main, G. *Tobacco Colony: Life in Early Maryland.* Princeton: Princeton University Press, 1982.

Main, J. *The Social Structure of Revolutionary America.* Princeton: Princeton University Press, 1965.

McCusker, J., and R. Menard. *The Economy of British America, 1607–1789.* Chapel Hill, N.C.: University of North Carolina Press, 1985.

North, D., T. Anderson, and P. Hill. *Growth and Welfare in the American Past.* 3d ed. Englewood Cliffs, N.J.: Prentice-Hall, 1983.

Parker, W. *Europe, America, and the Wider World: Essays on the Economic History of Western Capitalism.* 2 vols. New York: Cambridge University Press, 1984, 1991.

Perkins, E. *The Economy of Colonial America.* 2d ed. New York: Columbia University Press, 1988.

Price, J. *Capital and Credit in British Overseas Trade: The View from the Chesapeake, 1700–1776.* Cambridge, Mass.: Harvard University Press, 1980.

Schweitzer, M. *Custom and Contract: Household, Government, and the Economy in Colonial Pennsylvania.* New York: Columbia University Press, 1987.

U.S. Department of Commerce, Bureau of the Census. *Historical Statistics of the United States: Colonial Times to 1970.* 2 vols. Washington, D.C.: Government Printing Office, 1975.

Walton, G., and J. Shepherd. *The Economic Rise of Early America.* New York: Cambridge University Press, 1979.

———. *Shipping, Maritime Trade, and the Economic Development of Colonial North America.* New York: Cambridge University Press, 1972.

CAUSES AND CONSEQUENCES OF INDEPENDENCE

THE PRE-REVOLUTIONARY WAR ATMOSPHERE

Until 1750, British rule had imposed no appreciable hardships on the colonial economy. Indeed, it appeared preferable to any realistic alternative. While the French and the Spanish remained politically powerful in North America, the colonies could not hope to retain political independence if it were achieved. Their small populations, limited military capabilities, lack of unity, and wealth were a tempting combination to potential aggressors. This made colonial independence from all European powers most unlikely in the political climate of the eighteenth century. Under these circumstances, British colonial status appeared preferable to French or Spanish rule; it allowed the colonists far more control over their own affairs.

Mercantilism was never carried as far in Britain as it was in continental Europe, and for most of the colonial era, Britain made little sustained effort to enforce regulations that the colonists found irksome. For all practical purposes, the colonists made their own laws and obeyed only those British rules that appeared likely to increase colonial incomes. Colonial economies had developed largely as dictated by comparative advantage, devoting their resources to whatever uses produced the greatest income, with no regard for the mercantilistic ideals of the Mother Country. Parliament made few laws affecting colonial economic affairs and was not insensitive to colonial views on trade regulations and other matters, although it did tend to respond to colonial protests rather than incorporating American views in original legislation. Several laws that the colonists disliked had been modified or rescinded, and the colonies were allowed broad discretion in their application of British law. They made full use of it, both in their courts and in their choices between measures to enforce and those to ignore. In general, Britain followed a policy of benign neglect: Little attention was paid to colonial affairs.

Conditions in 1750

By mid-eighteenth century, then, few colonists had much basis for questioning the overall benefits of British rule. Colonial incomes were high by world (and British) standards, and rising. The explicit cost of British control was very low. The colonists paid no taxes directly to Britain, and as Chapter 2 indicated, few of any kind. Nevertheless, they were beneficiaries of the most efficient services provided by the British government. The colonists received protection on land and sea from the most effective military power of the era. At the same time, they were spared the most negative aspects of British government—the direct mercantilistic interventions in economic activity about which the economist Adam Smith complained so eloquently. Mercantilism furnished many opportunities for rent-seeking activity. Because the gains to its beneficiaries were less than the losses to the general public, rent-seeking reduced aggregate incomes in Britain.

American colonists enjoyed free access to the British market, by that time the largest single aggregation of purchasing power in Europe. They could obtain English manufactured goods and trade credit on terms that allowed them maximum benefits from British efficiency in these important activities. In dealing with other nations, the colonists could call on the British diplomatic service for support. For all these benefits the colonists paid very little in explicit terms and even less when all costs and benefits were considered.

Tax Burdens Colonial taxes were very low and devoted entirely to the support of colonial rather than British governmental activity. In the early 1770s, the British were spending 400,000 pounds sterling annually on governmental services for the American colonies, chiefly for military and naval protection. This sum represented perhaps 1 percent of colonial gross product; it was far more significant for the colonial trade balance than its aggregate dimensions indicate.[1] There is no doubt that the colonists found British military protection valuable; after achieving independence, Americans paid far heavier taxes to their own government than the British asked them to pay for similar services. From the British viewpoint, the colonists were "free riders," consumers of services for which they did not pay.

THE BACKGROUND TO REVOLUTION

Before 1750, Britain had paid little attention to the colonies because their economic importance had been slight; North America accounted for only a minor (though growing) portion of the Empire's overseas trade. But as incomes and populations increased, so did the economic importance of British America. By 1773, the colonies had become the largest single market for British exports and accounted for growing portions of British imports and re-exports as well.[2] Moreover, as previously noted, some colonial exports to Britain had economic and political significance greater than their quantitative dimensions might indicate.

■ Colonial tax protests, such as the tarring and feathering of royalist officials, vividly demonstrated the colonists' attitude toward England. The sympathy of the artist who rendered this sketch, however, is evident in the expressions of the subjects' faces.
Source: Library of Congress.

Other colonial trading activities were less well regarded. As the size and growth of colonial trade spurred British interest, it became clear that the colonies, or some of them, were the only regions within the Empire that did not fit comfortably into the mercantilist mold. Not only did these colonies trade outside the Empire, but they also competed with British producers and traders within it. Although these activities made the colonies better markets for English goods, that was an indirect result of an obvious violation of mercantilist

---

[1] G. Walton and J. Shepherd, *Economic Rise of Early America* (New York: Cambridge University Press, 1979), 102–103.
[2] P. Deane and W. Cole, *British Economic Growth, 1688–1959: Trends and Structure*, 2d. ed. (Cambridge, U.K.: Cambridge University Press, 1969), 87.

doctrine. And the groups injured by such activities had better access to Parliament than did the colonists.

The colonies' political situation also changed in a manner significant for both them and Britain. The conclusion of the Seven Years' War (known to Americans as the French and Indian War) ended the French and Spanish presence in eastern North America. England acquired both Canada and Florida, and with them all territorial claims made by France and Spain. The only remaining threat to the security of the colonies was the Indians, who by this time posed little or no danger to the bulk of the colonial population.

These developments made political independence a realistic possibility for the colonies. The war had major consequences for Britain as well. It had been enormously expensive. Large-scale military and naval operations had occurred in Europe and the Orient as well as in the Americas. Heavy wartime taxes levied on British citizens had not sufficed to finance the entire cost of the conflict. Borrowing had been necessary, and the British national debt had doubled during the conflict. Repayment of this debt implied the continuation of high taxes within Britain unless some other source of revenue could be found or government expenses could be reduced. Britain had borne most of the war's costs even within the colonies. British troops had done most of the fighting, especially in the final conquest of Canada. Much of what military spending had been undertaken by colonial governments had been subsidized either currently or subsequently by Britain. After the war, colonists had frequently used British reimbursements to reduce their own tax levels.[3] They had done little to endear themselves

to British forces during the war and had often benefited at the Empire's expense.

Colonists who sold supplies to British forces had charged what appeared to be high prices. Worse, their sales to the French delayed, or in the case of Haiti, even prevented eventual British victory.[4] Returning English veterans carried bitter memories of the colonists' role in what, from the British viewpoint, was a war fought for their benefit. They also brought better information about the actual levels of colonial wealth and income. Previously, British lack of interest in the colonies had been based on assumptions that the colonists were poor. It was assumed that the colonial tax base was small. But now it became known that the colonists were anything but poor. Understandably, Britain began to consider taxing them in order to relieve British taxpayers and reduce the national debt. When it became clear that defense of the colonies against the Indians would require continued heavy British expenditures, the case became even more compelling in British eyes. The colonists appeared both well able to pay and legally obligated, as citizens of the Empire, to do so. But at the same time, the results of the war gave the colonists a new alternative to British rule. The clash between these changed impressions on both sides eventually produced the American Revolution.

THE ECONOMIC BASIS OF REVOLUTION

Most American students have been taught to view the Revolutionary War as a protest against actual or proposed taxation by the

---

[3] E. Perkins, *The Economy of Colonial America,* 2d ed. (New York: Columbia University Press, 1988), 130–131.

[4] Walton and Shepherd, *Economic Rise,* 162.

British. These taxes supposedly threatened colonial well-being. But this no longer appears to be the case. If British rule did reduce the colonists' welfare, its impact was through other measures, particularly the laws imposed on the colonies' overseas trade.[5]

Trade Regulations

The Navigation Acts were a series of laws enacted by Parliament from 1651 onward. Their purpose was to extend and increase the maritime strength of the British Empire. Later the acts were extended to achieve a wider range of mercantilistic objectives. All trade between Britain and her colonies was reserved to ships built and owned within the Empire, and such ships' crews had to be at least three-quarters British. Foreigners could ship their domestic products only to British, not colonial, ports. They could only carry British exports directly to their own countries. Trade with countries unable to furnish their own shipping was reserved to British vessels. Colonial vessels, crews, and owners were regarded as British under the provisions of the Navigation acts.

Benefits and Burdens The purpose of the acts was to take as much of the international carrying trade from the Dutch as possible and to make Britain the trade center of Europe. The American colonists benefited from these laws, particularly before 1750. Because the Dutch were now less able to compete for the Empire's extensive carrying trade, the demand for colonial ships and shipping services rose. Colonial expertise in these areas, which had always been high, improved at the expense of

both the Dutch and the British. This apparently more than offset any resultant increase in the cost of imported goods. Thus, this aspect of the Navigation Acts stimulated colonial economic activity in an area to which colonial resource patterns were already well suited.

Other aspects of the Navigation Acts had less favorable impacts on the colonial economy. The acts required that certain colonial products, called "enumerated goods," be shipped through British ports regardless of their ultimate destinations. For goods ultimately consumed outside Britain, this law imposed the expenses of longer voyages, port fees, the costs of transshipping, and sometimes warehousing goods in Britain. These costs applied to both enumerated colonial exports and American imports from non-British sources. The burdens that resulted were shared between buyers and sellers. Because the extra costs raised prices to final purchasers, the quantities exchanged were lower and the prices received by the original producers less. This applied to both colonial exports and to imports from continental Europe. The difference between the prices paid by consumers and those received by producers accrued to British middlemen, whose services were necessary only because of the Navigation Acts. Regulations on non-British imports raised their prices to colonial consumers and improved the competitive position of British substitutes.

At first, enumeration affected only a few items, but by 1770 the list of enumerated colonial goods exempted only fish, rice, and breadstuffs among major colonial exports. Even in those cases, free export was allowed only to European points south of Cape Finisterre, a point in northwest Spain. For all practical purposes, direct trade between the colonies and industrial areas of continental Europe was illegal. Moreover, as time passed the laws were more strictly enforced. Because

---

[5] For an excellent summary of recent work on the issues motivating the Revolution, see J. McCusker and R. Menard, *The Economy of British America 1607–1789* (Chapel Hill, N.C.: University of North Carolina Press, 1985), Chap. 17.

a high proportion of enumerated exports originated in the Plantation colonies (especially tobacco, indigo, and some rice), the burden of these laws was especially great for that region.[6]

Enumeration benefited British shippers and distributors at the expense of the colonists and other Europeans, but the British recognized that these gains could only be had while trade continued; it would not pay to raise costs so high that the volume of trade fell sharply or ceased altogether. In some cases where the laws made it difficult for colonial exports to compete in world markets, the regulations were relaxed or eliminated. There was partial compensation: domestic production of tobacco was forbidden in Britain, and rebates were granted on duties paid by colonial products subsequently re-exported from Britain. The colonists reduced the burden of enumeration by smuggling, bribing customs officials, and a variety of other illegal actions. They were at least equally ingenious in obtaining European goods outside the law. Trade regulation burdens rested disproportionately on high-income groups in the colonies—planters and merchants—and on the towns, which benefited from the largest possible volume of shipping and maritime activity.[7]

Additional Regulations

In addition to the Navigation Acts, Parliament attempted to regulate or restrict other colonial economic activity. The regulations placed on banking have been described in Chapter 2. As of 1775, there was no evidence that these laws had any severe adverse impact (the colonial economy continued to thrive),

and the most restrictive acts had already been repealed, but the long-term consequences of such regulations could not be favorable. Further, as with many other regulations, they were applied to all colonies with no consideration of whether each had contributed to the problem or not.

Parliament also passed laws restricting colonial manufacturing or exports of manufactured goods, but these had little real effect. First, the colonial manufacturing sector was such a small portion of the economy that even effective prohibitions would have only a minute impact on aggregate colonial incomes. Second, nearly all of the manufactured goods the colonies did produce were for their own use, not export. The fact that potential incomes were much greater for the colonists in agriculture and maritime activity than they were in manufacturing was a much greater barrier to the growth of industry than was British trade policy. Nor did Parliament forbid manufacturing in general; its restrictions applied only to a few specific items, such as hats, for the export market. And the laws were widely evaded, ignored, or defied by the colonists, as were most other regulations they found inconvenient. Historical evidence strongly supports the conclusion that British regulation was not a major influence on American industrialization. Even after independence, manufacturing did not really get underway in the United States for 30 or 40 years, in spite of a legal climate that now aided rather than opposed it.

Tax Resistance

British taxes also had minimal real impact on the colonies. The tax laws that generated such vehement protests were in fact almost never put into effect. Most of the revenue measures enacted by Parliament after 1763 were rescinded after a few years and yielded little or

[6] Perkins, *Economy of Colonial America,* 30.
[7] Perkins, *Economy of Colonial America,* 35–36. See also M. Egnal and J. Ernst, "An Economic Interpretation of the American Revolution," *William and Mary Quarterly* (January 1972), for a somewhat different view.

Table 3.1   Index of Per-capita Tax Burdens in 1765 (Great Britain = 100)

Great Britain	100
Ireland	26
Massachusetts	4
Connecticut	2
New York	3
Pennsylvania	4
Maryland	4
Virginia	2

Source: Derived from estimates by G. Palmer as given in G. Gunderson, *A New Economic History of America* (New York: McGraw-Hill, 1976), 89. Quoted in Walton and Shepherd, *Economic Rise*, 163.

■ This piece of English creamware is a relic of American colonists' and their British sympathizers' disdain for the Stamp Act.
Source: Courtesy Essex Institute, Salem, Massachusetts.

no revenue while in force. The Stamp Act of 1765 required the colonists to purchase special stamps for all legal documents, even newspapers and playing cards. The act's burdens were largely on businessmen, planters, publishers, and lawyers; in short, on all the politically active and articulate groups in the colonies. It provoked massive opposition, including an effective boycott of British goods in most colonies, and was repealed the next year. No revenue was collected while the act was supposedly in force. Mobs (often including merchants, lawyers, legislators, and other members of the colonial "establishment") intimidated the men appointed to administer the act.[8] In 1767 the British tried again, this time with duties on paint, paper, glass, lead, tea, and other items (the Townshend duties). The taxes were accompanied by new measures to stiffen enforcement of the trade laws. The colonial response was boycotts so effective, especially in the Middle colonies, that British merchants petitioned Parliament to repeal the

taxes. The colonists won again; the Townshend duties were repealed in 1770 (with the exception of the tea tax).

Britain spent an estimated five pounds on tax collection in the colonies for every pound of revenue actually collected before 1768. After that date, the new laws and revisions in the rates of some longstanding duties on sugar and molasses raised approximately 17,000 pounds yearly. This was a minor burden, representing a maximum of 5 cents per colonist annually when yearly incomes were at least $100.[9] By the time the Revolution occurred, the colonists would appear to have resolved the question of British taxation in their own favor. No new British taxes had been proposed since 1770, and the burden of those actually imposed was infinitesimal. Table 3.1 indicates that the colonists could hardly be termed overtaxed relative to Britain. It also helps to explain British interest in raising revenues from the colonies.

[8] J. Hughes, *Industrialization and Economic History: Theses and Conjectures* (New York: McGraw-Hill, 1970), 106–110.

[9] J. Hughes, *Social Control in the Colonial Economy* (Charlottesville, Va.: University of Virginia Press, 1976), 158. See also Perkins, *Economy of Colonial America*, 137–138.

BENEFITS OF BRITISH RULE

Although British trade regulations imposed costs on the colonists, there were also benefits from British rule that went far to offset them. If we minimize the value of British naval, military, and diplomatic services by assuming that they were no greater than U.S. spending for the same purposes after 1789, we find that they were worth between $1 and $3 million dollars annually.[10] Because the forces provided by U.S. expenditures were far smaller and at least initially less respected abroad than their British counterparts, we may be quite confident that use of these figures understates the value of the British contribution. In addition, Britain paid subsidies to colonial producers of indigo, timber, and naval stores, increasing their incomes. Colonial incomes from shipping services performed outside the empire were reduced by the Navigation Acts, but one scholar has concluded that those obtained within the area of British rule were increased by about as much.[11]

Crushing Tax Burdens?

Attempts have been made to quantify the net impact (both benefits and costs) of British imperial policy upon the colonial economy. Although the necessary data for an exact determination do not exist, the conclusions of a number of careful studies are that the net burden per colonist could not have exceeded $1 per year, and there is some possibility that British rule *raised* colonists' incomes rather than reducing them. Because colonial per-capita incomes were about $100 per year in 1770 dollars, conclusions that Britain had imposed intolerably high costs on the colonists appear unjustified.[12] It is not even clear that the burden was increasing in the years immediately preceding the Revolution. The colonists had obtained concessions on nearly all British regulatory policies or taxes, and there is little evidence that new attempts were under consideration.

WHY A REVOLUTION?

Because the Revolution did occur, but its economic origins do not appear to be very firmly based, what was its cause? There was no guarantee that the Revolution would succeed. The first armed resistance by the colonists was apparently intended to force further British concessions rather than gain independence. Even after the war began, its eventual outcome was uncertain for years. The colonists could have held few illusions about the risks involved. There were many Highland Scots and Irish in America who could furnish grim firsthand accounts about British treatment of unsuccessful rebels. If potential risks were so great, the prospective gains so small, and colonial incomes both comfortably high and rising, why would the colonists rebel? If the Revolution is viewed as an economic proposition, either the colonists, or some of them, viewed the costs and benefits differently from the analysis presented here, the benefits and

[10] *Historical Statistics of the U.S.: Colonial Times to 1970*, 2 vols. (Washington, D.C.: Government Printing Office, 1975), 1:1115.

[11] R. Thomas, "A Quantitative Approach to the Study of British Imperial Policy upon Colonial Welfare: Some Preliminary Findings," *Journal of Economic History* (December 1964).

[12] Thomas, "Quantitative Approach." See also G. Walton, "The New Economic History and the Burdens of the Navigation Acts," *Economic History Review* (November 1971), and Perkins, *Economy of Colonial America*, 138–141.

burdens were unequally shared (or recognized), or our analysis has omitted something of importance to the colonists. Otherwise, we cannot view the American Revolution as an event whose causes were largely economic. There is support for all of these points.

Economic Factors

The costs of trade regulation were only too obvious to colonial planters and merchants. The Navigation Acts required that about three-quarters of all colonial exports be shipped through British ports. About 85 percent of these goods were subsequently re-exported. Thus, about two-thirds of all colonial exports were subject to laws that reduced both the volume and prices of exports. Approximately one-fifth of all colonial imports originated in continental Europe and cost the colonists more than was economically necessary because of the rerouting imposed by the Navigation Acts.[13] These are maximum estimates, because some of this trade, both exports and imports, would be (and after independence was) shipped through Britain even in the absence of legal compulsion. Britain was, after all, the greatest trade center in Europe. Large-scale traders were most heavily affected by the Navigation Acts. But planters were shipping a declining portion of colonial tobacco exports after 1740, and the portion of smaller farmers' income derived from tobacco was much less than that of the great planters.[14]

Political Economy or *Special Interests, 1775 Model*

Still, the great planters and the merchants of the colonial cities were the colonies' political as well as economic leaders; developments that affected them had a disproportionate impact on British–colonial relations. To some analysts, the changes in British regulations threatened both the monopoly power of the colonial elite (as distributors of imports and credit) and the political power on which it was based. These groups supported the nonimportation agreements of 1766 and 1768–1769, both to regain control over import markets from British firms' auction sales and tobacco factors and as a means of disposing of excessive inventories of imported goods.[15] The artisans and workers of the ports were also adversely affected by measures that reduced the volume of trade. Supposedly, they also saw increased colonial autonomy as a source of more jobs through increased manufacturing activity, the lifting of debt obligations to British exporters, and a greater voice in the domestic affairs of the colonies.[16] The latter point, however, does not appear well supported as an important cause of the Revolution. The "lower orders" influence was small because they were such a tiny portion of the population and were disproportionately under-represented because of property qualifications for voting. And it is difficult to understand how they felt injured by British policies that reduced the prices of both imported goods and credit. In the years immediately preceding the Revolution, trade volume was clearly influenced more by colonial actions (boycotts) than it was by British policy.

Open and Concealed Benefits The chief benefits from British rule were easy for most colonists to overlook. When the Royal Navy was most effective in protecting colonial shipping, merchants and sea captains seldom saw the

---

[13] Thomas, "Quantitative Approach."
[14] Perkins, *Economy of Colonial America*, 52–55.

[15] Egnal and Ernst, "An Economic Interpretation of the American Revolution."
[16] Egnal and Ernst, "Economic Interpretation."

frigates that drove pirates from the sea lanes. When the Navy was visible, it often appeared to be doing little but interfering with the pursuit of peaceful trade. The drastic fall in maritime insurance rates that the Navy's efforts produced in the eighteenth century was also easily taken for granted or attributed to other causes.[17]

Most colonists had a low opinion of the British Army's Indian-fighting ability. But their own record was also poor. The colonists may have suffered from 30 to 50 casualties for every one they were able to inflict on the Indians.[18] The Indians were generally able to control the time and place of battle, which was a major handicap to frontiersmen and militia with other claims on their time. After the British Army was withdrawn, Americans found it necessary to replace it with their own and support it with taxes. The United States Army also had to learn Indian fighting the hard way.

The costs and benefits of military protection were apportioned very unevenly over the colonial population. A frontier settlement with limited access to outside trade might gain as much in expanded sales to a nearby garrison as it did in improved security; its overall benefits would be great. New York or Philadelphia merchants might well take a different view. To them the taxes that Britain was attempting to collect might appear a greater threat than the Indians. More rigorous enforcement of trade regulations by customs officials able to call on the protection of a sympathetic British military might cost the towns more than they could earn by selling provisions and other services to the Army or Navy. The Quartering Act of 1765, which obliged colonial towns to house British troops in civilian dwellings if the towns

would not provide barracks, was probably the most unpopular single measure proposed in this era so rich in British "provocations."

THE PATH TO REVOLUTION

Perhaps the most alarming development from the colonial viewpoint was Britain's growing determination after 1763 that its regulations should be obeyed. In pursuit of this goal, the British developed increasingly sophisticated measures that grew more difficult for the colonists to evade. After 1763, no longer were the trade laws to be enforced by the colonists themselves in their own courts or by officials dependent on the colonists for salaries or security. Customs officials were ordered to their posts in the colonies (the necessity of such an order is eloquent testimony to the previous efforts at law enforcement), and informed that they would be paid from the revenues they collected. Colonial governors were given larger staffs and granted more freedom from the colonists' legislative and judicial control. Revisions were made in the tax laws that made evasion far more difficult. Taxes on tea and sugar were reduced, while more active customs efforts raised the cost of goods smuggled in from French or Dutch sources. Sometimes the result was a reversal of the relative prices of legal and smuggled goods and a redistribution of incomes among colonial sellers.

Political Considerations
In their attempts to influence the laws, the colonists had severe political handicaps. They were, of course, not represented in Parliament. Even had they been represented in proportion to their numbers, the colonial delegation would have been a minority voice, unable to

---

[17] Walton and Shepherd, *Economic Rise*, 120–121.
[18] J. Furnas, *The Americans: A Social History of the United States* (New York: Putnam, 1969), 38.

defend colonial interests in any straightforward clash of regional interests. In 1770, Britain's population was more than four times that of the colonies. Worse, although the colonists were not directly represented in Parliament, several groups strongly opposed to them were. British landlords, who paid the property taxes that furnished much of the government revenue, comprised the largest single group in Parliament. Merchants, whose interests wavered between efforts to expand their American markets and attempts to minimize the risks of existing trade, also formed a sizable portion of Parliament's members. Indirectly, even the British West Indies had a strong legislative voice.

Unlike the North American colonies, where immigrants remained for the rest of their lives, many British planters returned to England after making their fortunes in the Caribbean. In eighteenth-century England, politics was a socially acceptable hobby for a retired man of wealth, and there were many seats in Parliament more or less for sale to the highest bidder. The sugar interests were strongly opposed to competition from the French sugar-producing islands that colonial traders had found to be such lucrative sources of income.

Representation without Taxation—the British View

Englishmen paid taxes and, to a limited extent, voted in Parliamentary elections. The colonists did neither. They admitted that Parliament was the ultimate political authority within the Empire but disputed its right to pass laws with which they disagreed. They expressed their displeasure through (legal) boycotts and mob threats and violence, violating colonial as well as British law. Even Englishmen favorably disposed toward the colonists found it impossible to defend so self-serving a position.

British Land Policies

A final major source of friction between Britain and her colonies was land policy. Various colonial charters had either left the region's western boundary undefined or extended it to the Mississippi River or even the Pacific. Sales of western land had allowed colonial governments to raise revenue without taxation, which was understandably popular among Americans. The value of western land appreciated as colonial populations grew and settlement was extended. Also, it was thought, apparently without much factual evidence, that soil fertility near the seaboard had or might decline. Most colonists were land speculators. Early settlers or those with political influence could often obtain and hold land for virtually nothing, so the potential gains from its appreciation appeared to be limited only by the landholders' optimism.

Cheap Land or Expensive Security?

After the French surrender in 1763, the British faced a difficult decision. If peace could not be maintained between the colonists and the Indians, they would be faced with the expenses of yet another war, this time almost entirely for the colonists' benefit. The Indians were uneasy because their French allies were gone. But precisely because the French no longer supported the Indians' opposition to new settlements, the colonists were eager to extend the frontier westward. Faced with a choice between paying for more wars or incurring continuous expenses for keeping the antagonists apart, and under heavy domestic pressure to reduce taxes, the British decided to govern the lands west of the Appalachians along the lines pioneered by the French. Settlement west of the Atlantic watershed was prohibited, and colonial, though not British, land speculators' claims west of this "Proclamation Line" were denied.

To the British, this decision seemed better than any alternative. There had already been one serious Indian war (Pontiac's Rebellion) in 1763, which had been very costly in both money and the lives of British troops. If the colonists would not pay their own defense costs, they had to be kept out of contact with the Indians, even if this meant the abrogation of land claims. Colonial pressure induced Parliament to shift the Proclamation Line slightly farther west in 1768, but in 1774 the Quebec Act was passed. This legislation transferred ownership of all western lands north of the Ohio River to Canada, reserved large tracts south and east of that region for the Indians, and raised the price of land in the areas remaining open to settlement. As if to add insult to injury, French Canadians were granted liberal terms of government that upheld many of their political and religious institutions—a move the British hoped would further ease the costs of government. The colonists were outraged. Not only did most of them dislike Catholics and nearly all harbor an intense hatred of Indians, but their dreams of prosperity financed by land sales were abruptly replaced by the nightmare of higher taxes. The Quebec Act had a direct impact on far more colonists than did trade regulations. Even though there was a great deal of uncultivated land remaining within most colonies, rapid population growth and static agricultural technology apparently made access to additional land necessary for the long-term growth of the colonial economy. Because the colonists had no intention of paying taxes to Britain, the fact that the Quebec Act would reduce the Empire's defense costs had little, if any, offsetting weight.

The View from Whitehall

The British saw colonial relations differently. To them, the new regulations and attempts to raise tax revenues seemed not only legal but eminently reasonable. The colonists were British subjects and therefore obligated to provide support for the government. They were being asked to pay only about one-fourth the tax burden already imposed on Englishmen; even the desperately poor Irish paid more.[19] Most of the laws that the colonists were now to obey had long been on the statute books—a consideration that appeared very different to the colonists. One thing that Parliament could not accept was open defiance, especially in the case of laws that were intended to benefit both the colonists and the Mother Country. The English were not trying to raise taxes for their own sake; their program was an effort to keep overall taxes as low as possible by combining tax policy with laws that reduced the necessity for expenditures.

Efforts to separate the colonists and the Indians would, if successful, reduce military expenses and the taxes required to support them. The colonists had provided little aid to the British during the war; they could do so now. Parliament was willing to compromise on details. Taxes were changed and, in some cases, abolished in the face of colonial protests, which was possibly a serious error. What Parliament saw as flexibility, the colonists may have viewed as the ability to reverse any law they disliked. Moreover, the means employed by the colonists were extralegal, including protests and sometimes mob violence. The colonists had won the initial tests of will. Parliament had taken several stands on principal and had backed down in the face of colonial opposition each time; the Stamp Act and the Townshend Acts were both repealed. It may have been difficult for the colonists to realize that they could push too far.[20] Ominously, even in its revocation

---

[19] G. Gunderson, *A New Economic History of America* (New York: McGraw-Hill, 1976) 88–89. See also Perkins, *Economy of Colonial America*, 163–164.

[20] L. Harper, "Mercantilism and the American Revolution," *Canadian Historical Review* (March 1942).

of some measures the colonists opposed, Parliament had restated its ultimate authority over the colonies.

Colonial Defiance and Mutual Provocations

Other developments, minor in themselves, added to the colonists' list of grievances or to British conclusions that the colonists refused any of the responsibilities of citizenship while claiming all its privileges. The Royal Navy was often less than polite in its searches for contraband and in its insistence that colonial ships perform elaborate salutes to the flag. Some crews of British customs cutters, already unpopular for their very presence, helped themselves to colonial livestock, firewood, and other property. British troops in colonial garrisons were continually harassed, one instance (1770) provoking the Boston Massacre. The British needed tall, straight white pines for warship masts and spars. Timber cruisers were sent through New England forests to locate suitable trees and mark them with the broad arrow that designated them as government property. But often when the Navy crews arrived to cut the tree, only a stump remained, and no one in the neighborhood population had noticed that the tree had been cut. Because felling and moving such a tree required a large work force and from 16 to 100 yoke of oxen—the entire draft-animal force for miles—the British found colonial protestations of ignorance hard to accept at face value.

The inevitable challenge came in 1773. The East India Company, a British trading company with a monopoly on oriental trade, was in financial trouble. To increase its revenues, Parliament allowed it to ship tea directly from India to the colonies, and the tax on tea was reduced. These measures reduced the price of legal tea in the colonies to less than that of smuggled tea from Dutch suppliers. Colonial consumers benefited, but merchants and smugglers did not. In colonial ports, the tea ships met a hostile reception, and many returned to England without even attempting to land their cargoes.

The Last Straws In Boston, a mob boarded the tea ship *Beaver* and threw its cargo into the harbor—the famous Boston Tea Party. This was an affront that exhausted Parliamentary patience. The response was a series of laws making it clear Parliament was finally determined to show itself as the ultimate source of authority within the Empire and would brook no further colonial opposition (the Port of Boston Act). Boston was closed to all shipping until the East India Company received restitution for its tea. British officials charged with crimes committed in the enforcement of trade regulations were to be tried outside the colonies, the hand of the royal governor was strengthened, and more troops (whose expenses were to be paid by Boston) were sent to ensure the enforcement of the laws. There was no mistaking Parliament's intentions. Bostonians called these laws the "Intolerable Acts."

It now appeared that England was not merely trying to force the colonists to buy British goods (at the same time restricting their ability to pay for them). Boston could not exist without trade; the city depended on imported food. To compound matters, once again Parliament refused to notice variations in colonial behavior: Annapolis had burned its tea, ship and all, and only the discretion of tea-ship captains had prevented similar incidents in other colonial ports. Worse, there seemed to be no way to evade these penalties.

Other changes in trade regulations that occurred after 1765 outraged the colonists. Smuggling cases were now tried in Admiralty Courts. Because these courts were staffed by Royal Navy officers who received a share of

■ The British reaction to the Boston Tea Party in 1773 was very different from that of the cheering crowds depicted in this Boston drawing.
Source: Culver Pictures.

any confiscated cargo, their decisions were not characterized by excess leniency. Colonial merchants now lost cases with the same regularity with which colonial courts had once acquitted them. New search warrants called Writs of Assistance allowed customs officials to comb colonists' homes and warehouses for smuggled goods.

Revolt of the Masses

Even at this time, few Americans advocated more than the redress of what they regarded as legitimate grievances (regardless of British opinions on these questions). A year of armed conflict was required before even American activists concluded that no solution could be found short of independence. Still, they failed to convince a majority of the colonial population. The American Revolution was not a mass movement. Only about a third of the colonists supported it to varying degrees. A slightly smaller group, the Tories, was equally active in opposing the Revolution. The rest of the population tried to remain neutral. Although support for the Revolution was strong in the urban centers, with less than 5 percent of the aggregate population, the towns could not have achieved independence without rural support.

Trade regulations may have been important issues to colonial townspeople, but the overwhelming majority of colonists were small-scale farmers. This group's attitudes were determined largely on political, not economic, grounds. To them, the issue was that they had always made their own political decisions and now the British appeared to be challenging those rights. Another group of colonists had little choice about supporting the revolt. The frontier had normally felt itself oppressed more by colonial governments than by the British. But changes in land acquisition policy began to change this view, and after hostilities began the British recruited Indians to fight for them. The Indians attacked those colonists who appeared to pose the greatest threat to their interests: the frontier settlements. No doubt one colonist looked much like another to the Indians. In any case, the frontier found itself supporting the Revolution as a matter of survival.

Not all planters and merchants supported the Revolution. If they bore the greater portion of the burdens of British rule, they remained wealthy after such costs were met. Nor was their position determined on economic grounds alone; some had strong loyalty to the king. Even on purely economic grounds, the Revolution's appeal to the wealthy must have been limited. Where established authority is to be overthrown, the rich have much to lose. It could not have been clear that the interests of high-income groups would be improved by the Revolution.[21] Although many planters and especially the Middle-colony merchants had debts to British merchants, repudiating these by revolution was unlikely to help. In the long run their incomes depended on continued exports, and their British creditors were the best customers and suppliers available.

THE ECONOMICS OF THE REVOLUTION

Britain had many advantages in a colonial war: an experienced army; command of the sea, which allowed easy concentration of force;

and a home government whose authority was unchallenged—all sharp contrasts to the colonists' circumstances. Quantitatively, Britain had other assets: much greater population, manufacturing resources, and wealth. Even within the colonies, it was not likely that the Americans would be able to assemble superior forces. Total population was slightly over two million people, but only a small portion of these would be available to the Continental Army or to the state militias. Half the population was female, one-fifth were slaves, and of the remainder, two-thirds did not support the Revolution. Even if over half the resulting manpower pool was capable of military duty, this was perhaps 150,000 men. But only a fraction of this number could serve as soldiers. Because output per person was low, most had to continue their civilian occupations. Any large-scale diversion of manpower to the army would have resulted in a disastrous drop in the production of food and other goods.

The Logistics Nightmare The Patriots also had difficulty in concentrating large numbers of troops at any given point. Transportation and supply were especially difficult. The Royal Navy was strong enough to prohibit any large-scale movement of American troops by sea, and there were no means of transporting large numbers of men overland. Political difficulties added to the Americans' problems. Complete unity of purpose was an ideal the thirteen colonies never attained. There was no political authority that could compel individual colonies to send troops or even supplies outside their own borders. Even should their governments be willing, individual soldiers were often reluctant to serve far from home or for long periods. Consequently, Washington never commanded more than about 20,000 troops and usually led about a third of that number. Every change in the location of military activity resulted in both qualitative and quantitative declines in the Continental Army

---

[21] Egnal and Ernst view this as a point increasing the pressures on the colonial elite to regain political domination— which they did. "An Economic Interpretation of the American Revolution."

until men from the new area could be recruited, trained, and disciplined. America had to find its military leaders by trial and error. Many of the officers initially appointed owed their positions to political influence rather than military skill—and proved it in battle. The colonists also were dependent on access to foreign supplies of arms and munitions so control of some major seaports was essential to them. Fortunately, British forces were never sufficient to occupy all the major ports simultaneously.

The Sources of Victory

Despite all these handicaps, the Revolution succeeded. The Americans won because the British, for a variety of reasons, failed to make full use of their military potential. Because the British were fighting in many different parts of the world as well as in America, they were never able to commit troops in numbers sufficient to overwhelm the Continental Army. For the most part, the English sent second-rate generals to America. Some of these failed to live up to their reputations.

The Americans learned from a variety of mistakes, aided by British failure to follow up on advantages. They persevered under difficult circumstances, and they received efficient foreign help. The entry of France into the war in 1778 spread the conflict to Europe, the Caribbean, and even the Orient, weakening Britain's ability to concentrate her force on America. At sea, a rejuvenated French fleet required almost the full attention of the Royal Navy. Few British ships were available to blockade the American coast, and the Patriots could obtain supplies and military assistance from Europe.

The French Connection Saratoga (1777) and Yorktown (1781) were the two decisive battles of the war. Saratoga was won by the colonists with French arms and supplies. At Yorktown, a naval victory by the French was crucial; it trapped a British army and enabled a combined American and French force to beseige and defeat it.

In addition, swarms of American privateers attacked British merchant shipping. Over 1,600 letters of marque ("privateering licenses") were issued to Massachusetts ships alone.[22] Though they never threatened Britain's control of the sea, the privateers greatly increased the costs of Britain's overseas trade, even in European waters, and forced the Royal Navy to use warships for convoy duty. Cargoes captured by privateers helped to offset the reduction in American trade with Britain. Many Americans found privateering a means of combining patriotism and profit. Successful privateering ventures paid much better than service in the army and may not have involved greater risks.

In the end, the British found the cost of suppressing the Revolution more than any benefits it might have offered. Given the costs also incurred by the colonists, perhaps the British were more realistic. Britain's gains from political control of the colonies, if any, could not have been great, and it was obvious that the costs of enforcing exploitation would henceforth be much greater.

FINANCING THE WAR

The Revolutionary War lasted from 1775 to 1783, and there was considerable fighting in all but the last two years. Wars are always expensive, but the Patriots faced several unique problems. First, support for the war was not

---

[22] S. Morison, *The Maritime History of Massachusetts: 1783–1860* (Boston: Northeastern University Press, 1961 and 1979), 29.

universal among the colonial population. The Tories not only refused to help, they actively aided the British. Colonists living in areas under British control were in no position to offer aid, regardless of their sympathies. It was risky to press the neutral third of the people very hard. Even among the patriots, a revolution against British taxation was hardly the ideal basis for raising revenues. The taxes that were levied were imposed by state governments, not the Continental Congress, which had to depend on whatever funds the individual states were willing to allocate to it. They financed only 6 percent of the total cost of the war.[23]

Military demands diverted resources from other uses and thus reduced total output and incomes. War damage further reduced the base against which taxes could be levied. Borrowing was a time-honored method of financing wars, but for the patriots it was difficult. Americans were little more willing to buy war bonds than they were to pay taxes; state and national bond issues paid 28 percent of wartime expenditures. The value of such bonds to purchasers obviously depended on the buyers' assessment of the war's progress. A British victory would make bond sales more difficult just when the need for funds to replace lost equipment, train new troops, and, above all, to pay and supply those already enlisted was particularly urgent. Foreigners might be persuaded to lend to America, but again, their views of the military situation influenced their lending. In addition, the British would interpret such a purchase as an act of war, and only France was openly allied with the patriots before 1779. In total, domestic and foreign borrowing raised only about $14 million. Foreign lenders contributed 8 percent of war costs.

Paper Money Problems

Faced with soaring military expenses, the patriots tried a variety of expedients. Property seizures by the states raised another 18 percent, but this measure risked the Revolution's fragile popularity. Only one major source of finance remained to the Patriots: They printed money. The states issued $209 million in paper currency from 1775 to 1779, and the Continental Congress issued another $241 million. This amount was equal to nearly two years' income for every resident of the colonies at prewar prices; it was an enormous increase in the money supply, and it paid about 40 percent of total military expenses. Its inflationary potential was increased still further because not everyone would accept such currency, and the supply of goods and services available for purchase had been reduced by the diversion of resources to war purposes.

At the same time, the Continental Army's purchasing agents had to compete with those of the British and French, who paid in gold, not paper. The huge increase in the money supply resulted in runaway inflation. Because the Continental Congress was known to lack the power to tax, it could furnish no credible assurance that its paper money issues could ever be redeemed for their face value in goods or specie.[24] Paper currency rapidly lost value both in purchasing power and in relation to metallic money. By 1781, prices peaked at 135 times their prewar levels. Efforts at price controls during this period had little effect because the real source of the inflation was the increase in the supply of paper money relative to goods; higher prices were merely the result.[25] After 1781, prices fell rapidly as state money issues were repudiated and governments refused to

[23] Figures on Revolutionary finance are from C. Calomiris, "Institutional Failure, Monetary Scarcity, and the Depreciation of the Continental," *Journal of Economic History* (March 1988).

[24] Calomiris, "Institutional Failure."
[25] A. Bezanson,"Inflation and Controls: Pennsylvania 1774–1779," *Journal of Economic History* (Supplement, 1948), 1–20.

accept them in payment of taxes. As a result, the state money became unacceptable and ceased to circulate.

The Burdens of War

Who paid for the Revolutionary War? Little of the financial cost was paid by taxpayers per se: Only a small part of the total cost of the war was tax-financed. Those who bought bonds, then found that Congress was unable to pay even the interest on its obligations, let alone redeem them on the specified terms, obviously paid more than they had expected. When the bonds eventually were redeemed some years later, current bondholders gained at the expense of taxpayers who financed the redemption, but by 1792 the composition of both bondholding and taxpaying groups was very different from what it had been when the bonds were issued. Some bondholders had acquired bonds at a fraction (as little as one-eighth) of their original value. Those who accepted paper currency and underestimated the rate at which it would lose purchasing power

also paid for their errors. Taxation in the usual sense had been replaced by "taxation" through inflation, currency repudiation, and by the imposition of less favorable terms of debt repayment than those originally offered. Tories lost property through government confiscation. Most veterans also paid; they were promised rewards that were either never paid or long delayed. Obviously, some people paid in physical terms—they were killed, wounded, or imprisoned during the war, or they lost property. This group included Tories as well as Patriots and those who suffered confiscation of property or were coerced into accepting paper money in payment on terms that they would not have freely accepted. To the extent that the war reduced the economy's productive activity, the entire population incurred reductions in income below those potentially available.

THE WAR'S IMPACT

The war caused distortions within the colonial economy, but overseas trade expanded after 1777. There was now no reason to obey the Navigation Acts; the Royal Navy had few ships to spare for customs patrols. Even trade with Britain did not cease entirely. A small volume of trade from areas under British control continued, and the Patriots were able to obtain some British goods by smuggling and trading in neutral ports, such as St. Eustatius in the West Indies. Privateering and raids supplemented the goods received through voluntary exchange. Trade with continental Europe expanded.

There was a considerable expansion of colonial manufacturing activity in both military goods and substitutes for imported goods that were now more expensive and uncertain in supply. As is generally the case during periods

■ The large denomination of this Continental note indicates inflation was already severe in 1778. In prewar years, $20 would have equaled about two months' average income.
Source: Library of Congress.

of rapid inflation, economic activity was high, although efforts to offset the effects of higher prices meant that not all of it was productive. Nearly all of the new manufacturing depended upon the continuation of the war, which raised the prices of imported industrial products far above peacetime levels, allowing high-cost American producers to compete.

Human and Physical Costs

There was little permanent damage to productive resources. Human casualties were low in relation to the population and in comparison to later wars, although they were about one-eighth of the military personnel, a high portion in comparison to rates in subsequent military ventures.[26] The Loyalists who felt compelled to leave the country after the war represented a loss of capabilities much greater than their numbers would suggest; they were disproportionately members of highly productive groups. Because the war had been fought chiefly in the countryside, aggregate property destruction was not great. It was difficult to do lasting damage to agricultural areas with eighteenth-century weapons.

Regional Impacts The war's impact on geographic regions varied. New England was untouched after 1775, with a few exceptions in coastal areas. The South was the scene of much of the later combat, and the only area in which the British made efforts to employ economic warfare. Some 50,000 slaves were carried off by the British, and there was considerable deliberate destruction of buildings, crops, and livestock in the Plantation colonies. Markets for grain expanded, but those for rice and tobacco were sharply reduced, and indigo production dwindled

---

[26] S. Lebergott, *The Americans: An Economic Record* (New York: Norton 1984), 41.

without the British subsidy, which now went to West Indian producers.

Before 1781, overseas trade had expanded and a new maritime activity (privateering) appeared, but the war also hurt some maritime activities. American fishing and particularly whaling fleets proved as vulnerable to British privateers as the Empire's trade was to American letter-of-marque ships. Britain had been the colonies' principal market for whale oil, and this was now lost. The Middle colonies benefited from increased demand for their food exports.

The impact of the war was equally varied for individuals. Importers, those who supplied the French and British armies, debtors, and successful privateers all gained. Tories, those suffering physical damage, many shippers, creditors, and those few persons living on fixed incomes endured reductions in their standards of living.

THE POSTWAR SITUATION

Once the war ended, the citizens of what was now the United States of America quickly found that the absence of British rule was not a solution to all the country's problems. Indeed, some were worse. The British Navigation Acts no longer restricted trade outside the Empire, but they were now applied against Americans who wished to trade within it. Other European nations had mercantilistic regulations of their own, and these were often both more stringent and capriciously applied than the British laws had been. Shortly after the war's end, British manufactured goods reappeared in American markets and the protection that wartime trade disruptions had provided disappeared. The war-baby American industries found it impossible to match British efficiency. The specie balances that had accumulated in the last years of the war flowed out as payment for imports, and domestic prices fell.

Nor did the absence of British rule produce an alternative form of government. Even after their victory, Americans had not decided what form of government the United States would eventually adopt. Under the Articles of Confederation, which had been adopted in 1777, there was little central authority. Congress was unable to exert effective control over the economic activity of the individual states, either in their relations with foreign countries or with each other. It had no authority to levy or enforce a uniform tariff on imports, and the states could not agree among themselves. A low-tariff state would gain a high proportion of foreign trade, which would much more than compensate it for any loss in manufacturing income and employment.

Restoring International Commerce

Maritime activity was slow to recover from the war. Despite ample shipbuilding capacity, the wartime losses in the fishing and whaling fleets were not replaced for the first decade after the war, an indication of the lack of demand growth for the end products of these industries. In countries now open to American trade, it took time to develop contacts, adjust to different regulations, and obtain new sources of finance, because Americans had little prewar experience on which to draw. Because few countries extended full recognition to the United States, and only minimal American diplomatic services had yet been established, great uncertainty prevailed concerning the rules under which American overseas trade was to be conducted.

Debt Burdens and Reactions
Prices fell to prewar levels by 1785. A declining price level is seldom an encouragement to business, and deflation was particularly hard on debtor groups. In the United States, many small farmers, particularly those on the frontier, were debtors. States' policies toward the repayment of their war debts varied. Some states levied taxes to pay off the debts they had incurred during the Revolution; others did not.

In one instance, a state's effort to discharge its bonded debt led to serious trouble. Massachusetts imposed taxes to redeem the bonds it had issued during the Revolution. The taxes were levied on real estate, and thus bore most heavily on the agricultural regions of the state, but most bondholders were seaboard merchants. Deflation worsened the farmers' situation: A given amount of agricultural products now produced less money income, but the debt retirement required fixed sums. Thus, it took a larger amount of farm produce to finance a given amount of bond principal and interest, and tax burdens rose. Farmers' welfare was reduced by these changes but bondholders benefited; they received money whose purchasing power had increased. Some farmers in western Massachusetts refused to pay their taxes. In 1786 this group seized an armory and prevailed upon Daniel Shays, a former Continental Army captain, to lead them. The state militia, aided by Harvard students, was able to suppress the revolt, but Shays' Rebellion frightened many people. Had the state forces not been sufficient, there was no prospect of aid from the central government. In the same year, a similar incident took place in New Hampshire, arising from a dispute over proposed state paper-money issues. Southern states feared slave rebellions for the same reason. Deflation caused increasing political pressure on state governments for debt moratoria and paper-money issues—neither of which would further economic stability.

A Weak Central Government
The central government faced no more urgent problems than those that stemmed from its financial difficulties. Congress lacked the

power to levy taxes and could only ask the states for funds with which to carry out its duties. In one postwar year, its receipts from the states were enough to pay only one-third of the interest due on the national debt, with nothing whatever left over for other expenses of government. The United States' failure to pay even the interest on its foreign debt hardly encouraged international respect for the new country. Even if treaties could be negotiated with foreign powers, Congress could not require the states to comply with their terms. Britain and Spain continued to occupy territory that the Treaty of Paris had granted to the United States. The nation was no better equipped to secure respect abroad than it was to enforce the central government's authority at home. There was no navy, and the 718-man army was considering mutiny to recover its long-overdue pay.

Pirates found that U.S. shipping was no longer protected by a navy, or, in North African waters, by British bribes to the rulers of Algiers, Tunis, and Tripoli. Piracy depends on seizing opportunity, and some pirates achieved great success at U.S. expense. The resolution of other questions, such as relations with the Indians and the disposal of western lands, also required an effective central government. Even so, matters could have been worse. Despite the shortcomings of the Articles of Confederation, states acted responsibly in economic matters for the most part, particularly in regard to monetary policy. But there was little to assure the continuation of these trends, and fears persisted that, at best, the states might prove unable to enforce their laws or to relate them coherently to those of other states. Although the states had not enacted measures that would imperil economic stability and the long-term investment projects it facilitated, there was little to prevent such a change.

Postwar Progress

Even so, the U.S. experience under the Articles of Confederation was not entirely inimicable to economic development in either private or public sectors from 1783 to 1789. States provided some minor improvements in access to land and flexibility in its use through the breakup of some of the large estates previously owned by Tories (most, however, passed intact into the hands of wealthy patriots), and through laws restricting entail (which allowed heirs only the use but not the right to sell estates) and primogeniture. Quitrent payments to colonial proprietors were abolished. These developments, however, affected only a minor portion of the land; changes on the western frontier had greater significance.

Property Rights and Westward Ho
Frontier population and settlement were expanding rapidly in this period, especially in Kentucky, Tennessee, upstate New York, and northern New England. The Northwest Ordinances of 1784 and 1785 provided a highly favorable climate for the westward movement. Land in regions covered by these ordinances was to be sold only after accurate surveys had been done that established a township system and assured secure land titles. This aided dense settlement, promoted social stability by providing for the basic functions of local government, such as education, and increased the value of land by making it easy to sell. The states ceded their claims to western land to the central government. New states were to be admitted to the Union on an equal political footing with the original thirteen. One potential source of problems was thus avoided; the United States would have no colonies, at least within its contiguous area.

Incomplete Trade Recovery

American merchants began an active search for new trade commodities and routes that took their ships to the Baltic, the eastern Mediterranean, the East Indies, and even China and Arabia. The new markets represented only a minor fraction of overseas trade in this period, but some of them had potential for considerable expansion. The terms of trade immediately after the war moved in favor of the United States; a unit of exports would now finance more imports than in the prewar period, but by 1790 the terms of trade were at prewar levels.[27] Institutions that aided both internal and external trade, such as banks and insurance companies, now appeared. Population growth was rapid, and given America's chronic labor shortage, a larger work force enhanced the economy's potential. In international affairs, Dutch bankers were somehow persuaded to lend the United States government money with which to pay the interest on its foreign debts.

In assessing America's economic development in this era, we are forced to rely on indirect evidence; data on incomes are incomplete. Contemporary observers' conclusions about the United States' economic circumstances in the 1780s range from guarded optimism to the deepest pessimism, and in the absence of accurate statistics on per-capita incomes, cannot be fully resolved. Figures on the volume of international trade indicate that prewar trade volumes had been regained in physical terms by 1788, and in money terms the recovery was somewhat quicker. The prices of tobacco, wheat, and rice, the principal U.S. exports, all rose in relation to import prices. But trade recovery was uneven. Most of New England had regained prewar levels of per-capita exports and shipping earnings by the early 1790s, but New Hampshire

failed to share in this recovery. Rising exports of breadstuffs and meat benefited most of the Middle Atlantic states and wheat and its products replaced tobacco as the most valuable U.S. export at this time. Nevertheless, Pennsylvania experienced a serious economic slump. In the South, particularly the Carolinas and Georgia, conditions were less favorable. Increased prices for tobacco and rice did not generate rising output, and indigo production was declining, although it by no means disappeared.[28]

Aggregate trade volume is only one indication of economic welfare. Even though the United States had regained prewar volumes of trade and probably of shipping earnings by 1790, the country's population had grown to nearly twice its 1770 level. On a per-capita basis, then, foreign trade was still considerably below prewar levels, and because the structure of the economy had not changed significantly, it held the same significance as an indicator of individual welfare and income as it had in colonial times. Most of the "growth" of the 1780s was thus merely a recovery of lost ground, not an advance beyond previously attained levels of income, which may well not have been regained. The long-term outlook did not appear promising. Markets for the traditional plantation staples were not expanding, and incomes in the South were heavily dependent on exports. Slow urban growth produced scant prospects for internal markets for agricultural products. Some scholars have suggested that the economic prospects were even worse than suggested here.[29] Independence had proved no economic panacea for most Americans by

---

[27] Walton and Shepherd, *Economic Rise*, 185.

[28] Walton and Shepherd, *Economic Rise*, 182–189.
[29] G. Bjork, "The Weaning of the American Economy: Independence, Market Changes, and Economic Development," *Journal of Economic History* (December 1964).

1790, and there were both internal and external barriers to growth for which adequate responses had yet to be developed.

THE ECONOMICS OF THE CONSTITUTION

The internal problems, or at least those related to government, were addressed in 1789. With the Constitution, the United States provided an effective institutional framework within which economic activity could occur. Most of the previous failings of the central government were resolved by strengthening its powers relative to those of the states. Above all, the new federal government was granted the right to levy its own taxes; it would no longer be dependent on the states' largess—or crippled by their niggardliness. Treaties negotiated with foreign countries by the federal government superseded state laws, and the states were forbidden to interfere with interstate commerce. The federal government was also given control over monetary matters: The Constitution prohibited issues of money by the states. Thus, in the areas where the states' economic performance had been poor or a source of potential difficulties, economic controls were shifted to the federal government.

One immediate result of this transfer of powers was the formation of a "common market" consisting of the entire United States. Buyers or sellers in any part of the country were free to participate in the markets of all states without any government-imposed barriers to the movement of goods and services. This permitted maximum utilization of the available opportunities for specialization and economies of scale. As population grew and improvements in both transportation and production technology occurred, the provision of a common market among the states would encourage specialization and competition.

The Constitution strongly supported property rights, including, at least implicitly, property rights in slaves. The enforcement of contracts was upheld, and government was not allowed to change the provisions of existing contracts. Patent and copyright systems were established, giving the producers of new ideas the right to profit from them. These provisions provided incentives for productive change that some economists regard as the crucial element in economic development.

A system of federal courts was established with the power to hear appeals from state court decisions. Because the Constitution gave the federal government its own powers of taxation, the implicit control over the central government by the states was now ended; the states could not "veto" central government measures by refusing to fund them. The federal government could now support an effective standing army, and a navy was established. The federal structure of government was another potential aid to new economic activity; it reduced the possibility that established producers could forestall innovation and new competition.[30]

The Political Economy of the Constitution

The Constitution has been described as a class-oriented document, more protective of property rights than human rights, and especially tender toward the interests of delegates

---

[30] Diversity between political jurisdictions has received increasing attention as a source of long-term economic growth. See, inter alia, J. Hicks, *A Theory of Economic History* (New York: Oxford University Press, 1969); M. Olson, *The Rise and Decline of Nations* (New Haven, Conn.: Yale University Press, 1982); N. Rosenberg and L. Birdzell, *How the West Grew Rich* (New York: Basic Books, 1986); and E. Jones, *The European Miracle* (Cambridge, U.K.: Cambridge University Press, 1981).

■ On September 17, 1787, 39 of the 55 delegates at the Constitutional Convention in Philadelphia signed the Constitution after a lengthy debate over economic and property rights.
Source: The Bettmann Archive.

to the Constitutional Convention. This charge at least implies that such a slant came at the expense of other groups within the American population. Many of the convention delegates were wealthy, but the evidence indicates that the document that they produced found broad acceptance among the general population. The Constitution apparently represented an effective response to what most Americans saw as the major governmental problems of the day. By no means were all convention delegates doctrinaire conservatives; many had voted for paper-money issues and debt-relief measures as state legislators. Nor do their voting patterns indicate that they were motivated largely by the possibility of gains from redemption of

the outstanding debts of preceding governments. There is some evidence that delegates to ratification conventions had stronger personal interests in the adoption of the Constitution. Delegates with merchant interests or western land were prone to favor ratification. Personal debt, residence in the interior, or possession of slaves were linked to opposition.[31]

The concern with property rights that is illustrated in the body of the Constitution may

[31] R. McGuire and R. Ohsfeldt, "Self-Interest, Agency Theory, and Political Voting Behavior: The Ratification of the U.S. Constitution," *American Economic Review* (March 1989).

be explained by two factors. First, the vast majority of all American voters were property owners; the United States at this time was a nation of owner-occupied farms. Land values clearly depended on the security of property rights. Second, the Constitution was a response to failures of the previous system rather than an attempt to build on its successes. Human rights had been better protected under the Articles of Confederation than were property rights.

In any case, the Constitution was ratified by large majorities in both agricultural states and those where commercial interests were strong. Although no women, very few blacks, and, in some cases, only those white males who met property qualifications were eligible to vote, this was still a wider franchise than existed in any other country in 1789. There is no evidence that those excluded from the polls were largely opposed to the Constitution or its major provisions. A statement of human rights (the Bill of Rights, 1791) was added to the Constitution through a set of ten amendments to the main body of the document.

The Application of New Economic Powers

In economic matters, the Constitution is largely a permissive document. It defines what various levels of government *can* do but not what they *must* do or *how* they are to do it. Decisions were still necessary within the constitutional framework on how the federal government would use its new powers over money, taxes, and international trade, and toward what ends. Would the United States seek economic self-sufficiency or a continuation of the international specialization and exchange of the previous era? What would be done about the outstanding debts of all levels of government, state as well as central? This point was complicated; not only did the amounts of state indebtedness show wide variations, some states had already repaid at least part of their indebtedness, while others had

made no efforts toward this end. Further, the original purchasers of some government bonds, despairing of ever receiving payment, had sold their bonds to speculators at heavily discounted prices. If the bonds were redeemed at par, some bondholders would receive large windfall profits. The same considerations applied to some of the benefits promised to veterans. What type of taxes would be levied by the federal government? What type of money would the new country use? The federal government had inherited title to vast expanses of western land; how would it use this resource?

Decisive Actions and Federal Hegemony

The answers to many of these questions were interrelated. The policies established by the Northwest Ordinances were continued; the public domain would be sold by the government to private individuals. Revenues for the federal government would come from land sales, excise taxes on a few domestically produced goods, and from modest tariffs on imported goods. Several of these decisions had wider implications. The excise tax on whiskey provoked defiance by some producers—the "Whiskey Rebellion"—which the federal government suppressed with its new powers, backed by the army. One primary objective of the Constitutional Convention had been achieved; there was now an effective central government able to enforce its control against illegal opposition. The decision to use the tariff to produce revenue rather than for the protection of domestic producers indicated another policy. A tariff can protect domestic producers by raising the prices of foreign goods so high that few are sold, or it can yield revenue because goods on which the tax is levied continue to enter the country. It cannot simultaneously do both under normal circumstances. The decision to employ the tariff for revenue meant that the United States would continue to employ its productive resources along the lines of comparative advantage.

Solutions to the Debt Problem

In another momentous decision, the federal government assumed responsibility not only for the outstanding debts of central government, but for those of the states as well. These would be paid off at their face value rather than the much lower current prices that indicated financial markets' skepticism that they would ever be redeemed. In the long run, this decision proved very beneficial to the United States. Europeans reasoned that if Americans would pay taxes to allow their government to repay its debts, surely the citizens would also repay their private obligations. America and its people were now regarded as good credit risks, which enabled them to borrow in Europe's financial markets.

Because capital was particularly scarce under U.S. economic conditions, access to European money markets was a valuable asset. Most capital employed in the American economy was generated by its own citizens, who restricted their consumption and used the balance of their incomes to raise future output. The use of European savings allowed Americans to make smaller short-run sacrifices than would have been necessary if only domestically generated funds had been available.

The Monetary Standard

The monetary unit of the United States was defined as the dollar. The Spanish milled silver dollar had been the most common coin in circulation in the colonies, and the new monetary unit contained the same amount of silver. Unfortunately, the U.S. dollar was defined in terms of both gold and silver. This resulted in difficulty when the relative values of gold and silver as metal changed, as detailed in Chapter 8.

By defining the dollar in terms of a fixed amount of precious metal, its value in terms of the currencies of other countries following similar policies was determined. For example, a British pound could be exchanged for 4.56 times as much gold as an American dollar, therefore, the pound exchanged for $4.56. As long as American internal prices were free to rise and fall, this allowed Americans to readily compute the prices of foreign goods, as it did for foreign customers of American producers. Consequently, international trade and specialization were encouraged.

JEFFERSON VERSUS HAMILTON

The resolution of the questions just discussed provided a favorable climate for economic activity in the United States. Secure property rights, easy access to markets, and a defined currency all encouraged Americans to produce and to make long-term economic commitments. But the direction of economic development was not determined thereby. Two very different visions of America's economic future were proposed by Thomas Jefferson and Alexander Hamilton.

The Jefferson Ideal

Jefferson's ideal was a nation of owner-occupied farms, with each farm and the nation as a whole providing a high proportion of its own consumption needs. He wanted little, if any, urbanization and manufacturing and thought that foreign trade should be used only to obtain necessities that could not be produced domestically. Jefferson advocated a minimum of government intervention in the economy, and opposed concentrations of power in any form.

The Jeffersonian goal was a nation of informed, independent yeoman farmers who placed a major emphasis on individual freedom. Jefferson had been profoundly and unfavorably impressed by the conditions of life in European cities, which were horrible by modern standards or even relative to his own experience in contemporary rural America. Wage labor may also have implied a loss of personal independence to Jefferson.

Hamiltonian Mercantilism

Hamilton's views were more closely allied with those of European mercantilists. His goal was rapid American industrialization; accordingly, he proposed that the government serve as a development agency. Tariffs and subsidies were appropriate mechanisms for the encouragement of manufacturing and would, Hamilton thought, eventually produce an economically self-sufficient United States. To Hamilton, industrialization was the most efficient route to national power, and the sooner the United States chose it, the better. Hamilton's view emphasized the interests of the state rather than the individual.

Conflict between Flawed Models

Both visions were highly idealistic and contained a large element of political ideology. Like most other ideological proposals, they ignored some inconvenient realities. Jefferson's program glossed over the actual conditions of small-farm life in eighteenth-century America. People in that occupation had to work long hours with few mechanical aids to supplement their own muscles. Moreover, their lives were insecure. Farmers were vulnerable to weather, illness, injury, and adverse market conditions. (Even Jefferson realized that some goods

would have to be obtained from nonfarm producers.) The living conditions imposed by this type of life left little time for the individual expression so valued by Jefferson, and small farmers' incomes restricted their ability to change their circumstances. One wonders whether even informed and educated yeomen would have much interest in discussing the great issues of the day after a 14- to 16-hour workday at harvest time. It must be remembered that Jefferson's own agricultural experience was hardly that of a small farmer totally dependent on his own labor.

Had Jefferson cared to look, he might have found considerable evidence that many American farmers wanted something other than the self-sufficient life he advocated. Improved transportation, especially if it gave better access to markets, labor-saving devices, and a wide range of creature comforts were all sought by the agricultural population. This enthusiasm for change and material betterment was seldom tempered by thoughts that these developments increased farmers' interdependence with the rest of the economy. To most economists, the Jeffersonian program would risk long-run stagnation, in which incomes and opportunities never changed. The typical American viewed increased income as highly desirable and welcomed change if it furthered progress toward that goal. A crucial long-run deficiency was that the agrarian ideal had nothing to effectively offset diminishing returns resulting from population growth.

Even though North America was still an underpopulated continent in 1790, the Jeffersonian scheme could only accommodate population growth by using more land in the same way because it envisioned no change in technology or occupational patterns. Thirteen years later, when Jefferson signed the Louisiana Purchase, he thought he had provided land for a thousand years' growth. But U.S. territory as of 1803, plus more than a million square miles of additional land, were occupied (though not fully brought into use) in less than a century, largely by people born in America.

Hamilton's proposals involved the risks of major mistakes in direction as well as the certainty of high short-run costs. In 1790 the productive resources of the United States were not well suited to manufacturing. In particular, the human skills and large amounts of capital required for industrialization simply did not exist. Consequently, most American manufactured goods cost far more than European products. These costs reflected foregone alternatives; Americans could earn high incomes producing agricultural and primary products and providing shipping services. They had to be compensated accordingly if they were employed in manufacturing instead. Furthermore, the incomes already enjoyed by Americans were, if anything, higher than those of "more developed" economies; manufacturing wages might well have to be higher than those in Europe. Following Hamilton's ideas implied shifting American resources from high- to low-productivity uses. The result would have been a reduction in total output from the same resources—a fall in income. This was the short-run cost of Hamilton's proposals. The adverse effects might have been even greater than those directly induced by resource misallocation, because the diversion of resources away from export-producing occupations into making substitutes for imports would reduce the incomes foreigners could earn from trade with the United States. Thus, their demand for the remaining American exports would fall. American consumers would find the total volume of goods available to them reduced and their real incomes lower as a consequence of such programs.

If subsidies to American producers were employed instead of tariff protection, taxpayers would have to pay for them. Manufacturing might have developed faster under the Hamiltonian scheme than it actually did,

through "learning by doing" and higher rates of industrial investment, which would reduce America's shortages of industrial resources. But the program's short-run costs appear inescapable. Furthermore, the extent to which American manufacturing became efficient relative to foreign producers depended on the government's ability to direct its support only to industries whose efficiency would eventually equal that of overseas competitors. The government could not hope to support all industries simultaneously; it lacked the resources. But such a strategy involved many risks. Some of the industries selected to receive aid might never develop to the point where they could meet foreign competition without aid, and the price of American products from such industries would always be greater than that of imports. Even in sectors where American producers became competitive, Hamilton's proposals could not be deemed economically successful unless the aid or protection was then terminated. The history of government assistance programs offers little hope that such "infant industries" would ever willingly give up aid. If government-assisted industries never relinquished aid even after they had achieved full maturity, the aid recipients might benefit, but consumers and taxpayers would not. Finally, Hamilton's proposals, if their end result was to be economically efficient, assumed a degree of foresight and restraint that government has yet to exhibit in providing industrial aid.

THE NEW ECONOMIC ENVIRONMENT

Ultimately, the United States did little to foster either Hamilton's or Jefferson's ideas. As mentioned, the tariff was low and furnished only minimal protection to American producers. The fishing and shipbuilding industries received modest subsidies, and the market for coastal shipping was reserved to U.S. vessels. Only in arms manufacture did the government actually establish its own factories, largely for defense rather than economic considerations. These armories were a fertile source of new tools and techniques that proved to have important applications in other industries. But these limited efforts represented the total government aid to industrialization. Although the government continued to sell land to individuals and American support for education was strong by international standards, little else was done to further the Jeffersonian goals.

Property Rights and Progress

Instead, the United States presented its citizens with a highly permissive climate for all types of economic activity. People were largely free to produce whatever and however they pleased and to sell the results for whatever prices they could obtain. Their security in the proceeds of these market activities was guaranteed by the Constitution and a series of laws and court decisions. American markets allowed wide freedom of entry; the legal climate was opposed to monopoly.

Property rights established through the Constitution provided incentives to generate useful new ideas. If an inventor bore the full costs and risks of developing a new product or method only to discover that others were free to use the fruits of his work at no cost to themselves, the search for new goods and activities would be discouraged. Most inventive activity is undertaken with some anticipation of a reward for success, not merely to benefit society. Moreover, new ideas and their practical applications are necessary both to ward off diminishing returns and to avoid economic stagnation. This point is central to the recent work of several students of the development

process.[32] Other governmental measures that encouraged economic growth were the establishment of a postal system and the adoption of uniform weights and measures.

Promotion of Trade and Exploration

The new government sought information about the economic potential of distant areas and made it available to the public. The diplomatic service furnished reports on economic conditions in the countries where embassies and consulates were located. Within the United States, the government sent out expeditions such as those of Lewis and Clark (1804–1806) and Pike (1805–1807), and published their reports. These efforts supplemented the information gained by American merchants and the mountain men. The Army began (with varying success) to protect the frontier, and the Navy to extend protection to American merchant shipping in the Caribbean and Mediterranean.

Efficiency and Special Interests

Relations between government and the economy were not entirely along the lines dictated by economic efficiency, however. Sometimes goals conflicted. The desire to transfer western land into private hands and the desire to foster western settlement were tempered by the U.S. Treasury's need for revenue from land sales. Sometimes decisions were made on purely political grounds. Contracts to build the new

---

[32] D. North, T. Anderson, and P. Hill, *Growth and Welfare in the American Past: A New Economic History*, 3d ed. (Englewood Cliffs, N.J.: Prentice-Hall, 1983). Chap. 2. See also D. North, *Structure and Change in Economic History* (New York: Norton, 1981); D. North and L. Davis, *Institutional Change and American Economic Growth* (New York: Cambridge University Press, 1971); and M. Olson, *The Rise and Decline of Nations: Economic Growth, Stagflation, and Social Rigidities* (New Haven, Conn.: Yale University Press, 1982).

navy were allocated to as many shipyards as possible, instead of restricting them to those yards capable of building the types of warships actually required. The initial result was a number of small gunboats, all of limited military value and many not even oceanworthy. But the real product sought was votes from shipbuilders, not the most efficient naval protection for the United States.[33]

In general, the role of government in the American economy was determined by pragmatic rather than ideological considerations. There was little advocacy of laissez faire for its own sake. Americans were quite prepared to pursue economic goals through government action where it promised better results than the available private alternatives. If most economic activity was left to private markets, subject only to a framework of rules intended to improve the efficiency of markets, it was because this was deemed likely to result in the greatest total well-being. Political values occasionally ruled; the eventual technological efficiency of the armories in which the government produced its weapons was not the primary reason for their existence. Depending on Europe for arms imposed intolerable political risks, whatever the economic considerations. The Constitution's provisions indicate that Americans believed that government had a definite role to play in economic activity. The U.S. Treasury, under Alexander Hamilton, played a leading role in most of the activities of the federal government in the 1790s, helping to determine the form and extent of tax and tariff programs, the distribution of revenues, land disposal, banking, overseas commerce, and foreign relations.[34]

INDEPENDENCE

It has been claimed that the United States and its colonial predecessors were in fact independent long before this was formalized in the Treaty of Paris (1783) that ended the Revolutionary War. Alternatively, it has been argued that it was many years after 1783—perhaps not until after the American Civil War—that the United States achieved true independence from Europe. It appears that the proponents of these positions employ different criteria in reaching their conclusions.

For most of their history, the American colonies determined their own laws, subject to only the loosest British controls. When the British finally made a serious effort to impose their wishes against colonial opposition, they failed—the Revolution succeeded. In this largely political sense, independence was achieved long before 1776. But it is equally true that Americans maintained important economic ties with Europe and other parts of the world after the ratification of political independence. To the extent that American needs for European manufactured goods, credit, and markets imposed the necessity to respond to foreigners' preferences, independence was never fully attained. But Americans preferred to make such responses rather than bear the costs of self-sufficiency. The rest of the world was and is not fully independent of the United States. Events in Europe influenced the American economy before 1792, but their importance would greatly increase after that date, in both economic and political terms.

[33] A. Mahan, *Sea Power in its Relations to the War of 1812*, repr., 2 vols. (New York: Greenwood Press, 1969), 1: 187, 2: 154–161.
[34] L. Hacker, "Secretary of the Treasury," in *Alexander Hamilton in the American Tradition* (New York: McGraw-Hill, 1957), 127–146.

SELECTED REFERENCES

Beard, C. *An Economic Interpretation of the Constitution of the United States.* New York: Free Press, 1913.

Bjork, G. *Private Enterprise and Public Interest: The Development of American Capitalism.* Englewood Cliffs, N.J.: Prentice-Hall, 1969.

Henretta, J., and P. Nobles. *Evolution and Revolution.* Lexington, Mass: D.C. Heath, 1987.

Hughes, J. *The Governmental Habit: Economic Controls from Colonial Times to the Present.* Charlottesville, Va.: University of Virginia Press, 1977.

————. *Social Control in the Colonial Economy.* Charlottesville, Va.: University of Virginia Press, 1976.

Jensen, M. *The New Nation: A History of the United States during Confederation.* New York: Knopf, 1958.

Main, J. *The Social Structure of Revolutionary America.* Princeton, N. J.: Princeton University Press, 1965.

McCusker, J., and R. Menard. *The Economy of British America, 1607–1789.* Chapel Hill, N.C.: University of North Carolina Press, 1985.

McDonald, F. *We the People.* Chicago: University of Chicago Press, 1958.

Nettels, C. *The Emergence of a National Economy, 1775–1815.* New York: M.E. Sharpe, 1961.

North, D., T. Anderson, and P. Hill. *Growth and Welfare in the American Past: A New Economic History.* 3d ed. Englewood Cliffs, N.J.: Prentice-Hall, 1983.

North, D., and L. Davis. *Institutional Change and American Economic Growth.* New York: Cambridge University Press, 1971.

North, D. *Structure and Change in Economic History.* New York: Norton, 1981.

Olson, M. *The Rise and Decline of Nations: Economic Growth, Stagflation, and Social Rigidities.* New Haven, Conn.: Yale University Press, 1982.

Paul, E., and H. Dickman, eds. *Liberty, Property, and the Foundations of the American Constitution.* Albany, N.Y.: SUNY Press, 1989.

Perkins, E. *The Economy of Colonial America.* 2d ed. New York: Columbia University Press, 1988.

Walton, G., and J. Shepherd. *The Economic Rise of Early America.* New York: Cambridge University Press, 1979.

The Emergence of an American Economy, 1790–1865

Census figures refer to the year 1790.

PART II

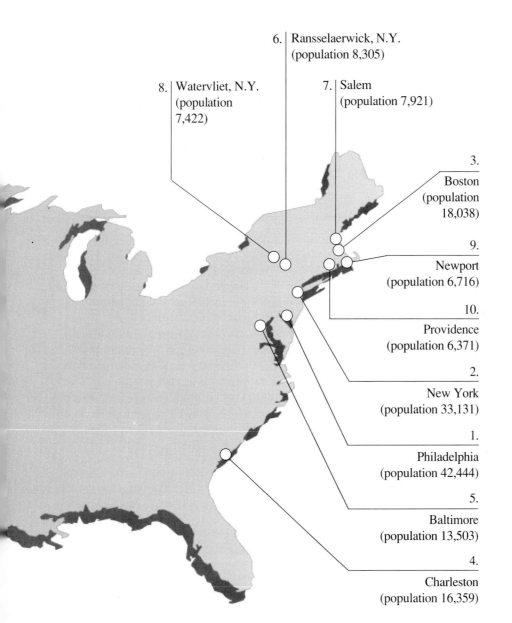

6. | Ransselaerwick, N.Y.
(population 8,305)

8. | Watervliet, N.Y.
(population
7,422)

7. | Salem
(population 7,921)

3.
Boston
(population
18,038)

9.
Newport
(population 6,716)

10.
Providence
(population 6,371)

2.
New York
(population 33,131)

1.
Philadelphia
(population 42,444)

5.
Baltimore
(population 13,503)

4.
Charleston
(population 16,359)

*T*here was little change between the economy of colonial America and that of the United States before 1815. Political independence had been achieved and some steam engines were in use—developments that would have appeared unprecedented in colonial eyes. There were other changes that were new to this country if not to the world: cotton cultivation in the South, a few factories in the North, and financial institutions (banks and insurance companies). The economy had expanded. Population was over 7 million by 1815, and the area of settlement had grown. Still, the basic elements of economic life in America were similar to those prevailing in 1700. The economy was overwhelmingly agricultural and rural, and most manufactured goods were obtained through trade with Europe. Tools and methods were basically the same as they had been in colonial days, and in most occupations output per worker was only slightly greater. Even location was much the same: Most Americans still lived close to the Atlantic coast.

DIMENSIONS OF ECONOMIC GROWTH

By 1860, however, there were great changes. First, the economy had expanded in all physical dimensions. Settlements now extended to the Pacific, and about one-fifth of the 32 million Americans were now urban dwellers. But the most significant differences involved increases in per-capita incomes, the rate at which they grew, and their sources. Real domestic output per person is thought to have risen 60 percent from 1800 to 1840, and the pace was quickening. According to one study, annual per-capita income growth rose from a range of 1.0–1.5 percent in the early decades of the nineteenth century to slightly over 1.5 percent in the 1840–1860 era. The increase was neither constant nor continuous; incomes may have fallen from 1807 to 1820 and again in the early 1840s.[1] By 1860, United States per-capita income levels were higher than those of at least half the world's population today.

Growth Sources
Increases in per-capita income of this magnitude imply qualitative changes within the economy; they are an indication that production methods and the ends toward which they were directed had changed. Between 1815 and

---

[1] P. David, "The Growth of Real Product in the United States Before 1840: New Evidence, Controlled Conjectures," *Journal of Economic History* (June 1967). See also R. Gallman, "The Pace and Pattern of American Economic Growth" in C. Davis et al., *American Economic Growth: An Economist's History of the United States* (New York: Harper & Row, 1972), and W. Rothenberg, "The Emergence of Farm Labor Markets and the Transformation of the Rural Economy: Massachusetts 1750–1855," *Journal of Economic History* (September 1988).

1860 there were three major sources of such growth. Labor shifted into jobs in which productivity was higher; a larger proportion of the population was in the labor force; and productivity rose within existing sectors of the economy. Although these gains in productivity were greater than those achieved in the colonial period, the pace was not high by modern standards. Most of the growth in aggregate economic output in this period was the result of improvements in factor (especially labor) productivity, rather than changes in factor proportions.[2] Interindustry shifts were less important. As population, usable natural resources (chiefly land) and capital increased, they generated more income.

The rate at which per-capita income growth accelerated and the time pattern of this development have been controversial matters. At one time it was thought that U.S. incomes had stagnated or perhaps even declined from 1810 to as late as 1830. Maritime activity was a shrinking portion of the economy, and other high-income activities were thought to have grown too slowly to take up the slack before 1830 or even 1840. Some economists thought that agricultural productivity might have declined as the movement to western lands might have failed to offset declining soil fertility in the East. Since no comprehensive figures on income have been developed for this period, the questions must be answered by theoretical inference from what data is available.

Shifts in the allocation of the labor force and growth in labor force participation rates increased per-capita income. Both these developments raised output per person—the first through the transfer from low- to high-productivity jobs, and the second by increasing the ratio of workers (and consequently aggregate output) to the total population. However, if agricultural productivity declined, the dominance of the agricultural sector in the American economy could offset more favorable developments elsewhere. Recent inquiries on this point, however, have concluded that the evidence points to an increase in the productivity of agriculture rather than a decrease. Moreover, the increase in farm efficiency was significant, perhaps as much as 30 percent from 1800 to 1840. When these gains are combined with those achieved in manufacturing, the results are increases in per-capita incomes of between 55 and 62 percent for the period. Growth was particularly rapid from 1800 to 1807, from 1820 to 1835, and again in the later 1840s. Rates of growth approached the modern pace as early as 1820.[3]

The Rise of Industry

By 1860, the United States ranked no worse than fourth and probably second only to Britain among the world's manufacturing nations. This must be

---

[2] S. Engerman and R. Gallman, *Long-Term Factors in the Economic Growth of the United States* (Chicago: University of Chicago Press, 1986), 190–191.
[3] David, "Growth of Real Product" and Rothenberg, "The Emergence," found similar increases in Massachusetts agricultural productivity from 1780 to 1840.

viewed in context, however; America was still primarily an agricultural economy. Manufacturing employed nearly one-fifth of the U.S. work force in 1860, and it accounted for about 30 percent of the value of aggregate output. The proportions are significant because the above-average incomes generated in the manufacturing sector imply that it would continue to grow faster than the overall economy and draw resources away from less productive applications. Manufacturing activity was concentrated in the cities and helped to account for their relatively rapid growth in this era. American manufacturers turned out a growing variety of products by 1860, and had begun to adjust both methods and products to the unique characteristics of the American market and resource endowment, just as agriculture had two centuries earlier. Some of their products and techniques were considered the best in the world.

Improvements in Transportation

By 1860, the cities of the United States were linked to each other and to their hinterlands by a network of canals, river transport, and railroads that made overland transportation of bulky goods practical for the first time. The new transport network also encouraged the development of commercial agriculture by reducing the cost of moving produce to market. Agricultural activity was now oriented toward markets rather than consumption by the farmer and his family. Reapers, steel plows, and many other implements unknown in colonial times were in widespread use. If it had ever been a reality, the Jeffersonian ideal of the independent farmer was fading rapidly as agriculture became tied to other sectors both for inputs and markets. In the South, the production of plantation staples, particularly cotton, was expanding in a highly commercialized farming sector.

The Role of Attitudes

After 1815, change became the rule rather than the exception in American economic life. People moved much greater distances than ever before, and increasingly they moved to new occupations and life-styles rather than simply to new farms. Even if they retained their initial residences and jobs, the tools and methods with which they produced goods, and even the goods themselves changed, sometimes almost beyond recognition. The increasing variety of products raised the standard of living, and the increasing variety of jobs gave better opportunities for efficient use of the varied productive talents of the work force and encouraged their further development. In general, the efficiency of both human and nonhuman resource allocation improved. Human mobility had always been a prominent feature of the American economy. With the greater variety in jobs, locations, and products, it became a significant advantage. The quick and enthusiastic response to new opportunities realized the potential inherent in new ideas. Many of the new ideas employed did not originate in the United States, but they were brought into use faster and more fully in this country than in those where they had first been developed.

MODELS OF ECONOMIC GROWTH

Rostow's Stages of Growth

Two well-known models of economic growth have been developed to explain the growth of the American economy in this period. The first is the "Stages of Growth" model of W. W. Rostow.[4] In this model, all economies pass through a series of distinctive periods in the course of economic development.[5] The critical stage is the "takeoff," which marks the transition to sustained economic growth from earlier periods in which economic stagnation or only episodic growth were the norm.

In Rostow's view, the takeoff period for the American economy as a whole was from 1843 to 1860, and railroads were the "leading sector" whose growth caused the rest of the economy to develop. Critics have noted, however, that the U.S. economy had begun to generate sustained growth in per-capita income (supposedly the distinctive feature of the takeoff) well before 1843, certainly by the 1820s, and, in all probability, much earlier.

Although both incomes and the proportion of income devoted to capital formation increased in the nineteenth century, the time pattern is not consistent with Rostow's theory, which views the takeoff as an abrupt departure from previous conditions, that is, an economic revolution. Instead, the empirical evidence now points to a gradual increase in the pace of growth extending over most of the century. Moreover, the railroads, which Rostow claimed were the leading sector, appeared well after growth was underway, and even then had only modest effects on the rest of the economy. Railroad construction and operations could not have influenced development that preceded them. Thus, there is little evidence that the U.S. economy (or any other) ever experienced anything resembling a Rostovian takeoff.[6]

The pattern of U.S. economic growth was a gradual acceleration, based on simultaneous development in many sectors, rather than an abrupt transition narrowly based in one or a few sectors of the economy. Still, it is true that the American economy was greatly altered over this period, and its

---

[4] W. Rostow, *The Stages of Economic Growth* (Cambridge, Mass.: Cambridge University Press, 1960).

[5] Rostow believes that a few countries, such as a few British overseas dominions and the United States, were "born free," skipping the traditional economy stage. See W. Rostow, *Stages of Economic Growth*.

[6] H. Rosovsky, "The Takeoff into Sustained Controversy," *Journal of Economic History* (June 1965).

capabilities for growth increased. The process was less dramatic than that posited by Rostow, but the consequences were no less significant.

North's Staple Model

The second model that has been developed to explain the economic growth of the United States in the pre–Civil War era was that of Douglass North. This explanation views the international cotton trade and its repercussions on the United States as the primary source of development.[7] Cotton made up more than half the value of all America's exports from 1815 to 1860, and it reached a peak of 63 percent in the 1830s. In North's view, American cotton production initially would increase rapidly in response to rising British demand for raw materials for the textile industry. Planters could shift land from other crops and bring previously unused acreage into production in no more than two years. But once almost all suitable land was already employed in cotton production, further increases in British demand for cotton would increase its price rather than the quantity produced. Because this phenomenon did not raise planters' costs of production, their profits would increase sharply. Higher profits increased the incentives to expand cotton production, resulting in land booms as planters bought more acreage and pushed settlement further west. Once the new lands' output came onto the market, however, the abrupt increase in supply would generate a sharp decline in cotton prices, lowering profits and altering planters' expectations. In the less euphoric circumstances, some growers would switch to other crops and to increased self-sufficiency, growing more of their own food. Efforts to bring new land into cultivation would be inhibited until British demand rose sufficiently to catch up with actual and potential cotton-growing capacity in America, after which the cycle would be repeated.

Cotton and the Business Cycle In this view, the cotton cycle influenced the rest of the American economy, because in periods when cotton prices were high, the South specialized heavily in its production, buying its food and draft animals from the Ohio Valley. Increased southern demand for western food in turn produced higher incomes in the West, and generated another land boom similar to those caused by the demand for cotton. Increased incomes in southern and western agriculture meant higher demand for the manufactured goods of the North and for its shipping and financial services. Prosperity also encouraged foreign investment in the United States, which increased the money supply and consequently economic activity. The three regions of the United States are interdependent in North's model, but it was the South's cotton exports that were the ultimate source of growth for

---

[7] D. North, *The Economic Growth of the United States, 1790–1860* (Englewood Cliffs, N.J.: Prentice-Hall, 1961).

all areas. Even though the influence of cotton was waning in the 1850s, North considered it to be the most important source of economic growth.

Critiques of the Staple Theory Critics of the North model charge that its view of the interdependence of the three areas of the United States is overstated, particularly that of the South on western food and northern manufactured goods. In fact, the South produced nearly all its own food even in boom times. Most of what food the southern planters did purchase was grown either on smaller farms within the South or in the border states, (which were southern in everything but their ability to grow cotton), rather than the West. Although shipments of western food down the Mississippi River were substantial, most such cargoes were for export or sought cheap all-water transportation to eastern cities.[8] For its requirements in shipping services, finance, and manufactured goods, the South had (and often employed) an alternative supplier in Britain.

The linkages between the North and the West, however, were strong and growing, particularly after 1845, when both western development and the completion of efficient rail and water transportation links encouraged interregional trade. Others have concluded that the price of cotton was influenced more by demand changes than by the "surges" and short-term restrictions in supply so prominent in North's model.[9]

BROAD-BASED GROWTH

American economic growth now appears to have been broadly based; no one industry, with the possible exception of transportation, appears critically important. Some development continued even when the cotton trade was depressed. Thus, although cotton was the basis of a major industry and had linkages to others, it cannot be presented as the mainspring of American economic growth prior to 1860.

Because neither of the models developed to explain the economic growth of this period appears to offer a complete explanation, we must look further at U.S. economic circumstances of this period. In terms of aggregate growth, the development of new sectors, and in the changes taking place within sectors, the pace and pattern of American economic development from 1815 to 1860 were quite different from anything preceding it. Not only had the

---

[8] A. Fishlow, "Antebellum Interregional Trade Reconsidered," in *New Views on American Economic Development*, ed. R. Andreano (Cambridge, Mass.: Schenkman Books, 1965), 187–200. See also "Postscript," 209–212. A more sympathetic treatment of the North model's views on interregional trade, at least for the period before 1840 (when its volume was not large) is L. Mercer, "The Antebellum Interregional Trade Hypotheses: A Reexamination of Theory and Evidence," in R. Ransom, R. Sutch, and G. Walton, *Explorations in the New Economic History: Essays in Honor of Douglass C. North* (New York: Academic Press, 1982).

[9] P. Temin, *The Jacksonian Economy* (New York: Norton, 1969), 91–112, and G. Wright, *The Political Economy of the Cotton South* (New York: Norton, 1978), 93.

scope of American economic capabilities broadened, but the influences on activity were much more heavily based on domestic events than had been true in the colonial era. The attitudes of the population fostered a response to the opportunities generated by technological change and the western movement that was both swift and widespread in comparison to that of any other nation. With the Constitution and the early legal interpretations of its clauses by the courts, the United States had developed an institutional setting that provided maximum incentives to individual economic effort. Its people had the attitudes that ensured an enthusiastic response to these opportunities in many different regions and industries.

SELECTED REFERENCES

Andreano, R. *New Views on American Economic Development*. Cambridge, Mass.: Schenkman Books, 1965.

Davis, L., W. Parker, R. Easterlin et al. *American Economic Growth: An Economist's History of the United States*. New York: Harper & Row, 1972.

Engerman, S., and R. Gallman, eds. *Long-Term Factors in American Economic Growth*. Chicago: University of Chicago Press, 1986.

Fogel, R. *Without Consent or Contract: The Rise and Fall of American Slavery*. New York: Norton, 1989.

Lee, S., and P. Passell. *A New Economic View of American History*. New York: Norton, 1979.

North, D. *The Economic Growth of the United States, 1790–1860*. New York: Norton, 1966.

———. *Structure and Change in Economic History*. New York: Norton, 1981.

Parker, W. *Europe, America and the Wider World: Essays on the Economic History of Western Capitalism*. 2 vols., Cambridge, Mass.: Cambridge University Press, 1991.

Ransom, R., R. Sutch, and G. Walton. *Explorations in the New Economic History: Essays in Honor of Douglass C. North*. New York: Academic Press, 1982.

Rostow, W. *The Stages of Economic Growth: A Non-Communist Manifesto*. Cambridge, Mass.: Cambridge University Press, 1960.

Temin, P. *The Jacksonian Economy*. New York: Norton, 1969.

MARITIME PROSPERITY AND "SECOND BEST" MANUFACTURING

POSTWAR ECONOMIC CONDITIONS

In 1790, prospects for the U.S. economy were not particularly bright. The nation still had roughly the same economic capabilities it possessed before the Revolution. The economy was not well equipped to undertake new types of economic activity. It lacked the capital, labor, and concentrated internal markets required for industrialization. Agricultural productivity was rising imperceptibly, if at all. There were a few bright spots: a growing population, territorial expansion, and the improved institutions either provided by the Constitution or legislated after its ratification.

International Trade Problems

Some of the most serious problems were centered in the country's foreign trade. As noted in Chapter 3, by 1790 trade had regained or slightly surpassed its pre-Revolution volume, but remained well below the old levels in per-capita terms. There appeared to be few prospects that it would soon return to its former levels.

Even though independence had freed U.S. overseas trade from the British controls imposed during the colonial era, Americans still had to contend with the mercantilistic restrictions imposed by other nations. In addition, British diplomatic assistance and trade credit were no longer available on favorable terms. Instead, the ex-colonists were treated as foreign rivals by the British. Even where trade with other nations was possible, access did not necessarily guarantee that trade would occur. American traders had to gain familiarity with other nations' product preferences, financial institutions, and legal climates. This required costly efforts, particularly in the political turmoil sweeping much of Europe after 1790.

Britain sharply limited U.S. trade with her West Indian possessions in an effort to de-velop Canada as a supplier of the fish, timber, food, and shipping services the islands had formerly obtained from this country. American indigo producers had lost their British markets as well as the subsidy. They were not permitted to compete with the British Caribbean for England's markets and found it difficult to develop new ones. Although the United States was accorded relatively favorable treatment in direct trade with Britain in comparison to that given other nations, its ability to export to the leading trade center of the world was reduced. Britain would no longer buy American-built ships, and U.S. shipbuilders found no markets elsewhere to replace this loss. U.S. trade with other nations' American colonies increased, but it encountered tariffs, prohibitions, and frequent changes in the laws.[1] In particular, Spain withdrew the trading privileges with its Caribbean possessions extended during the Revolution. The Navigation Acts of other nations restricted American access to the carrying trade.

Trade Prospects in 1790

Foreign trade was hardly near collapse, but European markets for traditional American exports did not appear to be growing. There were some improvements; selling directly to the nations that consumed American rice, tobacco, wood products, grain, and fish allowed U.S. producers a higher portion of the final price than they had previously received. But the United States had not increased its ability to export in proportion to its own population growth. Though Americans might want increasing quantities of European goods, the ability to pay for them was not expanding. From 1790 to 1792 there was no significant increase in U.S. exports. Only a slight increase in the proportion of that trade carried by American ships brightened the gloomy pros-

---

[1] C. Nettels, *The Emergence of a National Economy, 1775–1815* (New York: M. E. Sharpe, 1962), Chap. 3.

pects.[2] Since trade was still a major source of high and growing incomes relative to most domestic alternatives, this situation had serious implications.

THE WARTIME BOOM

In 1793, American trade prospects improved dramatically because of political developments in Europe. The Napoleonic Wars began and eventually involved nearly the entire continent. The hostilities continued with only brief pauses until 1815. The English and their allies, as well as the French, sought to destroy their enemies' overseas trade. Because the Caribbean islands and the Spanish Main lacked both the shipping and the resident merchants to respond to Europe's needs, the United States was in a uniquely favorable situation. While the United States was able to maintain its position as the only major neutral maritime nation, it reaped great gains from this turn of events. In terms of the familiar production-possibility frontier concept, the range of opportunities open to the American economy, particularly its foreign-trade sector, had increased; the curve had shifted outward. U.S. shipping services could now be exchanged for far larger quantities of European goods than had been the case before the advent of war.

The war created a huge increase in Europe's demand for U.S. shipping services and exports, and an entirely new market for re-exports. The Royal Navy and British privateers were able to drive French, Dutch, and Spanish merchant shipping from the seas. The demands of a major war and French privateers' attacks on shipping left the British merchant marine unable to meet that country's commercial needs. The war restricted or eliminated British access to grain, lumber, and other items traditionally imported from the Continent, just as continental Europe lost direct access to the products of its American colonies. It also reduced Europe's overall production and disrupted traditional patterns of trade. For both combatants, choices were reduced. They could buy American goods and services, do without, or obtain smaller quantities at higher prices from traditional sources. Almost overnight, the war increased demand for U.S. exports and even more for the services of American shipping.

Maritime Prosperity at Others' Expense

Both Britain and France found it expedient to change their trade regulations in order to allow American ships to carry their overseas commerce, particularly that of their colonies, which they had previously tried to reserve for their own shipping. Not only did the belligerents suspend their navigation laws to permit American carriage of their own goods, they also grudgingly allowed U.S. merchant shipping to carry goods between their European enemies and those nations' overseas colonies. A legal subterfuge was required under existing laws, but it was one that greatly increased the profits of American shippers. The trade was made indirect. For example, an American ship might load a cargo of sugar in the French West Indies for ultimate delivery to France. If the sugar were carried directly to France, it was considered an export of a French possession and was subject to seizure by the British. To avoid this, the sugar would first be sent to a U.S. port, American duty paid on it, and then re-exported to France. The American government would refund a large portion of the duties initially levied on the cargo to the shipper in such circumstances. On passage from the United States to France, the sugar would now

---

[2] G. Walton and J. Shepherd, *The Economic Rise of Early America* (New York: Cambridge University Press, 1979), 197–198.

be regarded as a U.S. export, protected by American neutrality from British interference. Trade between Britain and her colonies gained similar protection from French attacks through routing via American ports. The situation was a sort of mirror image of that which had prevailed under the Navigation acts.

The demand for American shipping increased not merely because it substituted for European vessels, but also because voyages were now longer. In addition, American ships were the only safe transport available, and shippers could charge monopoly rates. American shippers, port facilities, and tax coffers gained at Europe's expense. The terms of trade became more favorable: A unit of American exports now purchased a larger quantity of European goods.

Neither the British nor the French had any illusions about the re-export trade, but both found it too useful to stop American trade with their adversaries and risk a cutoff of their own trade in retaliation. But the temptation to strike at the enemy's supply lines grew stronger, especially after 1805, as the war appeared to reach a stalemate. The French were supreme on land, Britain controlled the seas, but neither nation was able to inflict crippling blows on its adversary.

The Trade Boom

While the opportunity for gains from such commerce existed, the United States took full advantage of it. Exports of domestically produced goods more than doubled from 1790 to 1807, the peak years of "maritime prosperity." Re-exports grew from negligible amounts—about 5 percent of domestic exports in 1790—to equal or exceed the volume of exports originating in the United States, despite the export boom. The aggregate value of American exports (including re-exports) more than quintupled over the years from 1790 to 1807.[3] Not

surprisingly, the earnings of American shipping also rose. Shipping prices increased and more cargo was carried in American vessels, producing a sevenfold increase in income from the carrying trade. The increase in gross income did not cause shipping costs per unit to rise; on the contrary, they fell. Ships spent more time at sea and less in port waiting for cargoes, and tended to carry full loads more often than they had in normal times. (See Table 4.1.)

Other Economic Activity

Foreign trade may have generated as much as 25 percent of U.S. GNP in the peak years of 1805–1807. The major ports (Boston, New York, Philadelphia, and Baltimore) benefited disproportionately from this commerce, apparently because of the economies of scale inherent in some of the services that supported overseas trade, particularly finance. The costs of insurance, banking, and information services do not increase in proportion to the number of customers. The larger ports also offered more competition, wider markets for imports, and shorter turnaround times.[4] Their populations rose nearly half again as rapidly as that of the entire country, and urbanization increased. By 1810, about 1 American in 14 lived in a "city" of 2,500 people or more.

Since imports also rose during the trade boom, distributional activities benefited as well. Specialized occupations requiring a large market to fully occupy their practitioners became more common. Shipbuilding, warehousing, and chandlers flourished when the shippers to whom they sold goods or services expanded their activity. The growth of the big ports was obvious to contemporary observers, who remarked on new buildings, luxury con-

---

[3] U.S. Bureau of the Census, *Historical Statistics of the United States: Colonial Times to 1970* (Washington, D.C.: Government Printing Office, 1975) 2:886.

[4] G. Taylor, "American Urban Growth Preceding the Railway Age," *Journal of Economic History* (September 1967).

sumption, and other signs of growing afflu-ence. Baltimore, with its services as a major port for the export of breadstuffs combined with flour milling and shipbuilding, enjoyed particularly rapid growth.[5]

Financial services that had been expanded largely to serve maritime activities also as-sisted the growth of the domestic economy. In 1790 there had been only three commercial banks in the entire United States; by 1800 there were 29, and in 1811, 89.[6] Banks can facilitate the transfer of funds saved from one type of economic activity to investment in an-other. They serve as a knowledgeable link be-tween savers seeking new areas of investment and borrowers trying to attract funds to new uses. Insurance activity in America antedated the Revolution, but it greatly expanded from 1792 to 1807. Insurance companies do more than reduce risks for those insured; they also serve as a link between savers and investors, using their premium income to buy securities of various types. The maritime boom was con-centrated in a few towns and on a small pro-portion of the population, so that it increased income spectacularly for those affected. But the rest of the economy was not stagnant.

THE RISE OF KING COTTON

A new export, cotton, began to gain a prom-inent position in American foreign trade. The new crop was the result of an invention that broke a technological bottleneck. Eli Whit-ney's cotton gin was unquestionably the most significant agricultural innovation of the early nineteenth century. The cotton gin had an enormous economic impact because it al-lowed rapid and extensive responses in both supply and demand. Prior to the cotton gin, cotton was a profitable American crop only along a narrow strip of coast in the Carolinas and Georgia. Nowhere else could sea island cotton be grown. This variety of cotton pro-duces long, soft fibers that are still valued for fine fabrics today. In the eighteenth century, however, the value of sea island cotton lay in the fact that the raw cotton could easily be separated from its seeds, allowing the fibers to be spun into thread. Other varieties of cotton grew well in the southern interior, but they were unprofitable because their seeds were so difficult to remove from the fiber. It was a full day's work to clean a single pound of upland cotton and, under American conditions, even slave labor was too expensive to be devoted to this task.

Whitney's cotton gin (1792) broke this bottleneck. The machine was a simple ar-rangement of screens and roller brushes. It was cheap and easy to construct and operate. And it worked: It may have increased productivity as much as fiftyfold. Like many other inno-vations, Whitney's machine was not a com-pletely new idea, but it was the first really successful response to the cotton-cleaning problem. Although Whitney patented his in-vention, the machine was so easy to build and initial profits from its use so high that he was unable to enforce his patent monopoly. Use of the gin spread like wildfire, and it was im-proved in the process, making cotton produc-tion still more profitable.

The Southern Cotton Boom

The cotton gin's reception in the South was linked to both supply and demand factors. It represented an obvious method of raising the income that other factors of production such as land and labor could produce. The soil and climate of the American South were ideally suited to cotton cultivation, and the region

---

[5] The picture of this era as one of unprecedented pros-perity has been questioned. See D. Adams, Jr., "American Prosperity and Neutrality, 1793–1804: A Reconsidera-tion," *Journal of Economic History* (December 1980).
[6] Nettels, *Emergence*, 296.

Table 4.1   Trade Statistics, 1790–1816
(In Thousands of Dollars)

Date	Total Exports*	Re-exports	Total Imports**	Net Income from Carrying Trade
1790	$20,205	$300	$23,800	$5,900
1791	19,012	500	30,500	6,200
1792	20,753	1,000	32,500	7,400
1793	26,110	1,750	32,550	11,900
1794	33,044	6,500	36,000	15,550
1795	47,989	8,300	71,300	19,000
1796	67,064	26,300	82,936	21,600
1797	56,850	27,000	77,379	17,100
1798	61,527	33,000	70,551	16,600
1799	78,666	45,523	81,069	24,200
1800	70,972	49,131	93,254	26,200
1801	94,116	46,643	113,364	31,000
1802	72,483	35,775	78,333	18,200
1803	55,800	13,594	65,667	23,700
1804	77,699	36,232	87,000	26,900
1805	99,566	53,179	125,525	29,700
1806	101,537	60,283	136,562	34,600
1807	108,343	59,644	144,740	42,100
1808	22,431	12,997	58,101	23,000
1809	52,203	20,798	61,029	26,200
1810	66,758	24,391	89,366	39,500
1811	61,317	16,023	57,888	40,800
1812	38,527	8,495	78,789	29,000
1813	27,856	2,848	22,178	10,200
1814	6,927	145	12,968	2,000
1815	52,558	6,583	85,357	20,600
1816	81,920	***	151,357	16,900

*Includes re-exports.
**Includes goods intended for re-export.
***Not available.
Source: D. North, *The Economic Growth of the United States, 1790–1860* (New York: Norton, 1961), appendices I and II.

had plenty of underused resources. In particular, the slave population had grown faster than the markets for traditional plantation crops. Not only was natural increase among the slaves equal to that of the free population, slave imports had been large in the previous decade.[7] A provision in the Constitution prohibited imports of slaves after 1807, and the

---

[7] R. Fogel, *Without Consent or Contract: The Rise and Fall of American Slavery* (New York: Norton, 1989), 248.

■ The cotton gin was a simple, easily constructed machine that revolutionized agriculture in the American South after 1793.
Source: The Bettmann Archive.

slave revolts in Haiti had caused many planters to flee to the United States, bringing their bondsmen with them.

Since cotton production required nearly year-round work with few peak work demands, it was well suited to production by slave labor. There were important economies of scale if production units were large enough to employ the "gang system" of closely supervised, routine labor. These gave large plantations a cost advantage, but the fiber could also be produced on smaller farms.[8] Cotton gave the South a new cash crop and a new export.[9] Production expanded rapidly. By 1807 the United States was Britain's most

---

[8] G. Wright, *Old South, New South: Revolutions in the Southern Economy Since the Civil War* (New York: Basic Books, 1986), 107–110. See also G. Wright, *The Political Economy of the Cotton South* (New York: Norton, 1978).
[9] G. Wright, *Political Economy,* 18, 28.

important source of cotton, and by 1810 it was the country's most valuable single export.

Cotton fiber was made into cloth in Britain. Cotton textile factories employed machinery and experienced rapid increases in productivity in a highly competitive industry. Consequently, producers were forced to pass their cost savings on to consumers in lower textile prices, which fell until cotton became the first really cheap cloth the world had ever known. Demand for cotton cloth proved to be highly price elastic; a decrease in price resulted in a more-than-proportionate increase in the quantity sold. So productive were the new spinning and weaving methods (and so large were England's supplies of female and child labor), that by the early nineteenth century Britain was able to sell cotton cloth even in India. There, textiles from British factories replaced the traditional handmade fabrics with cheaper and better substitutes.

The demand for raw cotton from the United States grew as textile sales increased, and cotton prices remained at levels highly profitable to U.S. planters. Throughout the nineteenth century, economic activity in the American South centered on cotton. At least one economic historian has claimed that the growth of the entire American economy was shaped by the requirements of cotton agriculture and the state of foreign demand for cotton prior to 1860.[10]

Transportation Innovations

The transmontane west, which previously had sent only a trickle of high-value, low-bulk goods back over the mountains, now began to ship bulky exports through New Orleans. There was great agitation for improvements in internal transportation to aid this trade. Roads could not be improved sufficiently to meet the transport needs, but a completely

new travel mechanism—steamboats—was a partial solution. These will be discussed in Chapter 5.

Trade's Backward Linkages

Because high profits were available in overseas trade, more investors were attracted to it than to manufacturing. But trade's expansion did affect industry. Some items essential to the merchant marine, such as sails, rope, cable, and anchors, were made in the United States. A rising portion of American wheat exports was processed into flour before leaving the country. There were also some attempts to make new products. Textile mills appeared in New England and some of the larger cities, attempting to copy British machines and methods. These developments, and rising demand for farm products in both domestic and foreign markets, caused widespread gains in income. Although farmers and processors did not obtain the spectacular gains that were achieved in maritime activities, the aggregate increase in incomes from these sources has been claimed to be greater than that generated by foreign trade.[11]

The Costs of Neutrality

Whatever the impact of the various sources may have been, it appears that American incomes rose substantially from 1790 to 1807. But the path to riches was neither smooth nor steady. In particular, changes in European political conditions could end America's favorable trade position as quickly as they had generated it. Trade activity fell off sharply in 1802–1803, when Britain and France temporarily ceased hostilities. (See Table 4.1.) And as the two great antagonists sought methods of ruining each other's economies and attempted to cut their enemies off from foreign

---

[10] D. North, *The Economic Growth of the United States, 1790–1860* (Englewood Cliffs, N.J.: Prentice-Hall, 1961).

[11] C. Goldin and F. Lewis, "The Role of Exports in American Economic Growth During the Napoleonic Wars, 1793 to 1807," *Explorations in Economic History* (January 1980) find that foreign trade may have furnished as little as one-fourth of the total increase in incomes.

trade, American cargoes bound to enemy ports were increasingly regarded as war contraband subject to seizure. Often the ship was confiscated together with its cargo. In all, some 2,000 U.S. merchant vessels were taken by the French and British between 1790 and 1812.[12]

Cargoes and ships were not the only items at risk. The British, desperately in need of seamen, often forced (impressed) crewmen captured from American ships into the Royal Navy, sometimes despite evidence that the sailors were U.S. citizens rather than British deserters (the legal pretext for impressment from foreign ships). The United States fought an undeclared naval war with France between 1796 and 1800. The pirates of the Barbary Coast had been preying on American shipping ever since the Revolution took away the shield of British naval protection and bribes. In 1805 the new U.S. Navy forced an end to these raids. There is no doubt that some American seamen paid a high physical price and some shippers suffered severe financial losses. United States protests at what were regarded (by this country) as violations of neutral rights were frequent. But in aggregate, American gains exceeded losses, and trade continued.

The Louisiana Purchase

Another development arising from political events in Europe was to have momentous consequences for the United States. Under the terms of the Treaty of Paris, which had concluded the Revolution in 1783, the southwestern boundary of the United States did not extend to the mouth of the Mississippi River or include the port of New Orleans. Spain controlled both, and in the 1790s had restricted American use of both river and port. Since the Mississippi was the only low-cost outlet for products from the rapidly growing agricultural areas of Tennessee and the Ohio Valley, restrictions on the use of the river, even if only

potential, impeded western settlement. Land had little value if there were no means of sending its products to market. After Spain ceded New Orleans to France in a secret treaty (1803), the United States offered to buy the city. The American diplomats presenting the offer were astounded when Napoleon's response was a proposal to sell the entire Louisiana Territory, a tract of 827,000 square miles. Acquisition of this region would nearly double the land area of the United States.

President Thomas Jefferson and his Secretary of the Treasury, Albert Gallatin, were able to overcome their distaste for deficit financing in the face of such a bargain (the French asked for $15 million). The government, making use of its newly developed creditworthiness, borrowed the funds before Napoleon could change his mind (or lose the territory to the British). The Louisiana Purchase must be considered one of the most productive triumphs of pragmatism over ideology in American history. Once the purchase was concluded, Jefferson sent expeditions led by Lewis and Clark and Zebulon Pike into the new territory to determine its economic potential.

The purchase gave the United States another new plantation crop. In 1795, French planters fleeing slave revolts in Haiti succeeded in growing sugar cane in the Mississippi Delta below New Orleans. Like rice, sugar was a capital-intensive crop restricted to a small area by natural conditions (in this case, climate). Productivity in sugar production benefited from rapid technological gains, and the industry generated huge fortunes for planters.

EMBARGO AND WAR

Foreign trade's contribution to U.S. prosperity came to an end with 1807. The war between Britain and France had been resumed in 1803, and by this time was a

---

[12] Nettels, *Emergence,* 324–325.

■ The Embargo Act, in effect from 1807 to 1809, led to widespread smuggling. The smuggler, on the right, exclaims, "Oh this cursed ograbme." "Ograbme" is, of course, backward for "embargo."
Source: The Bettmann Archive.

desperate struggle in which the opponents attempted to destroy each other by any means possible. Increasingly they began to strike at their rivals' foreign trade. The British proclaimed a blockade of all French-controlled ports in Europe, denying even neutral ships the right to trade there. Only if neutral shipping had received British permission and paid duties in England was trade with the Continent allowed, and then only in goods that the United States had exported before the war. The French forbade all trade with Britain. Napoleon's Milan Decree (1806) proclaimed that any neutral ship that entered a British port or even submitted to British search was subject to French seizure. The dilemma of the United States was obvious.

The price of continued trade with either country was the forfeiture of all exchange with its opponent. Still worse, there was a strong probability of war with the nation to which America denied its trade. To accede to the demands of either side would imply not only a surrender of U.S. sovereignty over its foreign commerce, but at least implicit support of the war against the other belligerent. The U.S. Navy was far too weak to protect American commerce against either party, especially in European waters. Under these circumstances, President Jefferson requested the authority to restrict American commerce with the warring nations. In December 1807 Congress passed the Embargo Act. This measure forbade practically all trade with foreign nations, and placed strict limits even on American coastal trade.

The Impact of the Embargo

To Jefferson, the embargo was the only U.S. response that might avoid a war for which the nation was not prepared. Neither Britain nor Napoleonic France was an attractive ally; both had inflicted grievous damage on U.S. shipping and seamen. The reasoning behind the Embargo Act appeared to be that because both Britain and France would lose more through the absence of American exports, shipping services, and markets than they could "gain" in damage to each other, they would withdraw their ultimatums to American commerce. But the emotions generated by all-out war are no aid to rational consideration, and the combatants were more concerned with the damage they might inflict on each other than they were with the injury imposed on their own economies.

The effect of the abrupt cessation of trade on the maritime sector of the economy, until then the locus of highly concentrated gains, was disastrous. Exports of both U.S. and foreign origins plummeted, as did shipping earnings. Unemployment was concentrated on the ports, where there was plenty of evidence of economic distress: idle ships and seamen, bankrupt merchants, and jails bursting with imprisoned debtors. The rest of the economy did not escape. The prices of many exports fell, reducing the incomes of middlemen and producers alike. Smuggling and loopholes in the act mitigated its effects somewhat, but the economy was severely and adversely affected. There had been no time to prepare for the embargo's impact; all the adjustments had to be made after the law was imposed.

Trade with nations other than France and Britain was resumed in 1809, and the Macon Bill (1810) reopened trade with those two countries as well, but only briefly. Trade with Britain was suspended again in 1811.[13] Still, as Table 4.1 indicates, trade volume never regained pre-embargo levels. With the onset of the War of 1812, U.S. overseas trade all but collapsed completely. After Trafalgar (1805), there was no French fleet to occupy the Royal Navy, and the British blockade of U.S. ports became increasingly effective. By 1814, it had become almost impossible for U.S. vessels to leave or enter their country's harbors.

ALTERNATIVES TO TRADE

Even before the political interferences with American overseas commerce that culminated in the War of 1812 became significant, there had been some diversion of resources into domestic economic activity. Some seaboard merchants had accumulated large fortunes, and in the face of increasing risks in trade, they sought new areas of investment. The production of substitutes for imported manufactured goods might now be possible; new technology and labor with few alternative employment prospects reduced America's traditional manufacturing disadvantages.

The Textile Industry

The largest single category of imported manufactures had long been textiles.[14] Factories were set up to produce woolen and especially cotton cloth in America. These were concentrated in New England and the port cities, where capital and cotton were available, and there were many underemployed or unemployed women and children (New England's

---

[13] Nettels, *Emergence*, 329–330.
[14] Walton and Shepherd, *Economic Rise*, 85.

■ New England became the center for textile production during the Industrial Revolution. *Source:* Yale University Art Gallery, Mabel Brady Garvan Collection.

agriculture was highly seasonal, and the ports had few jobs for such workers). New England had abundant waterpower sites close to the coast with which to power the new machinery. After the embargo was imposed, labor of all types became abundant. British machines and techniques were copied, often by persuading trained workers who had memorized machinery designs to leave British factories. Britain's mercantilistic regulations forbade both the export of machines and the emigration of skilled labor, but a number of men familiar with the new machines brought their knowledge to the United States. Americans also did some industrial espionage in their attempts to obtain British technology. Knowledge, especially if it promises large gains, has always been difficult to keep secret. Among the workers who emigrated was Samuel Slater. He came to Rhode Island in 1790 at the invitation of a local merchant who combined his capital with Slater's expertise to establish one of the first cotton textile factories in America. The first mechanized cotton textile mill in the United States, however, was built in South Carolina, just be-

fore Slater's venture. The Carolina mill was unsuccessful.[15]

Only after the embargo and war restricted textile imports did U.S. cloth producers make real progress. Despite efforts to copy British techniques, they were unable to compete with the originators. Even after meeting costs that domestic producers did not have, such as transatlantic passage and tariffs, British textiles sold at lower prices than American goods. When the embargo reduced imports to a trickle of high-cost smuggled items, the American industry grew rapidly. War emphasized the trend. By 1815 there were over 200 factories making cotton textiles; there had been less than 20 in 1800.[16] Production of woolen cloth also increased, but to a lesser extent, because woolens were less suited to machine production. Substantial amounts of woolen cloth were still produced by home manufacture in most regions of the United States, indicating that even the British had as yet not fully mastered factory production of that commodity.

The First Factories

The new textile establishments were noteworthy because they were true factories, employing powered machinery (driven by water) and the coordinated efforts of all the workers employed. They were not mere assemblages of labor using traditional methods to duplicate the techniques of the one-man shop or cottage production on a larger scale.[17] Since they were so different from the production methods previously employed in America, it is not surprising that time was required for the new methods to reach efficient operation.

Other Manufacturing

Other types of manufacturing appeared in addition to textiles. Some were developments from colonial beginnings, such as flour milling and iron and lead smelting. But progress also

[15] Wright, *Old South, New South*, 286.
[16] Wright, *Old South, New South*, 275.
[17] Wright, *Old South, New South*, 269.

occurred in paper, glass, leather, and gunpowder output, in printing, and in a variety of other processing and finished-goods industries. Rising population and income, as well as transportation improvements, increased the markets for these goods and traditional handicraft products. Lists of specialized occupations, particularly in the larger ports, grew longer. In many cases, factory production did not represent a net increase in commodity output; it often replaced goods that people had made for themselves in their homes. The increasing range of production utilizing new methods (at least by American standards) generated useful experience. In a few cases, the lessons learned allowed American producers to survive the return of British competition after 1815.

Arms

Another industry heavily affected by political considerations (in this case antedating the embargo) was the manufacture of arms. U.S. armories developed a number of ingenious wood and metalworking tools, such as lathes, milling machines, jigs, taps, and gauges. These plants developed and applied the idea of interchangeable parts, although they did not originate the basic concept.

Internal Transportation

War and the British blockade placed additional emphasis on the development of internal transportation. With coastal shipping now threatened by British frigates, New England built and used more roads, finding them a thoroughly inferior and vastly more expensive means of moving goods. The West, with its greater distances, bulky agricultural products, and extensive river systems, developed a wide variety of water craft, from simple rafts and flatboats to schooners and steamboats. Sometimes it proved possible to export both cargo and its container; the Ohio Valley built some ocean-going sailing ships and sent them down the rivers with loads of farm produce. In such cases both ship and cargo were exports, since sailing ships could not return against the current. Steamboats offered a solution to the problems of two-way travel on rivers. They were employed on the Ohio and Mississippi within a few years of Robert Fulton's voyage on the Hudson. The first steamboat reached Louisville from New Orleans in 1815.

Although most of the early efforts in manufacturing were premature, they illustrate once again the flexibility and rapid adjustment to new circumstances that characterized the American economy. Resources were switched to new and unprecedented uses in just a few short years. Moreover, the same willingness to learn from "strangers" that had served the country so well in colonial days was still evident. It cannot have been easy for Americans accustomed to very different work styles to accept the direction of foreigners in factories, or to entrust hard-earned fortunes to them. But it was done, and apparently with much less friction than accompanied the transfer of British technology to continental Europe a few years later.[18] We must remember that the people who adapted so readily had, in most cases, never encountered power sources other than the traditional muscle, wind, and water. They certainly were not accustomed to the work conditions imposed by factory production, where machines or the overall establishment controlled the pace, rather than the individual worker, as was true in agriculture.

THE WAR OF 1812

The usual cause cited for the outbreak of America's second war with England is British interference with American shipping, especially the impressment of American seamen.

---

[18] D. Landes, *The Unbound Prometheus* (Cambridge, U.K.: Cambridge University Press, 1969), Chap. 4.

The British had impressed about 4,000 American seamen and confiscated many ships, but the French were hardly innocent of the same offenses. Some Americans, particularly the "war hawks" of the western states, saw a chance to seize territory from Canada and Florida, then under British and Spanish control. American frontiersmen regarded both these areas as havens for fugitive slaves and arsenals for hostile Indians, as well as rich potential conquests. New England did not share the enthusiasm for war, and when the British blockade became an even more effective restriction on trade than all those suffered in the preceding years, some exasperated Yankees considered the idea of secession from the Union (the Hartford Convention, 1814) in order to regain the shipping incomes they had lost.

American war objectives were not achieved. At the war's end, the United States was on the defensive almost everywhere. Most of the victories gained by American armies were repulses of British invasion attempts. At sea, American privateers took over 2,000 British prizes during the war. The American Navy gained some stunning (particularly in British eyes) victories in single-ship actions. But by the end of the war, the weight of British seapower prevailed; few American ships remained at sea. Perhaps the results are best summarized by noting that Americans entered the war with the slogan "On to Canada!" and concluded it on a rather different note, "Not One Inch of Territory Lost or Ceded."

The Consequences of War

The War of 1812 generated the usual inflation. Real output fell as efficient uses of American resources were given up in favor of the demands of the military and even to civilian occupations that generated lower incomes than the alternatives available in peacetime. The government borrowed heavily to finance its military efforts. Borrowing from the banks increased the supply of paper money, while hard currency supplies did not rise. Banks outside New England "suspended payment" by refusing to redeem the paper currency they had issued for its face value in coin. Nevertheless, the banks continued to operate and their notes to circulate as money. Such currency's specie value depended on the public's opinion of the probability and imminence of its eventual redemption in coin.

New Banking Developments

One potentially useful result of the demands of war finance was the formation of the Second Bank of the United States. The First Bank of the United States had been chartered by the federal government in 1791. With its federal charter, the bank could and did operate throughout the country, rather than in a single state, but its charter had been allowed to lapse in 1811. Although neither the First nor the Second Bank of the United States was a central bank in the modern sense, their many branches and their position as government depositories afforded some measure of monetary control. The Second Bank of the United States failed to achieve one objective that had figured heavily in its establishment. Bank stock could be purchased with government bonds. The intent was to make it easier to sell these securities to finance the war. But the Bank did not receive its charter until 1816.

Political events had produced industrialization in the United States when peacetime conditions would not, but the return to normal conditions indicated that economic realities had changed far less than the political situation between 1807 and 1815. When the war ended and British goods once again became available to American customers, all but a handful of the war-baby domestic firms were unable to survive the competition. Only those firms that had gauged the nature of the American market correctly had a chance against British competition, which had the advantage of a decade's technological progress. At the same time, however, traditional American economic activity flourished after a brief period of adjustment to peacetime conditions. Both exports of American goods and carrying trade earnings were far above 1790 levels in 1815 and 1816. Thus, the wartime diversion of American resources into manufacturing was a "second best" use of their productive capacity that could endure only as long as political conditions prohibited their employment in the areas where their productivity was greatest. In other words, it was appropriate only under wartime circumstances. The example of the few American firms able to survive the return of British goods initiated a general search for effective competitive responses. It would not be long before the effort met increasing success.

SELECTED REFERENCES

Davis, L., R. Easterlin, W. Parker et al. *American Economic Growth: An Economist's History of the United States.* New York: Harper & Row, 1972.

Nettels, C. *The Emergence of a National Economy, 1775–1815.* New York: M. E. Sharpe, 1962.

North, D. *The Economic Growth of the United States, 1790–1860.* Englewood Cliffs, N.J.: Prentice-Hall, 1961.

North, D., T. Anderson, and P. Hill. *Growth and Welfare in the American Past: A New Economic History.* 3d ed. Englewood Cliffs, N.J.: Prentice-Hall, 1983.

Temin, P. *The Jacksonian Economy.* New York: Norton, 1969.

U. S. Bureau of the Census. *Historical Statistics of the United States: Colonial Times to 1970,* 2 vols. Washington, D. C.: Government Printing Office, 1975.

TRANSPORTATION FOR A GROWING ECONOMY

TRANSPORTATION DEFICIENCIES

*I*n 1808, Secretary of the Treasury Albert Gallatin proposed a series of transportation improvements to Congress. In Gallatin's plan, the federal government was to finance the construction of a major highway along the East Coast and four canals through the major peninsulas, allowing sheltered-water navigation from Cape Cod to the Carolinas. To facilitate east–west transportation, Gallatin proposed four improved river-and-road links between the Atlantic Coast and the Mississippi Valley, plus a canal connecting the Mohawk River with Lake Ontario. Within regions, canals would be built to circumvent major obstacles to river travel, such as Niagara Falls and the Falls of the Ohio at Louisville, and improved roads would be constructed in the West. Finally, in a gesture that modern politicians would appreciate, Gallatin proposed that $3.4 million be spent for internal improvements in areas not directly benefited by the other routes.[1]

Such "sweeteners" proved to be essential ingredients in large-scale governmental transport improvement schemes throughout the early nineteenth century. They may have persuaded taxpayers in regions distant from efficient transport routes to support construction, but often greatly increased the costs of government aid to transport projects.[2] The proposals were never carried out: The tariff revenues with which Gallatin had thought they could be financed were sharply reduced by the imposition of the Embargo Act.

Gallatin's proposal was a response to a very real need. The difficulty of overland transportation in the United States during the early nineteenth century probably ranks as the foremost obstacle to economic development. It is hard to appreciate the incredible obstacles to moving people, goods, or even information that confronted Americans at this time. For example, letters sent from Philadelphia to Boston required five days to reach their destination. But this was along the best-developed routes; elsewhere, conditions were worse. Mail carried by "express" riders took two to three weeks in passage from Philadelphia to Nashville. Communications, of course, could move no faster than the people conveying the information.

Overland travel was slow, expensive, and not infrequently dangerous. Thomas Jefferson had to swim his horse across five of the eight rivers between Washington and Monticello because there were neither ferries nor bridges. The travel conditions encountered by the President of the United States in Virginia, one of the longest-settled and most populous of all the states, were by no means unusually bad. Although the United States had about 20,000 miles of roads in 1800, these were neither surfaced nor drained. Many roads had been "constructed" with axes, not picks and shovels. Several regions had laws specifying that no stumps over 18 inches high were to be left in the right of way. In dry weather roads were dusty; in wet weather they became quagmires.

Some roads were impassable by wheeled vehicles, and even where wagon travel was possible, the loads that could be transported were severely limited. On the very best roads, stagecoaches could achieve speeds of six miles an hour. The cost of such haste was great discomfort; stagecoaches had only the most primitive springs to soften the shocks. Most wagons

---

[1] C. Goodrich, "National Planning of Internal Improvements," *Political Science Quarterly* (March 1948).
[2] S. Lebergott, *The Americans: An Economic Record* (New York: Norton, 1984), Chap. 10.

lacked any springs at all. In addition to frequent breakdowns and accidents, travelers might encounter bandits or hostile Indians.

Travel Costs

Travel was costly as well. One passenger reported spending $21 for 36 hours of continuous travel from Philadelphia to New York City.[3] Stagecoach lines typically charged about six cents per mile, and consequently their customers were only the wealthy. Food and lodging brought the total money costs of travel close to ten cents per mile. The real costs were much higher than these figures suggest, however. Not only were nineteenth-century prices far lower—perhaps only one-tenth their 1992 levels—but real incomes were lower still. Nor is this a full measure of the costs. Time consumed in travel could not be devoted to other purposes, and this constituted an additional expense. Table 5.1 gives some idea of speeds, but it should be remembered that by 1840 there had been substantial improvement in comparison with conditions a few decades earlier. Nineteenth-century travel costs were high even in comparison to the less efficient modern forms, such as one person driving a large car. The expense of transporting goods was even greater. Frequently, the charges for moving goods 100 miles or less exceeded the price at which they could be sold. Under such circumstances, most regions were forced to produce a high proportion of all that they consumed, even though other areas might make some of these items at much lower cost.

Small wonder that Americans preferred travel by water. Along the coast, virtually all freight went by sea. Inland, shippers utilized virtually any stream capable of floating even a canoe in approximately the right direction.

---

[3] H. Adams, "Physical Conditions" in Cochran and Brewer, *Views of American Economic Growth: The Agricultural Era*, vol. 1. (New York: McGraw-Hill, 1961). Professor Robert Gallman has suggested that this was an unusually expensive trip, at least in money costs.

Table 5.1 Passenger Speed, 1840

Transport Mode	Miles per Hour
Sailing vessels	2.5
Canal boats	3.9
Stages and sleighs	4.9
Railroads, horse-drawn	6.0
Steamboats, rivers	9.0
Steamboats, lakes	10.0
Railroads, steam	15.0

Source: The American Almanac, 1841, 87. Quoted in S. Lebergott, *The Americans: An Economic Record* (New York: Norton, 1984), 113. Based on a report by a "foreign gentleman" who travelled 10,330 miles throughout the United States.

Rapids, low water, ice, indirect routes, and the occasional attentions of river pirates notwithstanding, bulky goods could be moved less expensively by water than by any other means available. If goods were large or heavy, often it was physically impossible to transport them by any other means.[4]

Western Transportation Difficulties

Beyond the Appalachians, transportation was even more difficult than the descriptions already given imply. Only a few high-value, low-bulk items, such as ginseng, furs, and whiskey could be profitably shipped eastward over the mountains. Cattle and hogs could be driven to markets in the East, but they lost a good deal of weight, not a few of their numbers, and any vestige of tenderness their meat might ever have possessed en route. Most western produce was sent down the Ohio and Mississippi Rivers to New Orleans, where ocean-going ships could carry it to the Eastern Seaboard. The frontiersman who had sold a boatload of whiskey, flour, or preserved meat in New Orleans (and then the boat, to be broken up for lumber or firewood) faced the problem

---

[4] G. Taylor, *The Transportation Revolution, 1815–1860* (New York: M. E. Sharpe, 1962), Chap. 8.

of getting home with the proceeds. Neither a keelboat voyage up the Mississippi nor an overland journey along the Natchez Trace offered much certainty of a safe return. Ironically, the money obtained in New Orleans would, in large part, go to pay the costs of transporting goods over the same mountains that barred direct access to eastern markets. Shipping goods by wagon was often unprofitable; even a 40-mile journey might cost more than the load of grain or other crops would potentially bring.

Distances in America, even east of the Mississippi, were longer than those with which western Europeans had to contend. The land mass of the United States was far greater than that of any of the developed countries of Europe. Nor did Britain, the Netherlands, and northern France contain any geographic barriers comparable to the Appalachian Mountains.

Financial and Political Obstacles to Better Transportation

Although Americans recognized the need for improved transportation, providing it was difficult. The first problem was financial; the sums required to build roads, canals, and railroads were far beyond the ability of any single individual to finance. Institutions would have to be developed to pool the funds of many savers. Once this became apparent, Americans turned to the only institution with such capabilities already in existence. Government, with its taxing power allowing superior access to credit, was used to raise the large sums required for constructing many of the early transportation improvements. Another obstacle to private financing was the difficulty of collecting the full value of transport improvements from customers. The benefits of improved transportation are often far greater than the reduced charges for freight or passenger movement. Consumers pay lower prices for goods, and producers receive a

higher portion of the final price. The value of productive assets rises because their products can reach wider markets. In addition, there may be long-term benefits if improved access to markets results in improved production methods. Economies of scale may now be worth using, and costs may fall because of greater experience with the production process. But the users of transportation improvements and their customers tended to receive more of these benefits than the owners, which meant that the incentives to construct roads or canals were less than their aggregate economic contribution.

ROADS

Even road construction strained early nineteenth-century American capacity for capital generation. Partnerships were not well suited to road finance. Roads often required large sums, which in turn meant either an unworkable number of partners or high risks to the individual members of such an agreement. Returns from an investment in roads would be gained only over the long term, which increased the difficulties of partnership financing. To acquire the necessary capital, the corporate form was used. Groups of investors petitioned state legislatures for corporate charters giving them the rights to build roads and charge traffic for their use. By 1830, 22,000 miles of turnpikes had been constructed, mainly in New England and the Middle Atlantic states. But few of these proved to be profitable for their owners. Often the volume of traffic was insufficient to pay for the maintenance of the road, much less amortize the initial investment or provide a return to the turnpike owners.[5]

---

[5] L. Davis, R. Easterlin, and W. Parker, *American Economic Growth: An Economist's History of the United States* (New York: Harper & Row, 1972), 472.

One problem was technological: Even good roads allowed draft animals to pull only a minor fraction of the loads they could move over rails or along canals. Furthermore, roads were expensive to build and maintain, so at charges of 12 to 17 cents per ton-mile necessary to cover costs of construction and maintenance, only small volumes of high-value goods travelled by roads of any type. Those few roads built to serve large existing volumes of traffic, such as the routes between Lancaster and Philadelphia, and some New England turnpikes, showed good financial performance, but these were exceptional. Even where traffic was heavy, tolls were not easy to collect. Travellers could often detour around the tollgate where a "pike" was lowered across the road to make traffic stop and pay tolls. At best, roads could not provide a national transportation network. Most were short, and there was no incentive to link them. Roads simply were not capable of accommodating long-distance freight traffic at costs allowing a substantial volume of traffic.

Government's Role in Road Construction

Government played a limited role in turnpike construction and operation. Such roads were usually private ventures, although the governments of Ohio, Virginia, and especially Pennsylvania did make financial contributions to construction costs. The federal government built the National Pike,[6] which reached a western terminus in Vandalia, Illinois, in 1852, but this was the only federal road project. Even though the federal government had the ability to provide the large initial investment required for the construction of a first-class road through its tax powers and better access to credit than private investors, there were re-

strictions on the national government's role. Sectional rivalries, particularly objections from areas that had already built their own roads and did not want to be taxed for the benefit of other regions, were common. If these were resolved by providing government projects in return for votes, the result was an increase in costs. Some people had doubts about the constitutionality of federal road building. The role of the federal government was largely restricted to providing surveys and training engineers at West Point. It was more active in improving water transportation, and rivers and harbors bills became a favored means of obtaining federal funds for local projects very early in Congress' history.

The limited role of government in road building may not have been a disadvantage for the economy. As noted, most roads generated financial losses to the investors who financed them. The evidence that they developed compensating increases in income for the rest of the economy is slight. The location of economic activity does not appear to have been affected by turnpikes, nor did property values along such roads show increases above the average. As long as the traffic using roads was limited to animal power as a motive force, roads were not the answer to America's transportation problems.

STEAMBOATS

Most turnpike builders failed to recover their investments,[7] but the owners of steamboats enjoyed modest financial success in the antebellum era. Steamboats could be constructed by individuals or small partnerships. More importantly, they used waterways that were already available, and there were no problems in collecting for their services. At least in upstream travel, steamboats faced effective

---

[6] Davis, Easterlin, and Parker, *American Economic Growth*, 475.

[7] Davis, Easterlin, and Parker, *American Economic Growth*, 472.

competition only from their own kind for several decades. Before the advent of steamboats, American rivers had been extensively employed as transport routes. However, except for those few streams broad enough to allow the use of sails or slow enough to make rowing possible, river travel was largely with the current.

The Long Haul Upstream

On the Ohio and Mississippi Rivers, a wide variety of craft, ranging from simple rafts to some ocean-going sailing ships, could be sent downstream. But upstream passage was extremely difficult. Keelboats made the journey upriver from New Orleans to Louisville in from three to four months, with the crew rowing, poling, or towing the boat from shore. As a young man, Abraham Lincoln made the journey to New Orleans several times, travelling downstream via raft or flatboat, and taking keelboat passage or walking back to Illinois. But the only way to generate adequate muscle power for this feat was to employ a crew so large that there was little space left over for cargo or passengers. Losses from accidents were high, and the brawny, brawling rivermen were not famed for honesty. Under such circumstances, there was great interest in alternative means of upstream transport, and steamboats appeared on western waters soon after Fulton's successful voyage on the Hudson River in 1807. The first steamboat from Pittsburgh reached New Orleans in 1811. A few problems remained to be solved; the first boats lacked sufficient engine power to return against the current, but by 1815 two-way traffic had begun.

New Technology and Falling Costs Steamboat charges for upstream travel soon fell to less than 10 percent of keelboat rates for the same services.[8] The journey from New Orleans to Louisville took the first steamboats slightly more than a month, but this was reduced to less than a week by the 1850s. The circumstances are a classic example of the benefits of competition. Profits earned by the first boats were very high, but entry barriers in steamboating were low. When it was realized that some of the early boats had repaid the sums invested in them in just a few years, the number of steamboats increased rapidly. Freight charges were forced down to little more than costs. Furthermore, costs continued to fall; one study found that steamboats' productivity rose at an annual rate of 4 to 6 percent annually up to 1860.[9] Improvements in productivity in an open industry employing new technology might be expected; over time, boat operators could increase profits only by reducing costs faster than their rivals. The chief beneficiaries of these improvements in efficiency were the boats' customers.

Especially on western waters, steamboats were modified to increase speed and carrying capacity and to reduce the boats' draft, which increased their ability to operate in times of low water. The growth of markets allowed savings in capacity utilization and more trips per year. Improved ports and loading facilities also reduced costs.[10] By 1850, some steamboats on the larger rivers could achieve speeds of 15 miles per hour. Steamboats were practical on American rivers, where wood was available at every landing and their high fuel consumption made little difference. On the ocean, early efforts revealed that both fuel and payload for practical journeys entirely under power could not be carried, and most freight continued to cross the sea in sailing vessels until well after the Civil War. Passenger travel, at first in the coastal trade and later in transatlantic voyages, shifted to steamers.

---

[8] E. Haites, J. Mak, and G. Walton, *Western River Transportation: The Era of Early Internal Development, 1810–1860* (New York: Kennikat, 1975), 637.

[9] J. Mak and G. Walton, "Steamboats and the Great Productivity Surge in River Transportation," *Journal of Economic History* (September 1972).

[10] Haites, Mak, and Walton, *Western River Transportation,* 62–73.

■ Although one of his first steamboats was dubbed "Fulton's Folly," Robert Fulton's *Clermont* (1807) and its successors reduced the cost of river transportation.
Source: I. N. Phelps Stokes Collection. Miriam and Ira D. Wallach Division of Art, Prints, Photographs. The New York Public Library, Astor, Lenox and Tilden Foundations.

Steamboats' Limitations

Even though they were a marked improvement over previous modes of river travel, steamboats had their disadvantages. Like other river craft, they could be used only on natural bodies of water. Rarely was there a direct water route between two cities, and no route whatever existed between the Eastern Seaboard and the Ohio Valley. Steamboats could not be used on canals because the wake they produced eroded the banks. River travel had its hazards: ice, drought, snags, sandbars, and floating debris. The operating methods of many early steamboat captains created other problems. The quest for speed often caused overloaded boilers; the era's uncertain metallurgy and unreliable pressure gauges gave only the most drastic evidence of the limits of machinery. Boiler explosions, collisions, and fires—often during races—ended the careers of many riverboats. The average life of a steamboat on western waters was only about five years.

In the 1850s steamboats began to suffer from railroad competition. Although the absolute amount of tonnage carried by steamboats continued to rise, railroads were taking an increasing proportion of the total freight transported, and a disproportionate percentage of the more valuable cargoes. On the larger rivers, steamboats could still compete by 1860 (as could sailing ships on the Great Lakes), but on smaller streams they had lost the battle; railroads were faster and more dependable.

CANALS

Americans tried another approach to the high cost of overland transportation: They created man-made waterways. The canals that were built in three "booms" between 1815 and 1860 added significantly to U.S. economic development. Some were profitable to their owners as well. The most successful of these ventures was the Erie Canal.

The Erie Canal

In 1817, the state of New York began constructing a canal from Albany, at the junction of the Mohawk and Hudson Rivers, to Lake Erie. This project had been proposed several times before, and work had actually commenced at least once. This time, however, the project was not only completed, but was so successful that it touched off a canal boom that spread to those regions of the United States that considered their natural waterways to be inadequate avenues for commerce. The Erie Canal was an immediate financial success. Revenues from the first sections completed were used to finance construction of the final portions linking the Eastern Seaboard to the Great Lakes. When the canal was finished in 1825, New York City became the only eastern seaport with an all-water link to the interior. No project of comparable size had ever been undertaken in the United States before. The canal's construction symbolized the optimism, vision, and determination of early nineteenth-century Americans. It also illustrated the country's ability to allocate the right people to perform important tasks.

The canal's construction was supervised by two lawyers. In this era, lawyers' work was heavily concerned with land titles, so properly trained lawyers were also surveyors. Few engineers with formal training were available at this time; only West Point gave academic instruction in this field. The canal became a massive on-the-job training project for its builders. The only tools available were black powder and horsedrawn scrapers; most of the work was done by men with shovels. After construction was underway, it was discovered that some of the canal's locks would not hold water. The invention of waterproof cement solved this problem, and others were overcome by persistence, effort, and good fortune. The canal's route covered a distance of 364 miles and a vertical rise of 655 feet. Its locks were paired to allow continuous two-way traffic.

A Profitable Undertaking

The Erie Canal returned at least 8 percent on the capital invested in it by the state. The reasons for its profitability were obvious. It connected a major seaport with a rich and well-populated hinterland, initially in upstate New York and later with the entire Great Lakes Basin, and, with the help of additional canals, the Ohio Valley as well. Since the terrain crossed by the Erie was relatively level, traffic on the canal was unusually quick and convenient and construction costs per mile were low. From the first, the Erie Canal was heavily used. In the 1820s and 1830s, most of the traffic in both directions originated within New York State, but after 1846 a majority of the eastbound shipments had been generated farther west. The canal was an important factor in New York City's rise to preeminence among eastern seaports. It also contributed greatly to the growth of Buffalo at its western terminus, where cargo was transferred from lake vessels to canal barges.

Other Canals

The Erie Canal generated extensive external benefits for the state; population and industry grew rapidly in the regions that it served.[11] It spurred nationwide interest in canals. Once the Erie was built, other seaports had to find some way to match New York City's connections with the interior or forfeit both existing trade and a large share of the growth that could be expected as western settlement increased. New York State was already expanding its canal system (much less profitably) to Lakes Champlain and Ontario and the region south of the Erie Canal's route.

---

[11] Davis, Easterlin, and Parker, *American Economic Growth*, 477–485.

■ Canals, equipped with locks allowing passage over varied terrain, constituted America's first man-made transport system.
Source: Courtesy of The New-York Historical Society, New York City.

But nature had been less kind to Philadelphia and Baltimore than it had to New York City. Boston's geographic position was even worse; it could not hope to do more than eventually tap into New York's system, and it could not even do that until railroads became practical. Baltimore attempted to build a canal linking the Potomac and Ohio Rivers, but the Baltimore and Ohio Canal was never extended past Cumberland, Maryland, which it reached in 1850—too late and far short of its goal.

The Main Line Canal Philadelphia also attempted to build a route to the Ohio. The route was far more difficult than that traversed by the Erie Canal; the vertical rise in the Al-
leghenies was over 2,000 feet. The technical capabilities of the time could not construct an all-water route over such terrain. Construction on the Pennsylvania Main Line Canal began in 1826 and took eight years to complete. The engineer who was initially chosen to supervise the project recommended a railroad, but canal construction promised more construction jobs, and with an election in the offing, he was persuaded to change his plan.[12] When completed, the Main Line was a canal—and a horsedrawn railroad, and a series of inclined planes up which disconnected halves of canal boats were pulled by stationary steam engines.

-----
[12] Lebergott, *The Americans,* 107.

■ In 1820, passengers could be transported through the Erie Canal on packet boats. Speed: six miles per hour at best.
Source: The Penn Central Corporation.

There were no less than 174 locks. The frequent transitions between modes of transport slowed traffic, and the heavy construction expenses made the Main Line's tolls high. Although it did tap the Ohio River Valley, which was densely settled before the Great Lakes region, the Main Line never fulfilled its builders' expectations. Construction of a series of branches to other regions of the state added more expenses than revenues.

Ohio built two canals that linked the Ohio River with Lake Erie, one at each end of the state. Indiana constructed another, and Illinois connected Lake Michigan with the Illinois River and, through it, the Mississippi. The Ohio canals, particularly the Ohio and Erie, may have been financial successes. Most canals, especially those in the western states, were not. Canals in that region tended to be long, requiring much time and expense for completion. Many were built to promote settlement in sparsely populated regions rather than to link existing markets. Projects begun in the later 1830s and 1840s had little time in operation before encountering competition from the railroads. Many western canals failed to earn back their construction costs, and few, if any, generated returns equal to alternative uses of capital.

The Canal Boom

There were three cycles of canal building. During the first, between 1815 and 1834, 2,188 miles of canals were built. In the second, from 1834 to 1844, another 1,172 miles were added. The third era extended from 1844 to 1860, and 894 miles of new canals were added, but by the 1850s, existing canals may have been abandoned as rapidly as new ones were built. In all, some 4,200 miles of canals were built in the antebellum era at a total cost of $188 million.[13]

With the exception of the Erie Canal and a few others, canals proved to be poor investments for their owners. In some cases, tolls did not even cover operating expenses. But canals' impact on the economy was more positive than the private returns (or their absence) would suggest. Ton-mile shipping charges on the canals were a tenth or less than those charged for wagon transportation, and canals shipped some goods that wagons simply could not handle. Population density increased sharply and economic activity became more diversified in regions served by canals than in similar regions that lacked them. Regional specialization increased and local monopolies declined as the canal network expanded. This suggests that canal tolls did not represent the full value of the services that these waterways rendered to their users. Part of the rise in incomes produced by canals accrued to canal users, not to the owners. Calculation of the precise amount of these external benefits depends heavily on the analyst's assumptions about what would have occurred in the absence of canals. Little consensus exists on this topic, especially for individual canals. But canals' impact on the aggregate economy was almost certainly positive.[14]

Keys to Canal Success

Canals built between two areas that had already undergone some economic development—particularly if the areas specialized in different products—proved to have better economic records than those constructed into previously unsettled areas as incentives for settlement. Easy construction usually was a good indicator of economic success: Low construction costs resulted in modest tolls, greater speed, and higher traffic volume. Difficult, costly construction generally indicated that the canal would be inconvenient and expensive to use. The first canals (which were built in areas where the advantages were obvious) had longer operating periods before railroad competition appeared.

Some special-purpose canals also generated good financial records. Those linking eastern Pennsylvania coal mines with Philadelphia are examples. They were short, answered an existing demand, and the demand for fuel tended to be price-elastic, so that the reduction in the price of coal caused by lower transport costs resulted in large increases in the volume of traffic. Bulky, low-value items like coal were especially well-suited to water transportation.

Canal Benefits

The canals' contribution should not be underestimated. Without railroad competition, their financial record might have been better. But it was the canals, not the railroads, that produced the major portion of the fall in freight rates before the Civil War. The lower transportation costs allowed regional specialization and the utilization of comparative advantage. In a nation whose resource patterns were as varied as those of the United States, this yielded important income gains: The same resources could produce more output. Competition from larger numbers of producers meant that consumers paid lower prices. Over time, it also pressured producers to reduce their costs by improving the efficiency of their plants. Resources' value increased when their products could be sold in larger markets. Even though canals could not be extended to all regions of the country, they furnished the

---

[13] C. Goodrich, ed., *Canals and American Economic Development* (New York: Columbia University Press, 1961), 172–173.

[14] R. Ransom, "Canals and Development: A Discussion of the Issues," *American Economic Review* (May 1964); H. Segal, "Canals and Economic Development," in Goodrich, ed., *Canals;* and Davis, Easterlin, and Parker, *American Economic Growth,* 474–485.

first low-cost transport links between the East and the West, encouraging the development of both regions.

Canal Limitations

Canals had their limits as well. Transportation on them might involve low money tolls, but the time costs were still high; canal travel was very slow. Basically, the speed limit on canals was the walking pace that draft animals could sustain—two to four miles per hour, and even this pace was reduced if there were traffic congestion or many locks. Locks, low water, and floods slowed traffic. Canals' widths, depths, and lock dimensions varied, which often forced shippers to transfer their cargoes between boats of appropriate dimensions. Weather imposed another time delay; most of the canal network was in regions where winter closed the canals for several months every year. The result of delays was higher inventory costs, losses in shipment, and higher risks for those dependent on the canals than more rapid transportation would involve. Finally, canals could not be developed into a true national transportation system because terrain and water-supply constraints restricted the construction of east–west canals.

Government's Role in Canal Financing

Investment in canals usually required the commitment of a large sum, perhaps millions of dollars, and the certainty of a long wait before the investment would yield any return. Thus, canals were difficult to finance for private investors. The high proportion of income gains that were captured by customers rather than owners was another problem for investors. In the early years of canal construction, few institutions designed to raise large sums from private sources had been developed. In consequence, state governments played a prominent role in canal financing. The states

issued bonds that were to be redeemed by canal tolls and projected increases in tax revenues stemming from the economic development that the canals would promote. Although the federal government made several grants to the Baltimore and Ohio Canal, in general it played only a minor role in canal financing.

Canal bonds were sold to investors both in the United States and in Europe. Perhaps one-third of all canal construction funds were raised in Europe.[15] In the 1830s, the credit rating of the federal government was very high in Europe, and many investors there either did not understand the difference between federal and state governments or thought that the central government was responsible for the debts of the states as well as its own; it had, after all, assumed state debts at the time the Constitution was adopted. But when a number of states defaulted on their bonds in the early 1840s, these investors learned a painful lesson. European investors shied away from American securities for years after these defaults, or demanded high risk premiums. There was an internal reaction as well; many western states that had borrowed heavily to finance development programs now demonstrated a strong aversion to further government-financed projects and borrowing. Bonds had been very easy to sell in the euphoric atmosphere of the mid-1830s, and some canal projects were apparently launched for little more reason than the ready availability of funds.

RAILROADS

By 1860, railroads had become the dominant and most rapidly growing form of transportation in the United States. Nevertheless, the railroads' impact on the economy was not

---

[15] H. Segal, "Cycles of Canal Construction," in Goodrich, ed., *Canals*.

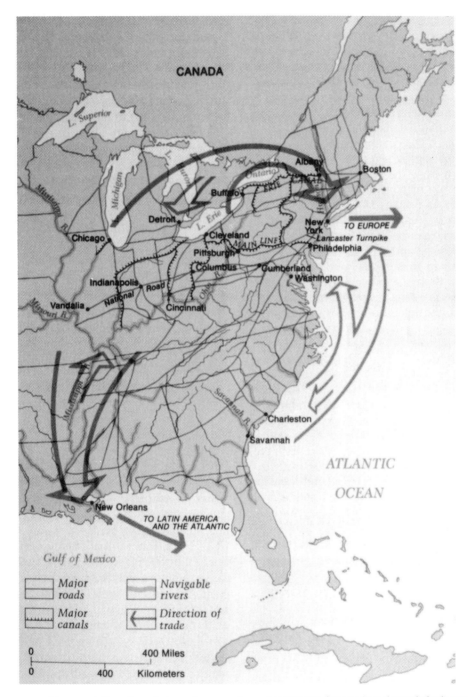

■ Commerce and transportation depended on rivers, roads, and canals moving goods and people both east to west and north to south.

Source: From *America Past & Present, Volume I*, by Robert A. Devine and T. H. Breen, 251. Copyright © 1984 by Scott, Foresman and Company. Reprinted by permission of HarperCollins Publishers.

really a different order of magnitude than anything that had preceded them. Antebellum railroads had surprisingly small effects, either through forward or backward linkages, on the rest of the economy.[16] They clearly did not cause American industrialization, since this was well underway when the first railroads appeared. Railroads consumed relatively small proportions of the economy's output of machinery, engineering services, and (until the 1950s) even iron. As we have seen, the railroads were not responsible for the large drop in transportation costs that occurred in the antebellum era; canals and steamboats generated much greater reductions in shipping costs.

Nevertheless, railroads were an advance over earlier forms of transportation. The fact that they were able to attract business away from other transport modes is proof enough. Railroads influenced more than just shipping costs and passenger charges. Competition, the structure of business firms, the location of industry, financial institutions, and the relations between government and the economy were all changed by the appearance of the railroads. But the U.S. economy was not static or technologically incapable of responses to transportation problems before the railroad era; the growth in per-capita incomes and growing diversity of activities that it produced indicate this. In sum, the railroads in the antebellum era facilitated, but did not instigate, economic growth.

The First Railroads

Before the invention of the steam locomotive, it had already been discovered that horses could pull far greater loads over iron rails than they could on even the best roads. England built the first steam railroad, the Stockton and Darlington, in 1825. Americans were quick to try out the new idea, and, in 1829, an English steam engine was imported and tested, though not very successfully. Still, the new mechanism showed promise, and America had an obvious need for improved transportation.

Once again, an idea from overseas required considerable modification and adaptation to achieve its potential under American conditions. The railroad had been invented in England, a country of short distances, relatively abundant labor and capital, and efficient water transportation. No point in Britain is more than 70 miles from the sea, and there are few real mountains or other obstructions. In addition, the English already had a system of canals and improved rivers. As a result, British railroads were built slowly and designed for a long life. English construction methods reflected resource patterns. Tunnels, bridges, and grades were all designed to minimize operating costs and to reflect the available alternatives. In Britain, really heavy or bulky goods continued to move by water.

American Adaptations
The circumstances were different in America. Distances were greater in this country, and water transportation was a less available alternative. Natural obstacles were more challenging, labor and capital were scarcer, and fuel was much cheaper than in Europe. By the 1840s, American railroads exhibited some distinct features that were responses to the conditions under which they operated. There was great emphasis on speed of both construction and operation. Wood was more extensively used than on English railways. Not only were American wood supplies large, wood required far less skilled labor than did other materials such as the stone the British employed for ties and bridges. In America, sometimes even rails were wood topped with a strip of iron. Grades and curves were sharper than those on British railroads.

[16] R. Fogel, "Railroads in American Economic Growth," *Journal of Economic History* (June 1962). A. Fishlow, *American Railroads and the Transformation of the Antebellum Economy* (Cambridge, Mass.: Harvard University Press, 1965), assigns greater impact to the railroads than does Fogel.

Experience yielded the appropriate methods, but only after a prolonged period of trial and error. There were many errors; few Americans (or any other nineteenth-century humans) had the formal engineering skills to make accurate predictions of the strength of bridges, the tolerable radius of curves in the track, or the slope of grades. Nobody at all had practical experience in operating machinery of such mass and speed—or the brakes required to stop it. Before the invention of the telegraph in 1844, the human eye was the primary instrument of traffic control. Wood-and-iron rails produced "snakeheads"; the iron would separate from the wood and curl up as trains passed over, often penetrating the floors of cars. Boilers were no safer than they were in steamboats, although at least the passengers were farther away. Perhaps, in part, because there was so much room for improvement, productivity gains with the new technology were rapid: Output per unit of input doubled in the railway industry between 1839 and 1859.[17] After prolonged experimentation, the "T" rail of solid iron replaced earlier varieties. Swivel trucks, improved brakes and signals, and more experience increased output and safety. Trains grew heavier, faster, and more powerful.

New Organizational Forms As railways grew longer, new forms of organization were necessary for efficient operation. Lines of authority had to be worked out because local agents often had to decide loads, adjust schedules, and keep track of rolling stock, while fitting local operations into an integrated whole. In addition, the requirements of railroad finance, in which large amounts of capital had to be obtained for long periods, put new emphasis on the corporate form.[18]

Man-made Barriers There was no lack of opposition to the railways. Canal boatmen, wagoneers, and the innkeepers and stable operators who supported their activities saw the threat to their jobs and reacted accordingly. Also, the railroads were obviously new and "unnatural" in an age where such phenomena were far less commonplace than in our own. Debates raged over the effects of prolonged speeds of 20 miles per hour or even more on the human body, or whether speed attained by such means represented a violation of divine law. Because railroads required government help in acquiring corporate charters, obtaining rights of way in settled areas, and often requested government aid in financing, social opposition could not be disregarded.

Railroad Advantages

It was soon clear that the railroads had advantages possessed by no other form of transportation. They could traverse land with too many hills or too little water for canals and carried far more than wagons. Railroads were easier and cheaper to build than canals. Once railroad operators realized that the efficient way to operate a railroad was to run their own trains rather than renting the tracks to others using their own rolling stock, fare collection posed no problems. Above all else, however, the railroads were faster than other forms of transportation. Speeds over the ground were greater than those of canals or most steamboats, routes were more direct, and the railroads ran all year.

Since railroad charges per ton-mile were two or three times those of canals,[19] it is obvious that the shippers who chose them in preference to water transportation placed a high value on time. Initially, most railroad business was passenger traffic, but as technology

---

[17] Davis, Easterlin, and Parker, *American Economic Growth*, 484.

[18] See A. Chandler, *The Railroads: The Nation's First Big Business* (New York: Harcourt, Brace, and World, 1965), and *The Visible Hand: The Managerial Revolution in American Business* (Cambridge, Mass.: Harvard University Press, 1977), Chap. 3.

---

[19] Davis, Easterlin, and Parker, *American Economic Growth*, 484.

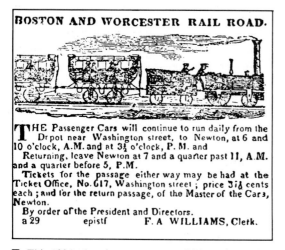

BOSTON AND WORCESTER RAIL ROAD.

THE Passenger Cars will continue to run daily from the Drpot near Washington street, to Newton, at 6 and 10 o'clock, A.M. and at 3½ o'clock, P. M. and Returning, leave Newton at 7 and a quarter past 11, A.M. and a quarter before 5, P.M.

Tickets for the passage either way may be had at the Ticket Office, No. 617, Washington street ; price 3½ cents each ; and for the return passage, of the Master of the Cars, Newton.

By order of the President and Directors.

a 29   epistf   F. A WILLIAMS, Clerk.

■ This 1834 advertisement promoted Massachusetts' first passenger train.
Source: History of the American Nation, by Andrew C. McLaughlin. (New York: D. Appleton, 1901), 316.

Table 5.2   Railroad Mileage and Construction, 1830–1860

Date	Total Mileage Operated	Construction (miles)
1830	23	40
1835	1,098	133
1840	2,818	491
1845	4,633	277
1850	9,021	1,261
1855	18,374	2,453
1860	30,625	1,500

Source: Historical Statistic of the United States: Colonial Times to 1970 (Washington, D.C.: Government Printing Office, 1975), 2:733–734.

improved, freight accounted for a growing portion of revenues. By 1850, freight constituted the majority of railroad business. Inventory costs fell as it was realized that additional goods could now be obtained with much less delay. Increases in traffic volume reduced ton-mile charges as fixed capital was more fully utilized. Railroads could be much more flexible in response to shippers' needs than canals; in many cases a spur could be constructed to the factory door. Speed gave railroads particularly great advantages in shipments of perishable cargoes, but canal barges continued to carry a large share of coal, grain, and other raw materials. As Table 5.2 indicates, the U.S. rail network expanded rapidly after 1845.

Expansion of the Rail Network

By 1840 there were almost 3,000 miles of railroad track in the United States, and all Eastern Seaboard cities were linked. A decade later, 9,000 miles of railroads extended into all re-

gions of the country, and by 1860, the United States could be said to possess a railway system. There were then 30,000 miles of railroad, and it was possible to travel by rail between nearly all the country's large cities, although not always directly. In the 1850s there was extensive construction in the West and South. Raw statistics give a somewhat misleading picture of the situation. Because there were neither standard track gauges nor central (union) terminals, both passengers and freight often had to transfer from one railroad to another, sometimes by wagon, in the course of their journeys. But by 1860 it was possible to travel from any of the great East Coast ports to Chicago or St. Louis and thence to New Orleans at speeds inconceivable only 30 years earlier.

State and Local Government Roles
The federal government was not active in financing the railways until it began to make grants of land to them in the 1850s. State governments played a major role only in the South, where they provided about half the funds required. Local governments contributed to railroads' construction expenses in

■ The first railroad to cross the Allegheny Mountains is shown in this 1863 re-creation of the event, which actually occurred 10 years earlier.
Source: Library of Congress.

various ways—land donations, favorable tax treatment, or guarantees of interest payments on railroad bonds. Cities and towns were quick to recognize that they could gain if a railroad served them, or they could lose population, industry, and jobs to rivals if they were bypassed. The railroads recognized this as well and were not bashful about requesting aid. Nevertheless, private funds furnished the bulk of the capital for antebellum railroad construction in America.

The Role of Private Investors

Financing railroads posed the same types of problems as had canals. A large sum had to

be raised, far beyond the means of even the wealthiest individual investors, and no returns could be expected for a long period. Since the primary source of funds was private savers, railroads were organized as corporations. The corporate form has many advantages as a device to pool the savings of many individuals in a common enterprise. Shares of corporate stock are transferable; they can be bought and sold, although securities markets were limited at this time. In a partnership, the entire agreement must be renegotiated each time a partner is added or deleted. Further, corporate shares carry limited liability. Shareholders cannot lose more than the purchase price of their stock or its face value, whichever is greater, no matter what happens to the corporation. Members of a partnership, on the other hand, are liable for its debts to the full extent of their personal wealth, regardless of the size of their investment or their participation in its management. Thus, corporations were better instruments for raising capital for new ventures such as railways. The lower risks involved in share ownership made it easier to raise the large sums necessary. Corporate charters had to be granted by state legislatures, initially on a case-by-case basis with strict limits on the type of activity permitted. Over time, however, states became more willing to grant wider powers to the holders of corporate charters.[20]

The European Connection Especially after 1850, when memories of earlier American investment defaults had begun to fade, Europeans bought large amounts of American railroad securities. The bulk of the investment remained American, but funds from Europe provided some advantages. The cost of raising a given sum was often lower in Europe, where wealth was more concentrated and financial markets better organized than in the United States. Western railroads, which had to build over long distances in regions where few investors had sizable amounts to invest, found access to European capital especially advantageous. Investors along the Eastern Seaboard of the United States had plenty of other promising alternatives and often were less willing to hazard their funds in the West than Europeans. As the interest in railroad securities increased, institutions to market them and facilitate the transfer of existing issues were developed. By 1860, most large cities had "stock exchanges" that dealt largely in government and railroad bonds rather than in stocks.

Low Costs and High Returns There were other means to minimize the initial investment required. The attempts to obtain government aid have already been noted. Most railroads, particularly those built in the 1830s and 1840s, were short. They served local markets, connecting complementary economic activities. At least in this period, railroads were not built ahead of existing settlement, and most were profitable shortly after they began operations.[21] This record made it easier to raise funds for later projects.

Federal Assistance
An indication of the future participation of the federal government in railroad finance occurred in 1850. The Illinois Central Railroad was given several million acres of federally owned land that year. The idea was that the railroad would sell most of the land to settlers (it had been granted far more than was needed for a right of way), and use the funds it obtained for construction. Since the land would eventually be close to a railroad, it could be sold at premium prices in comparison to similar land lacking transportation services. This procedure facilitated the achievement of several governmental objectives: Western settlement would increase and the railroad would be constructed. (It appeared that conventional sources of finance could not supply sufficient funds.) At the same time, sales of the remaining government-owned land in the region would be easier. The cost to the treasury was essentially zero, since the government then held more land than it could sell—in many cases because the land's produce could not be marketed. As with the corporate form, this procedure would be greatly expanded in the years to come.

---

[20] Chandler, *The Visible Hand,* 89–94.

[21] Fishlow, *American Railroads,* Chaps. 4–5.

CONSEQUENCES OF TRANSPORTATION IMPROVEMENTS BY 1860

The East

On the eve of the Civil War, little of the American transportation system had been in operation for more than a few decades, but it had already begun to influence regional specialization and interdependence. The Middle Atlantic and New England regions now devoted fewer resources to agriculture and more to manufacturing, commerce, and finance. A growing share of the food consumed in these regions came from the Midwest via the Erie Canal, the railroads, and coastal shipping. The remaining eastern farmers had been forced to react to the competition from more fertile western soils by switching from grain production to wool, dairying, and truck farming. Other eastern farmers had abandoned agriculture there and moved either to midwestern farms or to the cities.

The Midwest

In the Midwest, aggregate population rose sharply. Potential agricultural incomes in the region were now higher because food could be shipped cheaply to eastern markets. Not everyone found the changes desirable. Prior to the advent of efficient transportation, there had been a considerable development of small-scale, locally oriented manufacturing in the Midwest. When transportation costs declined, many of these firms were unable to meet competition from larger, more specialized producers.[22] Yankee farmers regarded the invasion of their markets by Midwestern pro-

duce with no more enthusiasm. The result, however, was that American resources produced more output because they were better allocated toward their most efficient uses. As Table 5.3 indicates, transportation costs were now as little as one-tenth their levels in 1815.

Returns to Transportation

Not only were regions now able to specialize in producing those items that were best suited to their resources, but lower transport costs forced them to pass on the gains in efficiency to their customers. Before 1860, most firms were tiny in comparison to their modern counterparts in absolute size, but not in terms of the markets in which they operated. Though small, they often had monopoly power both

Table 5.3 Average Freight Rates per Ton-Mile (Cents per Ton-Mile)

Mode	1816	1853	1860
Turnpikes	30.00	15.00	15.00
Mississippi–Ohio downstream	1.30		.37
Mississippi–Ohio upstream	5.80		.37
Erie Canal		1.10	
Ohio Canals		1.00	
Pennsylvania Main Line Canal		2.40	
New York Central Railroad		3.40	2.40
Erie Railroad		2.40	1.84
Western Railroads (Buffalo–Chicago)		2.50	
Pennsylvania Railroad		3.50	1.96

Source: Adapted from G. Taylor, *The Transportation Revolution* (New York: M. E. Sharpe, 1977), 442.

---

[22] North, *Economic Growth*, 157, 163.

as sellers of products and as purchasers of inputs. The workers with whom they dealt often had little bargaining power because there were only one or two potential employers within walking distance of their homes. The firms' customers had few more alternatives. Lower transportation costs increased the range of choices in many markets and reduced (but hardly eliminated) the power of many local monopolies. By increasing the number and incomes of potential customers for any single producer, they encouraged the use of techniques that increased the volume of output and often reduced its unit costs as well. The development of the mass market that transportation improvements did so much to produce was one of the distinctive features of the American economy and a major source of its further growth. As previously noted, the contribution of transport improvements is hard to quantify, but one study found that the railroads had produced a social saving of 5 percent of GNP by 1860; that is, aggregate U.S. income was 5 percent higher because of the railroads than it would have been in their absence.[23] Because the railroads' contribution built on the achievements of the canals and steamboats, it seems clear that the developments in antebellum transportation made very substantial differences in the economic alternatives available to Americans.

THE COMMUNICATION REVOLUTION

Passengers and goods could be transported at much greater speeds in 1860 than ever before, but the telegraph improved the speed with which information travelled far more. Invented by Samuel Morse (and simultaneously by two Englishmen) and patented in 1844, the telegraph provided nearly instantaneous communication over long distances. Rapid communication made transportation even more productive. It was the answer to railroad traffic control problems. The risks of dependence on suppliers in distant regions were now greatly reduced, fostering regional specialization and increasing the volume of goods traffic.

SELECTED REFERENCES

Chandler, A. *The Railroads: The Nation's First Big Business.* New York: Harcourt, Brace, and World, 1965.
———. *The Visible Hand: The Managerial Revolution in American Business.* Cambridge, Mass.: Harvard University Press, 1977.
Davis, L., R. Easterlin, W. Parker et al. *American Economic Growth: An Economist's History of the United States.* New York: Harper & Row, 1972.
Fishlow, A. *American Railroads and the Transformation of the Antebellum Economy.* Cambridge, Mass.: Harvard University Press, 1965.
Goodrich, C., ed. *Canals and American Economic Development.* New York: Kenikat, 1975.
Haites, E., J. Mak, and G. Walton. *Western River Transportation: The Era of Early Internal Development, 1810–1860.* New York: Kenikat, 1965.
Kirkland, E. *Men, Cities, and Transportation.* 2 vols. New York: Russell and Russell, 1968.
Klingaman, D., and R. Vedder, eds. *Essays in Early 19th Century Economic History: The Old Northwest.* Athens, Ohio: Ohio University Press, 1975.
North, D. *The Economic Growth of the United States, 1790–1860.* New York: Norton, 1966.
North, D., T. Anderson, and P. Hill. *Growth and Welfare in the American Past: A New Economic History.* 3d ed. Englewood Cliffs, N.J.: Prentice-Hall, 1983.
Scheiber, H. *The Ohio Canal Era.* Athens, Ohio: Ohio University Press, 1969.
Taylor, G. *The Transportation Revolution, 1815–1860.* New York: M. E. Sharpe, 1962.
U.S. Department of Commerce, Bureau of the Census. *Historical Statistics of the United States: Colonial Times to 1970* 2 vols. Washington, D.C.: Government Printing Office, 1975.

---

[23] Fishlow, *American Railroads*, Chaps. 4–5.

AGRICULTURAL EXPANSION AND CHANGE

M ore people earned their living in agriculture than in any other occupation from 1815 to 1860. Thus, developments in agriculture directly affected most Americans. Even so, agriculture's importance to the economy declined; in 1860, it employed 53 percent of the work force versus 79 percent four decades earlier.[1] Farming's share of the value of total output declined from 60 to less than 40 percent over the same period. The numbers indicate that the relative decline of agriculture within the U.S. economy was not over in 1860; resources were more productive (and earned larger incomes) in other sectors. Incomes had grown more quickly elsewhere in the economy, and would continue to do so.

AGRICULTURAL CHANGES

But agriculture was neither declining nor even static in absolute terms. From 1815 to 1860, both agricultural exports and the proportion of the U.S. population living in cities increased, indicating that output per farmer had risen. In 1860, each farmer supplied the food and fiber needs of a larger number of people than in 1815. Total agricultural production had increased sharply, but output rose faster elsewhere in the economy.

Two major trends characterized American agriculture from 1815 to 1860. First, there were huge aggregate increases in virtually all its dimensions: work force, total product, cultivated area, and in the amount of land available. Second, a variety of developments increased individual farmers' productive capacities. Productivity rose far more than it had in the colonial era.

In the first half of the nineteenth century, the United States increased its land area to 3.4 times that of 1789. A combination of purchase, coercion, and annexation added the Louisiana Purchase, East and West Florida, Texas, Oregon, and the vast territory taken from Mexico. The acquisitions, together with its initial area, gave the United States large areas of some of the richest agricultural land on earth and a vast endowment of timber and mineral wealth. In 1860, most of the new areas had not been settled, and more were still raw frontier. Yet settlement extended far beyond its previous boundaries. These new lands often required adjustments from their owners. Soil, climate, and productive capabilities differed from those along the Atlantic Coast. By 1860, appropriate responses to the new opportunities had barely begun to be learned, far less realized.

As Table 6.1 indicates, there had been very substantial population movement to the new areas. Both the Midwest and the "New South," the area west of Georgia, particularly the lower Mississippi Valley, had populations rivalling those of any of the older settled areas on the eve of the Civil War.

LAND POLICY AND THE PUBLIC DOMAIN

This vast area initially was the property of the federal government. Most of it was sold to private citizens on increasingly lenient terms, as Table 6.2 reveals. Widespread defaults forced the government to discontinue sales on credit after 1820, but by that time more than

---

[1] L. Davis, R. Easterlin, and W. Parker, *American Economic Growth: An Economist's History of the U.S.* (New York: Harper & Row, 1972), 187. See also T. Weiss, "Revised Estimates of the U.S. Workforce, 1800–1860, in R. Gallman and S. Engerman, *Long-Term Factors in American Economic Growth* (Chicago: University of Chicago Press, 1986).

Table 6.1   U.S. Population by Region

| Region | 1820 | | 1860 | |
	Number	Percentage of Total	Number	Percentage of Total
New England	1,660,071	17.2%	3,135,283	10.0%
Mid-Atlantic	2,699,845	28.0	7,458,985	23.7
East North Central	792,719	8.2	6,926,884	22.0
West North Central	66,586	.7	2,169,832	6.9
South Atlantic	3,061,063	31.8	5,634,703	17.1
East South Central	1,190,489	12.4	4,020,991	12.8
West South Central	167,680	1.7	1,747,667	5.6
Mountain	—	—	174,923	.5
Pacific	—	—	440,053	1.4
Totals	9,638,453	100.0	31,442,321	100.0

Source: U.S. Bureau of the Census, *Historical Statistics of the United States: Colonial Times to 1970* (Washington, D.C.: Government Printing Office, 1975), 1:22, 23.

enough land for a family farm could be obtained for $100. The land was sold at auction, and the prices listed were the minimum bids required. But so much land was available that prices seldom rose much above the minimum. Land purchased at government auctions had been surveyed and bore secure titles. It could be transferred readily, and land speculation was at least as widespread as it had been in the colonial era.

Table 6.2   Land Sale Provisions and Prices, 1785–1854

Year	Minimum Purchase Allowed (Acres)	Minimum Bid (Price per Acre)	Sale Terms
1785	640	$1.00	Cash
1796	640	2.00	1/2 cash; rest in 1 year.
1800	320	2.00	1/4 cash; rest over 4 years.
1804	160	2.00	1/4 cash; rest over 4 years.
1820	80	1.25	Cash
1832	40	1.25	Cash
1841	*	1.25	Cash
1854	40	**	Cash

* Preemption Act (see text).
** The Graduation Act (see text).
Source: E. Kirkland, *A History of American Economic Life*, 4th ed. (New York: Appleton Century Crofts, 1969), 86, 87.

Public Land Sale Policy

In 1841 and 1854, the Preemption and Graduation Acts eased the land-acquisition process still further. The first enabled "squatters" who had settled on surveyed land without purchasing it to buy up to 160 acres of the land they occupied at the $1.25 per acre minimum price. It more or less recognized reality; squatters were prone to discourage those who sought to gain their land through legal means by threats or outright force, and Congress had legitimized their acquisitions several times before. The second law provided that land that had gone unsold at $1.25 for more than 10 years would be sold on a sliding scale, reaching 12.5 cents per acre for land that had not been sold after 30 years. In itself, the Graduation Act indicated that there was plenty of top-quality land available at existing prices. Land could also be obtained from state and local governments, and military veterans were rewarded with warrants giving them the right to land. These were transferrable, often at per-acre prices below those charged for direct purchases from the government.

Although some people believed that the government should have given the land away to encourage the growth of family farms, the speed with which settlement occurred indicates that land costs could hardly have been a substantial barrier to farm formation. Since land sales were the second-largest source of federal revenue, the government would have had to develop an alternative fiscal resource to replace that forfeited. In addition, by 1860 the cost of land was only a small portion of the total expenditure necessary to develop a commercially viable farm. The amounts required for livestock, tools, building materials, land clearance, travel, and first-year maintenance of the settler and his family might total ten times the land's purchase price. Another question posed by the free-land proposal was the criteria by which land was to be distributed—who would receive how much? Obviously, each potential recipient had an incentive to overstate the quantity required or desired if the land's marginal costs were zero.

Land was not kept from small farmers by large-scale land speculators. It is quite true that many persons, including most small farmers, bought as much land as they could in hopes of reselling it at higher prices. But the market for land was highly competitive: Sellers had their choice of many parcels from a variety of buyers. As previously noted, the stable prices at which government land actually sold indicated that it was not growing scarcer. Also, the larger the number of speculators, the less their ability to drive up prices.[2] Since more land was settled in this 45-year period than in the previous two centuries, the overwhelming bulk of it by small farmers, it is difficult to make a convincing case for speculation's inhibiting effects on settlement. Tracts with special properties—already cleared, a desirable location, or special appeal to the buyer—might bring high prices, but, in general, it was a buyers' market for ordinary land.[3]

The Safety-Valve Theory
The availability of western land was once thought to improve the bargaining power of eastern workers versus their employers. According to this "safety-valve" theory, if wages

---

[2] See A. Bogue and M. Bogue, "Profits and the Frontier Speculator," *Journal of Economic History* (March 1957), and R. Swierenga, *Pioneers and Profits: Land Speculation on the Iowa Frontier* (Ames, Iowa: Iowa State University Press, 1968).

[3] The results of speculative activity are often confused with the intention of speculators–who certainly hope to resell the commodities they have purchased at higher prices than they paid. But when such activity has a significant effect upon markets, it tends to be self-defeating. By adding to current demand, speculators raise prices at the time they make their purchases. When they resell, they add to the (then) current supply, and this pushes prices down. Speculation might not influence prices at all if it is on a small scale, but it cannot fulfill its perpetrators' hopes if there are enough of them to influence prices. Speculation reduces the margin between current and future prices rather than increasing it. The foregoing analysis appears especially pertinent to the highly competitive land markets of the nineteenth century.

fell, workers could always leave their jobs, buy land, and become farmers. This idea is almost certainly invalid for individual workers and probably for the economy as a whole. Wages in manufacturing, on the average, exceeded farmers' incomes, and thus a move from industrial work to agriculture would be a switch from a sector where incomes were above the national average to one in which they were below it. Nor would entry into farming be easy for most urban workers by 1860. Years of saving would be required for the investment required to purchase a fully equipped farm, and this would be difficult indeed if the worker thought his wages too low. Credit was hard to obtain for the average individual at this time, particularly on the frontier. Finally, by 1860 commercial farming had become a specialized occupation requiring skills and specialized capital few urban workers or recent immigrants possessed.

Patterns of migration observed during this period tend to refute the safety-valve theory. Few, if any, city workers switched to agriculture, but some farmers, or their children, moved to the cities. The urban population of the United States rose from 7.2 to 19.7 percent of the total during this period.[4] Movement to the West was most pronounced during good times, not in periods of unemployment and falling wages. In short, population movements indicate that the western movement was a response to opportunity, not a flight from adversity.

Today it may be possible to romanticize life on a nineteenth-century farm, but the reality was less appealing. Work on farms in a time when power was supplied almost exclusively by human or animal muscles was brutally

hard, and hours at planting or harvest time were limited only by available daylight. Even contemporary factory jobs might look easy in comparison. Frontier farmers generally had fewer tools and some even more demanding tasks, such as land clearing and construction, than their counterparts in long-settled regions.

The thesis that the American frontier served as a safety valve for social nonconformists also has little empirical support. As the Mormons discovered at great cost, the frontier was not particularly tolerant of those with different social or religious views. Cities have always been more receptive to a variety of opinions and life-styles than has the countryside.

Despite this, the West had a significant impact on the economic life of the East. By furnishing a growing market for eastern goods, western economic growth increased demand for industrial workers, thereby raising their wages. Parts of the West were developing their own cities, and the demand for labor there was greater than it was in older areas. Cheaper food from the West also raised eastern workers' real incomes. For farm laborers in the East, the safety-valve theory may well be valid; the West offered higher wages and better access to land.

PRODUCTIVITY GROWTH IN AGRICULTURE

Although yields per acre changed very slowly, output per farmer rose, indicating that the average size of farms was increasing. Improved stock care and better organization apparently resulted in growth in output per New England farm worker after 1790.[5] Man-hours required

[4] U.S. Bureau of the Census, *Historical Statistics of the United States: Colonial Times to 1970* (Washington, D.C.: Government Printing Office, 1975), 1:12. See also F. Lewis, "Explaining the Shift from Agriculture to Industry in the U.S., 1869–1899," *Journal of Economic History* (September 1979).

[5] W. Rothenberg, "The Emergence of Farm Labor Markets and the Transformation of the Rural Economy: Massachusetts 1750–1855," *Journal of Economic History* (September 1988).

per unit of corn, wheat, and cotton had begun to fall after 1800.[6] Output of these three crops doubled from 1839 to 1859, a period in which the agricultural work force rose by about 65 percent.[7] Gains of this magnitude indicate that production methods had changed.

Technological Change

The sources of these productivity gains are varied. Western land was more fertile than much of the East, but movement to more fertile land accounted for only minor gains. Improved knowledge also made only a limited contribution. Farmers were now able to cultivate larger acreage, and the major factor in this development was the appearance of new machinery. Some improvement and innovation in agricultural tools had been apparent since 1800, but in the 1840s and 1850s new mechanical devices came into widespread use, giving farmers greater capabilities than they had ever possessed before.[8]

By 1860 the changing conditions of American agriculture had provoked a series of highly successful responses. Increased output could now be sold in larger markets to which farmers had better access, raising the incentives for commercial rather than subsistence farming. The chief barrier to increased production in American agriculture had always been the shortage of labor. Because land, if anything, became less scarce than it had been previously, productivity-raising innovation emphasized devices that allowed individual workers to farm more land, that is, labor-saving equipment. The new machinery allowed the application of a given number of man-hours to far more land than before.

The Search for New Techniques

There was scope for productivity gains in the introduction of scientific, or at least systematic, techniques in animal husbandry and other areas of agriculture, but efforts in these areas, although begun earlier, were as yet less productive than the introduction of mechanical implements. Without an understanding of the basic scientific principles of heredity and soil chemistry, progress in the selection of new breeds of stock, strains of seed, and fertilizers had to be achieved by trial and error. New breeds of sheep and cattle were introduced. In plant cultivation, attempts at developing strains that were resistant to disease and insect attack occurred.[9] Cotton cultivation may have been an exception, perhaps because of the influence of large production units able to maintain records of their innovative efforts and use control groups that increased confidence in the results obtained.[10] Despite the appearance of agricultural journals, fairs, and other devices for conveying information, innovations were likely to spread mainly after direct demonstration. If the new idea did not produce the same results for emulators that it had for its inventor, there was no way of determining why it had failed.

The Introduction of Machinery
Mechanical aids, on the other hand, could be devised by small-scale observation and utilized familiar concepts. They did not require the application of formal scientific principles. Particularly in wheat and hay cultivation, the results of mechanical innovations were easy

---

[6] *Historical Statistics*, 1:500.

[7] *Historical Statistics*, 1:512, 518.

[8] W. Parker and J. Klein, "Productivity Growth in Grain Production in the United States, 1840–1860 and 1900–1910," in *Output, Employment, and Productivity in the United States After 1800, Studies in Income and Wealth,* (Princeton, N.J.: Princeton University Press, 1966), vol. 30.

---

[9] I am indebted to Professor Robert Gallman on this point.

[10] S. Lebergott, *The Americans: An Economic Record* (New York: Norton, 1984), 164–167.

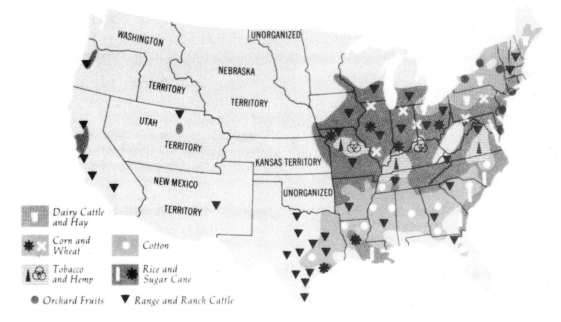

WASHINGTON

UNORGANIZED

NEBRASKA

TERRITORY

TERRITORY

UTAH

TERRITORY

KANSAS TERRITORY

NEW MEXICO

UNORGANIZED

TERRITORY

Dairy Cattle and Hay

Corn and Wheat

Cotton

Tobacco and Hemp

Rice and Sugar Cane

Orchard Fruits   Range and Ranch Cattle

■ This map indicates the distribution of American agricultural production in 1860.
Source: From *The American Pageant,* 7th ed., by Thomas A. Bailey and David M. Kennedy. Copyright © 1987 by D. C. Heath and Company. Reprinted by permission of the publisher.

to assess and attribute to the proper sources, so both invention and innovation were rapid.[11] Since the limits on farm production were imposed largely by the amount of labor available, especially for the harvest, efforts were concentrated on increasing output per labor hour and on harvesting rather than planting. Scythes replaced sickles early in the nineteenth century, and the cradle further increased productivity in grain harvesting.

Early plows were wooden, difficult for a team to pull, susceptible to damage, and incapable of deep plowing. Iron was gradually added to plows to reduce friction and increase resistance to wear. Improved designs allowed farmers to make straighter, deeper furrows

with less effort. In 1819, the first cast-iron plows appeared, and by the 1850s, John Deere's steel plow, better suited to western soils, was in widespread use. Seed drills, reapers, and threshers became common in the same decade. Reapers and threshers had been invented several decades previously, but considerable development was required before they became economically useful. Because labor was not usually available to harvest the crop if the reaper broke down, the machines had to be made reliable and easy to repair. In addition, producers had to build up organizations to market, finance, and service these expensive and complicated devices at the local level. The real impetus to mechanical reaping was the movement of wheat production to the larger, more level fields of the Midwest, where machines performed better. Harvesting machines' high initial cost could be spread over

---

[11] N. Rosenberg, *Technology and American Economic Growth* (New York: M.E. Sharpe, 1972), 25–26.

a greater volume of output, reducing capital costs per bushel of wheat harvested.[12] The relocation of production and its mechanization were linked to the development of a transportation network capable of carrying the larger volumes of grain to market. Horsedrawn rakes and cultivators reduced the amount of labor required to harvest hay and increased corn yields. Corn harvesting and shelling, however, remained a labor-intensive bottleneck throughout this era.

EASTERN AGRICULTURE

Prior to the improvement of transportation, eastern farmers had the markets of the seaboard cities to themselves. However, as western produce became more available at competitive prices, farmers in this region were forced to intensify the adjustments begun shortly after the Revolution. In general, animal husbandry improved and became more labor intensive.[13] The West's great tracts of fertile land were better suited to the utilization of labor-saving machinery than were the smaller, less level farmlands of the East. In grain production, the West's comparative advantage was so large that it was imperative for eastern farmers to find new products.

Eastern cities offered increasing markets for "truck" fruits and vegetables, hay, high-quality meat, dairy products, and, as the textile industry expanded, wool. The demand for dairy products in the cities exceeded the amounts that rural areas could deliver in this age of primitive cooling and preservation techniques. Improvements in distribution systems and in refrigeration were prerequisites to reallocating productive capacity to dairy products. Consequently, dairy herds were maintained within the cities.

Farmers in the East also attempted to compete with the West by improving the quality of both their output and their resources. Attempts were made to improve the quality of eastern farmland through experiments with fertilizers and crop rotation. Merino sheep, whose wool production far exceeded that of domestic breeds, were imported from Spain. Crossbreeding American and European cattle raised the productivity of beef and dairy strains, and horses and hogs were also improved. Animal weights rose substantially. Given the necessity for improved techniques, there was widespread interest in innovation. Devices to disseminate new ideas, such as agricultural magazines and county fairs (which were devoted largely to business rather than social purposes) appeared. After 1840 the gains from these sources declined.

In some cases, the response to western competition took a different form. Some farms, especially those on marginal soils, unsuited to the new methods, or badly located, were simply abandoned. This process was more widespread in New England than in the Middle Atlantic states. Despite the population movements of the 1970s, some rural areas in New England have yet to regain the population peaks recorded over a century ago.

---

[12] P. David, "The Mechanization of Reaping in the Antebellum Midwest," in *Technical Choice, Innovation, and Economic Growth* (Oxford, U.K.: Oxford University Press, 1975). David's conclusions have been the subject of some controversy. See L. Jones, "The Mechanization of Reaping and Mowing in American Agriculture: A Comment," *Journal of Economic History* (June 1977), and A. Olmstead, "The Mechanization of Reaping and Mowing in American Agriculture, 1833–1870, *Journal of Economic History* (June 1975).
[13] Rothenberg, "Emergence of Farm Labor."

THE OLD NORTHWEST

The valleys of the Ohio and the upper Mississippi contain some of the richest agricultural land on earth. Fertile, well-watered, and level, this area is immensely productive. Settlement of the region began in Kentucky and the southern Ohio Valley, with the first immigrants arriving from Virginia and the Carolinas in the 1770s.

After 1800, another stream of migration began. Originating in New England and upstate New York, and later strongly supplemented with immigrants, people in this group settled the northern halves of Ohio, Indiana, and Illinois, as well as southern Michigan and Wisconsin. When settlement reached the prairies, it faltered briefly. Farmers had traditionally assessed the soil quality of new land by the types of trees growing on it. But soon it was realized that the prairies were not inferior soil, but in fact were so rich that the grass smothered tree seedlings (or promoted prairie fires that killed them), and were far easier to bring into cultivation than forest land. Soon prairie grain and livestock production expanded rapidly.

Much of the actual pioneering effort was concentrated in a small group of frontiersmen, typified by Daniel Boone and John Sevier. After making the initial settlements, these specialists would sell their landholdings to those with more settled inclinations and move west again to repeat the process. While the frontiersmen practiced subsistence agriculture, lumbering, trapping, and trading, their chief source of income was land speculation.

Mixed Farming

The chief agricultural products of the Old Northwest were corn, wheat, pork, and, to a lesser extent, beef. The characteristics of these goods and the nature of the production processes they required shaped the region's economic development. Cattle could be driven east on the hoof, if distances were not too great, but mobility and food qualities were not easily combined in hogs. Pork was generally exported in preserved forms—smoked into hams or bacon, salted, or pickled. Grain crops,

especially corn, also required processing to improve their portability. Corn, wheat, beef, and pork were all well suited to production on farms worked by the owner and his family; there were no economies of scale open to larger units.

The region grew spectacularly. In 1800, the leading wheat- and corn-producing states were all on the Atlantic Seaboard. By 1840 Kentucky, Ohio, and Tennessee were challenging the previous leaders. In 1860, more than half of all the wheat grown in the United States originated in Illinois, Missouri, Indiana, Ohio, Michigan, and Wisconsin. The Midwest was a large-scale corn producer as well, but corn was grown almost everywhere that Americans farmed. It was widely used as food for both man and beast. Corn was not easily transported before a practical method of getting the kernels off the cob had been developed. Kentucky, Tennessee, and Missouri also produced tobacco, hemp, and mules.

Agriculture's Links to Urban Growth

The Midwest's chief crops could all be exported more easily if they were processed. Most corn left the Ohio Valley as fattened pork or whiskey. Before the railroads appeared, live hogs were more difficult to transport than was preserved pork. Wheat was more expensive to ship than was flour. There were economies of scale in the processing of all these items; unit costs fell when much larger amounts than the average farm turned out were milled, distilled, or slaughtered and packed by specialist firms rather than the farmers themselves. Once large-scale processing appeared, it paid to utilize such by-products as hides, tallow, mash, and bran. Plants making shoes, harness, soap, candles, lard, and feed were complementary to the mills, distilleries, and packing plants or combined with them. The large amounts of regional exports required containers—barrels at the time—and boats, especially since much of the region's output was sent to New Orleans on one-way flatboats or rafts. All these activities required sizable work forces that gave considerable impetus to the growth of towns. Urbanization increased the markets for foodstuffs and wood. The towns also served as distribution centers for manufactured goods from the East and Europe.

The Ohio Valley became thickly settled with a substantial urban population as a result of concentration on commercial agriculture. The Old Northwest depended on the eastern markets for its exports and on its factories for industrial goods. Thus, there was great interest in developing efficient transportation links to other areas. Initially, goods were sent down tributary streams to the Ohio and Mississippi Rivers and then to New Orleans for export or shipment to the East. Later, canals and railroads gave more direct access to seaboard markets. The numerous small-scale producers of basic export commodities required the services of concentration points for exports and distribution centers for the goods those exports purchased. Both local and regional centers were required.

The Stronghold of the Small Town
Few midwestern farmers were more than a day's wagon ride away from a town in which they could exchange agricultural products for other goods and services. Typically, the small town would have its general store, which did multiple duty as a tavern and social club. There farm products could be sold or bartered for tools, cloth, salt, whiskey, and other items. The town would offer specialists' services: There would be a blacksmith, sawmill, and gristmill, processing goods brought from the countryside. There might be a distillery and perhaps some small-scale manufacturing. Banks, churches, and lawyers (specializing in land sales) offered their services. Some local government functions would be available; at

least the circuit judge on occasion and more if the town were a county seat.

The town would also have a school, and there would probably be others scattered through the countryside. Education was valued in the Midwest. It enabled the new generation to read Scripture, but it also equipped them for economic activity. Each midwestern farm was a small business in which information had to be assimilated and evaluated, and decisions made about the type of crop to be produced and the techniques to be used under intensely competitive conditions. Farmers found the ability to read, write, and "cipher" useful. Land speculation required a knowledge of the law and surveying. Schools thus provided useful services to the population, and were established and supported by government. Before the financial debacles of the early 1840s, state government support was likely to be available for transportation improvements, and sometimes for banks as well. After that time, the basis of assistance shifted from state to local government and to private enterprise.

Regional Centers
The Old Northwest was not merely an agricultural region. The very nature of the area's agriculture and its products necessitated a very considerable urban development. Such cities as Cincinnati, Pittsburgh, Louisville, Cleveland, St. Louis, and Chicago began as lake or river ports and centers for processing and distribution, and they quickly developed further. Transportation and the processing industries encouraged a variety of other occupations linked to the primary activities. Overall population and income growth allowed scope for provision of an ever-expanding range of additional goods and services.

Because agricultural implements were bulky and difficult to ship, manufacturers of these items decided early to locate their production facilities near their midwestern markets, rather than in the more industrialized

East. Chicago, utilizing its position as a lake port for the prairies' exports as well as that of a regional distribution center, became the largest lumber market in the world. Here the forest products of the upper Midwest could be distributed to prairie dwellers who lacked local timber, or exported to the East. Other industry began to exploit the coal, copper, lead, and iron ore of the region. By 1860, Cincinnati was still a meat-packing center, but it was also making locomotives, a development of its early steamboat industry. Chicago was throwing out the network of railroads that would make it the regional metropolis. Major industrialization of the Midwest would occur after the Civil War, but the region's diversification from agriculture was underway.

The Innovative Environment

Grain and meat production from a host of small family-operated farms provided a receptive atmosphere for innovation. The limits to each farm's income were set by the amount of labor available; the more each produced, the higher its income. Since there were thousands of such farms, no one unit's production would have any influence on the price of the region's agricultural staples. Changes that increased productive capacity were therefore welcomed. Innovation was also a defensive procedure. Even though no single farmer's increase in output could reduce prices, a simultaneous rise in production by large numbers of farms might increase supply faster than demand, driving prices down. Under such circumstances, the individual farmer's only hope of maintaining or increasing income lay in reducing costs of production faster than prices fell. Thus, there was keen interest in any innovation that promised an increase in the amount of output each unit of labor could supply. Labor supplies themselves were difficult to increase; hired help was scarce and unde-

pendable, and even children would eventually grow up and leave home. Labor mobility was higher than it had been in the colonial era.[14]

If natural conservatism was a barrier to innovation, it was overcome by the highly competitive nature of midwestern agriculture and the demonstrated effectiveness of the new methods. It should not be forgotten that many of the new machines reduced the need for long hours of gruelling labor in addition to raising incomes; some might have been adopted even if they had no effect on money incomes. The nature of the land and the variety of commodities that it could produce also favored innovative responses. The shortage of wood on the prairies forced new solutions to building, fencing, and heating. Farther west, the lack of surface water would encourage another search for new methods. The midwestern farm was thus a training school for rational decision making.[15]

SOUTHERN AGRICULTURE

The antebellum South was vastly different from other regions of the United States. In its major exports, the nature of much of its agriculture, its relative lack of urbanization, and, above all, the existence of slavery, the agricultural economy of the South was unique.

The Cotton Kingdom

The southern frontier moved westward nearly as rapidly as did that farther north. (See Table 6.1.) Because of an almost total absence of cities in the South, its population density was

---

[14] D. Galenson and C. Pope, "Economic and Geographic Mobility on the Farming Frontier: Evidence from Appanoose County, Iowa, 1850–1870," *Journal of Economic History* (September 1989).
[15] Davis, Easterlin, and Parker, *American Economic Growth*, 396.

less than that of the North Central region. Both areas thus had many frontier characteristics in common, but there were also significant differences. Midwestern farmers produced a variety of cash crops and livestock products, but in the South, expansion was overwhelmingly centered on cotton. After the cotton gin had made upland cotton a profitable crop, its cultivation spread rapidly. Just as in the Old Northwest, yields rose as cultivation moved west. Upland Georgia was more productive than South Carolina, and Mississippi and Alabama soils were better still. The deep alluvial soil of the lower Mississippi Valley in Arkansas, Louisiana, and east Texas proved the best of all.

Cotton could be grown on farms of almost any size.[16] In most years from 1815 to 1860, prices made its cultivation highly profitable. Britain's appetite for raw cotton appeared insatiable, and the growing textile industries of the northeastern United States and continental Europe added to the demand. As a supplier, the American South had no peer among cotton-producing regions; Egypt and India could not match its productivity. Through this entire period, it was the largest single producer in the world. Cotton's importance among American exports has already been discussed.[17] The South's concentration on its principle cash crop shaped the entire region's economic development. While the region also produced and exported tobacco, rice, sugar, and hemp, and some areas produced surpluses of food and livestock, the combined value of all other antebellum southern exports was never more than a fraction of that represented by cotton. Even so, it is indicative of the productivity of nineteenth-century agriculture that corn cultivation required a larger amount of land than any other southern crop.[18]

Settlement Patterns in the South

Unlike the Midwest's agricultural exports, cotton required minimal processing to make it portable. The South possessed an extensive network of navigable rivers that allowed easy shipment to coastal ports for export. These characteristics gave little support to the growth of cities and towns. In the entire "New South," only New Orleans and Mobile were listed in the 25 largest cities in America, and Mobile was twenty-fifth. Even New Orleans owed its development to its status as the port of the Midwest rather than to regional activity. Most cotton was produced by plantations, not family-operated farms, further reducing the need for local concentration and distribution centers. Among all southern states, only Louisiana did not rank at the bottom of an index of urbanization, and Louisiana owed its rank almost entirely to New Orleans.[19]

Southern Industry

Because there were few cities and towns, the range of other economic activities was more restricted in the South than in either the Midwest or the East. There was much less manufacturing than in the East, although it has been claimed that southern industry compared quite favorably with that of the Midwest, particularly in cotton textiles,[20] and

---

[16] G. Wright, *The Political Economy of the Cotton South* (New York: Norton, 1978), 18, 28.

[17] D. North, *Economic Growth of the U.S. 1790–1860* (Englewood Cliffs, N.J.: Prentice-Hall, 1961), Table A-VIII, 233. See also the introduction to this section and Chap. 4.

[18] Wright, *Cotton South*, 18.

[19] D. North, *Economic Growth*, 130. See also A. Niemi, *U.S. Economic History: A Survey of the Major Issues* (Chicago: Rand McNally, 1975), 143–145.

[20] F. Bateman and T. Weiss, "Comparative Regional Development in Antebellum Manufacturing," *Journal of Economic History* (March 1975). Fogel claims that problems of census classification resulted in major understatement of southern industrial activity. See R. Fogel, *Without Consent or Contract: The Rise and Fall of American Slavery* (New York: Norton, 1989), 103–104. A thorough presentation of the view that southern markets and income distribution hindered economic development is given in W. Parker, *Europe, America, and the Wider World: Essays in the Economic History of Western Capitalism*, vol. 2 (New York: Cambridge University Press, 1991), Chaps. 3, 5, 6.

fewer and less varied service activities than existed in the other regions. The South might produce cotton, but its major crop was financed, insured, transported, and processed into cloth by Britain and the American North. Southern manufacturing also was handicapped by the region's concentration on cotton exports, nullifying any protection from competition that distance from foreign industrial centers might otherwise have provided. Cotton was very bulky in relation to manufactured goods. Consequently, ships travelled to southern ports only partly full, and might even make the trip in ballast, because they could be certain of obtaining a cargo there. Shippers would be willing to carry any freight that paid more than its cost of loading and unloading, and would charge very low rates for shipments to southern ports. The region's concentration on agriculture and the existence of slavery also reduced the potential industrial work force; the South had nothing comparable to the "mill girls" who staffed New England's cotton mills before 1840.[21]

Education

Education was also less developed in the South than elsewhere in the United States. Because of slavery, a smaller portion of the population was legally eligible for schooling in any case, and the area's lack of urbanization increased costs per student. Planters, who dominated the South's political as well as its economic life, were allegedly unwilling to support schooling that did little to benefit them, especially since they, as owners of most of the taxable property, would have to finance it.[22] Planters' children were taught by tutors or attended private schools. The point should not be overstressed: Literacy rates were lower

among free southerners than they were in the north, but the difference was on the order of 85 percent versus 95 percent.[23] Further, the immediate impact of lower levels of education is open to question; it may have hindered adjustment to changed conditions after the Civil War, but literacy was not a prime requisite for most nineteenth-century industrial jobs. It did, however, facilitate communication and response to opportunities, particularly after the Civil War.[24]

The Myth of Southern Underdevelopment

Much of the contemporary view of the antebellum South is inaccurate. The lack of cities, limited manufacturing and the existence of staple-crop agriculture, plantations, and slavery have allowed the persistence of deductions from these points that are not valid. First, most planters in the "New South" were not the heirs of ancient wealth. Apart from older areas along the Mississippi and the colonial settlements in Virginia and the Carolinas, most of the South resembled the Midwest; they were only a generation or so removed from primitive wilderness in 1860. There might be great plantation houses in the interior, but these were evidence of very recent ascents to wealth, often by the current inhabitants. Many of those who lived in the "big house" had settled the region when it was still raw frontier, and not a few had worked alongside their slaves clearing the land and planting the first crops. Income status in the South was not fixed. With luck and favorable cotton prices, it was possible to begin with a family

[21] G. Wright, "Cheap Labor and Southern Textiles before 1880," *Journal of Economic History* (September 1979).
[22] D. North, *Growth and Welfare in the American Past*, 2d ed. (Englewood Cliffs, N.J.: Prentice-Hall, 1974), 89–91. This point is not repeated in the latest (1983) edition.

[23] In 1860, literacy rates for free adult southerners ranged from 77 percent to 90 percent; the average for the United States was 91.7 percent. A. Niemi, Jr., *United States Economic History*, 2d ed. (Chicago: Rand McNally, 1980), 172–173.
[24] R. Margo, *Race and Schooling in the South, 1880–1951* (Chicago: University of Chicago Press, 1990), 93.

farm and expand it into a plantation, although this became more difficult after 1850. Many plantations were, however, offshoots of those on the seaboard, the direct result of migration by all or part of the work force of some Tidewater planter, perhaps under the direction of a younger son, to new and more fertile soil.

The South's income distribution was not particularly unequal by contemporary standards. The picture of the free southern population as a small class of planters and a much larger group of subsistence farmers who had little or no connection to the market economy is false. Most farms in the South (52 percent) were operated by owners and their families, with no slaves and little hired labor—a pattern quite similar to that in the North. Many planters, particularly those in the sugar region, would be millionaires in today's terms, but income distribution in the South was more even than it was in northern cities and differed little from that of the agricultural Midwest.[25] Plantations did not concentrate exclusively on cotton production; most produced enough food for their own labor forces, and some had surpluses for sale. Whatever food was needed beyond the plantations' output was purchased locally from smaller farms or from areas too far north for cotton cultivation, but still within the South.

The southern economy was rural and heavily concentrated on agriculture, but it was not static. Settlement and population were expanding, and, even more significantly, production of cotton per slave rose from 119 pounds in 1808–1810 to 759 in 1859–1860. There were comparable gains in other crops as well. The figures overstate actual productivity gains, since there was an increasing concentration on cash crops during the period and unusually favorable climatic and market conditions in 1859 and 1860.[26] But they do indicate that the South's economic efficiency was increasing, at least within its chief occupation.

The South was also able to reallocate its resources in response to market stimuli—again, within the agricultural context. There was a movement of cotton production toward more fertile land that paralleled a similar movement in the Midwest. Free nonslave-owning Southerners migrated to more fertile soil in much the same fashion and for the same motives as did northern farmers.[27] When necessary, the South could marshal resources for nonagricultural purposes. The region's extensive railroad construction after 1850 received more support from the planter-dominated state legislatures than did similar ventures elsewhere.[28] By the least favorable method of comparison, southern per-capita incomes were at least equal to those of the Midwest (an area often viewed as "dynamic") and rising more rapidly. In sum, the antebellum South was neither poor nor incapable of change.

[25] R. Fogel and S. Engerman, *Time on the Cross: The Economics of American Negro Slavery*, 2 vols. (Boston: Little, Brown, and Co., 1974), 1:254. As in many other areas, Fogel and Engerman's views have been contested. It is claimed that wealth distribution in the rural South was far less equal than that of the North, due largely to slaveholding, but income distribution among nonslaveowning rural southerners may have been quite similar to that of the rural North. See D. Yang, "U.S. Rural Wealth Distribution in 1860," *Explorations in Economic History* (January 1984); M. Schmitz and D. Schaefer, "The Parker-Gallman Sample and Wealth Distributions in the Antebellum South: A Comment," and D. Yang, "The Parker-Gallman Sample and Wealth Distributions for the Antebellum South: Reply," both in *Explorations in Economic History* (April 1985). For a contrary opinion, see W. Parker, *Europe, America, and the Wider World*, 2:Chap. 3.

[26] A. Conrad and J. Meyer, "The Economics of Slavery in the Antebellum South," *Journal of Political Economy* (April 1958). On the influence of the 1859 and 1860 crop years, see D. Schaefer, "The Effect of the 1859 Crop Year Upon Relative Productivity in the Antebellum South," *Journal of Economic History* (December 1983).
[27] D. Schaefer, "Locational Choice in the Antebellum South," *Journal of Economic History* (March 1989).
[28] O. Taylor, *Transportation Revolution, 1815–1860* (New York: M. E. Sharpe, 1962), 92.

The Economics of Slavery

Especially when it is inflicted by one race upon another, slavery is not an easy topic to analyze dispassionately. In the following discussion, words such as *efficient, profitable,* and *viable* do not have any connotation of good or bad, either in themselves or when used in conclusions about the economics of slavery. The involuntary servitude of black Americans was a monstrous injustice, but its economic and historical analysis requires more than moral judgments. This holds for any phenomenon that inspires strong emotions.

Profitability

After prolonged debate, consensus has been reached on the economics of slavery in the antebellum South. First, it was profitable, both to those who sold slaves and to those who employed them. Detailed studies have confirmed this for cotton, sugar, rice, and mixed-crop farming under a variety of conditions. The same results emerge from different methods of analysis.

Formerly it was argued that the observed trends in slave prices (which rose) and cotton prices (which fell) demonstrated that slave agriculture was unprofitable, or at least becoming so. Slavery served, it was thought, as a device for social control or as a manifestation of conspicuous consumption on the part of impractical planters.[29] But if slaves are regarded as a capital good, a human "machine" that could be used to produce income, the data indicate that under most circumstances slaveowners received income from the sale of slave-produced crops that was about equal to that obtainable from contemporary industrial securities of comparable risk. If the cost of food, clothing, shelter, medical care, taxes, tools, and other costs required to maintain a male

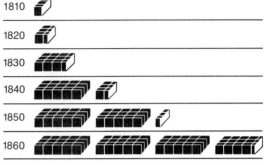

Cotton Production 1800–1860

1800	
1810	
1820	
1830	
1840	
1850	
1860	

= 200,000 bales of cotton

Slave Population 1800–1860

1800	
1810	
1820	
1830	
1840	
1850	
1860	

= 200,000 slaves

■ From 1800 to 1860, both the production of cotton and the number of slaves increased.
Source: Rise of the American Nation, Volume I, Liberty Edition, by Lewis Paul Todd and Merle Curti. (New York: Harcourt Brace Jovanovich, Inc., 1982), 298. Used with permission.

[29] Economics of Slavery," *Journal of Economic History,* June 1973.

slave's production (these expenditures may be viewed as the slave's income) are deducted from the value of the slave's output, there will still be a surplus in most years of the slave's adult life. If this surplus is discounted over the slave's entire life, an estimate of the value of the slave to his owner may be obtained. Quantitative studies indicate that this value was usually greater than the price at which a slave could be purchased. Alternatively, the returns on investments in slaves exceeded the rates charged to those borrowing to make such investments. Rental rates for slaves (whose short-term services could be purchased from their owners) indicate that slaveowners could obtain incomes from hiring out their chattels approximately equal to those received by owners of other forms of capital of equal value.[30]

The calculation is more complicated for female slaves because they produced children as well as field crops. Slave children began work at six years of age and produced more than the cost of their current upkeep at twelve. The value of these children, who could be sold or added to the work force, offset the lower field productivity of female slaves. The evidence on this point is quite conclusive: Hiring rates (rentals) were lower for female slaves than for males, but sale prices, which entitled the new owner to offspring, were about equal.

Returns to slave agriculture varied with soil fertility, the prices obtained for slaves' output, and slaves' mortality and birth rates; but in general, slave owners would be hard-pressed to find alternative investments yielding significantly higher returns. In areas where agriculture itself did not produce high incomes, slaveowners could sell their surplus slaves for additional income.

That slavery in the antebellum South was profitable should be no great surprise. An institution so widespread must have generated returns equal to alternatives to its participants, unless there were noneconomic reasons for its continuation. If slaves were investment assets that could be acquired by large numbers of owners, reasonably efficient markets would insure that the return on an investment in slaves would be approximately equal to that obtainable on other assets, holding risks of ownership constant.

Viability

Moreover, slavery was viable; the costs (including interest) of rearing slaves were less than the prices at which they could be sold, and the differential widened between 1815 and 1860.[31] There is no reason to doubt that slavery was primarily an economic institution. Slaves' prices rose and fell in accordance with those of major crops and the evidence of individual slaves' productive capabilities and skills. Since slave prices were at an all-time high in 1860 (both in absolute terms and in relation to their rental prices), slaveowners apparently expected the profitability of the institution to continue or improve; one does not pay more for a capital asset if the prospective return it will generate is becoming smaller or less certain.

The Prevalence of Slavery

Slaveholding was not universal among southern whites, and not all slaveholders were plantation operators. About half of all southern white families owned one or more slaves in 1860. But most of the slaves were held by only 12 percent of all slaveowners, and approximately half held no more than four slaves each.[32] The proportion of all slaves held by large-scale owners was rising by 1860; the pro-

---

[30] S. Lebergott, *The Americans*, 213–217. See also J. Reid, Jr., "Antebellum Southern Rental Contracts," *Explorations in Economic History* (January 1976).

[31] Y. Yasuba, "The Profitability and Viability of Plantation Slavery in the United States," *Economic Studies Quarterly* (September 1961).
[32] A. Niemi, *U.S. Economic History: A Survey of the Major Issues* (Chicago: Rand McNally, 1975), 149, 161.

portion of slaveowners within the white population was declining.

Slave Prices

Slaves were expensive: The price of a prime field hand rose from $700 in 1810 to $1,800 in 1860. (These figures should be compared to the per-capita income data in Table 6.3) The profitability of slaveholding and slaves' high prices were major influences on the treatment accorded slaves. Owners of such expensive and profitable assets might be expected to try to keep them productive. This would mean giving slaves adequate food, housing, and other maintenance. It would also mean that increases in slave numbers would be encouraged.

Trends in the Slave Population

The broad data are consistent with what might be deduced from economic theory. The slave population of the United States rose from 894,000 in 1800 to 3.954 million in 1860. This was a rate of increase roughly comparable to that of the domestic growth of the white population. Immigration further increased whites' numbers, but after 1808, imports of slaves into the United States were forbidden through a provision of the Constitution. Although some slaves were smuggled in after that date, the largest estimate for the 1808–1860 period is 250,000, and most are much smaller. Because slave productivity also increased at least as much as that of the general population, the conclusion follows that the treatment of slaves, at least in physical terms, was adequate to produce both population growth and productivity increases similar to those achieved by free Americans.

Most slaves were employed in agriculture, but some worked in mining, lumbering, manufacturing, and domestic service. Since there were fewer substitutes for slaves in plantation agriculture than there were in urban occupations where slaves were alternatives to free labor, urban populations fluctuated more than

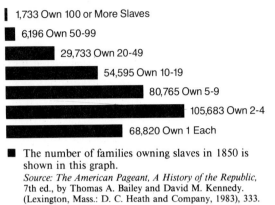

1,733 Own 100 or More Slaves

6,196 Own 50-99

29,733 Own 20-49

54,595 Own 10-19

80,765 Own 5-9

105,683 Own 2-4

68,820 Own 1 Each

The number of families owning slaves in 1850 is shown in this graph.
Source: The American Pageant, A History of the Republic, 7th ed., by Thomas A. Bailey and David M. Kennedy. (Lexington, Mass.: D. C. Heath and Company, 1983), 333. Used with permission.

did those of rural slaves. Nor should we assume that all slaves were unskilled, either in agriculture or in other occupations.

Slavery's Future in 1860: The Economic Indicators

Slavery on the eve of the Civil War was not threatened by economic factors. Not only was the institution profitable and viable at current costs and prices, the South had plenty of unused land suitable for plantation agriculture, and cotton prices remained high at least through 1890. Slaves could be (and were) profitably employed in nonagricultural occupations. So profitable was it to rear slaves that their prices could have fallen by one-half before the profitability of that business was endangered.

Evidence for slavery's profitability and viability, of course, is not an endorsement of the institution. But it does indicate that the major threats to slavery in 1860 were political, ethical, social, and those personified in John Brown and his supporters, rather than economic. From the viewpoint of 1860, the economic results generated by slavery constituted strong arguments for its continuation—from the slaveowners' position. Economic considerations, while not the only influence on

Table 6.3   Per-Capita Income and Rates of Increase by Region, 1840–1860

Region	Per-Capita Income with Slaves Considered As Consumers		Growth in Per-Capita Income over Period (Total Population)
	1840	**1860**	
North	$109*	$141	29%
Northeast	129	181	40
North Central	65	89	37
South	74	103	39
South Atlantic	66	84	27
East South Central	69	89	29
West South Central	151	184	22
United States	96	128	33

Region	Per-Capita Income with Slaves As Intermediate Goods		Growth in Per-Capita Income over Period (Free Population)
	1840	**1860**	
North	$110	$142	29%
Northeast	130	183	41
North Central	66	90	36
South	105	150	43
South Atlantic	96	124	39
East South Central	92	124	35
West South Central	238	274	15
United States	109	144	32

* All dollar values in 1860 dollars. In 1860, the purchasing power of the dollar was approximately ten times that of 1992.
Source: Adapted from S. Engerman, "The Effects of Slavery Upon the Southern Economy," *Explorations in Economic History* (Winter 1967).

slaveowners, explain a great deal of their conduct. Planters responded to changes in cotton prices, slave productivity, and other income opportunities like rational, well-informed, and economically motivated businessmen, rather than impractical romantics or "cavaliers." Few slaveholders could have doubted slavery's benefits to them.

For small farmers, even those without slaves, the most obvious route to wealth lay through the acquisition of a slave work force—a method they had seen enrich so many others. Planters with large work forces were wealthy men; 50 slaves in 1860 were worth at least $450,000 in 1992 dollars and would generate an income many times that of the average citizen. And yet 50 slaves did not constitute a large work force. The owners of such valuable assets could be expected to try to preserve and increase their productivity, just as contemporary capitalists care for expensive machinery.

New Slants on Established Views

About two decades ago, a book appeared that claimed that economic rationality drove planters well beyond the provision of adequate treatment to allow slaves to maintain their numbers and productivity. It claimed that slaveowners offered a variety of positive incentives for improved performance to their work forces.[33] Even more than this, the slaves responded to these incentives, in a sense cooperating with their masters. Fogel and Engerman do not deny that coercion was used—indeed, it is part of the very nature of slavery—but they claim that positive incentives were at least as commonly used to elicit greater effort as were whipping and loss of privileges. Bonuses, gifts, grants of leisure time, rights to garden plots, and the encouragement of a competitive spirit among the slaves, they found, were all both used and effective. Perhaps the strongest incentive available was one not normally associated with slavery: the chance to rise in status, as the driver of a work gang, a skilled worker, or even a plantation overseer. A high proportion of all work supervision on plantations was done by the slaves themselves, with virtually all work gang leaders and perhaps 75 percent of all overseers (the top non-ownership management on plantations) being bondsmen.[34] More recently, Fogel claimed that about 20 percent of all adult male slaves (but very few females) were artisans or managers.[35] In responding to positive incentives, and even more in directing the labor of others, slaves accepted their condition. This is not an indication that slaves welcomed their servitude. They took advantage of what limited opportunities their condition afforded.

The living conditions of American slaves described in *Time on the Cross* compare quite well with those of contemporary urban industrial workers. Diets, while monotonous and falling far short of modern standards of nutritional adequacy, were hearty, at least for adults. Slaves had opportunities to supplement their rations; most families had garden plots in which they could grow food for their own consumption or even for sale, and a chance to raise livestock as well. Some could use their leisure time for hunting or fishing. Hours of work were slightly shorter than those of free northern farm workers (58 versus 60 hours per week), although slaves' work pace was far more intense.[36] Housing, according to this view, was comparable to that of northern workers, although standards varied widely between plantations. Clothing and medical care were adequate by contemporary standards. The treatment of slaves was surprisingly mild: The typical slave was whipped perhaps once a year, and care was taken to avoid serious injury. While this is not "mild" treatment by modern standards, whipping and beating were by no means unknown as punishments for free Americans in the nineteenth century.

Fogel and Engerman also found that economic rationality governed slaveowners' attitudes toward slaves' family lives. They claim that the nuclear family was strongly supported by slaveholders. Although slave marriages had no legal standing, planters encouraged them because they made for a more tranquil and productive work force and a higher birthrate. In furtherance of these goals, slave marriages were seldom broken up by the sale of one of the partners. Most of the slaves sold were single young adults, and sales of young children were infrequent, perhaps no more than might result from the incidence of orphans. Promiscuity, forced marriages, and interracial sexual relations were strongly opposed by most

[33] Fogel and Engerman, *Time on the Cross.*
[34] Fogel and Engerman, *Time on the Cross*, 212.
[35] Fogel, *Without Consent*, 46–47.

[36] Fogel, *Without Consent*, 28–29, 77–78.

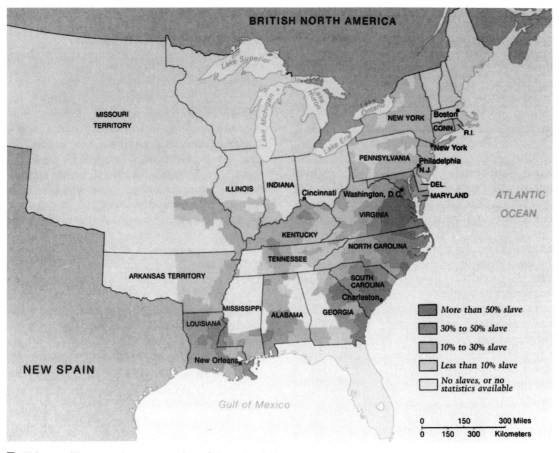

■ This map illustrates the concentration of slaves in 1820.
Source: From *America Past & Present, Volume I,* by Robert A. Devine and T. H. Breen, 330. Copyright © 1984 by Scott, Foresman and Company. Reprinted by permission of HarperCollins Publishers.

slaveholders because they reduced productivity—perhaps a stronger restriction than morality. Slaves were exploited, in the sense of receiving less than the value of what they produced (if they were not, there is no economic basis for slavery), but the extent of exploitation was surprisingly small if all costs of slave maintenance were considered. Slaves were also exploited, however, by their employment under working conditions that free laborers, either white or black, would not accept, that is, the gang system and the requirement that slave women perform field labor.

The Economic Efficiency of Slavery

The authors of *Time on the Cross* concluded that such treatment of slaves paid off. Slaves can be considered as an intermediate good in the production process. In this analysis, slave maintenance costs ("income") are subtracted from free southerners' incomes and slaves are deducted from the total southern population. This process considers slaves to be a productive asset, but not the consumers toward whose wishes economic activity is directed.

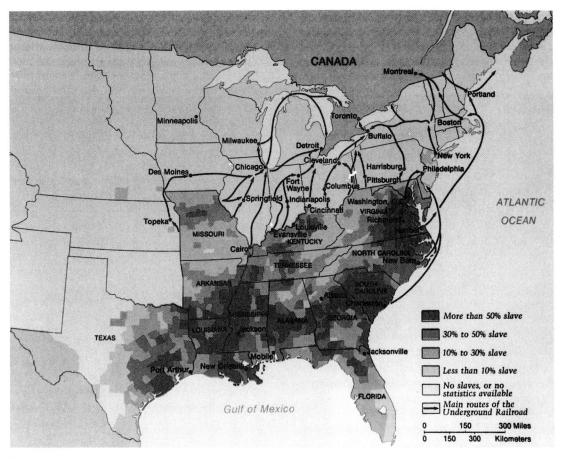

■ By 1860, slaves were more widely distributed than they had been in 1820.
Source: From *America Past & Present, Volume I,* by Robert A. Devine and T. H. Breen, 331. Copyright © 1984 by Scott, Foresman and Company. Reprinted by permission of HarperCollins Publishers.

With this approach, southern incomes compared favorably with other regions of the United States, both in amount and in rate of growth (see Table 6.3).

If slave incomes and population are incorporated in southern totals, that region's per-capita income figures for 1860 were exceeded only by Australia, Britain, and the northern United States. Even if, as has been claimed, Fogel and Engerman understated slave maintenance costs by 60 percent, these conclusions would not be substantially changed. By contemporary world standards, the South was wealthy, and by some criteria, it generated incomes equal or superior to those of any other area.

Southern Agricultural Productivity

Because these southern incomes originated in a largely agricultural economy and incomes in manufacturing were much higher than those in agriculture for the country as a whole, they imply that southern agriculture was considerably more efficient than that of other regions. In Fogel and Engerman's view, southern agriculture was in aggregate 35 percent more productive than that of the North (the South produced 35 percent more output per unit of input). Slave-using farms in general were 40 percent more efficient, and large plantations in the "New South," which combined efficiently organized slave work forces, economies of scale, and especially fertile soil, were a startling 53 percent more productive. Even southern farms employing only free labor were 9 percent more efficient than their northern counterparts.[37]

The portrait of the antebellum South and slavery that emerges from *Time on the Cross* departs considerably from the conventional picture. In the Fogel and Engerman study, slavery was not a retarding force in southern economic development; instead, it contributed strongly to the achievements of a wealthy and dynamic regional economy. The slaves themselves had a share in the incomes and opportunities produced (albeit a limited one in which many jobs were beyond the aspirations of even the most talented slave, and incomes, at least in the short run, were gained at the sufferance of the master and the form they took determined by him). Slaves responded positively to incentives. The South was agricultural and rural, but this structure was merely a logical response to the region's comparative advantages, and conveyed economic gains rather than imposing income penalties.

The Fogel and Engerman study is controversial, but it must be evaluated on the grounds staked out by its authors, rather than the distorted views attributed to it by others. In no way did Fogel and Engerman conclude that slavery was "good" or "justified" or that the slaves liked it.[38] Nor do they imply that the treatment of slaves gave them "fair" or "just" shares of the income resulting from their work.

The Conditions of Life under Slavery

Slavery reduced human beings to the status of intelligent work animals and was brutal by its very nature. Slaves were forced to work under conditions like the gang system (in which tasks were assigned to a work group supervised by a "driver") that free labor would not accept at any wage payable by the proceeds of such toil. In addition, slaves had only minimal control over their own fate. They could be sold, and they had no defense against a sadistic or lecherous overseer in the short run, or against a similarly inclined master in the long run. Above all, they were not free to choose their occupations or to succeed or fail on the quantity and quality of their efforts. Regulations in which they had no voice imposed ceilings on their attainments. The denial of education handicapped ex-slaves even after freedom was achieved in 1865. Slaves simply made the best life possible under the restricted opportunities open to them. If they could not change their circumstances, response to some positive incentives at least made their lives a bit more comfortable. It might even be said that the Fogel and Engerman view is less patronizing than those that stress blacks' "difficulties" in adjusting to freedom after 1865.

Achieving freedom by flight or revolt was not a very realistic possibility for slaves. Whether from fear of the unknown (often a powerful influence on the uneducated), or from a realistic assessment of the opportunities available to free blacks outside the South, incentives to escape were not strong. The famous "Underground Railway" apparently freed only some 25,000 slaves in the entire antebellum period. Plantations operated for half a century along the Ohio River, where a slave had only to find a boat or even a log to

---

[37] Fogel and Engerman, *Time on the Cross*, 192–196.
[38] See the "Moral Indictment of Slavery," (the final chapter of *Without Consent or Contract*).

■ Only some slaves spared the time to pose for the camera in this photo of them harvesting cotton in Georgia. *Source:* Library of Congress.

cross to free territory on a summer night. Although the prospects of slave revolts were widely discussed, there were less than a half-dozen instances of organized rebellions by slaves in the entire history of the institution in North America. Nor does the conduct of plantation owners indicate that they felt any serious threat. On the typical plantation, slaveowners were heavily outnumbered and had no means of summoning help rapidly. Yet

they slept in wooden houses among their slaves, and felt no compunctions about close contact with work forces using potentially lethal tools. Most adult white males had little hesitation over leaving their farms to fight in the Civil War.

It must be remembered that the conclusions in *Time on the Cross* and *Without Consent or Contract* are based on averages. The authors do not argue that there were no exceptions, for better or worse, to the averages they compiled, only that those averages give a more typical picture than do individual cases without context.

Opposing Views: The Critique of Time on the Cross

The work of Fogel and Engerman may be more valuable for the discussion and study that it provoked on the issue of slaves' treatment and response than for any claims initially made. Subsequent work has generated both support and criticism for their study, which provoked a detailed response by Fogel.[39]

Diets and Medical Care

Some points are now fairly clear. The conclusion that adult slaves received adequate diets for the work they performed is supported by both demographic data and analyses of the diet itself. Adult slave death rates were about the same as those of free southerners, and their population and output increased in a similar manner. Recent work by Fogel and others indicates that the diets of slave children below working ages were seriously deficient, even though those of their parents were adequate except in the case of pregnant women, who received neither special diets nor lighter workloads.[40] Despite several studies that indicate serious dietary deficiencies among slave infants and children under working age, some unresolved controversies remain. First, the cause of malnourishment among young slaves is held to be the gang system, under which

slave parents were fed communally, and their children received separate rations. Not all slaves worked under this system, and as yet no comparisons of small- and large-plantation health have been made.[41] In addition, it is generally agreed that slaves produced part of their food from their own garden plots, or by gathering and fishing (the portion of the total diet that these sources represent is unclear, but it was probably smaller on large plantations). Unless this food was under the master's control, would slaves starve their own children? Finally, records of the height and weight of West Point Cadets and students at Harvard also show evidence of dietary deficiencies, particularly in protein intake, during the 1850s.[42] The evidence of malnourishment among slave children and pregnant women seems compelling, but this problem was not confined to slaves, although it may have been more acute among them than in northern city dwellers. Adult slaves were well fed by contemporary standards, and slave children's height "caught up" with that of free children as they began to receive the adult diet. The cause was almost certainly not intentional mistreatment of slaves; the nineteenth century had almost no comprehension of nutritional needs. Similar criteria apply to medical care; nineteenth-century doctors might not be very effective, but what slaveowner who was able to calculate the changes in slave values caused by a quarter-cent variation in cotton prices would begrudge fifty cents for a doctor's visit?

Housing and Work Incentives

Fogel and Engerman's comparisons of slave housing and apparel with those of northern

---

[39] For an extensive summary of the debate, see P. Passell and S. Lee, *A New Economic View of American History*, (New York: Norton, 1978), Chaps. 8, 9. S. Lebergott, *The Americans*, Chaps. 18, 19, contributes a well-reasoned presentation of the quantitative data. *Without Consent or Contract* is Fogel's response.
[40] R. Steckel, "A Peculiar Population: The Nutrition, Health, and Mortality of American Slaves From Childhood to Maturity," *Journal of Economic History* (September 1986). See also Fogel, *Without Consent*, 142–147.

[41] Steckel, "Peculiar Population." Preliminary estimates indicate that slaves from areas in which small plantations predominated tended to be taller.
[42] J. Komlos, "The Height and Weight of West Point Cadets: Dietary Change in Antebellum America," *Journal of Economic History* (December 1987).

workers appear to be overstated. They apparently matched slaves against the poorest northern slum dwellers. Even at this time, such a basis seriously understates the living standards of most urban laborers: The typical worker did not live in what then was considered a slum, but *Time on the Cross* compares northern slums to slave quarters.[43] Likewise, that work is probably too optimistic on the subject of slave treatment and incentives. The available data are insufficient in quantity and probably of uncertain validity for firm conclusions on the incidence of physical punishment, and the reactions of slaves to it. Both sides appear to miss the real point regarding slaves' access to supervisory or overseers' jobs. It is not so much the portion of these actually held by slaves that is germane here, but whether the openings available to slaves were sufficient to furnish incentives for greater effort on their part. Fogel's recent work found that slaves' access to managerial positions was declining in the 1850s, largely for political reasons.[44]

Family Stability

Data on family stability and the degree to which slaveowners encouraged or discouraged it are insufficient to support a firm conclusion. The effect of sales on family stability appears suspect on both sides. Fogel and Engerman concluded that the majority of slaves entering the "New South" from the older plantation states came through the migration of entire labor forces moving as units with their owners. Their critics emphasize a much greater role for the sale of individual slaves, but their arguments rely heavily on data from Maryland, the one major slaveholding state whose slave population was falling in the mid-nineteenth century, which was an indication that slave sales or migration were much more common there than throughout the South. No firm conclusion has been reached on the question of slave family stability; studies since *Time on the Cross* concluded that as few as 16 percent to as many as 60 percent of slave marriages may have been broken by the sale of one party.[45] Still, whatever the statistical probabilities, slaves could not control this source of family disruption and it may have generated a great deal of fear.

Exploitation

The discussion on the amount of exploitation of slaves has reached little common ground, aside from a consensus that it existed. Fogel and Engerman view the question as an investment, as the slaveowner might. In this case, the costs of slaveownership include not only the current maintenance of adult slaves, but also rearing costs (including expenditures on slaves who died before reaching maturity) and whatever costs might be incurred for the nonworking elderly, plus interest on such expenses. Others have approached the problem from the viewpoint of the adult slave, and treated the entire difference between current maintenance costs and the value of the slave's production as the burden of exploitation.[46] This approach yields a much greater burden than does the Fogel and Engerman method. The largest beneficiaries of this exploitation were not the slaveowners, but the consumers

---

[43] The claim is not repeated in *Without Consent*.
[44] Fogel, *Without Consent*, 52.

[45] R. Sutch, "The Breeding of Slaves," in S. Engerman and E. Genovese, *Race and Slavery in the Western Hemisphere: Quantitative Studies* (Princeton, N.J.: Princeton University Press, 1978), and H. Gutman, *The Black Family in Slavery and Freedom* (New York: Pantheon Books, 1976). See also Fogel, *Without Consent*, 152, 167. The 60 percent figure is from M. Tadman, *Speculators and Slaves: Masters, Traders, and Slaves in the Old South* (Madison, Wisc.: University of Wisconsin Press, 1990).
[46] See Fogel and Engerman, *Time on the Cross*, 244–246, and R. Ransom and R. Sutch, *One Kind of Freedom: The Economic Consequences of Emancipation* (Cambridge, U.K.: Cambridge University Press, 1977), 3–4.

■ Reaping machines and other newly invented machinery increased agricultural output after 1840.
Source: Chicago Historical Society, lithograph, "The Testing of the First Reaping Machine Near Steeles Tavern VA A.D. 1831."

of cotton cloth, whose aggregate gains were far greater than those accruing to planters. Cotton planting was a highly competitive industry, and prices were continually being pushed down toward production costs. Cheap cotton cloth was in part a consequence of the exploitation of American slaves—and this fabric was used throughout the nineteenth-century world.

The Economics of Southern Agriculture

The efficiency of southern agriculture relative to that in other regions is another area of controversy. This point is linked with the fate of the southern economy after the Civil War as well as in the period under discussion. It has been pointed out that much of what Fogel and Engerman regarded as "greater southern efficiency in agriculture" might instead be credited to a variety of factors: the South's ability to produce semitropical crops to which the North was unsuited, the effects of two extraordinarily favorable crop years (1859–1860), and the fact that the working conditions of slave and free labor were different.[47]

Efficiency and Farm Size
The economies of scale of large plantations have also been downplayed, particularly by

[47] See Schaefer, "Effect of the 1859 Crop Year," *Journal of Economic History* (March 1989).

Gavin Wright. Since the large plantation could concentrate on cash crops more fully than could the small owner-operated farm, Wright hypothesized that planters could grow mainly cash crops and buy any food they were unable to produce. If crops or prices turned out less favorably than expected, the planter had access to credit, slaves for collateral, and possibly cash reserves to tide the plantation over to the next crop. The small farmer could only borrow against the farm itself, and risked losing his land if things turned out badly. In addition, the small farm maximized welfare while the plantation maximized chiefly money income. Leisure for the farm family had a very different value to the small farmer than did leisure for the slaves to the planter. Risk considerations and the limits imposed on total crop size by labor constraints reduced cotton's returns to small farmers, and leisure considerations reinforced this. Whatever the impact of the factors listed by Wright, they were powerfully reinforced by the patterns of direct economic gains. Recent work has emphasized the role of economies of scale in determining the patterns of cotton production.[48] Once allowance is made for variations in soil fertility and capital differences are made, Fogel and Engerman reduce the efficiency advantage of large slave-worked plantations to 34 percent.[49] The criticisms appear to have a good deal of merit, but they do not alter the fact that the South's agricultural system was able to generate incomes for its practitioners that were high by contemporary standards—and rising. At least by comparison with other farming areas, it is difficult to describe the South as inefficient.

Regional Incomes and Trends

A final point involves the comparative growth rates of northern and southern incomes. If the arguments for excluding slaves from income figures for the South can be accepted, income growth for the South as a whole is much higher than that for any subregion within it (see Table 6.3). This results from the relocation of resources from regions where incomes were low to those where they were high, in other words, from the Old to the New South. Gains from this source cannot continue indefinitely. Is this evidence of real growth in incomes? Was the southern economy capable only of reallocating resources between regions, but not between occupations? (It must be conceded that income growth in other regions of the United States also is increased by this factor, albeit not to the same extent.)

Income gains within subregions of the South, while lower than the U.S. average, were still respectable. Thus, this charge cannot be fully accepted; continued growth in southern productivity was possible. Whether such gains could have kept pace with the North is problematical. Some analysts have concluded that the South, burdened with slavery and its alleged inflexibilities plus a lack of educated labor that reduced the adaptability of the free work-force as well, would have found the transition to industry difficult, if not impossible. Others have pointed out that the South did not industrialize at this time because there was little economic incentive to do so; its comparative advantage in agriculture generated incomes and growth comparable to those of the manufacturing regions. The antebellum South *did* not change; but can it be concluded from this that it *could* not change? To free southerners in 1860, the need to industrialize cannot have appeared very pressing. Specialization along traditional lines did not appear to have handicapped the South at that time. Slavery would have to be abolished for noneconomic reasons, as it was.

---

[48] Wright, *Cotton South*, 3.
[49] Fogel and Engerman, *Time on the Cross*, 209–210. *Without Consent*, 72–80, credits the gang system with 39 percent greater efficiency than farms using either free or slave labor under other work systems.

GROWTH AND DIVERSITY IN AGRICULTURE

Agriculture remained the principle occupation in America in 1860, as it had been in 1815. But the pace of change was increasing rapidly for American farmers. Competition from distant producers now affected the markets where they sold their produce, and they sold a larger portion of their output than they had in the colonial era. Far more alternatives now had to be taken into account; the choices were wider in location, types of crops, access to markets, methods, and particularly in the range of machinery available to assist them. The growth of other sectors of the economy allowed farmers to consider movement to new jobs as well. Wider alternatives offered greater scope for efficient reallocation of people, and rising incomes indicated that even within agriculture, people were taking advantage of the new opportunities.

SELECTED REFERENCES

Bogue, A., and M. "Profits and the Frontier Land Speculator." *Journal of Economic History* (March 1957).

Conrad, A., and D. Dowd et al. "Slavery as an Obstacle to Economic Growth in the United States." *Journal of Economic History* (December 1967).

Conrad, A., and J. Meyer. "The Economics of Slavery in the Antebellum South." *Journal of Political Economy* (April 1958).

David, P., H. Gutman, R. Sutch, and G. Wright. *Reckoning with Slavery*. Oxford, U.K.: Oxford University Press, 1976.

David, P., and P. Temin. "Slavery: The Progressive Institution?" *Journal of Economic History* (September 1974).

Fogel, R. *Without Consent or Contract: The Rise and Fall of American Slavery*. New York: Norton, 1989.

Fogel, R., and S. Engerman. *Time on the Cross: The Economics of American Negro Slavery*. 2 vols. Boston: Little, Brown & Co., 1974.

Genovese, E. *The Political Economy of Slavery*. New York: Random House, 1967.

———. *Roll, Jordan, Roll: The World the Slaveowners Made*. New York: Random House, 1976.

Genovese, E., and S. Engerman. *Race and Slavery in the Western Hemisphere: Quantitative Studies*. Princeton, N.J.: Princeton University Press, 1978.

Goldin, C. *Urban Slavery in the American South*. Chicago: University of Chicago Press, 1976.

Gray, L. *History of Agriculture in the Southern United States to 1860*. Washington, D.C.: Kelley, 1933.

North, D. *The Economic Growth of the United States, 1790–1860*. Englewood Cliffs, N.J.: Prentice-Hall, 1961.

North, D., T. Anderson, and P. Hill. *Growth and Welfare in the American Past: A New Economic History*. 3d ed. Englewood Cliffs, N.J.: Prentice-Hall, 1983.

Parker, W., ed. *The Structure of the Cotton Economy of the Antebellum South*. Washington, D.C.: Agricultural History Society, 1970.

Ransom, R., and R. Sutch. *One Kind of Freedom: The Economic Consequences of Emancipation*. Cambridge, U.K.: Cambridge University Press, 1977.

Rosenberg, N. *Technology and American Economic Growth*. New York: Harper & Row, 1972.

Schlebecker, J. *Whereby We Thrive*. Ames, Iowa: Iowa State University Press, 1975.

Stampp, K. *The Peculiar Institution*. New York: Knopf, 1956.

U.S. Department of Commerce, Bureau of the Census. *Historical Statistics of the United States: Colonial Times to 1970*. Washington, D.C.: Government Printing Office, 1975.

Wright, G. *The Political Economy of the Cotton South*. New York: Norton, 1978.

Yasuba, Y. "The Profitability and Viability of Plantation Slavery in the United States." *Economic Studies Quarterly* (September 1961).

THE ORIGINS OF INDUSTRY

*I*n 1860, the U.S. economy was still centered on agriculture. Almost 53 percent of the work force earned its living from the land, and the total value of agricultural products exceeded that of any other sector of the economy.[1] But the economy had made noteworthy strides in manufacturing, and agriculture's preeminence was fading. One worker in seven was employed in industry, and almost as many others worked in distributing, financing, or transporting manufactured goods, or in construction. About one-third of the total value of U.S. output originated in manufacturing.[2]

This disparity between the shares of employment and production in industry is significant; it indicates that productivity in that sector and the incomes that it generated were about double the national average. The figures do not necessarily mean that the average manufacturing worker's wages were twice the average American income, but they do indicate that resources employed in the industrial sector produced higher incomes than did most alternative uses. Consequently, manufacturing was likely to continue to grow faster than the rest of the economy, as the owners of capital, labor, and raw material reallocated their inputs to uses in which they produced higher incomes. This is a typical pattern for new sectors of the economy: High resource productivity generates high rates of growth and low opportunity costs attract resources.

EARLY NINETEENTH-CENTURY MANUFACTURING

Accurate estimates of the value of aggregate output in the early nineteenth century are difficult to make. Most American families were far more self-sufficient then than they are today, making a large proportion of their capital goods as well as most of what they consumed. For example, land clearance was a major investment for farmers on new land and a major component of the country's total investment, but its value is difficult to calculate.[3] In this period, Americans, particularly farmers, made most of the clothing, tools, and other items used in their households. Sometimes they performed all operations from gathering raw materials to finishing the product. Often they combined purchase of some components with home finishing. Yarn or cloth might be purchased and made into clothing, or the metal parts of tools obtained from factories or the local blacksmith might be fitted with handles in the home. Housewives processed food into the form in which it reached the table. Specialists might be employed to process or finish homemade materials; masons might build a chimney; or travelling cobblers might make shoes or harness from leather the family had cured. Some manufactured goods replaced items formerly made in the home, others were substituted for imports, and a few had never been available before. From 1815 to 1860, industrial activity grew faster than the aggregate economy. After 1820, the importance of home manufactures declined, and the variety and state of finish of goods purchased increased.

There had been some American manufacturing for market even in colonial days. Ships, tar, iron, and salt were produced by special-

---

[1] U.S. Department of Commerce, Bureau of the Census, *Historical Statistics of the United States* (Washington, D.C.: Government Printing Office, 1975), 1:139, 1:239.
[2] *Historical Statistics*, 239.

[3] M. Primack, "Land Clearing Under Nineteenth-Century Techniques: Some Preliminary Calculations," *Journal of Economic History* (December 1962).

ized units that often employed considerable work forces. By the Revolution, flour milling and shoe production were developing along those lines as well. Especially in the North, farms often had a surplus of home manufactures available for sale or barter. By 1860, however, specialized manufacturers controlled the manufacturing of a much greater range of items than were manufactured just a few decades earlier. Only where transportation costs made factory-produced goods extremely expensive, as on the frontier, were home handicrafts still able to compete by 1860.

Sources of Economic Growth

Even though manufacturing's growth exceeded that of the aggregate economy and thus "pulled" it forward, it should not be assumed that industrialization was the only source of American economic growth. As Chapter 6 indicated, agriculture was also growing, although not at the same rate. Finance, banking, trade, construction, and transportation also grew, sometimes at rates as high as industry. In 1860, even after very considerable growth, the manufacturing sector simply did not have the relative size to account for all of the increase in economic activity over the previous decade. Total U.S. output was increasing at about 5 percent annually in the 1850s, and about a third of total value added was in manufacturing. Had industry been the source of all growth, it would have had to grow at three times the rate of the entire economy, or about 15 percent per year. This is a most unlikely rate of growth for any broadly defined sector to sustain over a decade or more, especially when it is recognized that industry was well established several decades previously. The growth of manufacturing undoubtedly increased the aggregate growth rate of the economy, but it was hardly the source of all economic development.

EARLY INDUSTRIALIZATION PATTERNS

The upswing in manufacturing activity apparently began quite early in the 1815–1860 period, probably in the 1820s. The cotton textile industry was definitely expanding rapidly then, and the production of woolen goods, carpets, paper, lead, refined sugar, salt, glass, steam engines, and preserved meat all appear to have risen faster than population in this decade. This list includes only those items for which reasonably conclusive data are available; there may have been others as well. Manufacturing activity in America not only began within 50 years of independence, from its inception it involved a wide variety of products.

Industrial growth continued over the next 30 years, although certainly not at a steady pace. Variations in industrial growth were caused by both supply and demand factors. Initially, especially for really new products, demand may grow very rapidly as consumers buy an item for the first time or substitute it for other goods. But once these needs are met, the rate of growth declines, and sales rise only at the pace of population and income growth, or even less. After a new industry's initial growth spurt begins to wane, the economy's growth leaders are other industries whose products are still being purchased for the first time by consumers and industrial users. Thus, the appearance of new industries is a vital element in long-run economic growth.

In 1860, the United States might still be primarily an agricultural economy, but so were nearly all other nations. Industrialization here compared quite favorably with the rest of the world. By most estimates, the total value of manufactured goods produced in the United States was second only to that of Britain, at that time the acknowledged "workshop of the world." Even the least optimistic view placed the United States no worse than fourth among the world's industrial powers.[4] America possessed a sizable, varied, and rapidly growing industrial sector from the 1820s on. This evidence refutes two widely held views: Professor Rostow's thesis that a "takeoff" into sustained growth, fueled by new industrial sectors, occurred in the two decades before 1860, and the idea that the American Civil War caused U.S. industrialization.

Adjustments after 1815

Manufacturing, especially as it had developed by 1860, was a new type of activity for most of the Americans it employed. The adjustments required for the transition were much greater than we might imagine today. As they had in agriculture, Americans began with European techniques and modified them to suit New-World conditions. American factor proportions and markets were different from those of Britain. British tools and methods were not ideal for American conditions in their original forms. Factory production required adjustments from managers, workers, and consumers alike. Considerable foresight might be required to see the potential in some innovations. Most Americans' incomes allowed little margin over basic needs in 1815, thus making completely new products very risky. Many of the first factories therefore concentrated on substitutes for imported goods, because markets for such items already existed.[5] Consequently, firms learned to compete with established manufacturers as they learned to produce.

Moving from farm labor with hand tools to industrial work with powered machinery required difficult adjustments for many individuals. Working under somebody else's direction was hard enough for people accustomed to the individualism of farming, but now the pace of work was set by other people or, worse, machines. Nor was the performance of early factory equipment always sufficiently better than older methods to "buy" immediate acceptance. Most new machines required a considerable period of testing and operation before they operated as expected, and even that performance might be only slightly better than the technology they replaced.

The reception innovations received could be crucial to their eventual success or failure. It makes a great deal of difference whether new machines are regarded as basically good ideas but with "bugs" that will have to be worked out, or as something new, different, and either inherently unworkable or a threat to established jobs. Workers had adjustments to make outside the factory as well; most industry was located in cities, and the contrast between rural and urban life was as great then as it has ever been. The American response appears to have been more favorable than that of other nations, including Britain.[6] New methods and products were generally welcomed. Attitudes and social institutions were modified to accommodate them, rather than vice versa.

The Putting-Out System

In part because of these difficulties in adjustment to new methods and new surroundings, in some industries there was an intermediate step between domestic production and the factory. Known as the putting-out system, it was especially prevalent in goods whose production required a great deal of hand labor. The putting-out system attempted to use

---

[4] D. North, *The Economic Growth of the United States, 1790–1860* (Englewood Cliffs, N.J.: Prentice-Hall, 1961), v.

[5] S. Lebergott, *The Americans: An Economic Record* (New York: Norton, 1984), 130.

[6] D. Landes, *Unbound Prometheus: Technological Change and Industrial Development in Western Europe From 1750 to the Present* (Cambridge, U.K.: Cambridge University Press, 1969), Chaps. 2, 3.

resources that had few or low-productivity alternative uses, because these might be obtained at low cost.

Many farms, particularly those in the North, had seasons in which agricultural tasks did not fully occupy the available work force. The putting-out system utilized this labor force without requiring it to relocate in towns. Further, the workers supplied their own tools. Manufacturers or their agents brought raw materials to the farms, left instructions for completion of the work, and returned later to pick up the finished goods and pay the workers. Labor retained a good deal of independence under this system; the pace of work and, to some extent, its timing were determined by the individual. At a time when both social attitudes and transportation difficulties made it difficult for women to work outside their homes, the putting-out system allowed them to earn a cash income. To the manufacturers, the putting-out system was a response to the chronic American shortages of capital and labor. Not only might wage rates be less than full-time workers would demand, but the investment in capital was far lower.

Drawbacks to the Putting-Out System

The putting-out system had disadvantages as well. It could be employed mainly in the production of items produced by traditional hand methods, such as shoes, textiles, and clothing. It was very difficult, if not impossible, to introduce new methods, because output came from numerous scattered workers who owned their tools. The system did not allow for any great degree of specialization, and in most cases it did not provide full-time work. Workers and their employers squabbled continuously over the amounts of raw materials furnished and the quantity and quality of goods made from them. Selling products made by these methods could be a nightmare; quality control and dependable delivery dates were all but impossible to achieve. Some historians view the development of factories largely as

attempts to achieve better control over scheduling and quality, with utilization of new technology appearing only after workers had been grouped under central direction.[7] In some seasons, the system competed with agriculture's demand for labor. For a few goods whose production could not be mechanized and that required large amounts of unskilled labor working to its own schedules, the system persisted for a long time. "Panama" hats, for example, were produced in this manner. But for goods suited to factory production, the putting-out system was an inferior technique.[8]

Regional Manufacturing Patterns

Manufacturing was not evenly distributed through the United States. It centered in the Middle Atlantic states and New England in this period. There was less activity in the Midwest, although indications of future growth appeared early. The South was not devoid of manufacturing activity,[9] but the high returns available in plantation agriculture deterred industrial investment there. Nevertheless, as Table 7.1 reveals, southern manufacturing activity compared well with nearly every region of the United States except New England, the nation's industrial heartland. The very low output-per-capita figure for the South, however, reveals that only a small portion of that

---

[7] D. North and T. Anderson, *Growth and Welfare in the American Past: A New Economic History,* 3d ed. (Englewood Cliffs, N.J.: Prentice-Hall, 1983), 77–78.

[8] For theoretical discussion of the economics of centralized and decentralized control of production, see A. Alchian and H. Demsetz, "Production, Information Costs, and Economic Organization," *American Economic Review* (December 1972). A more historical treatment is A. Chandler, Jr., *The Visible Hand: The Managerial Revolution in American Business* (Cambridge, Mass.: Harvard University Press, 1977), Chaps. 1–4.

[9] F. Bateman and R. Weiss, "Manufacturing in the Antebellum South," in *Research in Economic History,* vol. 1 (Greenwich, Conn.: JAI Press, 1976). See also T. Fogel, *Without Consent or Contract: The Rise and Fall of American Slavery* (New York: Norton, 1989), 102–105, on data problems for southern manufacturing.

Table 7.1   Regional Manufacturing Comparisons, 1860

Region	Number of Establishments	Capital (Millions)	Employees (Thousands)	Total Output (Millions)	Capital per Establishment
New England	20,671	$257	392	$469	$12,456
Middle States	53,287	435	546	802	8,164
Western States	33,350	174	189	347	5,216
Southern States	24,081	116	132	193	4,827
Pacific States	8,777	23	50	71	2,664

Source: Adapted from F. Bateman and T. Weiss, "Comparative Regional Development in Antebellum Manufacturing," *Journal of Economic History* (March 1975).

region's population was engaged in manufacturing. Figures for southern manufacturing, however, may misrepresent reality. The 1850 and 1860 censuses may have listed the processing of agricultural materials as agricultural activity in the South, but as manufacturing in the North. Since sugar and rice mills tended to be large-scale operations, both the scope and scale of southern industry would be understated by such policies.[10]

In the Northeast, population densities were high by contemporary standards; there was a substantial rural population as well as more urbanization than elsewhere. New England farms appeared to produce people with as much facility as they did crops. Although the South had a substantial population, it had few urban concentrations, a lower overall density than New England, and greater opportunities in agriculture. In addition, slave labor's prices to industrialists were conditioned by national rather than local conditions, because slave labor was far more mobile than were single females.[11] Large cities such as Philadelphia and New York combined access to labor, capital, and markets, as well as the services of specialists in finance, construction, engineer-

ing, and distribution required to build factories and distribute their output. As seaports, they also had good access to transportation. With the exception of power sources and fuel for the iron industry, access to natural resources does not appear to have been a major constraint on the location of most industrial ventures in the antebellum period. Many of the early factories either used materials that were available locally or took advantage of water transportation.

The Cotton Textile Industry

From eighteenth-century England to contemporary Korea and Singapore, the manufacture of cotton textiles has been one of the first industrial activities to appear in the process of economic development. The capital requirements involved are modest and technologically simple. The labor skills necessary for textile workers are readily learned by women and children, who are often less than fully employed in agricultural societies.

Textile production had other attractions: The demand for cotton cloth was expanding rapidly and, at least prior to 1833, was highly price elastic. Cotton cloth was more easily cleaned than wool and could be dyed in bright colors or even printed much like paper. In

---

[10] Fogel, *Without Consent*, 103–104.
[11] G. Wright, "Cheap Labor and Southern Textiles before 1880," *Journal of Economic History* (September 1979).

Region	Employment per Establishment	Output per Establishment	Output per Employee	Value Added per Employee	Output per Capita
New England	19	$22,669	$1,196	$569	$149
Middle States	10	15,057	1,168	656	96
Western States	6	10,395	1,838	769	38
Southern States	6	8,034	1,466	641	19
Pacific States	6	8,115	1,419	851	165

comparison to linen, the only other lightweight fabric then available, cotton was much cheaper. The appearance of the first really inexpensive cloth allowed ordinary people some variety in their clothing. Prior to this time, cloth was so expensive that persons making wills carefully listed every article of clothing they possessed and assigned it to an heir. Now other innovations, such as underwear, bedsheets, curtains, and a variety of ornamental and useful items, were within the reach of most of the population. Cotton cloth was initially a substitute for other materials, but as its price fell to within the means of more and more customers, it became practical for a growing variety of uses.

Machine-Made Cotton Textiles

Efforts to produce cotton textiles with machinery in the United States dated back to the 1790s. Copies of English machines were employed in these early efforts, with mixed results. The British had made breakthrough discoveries in the mechanization of textile production. In the latter half of the eighteenth century, they developed a series of machines, such as the spinning jenny, water frame, and mule, that produced unprecedented quantities of yarn and were soon adapted to water or

steam power. Later, after prolonged development, power-operated looms came into use. The new methods sharply reduced unit costs, especially at high volumes of output. Machine production increased both the quantity and the quality of cotton cloth, transforming it from a luxury fabric to an everyday material used by all economic classes.

The new textile machines were simple to build and operate, and the cost of a fully equipped factory was low enough to allow even men of moderate means, singly or in partnership, to enter the industry. Consequently, cotton textile production expanded very rapidly. Highly competitive conditions (entry was easy and there were few firms with a significant market share) forced producers to pass on the results of rapid technological progress to consumers. By 1820, Britain was selling its textiles all over the world.

The American Response

The English-style factories set up in the United States were not a great success at first. The machines so carefully copied from British originals were designed for an economy where capital and labor were more plentiful than in America. Given their higher costs for the required "mix" of inputs, American producers had great difficulty competing with imports from Britain. After 1808, embargo and then

■ Many of the first textile mills constructed in New England during America's industrial boom still exist today.
Source: The Bettmann Archive.

war furnished protection from overseas production, and the industry expanded rapidly, only to suffer a near-total collapse when British goods once again became available in 1815. By 1820, a few American producers were able to meet British competition within the American market—aided by transport costs and the U.S. tariff, plus a correct assessment of consumers' tastes. In doing so, they learned some valuable lessons.

American producers modified British machines to obtain higher operating speeds and developed new types of power-driven looms. Because American capital costs were higher, it made sense to maximize output per machine-hour, particularly since scarce American labor as well as technological limits made the addition of multiple labor shifts impossible. Apparently, the experience gained in early operations was an important source of further productivity increases through "learning by

doing."[12] The real price of cotton cloth fell steadily before 1860, a reflection of both productivity gains and a highly competitive industry.

The New Factory Work Force
Innovations were necessary in other areas as well. Prior to this time, America had only a tiny industrial work force, and almost no means of housing large numbers of workers in a limited area existed. Nor was it clear who should be recruited to work in the early factories. Two systems were developed. Factories from Rhode Island south along the Atlantic Seaboard hired entire families; husband, wife, and children all worked in the mills. From

---

[12] P. David, "Learning by Doing and Tariff Protection: A Reconsideration of the Case of the Antebellum United States Cotton Textile Industry," *Journal of Economic History* (September 1970).

Massachusetts north, the bulk of the cotton mills' labor force was single young women from rural areas. Few of these "factory girls" expected to spend more than three or four years in their jobs. In order to attract the women (or rather, to persuade their parents to allow them to take the new jobs), dormitories had to be built near the factories, and a full range of services—churches, stores, social facilities, and especially supervision—had to be provided. Recruiting a labor force in northern New England was made easier by the scarcity of alternative jobs for respectable young women who wished to leave home before marriage.[13]

■ Although the hours were long and the pay was low, factory work provided nineteenth-century women their first opportunity to reduce the wage gap between the sexes.
Source: Courtesy Massachusetts Historical Society.

A Formula for Success The Boston Manufacturing Company discovered the formula by which U.S. firms were at last able to meet the British challenge with some chance of success. Industrial espionage in Britain, improved looms at home, an integrated plant combining spinning and weaving, and a work force of young women were the main ingredients. Production was concentrated on a type of plain white cloth, which was a decision that maximized the protection afforded by shipping costs and tariffs. In addition, the firm was much larger and better capitalized than most American companies. It was founded in 1813, when the War of 1812 precluded effective competition during the critical shakedown period—another aid to survival. The Boston Company was one of just a handful of American textile firms to survive the British onslaught in 1815. Initially, many U.S. mills did not produce cloth. Instead, they made yarn, which was sold for home weaving. By 1824,

however, the mills wove all the yarn they produced into cloth within their own walls.[14]

The Importance of Waterpower

The new spinning and weaving machinery required power, and in this New England was well favored. The region had plenty of well-situated waterpower. Especially north of Boston, the fall line (the point at which stream gradients increase) is often directly on the coast, allowing the textile mills to combine cheap water transportation for raw materials and finished goods with a source of power for their machinery.

Setting up Shop

Would-be textile producers had to start by building their own machinery. England was more successful in prohibiting the export of machinery than in restricting the emigration of people who knew how to construct and operate it. British workers learned that Amer-

[13] C. Goldin, *Understanding the Gender Gap: An Economic History of American Women* (New York: Oxford University Press, 1990), 46–54.

[14] R. Zevin, "The Growth of Cotton Textile Production After 1815," in R. Fogel and S. Engerman, eds., *The Reinterpretation of American Economic History* (New York: Harper & Row, 1971).

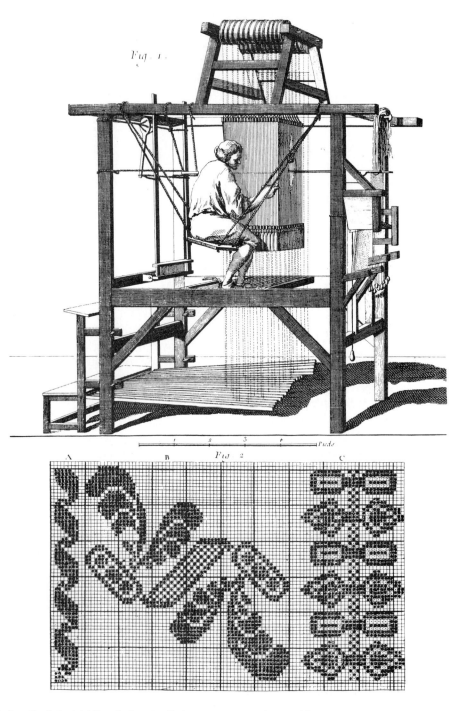

■ Even before the Industrial Revolution, textile looms were complex machines.

icans would pay well for technological expertise, and Samuel Slater was by no means the only English millwright to respond to Yankee dollars.

Machinery Production Once machinery was constructed and operating, firms discovered that smaller amounts of skilled labor were required to maintain than to install it. Textile producers found new uses for their millwrights' skills; they began to produce textile machinery, as well as cloth, for sale. Initially just a sideline to textile production, machinery construction paid off in two ways. Experience in construction yielded rapid technological progress; the basic designs became more productive, and the expertise gained in textile machine construction had other applications. A growing range of other tools were produced by the machine shops, even including locomotives. Improved machinery was instrumental in reducing cotton textile prices to one-quarter their 1815 levels by 1860.[15]

Originally machine production was carried out by large integrated mills, such as the Boston Associates' Waltham plant or the Amoskeag Mills in New Hampshire. By 1860, however, the numbers of textile producers had increased sufficiently to allow specialized machinery producers to appear. Increasingly, the textile factories "spun off" those functions for which they could not achieve full economies of scale and concentrated on those in which they were most efficient. In order to produce textile machinery, the shops had to develop tools that proved to have widespread applications beyond their initial uses, in addition to a growing range of finished products.

Meeting British Competition
American producers initially could compete with the British only in coarse fabrics, where their lower raw material costs gave the greatest offset to their disadvantages in labor skills and wages. Here too, shipping costs and the tariff,

which was levied on a per-unit basis, were larger portions of British firms' costs. By 1860, American mills had learned how to produce a variety of fabrics, including some of high quality. Significantly, they were now exporting some textiles to markets also open to British producers, so in these cases American textiles could survive in "fair" competition. Although the proportion of American textiles exported was not large, and many grades of American cloth could not compete in overseas markets, this indicated great progress from 1815, when American textiles could not hold their domestic markets.

Population growth as well as changes in supply worked to increase the production of cotton textiles. Incomes were rising and transportation costs falling, resulting in increased demand. The real price of textiles fell until 1860, indicating that supply was increasing faster than demand, particularly after 1833.[16] As they did in many other circumstances, American manufacturers responded to the growth of the market with innovations designed to increase production and to reduce unit costs.

Other Textiles

Cotton was more easily adapted to machine spinning and weaving than was wool, because cotton fibers were more easily straightened and twisted into yarn. Nor did the woolen industry fully solve the problems of using power-driven looms until 1840. Both coarse cloth from home industry and fine imported fabrics competed effectively with the products of American factories throughout this period. Even though American efficiency in woolen textiles apparently had not improved in proportion to that in cotton, the production of woolen cloth did rise sufficiently to keep that industry among the ten largest in the United

---

[15] Zevin, "Growth."

[16] Zevin, "Growth."

■ Powered machinery for both weaving and printing cloth was used in early nineteenth-century textile production.
Source: Courtesy of Museum of American Textile History.

States in 1860 (see Table 7.2). American woolen manufacturers developed several machines for carding (straightening) fibers and removing burrs during the antebellum period.

Production of other fibers also increased, as did some noncloth items made from them. Carpets, hemp bagging, rope, and twine were produced in large quantities. Linen was the only other fabric produced in the United States to any extent. Because its manufacture was not mechanized until just before the Civil War, linen suffered heavily in competition with cotton.

Cotton Spurs a Fabric Revolution

Momentous changes resulted from the availability of new, cheaper fabrics. Competition from cotton forced a response from the producers of the more traditional textiles, whose prices fell even as their quality improved. Cottons, which took dye more easily and could be printed in many patterns, must have been a welcome change from the often dull colors of traditional fabrics. Cotton could also be

washed without shrinkage, making higher standards of cleanliness possible.

Cloth produced by hand was more expensive to make and more uneven in quality than the machine-made article. The specialization in clothing production that increased textile output raised the quality of clothing, rather than lowering it, as is often assumed. With the advent of the sewing machine, another barrier to inexpensive clothing for the average citizen was reduced. More people could now afford a change of clothing, something many had previously not enjoyed.

Iron

In 1815 cheap metal was no more common than was cheap cloth. Wood was used instead of iron in an amazing range of applications in antebellum America. The list extended to the frames of steam engines and other machinery. Often all but the cutting or bearing edges of tools were made of wood. The reason behind this extensive use of wood was simple: In the early nineteenth century, iron and all other metals were very expensive. Iron was so scarce that many families burned their old homes when they moved in order to recover the nails used in their construction. An adequate supply of metal was an essential ingredient for successful industrialization. Despite American ingenuity in woodworking, that material simply could not be made to withstand the stresses produced by high-speed machinery.

In colonial times, America had been one of the world's leading producers of iron. Although American iron production increased faster than the population over the period from 1815 to 1860, particularly after 1840, domestic supply failed to keep up with increases in demand. The balance of the country's needs was made up by imports from Britain. This was especially so in the case of large items such as railway rails. Only in the late 1850s did

Table 7.2   United States Manufacturing Industries, 1860

Item	Number of Employees	Value of Product	Value Added by Manufacture*	Rank
Cotton goods	114,955	$107,337,783	$54,671,082	1
Lumber	75,595	104,928,342	53,569,942	2
Boots and shoes	123,026	91,899,298	49,161,124	3
Flour and meal	27,682	248,580,365	40,083,056	4
Men's clothing	114,800	80,830,555	36,680,803	5
Iron (cast, rolled, forged, and wrought)	48,975	73,175,332	35,685,275	6
Machinery	41,223	52,010,376	32,565,843	7
Woolen goods	40,597	60,685,190	25,002,489	8
Carriages, wagons, and carts	37,102	35,552,842	23,654,560	9
Leather	22,697	67,306,542	22,785,715	10

* Value added is calculated by deducting the value of raw materials from that of an industry's finished product. It is thus a measure of the contribution of the manufacturing process.
Source: Eighth Census of the United States: Manufactures. Reprinted in R. Robertson, *History of the American Economy*, 3d ed. (New York: Harcourt Brace Jovanovich, 1973), 220.

domestically produced rails begin to replace imports.

Limitations of Early Iron Technology
Antebellum iron production is a study in the limits of early nineteenth-century technology. Smelting iron ore requires a great deal of fuel. Because wood fires did not achieve the temperatures required, mankind had traditionally employed charcoal. Although charcoal's basic raw material is wood, which America had in abundance, charcoal manufacture is a highly labor-intensive process. Further, charcoal deteriorates badly if transported far in large quantities. Thus, furnaces had to be located near their fuel sources.

Coke Smelting Britain had the labor and skills necessary for iron production, but her supplies of wood for all purposes were becoming increasingly restricted in the eighteenth century. After prolonged trial and error, the British learned to use coke, a coal product, for smelt-

ing. Although the British coal supplies were ample, problems still remained.

Iron smelted with coke did not produce wrought iron (the soft, tough, nearly pure iron still used for ornamental railings) of quality equal to the charcoal-smelted variety. Cast iron, which contains impurities, could be made just as well with coke as with charcoal. Cast iron is hard and brittle and cannot be worked once cast. It could be used for kettles, stoves, pans, and other uses where rigidity was important, but much of the demand was for wrought iron. The reason for coke's partial failure as a smelting fuel was that it contained impurities that passed into the molten metal contacted by the fuel during the smelting process. Still, the price of British iron fell sharply. The cheaper fuel could be used to make at least one type of iron. Coke was better suited to the larger, more efficient blast furnaces that employed steam engines to increase the draft. Later, refining methods that avoided contact between the fuel and metal were developed.

Puddling and rolling, as the new methods were called, greatly increased the economies of scale in iron production.

Luck and Chemistry Unlike their counterparts in the textile industry, American ironmasters were slow to follow the British lead in smelting techniques, although they did adopt puddling and rolling. The reason was not conservatism, but the sulfur content of American coal. The only American coal available for blast-furnace fuel contained sulfur that combined with the iron to make metal that was all but useless. The coal used by the British contained no sulfur, and thus made satisfactory iron.[17] In addition, most of the bituminous (soft) coal yet discovered in America lay west of the Appalachians, while the major markets for iron were in the East.

American ironmasters did not know the chemical reason for the failure, but they quickly learned that British methods did not work west of the Atlantic. Consequently, they continued to use charcoal, and this limited the size of furnaces and restricted their location. Iron production could only be expanded by "more of the same" methods, and thus the price of domestic charcoal-smelted iron did not fall. American producers did adopt another British innovation—preheating the air blown through blast furnaces to increase combustion—within six years of its discovery. These "hot blast" furnaces allowed another innovation: They burned with sufficient heat to allow the use of anthracite (hard coal). Anthracite had been impossible to burn in earlier furnace designs, but there was plenty of it in eastern Pennsylvania, and it contained no sulfur. The new method spread rapidly, and by 1856 half of all the iron produced in America was smelted with anthracite.[18] By 1860, the iron industry was concentrated around its fuel

sources in Pennsylvania. The combination of hot blast and anthracite fuel allowed the use of larger, more efficient furnaces, and iron prices began to fall. Faced with this threat, the owners of older charcoal furnaces worked hard to improve their efficiency, with considerable success. This response is common when new technology threatens the very existence of older methods. Just before the Civil War, sulfur-free soft coal was discovered near Connellsville, Pennsylvania, allowing the use of British methods.

The Influence of Demand on Technology

The persistence of old-fashioned production methods may have owed a good deal to the nature of American demand for iron. Much of the charcoal-smelted iron in which American producers specialized was used for tools, nails, and other highly fabricated items whose buyers were willing to pay for performance. Once demand for large items, such as beams and rails, became a larger portion of the total, cost considerations weighed more heavily, and lower-quality British iron had an advantage, as did American anthracite-smelted iron. New methods' effects on the supply and price of cast iron (and rising prices for wood) allowed the production of cast-iron stoves to expand rapidly in the 1850s.

Iron firms, particularly after the introduction of the new methods, were sizable concerns, perhaps averaging larger than any other private organizations except the railroads. Developments in other sectors, such as easier incorporation, wider financial markets, and better transportation, were useful to them (see Chapter 8). The development of steam power had both forward and backward linkages to the iron industry. Steam engines and railroads consumed growing portions of the industry's production, and they were also important aids in the operation of large furnaces and rolling mills.

---

[17] N. Rosenberg, *Technology and American Economic Growth* (New York: Harper & Row, 1972), 78–80.
[18] Rosenberg, *Technology*, 79–81.

Steel

Through the antebellum period, the industry concentrated its productive efforts on iron, not steel. Steel is iron containing small amounts of carbon; it combines the most useful characteristics of cast iron and wrought iron. Cast iron contains more carbon than does steel; wrought iron, none. Steel had been produced in small quantities for at least a thousand years, but its cost was so high that it could only be used in applications where performance was paramount, such as springs, instruments, and weapons.

In 1860 steel making was still an art, rather than an applied science. It required vast experience and judgment, the only available substitutes for scientific knowledge. The process was not unlike that followed by a first-rate cook; the product may be of high quality, but the process may be difficult to duplicate with any degree of accuracy. Even when a process for large-scale steel making was simultaneously invented by William Kelly in America and England's Henry Bessemer, it did not come into widespread use for another decade. When others attempted to replicate the inventors' work, the results were imperfect, and the cause was unknown. Progress in industrial chemistry was necessary before steel making became a process in which systematic understanding allowed for predictable results.

THE APPEARANCE OF THE FACTORY

Everyone knows what a factory is. Unfortunately, as in many other instances of "common knowledge," the only common quality of individual definitions is diversity. If we define a factory as an aggregation of capital and labor performing interdependent tasks, using powered machinery toward the production of large amounts of some good, the essential features of the institution are captured.[19] (Boot and shoe production used almost no powered machinery.) In factory production, labor and capital must be integrated; each worker and machine is a part of a unified production process, not used alone to make finished items from raw material, and each unit of capital or labor performs only a part of the production process. This need not imply an assembly line, but that is perhaps the ultimate illustration of such integration. In relation to alternative production systems, factories are large-scale production units. The use of large amounts of capital is profitable only if the result is a large amount of total revenue ("sales"); hence, factories are normally practical only for large volumes of output.

Factories and Product Quality

Factories and some of the equipment used in them allowed people to accomplish tasks previously considered impossible. This was especially true in cases involving great weight of material or sustained high-speed operations. In addition, powered machinery made an important contribution to the increase in aggregate production. Human physical effort was greatly decreased, but even so, steam and waterpower had by no means completely supplanted muscles. In 1850, just over 70 percent of the total horsepower generated by nonhuman effort in the United States was just that—it was furnished by work animals.[20] Still, the

---

[19] Some authors regard coordination of labor as the essential element of factory production, with or without the use of powered machinery. See N. Rosenberg and L. Birdzel, Jr., *How the West Grew Rich: The Economic Transformation of the Industrial World* (New York: Basic Books, 1986), 161–163, and D. North, *Structure and Change in Economic History* (New York: Norton, 1981), 169.

[20] U.S. Department of Commerce, Bureau of the Census, *Bicentennial Statistics* (Washington, D.C.: Government Printing Office, 1976), 401.

demands on human muscles were now lower in proportion to output than ever before.

Adjustment Problems

Factories allowed more output per worker with less physical effort, but they also had their drawbacks. Control over the pace of work was no longer in the hands of the individual laborer, nor were hours of work for those in any integrated production process in which each step had to be performed in a fixed order. But this point should not be overstressed. Farmers, particularly those with livestock, have only limited control over their workdays (and no days free from all work). The seasons impose harsh penalties on those who fail to plant or harvest at the proper times, even though a uniform workday might not be necessary. Factory organization allowed higher wages than in agriculture; in 1849, industrial wages averaged more than twice the level of those in agriculture.[21] Despite high turnover, this appeared to be adequate compensation to maintain a factory labor force.

Waterpower versus Steam Power

Power for the new machines was furnished largely by falling water in the beginning, especially in New England. Initially, small- and medium-sized streams were harnessed; current engineering techniques could neither dam large rivers nor effectively utilize the power they produced. But by 1850 the problems had been overcome, and mills using the power of large streams, such as the Connecticut and Merrimack Rivers, were constructed. (One side effect, however, was the destruction of the Atlantic salmon fisheries.) So important was waterpower to the budding textile industry that whole towns, rather than just the mills themselves, were constructed at favorable sites, such as Lawrence, Lowell, Fall River, and Manchester.

Waterpower required a large initial investment; dams, particularly on large streams, were expensive. Once installed, however, waterpower's operating and maintenance costs were very low. Only a fraction of the power potential could be utilized, and waterpower operation was inflexible. Poor engineering and the inevitable losses to friction in power transmission further reduced actual yields. At the time there was no method of obtaining strength from shafts and gears other than to make them large and heavy, so much of the power generated by steam or water went to overcoming the inertia that accompanied strength. Waterpower was vulnerable to disruption by flood, drought, and ice, but its greatest disadvantage was its location. Machines had to be brought to the dam or falls, and this might be far from markets, inputs, or both. Though waterwheels were improved over time, and after 1850 the water turbine further increased the portion of waterpower captured, these problems remained. Until 1860, waterpower provided most of New England's needs, but nearly every potential site within 50 miles of the coast was in use.

Steam Power By 1840, another power source became available: Steam engines were competitive with waterpower even in New England.[22] Steam power was also far more mobile. It could be used anywhere that fuel and a little water were available; thus, many of the factories built in existing cities utilized it. Although the initial investment required for steam power was likely to be less than that for waterpower, operating costs were higher, particularly in regions where fuel was expensive.

[21] J. James and J. Skinner, "The Resolution of the Labor-Scarcity Paradox," *Journal of Economic History* (September 1985).

[22] P. Temin, "Steam and Waterpower in the Early 19th Century," *Journal of Economic History* (June 1966).

Nor were steam engines fully reliable until the 1850s.

In New England, fuel requirements were difficult to overcome: The region had no coal, and supplies of firewood were barely adequate for residential heating and cooking needs. Wood was very difficult to transport. For most of the antebellum period, the overall advantages appeared to lie with waterpower. In 1860, over half of all power generated for manufacturing came from water. Steam power was often used in the Midwest, a region whose rivers were far better suited to transporting the area's cheap coal than they were to driving waterwheels. This preference was undoubtedly reinforced by the region's high capital costs. But by 1860 the Midwest was far from the center of American manufacturing it later became.[23]

Steam Power and U.S. Adaptations

American steam engine design reflected the country's resource endowments as well as the uses to which it put steam power. Britain favored low-pressure steam engines, expensive to build but relatively fuel-efficient and long-lasting. In the United States, high-pressure engines, fuel-hungry and less durable, but cheaper to construct and better suited to transportation needs, were preferred. In Britain, capital was relatively cheap, fuel costs high, and most steam engines were in stationary installations. In the United States, the pattern of costs was reversed. So were the uses: In 1838, over 60 percent of American steam engines were installed in steamboats.[24]

An Overview of Antebellum American History

As Table 7.2 reveals, the major manufacturing industries of antebellum America fall into two groups: those that processed raw materials (lumber, grain milling, iron, and leather) and

[23] Temin, "Steam and Waterpower."
[24] Temin, "Steam and Waterpower." See also Rosenberg, *Technology*, 65, 71.

industries whose capital requirements were modest (textiles, boots and shoes, and clothing). The distribution reflects American resource endowments. Capital was scarce relative to Europe and Americans used it rationally, where it would produce a great deal of product per unit of capital. The machinery and transportation equipment industries may be less of an exception than they appear. These products, like iron smelting, required large "lumps" of capital and could be purchased from foreign producers whose capital and labor were lower than U.S. costs. But both were so expensive to transport that their delivered prices in America were higher than those of domestic producers. Nor were European machinery and transport equipment always well suited to American conditions.

Another point illustrated by the data is that value added per employee is low in textiles, clothing, and footwear, indicating the rather small amounts of simple machinery at each employee's disposal in those labor-intensive industries. Value added per employee in milling, where small work forces labored in highly mechanized mills, reflects very different conditions. Finally, by no means was all U.S. industry concentrated on light manufacturing. Nor had Americans been unable to generate capital. By 1860, there was an aggregate investment of over $1 billion in U.S. industry.

NEW TECHNOLOGY

Although American industrial technology had its roots in European methods, the United States developed distinctive patterns of production for many goods, as well as in the features of the goods themselves. The difference was one of degree rather than kind, but it was quite obvious to contemporary observers. Europeans observed and commented on American industrial methods, and by the end of the period had even copied a few of them. The "American System of Manufacturing," as the British called it, featured a series of machines developed in response to the technical problems that Americans found especially pressing.[25]

The reasons behind the development of these machines are unclear. American producers, operating in an economy where labor was scarce, generally have been thought to have substituted capital for high-priced labor. This raised production per worker and produced further increases in wages. There is no doubt that productivity increases allowed higher wages, but capital was also more expensive in the United States than it was in Europe, giving Americans an incentive to develop capital-saving methods as well. In any case, the source of any cost reduction is less important than its amount. Businessmen strive to reduce costs in general, rather than those of one particular input.[26]

Incentives for Productivity Growth

Because both capital and labor costs were higher in the United States than in Europe, it would seem that economic pressures would encourage increases in the productivity of both. But was capital substituted for labor in the United States to a greater extent than elsewhere? Output per worker would rise if hand-tools were replaced by powered machinery, and output per machine would increase if a second labor shift were added. The aggregate capital stock per worker was lower in the United States than it was in Britain before 1860, so it is difficult to maintain that, in general, capital was substituted for labor in the

United States.[27] The only available change in factor proportions that would increase the profits of American manufacturers was a rise in the proportion of raw materials relative to those of capital and labor.

Natural Resources in U.S. Manufacturing

Natural resources, particularly wood, were cheap in America and were used lavishly and for purposes unheard of in Europe. Wherever possible, natural resources were substituted for both capital and labor. Log-burning fireplaces economized on labor for woodchopping and required less capital than stoves. Once firewood prices began to rise, particularly in urban areas, and iron became more plentiful, the fuel-saving but capital-using properties of stoves were more widely used.[28] American woodworking equipment operated rapidly and required little maintenance, but it reduced what, in European eyes, seemed an appalling portion of the log to sawdust. European observers were impressed, but they did not adopt American woodworking techniques. Log cabins and balloon-frame houses are other examples of attempts to cope with short labor supplies. Log cabins economized on unskilled labor; balloon-frame construction saved on the highly skilled labor needed to construct a post-and-beam building.[29]

In some cases, the choice of factor proportions went beyond what might be indicated by current prices of inputs. For most of the nineteenth century, U.S. wage rates were rising and both capital and raw-materials prices were falling. Manufacturers' decisions in many cases appear to indicate that they expected these trends to continue, because the methods

---

[25] Rosenberg, *Technology*, 87–90.
[26] L. Davis et al., *American Economic Growth: An Economist's History of the United States* (New York: Harper & Row, 1972), 251.

[27] A. Field, "Land Abundance, Interest/Profit Rates, and Nineteenth-Century American and British Technology," *Journal of Economic History* (June 1983).
[28] Rosenberg, *Technology*, 29. It should also be noted that during winter in rural areas, the opportunity costs of woodchopping might be very low—a point reinforced by faster adoption of stoves in cities.
[29] Rosenberg, *Technology*, 27–29.

they chose tended to be even more capital and materials intensive and labor saving than existing prices would dictate. In addition, a bias toward raw materials also tends to produce a more capital-intensive technology.[30] A recent study concluded that there was no single "American System"; that industries employing skilled workers tended to be more capital intensive and those employing unskilled labor less so in America than in Britain.[31] The question of whether American industry was capital or labor intensive is still under discussion, and it appears that there may not be a single answer.

Another output-increasing option was to change the inputs themselves, such as better machines or more skilled workers instead of more machines. Efforts could also be made to use existing equipment and workers more efficiently. Both patterns were followed, and there was considerable interaction between the two.

Innovation as a Source of Lower Capital Costs

High capital costs in antebellum America have been thought to favor technological change. American machinery tended to be lightly built and to be operated at high speeds—features that increased output per investment dollar. One consequence was that such machinery had to be replaced more frequently than European machinery built and run with an eye to long life. It was thus easier to incorporate innovations as they appeared in America, and there was less of the fallacious but widespread view that any capital good, once purchased, had to be operated "until it repaid its cost." In any case, few American manufacturers hesitated to replace machinery of any age with capital that promised superior performance.

The high and rising rate of aggregate investment in the United States helped to insure that at any time a large portion of the nation's capital equipment was relatively new. The efforts to raise productivity were successful; real value added and output per worker rose two and one-half to three times in New England manufacturing over 1820–1860.[32] The primary source of productivity increase was a rise in factor (particularly labor) productivity, rather than changing factor proportions or interindustry shifts. The consequence was final-goods prices that fell relative to input costs. Productivity increases allowed higher wages for workers even while consumers paid lower prices for the goods produced.

SOURCES OF INVENTION

Throughout the antebellum era, the United States borrowed European ideas and adapted them to American conditions; but it also developed original ideas. The impressive list of American inventions from this period, with the important exceptions of the telegraph and vulcanized rubber, are applications of mechanics, involving rather straightforward principles of cause and effect. None is based on really sophisticated science, and most owe more to dogged trial and error than to mastery of fundamental principles.

In the area of basic science, and even in its formal applications in technology, the United States lagged far behind Europe in 1860. Until the middle 1850s, only the United States Military Academy at West Point offered formal training in engineering. One scientific journal was published in the entire country.

---

[30] L. Cain and D. Paterson, "Factor Biases and Technical Change in Manufacturing: The American System, 1850–1919," *Journal of Economic History* (June 1981).
[31] James and Skinner, "The Resolution."

[32] K. Sokoloff, "Productivity Growth in Manufacturing During Early Industrialization," in Gallman and Engerman, *Long-Term Factors in American Economic Development* (Chicago: University of Chicago Press, 1986), 679–736.

Nevertheless, the country had an ambitious, well-informed, and imaginative population, which went far to compensate for other deficiencies. Workmen tended to be literate and well versed in basic mechanical relationships. Further, they were eager to use new equipment, quick to learn how to repair and maintain it, and often able to make improvements or apply its basic principles in new areas. With its labor shortages, America welcomed both new ideas and new people, and tried to develop their potential.

Interchangeable Parts

The development of interchangeable parts typifies the American response to new methods. The basic idea of making many identical parts, each of which could easily be fitted into a complex mechanism in lieu of any other, originated in Europe. Its first really successful application, however, was in American arms manufacture. Although Eli Whitney's role in introducing this technique has been widely publicized, the real credit should probably go to Simeon North.[33]

Production of military weapons was a logical field for the first application of this principle. Until interchangeable parts were developed, each gun was literally custom-made. All but a few minor parts were hand-made and, more importantly, hand-fitted into the complete mechanism. The process was slow and required highly skilled hand labor; it took years of experience to learn to make and fit together a complicated mechanism such as a gunlock using only handtools and the crudest measuring devices. Even though defense needs might require large numbers of guns, it was impossible to expand production quickly while skilled labor remained such a bottleneck. This was hardly less true of wooden components than it was of metal. Irregular shapes, such as gunstocks, required large amounts of hand labor, and the result had to be painstakingly fitted to the metal parts. Repair of guns made by such procedures was equally time-consuming.

Two things were necessary to make interchangeable parts a practical possibility: machines capable of producing large quantities of components to a standardized design, and measuring devices and controls to insure that each unit of output conformed to standard dimensions. To meet the first need, a series of machines—lathes, milling machines, and grinders—were developed by 1845. Accuracy was achieved with the introduction of calipers, jigs, taps, and gauges. By 1860, irregular shapes in both wood and metal were being turned out in quantity by power-driven machines. The principle could be applied to many different products. The new technique did not merely increase the supply or reduce the price of the manufactured goods it produced, it made all but the most basic items of industry available to the average citizen for the first time.

Substitution of machine-produced uniformity for expensive hand fitting greatly increased productivity and reduced costs. After watching a workman at the Springfield Arsenal assemble ten muskets using only a screwdriver to fit together parts taken from guns made in ten different years, a British investigating committee paid the "American System" the most sincere compliment possible. It bought a complete duplicate plant and shipped it to England. The American workman had assembled one musket every 3½ minutes. Using traditional methods, a skilled workman could not make two such guns in an entire day's work.[34]

---

[33] R. Woodbury, "Eli Whitney and the Legend of Interchangeable Parts," *Technology and Cultural Change*, vol. 2: 1, 1960. Whitney apparently regarded the contract he had been awarded to produce muskets with interchangeable parts more as a source of funds for lawsuits over infringements of his cotton-gin patents than as a business venture in itself.

---

[34] Rosenberg, *Technology*, 90–91.

Linkages to Other Industries

Interchangeable parts could be readily adapted to the production of almost any complex mechanism, such as watches, clocks, furniture, agricultural machinery, and sewing machines. Entrepreneurs and customers quickly saw that interchangeable parts meant more than just low initial cost. If an item with interchangeable parts broke down, its owners could simply put a new part in place themselves. Previously, only a skilled workman—sometimes only the original producer—could make and hand-fit a new component, filing it to an exact fit with the other parts of the mechanism. The risks of employing machinery in place of labor fell because ease of repairs meant that "down time" was much less when breakdowns occurred. The cost of items made with such machines was also reduced.

Many of the new developments interacted. Sewing machines and cheaper cloth made more and better clothes possible for the average person, and allowed some attention to fashion. In turn, sewing machines benefited from interchangeable parts—no seamstress would buy such an expensive machine without assurance that it could be easily and cheaply repaired. Meat packing produced large quantities of hides, which could be combined with improved sewing machines in boot and shoe factories. Ready-made clothing still was handicapped by inadequate statistical knowledge: No accurate information about the proportion of people of different dimensions and sizes was available. The railroads benefited from the telegraph, an obvious aid to both traffic control and the problems of obtaining current information from distant station managers. Producers of all types of machines found cheap iron useful for rigid equipment that had to withstand heavy stress.

Machines developed in response to one industry's needs often proved to have even more significant applications in another. Some machines were equally effective in producing more machines. The United States began producing machine tools. These mechanisms are the very core of industry; they determine the technical limits within which users of their products can operate.[35] At first, machine tools had to be built by each industrial firm to meet its own needs, but specialized machine-tool builders enhanced the speed with which the new technology could be implemented throughout industry.

Better Goods or Cheaper Goods?

The resulting products should not be regarded as a flood of cheap and cheaply made goods that displaced the high-quality products of craftsmen. This may have been the case in a few instances, but goods made by the old methods generally remained available to those willing to pay for them. Far more often, the new manufactured goods, especially mechanical items, now made available to ordinary people what only the rich had previously been able to obtain. Before the machine age, low-priced goods could be produced only by skimping on materials or labor. The poor made do with inferior goods, attempted to make their own, waited for the cast-offs of the rich, or, most commonly, did without. Nor did quality necessarily decline. Machine-made items might be well designed; if a good or a component was to be produced in thousands, it might well pay to spend more care on its design than on one that was to be unique.

American conditions spurred innovative responses. Inventors with strong economic motives directed their efforts to areas of perceived need. Given the vast distances of the interior, the list of significant American contributions to transportation and communications improvements should not be surprising.

---

[35] Rosenberg, *Technology*, 96–100.

The Role of the Frontier

Frontier requirements also spurred innovative activity. Commanche warriors could keep a stream of six or more unpleasantly well-aimed arrows in the air from the back (or far side) of a horse at full gallop. Few riflemen could reload their weapons without stopping, and of course they could fire only one shot. The survivors of encounters with such formidable combat technology were highly receptive to the new technology furnished by Samuel Colt's six-shooters—although few were in any hurry for a return engagement.

In some cases the characteristics of new machinery spurred further innovation as experience was gained in its use. Increasing train weights and operating speeds stimulated the search for effective brakes and traffic control mechanisms.

The Influence of American Markets

The characteristics of the market for which the new goods were made were an important influence on both manufactured items and the technology with which they were produced. American population and per-capita incomes were both rising, and improving transportation further increased the markets open to most producers. In 1860, most Americans were still living in widely dispersed rural populations whose income distributions were considerably more equal than those of Europe. Such consumers wanted goods that performed their functions effectively, but they were not willing to pay for features that enhanced only appearance or the producer's sense of technical perfection. The fact that an item was already in widespread use did not inhibit American consumers as it might in Europe. This attitude was strengthened by the high proportion of tools among the new products; Americans were buying items they would use to make a living, not to display prestige.

The Importance of Price

Under such circumstances, price was a major consideration in most American markets. In most cases, several sellers competed for buyers' favor; thus, at least some competition was generally present. Consumers' interest in low prices resulted in ready acceptance of changes in design that made items easier to manufacture. The European consumer might insist on distinctive features and be willing to buy less at high prices if these could not be incorporated in machine-made items. The American counterpart felt differently. If changes in products that made them easier to manufacture reduced price, Americans were willing to adapt their tastes to what machines could produce.[36] American manufactured goods were seldom highly finished and their designs were often no more than adequate for their purpose, but they could be made by machines in large quantities and sold at low prices. Many of these simple, straightforward designs proved to be highly functional as well. American agricultural machinery, locks, clocks, and small arms performed better than European products, and proved it in international competitions.

Other Innovations

Where the product or the nature of inputs defied mechanization, innovations in organization were developed. Meat-packing plants could not use machines for butchering because animals are not uniform in size or proportions. However, if a large number of animals was to be processed, specialization and high productivity could be achieved through the introduction of a "disassembly line," a conveyor on which carcasses moved past workmen, each of whom performed one specific task. This system was well established before the Civil War.

---

[36] Rosenberg, *Technology*, 44–51.

Despite the advances detailed in this chapter, American manufacturing in 1860 was not a sector of giant firms using highly mechanized production techniques (see Table 7.1). On the eve of the Civil War, the typical manufacturing firm was an individual proprietorship or partnership, not a corporation. It employed fewer than ten workers, used methods that still relied heavily on human muscle, and served a local or, at most, a regional market. Only in a few industries (iron was one example) did firms represent exceptions to these generalizations.

NEW OPPORTUNITIES AND NEW RESPONSES

Periods of rapid economic growth tend to be periods of substantial technical change. The antebellum U.S. economy typifies this theory, particularly in industry, which for all practical purposes was a brand-new sector. The range of alternatives open to Americans expanded greatly in this era—in location, technique, and type of job within most sectors, and in the range of economic activities, to say nothing of products. There is abundant evidence that industrialization represented a massive response to new opportunities. New goods were made by new methods and sold under new conditions. Perhaps never before or since has the climate for entrepreneurial activity been so favorable in the United States. Population and income growth, as well as transport improvements, increased demand for most goods, and there was a highly favorable consumer response to new items, particularly in the period from 1840 to 1860. The new technologies in most cases allowed easy entry into new occupations; economies of scale were not great, and low capital costs and improving financial institutions eased access to capital. There were few large firms already entrenched in most in-

dustries. The legal and social climate was extremely favorable to new ventures; laws and court decisions strongly favored private property rights and competition. The improved communications of the period reduced some risks and made clear the success of others who might serve as role models.

Nor should it be assumed that this period was one in which only the owners of new industrial firms prospered. The range of occupations was far wider than it had ever been previously. Wider job choices always benefit individual workers; there is a better chance to locate an occupation that makes ideal use of individual talent. With more employers, especially from different industries, competing for labor, wage prospects are enhanced. There were as few barriers to entry for workers as for their employers. With many jobs in industries that a few decades before had not existed, lack of experience was expected. American manufacturing made very effective use of on-the-job training. Once on the job in new industries, productivity gains were typically high and firms small enough so their sources were recognized. Even within existing industries, work now produced higher and far more varied standards of living with less physical exertion. The gains were not great by modern standards, but those who achieved them had a different basis of judgment. Few of us can imagine the prospects of young adults in a world where the choice of jobs and location were as restricted as they were in rural life in the eighteenth century. America had always offered better opportunities than many people found in Europe. Now it offered improved choices to many of its own people as well.

SELECTED REFERENCES

Cain, L., and D. Paterson. "Factor Biases and Technical Change in Manufacturing: The American System, 1850–1919." *Journal of Economic History* (June 1981).

————. "Biased Technical Change, Scale, and Factor Substitution in American Industry, 1850–1919." *Journal of Economic History* (March 1986).

Chandler, A., Jr. *The Visible Hand: The Managerial Revolution in American Business.* Cambridge, Mass.: Harvard University Press, 1977.

Clark, V. *History of Manufactures in the United States.* 1929 Reprint. Washington, D.C.: Peter Smith, 1949.

Cochran, T. *Frontiers of Change: Early Industrialism in America.* New York: Oxford University Press, 1981.

David, P. "Learning By Doing and Tariff Protection: A Reconsideration of the Case of the Antebellum United States Cotton Textile Industry." *Journal of Economic History* (September 1970).

————. *Technical Choice, Innovation, and Economic Growth.* Cambridge, U.K.: Cambridge University Press, 1975.

Davis, L., R. Easterlin, W. Parker et al. *American Economic Growth: An Economist's History of the United States.* New York: Harper & Row, 1972.

Field, A. "Land Abundance, Interest/Profit Rates, and Nineteenth-Century American and British Technology." *Journal of Economic History* (June 1983).

Gallman, R., and S. Engerman, eds. *Long Term Factors in American Economic Development.* Chicago: University of Chicago Press, 1986.

Goldin, C. *Understanding the Gender Gap: An Economic History of American Women.* New York: Oxford University Press, 1990.

Habbakuk, H. *American and British Technology in the 19th Century.* Cambridge, U.K.: Cambridge University Press, 1962.

Hounshell, D. *From the American System to Mass Production, 1800–1932: The Development of Manufacturing Technology in the United States.* Baltimore: Johns Hopkins University Press, 1984.

James, J., and J. Skinner. "The Resolution of the Labor-Scarcity Paradox." *Journal of Economic History* (September 1985).

Kendrick, J. *Productivity Trends in the United States.* Princeton, N.J.: Princeton University Press, 1961.

North, D. *The Economic Growth of the United States, 1790–1860.* Englewood Cliffs, N.J.: Prentice-Hall, 1961.

Parker, W. *Europe, America, and the Wider World: Essays on the Economic History of Western Capitalism.* 2 vols. New York: Cambridge University Press, 1991.

Rosenberg, N. *Technology and American Economic Growth.* New York: Harper & Row, 1972.

Schmookler, J. *Invention and Economic Growth.* Cambridge, Mass.: Harvard University Press, 1966.

Temin, P. *Iron and Steel in 19th Century America: An Economic Inquiry.* Cambridge, Mass.: MIT Press, 1964.

U.S. Department of Commerce, Bureau of the Census. *Historical Statistics of the United States: Colonial Times to 1970.* 2 vols. Washington, D.C.: Government Printing Office, 1975.

Zevin, R. "The Growth of Cotton Production After 1815" in R. Fogel and S. Engerman, *The Reinterpretation of American Economic History.* New York: Harper & Row, 1971.

BANKING, FINANCE, AND COMMERCE

*T*he U.S. economy produced a much greater volume of goods and services in 1860 than it had in 1790. The variety of products was also far wider on the eve of the Civil War than it had been just after the basic institutions of the new republic were established. As specialized production of goods for sale replaced output for personal use, exchanges between individuals, industries, and regions became more common. A rising portion of those exchanges now involved a time dimension; goods were obtained in exchange for promises of future payment, or current payment was made for future deliveries. These changes increased the need for goods and institutions facilitating such transactions. For current trade, money and the institutions that produce and control it reduce transaction costs. Financial institutions are essential to exchanges with a time dimension.

MONEY AND THE ECONOMY

Economists have developed an equation that illustrates the relations between money and other economic activity. The equation of exchange, or quantity-theory equation, $MV = PQ$, summarizes a great deal in a few symbols. M is the supply of money; V is velocity, or the rate at which a unit of money is spent; P is the aggregate price level; and Q is the volume of transactions or real output.

Velocity is determined by individuals' demand for money balances and by the structure of monetary institutions, neither of which changes rapidly. Thus, changes in the money supply must affect the price level, output, or both. The level of prices times the volume of real output is a shorthand term for the money value of aggregate economic activity, and so the equation provides the link between the money supply and gross national product. The equation allows predictions to be made about the results of a change or variation in the rate of change in the money supply.

For example, if all resources are in use (the economy is at full employment), Q cannot rise much in response to increases in the money supply. Since V is stable, the effect of money-supply increases will be concentrated on the price level, which will rise. If unemployed resources are available, an increase in the money supply will raise both P and Q. Decreases in the money supply must decrease PQ, but it is important to distinguish between these two variables. If all prices fell in proportion, leaving real output unchanged, there would be no effect on overall welfare. But if real output declines, in a world where scarcity exists at least some people must be worse off. Not only will there be fewer goods and services available so that real incomes are lower, some of those employed in making the previous volume of output will lose their jobs. Economists' opinions on the relation between price and output declines have been altered several times in the past few decades. Today (1992) it appears that prices are more flexible than they were in the immediate past when they fell, if at all, only under conditions of severe unemployment. In the nineteenth century, prices both rose and fell, as Table 8.1 indicates; they certainly were not stable.

Short-term deflation might cause considerable distress, but it did reduce the decline in real output and employment otherwise necessary to accommodate decreases in the money supply.[1] Despite severe deflation, the

---

[1] P. Temin, *The Jacksonian Economy* (New York: Norton, 1969), 160–165.

Table 8.1   Wholesale Prices, 1815–1860
(1910–1914 = 100)

Year	Price Level	Year	Price Level	Year	Price Level
1815	170	1831	94	1847	90
1816	151	1832	95	1848	82
1817	151	1833	95	1849	82
1818	147	1834	90	1850	84
1819	125	1835	100	1851	83
1820	106	1836	114	1852	88
1821	102	1837	115	1853	97
1822	106	1838	110	1854	108
1823	103	1839	112	1855	110
1824	98	1840	95	1856	105
1825	103	1841	92	1857	111
1826	99	1842	82	1858	93
1827	98	1843	75	1859	95
1828	97	1844	77	1860	93
1829	96	1845	83		
1830	91	1846	83		

Source: U.S. Department of Commerce, Bureau of the Census, *Historical Statistics of the United States: Colonial Times to 1970*, 2 vols. (Washington D.C.: Government Printing Office, 1975), 1:201.

1839–1843 period was one of substantial real economic growth.

Bimetallic Money

In 1792 Congress had chosen the dollar as the U.S. currency unit. It defined the dollar as containing either 371.25 grains of silver or 24.75 grains of gold. A gold dollar, had such a coin been minted then, would have contained one-fifteenth as much metal as its silver counterpart. The government offered to buy and sell unlimited amounts of gold and silver at the 1 to 15 ratio in either coin or bullion form. Because American coins were pieces of pure metal, they were valuable for that reason as well as for monetary purposes. But the relation between precious metals' value in terms of each other and in monetary terms was a source of difficulty. As long as an ounce of gold exchanged for 15 ounces of silver in the bullion markets, where gold and silver were sold as commodities, all would be well. However, if the relative values of gold and silver as metal differed from the 1 to 15 ratio at which the mint exchanged them, people would exchange the overvalued metal for that which the mint undervalued. Early in the nineteenth century, gold brought 16 times its weight in silver in the bullion markets. It was possible, and profitable, to bring 15 ounces of silver to the U.S. mint, exchange them for an ounce of gold, use the gold to purchase 16 ounces of silver in the bullion markets, and repeat the transaction until the mint either ran out of gold or changed the ratio. Since U.S. gold coins were more valuable as metal than as money, they disappeared from circulation. After prolonged debate, Congress changed the mint ratio to 16 to 1 in 1834. But events had moved faster than political recognition; by this time the 16 to 1 ratio overvalued gold. Silver coins became so scarce that postage stamps and fractional paper currency were used as substitutes. Before the situation could be rectified, the discovery of gold in California in 1848 and in Australia three years later made it even worse.[2]

Aside from the difficulty of keeping both types of metallic money in circulation, the use of commodity money was inefficient. It is expensive to use any commodity that has higher-valued alternative uses for money with no consideration of opportunity costs. Gold and silver had other uses as commodities, and their production for monetary uses employed resources that otherwise might have produced other goods or metal for nonmonetary purposes. If other forms of money whose production required fewer resources were substituted for metal, the total output of the U.S. economy could be greater.

Until the California gold rush, precious metals were not produced within the United States in significant quantities. Gold and silver were obtained through international trade, as they had been in colonial times. Sales of U.S. goods or services to foreigners or foreign investment in the United States allowed the country to import specie or bullion—at the cost of other foreign products. There was a minor gold rush in the southern Appalachian Mountains in the 1820s and 1830s. It had little effect on the money supply, but it cost most of the Cherokee Indians their ancestral homelands, as gold seekers swarmed onto Indian lands in violation of treaties. Most of the Cherokees were forcibly removed to what is now Oklahoma by the army; many died on the journey.

International Monetary Considerations

When the United States defined the dollar as containing a specific amount of gold or silver, it determined the exchange rate between the dollar and foreign currencies whose metallic content was also fixed. Dollars would exchange for British pounds sterling in proportion to the rate at which each currency could be exchanged for gold. Gold in turn could be converted into sterling at known ratios. Prior to 1834, a pound sterling exchanged for about $4.58; after the change made at that time, the ratio was £1 for $4.87.[3]

The stable rate of exchange between the dollar and foreign currencies could affect domestic monetary and real activity. Precious metals not only furnished part of the U.S. money supply, they were also the reserves against which commercial banks issued their own money. If American prices rose, foreign goods would be less expensive to American purchasers, because the exchange rate would not vary. But U.S. inflation would raise the prices of American goods to foreigners. Thus, inflation would tend to increase imports and reduce exports, and gold would flow out of the United States. Deflation would have the opposite effect. As the monetary base changed in the United States, both price and real output changes might occur.

Foreign investment, mining activity, or changes in international trade flows might affect the U.S. money supply, interest rates, or investment by increasing or decreasing an important component of the U.S. money supply. The role of gold flows was magnified because

[2] There is some dispute over the disruptive effects of bimetallism. See M. Friedman, "Bimetallism Revisited," *Journal of Economic Perspectives* (September 1990).

[3] L. Officer, "Dollar-Sterling Mint Parity and Exchange Rates, 1791–1834," *Journal of Economic History* (September 1983).

changes in bank reserves could cause much larger changes in the amount of bank money in circulation. Since gold could move freely between nations, there was only a limited extent to which the United States could both control its own monetary affairs and maintain fixed exchange rates.

BANKS

Gold and silver coins were only part of the U.S. money supply. Most money was manufactured by commercial banks (see Table 8.3). Commercial banks, at least in aggregate, can create money. When an individual takes out a bank loan, he or she exchanges a personal promise to pay, which is not money, for the bank's promise to pay—a check or a credit to a checking account. Such bank debt is accepted as payment—it is money.

Prior to the Civil War, the use of checking accounts had already become widespread, particularly in eastern business transactions. But unlike today, banks could also print banknotes (currency) that they could lend.

From modest beginnings in the 1780s, banking became a growth industry after 1800. During the next 50 years, the number of banks grew at four times the rate of population growth, and banks' assets, note circulation, and deposits grew faster still.

Banking Fundamentals

Banks do not derive income from accepting deposits; indeed, deposits per se only increase banks' operating costs. A bank's income is derived from the interest paid on loans made by the bank or received on securities that the bank has purchased (which represent loans made by someone else). Bankers do not like to refuse loan applications; to do so costs them income (the interest that the loan would generate).

Since money's value depends on its scarcity, there are limits to banks' ability to increase the money supply. Nobody would incur any cost to obtain bank money if it were not accepted in trade. Bank money will not be accepted if it is not readily convertible into legal tender (forms of money acceptable in the discharge of debts). In the nineteenth century, legal tender meant specie—gold or silver. Banks had to be able to exchange their notes or the checking deposits held with them for legal tender on demand. Under normal circumstances, however, only a small fraction of any bank's outstanding note or deposit obligations would be presented for conversion on any given day. Usually deposits of coin

■ Before 1865, American banks issued their own currency.
Source: Culver Pictures.

roughly offset withdrawals, so that there was no net outflow of specie. Thus, banks needed to keep only one-tenth to one-third of their current note or deposit obligations in the form of specie; the rest could be loaned to increase the banks' income.

Banks do not like to hold larger reserves than are necessary to satisfy current transaction demands. Reserves in excess of requirements cost the bank interest on foregone loans, and large accumulations of specie attract the attention of bank robbers. The larger the portion of the bank's assets held as reserves, the smaller the bank's profits.

Fractional-Reserve Banking

Fractional-reserve banking allows banks to increase the money supply. If all banks hold 10 percent of their assets as reserves, a new deposit of $100 in gold coin will result in a $1,000 increase in the money supply as banks increase their loans. Under these conditions, each bank has a dollar in assets for every dollar of liabilities, but it has only ten cents in reserves immediately available to meet demands for conversion of bank money into other forms. Repayment of bank loans has the opposite effect. If all banks attempt to increase their reserves by calling in loans, the money supply will be reduced by the same multiple of the reserve ratio by which it was expanded. Banks' lending attitudes thus influence the money supply.

Usually people who believe that they can convert their bank money into legal tender are content not to do so. Both currency and checking accounts are safer and more convenient forms of money than large amounts of coin. But if for some reason a large portion of those holding bank money wishes to convert it into legal tender, they will not be able to do so simultaneously in any fractional-reserve system. Unless the banks can sell their non-reserve assets for legal tender or borrow funds, there is no way they can meet the unanticipated demand for conversion. Further, just as

any single depositor or banknote holder can convert bank money into other forms (but not all at once), so any one bank can sell or borrow from other banks (but not all simultaneously). If all banks try to sell their loans or securities at the same time, prices of such assets will fall, perhaps so much that their sale will not produce sufficient funds to meet the demand for legal tender. If all banks try to borrow from each other, the total amount of reserves (non-bank money) is not increased.

Banks loan money to people who use the funds for investment purposes. The activities of the lenders tend to increase the economy's capacity by facilitating commercial or other productive activity. In the nineteenth century, banks made virtually no other types of loans. Banks also serve as financial intermediaries, links between savers and investors, allocating funds to uses that generate the highest possible return. Since their information about investment possibilities is likely to be more comprehensive and accurate than that of individual savers, banks may allocate a given amount of savings more productively than could people with less information.

Antebellum Banking Practices

The history of American banking in the antebellum period is colorful. Banking was a new occupation, not yet well understood, in which profits could be very high. Banks appeared before effective operating rules had been devised or instituted. Banking attracted the ambitious and sometimes the unscrupulous. Because banks were usually corporations, states were able to impose restrictions on their operations through the terms embodied in bank charters. At this time, each corporation had to receive its charter through a separate act of the state legislature. Often the intent and enforcement of early regulations were deficient. Sometimes banks were required to keep reserves against their capital, the amount paid in by the banks' owners, or only against their outstanding note issues, not their checking accounts. Although the intent of such laws was to make banks safe (insure that depositors and noteholders could obtain legal tender on demand), laws requiring banks to maintain reserves against capital discouraged the formation of banks with large capitals. Capital provides a "cushion" of safety for depositors and noteholders. Requiring reserves only against notes in circulation encouraged banks to expand their checking liabilities instead; but checking accounts were the same type of current liabilities as were notes. In any case, formulating bank regulations is one thing; before 1860, enforcing them was quite another. Provisions for bank inspections were often designed to discover the extent of fraud rather than to prevent its occurrence.

Still, as Table 8.1 indicates, prices did not rise uncontrollably from 1815 to 1860, a period of very substantial real growth and generally low unemployment. To some extent, the large number of independent banks was a check on any individual institution's tendencies toward excess. If a single bank were to expand its loans much faster than the average of all banks, most of the checks and notes that it issued would be deposited in other banks. Banks receiving these deposits would return them to the bank of issue with a demand for payment in legal tender. This would tend to reduce the expanding bank's reserves, and hence its ability to meet further demands for conversion, either from its own customers or from other banks.

If a bank's ability to convert its own money into other forms was in doubt, that money would be accepted in trade and at other banks at less than its face value. The discount would vary with the degree of uncertainty about the issuing bank's eventual ability to redeem its obligations in full. Since information about the stability of banks generally became more difficult to obtain the more distant they were, most banks' obligations were dis-counted at rates rising with the distance from their point of issue. Local and regional clearinghouses, institutions for settling interbank debts through offsetting credits against one bank with debits against another so that only the net debt need be paid or credit received, also placed limits on individual banks' enthusiasm. They settled debts more quickly than was possible through transactions between individual banks, and the clearinghouse might threaten to exclude a bank that ran consistent deficits with other members.

Attempts at Regulation

Various attempts to regulate banks' performance—particularly in regard to note issues—were made in the antebellum era by both private and governmental agencies. States often contributed to a bank's capital and thus gained some control as stockholders. Indiana, Missouri, and Iowa established state-owned banking systems. At the other extreme, Wisconsin "regulated" banks by making them illegal.[4] In general, banking laws specified the amount of capital that had to be subscribed by the bank's owners, limited its note issue, and made some provision for inspections to insure compliance with these regulations. The extent of regulation and its enforcement varied; laws were stricter where merchant communities were well-established, for example, on the Eastern Seaboard and in Louisiana. In the newer states, laws often reflected a very imperfect understanding of banking, tending either to be lax or flat prohibitions. The Northwest was torn between two goals: It was a debtor region, eager for more capital, but also a stronghold of hard-money opinion, which frowned on banks and paper money.[5]

---

[4] B. Hammond, "Banking in the Early West: Monopoly, Prohibition, and Laissez Faire," *Journal of Economic History* (May 1948).

[5] T. Cochran and T. Brewer, eds., *Views of American Economic Growth: The Agricultural Era*, 2 vols. (New York: McGraw-Hill, 1961), 1:171. The point is made in a comment on the article by Hammond, "Banking."

The Suffolk Banking System

Led by the newly established Suffolk Bank, the Boston banking community developed one form of regulation in the early 1820s. Boston banks had to compete with those outside the city's limits. Since the rural banks kept a smaller portion of reserves and thus could make loans on more favorable terms than could Boston banks, their notes became the common form of circulating currency within the city. Time and travel were required to redeem the notes of rural banks, so they were discounted—accepted at less than their face value—by Boston merchants. Boston banks would not accept notes from rural banks at all, increasing the incentive to discount them. In retaliation, rural banks returned the notes of Boston banks for redemption in specie as they were received. Boston banks found it difficult to keep their notes in circulation under these conditions.

In 1820, the Suffolk Bank offered to accept the notes of any rural bank that would keep a permanent $5,000 deposit over and above the funds required for clearinghouse purposes, and to allow rural banks to redeem their notes at the same rate of discount that the Suffolk had accepted them. Rural banks that did not cooperate found that the Suffolk Bank would accumulate large quantities of their notes and present them for redemption at face value in specie with no prior notice. Such a practice was embarrassing to banks with low reserve ratios. The combined stick and carrot were effective, and most Boston banks joined with the Suffolk in enforcing the system. The Suffolk system did more than improve the competitive position of Boston banks. It caused the notes of all New England banks to circulate within the region at, or very close to, their face value. This made bank money a better and more easily used medium of exchange within the system and facilitated exchange.[6]

The Safety Fund System

One major source of the U.S. banking system's difficulties was that the many small local banks of which it was largely comprised were vulnerable to failure. In good times, they were tempted to issue too many notes in relation to their reserves, making it difficult to redeem currency in specie if large amounts were presented at once. Fractional-reserve banking is not secure against this type of difficulty unless most depositors think it is and act accordingly. Unfortunately, bank failures were too frequent (and suspensions even more so) for nineteenth-century Americans not to consider the possibility that their bank's money might lose part or all of its purchasing power. Small banks' loans tend to be heavily concentrated on local industry, adding to their instability. Some southern states allowed multibranch banks, whose risks were more diversified and total assets greater. Such large banks were able to devise effectively enforced agreements that reduced irresponsible action taken by individual banks.[7]

For depositors or noteholders, the risks were real and large. Even if the assets of a bank closed by a "run" were sufficient to cover its obligations, the process of liquidation could take months, with no certainty about the portion of the bank's debts that could be repaid. Such difficulties were real enough for local banks, but information on the solvency of distant banks was so hard to obtain that their notes might circulate only at large discounts, if at all.

New York State attempted to alleviate this instability through an institution similar to the modern Federal Deposit Insurance Corporation. In 1828, the state required that all banks in New York contribute 0.5 percent of their capital annually, up to a maximum of 3 percent, to a fund that would be able to make

[6] L. Davis, R. Easterlin, and W. Parker et al., *American Economic Growth: An Economist's History of the United States* (New York: Harper & Row, 1971), 35.

[7] C. Calomiris, "Is Deposit Insurance Necessary? A Historical Perspective," *Journal of Economic History* (June 1990).

good the notes of failed banks whose assets were not sufficient to cover their outstanding notes. Banks were required to join the system as a condition for the renewal of their corporate charters. The law provided for enforcement and contained provisions forcing banks to keep reserves against notes and checking deposits, not capital. The "Safety Fund" was an improvement over most contemporary banking laws, although it still based contributions to the safety fund on capital, not current liabilities. It had other deficiencies as well: It shifted some risk of loss from individual banks to the system, encouraging "free riding"; and, at least initially, it insured all creditors of the banks, rather than just depositors and noteholders.[8] Although the safety fund apparently was capable of protecting investors against the occasional failures of individual banks, it proved insufficient to deal with the widespread bank collapses of the late 1830s. The state government had to contribute nearly $1 million to make up the difference between the fund's obligations and its resources.[9] The safety fund did not fully repay its obligations until 1866. Indiana, Ohio, and Iowa established more successful systems.[10]

State Bank Instability and Its Consequences

Left to themselves, most state banking systems had serious weaknesses. Regulation varied greatly between states. Since most banks were small (many states forbade branch banking) and made most of their loans in the immediate vicinity, their solvency was closely linked to the health of the local economy. If local business was bad, the banks that served it would be forced to suspend payment or fail.

The entire U.S. banking system was unstable because there was no dependable source of additional reserves for the entire system. If enough people began to fear that their banknotes or checking deposits could not be converted into specie, the ensuing bank run would invariably prove them correct.

Banks faced difficult choices in responding to each others' requests for aid. It was risky for any bank to loan to another institution facing a run. To be effective, such loans had to be large. If such a loan allowed the other bank to meet its depositors' demands, well and good. If not, there was a strong likelihood that one bank's failure might spark runs on others, which would have to face them with depleted reserves.

Nevertheless, antebellum banks' inability to maintain the convertibility of their obligations was not always as catastrophic as this later became. If it appeared that the bank would be able to redeem its obligations at face value after it had time to sell some of its assets or call in loans, its notes and checks drawn on it would continue to be accepted, but at a discount. In this case, the bank had "suspended payment"; it was not redeeming its assets in specie. In "panics," all the banks in a region or even in the country might suspend payment, and specie would either disappear from circulation or command a premium over paper money.[11]

Without regulation, private, profit-seeking banks have a tendency to accentuate macroeconomic instability, to feed booms, and starve depressions. When business conditions are good, it is easy to find borrowers willing to pay high interest rates and offer good security. Consequently, additional bank loans may increase the money supply when full employment limits the economy's ability to increase real output, causing inflation. In bad

---

[8] I am indebted to Professors Thomas Ulem and Kenneth Ng, respectively, for this information.
[9] R. Robertson, *History of the American Economy*, 3d ed. (New York: Harcourt Brace Jovanovich, 1973), 180–181.
[10] Calomiris, "Deposit Insurance."

[11] Temin, *The Jacksonian Economy* (New York: Norton, 1969), 114–118.

times, each bank may wish to call in existing loans and make few new ones, because interest rates are low and risks high. Again, what makes sense for one bank may worsen the downturn when all banks follow the same practice. The record of growth and price changes over 1815–1860, however, does not indicate that these tendencies caused major difficulties for the American economy.

The Central Bank Concept

Central banks attempt to restrict private banks' destabilizing tendencies. The proper function of a central bank is not to make profits, but to regulate the money supply to insure that it does not contribute to macroeconomic instability. Ideally, central banks attempt to prevent rapid changes in the money supply, which tend to contribute to inflation or recession. Their main devices for this purpose are control over private banks' reserves and the ability to change them. Central banks often provide other services that aid the smooth functioning of the financial sector. They serve as government depositories and disbursing agencies and perform clearinghouse functions for the settlement of interbank debts. These institutions also transfer funds from one region to another and oversee international finance, whether under a gold standard or not. In the early nineteenth century, no nation had fully developed the central bank concept or devised mechanisms for carrying them out, but the United States had two banks with some central-bank characteristics.

THE BANKS OF THE UNITED STATES

In 1791, Congress had granted a federal charter to the first Bank of the United States. This institution was unique among American banks of its era because it had a number of branches and did business throughout the country. Because of this and its position as a government depository, the first Bank of the United States could return notes of other banks deposited with it for prompt collection. While this may have made currency values more uniform, it also restricted the lending of other, smaller banks, which did not endear it to them. It was a bone of contention between Hamilton and Jefferson, and its stock was largely owned by foreigners. Its charter expired in 1811, and the bill to extend it failed by a single vote.[12]

Origins of the Second Bank of the United States

The government's efforts to finance the War of 1812 were hampered by the lack of a large institution from which to borrow or use as an intermediary, so an attempt was made to establish one. In 1816, just too late for the war, Congress granted a charter to the second Bank of the United States, with much the same privileges and structure as its namesake had enjoyed. The bank was intended to aid the sale of government bonds for war finance. Bank stock could be purchased with bonds, and because the bank was expected to be profitable, it did increase bond sales.[13] The federal government contributed one-fifth of the bank's total capital of $35 million and appointed one-fifth of the bank's directors. The capital was an enormous sum for 1816, and only one-fourth of the privately subscribed capital was paid in specie. The bank was headquartered in Philadelphia, then the country's financial center, and had branches in all regions of the United States. It served as the federal government's depository, receiving all payments to

---

[12] S. Lee and P. Passell, *A New Economic View of American History* (New York: Norton, 1979), 112–113.
[13] C. Nettels, *The Emergence of a National Economy, 1775–1815* (New York: Harper & Row, 1962), 335, 340.

the government and handling many disbursals as well. The Bank of the United States also accepted deposits and made loans (issuing both checking accounts and its own notes) like any commercial bank. First and foremost, it was a profit-seeking private business dedicated to increasing its owners' incomes.[14]

The second Bank of the United States was much larger than any other bank in America. It also followed more conservative lending practices than other banks. Its reserves were large in relation to those of other banks. Because the Bank of the United States was a government depository, tax and tariff payments and the proceeds of land sales, usually in the form of notes issued by state banks, flowed into its vaults. Its own policies and its position as the government's depository ensured that the Bank of the United States consistently accumulated more obligations of other banks than those institutions did Bank of the United States liabilities.

The bank's start was inauspicious. Its first president was incompetent, and the second agreed to an accommodation with state banks from which the Bank of the United States was able to extricate itself only by a drastic and highly unpopular credit contraction. Fortunately, at least for the short run, in 1823 the bank came under the direction of Nicholas Biddle.[15] Under Biddle's presidency, the Bank of the United States assumed a role in which some scholars see central-bank characteristics.

Overseer of State Banks

The Bank of the United States began to use its position as a net creditor of the state banks (private bank corporations chartered by the states) to control their note issues. As it accumulated the notes of other banks, it returned them for payment in specie or its own notes. Its branches allowed it to transfer funds from one part of the country to another with far greater speed than was possible through alternative institutions. The state banks could do little about this policy; they could not prevent the use of their own notes for tax payments if they were to be acceptable at all.

Because of this policy, the state banks were forced to limit their note issues in relation to their reserves. They now had to anticipate that their notes might be returned to them rapidly even if they had been issued far from the bank. If they could obtain Bank of the United States notes, the state banks could return these instead of specie. However, the conservative lending policies of the large bank made its notes scarce. Because its reserves were so large, the notes were as expensive as specie. State banks had little choice but to hold larger reserves and reduce their loans.

An Unpopular Policy Bears Fruit

The Bank of the United States had many enemies. Bankers who had lost income and advocates of "cheap money" disliked it for purely economic reasons. But once the Bank's policy became effective, the notes of most banks circulated at close to their face value throughout the country. Prior to this, New England banks' currency had been accepted at par (face value), and this was only slightly less true for that of Mid-Atlantic states' banks. But the currency of Kentucky, Tennessee, and Alabama banks was accepted at 75 percent of its face value or even less. During the 1820s, this discount fell to no more than 5 percent.[16] State bank notes were now "a good traded in all markets," the classic definition of a medium of exchange. People conducting business far from home no longer had the difficulty and danger of carrying specie or suffering uncertainty about the exchange rate of regional currency.

---

[14] Temin, *Jacksonian Economy*, Chap. 1.
[15] Temin, *Jacksonian Economy*, 46–49.
[16] Temin, *Jacksonian Economy*, 48–50.

Was the Second Bank of the United States a Central Bank?

With its large reserves, the Bank of the United States could also function as a source of emergency reserves for state banks, as the "lender of last resort" that the American banking system had lacked. However, its performance in that role fell well short of the central-bank ideal. It did make specie loans to state banks that were in temporary difficulties, but the Bank of the United States loaned with an eye on its own reserve position and prospective profits as well as state banks' needs and the effects its actions had on the economy. Moreover, it sometimes acquired reserves to meet a crisis by selling bonds to the public for specie—a process that in itself reduced the money supply. This was the exact opposite of modern central-bank practice. Nor would it expand its loans sufficiently to become a net debtor to the state banks.[17] These were not classic central-bank operations.

As a result, the second Bank of the United States was able to regulate the quality of money (its convertibility into coin), and to exert some downward pressure on state banks' expansion ratios. By relaxing its practice of returning state banks' notes to them, it could, in effect, loan to these institutions, but apparently did not do so. However, its policies were ill-suited to lender-of-last-resort functions in a widespread banking crisis. Since the bank could not control the amount of reserves held by state banks, it could not expand the money supply. Nor could it contract the amount of bank money in circulation if state banks had ample hard-money reserves. In sum, the Second Bank of the United States could not fulfill the primary role of a modern central bank; it could not, in most circumstances, control the

money supply.[18] Its influence was nevertheless beneficial. The stability and efficiency of the American banking system were improved by its policies. The result was that banking became an aid rather than a hindrance to regional trade and specialization.

THE BANK WAR

In 1832, President Andrew Jackson vetoed an attempt to renew the federal charter of the Bank of the United States. Jackson's action apparently could have sprung from any or all of a long list of motives: his own dislike of banks, centers of private power, and Nicholas Biddle himself; considerations based on partisan politics; and some very confused economic analysis. When Jackson was overwhelmingly reelected after his veto, the bank's special relationship with the federal government was clearly at an end.

The "Pet Banks"

Although the Bank of the United States obtained a Pennsylvania charter and continued to operate until 1841, federal deposits were withdrawn and placed in banks owned by Jackson's political allies, the "pet banks."[19] After the Panic of 1837, in which the government lost much of the money deposited in such banks, government funds were kept in an independent treasury system. The federal government, it was decided, would avoid such losses in the future by collecting, holding, and disbursing all its own funds. Moreover, in 1836 the government refused to deal in bank money. The Specie Circular of that year an-

---

[17] Temin, *Jacksonian Economy*, 55.

[18] Temin, *Jacksonian Economy*, 50–54.

[19] The identity of the "pet banks'" owners is in some dispute. See H. Scheiber, "The Pet Banks in Jacksonian Politics and Finance, 1831–1841," *Journal of Economic History* (June 1963).

■ A number of nineteenth-century Americans held strong opinions about government debt.
Source: Culver Pictures.

nounced that henceforth only gold and silver would be accepted in payment of obligations (chiefly land, tariff, and tax payments) to the government.

The Distribution of the Federal Surplus

Another program not directly related to the demise of the Bank of the United States has been alleged to have affected the banking system. For most years after 1815, the federal government's budget had been in surplus. The excess of receipts over expenditures had been used to pay off the national debt. However, in 1835 the debt had been completely retired, and the accumulating surplus had grown embarrassingly large. Twenty-eight million dollars in federal surplus funds were distributed to the states in 1837. The panic of that year ended the program; trade and tariff revenues

were so diminished by the slump that the government had no further surplus to distribute.[20]

Economic Instability

Shortly after the veto of the Recharter Bill and during the other policies' implementation, economic affairs in the United States deteriorated sharply. After the government began to reduce its deposits with the Bank of the United States, there was a sharp credit contraction, possibly due to the bank's response (or overresponse) to the loss of government funds. In 1835 prices began to increase rapidly. A massive boom occurred, fueled by high crop prices and the resultant market in western lands. By 1837, prices were nearly one-third higher than they had been only two years previously. A

---

[20] Temin, *Jacksonian Economy*, 129.

severe panic with widespread bank failures developed, and after an unsteady recovery in 1838 and early 1839, an intensified slump began. Full recovery did not occur until 1843.

The Role of the Bank of the United States

To what extent were these events linked to the end of the Bank of the United States' control over state banks? Some scholars saw a clear causal chain. The termination of the bank's special relationship with the federal government removed the only restraint on state banks. Lacking the control of the Bank of the United States, the state banks expanded the money supply far beyond the safe limits of their reserves. The boom-time atmosphere encouraged speculation, particularly in land. This, plus the reckless monetary expansion, caused inflation. But the reserves of the state banks were not large enough to support the claims on them, and the situation was ripe for collapse. The final straw was the distribution of the federal surplus, which moved specie from the conservatively managed banks of the East and placed it in reckless western banks. They responded to this windfall by increasing their loans and hence the money supply still further. When the Specie Circular drew much of what little coin remained out of circulation, a banking collapse became inevitable.

This is what might be expected if a central bank's controls were removed suddenly because the proponents of monetary expansion found them too limiting. However, the monetary history of the late 1830s is now thought to be related far more to events taking place beyond U.S. borders than to President Jackson's attack on the Bank of the United States, misguided though that may have been. In particular, Jackson's ancient enemies, the British, played a larger role in the American inflation and the depression of 1839–1843 than did developments within the U.S. economy. British

actions were based on Far Eastern trade and the domestic harvest.

An Increased Money Supply

Inflation, as always, was a consequence of rapid monetary expansion; the money supply rose sharply between 1834 and 1836. As indicated in Table 8.1, prices rose by over 25 percent in that period. But the expansion in the money supply was not caused by an increase in banks' willingness to loan against given amounts of reserves (a rise in the expansion ratio). The ratios of reserves to bank money and of specie to all money did not fall. Moreover, reserve ratios were higher, not lower, in western banks than they were in the East (see Tables 8.2 and 8.3). Banks increased their loans and the money supply, but they did so on the basis of larger specie reserves.

The silver came from Mexico, where it was a commodity export. Furthermore, Mexican silver was being driven out of domestic circulation by the monetary policies of the Santa Ana regime. More silver came from Europe; British investors bought U.S. securities and France paid a war indemnity. Interest rates were higher in the United States than in Britain, and investment funds flowed to America as a result. Previously, much of the specie entering the United States had been used to finance trade with China, but now conditions in that trade changed.

Tea and Silver

Americans had long desired Chinese tea, silk, and porcelain, but the Chinese preferred silver to most American goods. However, in the 1830s the Chinese began to buy large quantities of opium from British India (and smaller quantities that Americans brought from Turkey). To pay for the opium, the Chinese wanted credit in London, rather than silver. American traders could now finance their purchases in China with drafts on London bank-

Table 8.2   Reserve Ratios of State Banks by Region, 1834–1837*

End-of-Year Treasury Data	New England	Middle Atlantic	Southeast	Southwest	Northwest
1834	.06	.22	.24	.13	.46
1835	.07	.16	.21	.15	.28
1836	.07	.14	.18	.14	.30
1837	.09	.19	.24	.13	.32
Van Fenstermaker's Data					
1834	.10	.21	.26	.21	.39
1835	.11	.16	.25	.17	.27
1836	.10	.16	.20	.13	.31
1837	.12	.26	.24	.13	.36

* Reserve ratios are the ratios of bank reserves to notes outstanding and demand deposits (current liabilities).
Source: P. Temin, *The Jacksonian Economy* (New York: Norton, 1969), 75.

ers. The Chinese used this credit to pay their drug bills.[21] While the British were buying large quantities of American securities and cotton, Americans had no difficulty in obtaining advances from London.

The silver that had formerly flowed to China now remained in the United States; the other developments noted previously increased the specie flow to this country. Part of the silver naturally found its way into bank reserves, and banks thereupon expanded their loans. There was a large, if incidental, British role in the decline after mid-1837 as well. The British increased their grain imports after a series of poor harvests, and their balance of trade deteriorated. Specie flowed out of Britain, and to prevent further loss of reserves, the Bank of England sharply restricted credit. Interest rates rose in Britain, offering better alternatives to foreign investment, and the British demand for American cotton also fell.

The Panic of 1837

The 1835–1837 expansion in the United States had been largely based on the boom in cotton production, and a major proportion of bank loans were linked to cotton in one way or another. When cotton brokers and the banks with which they dealt began to fail, runs on banks spread throughout the country. Twenty-three percent of all American banks failed, and many others suspended payment. The money supply fell by 34 percent from 1839 to 1843.[22] The surplus distribution and the Specie Circular apparently were only minimal influences on the situation. Transfer of specie from eastern banks did not cause them to fear for the adequacy of their reserves. Indeed, some eastern banks proposed to ship specie to England after the surplus distribution.[23] Given the pattern of reserve ratios indicated by Table 8.2, specie movements were

---

[21] Temin, *Jacksonian Economy*, 79–82.

[22] Temin, *Jacksonian Economy*, 157.
[23] Temin, *Jacksonian Economy*, 135.

Table 8.3 The Supply of Money and Its Determinants, 1820–1839

End of Year	Money (Millions)	Annual Rate of Change	Specie (Millions)	Reserve Ratio	Percentage of Money Held as Specie
1820	$85	—	$41	32%	24%
1821	96	12.4%	39	30	16
1822	81	−15.6	32	21	23
1823	88	8.6	31	25	15
1824	88	0.0	32	27	13
1825	106	20.5	29	19	10
1826	108	1.9	32	20	12
1827	101	−6.5	32	20	14
1828	114	12.9	31	18	11
1829	105	−7.9	33	22	12
1830	114	7.9	32	23	6
1831	155	36.0	30	15	5
1832	150	−3.2	31	16	5
1833	168	12.0	41	18	8
1834	172	2.4	51	27	4
1835	246	43.0	65	18	10
1836	276	12.2	73	16	13
1837	232	−19.0	88	20	23
1838	240	3.4	87	23	18
1839	215	−10.4	83	20	23

Source: P. Temin, *The Jacksonian Economy* (New York: Norton, 1969), 71.

toward regions where banks had high, rather than low, reserve ratios.

If the Specie Circular had any effect at all, it caused a flow of specie (potential bank reserves) into land purchases. But land purchases would reduce inflationary pressures rather than increase them. Given the huge acreage available, land prices were unlikely to rise, and the money devoted to land acquisition would be withheld from further circulation by the Treasury.

Had the second Bank of the United States retained in 1837 all the powers it possessed in 1832, events would not have turned out very differently—at least if its policies had resembled those employed before the withdrawal of government funds. The bank clearly could not have prevented an increase in the money supply based on a more-than-proportionate expansion of reserves Thus, it could not have prevented the inflation. Both British foreign lending and foreign policy, to say nothing of the British harvest, were beyond the Bank of the United States' control. The Bank of England's reaction to a gold outflow was a long-established policy. The demise of the second Bank of the United States did have domestic repercussions. In some states, regulations were to be still further eased before new and more effective rules were developed.

THE FREE BANKING ERA

In 1838, Michigan and New York passed laws that greatly eased the restrictions imposed on would-be bankers. No longer were new banks in these states required to obtain individual charters from the legislature, with at least some chance of scrutiny of their proposals. Instead, the deposit of approved securities of a stated face value with the state's banking officials and the observation of a few basic regulations entitled any individual or group to enter the banking business. Other states instituted their own "free banking" laws, and the number of state banks rose from 691 in 1843 to 1,520 in 1860.[24]

A Colorful History

State regulations often were not well designed, and enforcement might be lax. These conditions gave rise to some spectacular evasions of the basic financial responsibilities associated with banks. However, it now appears that some of the colorful tales about antebellum banking have survived precisely because the events described were unusual even when they occurred. Nevertheless, the stories are worth repeating.

The bonds of some states, particularly in the early 1840s, were all but worthless because the states were paying neither interest nor principal on them. (See Chapter 5.) But some "free banking" laws did not exclude such securities from those eligible for deposit with the state as surety for banks' performance. Unscrupulous individuals might put up only enough cash to allow the bank to acquire these "assets." The state might then allow the bank to begin operations, whereupon the bank's owners would print notes and begin to make

loans. The first loans might be to the bank's own stockholders, who sometimes used the proceeds to complete payments on their bank stock. Such a bank would have no real reserves—or even assets. Its success depended on receiving deposits or loan repayments in something other than its own currency.

"Wildcat Banks"

Some banks were called "wildcat banks" because they were located where there were "more wildcats than people." Another favorite location was among Indians whose pacification was uncertain. Like other banks, wildcat banks employed guards, but, in this case, the guards' duty was to discourage customers, not robbers, from attempting to make withdrawals. Failure rates among such banks were very high, and they affected customers as well as the banks' owners. People who were left holding the notes of failed banks found that the currency was now worthless, but their loans still had to be repaid, often to some distant financier to whom the bankers had sold them. One group of bank promoters had the audacity to note (as a selling point!) that 13 of the 27 banks they had already organized were still in business. In fairness, their rivals had experienced 41 failures in 43 tries.[25] Actually, although free banks' failure rates were above the norm for all banks, most failed free banks redeemed their notes, usually at their face value.[26]

Despite such tales, wildcat banking was not the norm, even on the frontier, as Table 8.2 indicates. Such practices became less prevalent as time passed. By 1860, both bankers and regulators knew that banks should keep reserves against all liabilities, not capital or merely their note liabilities. The enforcement of regulation improved, and some states

---

[24] Bureau of the Census, *Historical Statistics*, 1:1020.

[25] Hammond, "Banking."

[26] R. Rolnick and W. Weber, "New Evidence on the Free Banking Era," *American Economic Review* (December 1983).

provided for periodic examinations. Macroeconomic evidence strongly reinforces the conclusions of several modern studies that wildcat banking—or even all "free banking"—wreaked no serious damage on the aggregate economy. Economic growth was rapid over the 1843–1860 heyday of free banking, even in activities heavily dependent on bank financing. Prices changed considerably in this era, with an upward trend after 1848, but inflation appears to spring largely from the California gold rush, whose product raised bank reserves, rather than actions whose origins were within the banks themselves. The high reserve ratios of western banks are not entirely a reflection of unusual prudence; small banks have greater risks from any individual loan, and risks on the frontier were, in general, higher. Nevertheless, the evidence does not support the usual impression of high-risk or totally heedless frontier bankers.[27]

Currency Chaos

The demise of the second Bank of the United States left the country without a uniform national currency. In addition, there was now no agency as effective as the Bank of the United States to maintain the convertibility of state banks' notes. After 1836, virtually the only money accepted at its face value in all regions of the United States was gold and silver coin. The problem was not a lack of other types of money, but an overabundance. By 1860, the 1,500 banks in the United States had issued over 9,000 different types and denominations of notes that retained at least some value. There were many notes of failed banks and counterfeits in circulation as well.[28]

Persons offered unfamiliar currency in exchanges had several choices: The note could be refused, or its value could be determined either by bargaining with its current owner or by reference to one of the numerous bank note reference guides or "counterfeit detectors." These guides attempted to provide up-to-date information on the values of all notes in circulation and the latest discoveries of counterfeits. Some of these lists were remarkably comprehensive, but their information could never be either complete or current. Completed transactions required agreement on two sets of prices: first, that of the goods in "standard" money, and second, the value of the money involved relative to that standard.

The Burden of State Bank Currency

Traditionally, money has been considered to serve three functions: a medium of exchange, a store of value, and a standard of deferred payment. State banks' currency performed imperfectly in all these areas. Further, resources devoted to offsetting the disadvantages of such currency had alternative uses. But the damage to aggregate economic activity was not great; one study has estimated that social savings derived from the use of inferior paper money rather than specie declined by from one-tenth to one-hundredth of 1 percent of gross national product.[29] The cost resulting from impaired medium-of-exchange functions (including the time lost determining currency values) was almost certainly greater. But imperfect as they were, the responses Americans devised were effective, and the macroeconomic impact of the "rag bag" antebellum currency, while adverse, was not large.

[27] H. Rockoff, "Money, Prices and Banks in the Jacksonian Era," in Fogel and Engerman, *The Reinterpretation of American Economic History* (New York: Harper & Row, 1971), and "Varieties of Banking and Regional Economic Development in the United States, 1830–1860," *Journal of Economic History* (March 1975).
[28] Robertson, *History*, 192–193.

[29] M. Shuska, "The Antebellum Money Market and the Impact of the Bank War," *Journal of Economic History* (December 1976), and S. Engerman, "A Note on the Consequences of the Second Bank of the United States," *Journal of Political Economy* (July/August, 1970). The conclusions of Rolnick and Weber, "New Evidence" are similar.

Small Banks' Defensive Measures

The banking system as a whole was unstable, as indicated by bank failures and the erratic courses of the money supply and price levels. One effort to improve the stability of small banks was only partially successful. As noted earlier, banks sacrifice interest income by keeping large reserve balances in their vaults, but they sacrifice stability if their reserves are reduced. Small-town banks began to maintain some reserves in the form of checking deposits with banks in larger cities. The city banks in turn kept a portion of their reserves in deposits with banks in New York City. In normal times, if any individual bank foresaw an outflow of specie, it could obtain more coin quickly and easily by requesting funds from the bank holding its reserve deposit. Such deposits also facilitated clearance of interbank debts and they earned interest.

Continuing Instability

Unfortunately, the pyramiding of reserves in New York banks was an effective response from the viewpoint of individual banks, not the entire banking system. When many country banks demanded the funds they had on deposit in larger cities, the system might break down. The problem was that all the banks involved were private, profit-maximizing businesses, and no such bank was willing to hold large amounts of reserves that did not generate income. New York banks recognized that correspondent banks might suddenly request large withdrawals, so the investments to which such funds were devoted had to be highly liquid. Consequently, they lent the money "on call," which meant that the loans were repayable within 24 hours on the lender's request. Only borrowers who could convert assets into cash on such short notice would borrow under these terms. One such group was securities brokers. Further safety was derived from restricting the loans to a fraction (usually no more than one-half) of the value of the securities that they helped to purchase. Such loans appeared both safe and liquid.

Although any individual broker could count on selling securities for more than the amount owed the banks under such conditions, all brokers combined could not. If many brokers attempted to sell at the same time, securities prices might fall so far that the sale proceeds might not cover the loans. Even without broker defaults, the sudden decline in securities values might increase pressure on the banking system as a whole. Since it was known that banks invested in securities as well as loans, depositors and noteholders became uneasy when the news from New York or other money markets was bad.

MONEY-SUPPLY CHANGES AND THE ECONOMY

Today, there is widespread agreement among economists that the initial effect of a decline in the money supply or even of a sizable reduction in its growth rate would be a drop in real economic activity, that is, in production and employment. Recent history confirms this view, as witness the record from 1981 to 1983. While there might be disagreement over the time elapsing between cause and effect, most would agree that one to two years would have to pass under modern conditions before prices fell sufficiently to allow real output to recover. But through the nineteenth century, these conditions did not hold. First, the structure of the economy was different; most Americans were self-employed farmers who would feel the decline chiefly as a drop in prices received for their crops. (Most farms consumed a large proportion of their own output of foodstuffs.) The total amount of unemployment caused by a monetary contraction would be small in the farm sector. Although the impact would be greater among merchants, the manufacturing sector, and, of course, banks, these groups comprised a much smaller portion of the labor force than they do today.

Even where unemployment occurred, a variety of factors limited its duration. Joblessness might be severe among manufacturing workers and bankruptcies widespread among their employers, but price reductions were both quicker and more general than would be the case today. A worker with no savings and a family to support might have no alternative but to accept a cut in money wages, but the general reduction in prices would mean that his standard of living might not decline in proportion to the wage cut. If real wages did decline, wages are a price to employers, and this would increase employment. Flexible prices thus made the effects of monetary contractions both less and shorter than might be the case today.

FINANCE

Any economic activity in which time elapses between the start of production and final consumption involves financial considerations. Someone must forego the use of resources while they are being processed, transported, or held in inventories. If people are to continue to do so, and even more, to invest in capital goods whose returns are deferred, some form of compensation must be available. In addition, many people wish to consume more than their current incomes will permit. If they are to borrow, those lending to them will have to be paid for allowing others to use their funds. Finally, since the resources involved are scarce—they have alternative uses—some mechanism must be developed and employed to direct resources to the uses in which they produce more than their opportunity costs if incomes are to be maximized.

Banks as Sources of Capital

Commercial banks are imperfect devices for meeting some of the financial needs of new industries. Banks are better suited to providing loans for short-term working capital than they are to financing long-term projects. This holds with particular force where banks are small and local, as they were in the antebellum United States. Financing a railroad or factory involved the commitment of large sums for long periods. The payoff from such investments was likely to be spread over many years. Only a few loans of this type would be enough to tie up a large portion of a small bank's assets. Thus, the failure of any single such project might ruin the bank as well. Worse, commercial banks' liabilities tend to be short term; depositors are entitled to their funds on demand or in a short time after requesting them. Particularly where there is no source of emergency funds for banks, investments in fixed capital are not liquid; they cannot readily be sold at short notice. Hence, long-term loans involve high risks for commercial banks.

Early Capital Markets

In the early nineteenth century there were few sources of long-term capital loans other than personal relationships between borrower and lender. When the capital requirements of essential projects exceeded the resources of local merchant communities, the only alternative source of capital was government; the credit and taxing powers of state and local governments were frequently enlisted to raise funds for canal construction. Often, as previously discussed (Chapter 5), such methods of fund raising suffered from the lack of a market test.

Particularly in eastern cities, the tightly knit social structure of wealthy merchants who were invariably well acquainted and often related eased the problems of raising large sums. Nevertheless, the lack of an effective allocative mechanism for the entire economy limited capitalists' choices of investments. New England witnessed a notable redirection of activity from maritime ventures to manufacturing over the antebellum period, and by the 1850s New England funds were used to build railroads in that region and elsewhere. However, the reliance on local sources of investment capital and the necessity of combining the savings of many individuals in other parts of the country often resulted in high capital costs and an overemphasis on local projects that might not offer rates of return available on alternative investments.

Many early industrialists appear to have spent as much time searching for financial support as in producing and selling their goods. They obtained funds from friends and relatives, used the trust funds of widows, orphans, and churches, and demanded payment with orders rather than on delivery of products. Short-term bank loans might be taken out with an understanding that these would be continuously renewed. Nor were some would-be industrialists above marrying for money. Somehow, however, the necessary capital was generated.[30] The portion of income invested in the antebellum economy rose, and there were signs that the allocation of savings was becoming more efficient. These developments began on a local or regional basis, originating in Massachusetts even prior to 1800.[31] New legal concepts were required to make debts transferrable, and new institutions had to be developed to facilitate the reallocation of savings from agriculture to industry and transportation.

---

[30] L. Davis, "The New England Textile Mills and the Capital Market: A Study in Industrial Borrowing," *Journal of Economic History* (March 1960).
[31] W. Rothenberg, "The Emergence of a Capital Market in Rural Massachusetts, 1730–1838," *Journal of Economic History* (December 1985).

The Local Bias

The Massachusetts developments had by no means become universal by 1860. There was nothing resembling a national capital market by that date. Interest rates even in well-developed local markets, such as Boston and New York, diverged as often as they converged, and higher interest rates in the capital-starved West did not attract significant eastern investment until late in the period. Few people were willing to invest in projects outside their own communities or in those directed by persons they did not know personally. One Baltimore bank refused the loan application of a firm nine miles distant saying, "We know nothing of business conditions in the West."

The Rise of New Financial Institutions

Institutions that remedied some of these deficiencies were developed and utilized. By 1860, about half the states provided for general incorporation through laws granting charters on petition rather than by legislative approval of each application. Incorporation made pooling the funds of many investors easier, but many of its modern advantages were not yet fully realized. Corporate stock was sold almost exclusively to the same groups of lenders who had provided funds earlier, and was rarely traded. Stock exchanges appeared in most large cities, but they dealt largely in government bonds and, after 1850, in railroad bonds. Financial markets were very thin, with few securities changing hands each day, and price fluctuations were extreme. Prior to the Civil War, corporate stock other than that of the railroads was not sold on the stock exchanges.

The lack of large-scale financial institutions was not the barrier to formation of industrial capital that it might appear from a modern view. In most manufacturing industries, the scale of efficient production was small, and adequate capital could generally be raised by individuals or partnerships. As industry developed, firms' retained earnings became the chief source of additional capital; the rate of reinvestment was very high.

Savings Banks and Insurance Companies

Institutions suited to long-term lending had appeared by 1860, but most were still in their infancy. Savings banks and insurance companies were able to make long-term loans because they could count on retaining funds deposited with them for considerable periods. They pooled the funds of many savers and developed comprehensive knowledge of investment opportunities, reducing capital costs to investors and improving allocation. Both were capable of making large loans. These financial intermediaries operated in the East; they had little impact on western capital markets. As the importance of foreign trade waned and the institutions conducting it changed their fields of operation, trade credit from English merchants became less important than it had been in colonial days. Other forms of foreign investment achieved a new importance that will be discussed later in this chapter.

Southern Financial Institutions

In the South, capital mobility may have developed much further than formal market institutions would indicate. Capital in the form of slaves migrated with its planter owners to the rich lands of the New South. There was also some development of the inter-regional slave trade, although the extent is controversial. Working capital was provided to planters by cotton factors, specialized merchants who bought the crop from planters and sold it to British and New England textile firms. The cotton factors also provided loans and other services, sometimes on the security of next year's crop, obtaining their funds from En-

gland. Factors either bought cotton outright or sold it for planters on commission. They purchased supplies for planters with the proceeds. Planters and a network of retail and wholesale merchants collected the cotton produced by small farmers and retailed manufactured goods and other items to them.

INTERNAL COMMERCE

The Rise of the Middleman

As specialization spread from agriculture to manufacturing and then throughout the economy, the role of middlemen assumed greater importance. Specialized production gave rise to specialized distribution as markets grew and diversified. By 1860, there were people who handled only one or two distribution functions or dealt in a narrow range of items. During the colonial period, true distribution specialists had existed only for the major export crops, and most distribution functions were handled by the original producers. New opportunities appeared for warehousemen, draymen, salesmen, bookkeepers, clerks, and others, especially after 1820.

In colonial times, only the largest cities had markets sufficient to support stores selling less than the total range of imported goods. In the nineteenth century, population and incomes had grown, and urban populations were a larger portion of the total. The variety of items available was much greater than in the colonial period, and output came from larger numbers of producers. Incomes were now sufficient to allow some discretionary spending; consumers had something left after providing for basic food, shelter, and clothing. Because the technology of information gathering and transmission had changed little from the colonial era through the early 1840s, the initial

■ The cotton buyer was the intermediary between the cotton farmer and the manufacturer of cotton cloth. *Source:* The Bettmann Archive.

response came through increased specialization and increases in the numbers of middlemen that more or less paralleled the rise in the volume of business.[32]

---

[32] Chandler, *The Visible Hand: The Managerial Revolution in American Business* (Cambridge, Mass.: Harvard University Press, 1977), 48–49.

The General Store

The general store was still much in evidence in rural areas and the smaller towns, but even that hallowed institution was beginning to recognize that consumers had wider alternatives than previously. Commodity dealers, who bought wheat directly from the farmers and who utilized grain elevators, organized exchanges, grading procedures, and other

■ Land speculators often conducted business in the local general store.
Source: H. Armstrong Roberts.

new institutions, began to supplement sales to the general store in the 1850s.[33] Even frontier merchants now began to see the wisdom in viewing samples of goods before they bought, since customers who received cash for their crops were less tied to one store and the credit of its owner.

The Rise of Mass Markets

The attitudes of American consumers toward new products raised the returns garnered by those dealing in new commodities. Rising incomes allowed people to buy larger quantities

of the goods they had always purchased, but more importantly, it appeared that American consumers were interested in variety, in new items that made life different from what people had always known. In addition, as Chapter 7 indicated, production of many items now moved from the home—or from home finishing—to factory. Style and quality of finish became more important than in the days when few people bought more than staple foods, cloth, and tools. Competition became a real factor in many local markets as market size grew faster than the scale of production and distribution, and transportation broadened the choices of both consumers and individual producers.

---

[33] Chandler, *The Visible Hand*, 209–215.

New technology had increased the ability to produce, and it was soon apparent that new methods were at least equally necessary to distribute the increase in output. It became increasingly difficult to dispose of factories' entire output, especially of finished goods, by direct sale in local markets. As producers specialized, for example, in gingham rather than cotton cloth, this point gained additional importance. Marketing became vital to the success of producers whereas only a few decades before they could assume that if they could obtain financing and manage physical production, markets for their output could be taken for granted.

New Methods of Distribution

One marketing method was to sell through a commission merchant, who found retail outlets for the firm's production and received a percentage of the revenue they generated. Commission merchants did not take title to the goods they sold, leaving inventory financing to producers. Some producers sold their goods at auction.

Such methods did not answer all distribution needs. Commission merchants could not pay producers until they had sold the goods, and retailers often ordered far less than the quantity commission merchants had available. Later, jobbers intervened between commission merchants and retailers. Jobbers actually owned the goods they sold and were able to extend credit to retailers, with the assistance of bank loans. Jobbers also provided market information to producers, advising them about the characteristics that made goods sell. In turn, jobbers found information from the new credit-rating agencies useful. Few consumer goods were sold under brand names in the antebellum economy, and many wholesalers handled the output of several factories. Since few producers had experience in responding to consumers' wishes, marketing services were an important aid. Where markets were still small,

functions were less specialized; often large-scale retailers also served as wholesalers in selling to small-town merchants.[34]

FOREIGN TRADE

Foreign trade had been one of the two major sources of higher incomes and economic growth throughout previous American history. After 1815, however, the relative importance of foreign trade waned. Domestic substitutes appeared for many of the items previously obtainable only from overseas sources. As Table 8.4 reveals, the volume of foreign commerce increased, but the rest of the economy grew faster.

Changing Trade Patterns

The United States had traditionally exported raw materials to Europe in exchange for manufactured goods, a pattern that continued after 1815. But trade patterns were not static; cotton replaced tobacco and breadstuffs as the most important American export, and the balance of payments changed from that prevailing in the colonial era. In 1820, about three-fifths of U.S. exports were cotton, tobacco, and other crude materials. By 1860, crude materials comprised 68 percent of all exports, with cotton by far the largest single item. Manufactured items were only 6 percent of exports in 1820, but over 11 percent in 1860. In 1821, 56 percent of American imports were manufactured goods, and these still comprised 48 percent of the total in 1860. Britain was America's principal trading partner over the entire period, providing a market for one-third to one-half of all exports and supplying about two-fifths of all imports. Trade with other

---

[34] Chandler, *The Visible Hand*, Chap. 1.

Table 8.4 Foreign Trade, 1815–1860
(In Thousands of Dollars)

Year	Total Exports	Total Imports	U.S. Shipping Earnings (Net)	Net Capital Flows*	Net Debt	Specie Flows**	Dividends and Interest
1815	$52,558	$85,357	$20,600	$15,000	$94,000	$2,000	$5,000
1820	69,692	74,450	13,900	−1,000	86,700	0	4,807
1825	90,738	90,189	11,600	−7,000	80,300	−2,500	4,792
1830	71,671	62,721	10,500	−8,000	74,900	6,000	4,557
1835	115,216	139,499	8,800	30,000	158,100	7,000	7,042
1840	123,669	100,224	26,200	−31,000	266,400	0	11,888
1845	106,040	115,448	18,800	−4,000	213,000	−4,000	8,674
1850	144,376	180,450	8,600	29,000	222,100	3,000	13,326
1855	218,910	268,121	21,200	15,000	356,300	−53,000	22,320
1860	333,576	367,760	32,500	−7,000	379,200	−58,000	25,122

* Denotes an increased foreign purchase of U.S. securities if positive; American repurchase of U.S. securities held abroad if negative.
** Denotes imports of specie if positive; exports if negative.
Source: D. North, *The Economic Growth of the United States, 1790–1860* (Englewood Cliffs, N.J.: Prentice-Hall, 1961), 233–238, and U.S. Department of Commerce, Bureau of the Census, *Historical Statistics of the United States: Colonial Times to 1970*, 2 vols. (Washington, D.C.: Government Printing Office, 1975), 2:865–866.

nations of North and South America accounted for about 30 percent of imports through the period, but the identity of Western Hemisphere trade partners changed, with Canada, Mexico, and Brazil gaining at the expense of the traditional Caribbean trade.

Some new items became significant in American trade as others began to fade. In most years the United States imported more than it exported, just as it had from the late colonial period. Shipping earnings now offset a declining portion of the trade deficit. More and more American trade was carried by foreign ships, and freight rates fell.

The Importance of Foreign Investment

Foreign investment in the United States became an important component in the trade balance, with the exception of the early 1840s; some American imports were purchased by exports of securities. Never more than one-third as large as domestic investment, and usually far less, foreign capital was available in large amounts from Europe's more developed money markets at interest rates lower than those available in the United States, especially if the transactions cost of borrowing is included. In the case of repudiated securities, such as those of Mississippi, Pennsylvania, and Michigan, the costs actually incurred by Americans were very low indeed, because foreign investors were never repaid.

Foreigners were at least as willing to invest in the American West as were investors from the Atlantic Seaboard. Foreign funds, mainly from Britain, the Netherlands, and Germany, were invested in state bonds and railroad securities, allowing America to build its transportation system before domestically generated funds were available. The flow of dividends, interest, and principal to foreign owners of American capital increased with time. After 1850, two other factors contributed to the flow of money to Europe. The increased immigration of the previous decade generated a flow of remittances to the "Old Country." Often such payments became passage money for those still in Europe. And once the United States began to produce gold from its California mines, the yellow metal became a commodity export, another means of financing imports and paying for the services of foreign capital.

Tariffs

By the late 1850s, ocean freight rates were about one-fifth their 1815 levels, greatly reducing the delivered price of foreign goods. But by that time, Europe was no longer the only possible source of manufactured goods, and attitudes toward trade barriers had begun to change. As the physical barriers to foreign commerce were reduced, political obstacles replaced them. In 1816, Daniel Webster was a proponent of free trade, reflecting the views of his New England constituents—shipowners for whom the largest volume of trade maximized income. By the mid-1820s, Webster had become an advocate of tariff protection for his region's growing industry. John C. Calhoun, the great southern spokesman, opposed Webster on both occasions.

East versus South?
Attitudes toward tariffs have usually been presented as a contest between regional attitudes. The South, with its concentration on export crops and dependence on manufactured goods from other regions, supposedly favored free trade, which would raise the demand for its exports and reduce manufactured goods' prices either directly or by providing competition for Yankee industry. The East, and especially New England, was thought to be solidly pro-tariff after investment began to shift out of maritime activities. But an analysis

of congressional support for and opposition to tariffs reveals no such clear-cut regional divisions. Even the "Tariff of Abominations" over which South Carolina threatened secession in 1828 attracted majority or unanimous support from the congressmen of no less than seven Southern states. Massachusetts' delegation never gave majority support to any tariff proposal between 1812 and 1832, but Ohio congressmen supported each of these bills unanimously.[35]

Under generally poorly reasoned policies, tariffs were raised on all items in 1816. In the 1820s, duties on manufactured goods reached nearly prohibitive levels; in some cases, half the value of the imported goods. Initially, even goods that could not be produced in quantities sufficient to meet domestic demand were taxed together with items that competed with American products. After 1828, tariffs were gradually reduced to no more than 20 percent of the value of imports and more items were admitted duty-free. But no sooner had these levels been achieved in 1842 than they were increased in the next year. The 1846 Walker Tariff imposed import classification schedules, which levied different rates of duty on goods classified as luxuries, necessities, and raw materials. The Walker Tariff also reduced overall tariff rates to modestly protective levels again. (See Table 8.5.)

Tariff Fundamentals
The usual rationale for tariffs is that they encourage domestic production and thus provide jobs in the country that levies them. Tariffs may accomplish this, but only at the expense of employment in the country's exporting industries, since foreigners cannot buy unless they can also sell their own products. Generally, tariffs transfer resources from high- to low-productivity uses and reduce rather

---

[35] S. Lebergott, *The Americans: An Economic Record* (New York: Norton, 1984), 144–145.

Table 8.5   Tariff Rates and Proportion of Imports Subject to Duty

Year	Value of Imports for Consumption*			Rate of Duties Calculated to Total Imports		
	Total	Free	Dutiable	Duties Calculated	Free and Dutiable	Dutiable Only
1821	$44	$2	$22	$19	43.21%	45.0%
1825	66	4	63	32	47.72	50.54
1828	67	4	63	30	44.74	47.59
1830	50	4	46	28	57.32	61.69
1833	83	20	63	24	28.99	38.25
1835	122	58	64	26	21.25	40.38
1840	86	42	44	15	17.60	34.39
1845	106	16	90	31	29.34	34.45
1846	110	19	91	30	27.70	30.35
1850	164	16	148	40	24.50	27.14
1855	232	30	202	54	23.36	26.83
1860	336	68	268	53	15.67	19.67

* (Dollar values expressed in millions.)

Source: U.S. Department of Commerce, Bureau of the Census, *Historical Statistics of the United States: Colonial Times to 1970*, 2 vols. (Washington, D.C.: Government Printing Office, 1975), 2:888.

than raise the overall level of incomes. There may be one important exception. Protection for an industry in its early stages of existence may be economically justified if the tariff allows the domestic firms to gain skills and operating experience that allow them to compete successfully with foreign producers *in the absence* of tariff protection in the future.

The Impact of Tariffs

On balance, tariffs did little to encourage the growth of American industry. They probably did allow the survival of less efficient methods of production within the United States after free trade would have forced their elimination, for example, in the iron industry. There were few industries that owed their existence or formation to tariffs. Zevin, for example, found no significant effects from the tariff on domestic demand for cotton textiles from 1815

to 1833.[36] It is claimed that the demand for iron smelted with anthracite was sensitive to the price of competing imported British iron.[37] Since many American imports were mass-consumption goods, consumers paid for the tariff on such items.

The tariff generated over 90 percent of all the federal government's revenues in some years. Alternative sources of tax income would have had to be developed if tariffs were abandoned. A more cogent reason for the persistence of tariffs, then and now, was that the benefits of protection accrued to small, well-

[36] R. Zevin, "Cotton Textile Production After 1815," in Fogel and Engerman, *Reinterpretation*, 125–127. Lebergott, *The Americans*, 147–149, reaches similar conclusions.

[37] R. Fogel and S. Engerman, "A Model for the Explanation of Industrial Expansion During the 19th Century with an Application to the Antebellum Iron Industry," in *Reinterpretation*.

organized groups on whom monopoly power and profits were conferred, while the costs (greater in the aggregate) were borne by a much larger group, most of whom suffered only slight individual losses. This situation has always formed a political equation of formidable strength, and that was no less true in 1850 than it is in 1992.

Even though most economists would agree that there is some validity to the infant industry argument for tariffs, that defense does not appear very pertinent to the nineteenth-century United States. The argument presupposes that protection is only granted to those industries expected to outgrow the need for it, and that the government possesses both the foresight to recognize such potential and the forebearance to restrict protection to the groups that have it. Tariff protection was in fact granted for many other reasons and was seldom removed for purely economic considerations.

BUILDING A GROWTH INFRASTRUCTURE

Often we forget that economic growth entails much more than manufacturing, agriculture, and perhaps transportation. None of the sectors that produce or move physical commodities could function efficiently, if at all, without support from banking, finance, wholesaling, and retailing. As economic growth proceeds and the variety of goods produced increases, the volume of transactions grows more than in proportion, and the demand for specialized exchange services rises.

Initially, institutions that Europe had developed centuries earlier proved adequate for American needs. But with the increase in the volume and variety of production, the distances over which goods were transported, the reorientation to domestic markets, and the op-

portunities presented by improvements in transportation and communication, opportunities for new and better methods appeared. Americans were quick to grasp these. The innovations were particularly influential west of the Appalachians, where few entrenched proponents of older methods existed. Futures contracts, grading standards, credit agencies, and organized exchanges are not generally accorded prominent positions in economic history. Nevertheless, they may explain why Americans seemed to reap larger benefits from a pool of technology available to and largely developed by Europeans. The latter were less willing to transform the balance of their economies. America's human mobility and receptivity to new ideas may have contributed as much in the distribution sector as it did in factories and on farms.

SELECTED REFERENCES

Chandler, A., Jr. *The Visible Hand: The Managerial Revolution in American Business.* Cambridge, Mass.: Harvard University Press, 1977.

Davis, L., R. Easterlin, W. Parker et al. *American Economic Growth: An Economist's History of the United States,* New York: Harper & Row, 1972.

Fogel, R., and S. Engerman, eds. *The Reinterpretation of American Economic History.* New York: Harper & Row, 1971.

Hammond, B. *Banks and Politics in America from the Revolution to the Civil War.* Princeton, N.J.: Princeton University Press, 1957.

Kroos, H., and M. Blyn. *A History of Financial Intermediaries.* New York: Random House, 1971.

Nettels, C. *The Emergence of a National Economy, 1775–1815.* New York: Harper & Row, 1962.

North, D. *The Economic Growth of the United States, 1790–1860.* Englewood Cliffs, N.J.: Prentice-Hall, 1961.

Redlich, F. *The Molding of American Banking: Men and Ideas.* 2 vols. New York: Hafner, 1947, 1951.

Rockoff, H. *The Free Banking Era: A Reexamination.* New York: Arno Press, 1975

Studenski, P., and H. Kroos. *Financial History of the United States.* New York: McGraw-Hill, 1963.

Taussig, F. *Tariff History of the United States.* 7th ed. New York: G. Putnam's Sons, 1923.

Temin, P. *The Jacksonian Economy.* New York: Norton, 1969.

Timberlake, R. *Money, Banking, and Central Banking.* New York: Harper & Row, 1965.

U.S. Department of Commerce, Bureau of the Census. *Historical Statistics of the United States: Colonial Times to 1970.* 2 vols. Washington, D.C.: Government Printing Office, 1975.

INSTITUTIONS AND THE QUALITY OF LIFE

*T*his period, especially from 1820 to 1860, incorporates several contrasting developments. Per-capita incomes rose at a rate of 1.7 percent per year in the United States from 1820 to 1860,[1] and wages also increased. There is persuasive evidence that real prices of many manufactured goods fell as industrialization proceeded; Americans had better access to a wider variety of goods than ever before. At the same time, there are indications that income gains at best failed to generate gains in overall health and life expectancy for Americans; indeed, it appears that there was a decline from 1820 to 1860. The median height of American males (an important indicator of adult health), which had increased through the colonial era, registered much smaller gains after 1790, and then declined from 1820 to 1860. Data on Americans' life expectancy in the early nineteenth century are less conclusive, but also indicate a decline.[2] Income and wage trends at this time probably overstate the gains in the quality of life enjoyed by Americans.

Incomes rose, and almost undoubtedly at a faster pace than ever before. One study concluded that real per-capita product increased 60 percent over the first 40 years of the nineteenth century and a further 37 percent by 1860. Rates of increase varied, with the highest occurring in the 1830s and the lowest in the 1850s.[3] The record is affected by business cycles; 1839–1843 was a period of severe deflation, 1850 was a boom year, and the economy was enduring a recession in 1860. The data, especially for the first decades of the century, are not as trustworthy as those from later periods, so conclusions drawn from them should be regarded as best available estimates rather than facts. Nevertheless, they are in accord with what we know about productivity changes.[4]

THE DISTRIBUTION OF INCOME AND WEALTH

From 1815 to 1860, two opposing influences affected the distribution of income and wealth in the United States. The first was that the range of alternatives open to Americans grew steadily larger over this time, and there was considerable redistribution of people from low- to high-income occupations. This redistribution occurred both within and between occupations and regions. People and resources moved to regions where their efforts were more productive in the same work, and they also switched jobs in pursuit of higher incomes. This trend reduced the supply of resources in areas where they earned less-than-average rates of return, thus raising the incomes of those remaining. At the same time, it increased factor supply in high-income uses and regions, which reduced their prices there. Despite this, wage rates in different areas show only limited convergence after 1830. Midwestern wages decreased about 30 percent relative to those in the Northeast over 1820–1850.[5] During this time, the largest income

[1] P. David, "The Growth of Real Product in the United States Before 1840: New Evidence, Controlled Conjectures," *Journal of Economic History* (June 1967).
[2] R. Fogel, "Nutrition and the Decline in Mortality Since 1700," in Gallman and Engerman, eds., *Long-Term Factors in American Economic Growth* (Chicago: University of Chicago Press, 1986). See also J. Komlos, "The Height and Weight of West Point Cadets: Dietary Change in Antebellum America,"*Journal of Economic History* (December 1987).
[3] David, "Growth of Real Product."

[4] K. Sokoloff, "Productivity Growth in Manufacturing During Early Industrialization: Evidence from the American Northeast, 1820–1860," in Gallman and Engerman, *Long-Term Factors.*
[5] R. Margo and G. Villaflor, "The Growth of Wages in Antebellum America: New Evidence," *Journal of Economic History* (December 1987).

gains were in sectors of the economy that even in 1860 were fairly small in relation to the whole, and this tended to produce greater inequality. It must be kept in mind that the foregoing analysis refers to how the increases in aggregate output were allocated. There is little doubt that the majority of all Americans experienced at least some gains in real income. But some gained more than others.

Income Distribution

Some data on the functional distribution of income (the flow of output attributable to land, labor, capital, and other factors, respectively) are now available. A good deal is also known about the relationships between income (but not wealth) and age, skills, country of origin, and urban versus rural residence. From these we can derive a fuller, though still incomplete, picture of the levels and trends of income and wealth distribution in antebellum America. The evidence is inconclusive: Incomes and especially wealth were unevenly

distributed among the American population in 1815. It is not clear whether wages became even less so by 1860.[6] In one view, even when wealth in slaves is excluded and the data are adjusted for changes in the age, location, and national origin of the population, the concentration of wealth increased after 1820. To one proponent of this now-controversial view, the distribution of wealth in the United States may never have been more unequal than it was in 1860.[7] Professor Lebergott noted that the data from colonial days and from 1860, from which this inference is drawn by comparison, are not derived by the same methods and may tend to overstate income and wealth inequality at the later period.[8] Given the sources of new wealth, however, it would be surprising if some increase in concentration did not occur.

Landownership
Land was the largest component of aggregate wealth. American land was plentiful and cheap, and access to landownership was extraordinarily easy by European standards. Yet possession of land was by no means universal, even in rural areas. Although this was a country of small farms, only 42 percent of free male adults in the United States owned land in 1860. Only 60 percent of free Americans

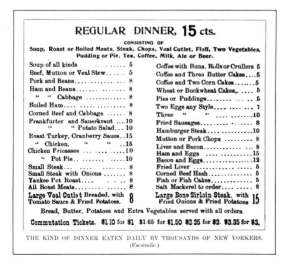

■ Although prices on this nineteenth-century menu appear very low today, incomes were relatively even lower at the time.
Source: Culver Pictures.

---

[6] P. Lindert and J. Williamson, "Three Centuries of American Inequality," in P. Uselding, ed., *Research in Economic History* (Greenwich, Conn.: JAI Press, 1976), 60, conclude that incomes became less equal. Margo and Villaflor, "The Growth of Wages," found no evidence of increasing wage divergence over the same period (the basis for the Lindert-Williamson conclusion that income inequality increased), and from that postulate that income inequality did not increase before the Civil War.

[7] Lindert and Williamson, "Three Centuries," 89.

[8] S. Lebergott, *The Americans: An Economic Record* (New York: Norton, 1984), 70–73, notes that while colonial income estimates were derived from probate records, those for the later period were obtained from government surveys, without verification. The nineteenth-century income data contain wide and seemingly inexplicable variations in claimed income and wealth among persons whose situations were apparently quite similar.

owned property (including land) valued at $100 or more.[9] Thirty percent of all U.S. real estate was in the hands of the wealthiest 1 percent of all property owners. Absolute figures do not tell the whole story. Comparisons with other nations are also useful. In England, the distribution of land was far less equal than in America. There, more than half the total acreage was owned by less than 1 percent of the population. However, we do not have comprehensive figures for any nation at this point in time.

Other Sorts of Wealth and Those Who Had It

Nonland wealth appears to have been less evenly distributed, especially in the cities.[10] Urban real estate and manufacturing assets or claims against them were largely new forms of wealth, and a few persons held most of them. The relationship between wealth and income is not linear; high incomes are possible even for individuals with little or no wealth. Wealth is defined by economists as stocks of productive goods. A lawyer who lives in a rented apartment and drives a leased car while spending every cent of a $100,000 annual income may have no wealth as it is conventionally measured, but we could not call such an individual poor. Still, there is no doubt that wealth was not equally distributed in America, and the distribution may have grown less equal than it was in the colonial era.

Demographic Influences

Even if disparities in wealth ownership increased, they may indicate to some extent the presence of economic opportunity in the United States rather than its absence. Individual wealth tends to be strongly linked with age. If all wealth were the result of individuals' saving, we would expect the young to have less than older persons. The data bear this out: The proportion of property ownership increases threefold between the ages of 20 and 60 in antebellum America.[11] Although the median age of the American population did rise slightly in comparison to the colonial period, part of the disparity in wealth can be derived from the rapid growth of population, which would make for a high proportion of young people. There was also some mobility among wealth holders—the identity of the top wealth holders in various cities changed even while the individuals listed remained alive.[12] But the demographic factors reduce rather than eliminate disparities in wealth. Trends in aggregate consumption, which grew at only slightly lower rates than did gross national product, indicate that gains in income, if not necessarily wealth, were widely distributed.

Growth and Income Distribution

Some trends in income distribution are related to changes occurring across the American economy. We would expect people who derived their incomes from rapidly growing sectors to fare better than those employed in areas where productivity grew more slowly. Even though the operation of the market system "pulled" resources into areas of above-average productivity and "pushed" them out of areas where performance was subpar, making for greater equality, the process was far from completed by 1860 (or today, for that matter).[13] Moreover, gains in productivity were quite

[9] L. Soltow, *Men and Wealth in the United States, 1850–1970* (New Haven, Conn.: Yale University Press, 1975), 22, 174. Because of the method by which the data for these statements was assembled, Lebergott suggests that they be viewed skeptically. See S. Lebergott, *The Americans*, 73.

[10] Soltow, *Men and Wealth*, 92–108, Passim. It must be remembered, however, that colonial wealth-distribution studies employed probate records subject to legal verification, while most of the nineteenth-century data is drawn from census questions that were not subject to any followup. Lebergott, *The Americans*, 73.

[11] Soltow, *Men and Wealth*, 28.
[12] Lebergott, *The Americans*, 72.
[13] Margo and Villaflor, "Antebellum Wages."

general and varied surprisingly little between industries.[14] Reallocation would continue as long as new opportunities were exploited. Patterns we would predict from theory appear in the historical data. Incomes in manufacturing were nearly twice the national average, and incomes of skilled machinists or experienced construction workers were higher still. Employment in both occupations rose in relation to the total over this period. Recent work, however, makes it less certain that the wages of skilled labor rose faster than those of unskilled labor from 1815 to 1856.[15]

Rural versus Urban Incomes

Urban incomes on average were higher than those of rural areas, though they were less evenly distributed. Property income in cities was more concentrated than in rural areas. Since the urban population was growing at nearly three times the rate of the total population, this would make for increased income inequality. Americans in the forefront of economic change, introducing new products or methods, might be expected to earn above-average incomes. Evidence from civilian wages at army posts throughout the United States, however, does not indicate wage disparities between regions or cities versus the countryside. (See Table 9.1.)

Women and children also increased their share of money incomes. Their wages might be well below the national average, but previously they had little or no opportunity to earn any wage. Before the appearance of factories and other sources of urban employment, the only occupations open to them were as low-powered, but easily trained, "work animals" on farms.

---

[14] Sokoloff, "Productivity Growth."
[15] Lindert and Williamson, "Three Centuries," 102–104. For contrast, see Margo and Villaflor, "Antebellum Wages."

Table 9.1   Real Wage Indices for the Northeast, 1820–1856 (1856 = 100)

Year	Skilled	Unskilled
1820	75.9	n.a.
1823	67.7	61.0
1825	70.1	72.2
1828	72.4	66.7
1830	70.0	66.6
1833	73.5	67.0
1835	80.7	75.4
1836	74.0	75.6
1840	84.4	64.1
1843	107.9	116.9
1845	115.7	118.1
1848	96.0	98.7
1850	99.8	113.2
1853	93.3	103.3
1855	84.2	90.0
1856	100.0	100.0

Decadal Averages (1821–1830 = 100)

1821–1830	100.0	100.0
1831–1840	109.5	105.2
1841–1850	145.2	157.8
1851–1856	132.7	148.4
Rate of growth	1.0	1.4

Source: Taken from R. Margo and G. Villaflor, "Wages in Antebellum America: New Evidence," *Journal of Economic History* (December 1989).

Income Distribution in the Rural South

There were some exceptions to the general rule that urban incomes and wealth exceeded those of rural areas. The ten counties ranked highest in average inhabitants' wealth in 1860 were all southern and rural. Most were in the sugar regions along the lower Mississippi River, where the economies of scale, rents of uniquely productive land, and the capital intensity inherent in sugar planting all accrued to plantation owners (but not to their slaves).

■ The opulent Shirley plantation in Virginia is indicative of the wealth accumulated by large-scale slaveholders.
Source: Library of Congress.

Much southern wealth was in the form of slaves, and the sugar plantations had unusually large work forces even by plantation standards.[16]

In 1860, an individual owning just two slaves and no other wealth possessed property valued at nearly twice the average held by all Americans. There were 10,659 planters who owned 50 or more slaves each in 1860. At an average price of $900 per slave, each such planter held a minimum of $45,000 in slave property alone, and, of course, these individuals possessed large amounts of land and other property as well. Since the dollar in 1860 had perhaps ten times its modern purchasing power, these planters were wealthy even by 1992 standards. With only about one-third the nation's population, the South was the home of 59 percent of America's wealthiest families on the eve of the Civil War.[17] In other forms

---

[16] Soltow, *Men and Wealth*, 167.

[17] Soltow, *Men and Wealth*, 101.

of wealth, however, the South was below the average for the northern industrial states.

Relative incomes of women rose from only 30 percent of men's to 56 percent with newfound female access to factory employment over 1815–1855.[18]

The Frontier

Generally, rural wealth was concentrated in more densely settled areas. Dense populations were indications that a high proportion of the land was cleared and under cultivation if the area were agricultural, or that the area had some type of capital–intensive activity. In either case, the inhabitants would have had some time to save. Frontier areas, thinly settled and with much of the land not yet in full use, had below-average wealth. Areas with heavy manufacturing employment and high proportions of native-born inhabitants fared better than did those whose populations were disproportionately young, foreign-born, or both. Low current wealth did not necessarily imply that such circumstances would continue. Investment rates were high on the frontier, and there was great opportunity for capital gains as land values appreciated.

Immigrants

Foreign-born urban residents generally had lower wealth than their American native neighbors, but in rural areas, national origin had little implication for wealthholding. In part, these conditions reflected the circumstances of the immigrants who chose each type of area. Those settling in the countryside were better equipped to take advantage of opportunities. Many of the immigrants in urban areas had been poor when they arrived, while those settling in rural areas were more likely to be educated and to have brought some cap-

ital with them. As noted in Chapter 6, the investment required for commercially viable farms rose substantially after 1840. Poverty was more common in American cities than it was in rural areas. With only about one-fifth of the nation's population, the cities sheltered 38 percent of the nation's poor in 1860. Because urban populations contained more than proportionate shares of the young, recent immigrants, and the illiterate, all factors that reduced incomes and wealth, this result is not surprising.

Urban Real Wages, 1820 to 1860

From 1809 to 1859, the real wages of unskilled American workers slightly more than doubled.[19] From what is known about wages, it seems that urban real wages probably rose in the 1820s and through the mid-1830s, declined through the early 1840s, then rose to a sharp peak in 1843–1846, and were almost as high in the early 1850s. Subsequently they declined, and they had not fully regained the lost ground by 1860.[20] At first glance, this is surprising, since per-capita incomes rose strongly from 1843 to 1860. Capital per worker and productivity both rose, factors that might be expected to increase wages. Even so, it appears that labor's bargaining power diminished. The causes are not completely understood, but three factors appear especially significant:

1. The price level rose by nearly one-third from 1851 to 1855. Wages often fail to keep pace with rapid inflation.
2. Immigration and, even more, the labor supply increased much faster than they had

[18] C. Goldin, "The Gender Gap in Historical Perspective," in P. Kilby, ed., *Quantity and Quiddity: Essays in U.S. Economic History*, (Middletown, Conn.: Wesleyan University Press, 1987).

[19] P. David and P. Solar, "A Bicentennial Contribution to the History of the Cost of Living in America," in P. Uselding, ed., *Research in Economic History* (Princeton, N.J.: Princeton University Press, 1977).
[20] Margo and Villaflor, "Antebellum Wages." See also S. Lebergott, *Trends in the U.S. Economy in the Nineteenth Century* (Princeton, N.J.: Princeton University Press, 1960), 490.

in previous years. Most of the new arrivals competed for urban jobs.

3. Industrialization increased the proportion of jobs held by women and children, whose wages were below the national average. Even so, the new jobs increased opportunities for women, and the gap between male and female wages fell as factory work became more common after 1815. Women's wages about doubled in relation to men's between 1815 and 1850. They continued this increase to 1890.[21]

A high proportion of the new immigrants were unskilled and destitute, with only minimal bargaining power, which would tend to drive down average wage levels. But real wages for specific jobs and individuals may not have declined, a point supported by the data in Tables 9.1 and 9.2. If the proportion of low-wage jobs rose, average wage levels might fall even though those for skilled jobs remained constant or even rose. The premium

for skilled over unskilled labor declined in the Midwest but not in the South from 1821 to 1856.[22] The overall evidence now makes dubious early conclusions that income inequality rose through this period.

Another indication of the probable course of income distribution and income levels is given by the increased production of certain types of goods. Furniture, textiles, rugs, stoves, tools, clocks, and amusement services in the cities were all produced in great quantities, an indication that economic gains extended to middle- and low-income groups.[23] The American rich already enjoyed these items and could hardly have increased their purchases sufficiently to account for the increased output.

The Demographic Paradox

Income and wage data generally indicate that most Americans' real incomes were rising. Yet other indicators point to a pervasive decline in average heights, life expectancy, and general

---

[21] C. Goldin, *Understanding the Gender Gap: An Economic History of American Women* (New York: Oxford University Press, 1990), 63.

[22] Margo and Villaflor, "Antebellum Wages."
[23] R. Andreano, "Trends in Economic Welfare, 1790–1860," in *New Views on American Economic Development* (Cambridge, Mass.: Schenkman, 1965), 131–167.

Table 9.2   Nominal Daily Wage Rates for Artisans and Unskilled Laborers

Year	Artisans		Unskilled	
	Northeast	Midwest	Northeast	Midwest
1820	$1.55	n.a.	n.a.	$.73
1825	1.32	$1.40	$.86	.56
1830	1.23	1.79	.74	.67
1835	1.54	1.78	.91	.85
1840	1.50	1.79	.72	.82
1845	1.55	1.48	1.00	.74
1850	1.45	1.70	1.04	.83
1855	1.73	2.11	1.17	1.05

Source: Data from R. Margo and G. Villaflor, "Wages in Antebellum America: New Evidence," *Journal of Economic History* (December 1989).

health after 1820. The changes were substantial; over three years life expectancy at age ten and an inch in adult height. At this time, no one has developed a full explanation of the deterioration, which apparently occurred among nearly all segments of the population. The first suspect might be nutrition, but mean heights of American rural dwellers fell more than urban residents'. Food production, especially of meat, apparently either did not keep pace with population or with increasing nutritional requirements due to greater work effort.[24] The largest reasonable values assigned to such factors as a larger portion of foreign-born among the population, urbanization, and its attendant dietary deterioration, exposure to epidemics, and less equal income distribution account for about half the observed changes.[25]

Fogel's hypothesis is that although food intake rose for most Americans, the intensity of work rose faster still. Even though diets improved absolutely, they became less adequate. There may also have been declines in the quality of prenatal and infant care that affected later health. Komlos postulates that even American farmers traded health for nonfood gains. His study indicated a decline in food production, especially protein, relative to needs. The urban middle class apparently escaped this demographic deterioration but was not large enough to offset the declines in laborers' health.[26] A full resolution of the problem awaits further research.

The Nature of American Prosperity

The previous discussion does not indicate that Americans' overall well-being declined from 1830 to 1860. Wage and income trends may overstate the improvements achieved, but these were real.[27] Foreign visitors all but unanimously recorded impressions of widespread, boundless optimism and a crude plenty. They observed fewer obvious differences in living standards between various income groups than were apparent in Europe. While such evidence is not the stuff of firm conclusions, it is at least consistent with the limited quantitative evidence available on income distribution. (The foreign observers' homelands were undergoing demographic trends similar to those in the United States, however.) Income shares may have changed, but if so, the variations were not large, and all groups gained in absolute terms. Diets aside, many goods had become available to middle- and lower-income groups for the first time. Real income gains were emphatically not restricted to a small wealthy minority.

Nonetheless, the antebellum economy was not egalitarian in terms of the results it generated. The gains of the poor were not at the expense of the rich, who apparently at least retained the share of income they had received in the colonial era. Despite the probable increase in income disparities, individuals found it easier to change their income status (to move up or down the income scale) in the United States than anywhere else. This is important, because it means that individuals' incomes could rise or fall in relation to the average, and hence there was constant pressure for efficient job performance on all individuals. The rewards for effort could be substantial in America and were much greater than those in Europe. Throughout American history, the opportunity to rise through one's own efforts has been a primary attraction to immigrants, and immigration rose at this point in time.

[24] See Komlos, "Height and Weight," and R. Fogel, "Nutrition."
[25] Fogel, "Nutrition." See also P. Lindert, "Comment," in Gallman and Engerman, *Long-Term Factors*, Komlos, "Height and Weight,"ascribes nearly the entire effect to protein deficiencies.
[26] Komlos, "Height and Weight."
[27] This is the preliminary conclusion of Professor Lindert in a review of Fogel's evidence. See P. Lindert, "Comment," in Gallman and Engerman, *Long-Term Factors*, 534–535.

The movements of people to new areas and new jobs indicate that the incentives were effective. Whether they moved from eastern farms to more fertile soil in the West, from rural areas to higher-income cities, or from low- to high-wage jobs in the same industry, the results obtained by mobile Americans were the same. Resources produced more in new uses, and those who moved increased the economy's aggregate production. Americans were as willing to change the nature of existing jobs as they were to move to new ones. Because of this, innovations were easier to introduce than they might be where the work force feared them as a threat to jobs. New forms of labor organization and increased intensity of effort contributed more to productivity growth than changes in factor proportions or technological change.[28] In addition, the full potential of new inventions was more nearly realized, and ideas spread rapidly from the areas in which they were first applied.

URBANIZATION

In 1815, one American in fourteen lived in a city or town of more than 2,500 people. By 1860, that proportion had nearly tripled, to one in five. Some individual cities had grown even faster. New York's 805,000 people in 1860 were more than the entire U.S. urban population of 1815, and Philadelphia's 565,000 were not much less.

Cities have certain advantages for economic growth. Markets and labor supplies are likely to be readily available to those seeking them. Information costs are lower—a point of special relevance before modern communication techniques appeared. Highly special-

ized resources of all kinds tend to locate where markets are large enough to allow them to exploit all existing economies of scale. A shop selling nothing but blue jeans would not be located in an isolated village, but even more specialized stores and workers are found in large cities. Supporting services, such as housing and shopping for workers, a transportation system to bring in raw materials and distribute products, and schools, churches, and cultural activities, can be taken for granted in large urban environments. So can at least the most basic governmental services—police and courts. As a city's population grows, the range of activities it can support generally grows even faster, particularly if transportation is improving as it was in nineteenth-century America. Because there are more opportunities for full utilization of specialists' skills, urban incomes are likely to average higher than those of the countryside, where such talents may not be fully exploited.

Conditions of Nineteenth-Century Urban Life

City life has disadvantages as well. With specialization comes a loss of self-sufficiency, although this, to some degree, is within the individual's control. But crowding, noise, pollution, and other results of life in close contact with large numbers of other people are unavoidable. In the middle of the nineteenth century, these problems had not been mitigated even to the extent they are today. Some had not even been recognized.

There were major disadvantages to urban life in all countries, and the United States was no exception. Only the rich could afford to maintain carriages within large cities. Since there was little or no public transportation, the bulk of the population had to live within walking distance of workplaces. The labor-intensive nature of most industry in this era

---

[28] Sokoloff, "Productivity Growth."

■ The streets of New York in 1855 are depicted.
Source: The Bettmann Archive.

exacerbated the situation. The poor lived in multistory tenements that were the only means of providing living space for large numbers of people within confined areas. Often, in the poorer areas, several families shared a room. For several decades after 1830, urban employment and population apparently grew faster than housing. This was a potentially lethal situation when the causes and transfer mechanisms of most diseases were unknown. Nor were people the only things in close proximity. Only in the 1850s did large American cities begin to build public water and sewage systems, and these were not extended to the entire urban population until long after 1860. Before the advent of water mains and sewers, wells and privies were only too obviously close together. New York City had one slum so

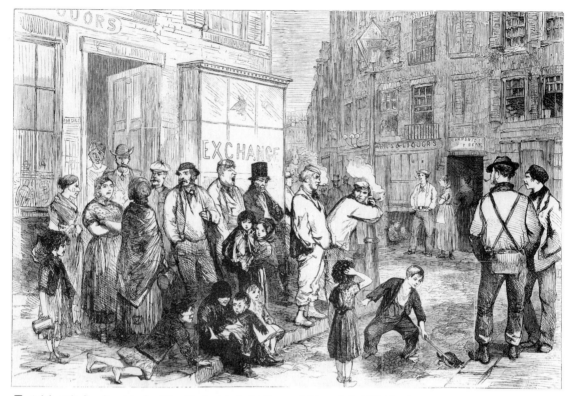

■ A leisurely Sunday morning New York-style is the focus of this artist's 1868 sketch.
Source: The Bettmann Archive.

crowded that there was no room for any sanitary facilities whatsoever; the city eventually purchased it and tore it down.[29]

Pollution

Most buildings were made of wood, and fires were frequent. Streets generally were unpaved and became seas of mud in wet weather. Worse, they were used as dumping grounds for every sort of refuse, which was picked over by children and the hogs that ranged freely through most cities. In 1900, horses deposited

24 tons of manure on New York City streets every day, and this source of pollution might well have been worse in the smaller but even more crowded cities before 1860.[30] Eventually, the mess would be trampled into the mud, or, rarely, cleaned up. Traffic was heavy, and accidents apparently were at least as frequent as they are today.

Poor Sanitation

Methods of preserving food had improved little from colonial times. Salting, smoking, drying, and pickling were used, and some ice was available, but little fresh food was within

[29] Davis et al., *American Economic Growth: An Economist's History of the U.S.* (New York: Harper & Row, 1972), 628.

[30] I am indebted to Professor Thomas Ulem of the University of Illinois for this information.

■ Urban traffic problems began long before automobiles were widely employed, as this mid-nineteenth century photo of Chicago shows.
Source: The Chicago Historical Society. Stereo by J. Carbutt.

the means of the poor for entire seasons. Food was often contaminated at its source or in processing. Since milk was difficult to transport long distances, many dairy cattle were kept within cities. Feed was expensive in the cities, so cows were fed whatever was available, and even the milk from diseased cows was sold.[31]

Disease

Ignorance and filth combined to produce incredible rates of disease, particularly among children. In the 1850s, 56 percent of all the deaths in New York City were children under the age of five. In an especially bad year in Chicago, 70 percent of all children less than one year old died.[32] Widespread epidemics

---

[31] Davis et al., *American Economic Growth*, 629.

[32] Davis et al., *American Economic Growth*, 629.

had previously been rare in America, but now cholera, tuberculosis, and various intestinal diseases, most linked to dietary problems, occurred frequently in the cities and sometimes affected rural populations as well.

Medicine provided no relief. Doctors could treat wounds or set broken bones with some chance of success, but for most diseases, they could at best relieve pain with drugs. Often their treatments made the affliction worse. Hospitals were mere warehouses for the dying. Maternal and infant mortality were high, in part because the most elementary principles of cleanliness were violated during childbirth.

The Economics of Urban Externalities

Urban problems stemmed from the lack of an organized response to them and the inability of the market system to provide one. If one citizen cut his or her personal contribution to the problem and others did not, there would be no noticeable reduction in pollution, and the "good citizen" would have incurred costs to no purpose. Even worse, the greater the voluntary cleanup of others, the less the economic incentive for anyone to follow suit if doing so involved costs in time, money, or changes in habits—the classic "free rider" problem. Lack of knowledge and means for effective responses made the problems even more intractable.

City governments were nearly as unable to cope with the problems of crime, fire, lighting, and education as they were with those of urban health. The rural background of most Americans was reflected in political institutions that were not designed to deal with costs inflicted on the general public by private actions that might be innocuous in more spacious environments. Changes would be required in political institutions as well as science and technology before effective responses to urban problems could be generated.

The Attractions of City Life

Given these conditions (the author has by no means presented the worst examples), why would any sane person choose city life? How could urban populations increase at three times the aggregate rate? There must have been some attractions to balance the grim picture just described, or possibly rural life had drawbacks as well. Both appear to be true. By no means did all city dwellers reside in slums, and urban life offered much greater variety in consumption and life-styles than was possible in the country. Urban occupations often had much better possibilities for advancement; rural laborers might save for years to obtain funds to buy a farm, but there the process stopped. In the rapidly changing cities, however, a dead end in one job might be avoided by changing occupations. Nor should we romanticize rural life at this time. Farm work was physically demanding and over the years offered little variety. And it was only relatively safer and healthier; life expectancy for the entire country was 35 to 40 years at best, or about half its present level.[33]

THE STRUCTURE OF THE LABOR MARKET

The employment of large numbers of people in manufacturing, transportation, and commercial firms was a new development. As had been the case in other areas of economic life, institutions had to be developed to deal with new situations, most of which had not existed before 1800. The requirements of the new jobs differed from those that had previously existed. Some placed emphasis on dexterity or

[33] *Historical Statistics of the U.S.: Colonial Times to 1970,* 2 vols. (Washington, D.C.: Government Printing Office, 1975), 1:56.

endurance rather than physical strength, or demanded skills that few, if any, people had previously possessed, such as those of a locomotive engineer. In some cases jobs appeared before any recognition of the skills required for them did, and answers had to be worked out by trial and error. Changing factor proportions and work organization made even long-established jobs different. In many instances employers had to recruit labor. Especially when locations of activity were dictated by power sources or raw materials, employers might have to build housing for their workers and sometimes entire towns.

Labor and employers also had to reach consensus on which aspects of work were areas of mutual concern and which were the primary interest of one party or the other. Absenteeism and tardiness could affect the performance of entire factories, so employers made rules and tried to instill desired behavior in workers accustomed to the less demanding schedules of agriculture. The pace and duration of work were matters that today would be acknowledged as legitimate, though not exclusive, concerns of employers. The basis and rates of pay were matters in which both sides had an obvious interest.

Initially, many employers appeared to believe that few, if any, aspects of workers' overall conduct could be trusted to employees' individual discretion. Some employers made it their business to regulate behavior off as well as on the job, requiring church attendance and contributions, regulating drinking, smoking, appearance, and other aspects of conduct. In many of these areas, however, employers were assuming roles previously filled by ministers, local governments, or public opinion, so their rules were not seen as the outrageous infringements on individual freedom that they appear today. Paternalism could have its positive side; most firms were small enough to put relations with the employer on a personal basis. Some employers might extend help to workers in times of personal trouble and take pains to

mitigate the effects of unemployment, but there was no obligation that they do so.

The "Mill Girls"

The first industrial firms appeared before large-scale immigration and while cities were still very small. Wholly new industries might have to create the pool from which to draw a work force under such circumstances. In northern New England, textile mills obtained a labor force by hiring the young unmarried women of the surrounding countryside. The "mill girls" were housed in strictly supervised boarding houses. These solved two problems: They eased parents' concerns over their daughters' moral and physical welfare, and they provided housing where none had previously existed. At this time (1815–1845) there was little difficulty in recruiting young women to work for 11 or 12 hours per day in the mills and live where their every action was subject to strict and unforgiving scrutiny, all for two or three dollars a week after room and board. Young women in this era had few employment alternatives outside their own homes. About all that was available was domestic service or possibly schoolteaching, and both involved life in another family's home. Domestic service meant the same type of work the girls had performed at home. Neither job provided much in the way of cash income. Large-scale manufacturing provided jobs in which the productivity of women and children was relatively high, and such firms employed large numbers of women and children.[34]

The mills offered higher wages, the chance to meet a wider range of people than was possible on the farm, and some control over one's own life.[35] Women might save for a dowry,

---

[34] C. Goldin and K. Sokoloff, "Women, Children, and Industrialization in the Early Republic: Evidence from the Manufacturing Censuses," *Journal of Economic History* (December 1982).

[35] Goldin, *The Gender Gap*, 63.

contribute to the support of their families, and obtain a few luxuries for themselves. Although life was tightly restricted by both social and economic limits, it offered more freedom than the farm. In their few leisure hours, the mill girls pursued literary and artistic endeavors, held debates, and followed many of the same activities that their more fortunate sisters might enjoy full-time at a boarding school. Most women spent only a few years in such jobs, which were widely viewed as an interval between childhood and marriage.[36]

The mill girls also organized one of the first employee strikes in American history. In 1828, the female employees of the Cocheco Manufacturing Company of Dover, New Hampshire "turned out" to protest a wage cut.[37] But the era of the mill girls was brief. By the 1840s, they encountered increasing job competition from immigrants willing to work for lower wages—in part because their personal conduct was not a matter of concern.

Unions

There were some formal labor organizations before 1860, but few aspired to permanence. Most were set up to achieve some short-term objective and lasted only until the issue had been resolved. The majority did not resemble modern labor unions. Often organizations appeared among skilled craftsmen who owned their own shops or were self-employed. The aims of these groups were reminiscent of the Medieval guilds. They sought to restrict entry into their occupations or to fix prices for their products. Craft journeymen attempted to organize both for higher wages and to restrict entry of additional employees. Such groups had little influence on the labor force as a whole. About 26,000 people—less than 1 percent of the labor force—were members of any type of labor organization in 1830. Later, membership declined, and the 1830 figure was not regained until 1860.[38]

Obstacles to Organization

Workers who sought effective bargaining power through organization faced formidable difficulties. In many of the new industries, workers were unskilled and readily replaceable. The structure of most industries was another barrier. Typically, there would be many small firms producing similar goods. Labor was a large portion of total production costs for these employers. Wage increases would force increases in product prices under competitive conditions, so that all firms in the same market would have to be organized simultaneously. If any single employer were to raise prices to cover a wage increase, he had to know that his competitors were facing the same situation before he would do so. Even then, firms outside the organized area might be able to invade its markets as transportation improved. If the employer's markets were distant from the plant, the entire industry might have to be organized.

Limits to Workers' Bargaining Power Wages were low, and labor organizations had no ability to sustain a strike. Lacking personal savings or strike benefits, most workers could strike only until they or their families got hungry. Workers' organizations were extremely vulnerable to the swings of the business cycle. If business conditions prompted an employer to cut wages, even the most militant employees might have little choice but to accept. Skilled craftsmen, who could not easily be replaced, enjoyed some bargaining success, but for most workers, the economic barriers to

[36] Goldin, *The Gender Gap*, 50–54.
[37] G. Taylor, *Transportation Revolution, 1815–1860* (New York: M. E. Sharpe, 1962), 276. The strike was lost because the mill owners were able to find other workers, and quickly threatened to do so.

[38] Davis et al., *American Economic Growth*, 220.

successful collective action were very strong. As the organization of work changed and mechanized, the proportion of unskilled jobs increased.

The Legal Climate The legal and political obstacles faced by would-be unions were even stronger. Government was invariably on the side of the employers, and was often willing to send police or militia to protect strikebreakers. Welfare payments were rare and not accessible to strikers; unemployment payments were unknown. Legal doctrine was, if anything, less favorable to unions. Until 1842, judges regarded labor unions as illegal conspiracies under the common law, an attempt to benefit members at others' expense. In that year, Judge Shaw ruled in *Commonwealth v. Hunt* that unions were not inherently illegal organizations and the purpose behind their actions had to be considered before the case could be decided. Since the courts took an extremely narrow view of the permissible range of union activities, the ruling did little more than allow unions to exist.[39] It did not grant them the freedom to organize and bargain as they wished.

Ineffectual Labor Leaders In some cases unions were not oriented to the interests of labor. Often the leaders of labor organizations were intellectuals whose goals lay more in the reform of society than in material betterment for workers within the current system. Many of these leaders advocated abolition of the wage system, with some form of utopian socialism or other social systems in which workers would control the entire economic system as alternatives. Even had they offered workable proposals, the reformers had little hope of success. They never succeeded in attracting more than tiny minorities of workers to their

views, and with good reason. They completely misunderstood workers' objectives, which were higher pay, shorter hours of work, improved working conditions, and the modification of laws that were not to workers' advantage. Even had their views appealed to the people to whom they were addressed, utopian proposals for labor's benefit might have been lost in the collective roar of propositions for reform of virtually every existing institution.[40]

Utopian Ideals

The antebellum era witnessed a burgeoning of panaceas—the world, or at least America, was to be improved or the millennium achieved through means ranging from the practical through the idealistic and on to the truly bizarre. Great things were to come if people would eat graham flour, wear woolen underwear, practice vegetarianism, create a utopian socialist state, or perform any of a thousand other religious, quasi-religious, or secular activities. All were stridently advocated as the answer to all questions their proponents considered important. Labor unions and the women's rights movement were not destined to do well in this climate. Would-be supporters within labor's ranks were deterred by early unions' association with such ideas. This experience with social reform left American labor with a lasting distrust of intellectuals or of any leadership not recruited from within its own ranks.

Not surprisingly, most of the attempts at new forms of social and economic organizations failed. Some of these advocated a return to agriculture and were attempted by people who tended to substitute romanticism for farming experience. Some groups had no agreement on the most basic goals. Others sought ends beyond their ability. A few efforts

---

[39] C. Gregory and H. Katz, *Labor and the Law*, 3d ed. (New York: Norton, 1979), 27–30.

[40] R. Robertson, *History of the American Economy*, 3d ed. (New York: Harcourt Brace Jovanovich, 1973), 233–237.

proved durable, usually in cases where the membership was united around strictly defined purposes. Religion was often the bond that held these groups together. Some groups (the Mormons) isolated themselves geographically; others (the Amish), socially. A few, such as the Onieda and Amana communities, succeeded in actively participating in the wider economy while maintaining group cohesion.

Some idealistically motivated projects for social betterment had positive, if limited, impacts. Savings banks were established to provide low-income individuals a place in which to keep their savings at interest (and to promote thrift among the "spendthrift" lower classes). Savings banks would accept very small deposits; other financial institutions would not. The real difficulty faced by persons with low incomes, of course, was accumulating savings in the first place.

Changes in Social Institutions

A few of the goals of American labor organizations and workers in general were achieved in this period. Imprisonment for debt was abolished, and the use of convict labor in competition with free workers was reduced. Mechanics' lien laws allowed workers to establish claims against the property of employers who failed to pay for services rendered. Education became more widespread and available to working-class children. Work hours were reduced: The average workday fell from 12 hours or more to 11 by 1860. Some states imposed laws restricting the workday of children to ten hours (usually with loopholes), and federal employees gained a ten-hour day in 1840. Long hours of work were partially mitigated by a slower pace of activity than that demanded by modern jobs, but the implications for leisure time are obvious.

These developments resulted from the efforts of many groups, only a portion of which could be regarded as representing organized labor or workers. Reductions in work hours and restrictions on the employment of children indicate growing affluence; society now felt it possible to sacrifice small amounts of production for leisure, or sought long-term gains through education rather than current output.

Occupational and Geographical Mobility

The U.S. work force had certain characteristics that distinguished it from those of European nations. The average age of workers was lower, reflecting both rapid population growth through natural increase and the influence of immigration; most immigrants were young adults. Above all, American labor was both occupationally and geographically mobile in comparison with that of Europe. The implications of this point were profound: Workers sought only their own betterment in moving, but reallocation of labor increased the efficiency of the American economy. It pressured employers to use existing work forces more productively and to pay them in proportion. Mobility was aided by high levels of education; most American workers were literate. Fewer people were stuck in jobs that did not suit them than was true of less flexible societies, and a larger portion of labor had an opportunity to develop and exercise whatever special talents it possessed. There was little reluctance to adopt labor-saving machinery; it was welcomed as reducing the load on human muscle. In the labor-scarce climate of the United States, there was less reason to fear displacement from a job when others were easy to obtain.

These work-force attributes also increased the productivity of innovations. Foreign observers noted repeatedly that American workers' response to a new machine was not merely to use it, but to try to understand its basic operating principles, and often to attempt to improve it. This attitude, when combined with labor's mobility and literacy, aided the rapid spread of new technology from its initial geographic and sectoral areas of application. Wide utilization and modification of inventions helped assure that their full potential was realized. Men trained in such nineteenth-century citadels of "high technology" as Colt, Brown & Sharpe, Waltham Watch, and the government arsenals were welcomed throughout American industry and their suggestions for change given serious attention. In addition, many small but cumulatively important improvements were made within existing plants through labor's efforts.

By no means was the American labor market perfectly competitive. Wide differentials in wages, sometimes even within the same city, occurred for basically similar jobs, and variations between geographic regions were still larger. Nevertheless, the mobility of the work force was a powerful mechanism for reducing income variations that were not based on productivity, and it was developed in this country far beyond the achievements of Europe even a century later. In a few cases, labor, whose mobility and bargaining power were especially limited, might face exploitation in the sense of being paid less than the value of its product, just as slaves were. The textile industry, which employed a high proportion of female and child workers who had few good job alternatives, is one such example.[41]

IMMIGRATION

Before 1830, immigration had been only a minor influence on U.S. population growth and the work force. It accounted for less than 5 percent of American population growth before that date. Not until 1828 did more than 25,000 people move to the United States in a single year. In the 1830s, the flow increased to almost 60,000 people annually, and in the 1840s it expanded even more. The peak for this era was between 1850 and 1855, a period in which over 2 million immigrants arrived in America, accounting for nearly half the total population growth of the period.

Most of the immigration still originated in northern Europe, but as time passed, immigrants' nationality began to change. The portion of the inflow coming from England, Scotland, and Wales diminished and that from Ireland and Germany rose. There was also an influx from eastern Canada, although its numbers did not compare with the European migrants.

It seems clear that the immigrants' primary motives were economic, but there were other causes. The Irish had endured centuries of social and religious persecution before the potato famines of the late 1840s. Wars, revolution, and repression were factors in the German migration, especially after 1848. Nevertheless, economic considerations were a primary motivation for the bulk of the immigrants. There were few restrictions on emigrants' choices of new homes. Even so, the United States, with its high levels and growth rates of income, attracted most of them. In addition, American immigration is correlated with favorable economic conditions in this country after 1830. Immigration increased in good times and fell off about a year after the beginning of slumps.

The Immigrants' Reception

Were the immigrants' hopes of a better material life fulfilled? How well did they fare in the new land? The new arrivals met hostility, discrimination, and sometimes violence.[42]

---

[41] R. Vedder, "The Slave Expropriation (Exploitation) Rate," *Explorations in Economic History* (October 1979).

[42] An excellent description of American workers' reactions to immigrants is R. Fogel, *Without Consent or Contract*, Chaps. 9–10.

■ Immigrants were sometimes the victims of mob violence incited by nativist groups.
Source: Library of Congress.

The Irish in particular were desperately poor, unskilled, illiterate, and willing to take almost any job even at low wages. To some Americans, they were an economic threat undermining the established structure and level of wages. To others, the Irish were Catholic, had no great love for established authority, and were easily identified. Any of these characteristics might be "reason" enough to hate them. As were many later immigrants, the Irish were derided for their life-styles and scorned for their poverty. The Germans often brought capital and skills, but their customs and language appeared strange to many Americans. In light of the reception they were accorded, it is hardly surprising that many immigrants tended to cluster in communities of their own. Often the core of such a group settlement would be earlier migrants from Ireland or Germany. Here the new arrivals found advice about jobs, housing, and other aspects of life; the transactions costs of adaptation were lower under such circumstances.

Those who disliked immigrants soon added another chorus to their complaints—immigrants were "clannish" and reluctant to associate with those who sought to deny them jobs and on occasion burned their churches. Opposition was particularly strong among unskilled workers with whom the new arrivals competed for jobs. Political groups, especially the American Nativist, or "Know Nothing party," were organized to oppose immigration. But the numbers tell the story. America's economic pull was stronger than the social opposition of some of its inhabitants.

In the U.S. economy, the demand for all types of labor was generally strong. Manufacturing, construction, and distribution could use workers of any degree of skill, and immigrants found jobs plentiful. Pay in these jobs was often low by American standards, and foreign-born urban residents had not achieved wealth equal to that of American natives by 1860. If immigrants were illiterate or unable to speak English, they would find it difficult to take full advantage of America's economic opportunities. Immigrant groups had more than their share of factors that were associated with poverty among all Americans: youth, illiteracy, and limited work experience. They were also likely to be poor people from countries far less affluent than the United States. Even without the discrimination that some of them encountered, it is not surprising that poverty was more common among immigrants than among native Americans.

In rural areas, especially those on the frontier or adjacent to it, immigrants apparently gained economic parity with those born in this country rather quickly. Even so, these were areas where average incomes for all inhabitants were below the national norm. Immigrants' average age probably remained below that of native Americans throughout the period, because so many were young adults who had arrived within a decade of 1860. As it did for all Americans, youth reduced both incomes and particularly wealth; there had not been time to gain job experience or accumulate assets.

The Irish and the Germans
The Irish tended to settle in urban areas. Most of them were too poor to start a farm immediately, and their experience with agriculture in Ireland could hardly have encouraged another try in America. Lacking funds for travel, the Irish tended to settle in the port cities of the Eastern Seaboard. German settlement reflected the better economic circumstances of migrants from that country; it was more evenly divided between sizable communities in growing western cities, such as Cincinnati, St. Louis, Milwaukee, and Chicago, and considerable farm settlement in the Midwest.

The "America Letters"
The incomes and living conditions achieved by immigrants did not equal those of native Americans, but they were undoubtedly superior to those the new arrivals had experienced in the nations from which they had come. Average per-capita incomes were higher in America, often considerably so. Even more important from the immigrants' viewpoint were two other considerations: American income distribution was more equal than that of Europe, so incomes here were likely to be closer to the national average; and there was far more opportunity to rise in the income scale (which itself was rising) than was the case in the "Old Country." Not only are immigrants' "America Letters" to those left behind full of references to the better life they now enjoyed, but the letters also urge those in Europe to come to the New World. More convincing still, the letters often contained money to supplement the incomes of European relatives or finance their voyage to America. Sometimes the letters contained prepaid steamship tickets. These are strong evidence that the immigrants could have returned to their native lands. Instead, they persuaded and assisted their friends and relatives to join them in America.

Apparently it required two to three years for a male Irish immigrant to save enough money to finance passage for his family.[43] In

---

[43] D. North, *Economic Growth of the U.S., 1790–1860* (Englewood Cliffs, N.J.: Prentice-Hall, 1961), 80–81.

Ireland, the accumulation of the same amount required much more time and greater sacrifice from lower incomes. The transatlantic flow of people was heavily in one direction—west. Although many people gave evidence that they had earned enough to return to Europe, few chose to do so. The new arrivals' actions were evidence that they were far better off in America.

The Value of Human Capital

Immigrants contributed far more than just unskilled labor to the American economy. According to one study, the human capital (in work skills and education) that America acquired through immigration in the 1850s almost equalled the value of physical investment in the same period.[44] The aggregate value of imported human capital thus far exceeded the sums Americans borrowed in European financial markets during the same period. As it had been and would be again, the immigrants were not typical of their native lands. They were largely young (which increased the potential benefits of emigration), and they possessed above-average skills and education. It is obvious that they were ambitious. In an economy that allowed personal mobility and rewarded responses to opportunity, such traits gave a welcome boost to the American economic growth.[45]

EDUCATION

Widespread literacy aids economic development by facilitating the exchange of accurate information. This reduces the risks of operations in new or distant markets and allows new methods and products to be more widely and quickly used. As noted earlier, it also hastens the adaptation of innovations to the needs of other industries.

Well before 1860, the United States was a world leader in basic education. The Northwest Ordinance of 1784 had provided land to finance public education in each township, and some existing states already had school systems by that date. Literacy and general school attendance in the United States equalled or surpassed those of any country in Europe. Not all of this was provided by public education: Only by 1860 did government provide the majority of educational expenditures.[46] By that time, 57 percent of all white children between the ages of 5 and 19 were enrolled, and over 90 percent of the adult white population was literate. Literacy rates were highest in New England and lowest on the frontier and in the South, but variations were not great (see Chapter 6). In the 1850s, southern and midwestern states followed the East's example in establishing public schools. Education accounted for about one-fifth of all state and local government expenditures by that time.[47]

American educational achievements should not be overrated. Few students received as much as what would be considered a junior high school education today. Very few attended high school, and only a tiny minority went on to college. Additionally, the school year was much shorter than it is today. In agricultural regions, planting and harvest seasons required children's full-time labor in the fields, and the school year was adjusted accordingly. Parents could sometimes be an obstacle to education. Poor urban families often tried to keep their children out of school; the opportunity cost of foregone income in this

---

[44] P. Uselding, "Conjectural Estimates of Gross Human Capital Inflows to the American Economy," *Explorations in Economic History* (Fall 1971).

[45] R. Gallman, "Human Capital in the First 80 Years of the Republic: How Much Did America Owe the Rest of the World?" *American Economic Review* (February 1977).

[46] A. Fishlow, "Levels of 19th-Century American Investment in Education," *Journal of Economic History* (December 1966).

[47] Fishlow, "Levels of 19th-Century."

■ In reality, most country schools were attended by a broader age-range of students than those shown in this 1860s-era painting; and the teacher, if she were female, was likely a teenager.
Source: Painting by E. L. Henry. Yale University Art Gallery, Mabel Brady Garvan Collection.

era of widespread child labor was at least equal to the direct costs of public education in 1860. Low-income families bore much of the burden of educational costs, particularly in the cities.[48]

Educational Quality

The quality of education was uneven. In some rural schools, children "graduated" when they grew large enough to beat up the teacher. Few teachers had much more schooling than the oldest of their students. In technical and scientific education, the United States lagged far behind Germany and France. Only one scientific journal was published in the entire nation before the Civil War. This may not have been the handicap it may seem, given the state of nineteenth-century science.

Blacks and Women

Nor was schooling universally available. Education was legally prohibited for slaves in most if not all southern states. Even in the North, only the bravest and most idealistic teachers would ignore public opinion and open the classroom to blacks. Women found it all but impossible to obtain advanced education. In 1850, school enrollment rates were about 10 percent higher for white males than for females, and those of whites were 20 times or more black rates.[49]

Yet the results were impressive. By stressing communications skills and arithmetic competence, schools made it easy for Americans to exchange information and approach practical problems with open minds. American formal education was more easily combined with that occurring on the job than in many other nations. In a world of such rapid

---

[48] Fishlow, "Levels of 19th-Century."

[49] *Historical Statistics,* 1:369–370.

yet basic technological change, perhaps such schooling was better suited to economic growth than any other. Although the quantity and quality of antebellum education compare unfavorably with those of today, we must remember that this is hardly the appropriate frame of reference.

GOVERNMENT'S INFLUENCE ON THE ECONOMY

Every form of government influences the economic activity that takes place under its jurisdiction. Indeed, without government to make individuals secure in their property and persons, it is difficult to see how any but the most elementary activity would occur. In addition, it is generally through government that people develop institutions that shape the process of economic development, even in market-oriented economies.[50] Government sets the limits of legitimate and illegitimate activity, and through tax policies, safety and environmental regulations, command over the money supply, and redistributional programs, it provides incentives or barriers to individual activity. By curbing two widespread, understandable, but basically harmful tendencies, government can aid economic growth. People will perform acts whose costs are borne by others if opportunities to do so arise, and they are also likely to try to benefit from activities whose costs have been paid by others, avoiding contributions even though these might be much less than the value of their personal benefits. Both lead to economic inefficiency. Persons are likely to push actions whose costs are borne elsewhere beyond the point where the benefits to society of additional action equal the costs of achieving them. Further, if most or all individuals can avoid contributing to the cost of providing services, these will not be performed even though their cost may be far less than the value of the benefits they produce. Government can increase economic efficiency in the short run and raise growth rates over time by instituting policies that equate private and social rates of return.[51]

At the same time, government can be used to further individuals' private concerns with no consideration of the costs to society or groups within it. Grants of monopolistic privilege are an example. These raise the monopolists' incomes, but at the cost of a larger aggregate reduction in the income of the rest of the economy. Economists term such activities "rent seeking." Whether, on balance, government actions will further or reduce economic efficiency cannot be determined by theory. The answer depends on the popular sense of proper activity and on government's response to the various groups seeking to use it for their own purposes.[52]

The Record of Antebellum Government

In the antebellum period, as in every other, the record of government was mixed. By providing strong support for property rights through the Constitution and extending these through a series of laws and court decisions, economic activity in general was encouraged. Contracts were enforced, and the producers of new ideas were given property rights to them—but not the right to extend their monopolies beyond the original patent, copyright, or use grants. Crime, even violent crime, was not

---

[50] See, for example, D. North, *Structure and Change in Economic History* (New York: Norton, 1981) and M. Olson, *The Rise and Decline of Nations: Economic Growth, Stagflation, and Social Rigidities* (New Haven, Conn.: Yale University Press, 1982).

[51] D. North, T. Anderson, and P. Hill, *Growth and Welfare in the American Past: A New Economic History*, 3d ed. (Englewood Cliffs, N.J.: Prentice-Hall, 1983), Chap. 2.
[52] North, Anderson, and Hill, *Growth and Welfare*, Chap. 2.

abolished, but most individuals apparently believed that their goods were secure enough to make long-term plans for investment and invention. Moreover, there was very little attempt to restrict individuals in either the generation or use of whatever incomes they might produce—a situation fostered by the multiplicity of legal jurisdictions within the United States. Taxes were very low, and there were virtually no laws designed to redistribute income from those who produced it. In addition, resources under government control (public lands) were rapidly transferred to private ownership.

There were instances in which government action or inaction reduced overall welfare; for example, the tariff. Government support for slavery cost the slaves more than the gains of slaveowners, textile producers, and consumers. The problems of urban life were another clear example of government failure to promote the general welfare. It might be argued that this reflected ignorance of effective countermeasures rather than lack of will or means, but measures to prevent fires and epidemic disease had become increasingly effective in Europe in the eighteenth century.[53]

Evaluation Criteria for Government Activity

In another area, government influenced the course of development by direct action; it invested in projects designed to raise aggregate income levels. Professors North, Anderson, and Hill have proposed three criteria by which this aspect of government's impact on the economy might be evaluated.

1. Was the social rate of return (the increase in aggregate income rather than that accruing directly to the causal factor) greater than the private returns? That is, were incentives to private activity less than

the true value they produced for the aggregate economy?
2. Were government investment policies concentrated in such areas of high social returns?
3. Was the overall level of government investment activity large enough to exert a significant effect on the economy?

They concluded that the overall contribution of government investment projects in the antebellum economy was not large. In general, government efforts were simply too small to have major effects, even had they consistently met the first two criteria.[54] Federal government spending accounted for less than 3 percent of gross national product in this period. Moreover, much federal spending could hardly be termed investment; over one-third was for national defense, which had few direct effects on economic development.

The State and Local Record

State and local government spending was considerably greater than federal spending in aggregate, but much of it failed the first and second criteria. The bulk of state government spending on canals, particularly after 1840, apparently reduced rather than increased aggregate income, although we lack a comprehensive evaluation of canals' social returns. Public subsidies to railroads were more productive, but these were a minor portion of government expenditure before 1860. Education did yield high returns, but the patterns of educational financing prior to 1860 suggest that much public spending would have been replaced by private efforts had government efforts been reduced. In sum, government investment was neither large enough nor consistently directed toward areas of high social benefits to have produced substantial

---

[53] E. Jones, *The European Miracle* (Cambridge, U.K.: Cambridge University Press, 1981), Chap. 7.

[54] North, Anderson, and Hill, *Growth and Welfare*, Chap. 8. See also earlier editions of *Growth and Welfare in the American Past*.

positive effects on income. Rent-seeking activity does not appear to have had substantial effects on the national economy.

Indirect Influences on Income Distribution

Government investment projects were not the only mechanism by which economic development was influenced. Government sets the framework of rules within which economic activity occurs. While there were no important attempts to redistribute income between groups on the basis of their previous incomes, federal government policies did redistribute income geographically as a consequence of collection and expenditure patterns. Because federal revenues were overwhelmingly derived from tariffs, they were collected largely in New England and the major ports, and spent in the South. Frontier states typically paid more to the federal government in taxes than they received, at least after their Indians had been pacified.[55] Patterns of federal taxation and spending indicate at best a minor role for the federal government in the redistribution of income. Funds were transferred from two capital-rich areas and one capital-deficient region to locales intermediate in this regard.

The Economic Climate of Antebellum America

The major economic impact of government on the antebellum economy was through its provision of a climate in which vigorous expansion by the private economy could and did occur. Government's role in capital formation diminished as private institutions were developed and expanded and as government influence over areas such as incorporation and contracts became more favorable to private enterprise. In cases such as bank regulation and the provision of social overhead capital

in the cities, an argument can be made that government's role was too small. Tariffs on balance probably reduced economic growth rather than aiding it as they were intended to do. For the Indians, of course, government policies for at least the first century of U.S. history were disastrous. Immigration policy, or the lack of one, may have had larger beneficial effects over time than any other single program.[56]

In this period, American attention was strongly centered on economic growth. In pursuing that goal, institutions were developed and expanded that proved admirably suited to their purpose. Both by the temperament of its people and in the institutions that affected and supported innovation, the United States offered an extremely favorable climate for expanded and innovative economic activity. The basic criterion for deciding on the appropriate agency for any purpose was pragmatism. Governments owned and operated arsenals, banks, railroads, and canals—which, of course, is socialistic—not out of ideological conviction, but through a perception that effective private institutions either were nonexistent or less effective than public agencies. The gradual abandonment of many semi-mercantilistic regulations, especially in the older cities, reflects no commitment to laissez faire, but a recognition that these were ineffective. If we compare the results actually achieved in this period with those that might be expected from the operation of a market economy with the absolute minimum of government intervention, it may be concluded that the overt effects of government activity on the U.S. economy were not great.[57]

---

[55] L. Davis and J. Legler, "The Government in the American Economy, 1815–1902: A Quantitative Study," *Journal of Economic History* (December 1966).

[56] Davis and Legler, "The Government." See also comments on this article by D. McDougal.

[57] J. Hughes, *The Governmental Habit* (Charlottesville, Va.: University of Virginia Press, 1976), is a proponent of greater governmental impact than those seen here.

SELECTED REFERENCES

Anderson, T., and P. Hill. *The Growth of a Transfer Society.* Stanford, Calif.: Hoover Institution Press, 1980.

Commons, J. *History of Labor in the United States.* 4 vols. New York: A. Kelley, 1918.

Davis, L., and D. North. *Institutional Change and American Economic Growth.* Cambridge, U. K.: Cambridge University Press, 1971.

Fogel, R. *Without Consent or Contract: The Rise and Fall of American Slavery.* New York: Norton, 1989.

Furnas, J. *The Americans: A Social History of the United States.* New York: Putnam, 1969.

Gallman, R., and S. Engerman. *Long-Term Factors in American Economic Growth.* Chicago: University of Chicago Press, 1986.

Goldin, C. *Understanding the Gender Gap: An Economic History of American Women.* New York: Oxford University Press, 1990.

Hughes, J. *The Governmental Habit.* Charlottesville, Va.: University of Virginia Press, 1976.

Lebergott, S. *The American Economy: Income, Wealth, and Want.* Princeton, N.J.: Princeton University Press, 1977.

Lindert, P., and J. Williamson. "Three Centuries of American Inequality" in P. Uselding, ed. *Research in Economic History.* Greenwich, Conn.: JAI Press, 1976.

———. *American Inequality: A Macroeconomic History.* New York: Academic Press, 1980.

North, D. *Structure and Change in Economic History.* New York: Norton, 1981.

Olson, M. *The Rise and Decline of Nations: Economic Growth, Stagflation, and Social Rigidities,* New Haven, Conn.: Yale University Press, 1982.

Soltow, L. *Men and Wealth in the United States, 1850–1970.* New Haven, Conn.: Yale University Press, 1975

———, ed. *Six Papers on the Distribution of Wealth and Income.* New York: National Bureau of Economic Research (distributed by Columbia University Press), 1969.

U.S. Department of Commerce, Bureau of the Census. *Historical Statistics of the United States: Colonial Times to 1970.* 2 vols. Washington, D.C.: Government Printing Office, 1975.

THE CIVIL WAR

*T*he American Civil War is often presented as a watershed event in political history. The war's influence on the economic history of the United States, though profound, is widely misunderstood, especially so since we can only compare the events that actually occurred in the war's aftermath with counterfactual hypotheses of "what would have happened if?..."

Some conclusions about the war are now well established. At one time, it was thought that the Civil War initiated U.S. industrialization, but economic historians now agree that the United States had developed a large manufacturing sector before 1860. Both the quantity and variety of manufactured goods produced in this country had been growing at impressive rates for three or four decades before the war. Nevertheless, in 1860 the United States was still primarily an agricultural economy. By 1890 it had become largely industrial. What role did the Civil War play in this transformation, and what were the mechanisms by which its influence was exerted? How significant were these effects?

THE COST OF FRATRICIDE

No other war of the United States has been more costly in terms of human lives than the holocaust that consumed the nation between 1861 and 1865. Over 600,000 men died—perhaps 6 percent of the work force. These deaths were disproportionately concentrated among young men who tended to be more productive as members of the work force and whose contributions might have been expected to grow still further. Additionally, there were hundreds of thousands of wounded as well as many civilian casualties. In relation to the total population, the military death rate was over 65 times that which the United States endured in Vietnam. Had the casualty rates there been equal to those of the Civil War, the Vietnam conflict would have cost this country 3.95 million American deaths. Even World War II, in which 405,000 Americans died in military service, pales in comparison, and the population of the United States in 1940 was four times that of 1860.

The direct monetary costs of the war, including measures of the loss to future output through premature deaths, have been estimated at as much as $6.6 billion in 1860 dollars.[1] Even though this figure is probably a maximum estimate, it is difficult to regard the war itself as anything other than a catastrophe for the United States. It has been pointed out, however, that some of the declines in income that occurred in the South after 1865 sprang from causes largely independent of the War.[2] In addition, some nonmonetary income gains produced by the war are difficult to quantify; we can assign a lower limit to the value of freedom to the ex-slaves, but the actual valuation of this change in circumstances cannot really be assessed through economic calculations.[3]

Long-Term Effects

Despite the limitations of the Goldin and Lewis study, a summation of its conclusions gives some idea of the possible effects of the war on the United States in subsequent years.

---

[1] C. Goldin and F. Lewis, "The Economic Cost of the American Civil War: Estimates and Implications," *Journal of Economic History* (June 1975). This figure is controversial because of data limitations and methodological problems. See S. Lee and P. Passell, *A New Economic View of American History* (New York: Norton, 1979), Chap. 11.
[2] P. Temin, "The Post-Bellum Recovery of the South and the Cost of the Civil War," *Journal of Economic History* (December 1976).
[3] However, see K. Ng and N. Virts, "The Value of Freedom," *Journal of Economic History* (December 1989).

■ The costs of the Civil War were great. Burying detail was among the typical soldier's duties.
Source: Photo by Alexander Gardner, U.S. Military History Institute.

Aside from the cost in lives, the effects of the war include the reduction in economic growth that occurred during the war and the loss in consumption required to catch up with the output levels that the continuation of prewar trends would have produced. The resumption of prewar economic growth rates after the war required higher levels of saving from lower incomes (greater consumption sacrifices) than would have been necessary in its absence. When these factors are included, the total cost of the Civil War may be as great as $9 to $15 billion in 1869 dollars. Full recovery, the study concluded, was not achieved until 1879 in the North (in terms of consumption levels), and the South reached the levels of consumption it might have enjoyed in the war's absence only in 1909.[4] Even though other estimates

reach more modest conclusions, by any one of them, the war produced a reduction in levels of physical welfare for most Americans that was both sizable and long-lived. We cannot know what might have happened to economic growth and per-capita consumption had the war not taken place, but even if only a continuation of prewar trends is assumed, the conflict reduced incomes to less than their potential for at least a decade and a half.[5]

The real market value of 3.9 million slaves at $1,000 each (probably a sizable overestimate) was almost certainly less than the direct cost of the war. Thus, the war was an expensive method of freeing the slaves; purchasing them out of public funds would have been cheaper. It is difficult to imagine

[4] Goldin and Lewis, "The Economic Cost."

[5] Temin, "Post-Bellum Recovery."

that compensated emancipation could have produced the social and political divisions that the war generated; these may still not be completely dissipated for any region or race. In addition, emancipation as it actually occurred imposed very substantial costs on the ex-slaves themselves.

CAUSES OF THE WAR

Because the Civil War was so incredibly costly in lives, wasted resources, property destruction, and it retarded economic growth, why did it occur? Was it a tragic mistake as well as a tragedy, or did some groups benefit even though aggregate well-being was reduced? Those who had been slaves before the war clearly gained from its outcome, but it strains credulity to suppose that they initiated the conflict. Could the war have been the result of calculation—even on faulty data or by flawed methods—that war was cheaper than available alternatives? Or were the causes wider than the slavery issue? Were tariffs, access to western land, the subsidization of a transcontinental railroad, the question of states' rights per se, or some other differences major contributors to the outbreak of war?

Slavery

Undoubtedly, the slavery question was the primary cause of the southern states' secession from the Union, which in turn was the immediate occasion for the war. The South had an enormous economic stake in slavery. Slaves comprised a major portion of southern wealth, and slavery raised the incomes of free southerners above the U.S. average. Slavery may not have benefited all or even most southern whites, and it certainly reduced the welfare of blacks. But slave owners had influence in southern politics far beyond that given by

their numbers alone, and slave owners reaped large gains from continuation of the "Peculiar Institution." So rapidly were slave prices rising in the 1850s that the capital gains on an investment in slaves at the beginning of the decade were in themselves more than sufficient to pay the costs of slaves' maintenance, even if the slaves were not employed in any form of production.[6] A threat to these levels of income and wealth would hardly fail to produce a strong response from their beneficiaries. It might also be supposed that slave ownership would not predispose planters toward acceptance of orders from others.

On no other topic was southern opinion so nearly unanimous as on the proposition that slavery must be preserved and shielded from any threat. As detailed in Chapter 6, market signals indicated that slavery was becoming more rather than less profitable. Even southerners who did not own slaves might see slave-based agriculture as their most promising avenue to riches. The danger came from political, moral, and social forces.

The Extension of Slavery

Congressional records show that no other issue engendered the same fierce unanimity of opposition from southern representatives as did any proposal for limitations, however slight, on slavery. Even the extension of slavery into new territories was a political rather than an economic question. Before 1860, there was no meaningful political challenge to slavery in the areas where it was already established. But the South was keenly interested in securing the rights of slaveowners (few were willing to risk a move into "unsecured" territories) to settle new areas. Only on the issue of slavery did southern views on states' rights differ significantly from those of other areas.

Since the South still had within its 1860 borders far more land than the existing slave

---

[6] Y. Yasuba, "The Profitability and Viability of Plantation Slavery," *Economic Studies Quarterly* (September 1961).

population could work, the extension of slavery to new territories might appear unimportant. The prices of slaves were rising in relation to those of land, which indicated the relative trends in supply of both inputs.[7] But if slavery were excluded from new territories, the admission of free states into the union might in time threaten the South's veto power in the Senate. Rapid population growth in the Northwest had already eroded the South's power in the House of Representatives. Southerners may well have thought that even if free states had thus far evinced no real antipathy toward slavery, they had no strong interest in maintaining it. Although there had been little nationwide support for John Brown and his efforts to raise a slave rebellion in 1859, northern opinions might change.

After Lincoln's election in 1860, only a scant one-third of Congress voted against a proposed constitutional amendment guaranteeing slavery's perpetuation where it already existed.[8] Not only were slave owners rich and getting richer, but the political threat to their property did not appear to be increasing. Yet the South attempted to secede over the issue of slavery. Why?

Maintaining Investment Values

One explanation has been offered by Professor Wright.[9] After noting the enormous wealth in slaves possessed by the South, he stated that each slaveholder's wealth was to a great extent dependent on the conduct of others. The market value of slaves to any single master was determined largely by the expectations of *all other* slaveowners, regardless of any individual slaveowner's views on the probability of emancipation, the future markets for slaves, or the crops they produced. If enough slaveowners offered their chattels for sale, prices would fall and the wealth of all would be reduced, whether they tried to sell slaves or not. To reduce the chance that any substantial group might become worried enough to sell slaves, Wright argued, the South continually sought new assurances from Congress that slavery would be maintained, even in cases where the challenges were trivial. Secession, in this view, would end any possibility of a political threat to slavery arising from those who had no stake in its continuation.

The Compromise of 1850, the Fugitive Slave Act (1852), and the Kansas–Nebraska Act (1854) were significant to the South, not because they affected sizable numbers of slaves or planters, but because they represented other regions' recognition of slavery as an institution, indicated the absence of current opposition, and thus raised the value of slaves by indicating the lack of opposition to slavery. The ownership of human property or the income derived from it were not seriously affected when slaveowners were prevented from pursuing runaway slaves through northern states or when they incurred the risk of changing their slaves' status if they brought their bondsmen to free states. These circumstances seldom occurred, and it was easy to avoid bringing slaves to free territory.

Opposition to Slave Import

The actions of the Confederacy itself lend strong support to Wright's thesis. No southern state, or even the Confederacy itself, supported measures to reopen the Atlantic slave trade. Indeed, there was widespread southern opposition to such a move. The articles of secession passed by several states specifically prohibited such actions, and the Confederacy refused to allow the importation of slaves from within the boundaries of the United States.[10] Either measure might have reduced the prices of slaves already owned by southerners by increasing the supply.

---

[7] G. Wright, *The Political Economy of the Cotton South* (New York: Norton, 1979), 131–134.

[8] Wright, *Political Economy*, 156.

[9] Wright, *Political Economy*, Chap. 5.

[10] Wright, *Political Economy*, 150–154.

Slavery's Prospects in 1860 Whether because of the political situation or because of favorable cotton markets, the evidence indicates that slaveowners were becoming increasingly optimistic about the future of slavery and plantation agriculture. Not only were slave prices rising sharply in the late 1850s, they were also rising in relation to the rental rates for the same slaves, indicating increasing confidence that slaves would be a profitable long-term investment.[11] Investors will not pay higher prices for capital assets they expect to lose in the near future. The North had no clear economic basis for opposition to slavery's continuation, although it may have had somewhat different feelings about its expansion. Although the abolitionist movement was not strong even in the North, it was growing, particularly among urban workers.[12]

Northern Views on Slavery

The political events of 1860 hardly indicate strong opposition to slavery outside the South. If Lincoln supported the abolition of slavery (and this was by no means certain at that time), he was a minority president. Although he received 59 percent of the electoral votes in 1860, Lincoln was the choice of less than 40 percent of the voters. He owed his election to a split in the Democratic Party.[13] The South underestimated the determination of the North and especially that of Lincoln to preserve the Union. The North underestimated the South's sense of insecurity. Once the fighting began, neither side felt able to lower its demands.

---

[11] R. Fogel and S. Engerman, *The Reinterpretation, of American Economic History* (New York: Harper & Row, 1971), 382–383.

[12] R. Fogel, *Without Contract or Consent: The Rise and Fall of American Slavery* (New York: Norton, 1989), Chaps. 9, 10.

[13] *Historical Statistics of the U.S.: Colonial Times to 1970*, 2 vols. (Washington, D.C.: Government Printing Office, 1975), 2:1074.

THE ECONOMICS OF WAR: THE SOUTH

Southern Weaknesses

It is ironic that many of the conditions that the South fought to preserve or further proved to be severe handicaps to Confederate war efforts. The prewar concentration on agriculture left the South largely dependent on foreign sources for arms and other manufactured goods. This should not be interpreted as an indication of economic weakness in the antebellum South, but only of the irrationality of war. Within the Confederacy's borders, only the Tredegar Iron Works in Richmond, Virginia, was capable of producing rails, artillery, and other heavy iron products when the war commenced. The Confederates built another foundry at Selma, in Alabama, but throughout the war, the South had to depend on prewar stocks, what could be brought through an increasingly effective Union blockade, captured from Union forces, or obtained in trade with the enemy. Partially because of the nature of warfare, and also because of the frequency of Union Army defeats early in the war, arms supplies were largely adequate, and blockade-runners' cargoes were largely civilian consumer goods until late in 1863.[14] Heavy-metal goods may have been an exception; by 1864 the South was forced to tear up branch railroads to obtain rails to keep its main lines in operation.

Population

The South was outnumbered two to one in population, but slavery deprived the South of more than one-third of its potential military manpower. The region's attitude toward

---

[14] S. Lebergott, "Through the Blockade: The Profitability and Extent of Cotton Smuggling, 1861–1865," *Journal of Economic History* (December 1981).

the possibility of slave revolts, however, is revealed by the fact that there was no hesitation in stripping some regions of virtually their entire white male populations. In its last desperate days, the Confederacy even began to employ slave troops long after the Emancipation Proclamation had been widely publicized.

Weak Central Government

Adherence to states' rights doctrines reduced the adequacy of given quantities of material in the South. The central government of the Confederacy was unable to compel state contributions toward the cost of the war. The Confederate government could only request men, funds, and supplies from the states. In 1865, Lee's forces were half-starved and facing hopeless odds not only because of the damage and casualties that the South had already endured, but also because some Confederate states would not release troops or supplies for use beyond their borders.

Finances

Finances were another of the Confederacy's crucial weaknesses. Since the central government had effectively no powers of taxation, it borrowed. But bond sales within the South did not raise the enormous sums required for the war. Borrowing abroad was only slightly more successful. Especially after mid-1863, European financiers wanted more assurance of success than the Confederacy could offer. Unable to obtain funds in any other way, the Confederate government resorted to the printing press. But as war needs grew and the area under Confederate control shrank, an increasing supply of money was applied to the purchase of declining amounts of real goods and services. Prices rose at accelerated rates as people learned to anticipate inflation and to spend money as soon as they received it. In terms of the equation of exchange, velocity rose. The result was the only runaway inflation since the American Revolution. Prices rose in terms of

Confederate currency until people began to refuse to accept such paper money, and the desperate army began to confiscate goods it could not buy, further disrupting the battered economy.

Crucial Miscalculations

Several miscalculations aggravated southern disadvantages. Britain's and France's dependence on southern cotton was overestimated. Many southerners had thought that a cutoff of cotton exports would force Britain and perhaps France to bring pressure on the Union government to allow secession. However, the 1859 and 1860 cotton crops had been enormous, and most of the cotton had already been exported when hostilities began. Although cotton prices rose outside the South, there were sufficient inventories in Europe to last until new sources could be developed in India, Brazil, Egypt, the Caribbean, and areas of the South now controlled by the Union. Initially, the South had tried to restrict its own exports of cotton, but by the time the failure of this policy was evident and exports were resumed, the Union blockade made the effort dangerous and expensive. Much of the cotton produced after that time could neither be consumed within the South nor exported; it was a waste of productive resources.[15]

There had been some hope in the South that the Midwest would remain neutral in any conflict over slavery, but that region's Union sentiment proved strong. As war proponents do in almost all cases, the South underestimated its military tasks and the resolution of its foes. Once the North learned to use its population and industrial advantages effectively, the southern cause was lost. In a long war, brilliant southern generals could not compensate for the fact that their troops were outnumbered and increasingly dependent on

---

[15] S. Lebergott, *The Americans: An Economic Record* (New York: Norton, 1984), 243.

defeating a stronger enemy to obtain supplies. After the North finally found military leaders who could exploit their advantages, southern prospects grew bleaker still.

THE NORTHERN ECONOMY IN THE CIVIL WAR

Northern Strengths

The North began the war no less optimistically, if perhaps with less enthusiasm, than the South. President Lincoln's first call for military volunteers was for 75,000 men for three months. Before the war ended, the total strength of the Union army exceeded one million. The North had population, industry, organization, and superior access to foreign goods on its side. Union control of the seas was never challenged. These gave it a margin with which to offset the many errors of the first years.

The North's transportation system improved while the South's deteriorated, and the South had no hope of breaking the blockade with its own resources. In addition, the North also enjoyed superior financial institutions and retained a strong central government that proved capable of marshalling resources for military purposes.

■ Even in 1861, patriotism had to be encouraged with cash. Note the bounties offered recruits.
Source: Leslie's, March 19, 1864. From John Grafton, *New York in the Nineteenth Century,* 2d ed. (New York: Dover Publications, Inc., 1980), 21.

Before the North could consolidate these advantages, piecemeal employment was not enough to offset timid or incompetent northern military leadership. Eventually the Union found generals who could exploit the disparity in resources effectively enough to overcome the great southern commanders. Union armies might lose battle after battle, but the Confederates always found yet another army facing them. Every battle was crucial to the Confederacy, but the Union army had only to avoid outright destruction to continue the pressure on the South. Confederate attempts to achieve conclusive victory earned only a costly draw at Antietam (1862) and a strategic defeat at Gettysburg (1863) in the East. In the West, the war became a series of disasters for the Confederacy. What victories the South won there were far too costly to offset the defeats that led to Union control of the Mississippi River (depriving the South of virtually all resources from its western regions) and ultimately to the loss of Atlanta (1864).

UNION WAR FINANCE

To finance the war, the Union government increased taxes. Tariffs were raised to levels well beyond those that had provoked southern protests earlier. Excise taxes were levied on a wide variety of domestically produced goods, and an income tax was imposed. Although these measures increased federal revenues from $56 million (including the South) in 1860 to $334 million from Union territory in 1865, expenditures rose much faster, from $63 million to $1.293 billion.[16] Less than one-fifth of wartime expenditures was tax financed.

To finance the unprecedented deficits of the war years, the Union government borrowed, selling large amounts of bonds. The national debt rose from $64 million to $2.678 billion. By the war's end, interest payments on the debt were almost three times total government expenditures in 1860.[17] Bond sales proved difficult, and the government turned to Jay Cooke. This financier organized teams of salesmen supported by newspaper advertising, testimonials, and appeals to patriotism to market the bonds both in the United States and abroad. Cooke also employed political pressure on the banks to further bond sales.

Paper Money

The Union government also printed money, both directly and indirectly. For the first time since the revolutionary war, Congress authorized the issue of paper money. In 1862, $150 million in noninterest-bearing notes called "greenbacks" was placed in circulation. These notes were declared to be legal tender for all private debts and most obligations of the government. Greenbacks were not redeemable in

■ Twenty-five-cent notes were printed by the North after coins were driven out of circulation during the Civil War.
Source: Brown Brothers, courtesy of Smithsonian Institution.

---

[16] *Historical Statistics*, 2:1106, 1115.

[17] *Historical Statistics*, 2:1104.

■ A woman receives her Saturday shopping allowance from her husband, controller of the household purse strings, in this nineteenth-century sketch. Their expressions reflect the burdens of rising Civil War inflation.
Source: H. Armstrong Roberts.

specie, and soon drove gold and silver out of circulation at their face value as money. "Hard money" continued to be available at a premium in currency. The total amount of greenbacks authorized ultimately reached $450 million. In 1860, the entire money supply of the United States had been $442 million.[18]

The National Bank Act

In a time-honored measure designed to increase the sale of federal bonds, Congress passed the National Bank Act in 1862. This time, however, it did not set up a single large bank. Instead, it offered federal charters to existing banks or to people forming new ones. The act allowed currently operating banks or

---

[18] *Historical Statistics*, 2:985.

groups of five or more individuals who wished to set up new institutions to receive corporate charters from the federal government if they would meet its requirements for paid-in capital. These varied with the size of the city where the bank was located. Each bank chartered had to deposit a portion of its capital with the U.S. Treasury in the form of government bonds. In return, the bank would receive National Bank notes to 90 percent of the bonds' face value. This currency could either be used as bank reserves, as specie had been, or the notes could be circulated as the banks made loans. National Bank notes were of standard design, although the identity of the issuing bank was indicated on one side. They were accepted at face value anywhere in the United States.

The National Bank Act contained provisions requiring banks chartered under it to maintain reserves as minimum proportions of their outstanding notes and deposits. Because the act's conditions imposed greater restrictions on banks' lending activities than state banking laws, few banks were chartered under the National Bank Act until 1865. In that year, Congress imposed a 10 percent tax on all outstanding state bank notes. The tax burden exceeded the interest income that state banks had received from loans made through currency issues and effectively ended state bank notes' use as currency. (A few state bank notes were kept in circulation for advertising purposes and prestige.) After the passage of the 1865 legislation, the number of banks chartered under the National Bank Act rose from 467 to 1,294—over 75 percent of all banks in the United States. The act solved one of the country's prewar financial problems: The United States now had a uniform currency, the National Bank notes. It also provided better designed and enforced regulation of banks. But the most serious failings of the banking system remained; there was neither a lender of last resort—a bankers' bank that could provide emergency reserves—nor a banking institution that could directly control the money supply.

The Effects of Inflation

Since the supply of money increased much faster than did that of goods and services during the Civil War, prices rose. By 1865, prices were 70 to 100 percent above prewar levels. In periods of rapid inflation, there are usually redistributive effects. Those who sell items whose price increases exceed the general rise, gain; those selling goods whose price changes lag, suffer losses in purchasing power. The same is true for purchases. If an individual buys items whose prices rise disproportionately, he or she is a victim of inflation; but gains result if purchases are concentrated on goods whose prices increase less than the overall average. Redistributive effects are especially likely if inflation is rapid and unforeseen. Although wages rose, they may not have kept pace with price increases, especially for imported goods. The extent of the decline is still under dispute, but it appears probable that real wages did fall during the war. At one time it was believed that profit recipients gained what workers had lost, but it now appears that the portion of income paid in wages rose slightly during the war.[19] Both workers and employers paid higher taxes during the war; the one certain beneficiary of inflation was the federal government, which greatly increased its command over the economy's output.

The law required that greenbacks be accepted in payment of debt. These notes were fiat money—defined as legal tender by the government. Greenbacks (and state bank notes until 1865) became the circulating medium.

---

[19] See R. Kessel and A. Alchian, "Real Wages in the North During the Civil War," *Journal of Law and Economics* (October 1959), and S. DeCanio and J. Mokyr, "Inflation and Wage Lag During the Civil War," *Journal of Economic History* (June 1975).

Gold and silver were worth as much as ever in terms of foreign currencies and foreign goods, so they were either exported or hoarded. Since specie could only be obtained by paying a premium in U.S. paper currency, foreign goods' prices in paper money rose.

The Abandonment of the Gold Standard

Specie flowed out of the United States, and the war made it impossible to reduce the domestic price level. Consequently, the United States was unable to remain on the gold standard; a paper dollar could no longer be exchanged for its face value in specie. The U.S.

■ An expanding money supply led to runaway inflation because real output in the Confederacy failed to keep pace. Five-hundred dollars represents more than a year's income at prewar prices.
Source: Culver Pictures.

■ The lower denomination of this Union bill is significant: Inflation within the Union was much lower than within the Confederacy.
Source: Brown Brothers, courtesy of the Smithsonian Institution.

mint could no longer sell gold for paper currency at the prices fixed before the war, at which there would have been an abundance of buyers, but no one willing to sell gold to the mint. The mint's gold stock would soon have been exhausted. Under the new conditions, the value of the U.S. dollar in international transactions was set by supply and demand; the exchange rate fell as Americans bought more foreign goods than their real exports would finance. At one time, the greenback exchanged for only 35 percent of its face value in gold. One traditional source of foreign exchange declined sharply. Merchant shipping tonnage fell as ships were lost to Confederate raiders or natural disasters or were sold to avoid capture. The industry had been declining before the war, but now it suffered a blow from which it never recovered.

DID THE WAR AID INDUSTRIALIZATION?

To some historians, the Civil War was a major economic as well as political divide.[20] To them, the antebellum United States was an agricultural nation, with institutions and values reflecting its peoples's occupations, and political control in the hands of southerners hostile to northern industry and western settlement. These historians believed that the war directly encouraged industrialization, as several later wars clearly did. They thought it also helped create a political climate much more favorable to the postbellum changes. In the absence of southern representatives, Congress could pass measures favoring transcontinental railroads; the Homestead Act, which

provided that government land be distributed virtually free of money charges to bona fide settlers; and steep increases in tariffs, which limited competition from foreign manufacturers. The National Bank Act, the financial markets developed through massive wartime sales of government securities and investors' greater familiarity with financial instruments, and the redistribution of income from labor to capital through "profit inflation" also aided postwar industrial financing, in the eyes of this group.

The "Beard-Hacker Thesis" developed by these scholars contends that repayment of the national debt after the Civil War further transferred income from those with a high propensity to consume to people who tended to save and invest large portions of their incomes. Even in the South, despite serious war damage, there were effects favoring this process. The abolition of slavery allowed more flexible and rational uses of labor because blacks were now freer to respond to economic incentives. Northern agriculture, it was thought, mechanized rapidly during the war to compensate for the loss of manpower to the military.

The Modern View

Implicit in each of these contentions is the idea that the result was both positive and significant for U.S. economic growth. However, today every one of these points is under severe challenge, if not totally refuted. Using statistics that were not available when the previous ideas were formulated, historians now increasingly view the Civil War as an event whose aggregate economic impact was negative, and possibly disastrously so.[21]

[20] See C. and M. Beard, *The Rise of American Civilization* (New York: Macmillan, 1930), and L. Hacker, *The Triumph of American Capitalism* (New York: Columbia University Press, 1940).

[21] T. Cochran, "Did the Civil War Retard Industrialization?" *Mississippi Valley Historical Review* (September 1961), was the seminal article in this reformulation.

The Revision of the Optimists' Views

The earlier, positive view of the Civil War's economic influence was based on impressions, not accurate data. Some writers tended to generalize from the U.S. experience in World Wars I and II, in which massive government spending eliminated prewar unemployment, and, at least in World War II, had some significant technological spinoffs that aided postwar civilian goods production. Some of the conclusions may result from two of the most common errors in economic reasoning: failure to assess alternatives properly (foregone options) and the belief that historical sequence implies causation. The massive economic transformation and growth of the United States after the Civil War are not proof that the war was responsible for these developments.

In general, the case against the view just stated is that the war used scarce resources and thus denied them to the alternatives foreclosed by such applications. Large numbers of men and horses that had previously been employed in agriculture, manufacturing, and distribution were transferred to military purposes. To employ these resources for war uses meant that their output in civilian uses was forfeited. The true gain (or loss) from their diversion is the difference in the value of their output in the two uses.

Economic Costs of Wartime Destruction

Because the primary "product" of resources' military employment was death and destruction, the war reduced overall welfare while it occurred. The cost was not only the direct result of military activity, but also the less noticeable forfeiture of civilian goods that were not produced. If men were replaced by less experienced or otherwise less productive workers, that is, women and children, the loss would not be total. But there must have been some overall reduction in output since these alternative (and lower-paid) labor sources were not used while men were available.

General Sherman's "Bummers," Sheridan's forces who devastated agriculture in the Shenandoah Valley, and General N. B. Forrest's raiders destroyed productive resources and left the areas of their attentions unproductive until the damage could be repaired.[22] Both the winners and the losers in the Civil War were Americans; the direct result of military action was that output from people, physical resources, and institutions was lost. Other resources had to be devoted to repair or replacement before the country regained its prewar productive potential.

The Demand for Industrial Goods

Modern war, which is waged at least as much with materials as with men, is capital intensive. The Civil War was not a modern war. Masses of men armed with rifles were the chief military instrument of both antagonists. There was little artillery and virtually no sophisticated machinery. This meant that the war imposed very light demands on industrial production and virtually none on heavy industry. Naval construction might constitute an exception, especially after the appearance of ironclad warships, but naval activity was only a minor part of the war effort. More iron was devoted to small-arms production than to any other item used by the Union Army. The second greatest use of iron was in horseshoes, and the two combined required only about 2 percent of total iron production during the war.[23] With the partial exception of weapons, both armies demanded much the same items for their troops as the men had consumed in civilian life. Only the inherent wastefulness of a military establishment in wartime increased

[22] General Sheridan is said to have assessed the results of his operations by saying that, "If a crow wants to cross the Shenandoah Valley, he had better carry his own rations."
[23] L. Davis, R. Easterlin, and W. Parker, *American Economic Growth: An Economist's History of the U.S.* (New York: Harper & Row, 1972), 56.

demand for food, clothing, and similar items above peacetime levels.

The Effects of Fiscal Policy

It might appear that a large expansion in government spending financed by such highly inflationary methods as were employed in the war by both sides would stimulate economic activity. If people obtained more money, they could be expected to spend most of it. However, although the volume of spending could rise almost indefinitely, once all productive resources are in use, little or no further increase in real production is possible without changes in technology, resource supplies, or the institutions governing their use. Such changes almost always require considerable periods of time to implement. The Civil War neither created more resources nor improved the efficiency with which existing stocks were used; indeed, the primary effects of the war were just the opposite. Approximately 25 to 35 percent of the labor force was diverted to less productive uses, if not outright destruction.[24] In the 1860 context, a large-scale increase in spending diverted resources from one use to another less productive employment. The increase in spending generated price increases rather than gains in real output. When the war began, the economy was at or close to full employment; there were few resources whose reallocation to military uses did not involve direct opportunity costs.

Wartime Growth

The U.S. economy did not cease to grow entirely during the Civil War, but the rate of growth was much slower than it had been in the two prior decades or would be again in the 1870s. The total output of goods and services had been growing at a 4.6 percent annual average rate from 1840 to 1860, and it grew at 4.4 percent from 1870 to 1900. The rate in the 1860s, however, was only 2 percent. Manufacturing's share of total production increased faster before the war than it did afterward.[25] Heavy industry became a larger portion of total manufacturing production during the war, but it did so largely by default; consumer goods output grew very slowly or in some cases even declined. There was no great spurt of growth in heavy industry.[26] Some important industries were badly hurt by the loss of southern markets, particularly boots and shoes and cotton textiles. The latter was also adversely affected by the restricted supply of raw cotton.

Despite the completion of the Union Pacific, the first transcontinental railway, railroad construction declined. In the 1850s, 20,000 miles of railroad track had been built in America; the next decade saw only 16,000 miles of new right-of-way, and most of that was built after the war.[27] In many other industries, the same pattern appears: growth, but at lower rates than the previous decade, or even absolute declines in production. Nor was slower growth in output offset by qualitative improvements. The 1860s was the only decade in the entire century in which labor productivity in manufacturing declined, an indication that the diversion of first-line workers to the military was not offset by the use of more or better capital.[28]

The war itself produced no innovations with profound impact on the productive potential of the postwar economy. Standardized clothing sizes and widespread use of canned goods were the most important new developments. In other sectors of the economy, the picture is similar to that in manufacturing. Northern agriculture did grow faster than industry during the war, but the pace of mech-

---

[24] Davis, Easterlin, and Parker, *American Economic Growth*, 56.

[25] Fogel and Engerman, *Reinterpretation*, 371.
[26] Fogel and Engerman, *Reinterpretation*, 372.
[27] *Historical Statistics*, 1:372.
[28] Fogel and Engerman, *Reinterpretation*, 372.

anization slowed down rather than accelerated. In any case, much of the increased production of wheat and corn was exported, and the growth in foreign demand can hardly be attributed to the war.

Southern agriculture was, of course, badly disrupted by the war and its aftermath. It did not fully recover for decades, although not all of the South's difficulties can be attributed to the results of the war.[29] Per-capita income in the South fell 38 percent from prewar levels, and much of this decline was due to the reduction in the labor force caused by the abolition of slavery.[30] Although the reduction in hours worked and labor force participation indicates a gain in leisure time or household activity for ex-slaves, and thus the loss in income is overstated by these figures, the drop in southern incomes was real and large.[31]

Delayed Effects?

It has been argued that the war's beneficial economic effects were delayed rather than immediate. The rapid economic growth of the economy in general and of manufacturing in particular in the 1870s is seen as deferred effects of the war. Whatever the immediate effects of the war may have been, proponents of this position believe that its long-run results were favorable. But growth rates in the 1870–1900 period were higher than those of the 1860s in part because of a catch-up effect; the economy grew faster because it had missed so many opportunities during the war. The postwar increase in growth rates would not have been necessary or could have proceeded from a larger base had growth in the 1860s been normal. In addition, it is not clear just how the war could have added to growth capabilities if it neither increased resource supplies (in the case of labor, it clearly reduced them) nor introduced important new technology. A new study by Professor Gallman indicates that previous estimates of antebellum capital stocks were too low, and thus postwar growth rates have been overstated, further downgrading arguments for the war's positive effects.[32]

THE BENEFITS OF WAR?

The strongest case for beneficial effects on economic growth related to the war appears to be in the area of financial and monetary developments. The claim that inflation transferred income from labor to capital during the war is weak, but postwar debt repayment may have had this result. During the war, the chief beneficiary of income transfers was the federal government; redistribution within the private sector during the war now seems unlikely to have had significant effects. Postwar retirement of public debt, which was financed largely by regressive taxes whose impact fell mainly on low- and middle-income groups rather than on the rich, did transfer income from consumers to investors. However, this accounted for no more than a fraction of the increase in investment that took place from 1866 to 1900. One study claimed these transfers caused no more than 3 percent of the increase in investment. Others are more generous, but all indicate that investment would have risen to 90 percent or more of the levels actually attained without the aid given

---

[29] Temin, "Post-Bellum Recovery."

[30] R. Ransom and R. Sutch, *One Kind of Freedom: The Economic Consequences of Emancipation* (Cambridge, U.K.: Cambridge University Press, 1977), Chap. 1. See also Temin, "Post-Bellum Recovery."

[31] Ex-slaves' incomes approximately doubled when both material income and the value of additional leisure are included. See Ng and Virts, "The Value of Freedom."

[32] R. Gallman, "The United States Capital Stock in the Nineteenth Century," in Gallman and Engerman, *Long-Term Factors in American Economic Growth* (Chicago: University of Chicago Press, 1986), 180–181.

by the form of debt repayment employed by the U.S. government.[33]

Banking and Investments

The National Bank Act did improve the banking system's operation to some extent. However, the evidence indicates that the ragbag currency of the antebellum period imposed only slight burdens on the economy or its rate of growth. (See Chapter 8.) The National Bank Act affected attempts to return to the gold standard in the postwar period in a manner that could not have aided economic growth. The money supply was restricted to the point of severe deflationary pressure, which resulted in real economic distress. Some rural areas' currency supply was so limited that barter transactions reappeared.[34] Nor did the act eliminate the instability of the banking system. Institutions similar to those provided by the National Bank Act could have been developed without the war, even though the legislation itself was spurred by the needs of war finance. If the war caused them to be introduced sooner than would otherwise have been the case, it was a horribly expensive catalyst.

The improved methods of securities marketing that appeared during the war were useful in the postwar period, but it is difficult to argue that the absence of that conflict would have done more than delay their implementation, nor can these methods have been the source of the postwar increase in investment. In fact, the proportion of gross national product devoted to investment had been rising before the Civil War, and its rate of increase

declined after the conflict.[35] On balance, the war-induced changes in monetary and financial institutions were favorable to investment and economic growth, but they reinforced trends that had already appeared, and their influence was not great. That the war was the immediate occasion for the introduction of these changes hardly makes their benefits greater than the costs of the conflict.

Politics

Few of the political arguments for the war's favorable effects on long-term economic growth now appear strongly based. The proposition that the war facilitated a shift in political control to groups more disposed toward industrialization and economic growth is weak. The war's immediate cause now appears to have been the realization that Dixie was *already* losing its veto power in Congress. Some of the consequences attributed to the shift in sectional control of Congress were not in fact points of contention between the North and South; indeed, there were almost no issues aside from slavery that united either area. The South was not opposed to government aid for the construction of a transcontinental railroad, although it wanted the eastern terminal to be located in New Orleans rather than St. Louis. Neither the North nor the South was united on the tariff issue. As Chapter 8 indicated, the trend in prewar legislation was toward lower rates, generally thought to be what the South desired. Easy access to western land was opposed by the South for political reasons, and the Homestead Act was passed during the enforced absence of southern representatives from Congress. But the point is not merely whether the South or the North favored or opposed legislation, but the actual effects of the laws in raising or reducing American economic growth.

[33] Fogel and Engerman, *Reinterpretation*, 378. This estimate (by Engerman) is the lowest. See also J. Williamson, "Watersheds and Turning Points: Conjectures on the Long Term Impact of Civil War Financing," *Journal of Economic History* (September 1974), P. Passell and S. Lee, *New Economic View*, Chap. ll, and Gallman, "The United States Capital Stock."

[34] I am indebted to Professor Price Fishback on this point.

[35] Fogel and Engerman, *Reinterpretation*, 373.

In the case of the Homestead Act, for example, the results were minor and probably adverse. Despite the reduction in money costs of government land, the act imposed non-money costs that apparently were at least as onerous; after 1862, most western land was transferred to private ownership under previous legislation requiring money payment. Even if the Homestead Act increased the temporary allocation of resources to agriculture, this was a transfer to low-productivity uses relative to other opportunities available to labor. As such, it reduced incomes rather than increasing them.

Tariffs

High tariffs increased the monopoly power of American producers, very much at the expense of consumers and probably of employment as well. It is difficult to view the continuation of the tariffs (which were instituted to raise revenue for the war) in the postwar period as stemming solely from their wartime origin. Attempts to measure the results of all the legislation so far discussed have concluded that none of these measures, including the transcontinental railroad, accounted for more than a fraction of 1 percent of U.S. economic growth. By 1865, the American economy was large and diversified. Even measures that doubled or halved the production of most sectors of the economy (and none of this legislation approached such an impact) would have a far less significant impact on the aggregate economy or its growth.

The Source of Industrialization

Another point made in defense of the war's economic impact is that it favored a shift from agricultural to business attitudes and thus allowed more rapid growth. The point is impossible to quantify, as are most psychological propositions in history. But it surely involves a misunderstanding of the attitudes of American farmers in general and southern planters in particular. These appear to have been typified by a high degree of economic rationality very much in conformity with what economic theory would predict. The contention that attitudinal shifts fostered economic growth would be strengthened had the South been ruled by values that consciously sacrificed economic advantage to other values or if the southern economy had been poor or stagnant in comparison with nonagricultural areas. But these were absent from the antebellum South. Incidentally, implications that such noneconomic values pervaded the South are seldom applied to midwestern agriculture, which had achieved less economic success than Dixie.

The American Civil War, then, was a costly diversion of resources to uses that reduced the rate of and potential for economic growth, and possibly even the level of current incomes. During the war, population growth slowed. Immigration was reduced. Birth rates fell because of soldiers' enforced separations from their families, and the heavy losses incurred by both sides meant that some of this population loss might be permanent. The labor-force reductions, it must be noted, occurred in an economy where labor was less plentiful and more productive than in Europe, and where increases in the labor force were the largest single source of economic growth.

THE WAR-DAMAGED ECONOMY

The Civil War, in aggregate, was no aid to U.S. economic growth. When it is realized that the war occurred after three or four decades of rapid economic growth and diversification, it is difficult to view it as anything other than a tragic interruption of increasingly successful peacetime pursuits. The war marked no transition to industrialization, because that process began 30 or 40 years before the conflict.

■ Atlanta was soon rebuilt despite its near-total devastation during the Civil War.
Source: Records of the Office of the Chief Signal Officer: National Archives.

The war's impact on various regions differed. It was, as we have seen, not beneficial to the northern economy. In the South, its effects were ruinous. Physical destruction, particularly of buildings, railroads, and other fixed capital, was widespread, but this was repaired in a surprisingly short time. Southern railroads and manufacturing apparently regained or exceeded prewar levels of production by 1870.[36] These sectors, however, were not the core of the southern economy. Agriculture was, and the South's agricultural recovery was much slower. The abolition of slavery did not immediately generate new methods of organizing agricultural production or employment. Persons unfamiliar with anything but the slave-operated plantation could only gradually work out new arrangements. Blacks found that the choices opened by freedom were sharply constrained by their lack of property and skills. Since freedmen did not obtain landownership with emancipation, they had little choice but to continue as agricultural labor.

---

[36] Ransom and Sutch, *One Kind of Freedom*, 40–42.

One consequence of emancipation was that black women and children greatly reduced the amount of time they spent in field labor. Destruction of the antebellum financial institutions and the extensive capital losses suffered by the planters all but eliminated any chance for the substitution of capital for labor or for investments in other sectors of the economy. Cotton prices were extremely high immediately after the war, which increased the incentives for a return to agriculture. But the long-term growth in demand for cotton was slowing, and this added to the difficulties generated by the disruptions in supply. The South did not regain prewar levels of per-capita income until the 1880s. (Incomes from the two eras are not really comparable due to the sweeping changes in the status of blacks.) It was this period, not the prewar years, that was the source of the South's relative poverty.[37]

SELECTED REFERENCES

Andreano, R., ed. *The Economic Impact of the Civil War.* Cambridge, Mass.: Schenkman, 1962.

Beard, C. and M. *The Rise of American Civilization.* New York: Macmillan, 1930.

Davis, L., R. Easterlin, W. Parker et al. *American Economic Growth: An Economist's History of the United States.* New York: Harper & Row, 1972.

Fogel, R. *Without Contract or Consent: The Rise and Fall of American Slavery.* New York: Norton, 1989.

Fogel, R., and S. Engerman. *The Reinterpretation of American Economic History.* New York: Harper & Row, 1971.

Gallman, R., and S. Engerman, eds. *Long-Term Factors in American Economic Growth.* Chicago: University of Chicago Press, 1986.

Hacker, L. *The Triumph of American Capitalism.* New York: Columbia University Press, 1940.

Lee, S., and P. Passell. *A New Economic View of American History.* New York: Norton, 1979.

Ransom, R. *Conflict and Compromise: The Political Economy of Slavery, Emancipation, and the American Civil War.* New York: Cambridge University Press, 1989.

Ransom, R., and R. Sutch. *One Kind of Freedom: The Economic Consequences of Emancipation.* Cambridge, U.K.: Cambridge University Press, 1977.

Studenski, P., and H. Kroos. *Financial History of the United States.* New York: McGraw-Hill, 1952.

U.S. Department of Commerce, Bureau of the Census. *Historical Statistics of the United States: Colonial Times to 1970.* 2 vols. Washington, D.C.: Government Printing Office, 1975.

Wright, G. *The Political Economy of the Cotton South: Households, Markets, and Wealth in the Nineteenth Century.* New York: Norton, 1976.

———. *Old South, New South: Revolutions in the Southern Economy.* New York: Basic Books, 1986.

---

[37] Ransom and Sutch, *One Kind of Freedom*, Chap. 3.

The Rise of an Economic Colossus

10.
San Francisco
(population 149,473)

1865-1920

Census figures refer to the year 1870.

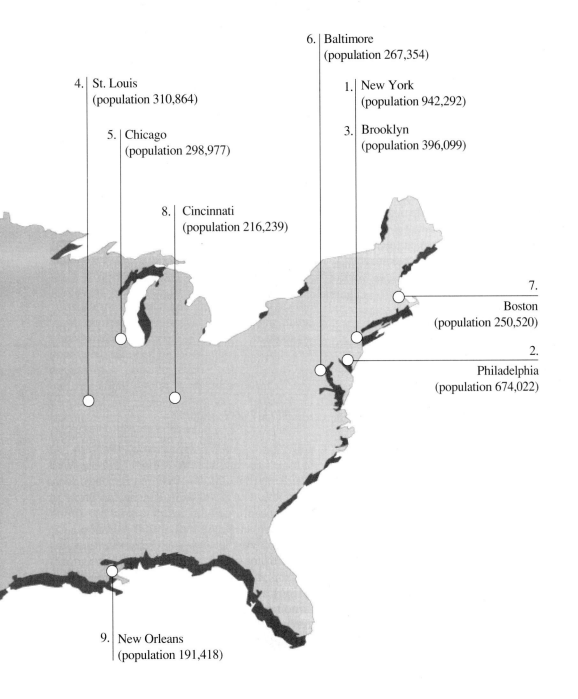

6. | Baltimore
(population 267,354)

1. | New York
(population 942,292)

3. | Brooklyn
(population 396,099)

4. | St. Louis
(population 310,864)

5. | Chicago
(population 298,977)

8. | Cincinnati
(population 216,239)

7.
Boston
(population 250,520)

2.
Philadelphia
(population 674,022)

9. | New Orleans
(population 191,418)

*P*hotographs depicting Americans at work in the period between the Civil War and the end of World War I often seem intended to convey an impression of capability and achievement. Typically, they show a construction crew, a factory work force, a shift of miners, or a group of lumberjacks posed in front of some product of their efforts. Another favorite pose is the business leader at his desk acting as the "Captain of Industry." The attitudes conveyed by both employers and workers reflect more than the conventions of portraiture in this era. American achievements over 1865–1920 were enormous, and knowledge of the feats was widespread. No other nation had done more in the economic sphere than the United States by 1910. Americans' pride in their economic attainments was justified.

In 1860, the American economy had been among the most productive in the world in terms of both aggregate output and per-capita incomes. By 1910, however, the U.S. economy was, in nearly all respects, the unchallenged world leader. Per-capita incomes were higher in the United States than in any other nation and growing faster than in most. In 1860, America had shown a talent for innovation, but it was still a technological and, especially, a scientific follower of Europe. A half-century later, American technology was the world's best in a growing range of applications, and the country's ability to generate new ideas was increasing rapidly. American economic leadership had already been achieved by 1910. The terrible losses and disruption that Europe endured as consequences of World War I meant that the United States no longer even had close rivals as the world's most productive economy.

THE DIMENSIONS OF GROWTH

American economic growth in this period was in part extensive; it resulted from increases in the amount of resources available. U.S. population growth continued to be rapid by world standards. The 37.5 million Americans at the close of the Civil War had grown to 99 million in 1914, and to 106 million in 1920. The expansion of economic activity into previously undeveloped regions continued for much of the period. The area of the contiguous United States had been stable since 1853, but many regions unsettled and unused at that time were now integrated into the national economy. The addition of Alaska (1867) and the acquisition of Hawaii and an overseas empire were less economically significant than the degree to which the entire continental area was brought into use. Even though settlement extended over the entire 48 states by 1910 and the frontier as a physical limit no longer existed, there remained enormous potential for further development of America's natural bounty.

Although population had nearly tripled, in part because of the greatest wave of immigration any nation had ever received, the total output of the economy had grown much faster. Real gross national product for the 1869–1878 decade had averaged 27.1 billion 1958 dollars. In 1914, the figure was $125.6 billion, and the 1920 gross national product reached $140 billion.[1] Table III.1 gives rough estimates of aggregate and per-capita GNP growth in 1990 dollars. Consequently, per-capita income in real terms had increased to nearly two and one-half times the Civil War–era level by 1920.

Americans enjoyed per-capita incomes about half again as large as those of the most successful European economies in the years just prior to World War I. American incomes were also growing faster than those of most other nations. Only Canada and Germany—both much smaller economies—came close to matching American per-capita income growth.[2] Sweden and Japan may have generated equal aggregate growth rates, but from much lower income bases. No other nation had achieved the American combination of rapid income and population growth.

Urbanization

Growth of these dimensions indicated changes, and changes were obvious in the American economy. Population patterns changed, both between geographic areas and between urban and rural dwellers. Cities grew much faster than the aggregate population. In 1860, 19.7 percent of the population lived in cities and towns of 5,000 or more. Two decades later, 28.1 percent of the population was urban, and by 1900, 39.7 percent. After World War I, the United States was an urban nation; just over half the population lived in cities.

The United States contained no cities of one million or more inhabitants in 1860, and only two with more than half that number. More than ten million people lived in such cities 50 years later, and the number of cities of all types had increased more than sixfold. As might be expected, this shift in living patterns was an indication of new employment patterns; the variety of jobs tends to expand at least as fast as urban populations. Perhaps more significantly, national health had improved despite urbanization; the decline in average adult heights was reversed in the last quarter of the nineteenth century.[3]

The proportion of workers engaged in manufacturing, transportation, and services was much higher than it had been in 1860, and the percentage

---

[1] *Historical Statistics of the United States: Colonial Times to 1975*, 2 vols. (Washington, D.C.: Government Printing Office, 1970), 1:224.
[2] *Historical Statistics*, 1:225.
[3] R. Fogel, "Nutrition and the Decline in Mortality Since 1700: Some Preliminary Findings," in Gallman and Engerman, *Long-Term Factors in American Economic Growth* (Chicago: University of Chicago Press, 1986).

Table III.1   Aggregate and Per-Capita Gross National Product

Date	Current Dollars		1990 Dollars	
	Total (Billions)	Per Capita	Total (Billions)	Per Capita
1870*	$7.4	$170	$283.4	$2,664
1880**	11.2	205	212.9	3,890
1890	13.1	208	264.9	4,200
1895	13.9	200	314.6	4,522
1900	18.7	246	386.5	5,078
1905	25.1	299	418.2	4,990
1909	33.4	369	565.4	6,248
1915	40.0	398	604.4	6,010
1920	91.5	859	670.0	6,292

* 1869–1878 average.
** 1879–1888 average.
Source: U.S. Department of Commerce, Bureau of the Census, *Bicentennial Statistics* (Washington, D.C.: Government Printing Office, 1976), 393.

in agriculture lower. The agricultural population had peaked in 1910; the number of people earning their living from farming has been declining ever since.[4] Construction and domestic service also showed declines in employment. Even so, agricultural production did not fall. Instead, it more than tripled from 1860 to 1900.[5]

New Regional Patterns of Production

The location of production changed within almost all sectors. By the close of this period, the Midwest, particularly the North Central states, had become an industrial region as well as the nation's agricultural heartland. Ohio, Indiana, Illinois, Michigan, and Wisconsin all exhibited faster industrial growth than the old centers in New England and the Middle Atlantic states.[6] Lumbering and mining shifted westward to a greater extent than did agriculture, but beef and wheat production were now centered west of the Mis-

---

[4] For all regions but the South, the agricultural population had begun to decline a decade or more before 1910. Only the very high proportion of the southern population engaged in agriculture kept the national figures from indicating this trend by 1900. See G. Wright, *Old South, New South: Revolutions in the Southern Economy Since the Civil War* (New York: Basic Books, 1986), Chap. 3.
[5] Wright, *Old South, New South*, 482.
[6] D. Meyer, "Midwestern Industrialization and the American Manufacturing Belt in the Nineteenth Century," *Journal of Economic History* (December 1989).

sissippi River. The West became a region of cities and diversified, highly productive agriculture. After 1900, the natural resources and low-wage labor of the South began to attract industry, even as southerners began to migrate to northern cities in search of higher incomes.[7]

These reallocations, which indicated a degree of human mobility greater than even the United States had ever seen before, began to reduce regional differences in wages. Capital too became more mobile as financial markets improved, and after 1900, regional interest rate differentials fell, with rates over large areas indicating nearly complete integration into national markets.[8] Relocation of people and industries toward the areas of highest returns led to increasing regional specialization. As Adam Smith had pointed out a century before, with specialization came interdependence. In nearly all walks of life, Americans used tools, raw materials, and services produced by others as essential elements in their jobs. Most of their consumption was now goods made by other specialists, wholly, or as in the case of food and clothing, through a larger share of the initial processing and preparation.

International Economic Relations

Domestic changes were paralleled by alterations in the economic relations between the United States and the rest of the world. Traditionally, this country had been an exporter of raw materials and semiprocessed goods, and an importer of manufactured goods. Its trade deficits were balanced by borrowing abroad. After 1874, the chronic U.S. trade deficit became a surplus as manufactured exports increased. After 1900, the United States had become an exporter of capital with growing investments in other countries, and its international indebtedness had begun to shrink. By 1914, America was an industrial power without peer. The country's manufacturing output was equal to that of Britain, Germany, and France combined.[9] In the next half-dozen years American industrial preeminence would grow even greater.

THE SOURCES OF GROWTH

Natural Resources

Before 1860, most U.S. natural resources had yet to be utilized. Many had not even been discovered or uses for them found. After the Civil War, exploitation of the nation's mineral and agricultural potential proceeded rapidly. Ample deposits of almost every mineral important to contemporary

---

[7] Wright, *Old South, New South*, stresses that this migration encountered formidable barriers.
[8] L. Davis, "The Investment Market, 1870–1914: The Evolution of a National Market," *Journal of Economic History* (September 1965).
[9] J. Hughes, *Industrialization and Economic History: Theses and Conjectures* (New York: McGraw-Hill, 1970), 126.

industry were discovered and exploited. Moreover, in many cases, these resources were easy to use where they were, or transportation links could readily send them to the points where they were needed.[10] For example, in the southern Appalachians, coal and iron ore were discovered in the same geological formation, which after 1871 gave rise to the great steelmaking center in Birmingham. Elsewhere, natural resources were conveniently located for water transportation. Where minerals, water resources, or soils were not so readily combined, Americans developed tools and methods to make them productive. Improvements in transportation, both extensive (the railroads were extended to nearly every corner of the country) and intensive (innovations such as refrigerated railway cars), made the cost of products from distant regions much lower after 1900, encouraging regional specialization. Other aspects of distribution also improved, and the proportion of final goods' prices that reflected wholesaling and retail charges fell.

Labor and Capital

America's generous raw materials endowment contributed less to economic growth than did increases in the nation's labor force and capital stock. The labor force grew even faster than the population; the declining birthrate produced an increase in the proportion of adults in the native population, as did longer life spans. Immigrants, as previously noted, tend to be young adults, and immigration, particularly in the 1900–1914 period, was enormous. Social changes also contributed to the growth of the work force: The portion of women employed outside the home rose from 18.9 to 25.4 percent of the female population over 1890–1910.[11] In the early decades of this period, children worked in factories and other urban jobs, but the portion of children so employed declined after 1900.

Qualitative changes, which had begun to contribute significantly to economic growth in the previous era, assumed a greater importance. The work force gained increased industrial experience and skills, education was extended to more children and the time spent in schooling grew, and more sophisticated management techniques appeared. Not only did each worker have twice as much capital with which to work in 1909 as in 1869, but the capital was improved.[12] Such changes in factor proportions contributed a substantial share of the increase in output per worker. Gross investment as a portion of American GNP has never been higher than it was at the turn of the century—some 30 percent. Recent studies have concluded that gross investment's contribution to growth doubled from 1840 to 1900.[13]

---

[10] To one researcher, this was a key element in American industrial development. See G. Wright, "The Origins of American Industrial Success," *American Economic Review* (September 1990).
[11] *Historical Statistics*, 1:133.
[12] R. Higgs, *The Transformation of the American Economy, 1865–1914: An Essay in Interpretation* (New York: John Wiley and Sons, Inc., 1971), 33.
[13] Gallman and Engerman, *Long-Term Factors*, 203.

According to one investigator, growth of the labor force accounted for about half of all American economic growth between 1840 and 1900. Capital accumulation produced another quarter of the total, and the increased development of natural resources under one-tenth. The remaining source of growth, about one-fifth of the total, was obtained through productivity increases, that is, through raising the amount of product each unit of inputs turned out.[14] (See Table III.2.) Much of the new capital was designed for the production of very large amounts of output; that is, it offered economies of scale. Often such capital had to be combined with extensive support facilities and large amounts of labor. Consequently, large firms became increasingly common in manufacturing, transportation, and, at the very end of the period, in distribution.

Economic Mobility

Growing interdependence, new technology, urbanization, and easier, cheaper transportation than ever before increased the range of jobs open to the typical worker. Since many of the jobs were new, either to the areas in which they appeared or often to the entire economy, there were few barriers to occupational mobility. As might be expected in a period of rapid economic growth, economic mobility was a noteworthy feature of the American economy. Those clinging to old production methods or old products often found their incomes falling in relative if not absolute terms, while workers

Table III.2   Percentage Contribution of Inputs and Productivity to Growth of Net National Product, 1840–1960

	1840–1960	1840–1900 Old	1840–1900 New	1900–1960
Annual growth rate	3.56%	3.98%	3.98%	3.12%
Labor	42.7	47.2	47.2	34.8
Land	5.9	9.6	3.3	2.5
Capital	22.8	23.6	28.1	18.6
Productivity	28.6	19.6	21.4	44.1
	100.0%	100.0%	100.0%	100.0%

Source: R. Gallman and S. Engerman, *Long-Term Factors in American Economic Growth* (Chicago: University of Chicago Press, 1986), 190–191.

[14] Gallman and Engerman, *Long-Term Factors*, 190–191.

opting to reinforce change by making new goods in new ways moved up the income ladder. The aggregate effect of millions of modest changes in American use of its human talent was more significant than the occasional spectacular gains from new jobs.

New Technology

As time passed, new growth sectors replaced those whose rapid initial growth had "pulled" the economy forward. Steam power, steel, and the railroads had figured largely in early growth. Before 1914, these had given way to a new technology based on industrial chemistry, electricity, and the internal combustion engine—techniques and tools geared to the needs of the wealthy, urban society that consumed their products. The formal application of scientific methods to economic activity had previously been limited to some types of engineering, marine navigation, and little else. Now such approaches paid dividends in large-scale manufacturing, public health, and even agriculture. The employment of scientific procedures made it easier to identify cause and effect, permitting a rapid dispersion of productive ideas through the economy, and their successful adaptation to circumstances different from those where they were first employed.

Another feature of the economic growth of this period that may appear surprising to modern students is that much of it occurred during a period of sustained deflation. From 1865 to 1896, the average level of prices fell by about one-half. After 1896, inflation appeared, but at modest rates—1 to 3 percent annually. In World War I, inflation was severe; prices doubled in less than four years, and prices were still rising in early 1920.

THE USES OF WEALTH

Higher real incomes increase individuals' well-being in two ways. First, they allow recipients more of the things they were already consuming. Were this their total effect, the attractions of greater purchasing power might quickly pall for most persons. But increased incomes also allow people to obtain variety, and this is an item for which wants are insatiable. It appears that this is no less true of nations than it is of individuals. The United States used most of its new productive capacity to increase private consumption and investment, so that the amount and variety of consumer and capital goods rose. But there was something left over to devote to new purposes. Child labor could be reduced, either because people now felt wealthy enough to forego output produced in such a manner, or because it was recognized that investing in more education would increase long-run productivity. As wealth and technological capabilities increased, the cost of imperialistic ventures as a portion of income fell, tempting Americans and their leaders into a new role in world politics.

Government's Role Expands

The role of government also expanded at home. Growing urbanization made responses to problems of public health, police and fire services, lighting, and utilities more essential. The growth of interdependence made accurate information more necessary, and government agencies appeared or were expanded to provide it.

Laws regulating working conditions, restricting monopoly, and protecting natural resources were also passed in this period. So too were new types of laws—those designed expressly to redistribute income. Cities, and to a lesser extent states, had always provided some support for the needy, even in the colonial era. Now, however, the first laws intended to change the overall distribution of income toward greater equality appeared. In the view of some scholars, a fundamental change in the legal climate took place. Instead of protecting individuals' property rights, the law now began to encourage rent-seeking—the use of government to transfer income from its producers to special-interest groups (which might or might not be poorer than those from whom the income was transferred).[15] The redistributional process in 1920 had not begun to reach the dimensions it has attained today.

American economic success and the ability to extend it to a large proportion of the entire population perhaps caused many people to consider their economic and political system superior to any other. This sometimes led to attempts to impose it on people who might have different values, such as American Indians and Filipinos. Efforts expended in such causes might better have been devoted to problems that remained within the American economy and society.

The Mixed Blessings of Progress

Nor was the economic achievement without its costs; people faced pressures to adjust to new circumstances at a pace never previously imagined. Some found the demands of new situations difficult or impossible to meet. Economic expansion offered opportunities for most people and ruin for those who found it difficult to change. Like any economic process, change involved both costs and benefits. Nevertheless, the gains achieved by most Americans during this period were real and substantial. Considerable evidence indicates that by 1920 even some traditional "have-not" groups such as southerners, blacks, farmers, and immigrants were beginning to share in the increases in output. Gains in life expectancy, literacy, the conquest of many epidemic

---

[15] T. Anderson and P. Hill, *The Growth of a Transfer Society* (Stanford, Calif.: Hoover Institute Press, 1980). See also D. North, *Structure and Change in Economic History* (New York: Norton, 1981); and M. Olson, *The Rise and Decline of Nations: Economic Growth, Stagflation, and Social Rigidities* (New Haven, Conn.: Yale University Press, 1982).

diseases, and drastic declines in infant and child mortality were unarguable improvements in living standards in which the entire population shared.

SELECTED REFERENCES

Anderson, T., and P. Hill. *The Growth of a Transfer Society*. Stanford, Calif.: Hoover Institute Press, 1980.

Chandler, A., Jr. *The Visible Hand: The Managerial Revolution in American Business*. Cambridge, Mass.: Harvard University Press, 1977.

Davis, L., R. Easterlin, W. Parker et al. *American Economic Growth: An Economist's History of the United States*. New York: Harper & Row, 1972.

Fogel, R., and S. Engerman. *The Reinterpretation of American Economic History*. New York: Harper & Row, 1971.

Gallman, R., and S. Engerman. *Long-Term Factors in American Economic Growth*. Chicago: University of Chicago Press, 1986.

Higgs, R. *The Transformation of the American Economy, 1865–1914: An Essay in Interpretation*. New York: John Wiley and Sons, Inc., 1971.

Kirkland, E. *Industry Comes of Age: Business, Labor, and Public Policy, 1860–1897*. New York: Holt, Rinehart and Winston, 1961.

Olson, M. *The Rise and Decline of Nations: Economic Growth, Stagflation, and Social Rigidities*. New Haven, Conn.: Yale University Press, 1982.

Niemi, A., Jr. *State and Regional Patterns in American Manufacturing, 1860–1900*. Westport, Conn.: Greenwood Press, 1974.

North, D. *Structure and Change in Economic History*. New York: Norton, 1981.

North, D., T. Anderson, and P. Hill. *Growth and Welfare in the American Past: A New Economic History*. 3d ed. Englewood Cliffs, N.J.: Prentice-Hall, 1983.

Rosenberg, N. *Technology and American Economic Growth*. New York: M. E. Sharpe, 1972.

Rosenberg, N., and L. Birdzell. *How the West Grew Rich*. New York: Basic Books, 1986.

U.S. Department of Commerce, Bureau of the Census. *Historical Statistics of the United States: Colonial Times to 1970*. 2 vols. Washington, D.C.: Government Printing Office, 1975.

Vatter, H. *The Drive to Industrial Maturity: The U.S. Economy, 1860–1914*. Westport, Conn.: Greenwood Press, 1975.

Wright, G. *Old South, New South: Revolutions in the Southern Economy Since the Civil War*. New York: Basic Books, 1986.

AGRICULTURAL ADJUSTMENT AND CHANGE

Before World War I, farmers had gained access to virtually all the high-quality agricultural land in the United States. By 1920, they had adjusted local patterns of production to fit the characteristics of each area. The agricultural implements developed before the Civil War were further refined and modified and brought into widespread use. There was no longer any question of whether agriculture was integrated into the rest of the economy or independent of it. The value of implements and tools used on American farms had risen thirteenfold while the number of farms had little more than doubled in this period. In contrast to the colonial period, few of the tools and a declining portion of the techniques employed had been developed on the farms or produced there. The output of American agriculture grew, both in aggregate and per-capita terms. Nevertheless, agriculture's share of gross national product declined over the 1865–1920 period.

GROWING ECONOMIC INTERDEPENDENCE AND INTEGRATION

With the exception of cotton, the centers of production for most crops had reached their modern locations by 1920. The techniques of production, however, have continued to change at ever-accelerating rates. The influence of markets was now pervasive throughout agriculture. Not only did farmers employ tools and techniques from the rest of the economy, their output was largely for sale rather than personal consumption. As regional specialization increased, farmers grew dependent on a growing chain of specialists to transport, process, and market their produce.

One example of the growing interdependence of agriculture with other sectors will illustrate the point. After the Civil War, the northern Great Plains were found to be particularly suited to the production of spring wheat if more disease-resistant varieties could be found and a method of transporting the crop to market developed. A search by the new Department of Agriculture discovered a type of eastern European wheat that flourished in the Great Plains environment and had greater resistance to plant diseases than previously grown varieties. The Great Northern Railroad solved the transportation problem, but it was then found that the application of existing milling methods to the new wheat produced gray flour unacceptable to consumers. Another search resulted in the adoption of roller milling, a Hungarian innovation.

Productivity Improvements

Particularly before 1900, most of the growth in output originated in extensive growth in agriculture—it was the product of increases in the amounts of land, labor, and especially capital.[1] But after 1900, little good land remained unused, and after 1910 the farm labor force ceased to grow. Thereafter, productivity improvements became an increasingly important source of production increases. The productivity of farm labor, aided by increases in the amounts of land and capital per farmer, had already shown considerable improvement, as indicated in Table 11.1. In 1870, the average U.S. farmer produced food and fiber sufficient for 5.1 people. By 1920, the figure had risen to 8.3. Output had risen faster than population and domestic markets; the proportion of farm

[1] L. Davis et al., *American Economic Growth: An Economist's History of the United States* (New York: Harper & Row, 1972), 374, 377.

Table 11.1 Farm Productivity

Year or Annual Average	Wheat			Corn for Grain			Cotton		
	Man-Hours per Acre	Yield per Acre (Bushels)	Man-Hours per 100 Bushels	Man-Hours per Acre	Yield per Acre (Bushels)	Man-Hours per 100 Bushels	Man-Hours per Acre	Yield per Acre (Pounds)	Man-Hours per 100 Pounds
1800	56.0	15.0	373	86.0	25.0	344	185	147	601
1840	35.0	15.0	233	69.0	25.0	276	135	147	438
1880	20.0	13.2	152	46.0	25.6	180	119	188	303
1900	15.0	13.9	108	38.0	25.9	147	112	189	284
1910–14	15.2	14.4	106	35.2	26.0	135	116	201	276
1920–24	12.4	13.8	90	32.7	26.8	122	96	155	296

Source: U.S. Department of Commerce, Bureau of the Census, *Bicentennial Statistics* (Washington, D.C.: Government Printing Office, 1976), 407.

Table 11.2 Agricultural Growth, 1860–1920

Year	Number of Farms (× 1,000)	Farm Acreage (× 1,000)	Total Value of Agricultural Produce*	Wheat**	Corn**	Cotton (× 1,000 Bales)
1870	2,660	407,735	$2,694	254	1,125	4,352
1880	4,000	536,082	4,129	502	1,170	6,606
1890	4,565	623,219	4,990	449	1,650	8,653
1900	5,740	841,202	6,409	599	2,662	10,124
1910	6,366	881,431	7,495***	625	2,853	11,609
1920	6,454	958,667	15,944***	843	3,071	13,429

Year	Cattle (× 1,000)	Hogs (× 1,000)	Horses (× 1,000)	Mules (× 1,000)
1870	23,821	25,135	7,145	1,125
1880	39,676	49,773	10,357	1,813
1890	57,649	57,427	15,266	2,253
1900	67,719	62,868	16,965	3,039
1910	61,804	58,186	19,823	4,101
1920	66,640	59,346	19,767	5,432

* Millions of 1910–1914 dollars
** Millions of bushels.
***Realized gross farm income, millions of current dollars.
Source: U.S. Department of Commerce, Bureau of the Census, *Historical Statistics of the United States: Colonial Times to 1970*, 2 vols. (Washington, D.C.: Government Printing Office, 1975), 1: 456–5200.

production exported had approximately tripled (see Table 11.2).[2]

The International Connection

As the increase in exports indicates, a growing portion of American farmers' production was consumed abroad. The demand for food is price-inelastic, so the prices of farm products would have had to fall more than in proportion to the increases in output to allow the domestic sale of all that American farmers turned out. The demand for most farm products is also income-inelastic; the quantity demanded changes less than in proportion to income variations. Thus, even growing percapita incomes within the United States did not assure a market for all that farmers were now producing unless domestic prices fell.[3]

U.S. farmers soon discovered that export markets exhibited the same problems. World production of grain and meat was growing faster than population at this time, as it was in America. Conditions in the export markets exerted a strong, even dominant, influence on domestic prices. Bumper crops elsewhere in the world might severely reduce grain prices within the United States, even though the domestic crop was small that year; or crop failures in other major food-exporting areas might mean high prices for American grain and meat despite a large harvest in this country. Political considerations also affected export markets. Some food importers gave protection to domestic producers or favored imports from colonies or political allies, a problem that became more serious after 1920.

Output per acre rose only modestly for most crops (see Table 11.1), reflecting the re-

location of agricultural activity to the Great Plains. Soil fertility was lower than the Midwest there, but farmers compensated by cultivating larger acreage to maintain or increase their incomes.

As urbanization, higher incomes, and better methods of preservation and transportation affected markets, some crops acquired new importance, and others began to lose markets. The demand for meat, fruit, vegetables, poultry, and dairy products increased relative to population, while that for grain and other starchy foods leveled off. Pork lost ground to beef. Prepared foods, such as canned goods and bakery products, increasingly supplanted items made in the home from basic ingredients. In consequence, the farmer was separated from consumers by another layer of specialists.

THE END OF THE FRONTIER

At the onset of the Civil War, settlement extended approximately to the western border of Iowa and into eastern Kansas in the north. The southern frontier was in eastern Texas. Beyond that line there were a few pockets of farmers, miners, and ranchers in Oregon, California, and Utah. Gold rushes had just begun to swell the populations of Colorado and Nevada. Elsewhere, the West was still the domain of the Indian and the buffalo, little travelled and not much better known than a half-century earlier.

This situation changed with amazing rapidity. By 1890, the Department of the Interior issued its famous, though premature, announcement that the frontier no longer existed. Between 1900 and 1910, pronouncement became reality. Although there were large areas where settlement was very thin and considerable pockets that were still essentially wilderness, the frontier as a contin-

---

[2] U.S. Department of Commerce, Bureau of the Census, *Historical Statistics of the United States: Colonial Times to 1970*, 2 vols. (Washington, D.C.: Government Printing Office, 1975), 1: 374, 377.

[3] A full discussion of this issue is F. Lewis, "Explaining the Shift of Labor from Agriculture to Industry in the U.S., 1869–1899," *Journal of Economic History* (September 1979).

■ A couple enjoys a roadside lunch in this photo from the 1870s: Note the absence of anything resembling a modern road.
Source: Kansas State Historical Society.

uous line beyond which population density was no greater than two people per square mile no longer existed. By eastern standards, the West was not densely populated; nor is most of it even today. But by the eve of World War I, very little land remained unsettled because its potential had not been examined.

Natural Resources

The end of the frontier emphatically did not mean that America had exhausted or even discovered all its usable natural resources. Gradually, developments in this period began to make clear that the supply of economically usable natural resources depends far less on the earth's total endowment than it does on resource prices and the technology by which they can be exploited. Even though the number of cultivated acres has declined in recent years, the volume of crops produced has increased as farmers substituted knowledge and other forms of capital for raw labor and land. Output per acre has risen more than enough to compensate for the reduction in tillage.

In general, as the value of any privately owned resource increases, its owners find it more profitable to safeguard it and increase the care with which it is used. America's

■ Workers labored to construct mining sluices. By the late nineteenth century, mining was capital intensive.
Source: U.S. Signal Corps Photo No. 111-SC-8302 in The National Archives.

richest and most accessible mineral deposits were the first to be mined, and initially no attempt was made to extract every bit of metal from ore. It was cheaper to increase overall output by exploiting new mines. But as demand for such resources increased faster than supply, their prices began to rise. Raw materials users found it in their interests to use inputs more productively and to look for substitute materials. Simultaneously, increased raw materials prices made it possible to use more distant, lower-quality, or less accessible deposits. Higher prices, by increasing the rewards for discovery of new deposits, not only encouraged efforts to make new discoveries, they also gave incentives to develop new tools to aid in exploration and production. As we have discovered in the case of oil and natural

gas in the past decade, the amounts of any raw material currently available reflect the intensity of the effort to find and exploit it. To the present day, these market responses have more than offset diminishing returns for the majority of raw materials. New discoveries continue to be made, and the efficiency with which existing materials are produced and used increases as well.

MINING

Many of the earliest western settlers were not farmers. Transportation in the region was initially so poor that there was little economic point in anything but subsistence farming;

■ Mining "strikes" briefly created towns but had little permanent effect on settlement.
Source: Courtesy of the Nevada Historical Society.

costs of moving farm products to market were often greater than the goods' value to final consumers. Gold and silver mining attracted numbers of people to areas where "strikes" had been made, but the precious metals had a limited impact on settlement patterns. As the scores of western ghost towns indicate, once the rich ore bodies were worked out, mining activities moved on because this was cheaper than working lower-grade ore. Precious metals are relatively easy to transport; they combine high value with limited bulk and weight. This had two implications: First, there was little incentive to develop transport links to mines; and second, any single producer was in competition with others throughout the world. If production costs rose, it might be more profitable to seek new deposits than to improve efficiency in the current location.

The characteristics of gold and silver mining had influences on other forms of economic activity in addition to their limited development of transportation. Mining created a local demand for food and lumber, but little else. Gold and silver furnished the initial impetus for settlement in Colorado, Idaho, Montana, and Nevada, but long-term population growth depended on activities with stronger links to the rest of the economy. In later years, copper, lead, and coal were also mined in the Rockies, and these minerals, which required larger quantities of inputs and better-developed transportation, furnished a basis for diversified activity.

LUMBERING

In this period, the center of lumber production relocated several times. Its original strongholds were in Maine and the Maritime Provinces of Canada. Timber production was incidental to land clearance for farming in much of the East, Midwest, and South. But as the eastern woodlands were cut, timber production shifted first to the upper Great Lakes region, and as that area in turn was depleted after 1910, to the Pacific Northwest, the South, and the higher slopes of the Appalachian Mountains. Lumbering required transportation for its bulky, low-valued product, but it too was a short-lived industry, at least locally. It was cheaper to move on to new areas than to manage existing forests for sustained yields, so the prevailing philosophy among lumbermen was "cut and get out." This was furthered by institutions reflecting the historical fact that land where timber stood had higher values in other uses, and lumber was cheap. Only as primeval timber stands were depleted and wood prices rose did it become profitable to manage forests for sustained yields. Some forest land had little or no alternative use; it would not produce crops at costs allowing competition with more fertile or advantageously located acres. As timber prices rose after 1900, conservation efforts, both private and public, began to appear.

RANCHING

Cattle ranching had long been a frontier activity in America, even before settlement reached the Appalachians. The abundance of unclaimed land gave plenty of cheap, wild pasture on which free-ranging cattle flourished. Nowhere was this more evident than in Texas. There the Spanish and Mexicans had developed ranching methods that were later imitated all over the West.

Great numbers of wild longhorn cattle, descendants of strays from the original Spanish herds, roamed central Texas. These animals were legally the property of whomever could capture them and drive them to market. Doing so, however, required considerable effort. Natural selection over the centuries had produced an animal well adapted to survival in a harsh environment without human assistance. The longhorns' primary attributes were mobility and toughness; they prospered even on the scant vegetation of this drought-plagued region. An adult bull was no mean adversary for a grizzly bear, and sometimes more than a match for inexperienced cattlemen. If wild cattle could be rounded up and marketed, those who did so might garner high profits.

Although wild longhorns had no human owners, the costs of getting them to market were not negligible. Well before the Civil War, herds of longhorns had been driven to New Orleans and even as far as Chicago. But losses of both men and cattle were high on the long drives, and better forms of transportation were sought. As railroads were extended west, the herds were driven to the railhead towns, shortening the drives and reducing costs. Towns like Dodge City and Abilene quickly developed atmospheres that no television serial would dare to portray realistically even today. The men who made the long drives had to be tougher than the cattle they herded and the hazards of the trail. In these towns the surviving cowhands received their pay and sought their own vivid forms of relaxation.

After 1865, lush grazing lands were discovered—and their Indian inhabitants evicted or killed—at the foot of the northern Rockies. Shortly thereafter, herds of longhorns were driven north from Texas to stock the Montana and Wyoming ranges. The range-cattle industry soon began to experience technological change. The qualities that enhanced the longhorns' survival on the range did not make them tender on the steak platter. Worse, the breed not only grew slowly, but it put much of its growth into bone and sinew. After 1880, new breeds were introduced, sometimes in crosses with the longhorn. These cattle required more care and could not be driven great distances without heavy loss of weight and life, but they grew faster and their beef was more palatable. In addition, the railroads had now been extended into the northern plains, reducing the necessity for long drives.

The End of the Open Range

In the first years after ranching began in the high plains, cattle were allowed to graze on the open range. Technically this land still belonged to the government. As long as the government did not enforce its exclusive rights to such property, and settlement was scattered enough to allow ample grazing for each herd, such methods were practical. But the development of highly specialized meat-packing plants and refrigeration rapidly increased the demand for western beef, and it was easy to enter the ranching business. With luck and some knowledge of the country and the ways of cattle, a small herd might be expanded into the basis of a fortune. But this also made free rangeland a thing of the past; as cattle numbers grew, one herd's grazing and water requirements might infringe on those of another. Private ownership of land supplanted the earlier institutions.

Some of the "cattle kings" acquired ranches whose dimensions appeared princely even to the European noblemen who visited them and occasionally tried their own hands at ranching. But the era of the cattle kings was brief. Overstocking the range drove beef prices down and increased competition for grazing land and water. In the late 1880s, a series of disastrous winters killed thousands of cattle already weakened by inadequate pasturage.

New competitors for the land appeared—sheep ranchers and farmers. By 1890, the open-range cattle industry had largely been replaced by fenced, privately owned ranches where natural grazing was supplanted by hay and other feed, often grown locally under irrigation. After considerable and often violent conflict, sheepherding became concentrated in the mountains and the Great Basin, the region between the Rockies and the Sierra Nevada. Farming in this region was restricted to small areas with favorable soil and water conditions.

Western Institutions and Innovations

As mining and ranching spread through the West, they required new institutions, both physical and legal, to meet the problems encountered there. Laws had to be developed or adapted from those of other regions to determine which mine had the right to follow a vein of ore beneath the earth's surface. Ranchers had to find new ways to care for cattle and methods of sharing grazing land. In this region, access to water was crucial to success in ranching as well as farming. Some ranching operations were more effectively carried out in cooperation with neighbors, and it was better to have commonly accepted property rights than to work out individual agreements with every neighbor. The registry of cattle brands, quarantine laws, rules for division of new calves between various owners at roundup time, and laws on water rights allowed ranchers to operate in close proximity even before the land was fenced.[4]

Several physical innovations also figured prominently in western settlement. Barbed wire was an effective fencing material in areas with limited timber, and it also permitted farming in close proximity to livestock—a

---

[4] T. Anderson and P. Hill, "The Evolution of Property Rights: A Study of the American West," *Explorations in Economic History* (April 1975).

consideration of growing importance to ranchers dependent on raising feed as well as to farmers. Windmills and the pumps they drove gave farmers and ranchers greater access to subsurface water, allowing more intensive agricultural activity on the Great Plains. The new laws, institutions, and innovations did not always appear in time to prevent bitter and sometimes violent conflict over access to water, land, and minerals.

THE GREAT PLAINS

The primary crop of the Great Plains was wheat. As far west as eastern Montana, the northern Great Plains were well-suited to spring wheat, and the Kansas–Nebraska region to winter wheat. Corn, as the new settlers discovered, required too much water to grow well on the Plains, and the centers of corn production remained further east, particularly in Illinois and Iowa. The vast, level lands of the Great Plains were not as fertile as the Midwest, nor was rainfall as heavy. But low land costs made it possible to substitute extensive land for high output per acre, and the area was ideal for agricultural machinery that allowed a farmer to spread his labor over large amounts of land. Consequently, the typical farm was large in comparison to those farther east. But economies of scale were not unlimited. Early attempts at truly large-scale agriculture, the so-called "bonanza farms," comprised thousands of acres of land farmed by hired labor. But these soon disappeared; they had no cost advantages over smaller farms operated by the owner and his family, usually with extra help at harvest time.

By 1909 the chief wheat-producing states were the Dakotas, Nebraska, Kansas, and Minnesota. These were far from markets and depended on railroads as a link to suppliers and customers for their crops. A second major center of wheat production developed in the 1890s. The "Inland Empire" of eastern Washington and Oregon was even farther from markets than were the Great Plains. Its wheat was shipped halfway around the world to Europe or to the eastern United States. The ability of these regions to compete in world markets is testimony to the efficiency of ocean transportation by this time.

Innovations Shape Great Plains Farming

A number of innovations aided Great Plains farming. Some may even have made it possible. The variety and efficiency of agricultural implements grew steadily. By the late 1880s, a single machine both reaped and threshed wheat. These "combines" were vast, unwieldy implements, often powered by steam engines and pulled by a score or more of horses. Since efficient harnessing and control of such large teams were difficult and the feed they consumed costly in both land and effort, farmers were very receptive to new and more compact sources of power when these appeared after 1910.[5] By 1920, about 20,000 tractors were in use on American farms. Note the increase in farm output in proportion to that of draft animals after 1910 revealed in Table 11.2.

Plows, rakes, cultivators, and other agricultural machines became more efficient and numerous. But the two great barriers to agricultural development on the Plains were the difficulty of keeping livestock out of field crops and the provision of dependable water supplies. As Table 11.2 and pictures of farm life at this time indicate, even farms that raised no cattle, sheep, or hogs required motive power: draft animals were indispensible. Barbed wire solved the fencing problem sim-

---

[5] Davis et al., *American Economic Growth*, 386.

ply and economically, requiring neither the wood used for the traditional split-rail fence nor the labor needed to construct ditches, hedges, or board fences. The barbs effectively restrained livestock. Springs and streams were few and far between on the Great Plains, and windmills provided a power source to pump subsurface water for irrigation and other farm needs and uses.

Other innovations appeared off the farm, but had no less impact in raising the efficiency of Great Plains agriculture. In addition to the railroads, an efficient system of grain elevators and market innovations, such as grading systems, futures contracts, and other developments, allowed for the concentration of many farmers' output and its transportation to distant markets at steadily decreasing costs. Ocean transport rates fell sharply through this era, extending the market for American agricultural products to most of western Europe. Railroad rates in the West, however, did not decline decisively until after 1896.[6] Nevertheless, farmers received a rising portion of the price paid by the final consumers of their products, despite a more elaborate chain of distribution.[7]

■ A horse team pulls a harvester through an Oregon wheat field in 1880. Note the complexity involved in adding horsepower.
Source: The Bettmann Archive.

THE CORN BELT

The movement of wheat production from its antebellum centers in the Ohio and upper Mississippi River valleys caused these areas to concentrate on the production of corn and the livestock that ate most of that crop. The area from Ohio to eastern Kansas and Nebraska became one of the world's most productive agricultural regions. It had many natural advantages: deep, highly fertile soil, abundant and dependable rainfall, and a lengthy growing season with warm summer nights. These allowed the production of a wide variety of crops, but conditions were particularly well suited to the cultivation of corn, which had no rival as the region's chief crop. Corn is an ideal food for livestock, but less portable than other grains; much of the crop was used to fatten cattle and hogs on the farms where it was grown.

The inhabitants of the Corn Belt developed institutions and attitudes that made the most of the region's natural advantages. On the typical Corn Belt farm, the owner faced a continual stream of business decisions. First was the choice of product: Corn or possibly another field crop could be grown, or cattle or hogs fattened for market. These operations occurred in a highly competitive market,

[6] R. Higgs, *The Transformation of the American Economy, 1865–1914: An Essay in Interpretation* (New York: John Wiley and Sons, 1971), 99–101.
[7] D. North, T. Anderson, and P. Hill, *Growth and Welfare in the American Past: A New Economic History*, 3d ed. (Englewood Cliffs, N.J.: Prentice-Hall, 1983), 107, 129.

■ Farmers may have thought grain elevator operators possessed monopoly power, but there is little evidence they did.
Source: Harper's Weekly, December 22, 1877. Drawn by W. P. Snyder from a sketch by Theodore R. Davis. From John Grafton, *New York in the Nineteenth Century,* 2d ed. (New York: Dover Publications, Inc., 1980), 229.

where the chief hope for higher incomes lay in the rapid adoption of cost-reducing innovations. Such an environment encouraged economic rationality and response to innovations among farmers.[8] The regions's arable land was fully utilized by 1900, so there was little hope of increasing income through "more of the same" expansion. Farmers sought lower production costs both through mechanization and rapid adoption of new techniques. As farmers had always done, they utilized the fruits of their own experience. But they also began to find the new ideas based on research done by the region's agricultural schools, the Department of Agriculture, and the farm implement companies useful. Innovation had its rewards; by 1920, the value of output per farm in Iowa and Illinois was equalled or exceeded only by states where the average farm was much larger, or by regions producing high-priced specialty crops, such as California and Hawaii.[9]

[8] Davis et al., *American Economic Growth*, 393–395.

[9] *Historical Statistics*, 1:458–464.

THE NORTH AND EAST

Other regions felt the competition from mid-western and Great Plains agriculture to a much greater extent than in the antebellum period. Newer regions' great efficiency and declining transport costs forced continuation of the readjustments that began in the previous era. If agriculture was to survive in regions less favored in soil and climate, new crops or new methods would have to be discovered. Some farmers took advantage of their proximity to large urban populations by specializing in dairy products, poultry, fruit, and vegetables—all items with relatively high income elasticities of demand. As incomes grew in eastern cities, these adjustments proved lucrative. In other areas, even the activities chosen as responses to western competition were displaced. Sheep flocks in New England and New York dwindled. As it became possible to ship meat from the great packing plants of Kansas City and Chicago, livestock raising became less profitable on the Atlantic Coast. Feed prices fell as cheap western corn flowed into eastern markets, aiding the region's dairy and poultry farmers.

Changing Agricultural Markets

Just as they had in productive capabilities, developments elsewhere in the economy affected eastern farmers' welfare. Canning was now practical for a wider range of items than it had been before the Civil War, and specialization in such crops was now practical. What was not sold for consumption as fresh produce could be vended to canning factories. Dairy farming benefited from cheap feed, as well as from developments in agricultural research, which developed breeds of cattle with higher milk and butterfat yields and improvements in butter- and cheesemaking. Some regions found that

the development and enforcement of grading standards for their products more than repaid the cost. Transportation of fresh milk was now possible and the cities gained as the number of cows stabled within them diminished.

Foods that only decades previously had been special treats for holidays or beyond the purses of all but the very rich now became regular items in the general diet. Areas with favorable climates, such as California and (later) Florida, began to supply citrus fruit and "out of season" vegetables to the cities. Demand for these items stemmed both from rising per-capita incomes and from changes in life-styles, particularly among urban residents. Fewer city folk now performed constant heavy labor, and per-capita demand for grain and other starchy foods declined. As always, one of the things people bought with higher incomes was variety—in diets as in other goods.

The Dairy States

The upper Midwest has shorter growing seasons and more rolling terrain than regions farther south and west. Thus, it was not as well suited to corn (at least as a grain crop) as the Corn Belt, nor were its fields as receptive to machinery as those of the Great Plains. But the region was well suited to hay and other forage crops, including silage corn, and parts of Minnesota, Wisconsin, and Michigan became specialized dairy regions. Many of their farmers had been dairymen either in the East or in Europe. Once again, growing urban markets and improved transportation allowed another opportunity for income-raising specialization. Institutional changes also aided the region: Its great land-grant universities produced a variety of useful agricultural innovations after 1900, and quality control standards administered by state government assured ready markets for the region's products.

POSTWAR SOUTHERN AGRICULTURE

The South exhibited similar developments to those of other agricultural regions. Agriculture became more specialized, with greater dependence on other regions and sectors for inputs and markets. But the South showed far fewer signs of agricultural prosperity. Its performance slipped badly in comparison to that of other agricultural regions in most indices. In 1860, the average value of output per farm in the South had been $3,455, a figure slightly above the national average. In 1870, southern farms averaged only $1,456 of output, a figure that did not rise significantly until after 1910, by which time farms in the South averaged only 43 percent of per-farm national output. Even if it is acknowledged that the definition of a farm in the South changed as a result of the abolition of slavery, the increase in the number of southern farms is not great enough to account for such a difference. Even the figures quoted fail to indicate the full decline in some subregions within the South, for they are inflated by the inclusion of border states, such as Kentucky and Maryland, and by areas settled after the war, such as central Texas, Florida, and Oklahoma. These regions performed better than the centers of antebellum cotton culture.[10]

The antebellum South had been self-sufficient in foodstuffs or more, but now the cotton-producing states became heavy net importers of food. The stagnation of southern agriculture might have had no more serious implications for the region than did that of New England had there been employment alternatives to farming. But developments within agriculture largely determined southern incomes because manufacturing was a minor employer until after 1900. Southern industrial wages were heavily influenced by agricultural incomes. In other regions, sizable nonagricultural sectors typically generated larger incomes than did farming. The roots of the South's poverty lie in two facts: Not only was the region heavily concentrated on agriculture, but that agriculture fell far short of matching the performance of farming elsewhere in the United States.

The dimensions of the southern income debacle are not completely clear. Income figures for free southerners in 1860 and 1870 are not really comparable because of the abolition of slavery. If we use Easterlin's 1860 figures, which include all persons, free and slave alike, southern incomes had been about 80 percent of the national average in 1860 (see Table 6.3). By 1870, southern incomes were only 51 percent of the national average, and they grew no faster than the national rate until after 1900. For at least 35 years, the gap between southern incomes and those generated elsewhere either increased or remained constant in relative terms, and the gap increased in absolute numbers.[11] When slaves are included in the prewar population and their maintenance added to income, postwar income declines diminish but by no means disappear, and the rate of recovery is no different.

The Economic Consequences of Abolition

There is little doubt that the Civil War and the conditions and consequences of emancipation explain much of the South's decline. Incomes fell most in those states where plantation agriculture had been most prevalent before the war. Physical damage done by the war explains little: The South sustained no destruction that it found impossible to repair,

---

[10] *Historical Statistics*, 463.

[11] R. Fogel and S. Engerman, *The Reinterpretation of American Economic History* (New York: Harper & Row, 1971), 40–44.

nor did it suffer a permanent reduction in its potential male labor force. In fact, manufacturing output in the South exceeded prewar production by 1870; but manufacturing was only a tiny portion of the southern economy.[12] Livestock losses took longer to make good, but the evidence that this caused any real handicap to agriculture is at best very weak; mule price trends do not indicate growing scarcity. As in more recent instances, it appears that developed economies have surprisingly little difficulty in putting the pieces back together again after wartime destruction. The job is done much more rapidly than was the initial growth process: witness Germany and Japan after World War II. The most serious casualties for the South were antebellum institutions. Those that replaced them may have been significantly less productive at least in measurable terms.

The abolition of slavery freed blacks, but emancipation gave them no land, capital, or skills other than those they already possessed. Only half-hearted attempts were made to provide blacks with education, although their response was noteworthy; by 1900, most were literate, largely through the schooling of new-age cohorts, not adults.[13] Blacks' skill acquisition and job mobility were hampered, though certainly not prohibited, by racism. Emancipation did give freedmen much more bargaining power. Wages and the value of increased leisure time more than doubled the "incomes" they had received under slavery.[14]

At the same time, the war had been very destructive of both some forms of antebellum capital and the institutions through which other types were allocated. Nearly every bank in the region was ruined, and the antebellum system of cotton factors had disappeared. Prewar landowners retained title to their soil, but they lacked both labor and credit necessary to resume production. The investment in slaves, of course, no longer existed.

The New Environment of Labor

Not surprisingly, the ex-slaves desired above all else the control over their own lives that servitude had denied them. Freedom allowed them to claim a larger portion of the value of what they produced (it reduced exploitation), but equally important, it gave them a voice in determining their new conditions of labor. One immediate response was that the characteristics of the black labor force became similar to those of whites. Black women and children were no longer available for field work at the landowner's discretion. There may have been some reduction in the hours and number of days worked by adult black men as well, although the work-year under slavery is not a settled matter. The reduction in labor force participation occurred regardless of the wages offered, and is therefore a comment on slavery. The additional hours of work required of them as bondsmen were worth more to blacks as leisure or opportunity for household duties than was the money income generated by the extra hours of labor. Thus, a fall in money incomes in this voluntary form would not indicate a reduction in the welfare of the ex-slaves, had such a decline occurred.[15]

Freedmen's labor responses indicate that a good part of the apparent economic efficiency of plantation slavery was its ability to coerce slaves into efforts and conditions of labor for which they could not receive adequate compensation as free people. The gang system used so effectively on large plantations was ultimately based on coercion; the economies of scale it produced were not attainable in free

[12] R. Ransom and R. Sutch, *One Kind of Freedom: The Economic Consequences of Emancipation* (Cambridge, U.K.: Cambridge University Press, 1977), Chap. 3.
[13] R. Margo, *Race and Schooling in the South, 1880–1951* (Chicago: University of Chicago Press, 1990), Chap. 2.
[14] K. Ng and N. Virts, "The Value of Freedom," *Journal of Economic History* (December 1989).

[15] Ransom and Sutch, *One Kind of Freedom*, 2–9. For an even larger estimate of freed slaves' gains, see Ng and Virts, "The Value of Freedom."

labor markets. The changes, plus reductions in the amount of field labor performed by women and children, caused a substantial reduction in the work force of the cotton–growing South. One study estimates the reduction as between 28 and 37 percent.[16] Blacks also wanted to free themselves from another vestige of slavery; they preferred to live in homes scattered among the fields rather than in closely grouped cabins in what had been the plantations' slave quarters. These changes, however, largely indicate what blacks would no longer do. The institutions and conditions of labor that would replace them were yet to be determined in 1865.

Participation in a (Relatively) Free Labor Market

Immediately after the war, cotton prices were very high, giving great incentives to resume production. Blacks had no option but to work for their former owners; their only asset was their labor. Landowners equally clearly needed blacks' labor services; the ex-slaves were the only work force available, and without their efforts the land would not produce. But new conditions of employment and payment had to be worked out.

In the first few years, landowners attempted to hire blacks under much the same conditions as those before the war; they simply offered cash wages in addition to the food and lodging that had traditionally been provided. The survival of large production units whose

labor was under central supervision is in part a matter of definition. One investigation concluded that large farms with many characteristics of antebellum plantations still produced between 24 and 39 percent of the cotton crop in 1880.[17]

Blacks disliked wage labor, especially under close supervision, because there was so little change in working conditions from those of slavery. They preferred to work on a more individual basis. Mobility added a new dimension: Landowners in regions with acute labor shortages proved willing to offer them higher wages. Landowners' first response to the new conditions was an attempt to compel blacks to remain on the plantations through the season, and to collude to keep wage levels low. But the "Black Codes" proved unworkable. Even where state laws could be passed, no state with a labor shortage respected the regulations of another. Individuals within such jurisdictions might prefer labor at illegal rates to none at all. In addition, the federal government soon rescinded these laws.

Adjusting to Labor Mobility

Planters were little more satisfied with the new system than their new employees. Some workers left for better offers; others demanded higher wages for the arduous work involved in picking the crop. Landowners might have difficulty in providing cash wages, food, and other supplies before the crop was sold, because of the destruction of normal channels of credit. They had lost one major item of loan collateral, and the widespread decline in southern land values indicates that land was not the loan collateral that it once had been.

---

[16] Ransom and Sutch, *One Kind of Freedom*, 45. Because work efforts under both slavery and free labor markets are by no means settled and some estimates conflict with output figures, the absolute and proportional work reduction is controversial. Others see about half the decline in southern per-capita incomes stemming from the loss of scale economies, one-third from lower rates of labor force participation, and the remainder to slower growth in demand for cotton than in the antebellum period. See C. Goldin and F. Lewis, "The Post-Bellum Recovery of the South and the Cost of the Civil War: Comment," *Journal of Economic History* (June 1978).

---

[17] N. Virts, "Estimating the Importance of the Plantation System to Southern Agriculture in 1880," *Journal of Economic History* (December 1987).

Sharecropping

With the reduction in the labor force, output was lower, at least for the first decade,[18] and the losses were especially pronounced on large- to medium-sized plantations, where the coercive force of slavery had been greatest.[19] However the advantages of large-scale production units had been achieved in the antebellum period, they no longer existed, and by 1868 a new arrangement between landlord and farmer had appeared. A sizable portion of plantation land was divided into plots, each of which could be farmed by a single family. A contract was made between the landlord and the farming family: The landlord agreed to supply a house, tools, work animals, and (usually) seed. The tenant provided labor and his own subsistence until the crop was harvested. After the deduction of the expenses incurred by both parties, the proceeds of the crop were shared—usually half to each party. If either made unusual contributions to the joint effort, the division could vary. Farm workers could still work for wages, rent land for fixed payments, or buy their own land, but sharecropping became the most common single form of farm organization under which black farmers labored in the postbellum South. Nevertheless, it was neither universal nor confined to blacks. The method by which land was cultivated was determined by transaction and monitoring costs, human capital accumulation (skills), and the portion of physical capital contributed by landlord or farmer. For example, on large plantations, where landlord supervision was difficult, land tended to be worked by fixed-rent tenants, who bore most of the risks, rather than by wage laborers (in which case the landlord assumed all risk), or sharecroppers.[20]

New Methods of Agricultural Finance

Since few sharecroppers had money to buy food and other subsistence needs before they received income from cash crops and harvested food they had raised for themselves, they made a second contract, borrowing against their share of the crop at the nearest country store. Such a loan would be secured by a lien against the crops. Sharecropping allowed a division of risks between the landlord, who would bear them all if he hired labor for wages, and the sharecropper, who would shoulder the entire burden if he rented the land. The storekeeper who held the sharecropper's lien also shared risks. All parties benefited if the crop were good or prices high. Although the sharecropper was hardly an independent farmer under such an arrangement, the system gave him more control over his own work than he had previously enjoyed. Landlord or storekeeper might keep a close eye on croppers whose abilities were unknown, but those with established reputations were largely left to their own devices.

These basic features of sharecropping mask considerable diversity in individual cases, as well as some fundamental differences in the interests of the concerned parties. Because landlords had a fixed quantity of land, they tried to make each sharecropper's farm as small as possible, so that the only way the cropper could get a large income would be to produce a great deal per acre. The sharecropper, on the other hand, wanted the largest possible amount of land, because he received a fraction of the total crop. There might also be disagreements over the division of the crop, provisions for emergencies, the quality of

---

[18] *Historical Statistics*, 1:517–518. For 1870–1875, production increased 8.5 percent over the best five-year prewar period, and for 1875–1880, 48.2 percent.

[19] Ransom and Sutch, *One Kind of Freedom*, Chap. 4.

[20] L. Alston and R. Higgs, "Contractual Mix in Southern Agriculture Since the Civil War: Facts, Hypotheses, and Tests," *Journal of Economic History* (June 1982).

land, tools, and animals, and the division of the tenant's efforts between raising cotton for sale and corn or other food crops.

The Controversy over Sharecropping

Sharecropping is a controversial topic; it has been blamed for most of the South's agricultural problems by some historians and absolved or viewed positively by others. Several myths should be dispelled early in any discussion of this institution. First, sharecropping was only one of several commonly used types of agricultural organization. In 1880, only 15 years after emancipation, 20 percent of all southern black farmers owned their own farms. Another 26 percent rented. By 1900 these figures had increased to 27 and 36 percent.[21] Thus, sharecropping did not become more prevalent with time, at least for blacks. Second, sharecropping was not restricted to blacks or even to the South alone. Whites performed an increasing share of the field labor necessary to harvest cotton; a share that nearly quadrupled (to 60 percent of the total) by 1900.[22] Finally, the incomes of southern blacks were not reduced after emancipation: They rose by from 14 to 29 percent in material terms and more if the value of leisure and work conditions (for which they sacrificed money income) is considered.[23]

Other conclusions about the institution hold only under special circumstances. Sharecropping was claimed to provide no incentives to croppers to increase productivity, particularly if the lease were renegotiated each year. If an especially good crop were produced, the landlord would increase his share of the following year's crop, which committed the tenant to additional effort for no increase in income. But if tenants were free to move to other landlords, good farmers would be able to play one landowner off against another. Further, *both* parties gained from a good crop. Rational landlords were not likely to remove all incentives from the actual producers.

Sharecropping was also thought to reduce long-term investment on the part of either landlord or tenant. Tenants would be unwilling to incur costs for improvements whose yields would be received in future years because they feared the landlord would evict them after they made the improvement, effectively confiscating it. Landlords might be reluctant to make improvements themselves if tenants were mobile, because in this case the tenant might abuse the improvement or neglect maintenance to increase his short-term gains. These arguments ignore the point that gains from greater productivity were shared between landlord and tenant. As long as there were opportunities for gains from investment, either party had an incentive to make the investment and "bribe" the other with anything short of the improver's full share of the increased net income. In any case, landlords had a strong incentive to at least maintain land fertility over time. There is ample evidence that terms of sharecropping and rental agreements reflected the contributions of both landlord and farmer, as well as the costs of enforcing contracts.[24]

The Influence of Southern Labor Force Characteristics

The question of sharecropping's effect on incentives is thus tied to the nature of labor markets. If labor is mobile and informed, landlords will find it difficult to pay tenants less than the value of their output. If the supply of labor rises relative to that of land, share-

---

[21] S. Lebergott, *The Americans: An Economic Record* (New York: Norton, 1984), 253–255.
[22] Lebergott, *The Americans*, 260.
[23] The size but not the direction of blacks' income gains from emancipation is still unsettled. See Ransom and Sutch, *One Kind of Freedom*, 210, and Ng and Virts, "The Value of Freedom."

[24] Alston and Higgs, "Contractual Mix." See also J. Reid, "Sharecropping as an Understandable Market Response: The Postbellum South," *Journal of Economic History* (March 1973).

croppers' bargaining position will deteriorate; it is now in the landlord's interest to increase the number of workers per unit of land. Workers will still receive the value of their output, but under constant technology, this will be less per worker.

When the theoretical view of sharecropping is compared to postwar southern reality in which the supply of labor was rising in relation to that of land, sharecroppers' incomes might be expected to fall as a portion of the value of total agricultural output. Also, southern labor markets fell short of the conditions required for perfect competition between sharecroppers and landlords, particularly for blacks. Information about employment conditions elsewhere was obviously imperfect, especially before the achievement of widespread literacy. There were attempts to coerce both blacks and landlords to keep black incomes low and black labor immobile.[25] Evidence on blacks' purchases of land and mobility at least within the South, however, indicates that coercion fell far short of its goals. A recent study has found that labor mobility—at least between agricultural employers—was quite high. For blacks, the difficulty was that there were few jobs outside of agriculture.[26] The growing portion of white sharecroppers and black land purchases indicate that black labor was not so abundant that landlords were able to dictate any terms allowing minimal subsistence to blacks.

The Structure of Southern Credit Markets

The role of the country stores has also figured in the critique of sharecropping. Professors Ransom and Sutch, among others, have alleged that sharecroppers, both black and white, were seldom able to pay off their obligations once they had fallen into debt to the country stores. Worse, they could not leave the sharecropped farm or control their own production activities until they did. More recent work, however, found that Georgia sharecroppers in the 1880s were generally able to discharge their debts in full after the harvest, and that total debt was declining in most counties.[27] Nor, as Ransom and Sutch claim, did external developments favor sharecroppers. Farm technology was nearly static, cotton prices low until 1900, and population pressure on the land increasing. Debt tended to increase because storekeepers insisted that sharecroppers produce the cash crop (cotton) once they had fallen into debt, and the result was that total cotton production rose and the price fell even more. This would increase sharecroppers' dependence on the stores for food. The credit market, in this view, was highly imperfect: It might cost the farmer a full day's travel to visit only two or three stores. Thus, each store had considerable monopoly power and used it to charge very high rates of interest on loans—an average of 60 percent per year.[28]

The process, in the opinion of Ransom and Sutch, made for a vicious downward spiral of incomes. Storekeepers' insistence on cotton production in the face of an inelastic demand for the fiber resulted in lower net income from its production, because total revenues were reduced and total costs increased. Southern banks, which might have offered an alternative source of credit and more far-sighted regulations on tenants' production, were very slow to recover after the Civil War and confined their loans to urban borrowers. They had little interest in agriculture. Nor would the stores' extremely high interest returns attract competition; they were not large

[25] Ransom and Sutch, *One Kind of Freedom*, 86–87, Chap. 9.

[26] G. Wright, *Old South, New South: Revolutions in the Southern Economy Since the Civil War* (New York: Basic Books, 1986), 65, 177–186.

[27] P. Fishback, "Debt Peonage in Postbellum Georgia," *Explorations in Economic History* (April 1989).

[28] Ransom and Sutch, *One Kind of Freedom*, 131–132.

■ Historians' assessments of the economic influence of southern country stores are not yet conclusive.
Source: Chicago Historical Society. Photo by Carrie Ellen Mears. (Photograph cropped.)

enough in aggregate to induce entry into the rural credit market.[29] Credit was so expensive and returns in cotton markets so unpredictable that neither landlords nor tenants had incentives to invest in long-term agricultural improvements. Only fertilizer, which yielded an immediate return, was a worthwhile investment, and the South used far more of it than any other area. But fertilizer merely kept soil fertility from declining.

In this view, the South was thus locked into cotton cultivation more securely than it had been in the antebellum period. Now, however, the only beneficiaries of the situation were the owners of the country stores. Share-croppers' futures were bleak as their numbers rose. Only after two developments external to this system did southern incomes improve. The boll weevil forced agriculture to shift from its concentration on cotton, particularly after 1910, and industry moving to the South created jobs outside farming. Neither had much impact before 1900.

Every main point of Ransom and Sutch's views on sharecropping and the causes of postbellum Southern poverty have been attacked.[30] It has been shown that southern banks recovered from the war quite rapidly and even grew faster than the national average after 1880. The banks had at least the capacity

---

[29] Wright, *Old South, New South,* Chap. 7, and Ransom and Sutch, "Debt Peonage in the Cotton South after the Civil War," *Journal of Economic History* (December 1972).

[30] W. Brown and M. Reynolds, "Debt Peonage Reexamined," *Journal of Economic History* (December 1973), and Lebergott, *The Americans,* Chap. 21.

to provide agricultural loans.[31] However, no one has as yet shown that the banks actually extended agricultural credit, and one study indicates that Knoxville banks, at least, did not.[32] Credit markets in the South appear to have offered few barriers to entry, and if this is the case, returns as far above competitive levels as those Ransom and Sutch claim the country stores obtained should have attracted competition. Ransom and Sutch found no reduction of credit charges over time, but others are reluctant to accept the combination of rates and trend that they portray.[33] The agricultural labor mobility noted by Wright and others does not conform to the "debt peonage" structure postulated by Ransom and Sutch, nor does the growing portion of total Georgia wealth held by blacks over nearly the entire 1865–1914 period.[34]

Some scholars have seen the shifts toward lower food production and the consequent loss of self-sufficiency as rooted in causes other than merchants' insistence on cotton production. Certainly under sharecropping neither landlord, merchant, nor sharecropper gained from policies that increased output of a less profitable crop (cotton) at the expense of one yielding greater income (corn or other food). Merchants, especially, would gain from greater food production. Not only could they market a more valuable commodity than cotton, but their customers' incomes would rise, and they would sell more goods at their mo-

nopoly markups. Nor were landlords, with far greater wealth and influence than merchants, likely to accept policies so disastrous to them without protest; but no such outcry is discernible for three or four decades.[35] Regional specialization was increasing in all regions, and the South was not exempt. In addition, a larger share of total cotton production now came from highly specialized areas, such as east Texas. The smaller size of production units under sharecropping might also reduce food production, but it has been claimed that the average sharecropping unit had ample capacity in both land and labor time for self-sufficiency in food.[36]

U.S. monetary policies, which caused the dollar to appreciate against the British pound until 1879, have been viewed as slowing southern recovery, because the price of cotton to British purchasers rose.[37] But this argument would be more cogent were the British demand for cotton price-elastic. As reported by other investigators, the elasticity of demand for cotton was quite low, implying that increasing output in the face of such a demand (which rose only slowly) made cotton production less profitable.[38] One effort to test the responsiveness of cotton production to price changes has failed to support the thesis that the South was "locked into" cotton production regardless of changes in its price. Rather, it appears that the supply of cotton was as price-elastic as that of wheat.[39] The South's

---

[31] Brown and Reynolds, "Debt Peonage."

[32] J. Campen and A. Mayhew, "The National Banking System and Southern Economic Growth: Evidence From One Southern City, 1870–1900," *Journal of Economic History* (March 1988).

[33] Lebergott, *The Americans*, 263–267 is particularly outspoken on this point.

[34] R. Higgs, "Accumulation of Property by Southern Blacks Before World War One," *American Economic Review* (September 1982). Higgs' conclusions have been extended to four additional states by R. Margo, "Accumulation of Property by Southern Blacks Before World War One: Comment and Further Evidence," and R. Higgs, "Reply," *American Economic Review* (September 1984).

[35] Higgs, "Accumulation." My colleague David Bradford informs me that, in Mississippi, stores were commonly owned by large landowners, rather than by independent merchants.

[36] Higgs "Accumulation."

[37] M. Aldrich, "Flexible Exchange Rates, Northern Expansion, and the Market for Southern Cotton," *Journal of Economic History* (June 1973).

[38] G. Wright, *The Political Economy of the Cotton South* (New York: Norton, 1978), Chap. 6; and Fogel and Engerman, *Reinterpretation*, 330.

[39] S. DeCanio, "Cotton 'Overproduction' in Late 19th-Century Agriculture," *Journal of Economic History* (September 1973).

failure to regain high incomes cannot be attributed entirely to sharecropping. The southern state economies that grew most rapidly over 1879–1899 were Florida, where sharecropping was much less common than in the rest of the South, and Texas, where it was more prevalent than usual.[40] The Midwest, where sharecropping was significant and increasing, was a region of vigorous agricultural growth, although that area featured diversified agriculture.

The Causes of Southern Poverty

Where does all this discussion leave the debate? It appears difficult to place the entire weight of southern poverty on sharecropping in the postbellum South. The mechanisms by which it has been alleged to have reduced incomes appear to be dependent on an unlikely combination of economic irrationality by those involved, especially the merchants, and failure to respond to opportunity on the part of others. These phenomena do occur, but among millions of people for 35 years? Given the rate, if not the volume, of country merchants' alleged profits, where is the evidence that they achieved great wealth?

Clearly, even though the incomes of southern blacks were higher after emancipation, poverty among them and their white neighbors was real. Blacks received below-average incomes in a society that was poor by the standards of the rest of the United States. At least in one Arkansas community, there is evidence that blacks' health, especially that of children, deteriorated after the war.[41] Their

ability to record the gains in landownership, wealth, literacy, and income achieved under such circumstances is testimony to their ability and determination.

The causes of the South's poor economic performance between 1865 and 1900 appear to lie in its lack of diversification and in its demographics. The South did not begin to develop significant employment alternatives to agriculture until the turn of the century. At the same time, its population growth was nearly equal to that of regions offering their people wider alternatives. The South put too many people into its major industry, and labor costs were so low that there may have been little incentive to mechanize agriculture, regardless of the credit situation. Both southern and northern capitalists invested in manufacturing rather than agriculture in the postbellum South. Finally, conditions were not uniform across the entire South. Incomes for the region as a whole were growing at the nationwide rate after 1880, but this is a composite of rapid growth in frontier and border states (Florida, Texas, and Virginia) and very low rates for the Southeast.

Southern Labor Mobility—or Its Absence

Another mystery is the very slow rate of migration from the South before 1900. Relocation was a well-tested mechanism for income gains, but it was not employed by the poorest region of the country to anything approaching the extent it was elsewhere in America. It is true that southern agricultural labor would have had to forfeit most of its skills, even if it shifted to farming in other regions; but many Americans and immigrants made much greater transitions. Unlike many immigrants, southerners spoke English, most were literate, and they came from a much more advanced economy than did many eastern European immigrants at this time. Lower levels of education in the South hardly seem a full explanation, even if their effects, particularly on mobility and response to new opportuni-

[40] R. Easterlin, "Regional Growth of Income: Long-Term Tendencies 1880–1950," in S. Kuznets, A. Miller, and R. Easterlin, eds., *Population Redistribution and Economic Growth: United States 1870–1950*, vol. 2 (Philadelphia: American Philosophical Society, 1960).

[41] J. Rose, "Biological Consequences of Segregation and Economic Deprivation: A Post-Slavery Population from Southwest Arkansas," *Journal of Economic History* (June 1989).

ties, must have been adverse. Poverty made saving to finance a move difficult, but many immigrants from overseas overcame far greater barriers. Recently, it has been claimed that the American South constituted a separate labor market from that of the rest of the United States, with weaker ties to the national economy than even foreign labor.[42] For whatever reasons, the South failed to make the same use of its people's talents as did other regions, and the cost of neglect was high.

GOVERNMENT LAND POLICIES

The land policies of the federal government as well as the market for agricultural commodities played a significant role in the postwar development of American agriculture. The major changes in government land policy from antebellum procedures were the Homestead Act, subsequent legislation expanding and modifying that law, and land grants to railroads. Under the Homestead Act, anyone who would live on a plot of land, cultivate it for five years, and erect a house would receive title to 160 acres (320 for a married couple) after paying only nominal monetary filing fees. Later amendments modified the act to encourage settlement in areas where 160 acres were not sufficient for a viable farm, provided access to timber or stone for settlers' personal use, encouraged irrigation or tree planting, or allowed even larger acreage grants in regions suited only to livestock grazing.

In the period between 1850 and 1871, the railroads were granted almost 200 million acres of government land; they actually took title to about 131 million acres, an area roughly twice the size of the state of Colorado. This land was given as a construction subsidy; it had not yet been settled.

Both policies have been the subject of intense controversy, not lessened because they appeared to operate at cross purposes. On one hand, the government made "free" land available to final users; on the other, it gave land to the railroads to sell to these same final users at the highest possible price.

The Economics of the Homestead Act

The Homestead Act and other related legislation resulted in the transfer of almost 250 million acres into private ownership between 1862 and 1920. All of the land distribution acts were poorly drawn, loosely enforced, and widely abused. It should be obvious that land was not "free" under such policies; the costs of obtaining land legally were compliance with the conditions in the acts. Many settlers apparently considered the costs of land acquired through compliance with homesteading requirements higher than those under previous land-purchase laws, because more than three times as much land was purchased under older laws than was homesteaded in the first four decades after 1862, and the costs of evading the act or complying with its requirements may have dissipated much of the potential grants of income from the land.[43]

Mining, timber, and ranching firms filed homesteading claims through their employees or obtained land through a variety of fronts. Although one requirement of the Desert Land Act of 1877 required the settler to provide irrigation, the law failed to specify what constituted irrigation. The Homestead Act required the construction of a permanent dwelling "twelve by fourteen," with no units of measure. The construction of a cabin of

---

[42] Wright, *Old South, New South.*

[43] T. Dennen, "Some Efficiency Effects of Nineteenth-Century Land Policy: A Dynamic Analysis," *Agricultural History* (October 1977); and G. Libecap and R. Johnson, "Property Rights, Nineteenth-Century Timber Policy, and the Conservation Movement," *Journal of Economic History* (March 1979).

those dimensions in inches and the use of a house mounted on wheels so that it could be moved from one plot to another to be witnessed as meeting the law's requirements were two of the more common frauds. Laws allowing settlers to cut timber on government land for local use were often flagrantly violated. Eastern legislators consistently ignored the importance of water rights to western land values in both land allocation and the determination of political boundaries. After 1890, the most convenient vehicles for fraud were repealed or altered. In the face of lax enforcement efforts, these violations of the law's letter and intent are not surprising. Given the chance to reduce the cost of obtaining a valuable commodity, many people furthered their own interests.

The real controversy over the Homestead Act concerns its efficiency as a vehicle for the transfer of government land into private ownership. Here the question is confused by various scholars' views of the ultimate goal: Was the act to promote efficient economic use of the land, or was it directed toward another, perhaps noneconomic, goal? Still other critics regard the Homestead Act as entirely too successful in promoting noneconomic ends; to them, the prospect of free land attracted too many resources into agriculture rather than too few. In this view, the act wasted human labor and capital that would have been more productively employed in other sectors of the economy. By attracting ill-qualified farmers, it may have caused irreparable soil damage. One point seems clear today: Homesteading was not an escape outlet for poverty-stricken people from the urban East. Farming by this time required investments in both knowledge and physical capital that were beyond their means, and in addition, the movement to the West occurred in good times, not in periods of economic distress. If settlers were the best judges of their own welfare, the fact that they bought more land from federal, state, and local governments, the railroads, soldiers' warrants, and private sellers than they homesteaded indicates that the Homestead Act was not the only efficient land-transfer mechanism—or even the lowest-cost. These points gain weight for areas where the minimum size of a viable farm exceeded the Homestead Act limits, or where land was not suited to the uses required by the law.

Neither abuses of the Homestead Act nor the restrictions it required made much long-run difference. Land acquired under the act was freely transferrable after title was obtained. The large quantities of land available from a variety of sellers insured that prices would remain close to the $1.25 per acre minimum required for government land sold at auction. Any settler wishing to buy land of given characteristics and willing to search for it (or finance others' searches) generally had a choice of land and methods of acquisition. In such a market, the role of land speculators had no adverse effects, whether it was done by the railroads, by land companies organized for the purpose, or by the many individual speculators, large-scale and small, dealing in raw land or that developed and worked for decades. There was a great deal of competition in land markets, and informed buyers did not pay more for land than its expected value. Often, final users paid less.

Land speculation was widespread (and homesteaders participated in it), but there is substantial misunderstanding of the nature and effects of speculation by some scholars. Speculators do not gain by buying assets or by withholding them from the market; their gains come from selling. Holding land, even land acquired without a cash outlay, involved costs. Only if land values are appreciating faster than the rate at which interest would accumulate on money obtained from the current sale of land is it profitable for a speculator to hold land instead of other assets. Few speculators acquired land at no cost, so to the costs already mentioned we must add interest foregone on any money tied up in the land. There were few opportunities for speculators to obtain income from their land while they waited for land values to increase; very few settlers wanted to rent. Speculators gained most by selling soon after they had acquired land, especially in cases where large amounts of land were available from other sellers, and thus long-run gains were likely to be small.

A few speculators, particularly those who were able to obtain accurate information about the lands they purchased, were able to obtain above-average rates of return on their investments, but this is normal in any activity—superior information is likely to produce better results.[44] Speculation, whether large-scale or small, would not change the land's physical properties. If land were best suited to small-scale farming, it would not be in the speculator's interest to sell only large plots, and if it were only suited for uses requiring a great deal of land, selling small parcels would reduce the return to sellers. Much of the land that was originally homesteaded was eventually sold and consolidated into large parcels, an indication of its highest-value use.

The Homestead Act and U.S. Income Distribution

Whether the land distribution favored the rich or the poor is unclear. Obviously, the program favored land recipients over taxpayers because the land policies sacrificed land-sale revenues. Whether the actual recipients were richer or poorer than average is unknown.

The structure of federal taxes at this time was regressive. (Federal revenues were derived from excise taxes and tariffs, which raised the cost of commodities adversely affecting low-income consumers.) More extensive land distribution under the Homestead Act would probably have increased tax burdens on the American poor. In addition, agricultural incomes were lower than those earned in most other sectors of the economy, and increasing the number of small farmers still further was hardly the way to raise them. As long as the land's value to its owners depended on how they used it, either giving land away or selling it in competitive markets would be likely to produce an efficient allocation over time if land were transferrable. The only difference in results would be the identity of the recipients of land's rental value. The government would obtain the rental values if the land were sold at auction, because prices would be bid up to the land's capitalized value. If land were given away with no charges in money or otherwise (as it was not), the new owners would receive the rents. Even the charge that the act misallocated resources has only short-run validity. High rates of failure on homesteaded land transferred its ownership to more efficient users. Damage to the land's productivity from inappropriate use may be another question.

Railroad Land Grants

Much critical attention has been directed at government grants of land to the railroads. Typically, the federal government land grants followed a checkerboard pattern along the right of way. Railroads thus obtained only half the land fronting on their proposed routes; the rest remained in government hands for disposal by either sale or (less often) homesteading. The idea behind the land grants was that the railroads could sell most of the land they received to obtain funds with which to actually build the railway. Lands adjacent to a railroad sold for higher per-acre prices than those at some distance away, especially in the Great Plains. In that region, the distances to market were enormous, and no alternative means of transportation were available.

The Distribution of Benefits from Land Grants

The charge frequently made is that too much land was given to the railroads, who sold it at prices so high that the farmers who purchased it received little or no benefit from their access

[44] A. Bogue and M. Bogue, " 'Profits' and the Frontier Land Speculator," *Journal of Economic History* (March 1957).

to transportation. Allegedly, the railroads not only charged very high prices for land, but their freight duties were so steep that farmers paid out all the gains that accrued from proximity to the rails. The evidence belies this contention. First, land adjacent to the railroads was eagerly sought by farmers, even though land of similar physical qualities was available at lower prices elsewhere, and the process continued long after farmers had gained experience with railroads' freight rates. Second, government land close to the railroads was also available, and buyers bid up prices to levels comparable to those charged by the railroads. Such land was expected to produce higher incomes than more remote acreage. The value of lands in private ownership along the railroads rose in value relative to that elsewhere, an indication that such land returned higher incomes. Finally, transportation costs for wagon freightage were so high that even land purchased at more than three times the government minimum of $1.25 per acre yielded a higher return than did "free" homesteaded land requiring a long wagon trip. This holds even when interest on the price of railroad land is included in its cost.[45]

Land Grants' Effect on Economic Growth

Several careful studies have concluded that railroad land grants had positive effects on economic growth. The grants' importance is increased when it is realized that western settlement might have been considerably delayed without them. Because the social rate of return on the western railroads was nearly double the private rate of return, the economy benefited from the grants by much more than the returns they generated for the railroads.[46] The railroads were not able to capture the full value of the increase in land values for themselves;

most of it accrued to the farmers. The government also benefited from increased land sales revenues and from the railroads' carriage of troops, mail, and government freight at below-market rates. By 1940, the value of these services is claimed to have more than equalled that of the land grants at prices adjusted to the current time.

If the goal of land grants and the Homestead Act was the rapid settlement of the West, they must be judged a huge success. In 40 or 50 years, an enormous area was settled, about as much as in the entire previous history of the country. The speed with which settlement occurred makes it difficult to envision an alternative method that could have done the job faster. It constitutes a strong argument against the view that there were substantial barriers to land acquisition and settlement.

THE AGRARIAN PROTEST

At many times in the three decades after 1865, the most rapidly increasing crop appeared to be farm discontent. Especially from the 1870s to the mid-1890s, farmers' unhappiness with their circumstances supported a series of political, social, and economic protests and proposals for change in American institutions. Led both by established politicians and such colorful types as Mary Lease, "the Kansas Pythoness," "Sockless Jerry" Simpson, and "Pitchfork Ben" Tillman, farm protest was a feature of American politics. The movement culminated in the populism of the 1890s, almost as much a crusade as a political movement. Although they differed in emphasis, groups such as the National Patrons of Husbandry (the Grangers), the Greenback Party, the various Alliances, and the Populists, all agreed about the source of farmers' difficulties and what should be done about them.

---

[45] Lebergott, *The Americans*, 271.
[46] L. Mercer, "Rates of Return for Land-Grant Railroads: The Union Pacific," *Journal of Economic History* (September 1970).

■ This cartoon reflects the popular belief of the time that Congress was under the influence of special interest groups and ignoring the plight of the farmer.
Source: The Granger Collection, New York.

Sources of Agrarian Discontent

To the farmers, the highly commercialized agriculture of the postwar period, with forward and backward linkages that tied farming to the rest of the economy, had exacerbated some old problems and created some new ones. They believed that the prices they received for their crops were falling in relation to those of the goods and services they bought. To the farmers, the reason was clear enough: They sold their produce in competitive markets, but nearly everything they bought came from sellers who seemed to possess greater or lesser degrees of monopoly power. Railroads, grain elevators, farm implement producers, banks and mortgage companies, and even the sellers of consumer goods all were far less numerous

than their customers. They seemed able to raise their prices while simultaneously reducing those received by farmers. Speculation was also viewed as a special source of farmers' ills. It seemed wrong that someone might be able to gain from buying or selling goods that he had not grown, transported, or processed, particularly when such a person might profit from a reduction in farmers' incomes.

Prices of the major grain crops, such as wheat and corn, as well as those of beef and pork, were now heavily influenced, if not determined, by supply and demand in international rather than domestic markets. Nor was the macroeconomic situation to growers' advantage. Farmers, especially those in newly settled regions, tend to be debtors. In any case, it appeared to many farmers that the interest

■ The Grangers believed that agriculture was the base upon which the American economy depended.
Source: Library of Congress.

rates that lenders charged them were higher than those paid by other borrowers—yet another indication of the monopoly power that they believed was exploiting them. The general deflation of 1865–1896 added to their burdens. As prices fell, farmers had to repay debt in dollars of greater purchasing power than those borrowed. If farm prices fell faster than others, this meant that it would take more units of farm goods to buy a given quantity of nonfarm commodities.

Proposals for Reform

The solutions advocated by farm groups generally involved some mechanism to curb or eliminate monopoly among the groups from whom farmers bought. Regulation of railroads and grain elevator charges by state commissions was proposed by the Grange. Other groups proposed that the government should operate some railroads and use its experience to set "fair" rates, or that all railroads should be nationalized and operated in the public interest. Curbs on monopoly power throughout the economy were to be sought through regulation, public ownership, or cooperative action by farmers to provide their own supplies and services. Banks and mortgage lenders of all sorts were special targets of reform and control proposals. Farmers were often joined by other advocates of institutional reform. At this time, some urban groups were agitating for municipal ownership or regulation of the new firms that had appeared to provide cities with water, gas, and other essential commodities and services.

Monetary Expansion Many farmers thought that if the money supply could be expanded, they would benefit as prices rose (obviously they thought farm prices would rise at least as fast as all others). The Greenback Movement, which attained the status of a political party in the late 1880s, advocated an expanded supply of the greenback currency that had been issued during the Civil War. Since that time,

■ Nineteenth-century Americans familiar with the quantity theory of money opposed increases in the note issue, as this cartoon illustrates.
Source: Culver Pictures.

the number of greenbacks in circulation had either been reduced or held constant. The political appeal of a rapid expansion of inconvertible paper currency was not great while memories of Civil War inflation remained fresh. At its high point, the Greenback Party won 22 electoral votes in the presidential election of 1892 and gained a handful of congressional seats.

Silver offered another route to the goal of monetary expansion. After 1860, most of the great mining discoveries in the American West had been of silver rather than gold. Consequently, the value of silver had declined relative to that of gold. The Populists, or at least the party's western wing, advocated the coinage of silver in unlimited amounts. Understandably, this idea was enthusiastically supported by western miners, but it too found only limited success.

Several other agrarian ideas have a distinctly modern ring. The Alliances proposed that the government set up a system of warehouses in which farmers could deposit their crops and receive loans of up to 80 percent of the crops' value in the form of greenbacks. They also proposed that the federal government enter the farm-financing business by offering greenback loans of half the value of any farmer's property.

Until the early 1890s, few of these proposals were put into operation. The courts endorsed the idea of regulation (in *Munn v. Illinois*) in 1877, allowing states to impose regulations on businesses "imbued with a public purpose" within their own borders. But in 1886, the Supreme Court forbade state regulation of interstate commerce, which effectively removed the railroads from their control. Cooperative efforts in both supplying inputs to farmers or marketing their products met with little success. Farmers learned that replacing a middleman who serves no useful function or charges monopoly prices for his services is one thing, but doing without or replacing those whose charges reflect the cost of service is quite another, particularly in cases where economies of scale or highly specialized inputs were involved.

The Populists

Political efforts were the most visible portion of the Populist effort. This group was an amalgam of farm protest with the reform movements then active in large cities. As such, it gained considerably more strength than its rural predecessors, which had never so much as succeeded in uniting the agrarian population.

The Populists advocated control over monopolies by the whole range of devices suggested by their predecessors. But it was the advocacy of the free coinage of silver, given voice by the passionate oratory of William Jennings Bryan, for which the Populists are best remembered. Despite the Populists' fusion with the Democratic Party, they were defeated. William McKinley, the Republican advocate of "sound money" and a gold-based currency, won the election of 1896. Bryan proved unable to carry areas like the Midwest, where agriculture was well established. Ironically, the long decline in prices was reversed in 1896, for reasons having little to do with politics, and for the next two decades farm prices rose faster than the general rate of inflation. The years from 1900 to 1914 were an era of prosperity for American farmers, in which the evidence of unrest rapidly disappeared.

Were Farmers' Complaints Justified?

There is little doubt that farmers thought they had legitimate grievances. The numbers of farmers involved in the protest movements and the fervor they exhibited were evidence of that. But moral outrage is a poor substitute for accurate information or coherent analysis. Much of the data related to farmers' complaints does little to support them.

Changes in Relative Prices

Prices received by farmers for their products continued to fall for three decades after the Civil War, but so did all other prices. Farmers still had a grievance if the prices of their products were declining faster than the average. But it now appears that the prices of goods farmers bought declined slightly relative to those of the goods they sold (see Table 11.3). Since farm produce remained essentially unchanged over this period while there were substantial improvements in the quality of both capital and consumer goods, the actual trends in real prices favored the farmers.[47] These price trends also refute the farmers' contention that manufacturers were exploiting them through the exercise of monopoly power. On the other hand, despite the long-term trends noted above, there were periods, especially in

---

[47] R. Robertson, *History of the American Economy*, 3d. ed. (New York: Harcourt Brace Jovanovich, 1973), 315.

Table 11.3   Farm Prices Received and Paid (1870 = 100)

Year	Prices Received for Livestock and Crops	Prices Paid for Farm Machinery	Midwest Interest Rates	Freight and Distribution Cost of West North Central Wheat
1870	100	100	100	100
1880	76	68	83	60
1890	64	48	68	45
1900	63	45	55	35
1910	95	45	52	24

Source: S. Lebergott, *The Americans: An Economic Record* (New York: Norton, 1984), 302.

the 1870s, when farm prices fell sharply. In general, farm goods' prices were far less stable than those of other goods.[48] Thus, while the data does not indicate that farmers were consistently injured by relative price movements, it would hardly be surprising if they were moved to public outcry when prices moved against them.

The Role of the World Market

In addition, the 1870–1900 period was the heyday of U.S. exports of grain and meat. The farmer was now participating in a world market, where prices might change for no reason visible to him. Moreover, such changes were impossible to predict. Bountiful crops in the United States might bring high prices and prosperity to American farmers if those in Argentina, Australia, Canada, and eastern Europe were poor; if foreign producers enjoyed large harvests, prices might be very low. There might be some compensation for poor American harvests if prices were high, but abundant crops overseas could compound American farmers' difficulties. Uncertainty over prices

might have been as great a burden—if not more—than the price changes themselves.

Railroads

The "exploitation" of farmers by railroads and middlemen, particularly grain brokers, was another source of complaints. Rail freight charges fell at about the same rate as all prices and continued to decline thereafter (see Table 11.3). However, especially in the Great Plains, they showed no tendency to decline in relation to grain and cotton prices prior to 1897.[49] Freight rates varied widely from year to year and often between regions as well. During the early 1890s, high rail freight charges coincided with farm protests. Such protests centered in the West, where freight charges were largest in proportion to the value of the goods shipped, and rate changes could make the difference between a good year and a bad one for many farmers.[50] Whatever the overall trend or level of rail charges, few railroads hesitated to employ whatever monopoly power they might possess in local markets or to price their services at or below cost to customers with good alternative means of shipment. The rising

---

[48] J. Bowman and R. Keehn, "Agricultural Terms of Trade in Four Midwestern States, 1870–1900," *Journal of Economic History* (September 1974).

[49] Higgs, *Transformation*, 89.
[50] Higgs, *Transformation*, 99–101.

value of farm land near railroads suggests that despite their best efforts, the railways were unable to squeeze the full value of their services from customers. But it was not for lack of effort.

The Impact of Middlemen on Farm Income

The farmers' case against commodity speculators and other middlemen appears to have little factual basis. The essence of speculation is the purchase of an asset at low prices in the hope of future sale at higher prices. In pursuing this goal, speculators add to current demand, which increases prices then, and also to future supply, which reduces prices later. For farm commodities, speculators' actions tended to raise prices immediately after the harvest, when most farmers were eager to sell, and to reduce those paid by consumers later. While speculators certainly wished that prices received by farmers might be very low, their actions produced just the opposite effect. Also, grain speculators suffered losses before 1897.[51] During the period in which agrarian complaints were at their loudest, the difference between the final prices paid for grain and meat and those received by farmers fell substantially, indicating that the efficiency of transportation, processing, and distribution of those commodities increased—and that the savings were passed on to farmers and consumers. Farmers may have compared their own incomes with those of middlemen serving hundreds or even thousands of farmers, and from this perspective, the middlemen might have appeared to be receiving huge (and unjustified) incomes.

Farm Debt

The actual burden of farm debt fares little better in the light of historical evidence. Falling prices make it harder to repay debts, especially if the prices of products from which repay-

ment is derived fall. However, the severity of the injury depends on the rate of decline in prices and the period of the loan. Nineteenth-century farm mortgages were for only three to five years, a period too short for deflation to add much to debt burdens. Still, in such a short time, one bad year might have a critical impact on income from which the loan was to be repaid, and as previously noted, there were wide swings in the prices received by farmers. A poor crop, due to any of the myriad business, environmental, or personal circumstances afflicting western farmers, could reduce incomes by from one-fifth to one-third.

Mortgages rates were higher for farms in the West than they were in the East, and highest of all on the frontier. This reflects two very real considerations: Demand for loans was high in relation to supply in areas where few people had had time to accumulate wealth; and the higher risks due to distance, lack of information, and the vagaries of western agriculture and ranching. Drought, blizzards, fires, insects, or even wolves and bears with tastes for sheep and cattle could turn an apparently sound investment into a total capital loss in incredibly short times. All of these dangers were either new or far more acute than they had been in the East.

Western interest rates may have exceeded those in the East, but the evidence indicates that, if anything, the differential was insufficient to compensate for the greater risks of lending in the West. By the 1880s, there was considerable competition among western mortgage lenders.[52] A classic study of western agricultural finance indicates that most farm borrowing was for expansion, rather than caused by distress. In the 1890s, bankruptcies among farm mortgage companies were frequent, and this is an indication that they had

---

[51] Higgs, *Transformation*, 87–90.

[52] D. North, *Growth and Welfare in the American Past*, 2d. ed. (Englewood Cliffs, N.J.: Prentice Hall, 1974), 133.

charged too little, rather than too much.[53] Nor were all or even most western farms mortgaged, although it is significant that the proportion of farms mortgaged was greatest and the interest differential highest in Kansas and Nebraska, both hotbeds of political activism. In most areas, less than half of all farms were mortgaged, and not a few midwestern farmers were lending money rather than borrowing. This may explain Bryan's poor showing in the older agricultural regions.[54]

Farm Incomes
The evidence on both capital gains and trends in farm incomes per se indicates that farmers' incomes and the value of farm property rose in every decade if not in every year. Gains were less (and short-run losses worse) in the 1870s than in other decades, but the general trend of farm incomes was upward. Farmers were receiving capital gains, even after deducting the burdens of their mortgages.[55] Agricultural incomes were not rising as rapidly as those of other occupations because productivity increased faster in other sectors of the economy. Moreover, there were differences in the experiences of farmers in various regions.

Regional Income Disparities
Incomes rose substantially in the Midwest and the West, but farms in the South and East recorded lesser gains or none at all during the protest era. After 1896, the general improvement in farm incomes was again unequally shared, and it failed to keep pace with income trends elsewhere in the economy. While additional land of good quality remained unused, there was little prospect that agricultural incomes would show substantial long-term gains. Farming was a highly competitive industry with few barriers to entry, so that any short-term improvement in farmers' prospects would spur a flow of resources into the activities in which they were generated. Only after the supply of usable land became less elastic would an increase in demand for food result in a permanent rise in real food prices. This apparently occurred after 1900, as population continued to increase rapidly and the number of farms rose at a much more modest pace.

The Burdens of Interdependence
Commercialization of agriculture, particularly in the West, may have been a factor in farm complaints, if not necessarily in the real difficulties of farmers. As agriculture became more market-oriented, farmers may have felt that their control over their own activities was reduced. They were more dependent on specialists to market crops; provide tools, credit, and supplies; and to provide the transportation necessary for these linkages. In earlier times, farmers had been able to perform many of these functions for themselves, and, in any case, were far less dependent on production for the market. The new conditions provided "outsiders" on whom farmers could focus discontent.[56] They also increased the impact of uncertainty; farmers could no longer trade off money income for self-sufficiency, as they might (but seldom did) in earlier times.

Farmers were losing their social and political position as well. From being regarded as the backbone of the nation and the embodiment of all its virtues, they became the butt of city jokes about hicks and hayseeds. Others lived better than the farmer, and any photograph of small towns on market days

---

[53] A. Bogue, *Money at Interest: The Farm Mortgage on the Middle Border* (Ithaca: Cornell University Press, 1955, 1968 reprint).

[54] Higgs, *Transformation*, 96–97.

[55] R. Fogel and J. Rutner, "The Efficiency Effects of Federal Land Policy, 1850–1900: A Report of Some Preliminary Findings," in W. Aydelotte et al., *Dimensions of Quantitative Research in History* (Princeton, N.J.: Princeton University Press, 1972).

[56] A. Mayhew, "A Reappraisal of the Causes of Farm Protest in the United States," *Journal of Economic History* (June 1972).

reveals only too clearly who lived in town and who did not. The conditions of urban life improved rapidly during this era, but those on the farm gained less, and in some regions, especially the Great Plains, they may have deteriorated. Farming in that region meant an insecure life of unending hard work, incredible isolation, and little variety. Women on Great Plains farms might literally never see friends or anyone outside their immediate families for six months at a stretch. That such a life was the reward for farmers' efforts might well occasion protest when others apparently did less and gained more.

It may have been that while entry into farming was easy, exit was difficult. If farmers felt themselves "locked into" an occupation where market forces offered little hope for rises in income status, the protests may be viewed as an attempt to seek income transfers (rents) outside the market. The early attempts largely failed, except in the case of railroad regulation,[57] but they may have encouraged farmers in more successful rent-seeking efforts several decades later.

THE BEGINNINGS OF CONSERVATION

For two and a half centuries, Americans had been accustomed to regarding natural resources as, if not locally, at least nationally, inexhaustible. For most of that period, natural forces had been enemies to be conquered by any means coming to hand. As representatives of the natural order, the Indians bore the burden of this attitude. They were regarded as obstacles to progress, to be destroyed or barely

tolerated if they converted to the "superior" ways of their conquerors. The Plains Indians were subjugated as much through the destruction of the buffalo on which their economy was based as they were through direct military action. In both cases, the job was thoroughly done: The Indians were decimated; and from herds estimated at from 25 to 60 million in 1800, only 541 wild buffalo remained in the entire country in 1889.

Vast areas were stripped of timber, and in the process, forest fires sometimes destroyed as much timber as was harvested. A single forest fire in Wisconsin burned several thousand square miles and took 1,500 lives in 1871. It went almost unnoticed, because at the same time the great Chicago fire destroyed most of that city.

Increasing Resource Costs

By 1900, it appeared that some resources might not last forever under current rates and practices of use. It was also realized that some were being used in a manner that reduced incomes in other sectors, that is, there were social costs. All too often erosion and massive flooding resulted from mountainside lumbering. Lumbermen who owned only the lands they cut (if those) were not liable for reductions in the productivity of farmland downslope from their operations. Previously, even though this had occurred, the aggregate costs were slight, because there was plenty of new agricultural land that could be settled if older regions' fertility was impaired. But after 1900 this was less so. Urban pollution was a similar problem.

In the first tentative steps, a few areas were reserved from settlement as national parks, which were to remain forever in their natural state. Yellowstone National Park was established in 1872; by 1914, seven others, all in

---

[57] A. Martin, *Enterprise Denied: Origins of the Decline of American Railroads, 1897–1917* (New York: Columbia University Press, 1971).

the West, had been set up.[58] More important than the parks was the idea that some resources, particularly timber, could be produced indefinitely if methods were changed. This thought began to influence both private and public attitudes. As timber resources dwindled and wood prices increased, lumber companies began to acquire forestland and manage it for sustained yields—sometimes over the opposition of the government.[59] In 1891, some of the more flagrantly abused land acquisition acts were repealed and enforcement tightened. During the second Cleveland administration, the federal government began to set aside mineral and timber reserves and to lease waterpower sites rather than selling them outright. Forest reserves (national forests) outside the national parks were to be managed for continuous production.

The federal government began a series of irrigation projects in the West and a program of navigation and flood control improvements in the rest of the country. While some of the latter projects may have generated social benefits, in large part they have now become the center of congressional "pork barrel" legislation, designed more to protect incumbent congressmen from floods of votes for the opposition than for economic benefit to the country. In 1911, Congress approved a program of land acquisition under which the government purchased mountain land in the East to preserve its forests and prevent floods.

The early conservation measures were heavily oriented toward timber and the preservation of resources rather than their intelligent use. They paid little attention to soil erosion and pollution control except in cases

■ Theodore Roosevelt is pictured at Yosemite National Park with John Muir, the pioneer naturalist.
Source: Culver Pictures.

where needs were overwhelming. In many cases, they may have been too chary of infringing on the "rights" of private property even where social costs were involved. Nevertheless, they marked the inception of a new attitude.

State governments also began to develop some concerns for conservation. Wildlife was protected through the regulation of hunting, and later by the establishment of game refuges. Previously, wild animals belonged to whomever could kill or capture them, especially from public land. There had been little incentive to refrain from securing all that one could, any way one could. If private property rights were not to be established for game animals, government intervention was required. Ecological relationships were still unknown, however, so most of these measures were directed only at game species.

It may be that such concern for the future could only be generated by the forces that brought it into existence in the United States—the evidence that wildlife, if not all natural

---

[58] One of the first tourist parties to visit Yellowstone found it considerably more "natural" than they had bargained for. They were attacked by Indians and one person was killed and several others scalped. My thanks to Professor Robert Gallman and the Grand Teton National Park Museum for this anecdote.

[59] Lebergott, *The Americans*, 273.

resources, could be destroyed permanently. There was also a sense that Americans were now wealthy enough to view some natural resources not merely as potential sources of immediate money income, but as something to give value to the leisure time that increasing numbers of Americans now possessed. At no time were the overall costs and benefits of conservation or preservation ever assessed: This was not an economic movement. But it bought time to allow more scientific analysis to be developed.

SELECTED REFERENCES

Arrington, L. *Great Basin Kingdom*. Cambridge, Mass.: Harvard University Press, 1958.

Atherton, L. *The Cattle Kings*. Bloomington, Ind.: Indiana University Press, 1962.

Bateman, F., and T. Weiss. *Deplorable Scarcity*. Chapel Hill, N.C.: University of North Carolina Press, 1981.

Bogue, A. *From Prairie to Corn Belt: Farming on the Illinois and Iowa Prairies in the Nineteenth Century*. Chicago: University of Chicago Press, 1963.

———. *Money at Interest: The Farm Mortgage on the Middle Border*. Reprint. Ithaca, N.Y.: Russell, 1968.

Davis, L., R. Easterlin, and W. Parker. et al. *American Economic Growth: An Economist's History of the United States*. New York: Harper & Row, 1972.

DeCanio, S. *Agriculture in the Postbellum South: The Economics of Production and Supply*. Cambridge, Mass.: M.I.T. Press, 1974.

Hicks, J. *The Populist Revolt*. Lincoln, Neb.: University of Nebraska Press, 1961.

Higgs, R. *The Transformation of the American Economy, 1865–1914: An Essay in Interpretation*. New York: John Wiley and Sons, 1971.

———. *Competition and Coercion: Blacks in the American Economy, 1865–1914*. Cambridge, U.K.: Cambridge University Press, 1977.

North, D., T. Anderson, and P. Hill. *Growth and Welfare in the American Past: A New Economic History*. 3d ed. Englewood Cliffs, N.J.: Prentice-Hall, 1983.

Ransom, R., and R. Sutch. *One Kind of Freedom: The Economic Consequences of Emancipation*. Cambridge, U.K.: Cambridge University Press, 1977.

Schlebeker, J. *Whereby We Thrive*. Ames, Iowa: Iowa State University Press, 1975

Shannon, F. *The Farmer's Last Frontier: Agriculture, 1860–1879*. New York: M. E. Sharpe, 1977.

Swierenga, R. *Pioneers and Profits: Land Speculation on the Iowa Frontier*. Ames, Iowa: Iowa State University Press, 1968.

U. S. Department of Commerce, Bureau of the Census. *Historical Statistics of the United States: Colonial Times to 1970*. 2 vols. Washington, D.C.: Government Printing Office, 1975.

Walton, G., and J. Shepherd. *Market Institutions and Economic Progress in the New South, 1865–1900*. New York: Academic Press, 1981.

Wright, G. *The Political Economy of the Cotton South*. New York: Norton, 1978.

———. *Old South, New South: Revolutions in the Southern Economy Since the Civil War*. New York: Basic Books, 1986.

INDUSTRY, TRANSPORTATION, AND THE RISE OF BIG BUSINESS

Manufacturing had been established in the United States before the Civil War, but in the half-century after 1865, it became the dominant sector of the economy and a chief source of growth. In 1859, agriculture had contributed about 62 percent of total value added in U.S. commodity production. Industry (broadly defined) produced 38 percent. By 1880, the contributions of the two sectors were about equal. In 1909, however, industry's share was almost three times that of agriculture: 74 versus 26 percent.[1] Since agriculture expanded very substantially over this period, the figures indicate that industrial growth must have been more rapid than that of the overall economy. And so it had been. American industrialization had made this country a giant among the world's manufacturing nations.

In 1914, not only was the United States primarily an industrial economy; its manufacturing output dwarfed that of any other single nation. With about 36 percent of the world's industrial capacity, the United States equalled the combined production of Germany, Britain, and France, its three closest rivals. American industrial primacy was not merely quantitative. In many types of manufacturing, the United States was now the world's technological leader. In 1860, the country had been an importer of capital goods and the ideas embodied in them. Now it exported both capital goods and expertise in production methods. American technical leadership was not universal; German performance in industrial chemistry, for example, was still unrivaled. But the previous picture of the United States as an economy weak in basic and applied science was no longer valid.

Developments in transportation were scarcely less impressive. Before the end of the nineteenth century, railroads had been extended throughout the United States and their operating efficiency greatly improved. Mileage of main railway track had increased more than sevenfold from 1865 to 1914, and the carrying capacity of the new lines had risen even more because of steady technological progress. Railroads had important forward and backward linkages to the rest of the economy; they were major consumers of steel, other heavy industrial goods, and coal; and their services had transformed the nature of competition and distribution in America.

EFFECTS OF POSTWAR GROWTH

As always, sustained growth within any economic sector meant change. The location and type of industrial activity, as well as the types of goods produced, were altered. Increasing portions of American industry were now in the Great Lakes region. That area's abundant coal, iron ore, and natural waterways, which allowed easy transportation, fostered more rapid industrial growth than New England or the Middle Atlantic states recorded. As the North Central states became centers of iron and steel production, they converted the metal into a growing variety of finished goods. After 1900, the South increased its industrial growth, mainly in labor-intensive commodities such as textiles and tobacco products, but also in iron and steel.[2]

Both capital and labor showed greater mobility than in previous eras, responding to the opportunities revealed by factor price differ-

[1] R. Fogel and S. Engerman, eds., *The Reinterpretation of American Economic History* (New York: Harper & Row, 1971), 27.

[2] G. Wright, *Old South, New South: Revolutions in the Southern Economy Since the Civil War* (New York: Basic Books, 1986), Chaps. 5, 6.

ences. The Midwest had developed industry serving local markets over 1850–1880. When transportation improvements produced national markets, the region had the infrastructure and entrepreneurial experience to compete in wider arenas.[3] The South had abundant labor and some types of raw materials, but capital was scarce. Consequently, wages were low, and the return on capital high. Capital was transferred to the South, although most southern industry was locally financed.[4] Southern workers began to migrate to the North, where greater capital endowments per worker raised productivity and wages. In the tight labor markets of World War I, this trend accelerated, particularly for blacks.

Leading Industries

The identity of leading industries and their production processes also changed. In 1860, most American manufacturing involved either raw materials processing or was characterized by modest capital requirements, as in textiles or boots and shoes. Although some of the leading industries of 1860 retained their importance in 1910, a number of new manufacturing aggregations had gained prominence. (See Table 12.1.) The figures do not indicate another important development—the decline of home manufacturing. Consumers now bought larger quantities of manufactured goods in finished or more nearly finished forms, ready-to-wear clothing rather than cloth, and bakery products rather than flour.

The development of the new industrial sectors reflected the changes that had occurred in demand and supply. New technology, increases in capital, and improvements in mechanisms for its allocation affected supply.

Demand was influenced by increased population and incomes and by changes in products, which increased the demand for industrial commodities as intermediate goods. Machinery and railroad car manufacturers needed steel; printing and publishing required paper, dyes, and specialized machines. Changes in the nature of the population also influenced the rank of industries. Heavy northern and eastern European immigration affected the growth of the brewing industry.

The lists of leading industries from 1860 and 1920 mask as many changes as they reveal. Growth rates between industries varied. The late 1860s and early 1870s witnessed a continuation of antebellum trends in both products and techniques. In the 1870s, the era of iron, firewood, and waterpower began to give way to steel, coal, and steam engines. In turn, coal and steel primacy was superceded by an era in which the major sources of industrial growth were factories powered by electricity, producing chemicals and capital goods. The new motive force was well on its way to supplanting steam as the chief source of industrial power by 1910; by 1929 it had done so. A decade into the new century, automobiles plus petroleum and its ever-widening range of products were leading industrial growth. Older industries showed continued growth and technological progress after their primacy had passed. Many others showed very rapid growth even though the value of their output never placed them in the "top ten."

New Products and Methods

Typically, newly introduced products show very rapid growth as customers become more familiar with the new item and find additional uses for it. Then, as supply increases through increased competition, better knowledge of production processes ("learning by doing"), and utilization of economies of scale, prices

---

[3] D. Meyer, "Midwestern Industrialization and the American Manufacturing Belt in the Nineteenth Century," *Journal of Economic History* (December 1989).
[4] Wright, *Old South, New South*, 131.

Table 12.1   The Largest Industries in 1910

Industry	Value Added (Millions of Dollars)	Employees (Thousands)	Value Added per Worker (Thousands of Dollars)
Machinery	$690	530	$1.29
Lumber	650	700	.93
Printing and publishing	540	260	2.06
Iron and steel	330	240	1.37
Malt liquors	280	55	5.01
Men's clothing	270	240	1.18
Cotton goods	260	380	.68
Tobacco manufactures	240	170	1.44
Railroad cars	210	280	.73
Boots and shoes	180	200	.91
All manufactures	8,529	6,615	1.29

Source: L. Davis, R. Easterlin, and W. Parker et. al., *American Economic Growth: An Economist's History of the United States* (New York: Harper & Row, 1972), 447.

fall and larger quantities are demanded, both by previous customers and those only now able to buy. After this period of rapid initial expansion, the industry's growth rate is likely to slow to that allowed by increases in population and incomes, or perhaps less. Increases in supply now are more likely to stem from refinements of existing technology, not the breakthroughs of the industry's early years. For these reasons, the continuous growth of an economy is contingent on the appearance of new sectors to supplement or replace those whose growth rates flag, cease, or even become absolute declines.[5]

Obviously, economies in which people are receptive to new ideas both as producers and consumers have a major edge in the process of long-term growth. Such an environment fosters efforts to produce new commodities, introduce new methods, and find new markets for existing goods. It also favors resource reallocations and changes in consumer demand that are critical to the acceptance of new products. Economic development is critically dependent on change in the long run. In all these areas, the United States enjoyed advantages over more rigid societies.

The new products, methods, and fuels were economically significant to a much greater extent than indicated by their immediate effects on total production and incomes. Many had important linkages to other sectors and fostered growth there. Most of the new growth sectors were highly capital intensive, allowing the achievement of low unit costs only at large volumes of production. Often they demanded the coordinated efforts of large quantities of capital and labor. Still, it would be inaccurate to describe American industry as being typified by huge factories in 1914. As late as 1900, the average American factory had about two dozen employees. This was more than twice the figure for 1859 (although the

---

[5] For a survey of the new products and methods that appeared after 1865, see A. O'Brien, "Factory Size, Economies of Scale, and the Great Merger Wave of 1898–1902," *Journal of Economic History* (September 1988).

earlier data include handicraft shops not counted later), and growth in firm size apparently was speeding up. By 1921, the average factory employed almost 40 workers, a two-thirds increase.[6] But even the 1921 figure implies the existence of many small- and medium-sized plants as well as the highly visible giant firms.

New Business Practices

With larger firm size and more complex operations, new methods of organization, information collection, and decision making were required. In earlier times, the firm might be small enough, the range of products sufficiently limited, and operations straightforward enough to allow the owner to supervise production from the shop floor. Now, however, firms produced a variety of products and sold them in markets having very different characteristics, and the pace of technological as well as market change was faster. The nature of the products and the markets in which they were sold were the primary determinants of the changes in the structure and organization of firms.[7] Improved accounting methods were nearly as important as new engineering techniques for firms producing a variety of

items or performing many operations, both developments that became more common in this period. Marketing assumed a new and greater importance as customers' choices between sellers and products increased. Advertising and other forms of product differentiation, such as brand names and packaging, were used to establish and maintain sellers' reputations for quality. Again, the marketing approach varied with the type of product. In marketing capital goods, emphasis was placed on designing goods to meet the customer's specific needs and on terms of sale rather than on attempts to persuade along other lines. Finally, as the number of firms, output per firm, and the transportation network grew, firms were forced to respond to new competitive circumstances that many had never encountered before.

The enormous increases in the production of manufactured goods caused the prices of industrial products to decline relative to other commodities throughout this period. In some cases, price declines were spectacular. Metal goods in 1910 cost consumers little more than half their 1865 prices in real terms, and the modern goods' quality was far superior. The absolute price declines for manufactured goods exceeded those for farm products, reflecting a much more rapid rate of productivity growth in industry than in agriculture.[8]

OLD AND NEW INDUSTRIES

Rapid growth in manufacturing in the latter half of the nineteenth century produced many varieties of change. Some established industries grew at relatively stable rates. Others employed, or were affected by, innovations that drastically altered their growth. In other cases, entirely new industries appeared, some

[6] U.S. Department of Commerce, Bureau of the Census, *Historical Statistics of the United States: Colonial Times to 1970* (Washington, D.C.: Government Printing Office, 1975), 666. The first edition of *American Economic History* included an erroneous interpretation of the data on the number of employees per firm. My thanks to Professor A. O'Brien of the University of Georgia for calling this to my attention. See A. O'Brien, "A Note on the Increase in Factory Size in Manufacturing, 1849–1919," Working paper, Department of Economics, University of Georgia.
[7] The following discussion owes much to the work of Alfred D. Chandler, Jr. See "The Beginnings of 'Big Business' in American Industry," *Business History Review* (Spring 1959); *Strategy and Structure: Chapters in the History of American Industrial Enterprise* (Cambridge, Mass.: Harvard University Press, 1962); and *The Visible Hand: The Managerial Revolution in American Business* (Cambridge, Mass.: Harvard University Press, 1977), among others.

[8] *Historical Statistics*, 1:200, 201.

producing products that had never been seen before and others turning out familiar items in unheard-of quantities.

Textiles

Factory production of woolen and cotton cloth had been one of the earliest manufacturing industries to appear in the United States. The growth rate of cotton textile production had peaked and was already declining in the 1830s. The industry's postwar growth was only slightly more than could be accounted for by the rise in population and per-capita income. Cotton textile prices did not fall in real terms, indicating an absence of technological breakthroughs. But the industry was not stagnant. New machinery was introduced and widely adopted. Ring spindles, more nearly automatic looms that replaced empty yarn bobbins without human intervention and stopped if the yarn broke, and other innovations allowed the employment of less skilled labor. The new features allowed one worker to tend several looms.

Because technological change was limited, other means of lowering production expenses were sought. The industry began to relocate, seeking lower input expenses. In New England, output continued to grow. But the pace was faster elsewhere. By 1910, the southern Atlantic Seaboard had two-thirds as many spindles as New England. The causes of this relocation are not clear. The postwar South had large quantities of labor not really required in agriculture (where its marginal product and wages were low). The South also had a relative shortage of capital, so that returns on investment were higher there than in other regions. These two inducements help to explain the movement of northern capital into southern manufacturing, but do not explain why investment concentrated so heavily on textiles. Wright's view that most southern textile investment was locally financed would

help to explain this through the industry's low capital requirements, as would the region's risk-averse lenders and poorly developed capital markets.[9] The shift in textile expansion away from New England is not difficult to understand. New England had no coal and had utilized nearly all its high-quality waterpower sites by 1900. Labor costs were growing. Further growth would require either higher costs or some technical breakthrough.

Relocation of textile production in Georgia and the Carolinas, rather than throughout the South, provides one indication of the answer. Agriculture was less profitable in those states than farther west, encouraging a diversion of local investment from agriculture to industry. Prior to emancipation, landowners in the Old South could either move to more fertile areas or compensate for inferior soil by selling another commodity—surplus slaves—to more productive farming areas. Now, of course, this was no longer possible, and landlords may have sought new directions for investment.[10] Developments in textile machinery facilitated the employment of unskilled labor, especially women and children. Given the reduced labor requirements, the South's educational deficiencies were a lesser handicap than might have been the case for other types of work.

Steel

More than any other single product, steel typifies the late nineteenth-century development of American industry. No other single product aided in the development of so many other

[9] Wright, *Old South, New South*, Chap. 5. See also D. Carlton and P. Coclanis, "Capital Mobilization and Southern Industry, 1880–1905: The Case of the Carolina Piedmont," *Journal of Economic History* (March 1989).

[10] L. Davis, R. Easterlin, and W. Parker et. al., *American Economic Growth: An Economist's History of the United States* (New York: Harper & Row, 1972), 438–441. See also Carlton and Coclanis, "Capital Mobilization."

industries, or increased capabilities beyond those possible with substitute materials. And with no other product did America rise to such total dominance before 1900.

Steel was not a new commodity in the latter half of the nineteenth century; the sword blades of Damascus, Toledo, and the Japanese Samurai indicate that fine steel had been made for many centuries. But it had always been so expensive and difficult to produce, particularly in large quantities, that it was only used in applications where quality of performance had a high priority over price. Steelmaking was an art whose intricacies could only be mastered through long experience. The crucible process by which it was made involved the addition of small amounts of carbon to molten wrought iron. It was all but impossible to make large quantities of uniform-quality steel, since each crucible had a limited capacity and each was prepared individually. The scientific nature of the process was only vaguely understood, so procedure was by rules of thumb and experience. Steelmaking bore a closer resemblance to the work of a skilled cook than it did to modern industrial processes. And just as in cooking, great variations between individual batches of steel might occur.

In 1850, no single alternate metal combined all the properties of even crucible steel. Wrought iron is tough, but soft and malleable, and cannot be given tensile strength. Thus, it was not suitable for applications involving high speeds or heavy stresses. Cast iron was hard, but brittle, and could not be worked once cast. Nor could it resist shock. Iron tools and machinery could be given additional strength only by adding material, a self-defeating process for moving mechanisms. Too much energy would be required to move heavily reinforced machinery parts, with little remaining for the task on which the machinery was employed. No other metal was cheaper or physically superior to iron.

Bessemer Steel

In 1856, it was discovered that steel could be produced by blowing air through molten pig iron, a process that removed most of the impurities from the metal. The discovery was made independently by William Kelly, an American, and Henry Bessemer of England. Kelly failed to make his discovery commercially successful, but Bessemer found a ready market for the steelmaking process named for him. The new process was rapid, requiring only about a quarter of an hour, and it greatly increased the quantities that could be made in a single batch.

Soon thereafter, those who tried to use Bessemer's steelmaking process were unable to repeat his success (see Chapter 7). After the source of the difficulty was identified as phosphorous in the iron ore, it became possible to counteract its effects. The United States had

■ By 1914, the steel industry was highly capital intensive.
Source: Library of Congress.

large, though highly localized, deposits of suitable ore, and further chemical research developed new linings for furnaces that permitted the utilization of a wider range of ores. Still more research resulted in changes in the Bessemer process that allowed more exact control of the metal's carbon content and the production of true steel. With the initial difficulties overcome, production of Bessemer-process steel increased rapidly in both Europe and the United States.

Initial Steelmaking Problems Although Bessemer steel was ideal for some applications, such as railroad rails, both it and its manufacturing process had some drawbacks. Bessemer steel was subject to mysterious fractures, now known to be the consequence of nitrogen dissolved in the iron by the air blown through it during the refining process.[11] At the time, however, discovery of the cause of this problem was beyond the scope of industrial chemistry. In addition, the Bessemer process could employ only a limited range of ores. American deposits of suitable ore were highly concentrated geographically and thus subject to monopoly control.

Open-Hearth Steel

Shortly after the Bessemer process came into widespread use, a second method was developed. The Siemens-Martin (named for its German-English and French inventors), or open-hearth process, used a huge open pan in which the heat from exhaust gases that previously had been wasted was employed to raise furnace temperatures. The open-hearth method could use both scrap iron and a wider range of ores than the Bessemer process, and the chemical composition of the steel could be more precisely controlled. Initially, however, the process was less efficient than Bessemer's

method. As Table 12.2 indicates, the open-hearth process was not widely used until the latter 1890s, but after that, open-hearth steel production expanded rapidly.[12]

The Steel Revolution

Steel supplied its users with increased capabilities compared to iron. Steel railroad rails, for example, lasted up to 17 times as long as iron rails. In addition, their greater strength allowed the passage of heavier, faster trains with greater safety. Railroads were now able to increase train speed and carrying capacity (steel cars had greater payloads per unit of car weight) and lost far less time to track replacement. Steel ships were stronger and safer than iron vessels, had greater carrying capacity per ton of displacement, and steel engines produced greater speed and higher fuel economy.

In construction, the use of steel produced a veritable revolution. For the first time, structural strength could be achieved without resorting to huge masses of wood or stone. Buildings made from traditional materials had practical height limits of no more than six or eight stories, because the supports for the upper floors had to be so large that the lower stories had little usable space. Steel frames greatly reduced this limitation. Cities could now expand up as well as out.

Steel was also well suited to high operating speeds and could be worked to much closer tolerances than were possible with iron. These properties made possible both improved machine tools and better-functioning products. As time passed, steel prices fell until they were below even the previous price of iron, encouraging still wider use of the world's first really cheap metal. Industrial chemistry produced a growing range of new alloys, and steel could be given properties that no metal had possessed before.

---

[11] Davis, Easterlin, and Parker, *American Economic Growth*, 443.

[12] Davis, Easterlin, and Parker, *American Economic Growth*, 442–443.

Table 12.2   Steel Production in the United States
(Thousands of Tons)

Year	Total	Bessemer	Open-Hearth	Crucible	Electric
1860	13			13	
1865	15			15	
1870	77	42	2	34	
1875	437	376	9	52	
1880	1,397	1,203	113	81	
1885	1,917	1,702	149	66	
1890	4,779	4,131	566	82	
1895	6,785	5,494	1,219	72	
1900	11,227	7,481	3,638	109	
1905	21,880	12,231	9,537	112	
1910	28,330	10,478	17,672	122	58
1915	35,180	9,178	25,838	108	55
1920	46,183	9,841	35,846	79	417

Source: U.S. Department of Commerce, Bureau of the Census, *Historical Statistics of the United States: Colonial Times to 1970* (Washington, D.C.: Government Printing Office, 1975), 2:695–696.

Productivity Gains in a New Industry

As with most new industries, productivity grew rapidly in steelmaking, and costs fell dramatically. After 1880, the real price of steel fell, making it not only physically superior to most other materials, but steadily cheaper as well. Producers learned to build plants that reduced heat loss between operations and used previously unwanted by-products, such as furnace linings and coke-oven gases. American engineers developed integrated plants utilizing the new technologies, which were unmatched elsewhere. In this, they were aided by the extremely rapid growth of the industry; large numbers of new plants were being constructed, most of them completely new ventures. Steelmaking also produced experience with the problems involved in moving great masses of material, shaping and finishing metal, and other tasks with applications outside the industry. Energy conservation yielded double dividends; not only was a fraction of the coal required to smelt a ton of iron in 1860 needed to produce a ton of steel by 1900, but materials handling, waste disposal, and other expenses were also reduced. Such developments taught plant designers to view the steelmaking process as an integrated whole rather than a series of separate operations.

The market for steel rails flagged as the pace of railroad construction fell in the 1880s, but demand for sheets, plates, and structural shapes more than filled the gap.

Industry Relocation

The pattern of natural resources in the United States was highly favorable to the steel industry. Steelmaking requires iron ore, coal, and limestone. Limestone is widely available, but many regions of the earth lack one or both of the other two. Great deposits of iron ore were available in the upper Midwest, and the huge ranges of northern Minnesota could be worked with steam shovels rather than expensive deep-mining techniques. After the construction of the Sault Sainte Marie Canal

■ Construction of the Brooklyn Bridge was a technological triumph for its time (1868).
Source: Library of Congress.

connecting Lake Superior with the other Great Lakes in 1855, the ore could be shipped by cheap water transportation to ports on the Lakes' southern shores, from which it could be easily transported by rail to the coal of the Ohio Valley. (Initially, a greater weight of fuel than ore was required to produce a ton of steel.) Toward 1900, coal was sent to lake ports such as Cleveland, Erie, and Toledo on the return trip of the ore cars. Another great steel center developed at the southern tip of Lake Michigan, utilizing the coal of Indiana and central Illinois, in Gary, Michigan City, and other steel towns. Near Birmingham, Alabama, coal and iron ore were found in alternating layers in the same geological formation, allowing the development of yet another steel-producing location.

Automobiles

The automobile is the twentieth-century economic counterpart of nineteenth-century steel. Like steelmaking, automobile manufacturing was a rapidly growing industry with major links to other sectors of the economy. No other nation has developed its production or altered the other features of its economy so fully in consequence of the mass-produced automobile as has the United States.

By the end of the nineteenth century, several reasonably practical automobile designs had been developed. Europe was an early leader in invention, but the United States was very strong in innovation. Developing cars suitable for everyday use was a formidable task.

■ Streetcar works such as this one were just beginning to feel competition from a new form of transportation—the automobile.
Source: Great Industries. From *The Picture Reference File,* Volume 1. (New York: Hart Publishing Company, Inc., 1976), 134.

Early Automobiles: The Toys of the Rich

The early cars were expensive. When contemporary income levels are taken into account, they cost far more than most modern counterparts. Early autos were even more expensive to maintain. Only the rich could afford to operate automobiles in 1900; the early cars were so unreliable that prudent owners who were not experienced mechanics required the full-time services of a combined chauffeur-mechanic. Service was all but unobtainable except in large cities, and repairs might require that the owner make and install replacement parts. Gasoline was initially sold by drugstores, in quart bottles, as cleaning fluid. Tire life was measured in hundreds rather than thousands of miles, and drivers carried several spares plus a patch kit and pump as a matter of course. Roads were unbelievably bad, almost totally bereft of either hard surfaces or road signs.

These barriers to ownership were gradually reduced. Auto manufacturers found that sales were increased if they provided service. Sources and normal sales units of gasoline became better suited to motorists' needs. Organizations of car owners allied with bicyclists to press for improved roads; by 1910, they had achieved some success.

Henry Ford's "Better Idea"

The real breakthrough for the automobile industry came from Henry Ford. But Ford's major contribution was not the moving assembly line, which he neither originated nor introduced into the auto industry. Rather, it was Ford's recognition that a truly low-priced car could be sold in vastly greater quantities than were possible while cars remained high-priced toys for the rich and adventurous. The moving assembly line, with its enormous volume of fixed investment, made sense only if its costs could be spread over unheard-of numbers of cars. Ford's vision of a mass market for automobiles was not widely shared. One banker told W. C. Durant, one of the founders of General Motors, that no responsible person would ever lend him money until he ceased his wild talk about the United States eventually producing 50,000 cars in a single year—and

■ Poor road conditions such as these shown frequently hampered U.S. travel before 1920.
Source: Auto Club of Western New York.

refused him a loan.[13] After similar encounters, Ford eventually got his financing from non-bank sources. In the process, he developed a lasting distaste for banks.

The Model T: An American "People's" Car In 1908, the Ford Motor Company began to produce a light, simple motor car called the Model T. In that year, despite the banker's views, the American auto industry produced and sold 63,500 cars, 5,986 of which were Fords. The differing versions of the Model T were priced at from $825 to $1,000. In the following year, Ford announced that henceforth he would simplify his model line: He would produce only Model Ts in two versions and "any color the customer wants, as long as it's black." In 1909, Ford production was 12,292 cars. Two

years later Ford began to build a new plant, and by 1914 the moving assembly line was in operation, turning out 260,720 Model Ts. Prices were $440 for the runabout and $490 for the touring car. Just as with modern cars, there was an optional-accessories list. If the customer did not wish to start his car with a crank, he could buy an electric starter for $15. That began and ended Ford's list of accessories. By 1916, Ford sold over half a million cars at $345 and $360. This was nearly 40 percent of all U.S. auto production. By 1924, despite the inflation caused by World War I, Ford was able to reduce the price of a Model T roadster to $260.[14]

The Model T was a simple car; many people could perform all their own maintenance work. Ford established a chain of deal-

[13] T. Cochran and W. Miller, *The Age of Enterprise: A Social History of Industrial America* (New York: Harper & Row, 1968), 186.

[14] A. Chandler, Jr., *Giant Enterprise: Ford, General Motors, and the Automobile Industry* (New York: Harcourt, Brace, and World, 1964), 32–33.

erships that were obligated to maintain service facilities for those unable to maintain their vehicles. Model Ts were rugged and reliable, safe and easy to drive, that is, ideally suited to American conditions. Above all, the Model T was cheap, a car for the middle class and even for many who could lay no claim to such status.

The Economic Consequences Ford, who had bought out his initial partners, earned a huge fortune from the production of the Model T. But the Ford Motor Company gave the people of the United States far more than just affordable cars. The mass-produced automobile gave Americans greater freedom than any other people had ever experienced. Possession of a car conferred a wider range of choices of places to live, shop, and work—and these choices meant greater freedom. Workers were no longer forced to deal only with those employers within walking distance of their homes (or to live in areas having only proximity to jobs to recommend them). Farmers no longer had to face the "take-it-or-leave-it" offers of a single grain elevator or general store.[15] The automobile made a huge contribution to the American specialty of efficient human resource allocation. It literally made it easier to put people and resources to work in the most suitable ways. Compared to this, the automobile's contribution to American lifestyles and leisure hours was unimportant.

Further Consequences
The automobile industry and its product had enormous forward and backward linkages. Manufacture required large amounts of steel, rubber, glass, paint, and other materials, and automobiles' special characteristics (together with those of bicycles a few decades earlier) spurred the development of alloy steels, bear-

ings of several types, and other innovations that had wide application in other types of manufacturing. Engineers from other industries studied the moving assembly line and adapted it to make new types of goods, just as Ford's engineers had. The automobile increased the demand for fuel, tires, service, and roads as consumer goods. Less directly, it made the suburbs possible, although this was not really apparent until after 1920.

Automobile production by all America's car manufacturers grew rapidly after 1908. Unit sales exceeded 500,000 in 1914. By 1916, they were over 1.5 million. In 1900, only 4,000 cars had been sold in the United States. The moving assembly line's introduction was eased by the use of some other American production specialties, such as interchangeable parts. In 1906, the Cadillac factory created a sensation in Europe by shipping three cars to England, disassembling them and scrambling the parts, and then reassembling the three autos with only hand tools and no fitting, a feat impossible for European carmakers at that time.[16] Note that this feat occurred before Ford built either his new car or the assembly line.

New Industrial Linkages

The foregoing industries are only well-known examples of the widespread industrial development sweeping the United States after 1865. Table 12.1 indicates that no single American industry produced as much as one-tenth of total value added by manufacturing, nor employed more than one-ninth of all industrial workers. Not only did the range of products from American factories expand, developments in one sector often spurred growth in

[15] J. Hughes, *The Vital Few: American Economic Progress and Its Protagonists* (New York: Oxford University Press, 1973), 291–294.

[16] D. Landes, *The Unbound Prometheus: Technological Change and Industrial Development in Europe from 1750 to the Present* (Cambridge, U.K.: Cambridge University Press, 1969), 315.

■ The advent of mass production led to long assembly lines like this one at Ford Motor Company in 1923.
Source: From the collections of Henry Ford Museum and Greenfield Village. Negative number 833.35688.

another. Customer acceptance of foods in more fully processed form allowed the rise of canning and baking firms. The great meat-packing companies such as Swift, Armour, Hormel, and Cudahy owed their formation to the development of western railroads and re-frigerated cars. There was great opposition by local slaughterhouses to competition from meat killed a thousand miles from its markets. To assure their products' access to consumers, the western packers were obliged to build up their own marketing organizations. Boot and shoe production benefited from improvements in sewing and cutting machines, and began to relocate in the Midwest to be near the supply of hides from the large meatpacking plants there. The use of standardized sizes and variations of the new machines also employed by the shoemakers allowed factory production of many articles of men's clothing to replace custom tailoring or home production for all but the very rich—a development that allowed ordinary people greater variety and often better-quality clothing than they had previously enjoyed. Some items of women's clothing were also produced in factories, but hand labor was still widely employed in making garments for both sexes.

Communications and Publishing

Increases in income, leisure time, and education stimulated the market for books, magazines, and especially newspapers. The publishing industry benefited from cheaper paper made from wood pulp rather than rags and new production devices, such as the linotype machine. Communications improved as the telegraph network was extended and incorporated new advances. In the 1890s, telephones came increasingly into common use. There were over a million telephones in use by the turn of the century, and that figure would rise thirteenfold by 1920. It was possible, although very expensive, to make a coast-to-coast long distance call by 1915.

Electricity

Electric lighting became practical with the development of the first central generating stations in the 1880s. Once the superiority of alternating current over direct current was established (an argument in which Thomas Edison found himself, uncharacteristically, on the wrong side), the lighting of American cities, both indoors and out, could be greatly improved. Steam-powered street railways could be replaced by quieter, less pollution-prone electric trolleys. Growth in industries associ-

ated with electrical manufactures plus power generation and distribution spurred copper production. With the aid of new refining methods that recovered copper from much lower-grade ore, copper output rose from 9,520 tons in 1865 to 744,036 tons 50 years later. Electric motors revolutionized the design and layout of many American factories after 1900, allowing for much greater productive efficiency in many industries. The use of electric motors facilitated the orderly flow of material through the factory and eliminated the dangerous and power-consuming maze of belts, shafts, and gears by which power had been distributed through plants using steam or waterpower. The electrical industry was the first science-based manufacturing establishment in the United States. Its research operations developed a variety of alloys, insulating materials, and plastics that were useful in other industries as well as to their originators.

Machine Tools

As they had earlier, machine tools and their makers played a central role in the dissemination of new technology through the economy. Machines themselves were improved as steel allowed higher operating speeds, closer tolerances, and greater strength. New developments in metal cutting, grinding, finishing, and polishing were widely employed. More importantly, the machine tool manufacturers served as specialized problem solvers for their customers, producing machines that addressed buyers' new requirements. Often the solution to one industry's needs proved to be just what another required in a different application, or it could be adapted for use in another context.[17] Yet another indication of the diversified growth of industry was that the American machine tool industry became highly specialized, with many producers

---

[17] N. Rosenberg, *Technology and American Economic Growth* (New York: Harper & Row, 1972), 100–102.

■ An early example of advertising is shown, from the *Daily Territorial Enterprise,* Virginia City, Nevada, 1892.
Source: The Bettmann Archive.

making only a narrow range of tools. As many others did, the machine tool industry relocated to be near its customers. Firms moved to the Midwest, seeking proximity to the steelmakers, to whose product their own was applied.

NEW FUELS AND POWER SOURCES

In 1865, the most common form of nonhuman energy used in American industry was waterpower. Wood was the most widely used fuel, furnishing 81 percent of all fuel-generated energy for the economy at that date. Fuel and energy sources changed rapidly; by 1880, coal had largely replaced wood as the fuel for steam engines, and steam power had supplanted waterpower in manufacturing. By 1900, steam generated about 80 percent of all the power used in factories. Waterpower accounted for 15 percent, but it was important only in textile, paper, and lumber production. Coal now furnished about three-quarters of the fuel energy required by the entire economy, and a still higher portion of that used in manufacturing. Thenceforth, coal's share remained approximately constant, while that of wood declined in favor of petroleum in the form of both oil and natural gas.[18] Although we are accustomed to a world powered by mineral fuels, these sources of energy have been in widespread use for little more than a century.

The application of power also changed. Replacement of waterpower by steam allowed more flexibility in plant location and reduced interference from weather. Steam power sources could be divided into smaller units, a very difficult proposition with waterpower. Even so, there was a minimum practical size for steam engines, and conversion of steam

engines' to-and-fro motion into rotary movement and varying the speed of operation wasted energy. Power-transmission devices in steam-driven factories were both inefficient and a major source of industrial accidents. Because of the limits of power transmission, all machines performing a certain function had to be grouped together, working off a shaft turning at the proper speed. Material had to be transferred from these machines to those grouped around another power source for the next operation, losing time in the process. It was difficult, if not impossible, to design a plant where materials could be moved from one machine to another in a continuous line.[19]

Electric power changed this. Even though the ultimate source of electricity might be mineral fuel or (much less likely) waterpower, it could be utilized in vastly more flexible forms. Electric motors could be designed to meet the specific requirements of any operation, eliminated most of the energy loss through transmission, and, most of all, allowed the rearrangement of materials flows through factories along lines most conducive to continuous operations. This was especially important in the production of items requiring many successive stages of manufacture. The moving assembly line is hardly conceivable without electric motors. Electric power was far more flexible than steam; it was now possible to transmit power economically over long distances from its point of generation.

PLANT SIZE AND NEW MANAGEMENT TECHNIQUES

The growing size and complexity of many industrial plants and the increasing need for integration of all operations caused men to begin the study of the plant as a whole rather than

---

[18] Rosenberg, *Technology*, 158–160.

[19] Rosenberg, *Technology*, 161.

a series of individual operations whose relationships to each other were unimportant. Many firms found that growing competition made it increasingly difficult to pass on production inefficiencies in the form of higher product prices, as had once been possible.

The New Managers

After 1900, a new generation of plant managers appeared, more oriented toward improving the efficiency of production than the previous owner–managers had been. The early managers had paid little attention to production once the plant was in operation; they spe-

■ Frederick Winslow Taylor introduced scientific management in 1895.
Source: Dictionary of American Portraits. (New York: Dover Publications, Inc., 1967), 610.

cialized in obtaining finance and in sales. The new men combined engineering with management skills, and their efforts resulted in the development of more efficient factories and improvements in the productivity of existing plants. Smaller amounts of fuel, labor, and raw materials were used per unit of output as a result of better plant organization, reduction of heat losses, increased use of by-products as inputs in the basic production process or as separate products, recovery and reuse of scrap, and a host of other measures. Often these measures had not been taken previously because they were worthwhile only at high volumes of output.

Mass Production

One result of these systematic changes in production was the development of mass production: the manufacture of large amounts of a uniform commodity through the coordinated efforts of many workers employing much highly specialized capital. The key element in mass production is coordination. When every worker performs as part of a larger team, there are no small mistakes. Any error affects the flow of product farther down the line, and possibly behind the point where the mistake occurred as well. If costs are to be minimized in such an organization, it is essential that each task fully occupy the labor and machine time available to perform it. Any slower pace wastes production potential and raises costs; any attempt to exceed capacity causes breakdowns, errors, and spoiled work.

"Scientific Management"

With these principles in mind, engineers began to study each worker's job and note how it fit into the whole. Led by F. W. Taylor, who developed what he called "scientific management" (the term was first used in an 1895 paper he presented), they tried to apply production theory to the workplace. The task involved a study of the mechanics of each worker's job, attempts to improve performance either by the use of specialized tools or work methods, and using incentives to motivate workers to accept the new methods. Because scientific management, where successful, increased production rates, workers might—and often did—regard it as a speedup. But scientific management was far more than just a faster work pace. Taylor opposed work rates that unduly taxed workers' stamina, because a pace that was beyond laborers' ability to maintain efficiently resulted in mistakes and accidents. Nor did scientific management necessarily reduce the worker to a high-speed automaton. Really simple repetition was better delegated to machines than to men, Taylor thought, and his system was designed to avoid worker fatigue and boredom. The new system's results did not accrue only to management. Taylor and his disciples were aware that few employees would be willing to change their work patterns just to set production records, so a fundamental tenet of scientific management was that improved performance must be recognized and rewarded. Thus, the new methods resulted in higher pay and shorter hours for workers. Scientific management also reduced physical effort and accident rates.[20]

As often occurs with innovation, many employers were not willing to accept the full spectrum of changes recommended by Taylor and his students. Nor was it always possible to persuade workers to accept them. The changes did, however, reduce workers' control over the pace of their efforts and often the manner in which they were performed.

The American Industrial Environment This attention to plant design and detailed management was uniquely American. It was developed earlier and to a far greater extent in this country than abroad. Various aspects of Taylor's ideas, but never his complete system, were utilized by railroads, the Remington Typewriter Company, Yale and Towne, and the steel and machine-tool industries. Possibly scientific management's American reception was greater than in foreign countries because it was easier to introduce changes in methods, tools, and compensation where the tasks were new. In the United States, many new plants were being built in which Taylor's ideas could be incorporated from the start. American workers were less threatened by the introduction of new machines and methods in the labor-scarce environment of the United States than were European workers. There was also less owner and managerial inertia to overcome. Heavy financial or psychological investment in older methods often make it difficult to institute change and realize its full potential. Even so, there was seldom any effective opposition to someone else's efforts to produce change in the United States. The promoters of managerial changes in America sowed their seed in fertile soil.

NEW BUSINESS STRUCTURES

The structure of American firms began to change along with the nature and volume of their output. In 1865, with the exception of the railroads and a few companies producing large metal goods, American manufacturing firms tended to be engaged in the processing of agricultural products or other raw materials and dependent on local markets for both inputs and sales. Typically, they produced consumer goods that required additional finishing before they were ready for final use by purchasers. Most firms were small in absolute size as measured by sales volume, number of employees, or the amount invested in them. After the Civil War, the completion of the railroad system and rapid urbanization frequently resulted in regional or national rather than local

---

[20] Chandler, *The Visible Hand*, 275–277.

markets. By the turn of the century, electricity and the internal combustion engine created a new set of pressures for change.[21] All of these developments created or reflected new linkages as well as changes in the firms most directly affected.

The Birth of "Big Business"

The transition to "big business" in the modern sense of large corporations selling their goods in national markets began in the consumer goods industries.[22] By the early 1890s it was well established. As transportation improved and new production methods appeared offering lower unit costs only at much larger volumes of output than previous rates, firms often attempted to expand their sales areas. Often these efforts resulted in a head-on collision with other similarly inclined producers. Where the products of various firms were standardized or similar, as many consumer goods were, the usual initial response to the appearance of rivals—attempts to destroy them—often gave way to efforts designed to eliminate competition.

Firms made agreements either on price and output or else on the division of markets between them. These developments appeared first among the railroads and spread to producers of standardized consumer products, such as flour and cigarettes. Occasionally, the erstwhile competitors formed pools in which they agreed to share profits on the basis of sales or some other formula. But such "gentlemen's agreements" were illegal under the common law, and there was no method of enforcing them. Worse, it paid any individual firm to make such an agreement with its rivals in hopes that the other parties to the agreement would keep it. If they did, cheating on the compact was highly profitable. The prices fixed by such arrangements were, of course, higher than those prevailing before the agreements were reached. At least some of the parties to such price-fixing would have unused productive capacity that could be employed producing goods to be sold for less than the agreed-upon price. As might be expected, the businessmen who made such illegal agreements did not become any more scrupulous when a profitable opportunity to break them was revealed. So long as individuals retained their freedom of individual action, they were likely to use it for their own benefit.[23]

Mergers

A more successful response to the problem of competition was mergers, which eliminated independent action by bringing firms under common management. But mergers changed, rather than eliminated, competition in consumer goods industries. Instead of many small firms, there might be a few large ones sharing the market. It is not even clear that actual competition was reduced, a point to be discussed later.

In addition to their attempts to combine horizontally, firms in consumer goods industries soon began to integrate into other stages of production and distribution. Producers buying their inputs in competitive markets chose to integrate forward rather than back; they purchased retail outlets to assure their access to customers.[24] Producers of new consumer goods often found it necessary to set up their own marketing organizations to assure presentation of their goods to consumers, as did sellers of cigarettes and bananas. Manufacturers of items for which service after the sale was important—sewing machines, bicycles, and, later, automobiles—developed

---

[21] Chandler, "Big Business."
[22] Chandler, "Big Business."

[23] Not all pools were immediately unsuccessful. See T. Ulen, "Railroad Cartels Before 1887: The Effectiveness of Private Enforcement of Collusion," in *Research in Economic History* (Westport, Conn.: JAI Press, 1983).
[24] Chandler, "Big Business."

closely controlled dealer networks and sometimes furnished their own credit arrangements as well. Retail outlets established to sell one item were sometimes profitably diversified. Meat packers discovered that stores they had founded to sell pork, beef, and mutton could also market poultry, eggs, and dairy products.[25]

Firm Structures

The nature of the product affected the firm's internal structure. If a company sold only one item or a narrow range of similar goods, its operations tended to be tightly controlled by a central office. The firm's divisions would be along functional lines, such as sales, production, accounting, and so forth.[26] Firms selling a variety of goods tended to be organized by product divisions; their structure and operating methods will be discussed later.

Changing Competitive Patterns

In addition to the difficulty of forming complete or cohesive combinations, the entry of new firms into established industries remained possible throughout the period. One attempt at monopolization that failed to make an adequate response to entry possibilities ended in disaster. In the 1890s there was an attempt to form a monopoly in the distilled liquor industry. The would-be monopolists purchased nearly all the existing distilleries. Although the liquor trust was able to gain control of over 90 percent of distilling capacity at one point, it attempted to defend its position by buying out any new firm that appeared. Unfortunately for the monopolists, an efficient distillery could be constructed for a modest investment. When it became clear that all such plants were certain to be purchased by the liquor trust, a new industry was born—the production not of liquor, but of distilleries. Eventually, the trust failed.[27]

Vertical Integration

Firms in the capital goods industries faced a different situation. They were not affected by market changes as early as were the consumer goods industries, and there were no attempts at consolidation among firms until the 1890s. Vertical integration among capital goods producers was generally backward, into sources of inputs, crucial transport links, and preliminary fabrication and processing.

The buyers of most capital goods were well equipped to judge quality for themselves; indeed, many capital goods were designed to customers' specifications. Sales in these circumstances were made on the basis of price, delivery terms, and product performance; there was little point in elaborate marketing efforts. As it had elsewhere, vertical integration generally followed a combination movement. In these industries, Chandler considered vertical integration to have been a largely defensive measure, designed to assure the firms' access to resources needed for continued operations, not to increase monopoly power.[28] A more recent study concluded that some firms, particularly U.S. Steel, found vertical integration provided useful barriers to the entry of new firms into the industry.[29]

In most industries, vertical integration was also designed to increase operational efficiency by improving coordination between successive stages of production and reducing

---

[25] Chandler, "Big Business."
[26] See also Chandler, *The Visible Hand*, Chaps. 12–14.

[27] Chandler, *The Visible Hand*, 328. See also N. Lamoreaux, *The Great Merger Movement in American Business, 1895–1904* (Cambridge, U.K.: Cambridge University Press, 1985), 181.
[28] Chandler, "Big Business." Others see greater roles for attempts at monopolization. See A. O'Brien, "Factory Size."
[29] N. Lamoreaux, *Great Merger*, Chap. 5. On U.S. Steel and its attitudes toward potential competition, see T. McCraw and F. Reinhardt, "Losing to Win: U.S. Steel's Pricing, Investment Decisions, and Market Share, 1901–1918," *Journal of Economic History* (September 1989).

scheduling difficulties.[30] Capital goods often passed through many stages of production before reaching finished form, and actual or threatened vertical integration might give users of inputs such as steel and copper bargaining power with their producers or with the ultimate users of electrical goods, bridges, pipe, and other items.

Diversification

Integrated firms, particularly after 1900, began to sell a greater variety of goods. The optimum (cost minimizing) scale of operations in successive stages of production might vary. One level of the firm might need to produce a larger volume of output than the next division could use to minimize unit costs. Finished capital goods might require some inputs that had simply never been produced elsewhere. These developments were especially prevalent in new industries, such as electrical goods, automobiles, oil refining, and chemicals, that began to sell not only the goods for which they were named, but also alloys, insulation, plastics, farm machinery, diesel engines, locomotives, tractors, dyes, and other goods.

Some firms discovered that the engineering talent necessary to design and build their production facilities was more than sufficient to operate them; they diverted part of it into research and development activities. The electrical industry began to produce not only the heavy generating and power-distribution equipment in which it originally specialized, but also consumer appliances. These were not only profitable in themselves, they increased demand for the firms' primary output.

Other firms diversified out of desperation. As the scale of operations increased, problems of waste disposal often rose more than in proportion. When the quantity of waste products was less and governments were more obliging, waste was simply thrown away. But as the greater volume and rising public concern over certain types of pollution made this more expensive, firms tried to reduce the amounts of waste. Meat-packing plants turned offal, bones, horns, and hooves into products ranging from pharmaceuticals to fertilizer. Steel firms sold used furnace linings as high-phosphorus fertilizer.

Firm Structure and the Nature of Production

In diversified firms, the head office exercised little control over the divisions' day-to-day operations. Divisions were generally organized along product lines rather than by function. The head office handled finance and made basic decisions, such as whether to construct a new plant, but production and often marketing were handled by the individual divisions almost as though each were a separate firm.[31]

The pathbreaking studies of Alfred D. Chandler, Jr., concluded that the primary influence shaping the development of American industry before 1900 was the establishment of the large corporation. In turn, this resulted from the appearance of a national market as transportation and communications improved. After 1900, Chandler found that the primary influences were innovations in products and in research.[32]

THE RAILROADS

From 1865 to 1915, the total length of railroads in the United States grew from 35,000 to 250,000 miles. These figures include only main track outside railroad yards; the railroads had another 140,000 miles of tracks in

---

[30] Chandler, "Big Business." See also O'Brien, "Factory Size."

[31] Chandler, "Big Business."

[32] Chandler, *Strategy and Structure*, and *The Visible Hand*.

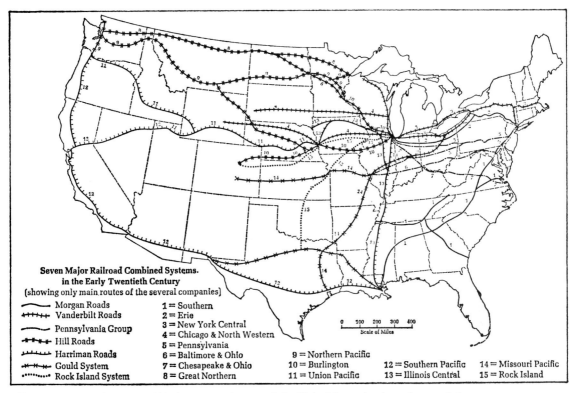

**Seven Major Railroad Combined Systems.
in the Early Twentieth Century**
(showing only main routes of the several companies)

Morgan Roads	1 = Southern	
Vanderbilt Roads	2 = Erie	
Pennsylvania Group	3 = New York Central	
Hill Roads	4 = Chicago & North Western	
Harriman Roads	5 = Pennsylvania	
Gould System	6 = Baltimore & Ohio	
Rock Island System	7 = Chesapeake & Ohio	9 = Northern Pacific
	8 = Great Northern	10 = Burlington

9 = Northern Pacific   12 = Southern Pacific   14 = Missouri Pacific
10 = Burlington   13 = Illinois Central   15 = Rock Island
11 = Union Pacific

■ Seven major railroad combined systems crisscrossed the United States by the early twentieth century.
Source: From *The Life and Decline of the American Railroad* by John F. Stover. Copyright © 1970 by Oxford University Press, Inc. Reprinted by permission.

double lines and yards.[33] Transcontinental lines, beginning with the Union Pacific in 1869, linked the West Coast with the rest of the country; trunk lines served new areas or paralleled existing routes; feeder lines connected local markets with the national economy; and special-purpose roads served isolated logging and mining camps.

Railroad efficiency improved as a result of standardized track gauges, the use of steel in boilers, track, and couplings, better brakes, telegraphic traffic controls, and centralized or "union" stations. Pullman cars made long-distance travel more comfortable. The speed and weight of trains rose, an indication of the increase in carrying capacity resulting from more miles per unit of rolling stock and larger loads per trip.

Railroads' Economic Impact

The advent of the railroad, America's first really efficient overland transportation, aided the economic unification of post–Civil War America, furthering regional specialization and interdependence. Railroads fostered the growth of regional hubs such as Atlanta, Chicago, and Kansas City. Until 1900, the railroads absorbed a larger share of aggregate investment funds than any other single use.

[33] *Historical Statistics,* 2:728.

■ In 1869, the famous meeting of the Union Pacific and Central Pacific railroads at Promontory Summit, Utah, took place, marking the completion of the first U.S. transcontinental railroad.
Source: Union Pacific Railroad.

Foreign investment in American railroads had been significant in the antebellum period, and much of the railways' equipment (particularly rails) had been imported in that era. But now the railroads' linkages were to the domestic economy, although foreign investment was still sizable. Rails and other equipment were now manufactured within the United States and sometimes exported. The role of foreign investment also declined.

The Indispensability Controversy
The measurement of the railroads' contribution to the American economy has drawn attention from many scholars. All have concluded that the railroads were indeed im-

portant in the economic growth of the United States. One study by Robert Fogel, however, has attracted a great deal of critical attention.[34] To test what he termed the "Axiom of Indispensability"—the idea that American economic growth would have been impossible, or at least seriously reduced, without the nineteenth-century railroad system—Fogel constructed a model of the U.S. economy identical to historical reality with one impor-

---

[34] R. Fogel, *Railroads and American Economic Growth: Essays in Economic History* (Baltimore: Johns Hopkins University Press, 1964). Fogel's latest response to his critics is "Notes on the Social Savings Controversy," *Journal of Economic History* (March 1979).

■ The construction of this railroad in Virginia in the late nineteenth century involved plowing up Civil War trenches.
Source: Richmond Newspapers, Inc.

tant exception: The hypothetical economy did not contain railroads. Fogel assumed that the transportation system of his hypothetical economy consisted of the best alternative methods of transportation then available: a greatly expanded network of canals and improved rivers combined with a system of feeder roads. By comparing the national product of his hypothetical economy with that actually achieved in 1890, Fogel hoped to measure the railroads' contribution to economic growth.

Surprisingly—and to many historians, not conclusively—Fogel discovered that his postulated road-canal-river transportation network was technically feasible well out into the Great Plains. This would have placed about 98 percent of all the agricultural land actually in use in 1890 within 40 miles of water transportation, a distance over which wagon transportation was economically possible. To maximize his estimate of the railroads' impact, Fogel assumed that the locations of eco-

nomic activity were the same as those that actually developed with the aid of the railways. Presumably there would have been some relocation of activity away from areas where alternatives to the railroads were especially poor.

The next step was the computation of the costs of transporting 1890's agricultural output from production to consumption points and a comparison of the costs of doing so with those actually incurred. Ton-mile charges would have been lower, not higher, on the water and wagon system, but direct freight charges alone understate the railroads' contribution. When allowances are made for the costs involved in using a slower form of transportation (inventories, insurance, and losses), and the effects of seasonal shutdowns on many water routes, the savings made by the railroads are positive, as they logically had to be. But the study found they were quite modest. Fogel concluded that national income in 1890 was only about 5 percent (4.7 percent) higher in the presence of the railroads than it would have been in their absence, even when the costs of transporting all goods, not merely agricultural products, were considered. (Fogel never actually computed costs for nonagricultural products, and his study excluded passenger transportation. He based the aggregate estimate on the proportion of agricultural to total income.) Five percent of national income was less than two years' economic growth at late nineteenth-century rates. If there had been no freight railroads available in 1890, Fogel concluded, the United States would have achieved only the income actually produced sometime in 1888. Railroads were important, Fogel stated (no other industry's absence would have caused as large an effect), but they could not be termed indispensable.

The Critical Response Some criticisms of Fogel's work are methodological. Specifically, some critics objected to his employment of a counterfactual proposition (the railroadless economy). Since this never occurred, they said, it could not be used in historical analysis. However, such counterfactual propositions are in fact implicit in every statement of cause and effect, historical or otherwise.

The more interesting debate is over the dimensions of the railroads' contribution. Fogel has been attacked on virtually every aspect of his procedures. Critics are not convinced that water transportation could have been expanded to the network Fogel assumed, nor do they believe that such canals could have handled the volume of traffic that Fogel assigned to them. The rates charged by various forms of transportation have been challenged, as has the extrapolation from agricultural products to all freight. Others have pointed out that another study concluded that the railroads were already contributing 5 percent of national income as early as 1860,[35] and that it was highly unlikely that railroads' impact was not greater when they served large regions in which access to water transport was much poorer than it was for the settled area of 1860.

The consensus of one group of critics is that the railroads' contribution was considerably greater than Fogel's estimate—perhaps 9 to 14 percent of national income in 1890, rather than 5 percent.[36] Another group, impressed by the very high social rates of return generated by the transcontinental railroads, has argued that the true benefits were greater than 14 percent, perhaps even over 20 percent of national income.[37] Whether even the latter conclusion would have made the railroads literally indispensable is still a matter of debate. There is no doubt, however, that the railroads' role in American economic growth during this period was greater than that of any other single industry.

Railroad Finances

Much postwar railroad construction took place under very different circumstances from that done before 1860. The earlier lines were built to serve regions that were already settled and in which markets for transportation services already existed.[38] Many postwar railroads, especially in the West, were built in undeveloped, sometimes almost unpopulated, regions. The output potential of these regions assured that they would remain undeveloped until transportation facilities were available to send their bulky, low-unit-value products to market. No accurate measure of the volume

[35] A. Fishlow, *American Railroads and the Transformation of the Antebellum Economy* (Cambridge, Mass.: Harvard University Press, 1965).

[36] S. Lebergott, "United States Transportation Advance and Externalities," *Journal of Economic History* (December 1966), and M. Nerlove, "Railroads and American Economic Growth," *Journal of Economic History* (March 1966).

[37] H. Boyd and G. Walton, "The Social Savings from 19th Century Rail Passenger Service," *Explorations in Economic History* (Spring 1972), and J. Williamson, "The Railroads and Midwestern Development: A General Equilibrium History," in Klingamen and Vedder, eds., *The Old Northwest* (Athens, Ohio: Ohio University Press, 1975).

[38] Fishlow, *American Railroads.*

of traffic that railroads would generate in such regions could be made. The extent of the settlement that the railroads would eventually attract was unknown, as was the rate at which it would proceed. Competing rail lines might be built into the same region. Under such circumstances, investments in railroads built into unsettled areas were viewed as risky. Strengthening this impression was the fact that it might be years after funds had been committed and construction commenced before an accurate assessment of the returns could be made.

Either optimistic or pessimistic conclusions could be reached under these conditions, and those who built the railroads tended to be optimists. They apparently overestimated the amount of development that would take place along the lines they built and underestimated construction costs, the competition that new railways would face, and the time required for both construction and settlement. Investors, on the other hand, tended to be pessimistic. Very high rates of return were demanded on funds invested in western railroads, an indication that such projects were deemed risky. Some of the methods used by railroad promoters to obtain funds for construction raised the costs of capital still higher. As a result, although the railroads generally earned at least a competitive rate of return on the funds actually used for construction, the costs of obtaining these funds were so high that the railroads' overall financial record was poor. One source of later difficulties was that the people who built the railroads did not intend to operate the lines once completed. They received payment for their efforts when construction was completed, rather than from the proceeds of railroads' operations. As a result, the railroad network was overbuilt.

The construction companies that actually built the railways were paid largely in bonds, not cash. These bonds were accepted by the construction companies at far less than their face value. Other bonds were issued to "sweeten" sales of corporate stock, sometimes for no cash payment whatsoever. The deflation of 1865–1896 added to railroads' interest and debt burdens, and the depressions of the 1870s and 1890s reduced their earnings. As noted above, the railways' earnings on the sums actually expended to build them were adequate, but the sums earned were far less than sufficient to discharge the obligations they had contracted. Construction companies might skimp on their work, increasing operating cost; one railroad was described as "two streaks of rust across the prairie" only a few years after its completion. The result was that the railroads were burdened with enormous fixed debts on which interest had to be paid before any dividends could be paid to stockholders. Often operating income did not cover interest and principal payments on bonded debt. The social benefits of many western railways were quite high; they raised the incomes of their customers by considerably more than the sums paid for their services. But returns to investors, particularly stockholders, were often low or nonexistent.[39]

Rate Wars In addition, debt burdens left the railroads vulnerable to any development reducing the volume of traffic, whether competition from other roads or cyclical slumps in economic activity. Railroads had no choice but to retain traffic by any means available in adverse conditions. Since railroad transportation is essentially a homogeneous good, they had to compete in price. The result was a series of rate wars in which railroads attempted to undercut each other. Attempts to collude and fix profitable prices were seldom successful. Rate cuts would attract a large volume of traffic to roads offering them, provided all others maintained their rates at agreed-upon levels. Any traffic that more than paid the costs of loading and unloading it at least

[39] L. Mercer, "Building Ahead of Demand: Some Evidence for the Land Grant Railroads," *Journal of Economic History* (June 1974).

produced something to apply against the railroads' fixed costs and helped to avoid bankruptcy.

The burden of financial problems pressured the roads to engage in tactics that customers dependent upon a single railroad found incomprehensible—or infuriating. The railroads' actions may have been merely attempts to survive in an uncertain environment while carrying heavy fixed costs, but they provoked punitive legislation from outraged state legislatures. One authority claims that the rates allowed railroads under regulation by the Interstate Commerce Commission (controlled by shippers) eventually proved insufficient to maintain their equipment in proper working order after 1900.[40] At one time or another before 1914, nearly every major American railroad declared bankruptcy, and the industry was in constant turmoil.

OTHER FORMS OF TRANSPORTATION

The railroads' expansion in part was at the expense of older forms of transportation. Steamboat traffic declined, particularly on the smaller rivers where their disadvantages relative to railroads, were greatest. Many of the canals so laboriously constructed before the Civil War were now abandoned. In some cases their towpaths became railroad rights-of-way.

Faded Glory: Barge and Steamboat Traffic

There were exceptions to the general decline in water transportation. Where cargo volumes were large or values per unit low, water travel was still cheaper. Traffic in grain, ore, coal, and building materials on the Mississippi and Ohio Rivers continued to increase for several decades after 1860. But only two canals remained important commercial arteries after 1870. Traffic on the New York State Barge Canal System, which included the Erie Canal, continued to increase until 1880. After that, despite improvements that reduced shipping costs, and even the abolition of tolls, traffic declined to only half its 1880 peak by 1900, and failed to rise thereafter.[41] The Sault Sainte Marie Canal, which linked Lake Superior with the other Great Lakes, experienced a rapid increase in traffic when the iron mines of northern Minnesota and wheat from the prairies of the United States and Canada furnished "exports" after 1885. Settlement of these regions furnished markets for the coal the ore boats carried on their return trips. Traffic on the other Great Lakes also increased. In the main, lower prices charged by water carriers were insufficient compensation for their lack of speed and convenience relative to the railways.

The Decline of the U.S. Merchant Marine
Coastal commerce continued to grow, even as the U.S. Merchant Marine declined in overseas trade. The carrying trade between U.S. ports was reserved to vessels built and operated by Americans by a law reminiscent of seventeenth-century mercantilism. But the gains in coastal traffic were insufficient to offset the losses in overseas commerce. The volume of merchant shipping built in American shipyards after 1865 never approached the levels of the 1850s and was often only one-third to one-half that built in the glory days of American clipper ships.[42] Technological backwardness hastened the decline of U.S. shipbuilding. American wooden sailing ships were the best in the world in the antebellum

[40] A. Martin, *Enterprise Denied: Origins of the Decline of American Railroads* (New York: Columbia University Press, 1971).

[41] *Historical Statistics*, 2:765.
[42] *Historical Statistics*, 2:749–750.

period, and their sailing records and ready markets abroad proved it. But when construction shifted to steam-propelled iron and then steel ships, American yards were slow to switch to the new techniques. This may have been due to their location: Downeast Maine had plenty of wood and men skilled in working it, but it was far from supplies of metal and had few men trained to build with that material. Foreign countries subsidized their vessels, sometimes with lucrative mail contracts, and American shipping costs, particularly for labor, were high.

Urban Railroads

Railways had their urban counterparts. Even before the Civil War, some cities possessed systems of horse-drawn cars running on rails set in the streets. Steam power was a logical replacement for horses, and after 1890, electric traction was used. As cities grew more congested, some elevated their street railways, creating "els." Urban railways became an important component of aggregate investment after the construction of interregional railways slackened in the 1880s. Cheap and reasonably efficient mass transportation allowed better housing for city dwellers, who could now reside further from their jobs. Another result was the development of specialized financial, shopping, and industrial districts within cities.

Few, if any, of the interurban and urban railroads survive today, but the system was extensive in the early twentieth century. There were lines in all large and most middle-sized cities, and there were many connecting different urban areas. It was even possible, although certainly not comfortable, to travel the entire Eastern Seaboard from Portland, Maine, to Richmond, Virginia, via interurban railway.

The Road System

Before 1900, little had been done to improve the quality of roads since the early national period. The road network had been extended with settlement, but that was about all. Farmers' use of the roads was concentrated in seasons when there were few other demands on their time, such as after the harvest, and they would have borne a large share of the property taxes used to improve roads. Consequently, rural areas exerted little pressure for better roads before the twentieth century. American roads tended to be dirt- or, at best, gravel-surfaced, poorly drained and graded, and without signs. Tales of potholes so large that horses drowned in them may be apocryphal, but most roads did become all but impassable in wet weather. In 1910, the United States had almost five million miles of rural roads, only 200,000 of which were surfaced.

Under pressure from bicycle and automobile owners, states began to construct roads and mark and maintain them. By 1914, most states had organized construction programs and highway departments. In 1916, the federal government began making grants to the states for highway construction. Only after World War I did the combination of improved motor trucks and adequate highways begin to offer a practical alternative to railway transportation, and even then only for short distances.

NEW COMPETITIVE PATTERNS

The opportunities revealed by new manufacturing techniques and access to more distant markets made firms increasingly aware of competition from other producers. Many of the new methods of production involved high fixed costs. This meant that large production volumes were necessary to gain the reductions in unit costs that such methods made possible. Moreover, it was costly either to produce at lower volumes or shut down. Thus, when competition appeared, some response had to be made; it was suicidal to simply reduce production. For many industrial firms there was no place to hide, even if they had no interest in new markets. Often there were compelling reasons to expand.

Growth in firm size offered several advantages. Often there was no other way to profitably utilize the new, highly capitalized production methods. Lower unit costs achieved by these techniques offered higher profits if prices remained stable, and constituted the ultimate defense against competitors. If firms' size increased relative to their markets, they might also gain some degree of monopoly power. Labor-saving, capital-intensive changes accounted for some, but by no means all, of the changes in market structure that occurred in this period.[43]

If a firm's size increases to allow utilization of economies of scale under competitive market conditions, the firm will be forced to pass its lower costs on to consumers. Such changes are beneficial to the entire economy. On the other hand, when firms become large in relation to their markets, they may be able to increase profits by selling smaller quantities at higher prices than under more competitive conditions, reducing overall welfare through the exercise of monopoly power. Monopoly of any type is thus likely to be far more popular with its owner than with those forced to pay its price or do without its products.

The Effects of Monopoly

Compared to competition, monopoly creates an artificial shortage. Under the same cost and demand conditions, monopolies produce less and charge higher prices than do competitive industries, even though their productive ability is the same. Such policies add to the monopolist's profits, but the monopolist gains

less than the aggregate economy loses. To retain the profits achieved by these means, a monopolist must be able to prohibit entry and prevent the market system from reallocating resources to uses where the value of their output is greatest.

In one instance, that of "natural monopoly," the results produced, while still short of ideal economic efficiency, may be superior to those resulting from competition within the industry. If the most efficient scale of operations—that which minimizes unit costs—is very large in relation to the market for the product, then a single seller may be able to reduce production costs so much that his price (which might nonetheless include a substantial monopoly profit) is lower than those reflecting smaller firms' costs. It is important to note, however, that economies of scale are generally available only within a single plant. The acquisition of additional plants, especially if it is done through mergers rather than new construction, will not reduce unit production costs significantly. When we note that the number of employees per plant rose only modestly in U.S. industry before 1900, and more slowly after the merger movement began than prior to it, the conclusion that the primary goal pursued by increasing the size of firms was increased market power rather than economies of scale is strengthened.[44]

The Competitive Jungle
Attempts to gain monopoly power were as varied as the results they produced. Rarely was a firm able to achieve economies of scale more rapidly than its rivals and drive them from the market by sheer superior efficiency. More commonly, there was a sequence of responses to rivals. Firms initially tried to destroy their competitors—sometimes literally rather than in a business sense—and, when these efforts

---

[43] J. James, "Structural Change in American Manufacturing, 1850–1890," *Journal of Economic History* (June 1983).

[44] James, "Structural Change." See also O'Brien, "Factory Size."

failed, were forced to adopt other tactics. "Cutthroat competition" (sales at less than rivals' costs of production in an effort to bankrupt them) was sometimes attempted. However, cutthroat competition works only if the price-cutting firm has either lower costs or the financial reserves to survive short-run losses. Further, if rivals are driven out, the victor must acquire their assets; if these are sold at bankruptcy-proceedings prices to new owners, all that has been accomplished is to create a new, more dangerous rival whose costs are lower than his predecessor's. Even where such tactics were successful, there was no assurance that the victor could recoup the costs of eliminating competition, nor that there would be no further attempts to enter the industry. Tactics such as suborning rivals' employees, arson, buying labor unrest for rivals from corrupt union officials, impugning the quality of rivals' products (Royal Baking Powder encouraged rumors that alternatives to its product contained poisonous ingredients),[45] or selling spoiled goods under rivals' trademarks had drawbacks as well. They were illegal, their outcome was uncertain, and they invited retaliation in kind.

Price-Fixing

The usual results of attempts to destroy competitors was a conclusion that those who could not be beaten might more profitably be joined. If all firms in an industry can agree on a common price and are able to restrict output to no more than the market will absorb at that price, they may obtain nearly the same total profit as a single-firm monopolist. The first attempts at collusion involved agreements on price, output, or both. These seldom succeeded for long; if only price *or* output were controlled, even colluding firms would alter the other dimension, and it would be impossible to sell total output or maintain all firms'

market shares. Even if agreements covered both price and output they were unenforceable under the common law and contained irresistible incentives to cheat. Pressures to undercut collusive agreements on prices were increased by the general deflation prior to 1896 and the boom-and-bust business cycle. When demand for an industry's product fell during a depression, individual firms were sorely tempted to regain lost sales through price cuts. If firms had high fixed costs and the industry had not existed long enough for its members to gain competitive experience, such actions were especially probable.[46] Even so, the short-run profits from a price-fixing agreement could be high, and attempts to collude were frequent.

Trusts and Mergers

Because agreements between independently managed firms were so unstable, even when they were merged into "pools" in which the parties agreed to share total profits under some agreed-upon formula, other institutions were developed. Trusts were one response to the cheating problem. Stockholders of competing firms would transfer voting control of their shares to a central group of trustees in return for certificates on which they would receive dividends. Since the trustees now controlled the stock of all participant firms, they could manage the industry as a multiplant monopoly. Trusts were organized in a number of consumer goods industries from 1880 to 1900. Holding companies (firms whose assets were the stock of other corporations) were a logical extension of the trusts. The purpose of such devices was transparently anticompetitive, and they began to encounter difficulty in state and federal courts almost as soon as they appeared.

Mergers might be employed as another route to increase market power. A merger is

---

[45] Lamoreaux, *Great Merger*, 157.

[46] Lamoreaux, *Great Merger*, 61–62, 87.

the acquisition of one firm by another, a combination of two or more firms into one. The merger of firms previously in competition with each other must always reduce competition if it has any effect. If there had been only two firms in the market, a merger would obviously eliminate competition. Such mergers are unlikely to produce offsetting benefits through increased efficiency; mergers change only the ownership of physical assets, not their productivity. Unless the acquired firm was badly managed, horizontal mergers will not reduce production costs.

Vertical mergers occur between firms that previously bought from or sold to each other. A paper mill might integrate backward by obtaining a pulpwood company, or forward through the purchase of a factory that made shopping bags. Both these types of mergers increase firms' absolute size, but only horizontal mergers increase firm size relative to the markets in which they operate. Vertical mergers increase the *number* of markets in which the firm operates. A merger movement in American industry began in the 1880s and ended by 1905. Its changing features indicate the motives behind mergers and their effects on competition.

The first great wave of mergers occurred among firms producing long-established consumer goods. Typically, there had been many such firms in each industry, most of them serving local markets. Expanded output in these industries caused supply to rise faster than demand, and prices fell. Often after the failure of less formal attempts at restricting competition, firms began to merge.

Standard Oil

Once the mergers were complete, the larger organizations sought improved operating efficiency through rationalization and centralizing those functions in which economies of scale were available. Oil refining was consolidated by John D. Rockefeller and his associates into the Standard Oil Company, which by 1870 controlled 96 percent of all refining capacity in the United States. Contrary to popular belief, Standard Oil was able to achieve this dominance in oil refining through a series of purchases in which owners of independent firms were often at least as eager to sell out as Standard Oil was to buy, rather than by cutthroat competition.

The assets of competing firms were worth more to Rockefeller as components of a monopoly than they were to their original owners as competing firms. Thus, Standard Oil's first move in an attempt to acquire an independent oil company was an offer to buy it at a price that was highly favorable from the owner's viewpoint. This was generally sufficient.[47] Rumors of cutthroat competitive tactics (or worse) were undoubtedly useful to Standard Oil, but there is little evidence that they were widely employed. Once its control was established, Standard Oil improved plants' operating efficiency. This was the primary basis of the firm's market power. Standard Oil was able to force railroads to grant it rebates on shipments of both its own oil and (very briefly) those of its competitors as well. Largely as a result of Rockefeller's cost-cutting efforts, the prices of refined oil products fell to one-seventh of their 1865 levels by 1884.[48]

Once new sources of oil began to appear and refining techniques changed in response to new uses of petroleum, Standard Oil's monopoly eroded. Standard Oil was unusual in achieving virtually complete, if temporary, control over its industry through mergers. In most cases, the first merger wave resulted in oligopolistic market structures in which from three to six firms controlled a large part of the industry's total production.

---

[47] J. McGee, "Predatory Price-Cutting: The Standard Oil (N.J.) Case," *Journal of Law and Economics* 137 (1958).
[48] S. Lebergott, *The Americans: An Economic Record* (New York: Norton, 1984), 325–334.

Changes in the Merger Movement

According to Chandler, the characteristics of merger activity changed in the decade after 1895. The second wave of mergers took place among the producers of capital goods and newer types of consumer goods, particularly those for the urban market. While some horizontal mergers occurred as they had earlier, the emphasis was now on vertical mergers. These were intended to protect sources of supply or access to final markets. Capital goods producers tended to integrate backward to protect their sources of inputs and crucial transportation links, while the producers of new consumer goods integrated forward, buying outlets to maintain their access to markets.[49]

Recently, this view has been challenged. According to Naomi Lamoreaux, horizontal mergers intended to produce monopoly or at least greater market power predominated in the post-1895 merger wave. Of 93 consolidations, 72 percent controlled at least 40 percent of the product market, and nearly one-third obtained a market share of at least 70 percent.[50] Her study concluded that mergers were especially prevalent in oligopolistic industries that had been growing rapidly before the depression of 1893, had high fixed costs, and had experienced traumatic price wars in that slump. In most cases, there was also a record of unsuccessful collusion prior to the merger activity.[51]

The Role of Financiers

Especially after 1897, a new motive for mergers appeared. Before then the desire for mergers had originated within the participating firms, but now financiers took an active role. Previously, financiers had dealt mainly in railroad and government securities, with little interest in industrial stocks and bonds. But railroad issues had compiled a dismal record in the depression of the early 1890s; industrial stocks had fared better. Equally important to financiers were that mergers often involved the issue of large volumes of additional securities and invariably required the performance of services on which fat commissions and fees could be obtained. Thus, financiers may have been more interested in the mergers themselves than they were in the firms that resulted from them. The high rate of failures among the firms so formed does little to dispel this view. In some cases, the mergers resulted in the issue of "watered stock," securities backed neither by tangible assets nor by justifiable hopes for increased monopoly profits. In most cases, however, it now appears that financiers facilitated but did not initiate such mergers; the motive forces were within the industries concerned.[52]

The Great Steel Consolidation

The financiers' ultimate triumph was the formation of the United States Steel Corporation in 1902. Companies whose assets were valued at $700 million before the consolidation were combined into a single firm controlling well over half the steelmaking capacity of the United States. The same assets now had a book value of $1 billion, reflecting their increased value because of the reduction in competition within the industry. The steel corporation fulfilled the financiers' hopes; it earned handsome profits even on the new asset valuations.

Central to the great steel consolidation had been the acquisition of Carnegie Steel Corporation. Andrew Carnegie had operated as a ruthless competitor who used his firm's superior operating efficiency to undercut his rivals' prices. Carnegie scorned attempts at price fixing; if his representatives attended collusive meetings, they did so largely to learn the level of prices that Carnegie Steel would

---

[49] Chandler, "Big Business."
[50] Lamoreaux, *Great Merger*, 2.
[51] Lamoreaux, *Great Merger*, 100.

[52] Lamoreaux, *Great Merger*, 112–115.

undercut.[53] The new United States Steel Corporation was formed with very different goals in mind: It was designed to reduce, if not eliminate, price competition in steel. Prospects for success in this endeavor enhanced the value of its stock. In one view, however, the changing antitrust climate constrained U.S. Steel from aggressive pursuit of maximum monopoly profits or even cost reduction.[54]

The Merger Era Ends

After 1905, merger activity was greatly reduced. Some mergers had failed outright or produced only disappointing profits; and the really promising merger opportunities had largely been utilized. Changes in technology and resource supply favored new firms, further reducing the attractions of mergers. Since potential entrants often had lower costs than the consolidated firms, there might be no effective barriers to entry. Lamoreaux found that in many cases high short-run profits from consolidation had provoked successful entry into the industries where they occurred by 1904.[55] Economic growth was rapid after 1900, and under such conditions there is little need to reduce output to generate higher profits.

The federal government did break up two large firms built by merger (Standard Oil and American Tobacco). It also used the Sherman Act to prevent a merger between two railroads (the *Northern Securities* case, 1904). Legal pressures appear to have played a smaller role in the decline of mergers than did economics. Probably the most significant legal development affecting competition was the *Addystone Pipe* case (1899), in which the Supreme Court ruled that price-fixing was illegal under any and all circumstances. The ruling made collusion between firms more difficult. Although it did not change the structure of existing industries, *Addystone Pipe* provoked a greater degree of competition from the industrial economy. In at least one view, however, the impact of antitrust rulings favored vertically integrated firms by allowing barriers to entry stemming from intrafirm practices that were prohibited between independent firms.[56]

DID COMPETITION DECREASE?

In the 1870–1914 era, many U.S. manufacturing and financial companies became larger than any previous business firms had been. Obviously, the managers of many of these new large firms sought control over the markets in which they operated. The results of these changes in size and (perhaps) in business leaders' intentions, however, are less certain.

Any introductory economics text states that monopoly produces less and charges higher prices than would occur under similarly circumstanced competitive firms. Except in the case of natural monopoly, the monopolist's gains come at the expense of the economy in which he operates. However, even while the drive for monopolization was at its peak from 1865 to 1914, prices of manufactured goods and transport and financial services (the products in which efforts to gain monopoly power were centered) fell in real terms, and their output rose much faster than aggregate economic growth.

Dynamic versus Static Monopoly

The results appear to be exactly the opposite of the textbook prediction, but they may not refute its conclusions as decisively as a first reading would indicate. First, there is some

[53] J. Hughes, *The Vital Few*, 231, 238–239.
[54] McCraw and Reinhardt, "Losing to Win."
[55] Lamoreaux, *Great Merger*, Chap. 5.

[56] Lamoreaux, *Great Merger*, 191.

question as to whether most firms actually gained market power or merely operated in new and larger markets. The size of individual firms undoubtedly increased, but it did so in an economy rapidly enlarging its aggregate dimensions. It is the firm's size relative to the market that constitutes the basis of monopoly power, not absolute size.

Second, it is a serious mistake to think of the antebellum economy as perfectly competitive, or close to it, just because the average size of firms was small. Before 1865, most industrial firms served only local markets, and typically there would be few if any substitutes available for the products of any one manufacturing company except in the largest cities. In such circumstances, individual sellers had very considerable market power. With the advent of regional or even national markets after the Civil War, the number of sellers actually competing in each local market may have risen, even in cases where the number of producers in the United States remained static or even declined—as it rarely did. Competition may well have increased despite the growth in firm size.[57]

Third, if the structure of industries is examined, it becomes apparent that although many firms sought monopoly power, few attained it and even fewer managed to retain profitable monopoly positions for long.[58] Most industries retained a number of sellers; even the most concentrated markets were oligopolistic rather than monopolistic. In such markets, the number of sellers may have been greater than in the more fragmented local markets of the antebellum era.

Finally, modern studies on the actual impact of monopoly power on the economy have shown its impact to be surprisingly small. The chief cause of this phenomenon appears to be the diversity of the American economy; few

people spend a large portion of their incomes on the products of any single industry, or even any small number of industries. Table 12.1 indicates that this point had considerable validity even in 1910. No modern study has concluded that the cost exacted by the exercise of monopoly exceeds 6 percent of national income, and most found the toll considerably lower.[59]

A Dynamic Economy

Also, the textbook case against monopoly is static. It assumes that technology, demand for the product, and consumer alternatives do not change. The economy in which these developments actually occurred over 1870–1914 was one of far greater change in all factors than had ever occurred before. It is difficult to imagine less favorable circumstances for the practices of static monopoly than a falling general price level, rapid growth in both technology and the aggregate economy, and a legal and social climate that favored the growth of new firms. The number of new corporations formed during the merger wave was more than ten times as great as the number that disappeared through merger or acquisition.[60]

Consumers were not helpless in their struggles against large firms at this time. Many of the new goods produced by large firms were objects of discretionary spending, not necessities. In these cases, attempts to exert monopoly power in sales of one good, even though no exact substitutes were available, would lead to a shift in consumer demand to

---

[57] Some authorities have little doubt of this See, for example, Lebergott, *The Americans*, 310–316.
[58] Lamoreaux, *Great Merger*, 189.

[59] The maximum (6 percent) estimate is from D. Worcester, Jr., "New Estimates of the Welfare Loss to Monopoly, United States, 1956–1969," *Southern Economic Journal* (October 1973). See also D. Kamerschen, "An Estimate of the Welfare Loss for Monopoly in the American Economy," *Western Economic Journal* (December 1966). Since these estimates were made, competition has clearly increased within the American economy. See Table 20.2 in this book.
[60] N. Rosenberg and R. Birdzell, *How the West Grew Rich: The Economic Transformation of the Industrial World* (New York: Basic Books, 1986), 286.

other goods meeting the same broad consumer desires. Sellers of sporting goods (a broad category in itself) might find that their customers considered live entertainment, books, magazines, the local beer parlor, card games, and even gossip as substitutes in better or less degree. In sum, the historical data as well as economic reasoning provide little support for any claim that monopoly power seriously reduced the welfare of the typical citizen in this period. The balance of the evidence would appear to indicate that competition grew rather than declined.

THE ROBBER BARONS

When business activity in the late nineteenth century is discussed, the names of those who founded and directed the great industrial firms, banks, and railroads invariably crop up. Many of these business leaders achieved wealth beyond the dreams of most Americans, and some were better known for flamboyant life-styles than for their business success. To at least one author, these men were "Robber Barons," a title that has endured with little consideration of the evidence supporting the appellation. In this view, the gains made by the Robber Barons had come at the expense of the rest of the population. They owed far more to their lack of scruples than to conventional business ability.[61]

The Morals of the Gilded Age

Some of the tactics used in business at this time would not be credible in the most lurid television serial shown today. Fraud, bribery, forgery of securities, deliberate destruction of

one's own firm for private gain, mob violence, arson, and even an occasional murder (in labor relations murder was not occasional), were all employed frequently enough so that even businessmen who would not and did not use such methods had to learn to deal with those who did. The last battle involving artillery fought in New York involved two gangs of hired thugs contesting the ownerships of the Susquehanna Railway. The law was not an effective shield. The New York State Legislature once publicly censured one of its members in a bribery case. In the opinion of his fellows, the legislator had sold his vote for too little, which might endanger the collusive rates fixed for bribery fees charged by other assembly members. In many other states, standards of political morality were no better. Judges might decide cases in favor of whatever party offered the largest bribe. In general, the moral standards of the Gilded Age do not compare favorably with any other period, including our own period.[62]

The values of this era put considerably more stress on the accumulation of wealth than on the details of its generation. Neither law nor social usage imposed many restrictions on business activity, and some men did not bother to develop their own. The business world was a complete jungle, and those who succeeded in such an environment often reflected the environment in which they operated.

The Robber Barons: An Assessment

It would be a serious error, however, to regard all successful business leaders of the period as a pack of thieves whose influence was entirely negative. They were hardly saints, and there were some for whom the preceding paragraphs constitute unduly generous praise, but for the

[61] M. Josephson, *The Robber Barons: The Great American Capitalists, 1861–1901,* Reprint (New York: Harcourt Brace Jovanovich, 1962).

[62] For a survey of political corruption in this period, see Cochran and Miller, *The Age of Enterprise.*

most part, the impact of these entrepreneurs was beneficial. The economy in which their activities figured so prominently was the scene of rapid economic growth, and this growth was most notable in manufacturing, finance, and transportation, all of which grew faster than sectors not afflicted with such leaders. Output increased, quality of products improved, and real prices fell in these sectors, in relation to the rest of the economy. Further, workers' real wages rose and their hours of labor were reduced; by no means were all the gains restricted to the rich.

None of the foregoing should be interpreted as an argument that these developments were solely due to the efforts of business leaders, or even that these developments reflected their primary intentions. But the gains did occur, and they were concentrated in the sectors where these men's activities were prominent. It appears difficult to conclude that the great entrepreneurs' impact was both significant and wholly negative.

Ford, Morgan, and Carnegie
Many of the business leaders exhibit a curious combination of traits. Aside from his one truly better idea, Henry Ford contributed very little. He was a narrow, inflexible man whose passion for independence from outside sources of supply and inability to tolerate opposition contributed as much to the near ruin of his great firm as much as his vision of the automobile market had done to build it. In company with many other businessmen of his generation, Ford saw only one appropriate response to organized labor—total opposition. J. P. Morgan's mathematical training may have reinforced his love of order, and competition is not an orderly process. Morgan's penchant for mergers and high returns on investment reduced competition in the industries in which he was active. But "Morganization" improved the operating efficiency of industry, financial markets, and railroads, reducing the instability that had plagued the lat-

ter two. Carnegie's record—or that of his lieutenants—with organized labor is brutal, but his operating methods, like those of Rockefeller, made the product of his industry cheaper than ever before, and consumers achieved a large share of the gains.

Even the enormous fortunes that some of the "Robber Barons" acquired must be viewed in the light of their achievements. Often they succeeded in efforts where it was plain the rewards for success would be great, entry was easy, but accomplishment extraordinarily difficult. In short, they did what no one else could. Henry Villard raised $60 million to build the Northern Pacific Railway. For two years' work, Villard received a commission of $3 million. This sum would be equivalent to perhaps $30 million today and was not subject to income taxes. But the railroad raised the incomes of those living in its operating area by many times the amount Villard received and continued to do so every year. Furthermore, Villard was by no means the first to attempt to raise funds for the railroad—only the first to succeed. The point is not whether such men were worth every penny they received—that is really a moral, not an economic judgment—but that their contributions were both substantial and unique.[63] Some of them engaged in extensive philanthropy, but that pales in comparison to the contributions they made in giving America cheap steel, oil, and automobiles.

The Rogues Gallery
There were, of course, business leaders of this era who can be charged with considerably more than perhaps being overpriced. The legacy of men like Drew, Fisk, and Hyde was less perfect financial markets because investors (rightly) hesitated to venture their savings in markets where such men were free to hatch

---

[63] Hughes, *The Vital Few*, is an excellent assessment of the careers and contributions of some of the business leaders of this period.

their schemes. Nevertheless, the business community was not composed solely or even largely of such types.

The introduction of new goods, processes, and applications substantially increased the income, wealth, health, and education of the average American while the business leaders were piling up their fortunes, so perhaps the most sweeping charge that can be levied is that welfare might have improved even more without them. Given the accomplishments of some of them, even this is dubious. Even to the extent that some of them were thieves, they tended to rob each other; the rich attract such attention more than the poor because the costs per dollar stolen are lower. We must also judge such men, if we can, against the background of their era, not ours, and in light of its ideals and standards. They gained much, but they also took enormous risks that daunted many others. Their vision, or that of most of them, made the new ideas work.

SELECTED REFERENCES

Chandler, A., Jr. *Strategy and Structure: Chapters in the History of American Industrial Enterprise.* Cambridge, Mass.: Harvard University Press, 1962.

———. *The Railroads: The Nations's First Big Business.* New York: Harcourt, Brace, and World, 1965.

———. *The Visible Hand: The Managerial Revolution in American Business.* Cambridge, Mass.: Harvard University Press, 1977.

Cochran, T. *200 Years of American Business.* New York: Basic Books, 1977.

Cochran, T., and W. Miller. *The Age of Enterprise: A Social History of Industrial America.* New York: Harper & Row, 1968.

Davis, L., R. Easterlin, W. Parker et al. *American Economic Growth: An Economist's History of the United States.* New York: Harper & Row, 1972.

Fishlow, A. *American Railroads and the Transformation of the American Economy.* Cambridge, Mass.: Harvard University Press, 1965.

Fogel, R. *Railroads and Economic Growth: Essays in Economic History.* Baltimore: Johns Hopkins University Press, 1964

———. *The Union Pacific Railroad: A Case of Premature Enterprise.* Baltimore: AMS Press, 1960.

Gallman, R., and S. Engerman. *Long-Term Factors in American Economic Growth.* Chicago: University of Chicago Press, 1986.

Hounshell, D. *From the American System to Mass Production, 1800–1936: The Development of Manufacturing Technology in the United States.* Baltimore: Johns Hopkins University Press, 1984.

Hughes, J. *The Vital Few: American Economic Progress and Its Protagonists.* 2d ed. Cambridge, U.K.: Cambridge University Press, 1986.

Josephson, M. *The Robber Barons: The Great American Capitalists, 1861–1901.* Reprint. New York: Harcourt Brace Jovanovich, 1962.

Lamoreaux, N. *The Great Merger Movement in American Business, 1895–1904.* Cambridge, U.K.: Cambridge University Press, 1985.

Martin, A. *Enterprise Denied: Origins of the Decline of American Railroads.* New York: Columbia University Press, 1971.

Nelson, R. *Merger Movements in American Industry.* Princeton, N.J.: Princeton University Press, 1959.

Porter, G. *The Rise of Big Business, 1860–1910.* New York: Thomas Crowell, 1973.

Rosenberg, N. *Technology and American Economic Growth.* New York: Harper & Row, 1972.

Rosenberg, N., and L. Birdzell. *How the West Grew Rich: The Economic Transformation of the Industrial World.* New York: Basic Books, 1986.

Scherer, F. *Industrial Market Structure and Economic Performance.* Chicago: Rand McNally, 1970.

Temin, P. *Iron and Steel in Nineteenth-Century America: An Economic Inquiry.* Cambridge, Mass.: M.I.T. Press, 1964.

U.S. Department of Commerce, Bureau of the Census. *Historical Statistics of the United States: Colonial Times to 1970.* 2 vols. Washington, D.C.: Government Printing Office, 1975.

Vatter, H. *The Drive to Industrial Maturity: The U.S. Economy, 1860–1914.* Westport, Conn.: Greenwood, 1975.

MONEY, BANKS, AND FINANCIAL INSTITUTIONS, 1865–1920

*T*he close of the Civil War found the United States with a monetary situation and financial institutions very different from those with which it had entered the conflict. The cost of the war had forced the Union government to borrow and print money. The expansion in the money supply had caused inflation, abandonment of the gold standard, and changes in financial institutions. For at least half this period, financial and monetary developments were influenced by the legacy of the Civil War. The long-term result was a series of remarkable changes: By 1920 the country would have a new central bank, a new currency, and a vastly expanded role for financial intermediaries.

WAR-INDUCED CHANGES

As a result of war-induced changes in monetary institutions, two new types of paper currency were in circulation in 1865. State bank notes, the previous (if heterogeneous) medium, were rapidly being withdrawn. The United States was no longer on the gold standard; paper currency no longer exchanged for gold at fixed rates. In foreign commerce, the exchange rate of the dollar for foreign currencies was determined by international trade and investment flows and relative price level changes within nations, rather than by fixed gold prices.

A new type of commercial bank had also appeared. Banks could now receive charters either from state governments, as formerly, or from the federal government—a privilege hitherto accorded only to the two Banks of the United States. With the appearance of the National Banks came changes in banks' ability to issue paper currency, a development that eventually produced important changes in the composition of the nation's money supply.

The Greenback Controversy

The Civil War had not been funded on a pay-as-you-go basis. The union government had sold bonds, but revenues from this source had become increasingly uncertain in the early years of the war, and there was opposition to the government's dependence on supersalesman Jay Cooke for bond sales. In 1862, the federal government had begun to print and issue a new form of paper currency officially called United States notes. The public termed these notes "greenbacks," because one side of the notes was green. About $414 million in greenbacks was in circulation in 1865. This amount was slightly greater than the entire currency circulation (including gold) in 1860, and about two-thirds of the entire money supply for the last prewar year.[1] Greenbacks were "fiat money"; Congress had declared them to be legal payment for debts, but they were not legally redeemable for their face value in specie. In effect, they were money because the law declared them to be money. Greenbacks did exchange at face value for bank money (state bank notes and deposits).

As explained in Chapter 11, real output could not increase at a pace even remotely similar to the rate at which the money supply rose during the Civil War, and consequently inflation approximately doubled the overall price level. Since the supply of greenbacks had increased so rapidly, their purchasing power and that of other forms of inconvertible paper money (banks suspended payment during the war) declined.

---

[1] U.S. Department of Commerce, Bureau of the Census, *Historical Statistics of the United States: Colonial Times to 1970*, 2 vols. (Washington, D.C., Government Printing Office, 1975), 2:993, 1020.

■ By 1865, U.S. currency consisted of national bank notes and greenbacks.
Source: Records of the Public Buildings Service: National Archives.

Suspension of the Gold Standard

The supply of gold had not increased, and gold retained its value in terms of foreign currency and thus of foreign goods. Although foreign goods' prices in U.S. currency had soared, owners of gold could still buy imports at prewar exchange ratios. Consequently, gold could be obtained for greenbacks only by paying a premium over the $20.67 per ounce price in standard prewar currency. The price of gold varied with the fortunes of the Union Army and the trade balance. At one time the greenback price of gold reached nearly $60 an ounce—another way of saying that $1 in greenbacks exchanged for approximately 35 cents in gold at prewar prices. In California, gold was the normal medium of exchange, and greenbacks circulated there at a discount from their face value. Elsewhere, gold disappeared from normal circulation within the United States.

Because the major trading partners of the United States had not experienced similar domestic inflation, the high prices occurring within the United States did not allow immediate postwar resumption of free convertibility of paper currency into gold at $20.67 per ounce, the antebellum price. Had this been attempted, there would have been swarms of buyers for gold and no sellers, because gold would be one of the few commodities whose paper-money price had not risen since 1860.

■ Recalling the monetary woes of the Civil War, many Americans, fearing inflation, were wary of proposals to expand the money supply.
Source: The Bettmann Archive.

As a result, the U.S. Mint would have exhausted its gold stocks. In addition, this policy would have reduced the prices of foreign goods to Americans by over 40 percent, an opportunity too good to pass up. Before resumption at prewar rates could be successful, the United States' internal price level would have to be reduced.

Greenbacks had clearly been a major cause of the wartime inflation, the reason convertibility of paper money and resumption of the gold standard at prewar rates could not be achieved. Stable convertibility could have been regained in several ways. The simplest, from a modern perspective, would have been to ratify the existing situation by increasing the official dollar price of gold to a level corresponding to that set by the market. This was politically impossible in the nineteenth cen-

tury; it would have been considered a violation of previous commitments made by government. With devaluation impossible, the practical alternatives were limited to measures that either reduced the supply of money in relation to that of goods or raised the supply of goods in relation to that of money. Either would reduce the level of prices within the United States. There was no method by which the supply of gold could be raised in the United States alone. Whether it was mined in California or obtained through international trade, gold would flow out of the country as long as its purchasing power was greater overseas. If gold had exchanged for greenbacks whose purchasing power was no greater than it was in the immediate postwar period at $20.67 per ounce, this would have been the case.

Attempts at Deflation

Congress first attempted to reduce the quantity of greenbacks in circulation. The reasoning was straightforward; as the supply of paper money dwindled, it would become scarcer in relation to other goods and services, and its purchasing power would rise, reducing and finally eliminating the premium on gold. Deflation was already underway in 1865: A slightly reduced supply of greenbacks had to cover transactions in the South as that area came back under Union control. Thus, a smaller amount of money serviced a larger volume of transactions, and the price of money in terms of goods rose. The government ran surpluses in the immediate postwar years, enabling it to reduce the quantity of greenbacks in circulation to $356 million by mid-1868. At the same time, several other types of government currency totalling about $208 million were retired.[2] The result was deflation, but the cost was high. The level of

---

[2] J. Kindahl, "Economic Factors in Specie Resumption: The United States, 1865–1879," *Journal of Economic History* (February 1961).

economic activity decreased, accompanied by unemployment and general economic distress. As the results of the greenback retirement program became clear, Congress limited the rate at which greenbacks were withdrawn in 1866, and stopped withdrawal entirely in 1868. The lesson was not forgotten; in a severe depression in 1873–1874, Congress even raised the legal limit on the number of greenbacks in circulation.

Resumption of the Gold Standard

Congressional reluctance to reduce the volume of greenbacks in circulation left only one policy available. The expansion of the money supply was restricted to less than real economic growth. The supply of goods and services rose faster than that of money, and prices fell. This approach took time, but it was ultimately successful. It may, however, have been overdone. In 1875, a lame-duck Republican Congress, fearing what the incoming Democrats might do, committed the Treasury to redemption of greenbacks at par in specie (meaning gold) on demand not later than the first day of 1879. Over the interval between the passage of the Resumption Act and its scheduled implementation, the supply of high-powered money (currency and commercial bank reserves, the basis on which the supply of bank money could be increased) did not rise. The money supply in all its forms (bank money, government money, and gold) rose only slightly.[3] Prices fell, but at a real cost. In 1879, the goal was achieved: Gold and greenbacks exchanged at par. There was a sharp recession as the policy was instituted, but real growth in the later 1870s was rapid despite the deflation. By selling bonds for gold, the government was able to accumulate a gold reserve to satisfy those who might wish to test greenbacks' convertibility, but after redemption became possible, the reserve was not needed under normal circumstances.[4] The United States was effectively back on the gold standard.

National Banks and Notes

In 1863 and 1864, Congress had passed the National Banking Acts. While the real purpose of this legislation was to aid the wartime sale of government bonds, the acts contained provisions that continued to be influential long after 1865. Banks had been offered the privilege of federal charters and the right to issue a new type of bank note, the national bank notes, but these were contingent on compliance with much more stringent federal regulations on capital and reserve requirements than most states imposed on banks. These laws reduced banks' prospective profits, so the 1863 act found few banks willing to accept the new charters.

The total amount of national bank notes in circulation was to be restricted to $300 million, and this sum was to be apportioned among the states on the basis of population. Within the states, banks were required to deposit government bonds equal to one-third of their capital with the comptroller of the currency, a new federal officer. In return, the banks received national bank notes. No bank's note issue was to exceed 90 percent of the par value of the government bonds that it had deposited with the Treasury. Since the 1863 legislation resulted in few charter applications and little increase in bond sales, Congress reduced banks' alternatives. In 1865, the tax on state bank notes was quintupled, to 10 percent. At this rate, it was no longer profitable for banks to make loans in currency.

In the short run, this policy had the desired effect: The number of banks converting to national charters rose sharply (see Table 13.1). In less than a year, the majority of all

---

[3] *Historical Statistics*, 2:993.

[4] Kindahl, "Economic Factors."

Table 13.1   U.S. Commercial Banks and Assets, 1860–1920

Year	State Banks	Total Assets (Millions)	National Banks	Total Assets (Millions)
1860	1,562	$1,000	—	—
1865	349	231	1,294	$1,127
1870	325	215	1,612	1,566
1875	586	395	2,076	1,913
1880	650	482	2,076	2,036
1885	1,015	802	2,689	2,422
1890	3,594	1,539	3,484	3,062
1895	5,086	2,085	3,715	3,471
1900	8,696	4,115	3,731	4,944
1905	12,488	7,217	5,664	7,325
1910	17,376	9,432	7,138	9,892
1915	19,793	12,316	7,597	11,790
1920	22,267	24,242	8,024	23,267

Source: U.S. Department of Commerce, Bureau of the Census, Historical Statistics of the United States: Colonial Times to 1970, 2 vols. (Washington, D.C.: Government Printing Office, 1975), 2:1025–1031. The series on state banks is not complete.

banks were operating under federal charters. In the long run, however, banks placed additional emphasis on an alternative to currency loans; they extended their own credit in the form of checking accounts. The limits on real estate and securities lending, reserve requirements, and inspection standards to which national banks were subject encouraged renewed growth of state banks. National banks remained somewhat larger on average than state banks.

A New Currency

National bank notes and greenbacks replaced state bank notes as the country's circulating currency. Such notes were uniform currency whose value did not depreciate with the distance from the bank of issue, which made long-distance transactions and regional specialization easier. The waste motion (bargaining over the value of currency in "standard" money) involved in the old heterogeneous

state bank note issues was abolished, but as Chapter 8 indicated, the real significance of this problem had been much less than persons accustomed to modern institutions might imagine.

The supply of the new paper currencies was fixed. As previously noted, the volume of greenbacks in circulation was held constant or reduced, with one minor exception in 1874, and the supply of national bank notes was originally fixed at not over $300 million. Although this ceiling was removed in 1875, the actual supply of national bank notes might not even reach the original legal maximum. The amount of national bank notes in circulation depended on Treasury policy and the loan prospects of national banks as well as the limit on total issue fixed by Congress. To obtain national bank notes, the banks had to buy government bonds and deposit them with the Treasury. As profit-seeking institutions, they would not buy bonds unless their yield, plus

Table 13.2   U.S. Money Stock, 1867–1920
(in Billions)

Year	M2 (Currency plus Deposits)	Monetary Gold	Silver*	Greenbacks	National Bank Notes	Federal Reserve Notes
1867	$1.28	—	$.01	$.319	$.287	
1870	1.35	$.23	.01	.325	.289	
1875	1.72	.09	.02	.350	.341	
1880	2.03	.33	.07	.328	.327	
1885	2.87	.54	.184	.331	.309	
1890	3.92	.64	.408	.335	.182	
1895	4.43	.53	.549	.319	.207	
1900	6.60	.93	.626	.318	.300	
1905	10.24	1.24	.639	.332	.480	
1910	13.34	1.66	.690	.335	.684	
1915	17.59	2.00	.689	.310	.782	$.07
1920	34.80	2.88	.425	.278	.690	3.064

* Includes silver certificates, Treasury notes of 1890, and all silver coinage.
Source: U.S. Department of Commerce, Bureau of the Census, *Historical Statistics of the United States: Colonial Times to 1970,* 2 vols. (Washington, D.C.: Government Printing Office, 1975), 2:992–995.

that on loans made with the currency so obtained, was at least equal to that obtainable on other types of investments.

The Role of Treasury Policy   Treasury policy was important because it influenced the prices of outstanding bonds and hence the rate of interest that could be obtained by purchasing them. If bond prices rose, their interest yield fell; the fixed amount of interest payable was a smaller percentage of their price. If bond prices fell, the rate of return rose.

Through much of this period, the government ran surpluses and used the proceeds to retire Civil War debt. This reduced the supply of bonds and consequently their prices rose. As Table 13.2 indicates, the volume of national bank notes in circulation rose through the early 1870s, and again in the early 1880s, attaining a nineteenth-century peak of $352 million in 1882. It fell to less than half that

amount by the early 1890s. Thereafter, the volume of national bank notes began an increase that ended only when this type of currency was replaced by federal reserve notes after 1915. Changes in regulations in 1882 (reducing required deposits with the Treasury) and 1900 (lower taxes and capital requirements for rural banks, plus an increase in note issues to 100 percent of banks' Treasury deposits) caused first a reduction, then (after 1900) a steady increase in National Bank note circulation.[5] National bank notes had an importance far beyond their value as currency: They were a major component of state banks' reserves. As such, they were an important factor in the growth of the money supply, since banks in aggregate could increase the amount

[5] B. Hetherington, "Bank Entry and the Low Issue of National Bank Notes: A Re-examination," *Journal of Economic History* (September 1990).

of checking accounts they held by a multiple of their reserves.

The Money Supply and the Economy, 1865–1920

As the Civil War experience had shown, a rate of monetary growth that exceeds that of real output, at least for any extended period, will result in inflation unless the demand for money (to hold rather than to spend) also rises. Extreme inflation, as the Confederacy discovered, can result in a collapse of the exchange system, because that institution is built on money as a medium of exchange. Too slow a rate of monetary increase will reduce the pace of real economic growth unless prices are flexible downward (as they were at this time). Even with flexible prices, however, sudden large changes in the money supply or its rate of change can outpace the ability of prices to respond, and produce declines in real output and consequently employment as a first effect. A major study of the events of this era concluded that all major declines in economic activity occurring in the period were associated with prior declines in either the money stock or its rate of growth.[6]

The composition of the money supply, as well as its amount, changed over this period. The data reveal that the proportion of "bank money," or deposits, rose over this period from about 52 percent of the total money supply in 1867 to 67 percent in 1900, 78 percent in 1915, and 79 percent in 1920. The aggregate supply of money rose at a considerably faster long-term rate than that of real output over the entire period. The pace was uneven, with aggregate monetary growth considerably faster after 1897 than before that date. A particularly rapid increase occurred during World War I,

once again because of the demands of wartime finance. Growth was very slow in the mid-1870s and early 1890s, and prices fell sharply in both periods.[7]

The equation of exchange ($MV = PQ$) indicates that increases in the money supply that exceed those of real output must produce inflation. There are physical limits to the available stocks of goods and the ability to increase them at any given time; and velocity tends to be quite stable, varying only in response to private attitudes toward holding money and changes in monetary institutions. However, both the latter variables did change.

Despite increases in the money supply, prices fell from 1865 to 1896, with only one short exception in the 1880s. Velocity must have fallen to produce these results, and it did, to only about 42 percent of its 1869 value by 1915.[8] This rate of decrease in velocity of circulation was sufficient to more than offset increases in the money supply from 1879 through the early 1890s. The decline in velocity resulted from the growing proportion of bank money in the aggregate money supply. Bank deposits earned interest and so were likely to be spent more slowly than currency or coin. There was also growing public confidence that prices would continue to decline in the period before 1896. These factors reduced the costs of holding money, contributing to the decline in velocity. After 1896, faster money-supply growth overcame the decline in velocity, and mild inflation replaced the long post–Civil War deflation.

Gold and the Gold Standard

The achievement of convertibility between paper currency and gold at prewar rates in 1879 did not end the controversy over gold's role in the American monetary system. Even

---

[6] M. Friedman and A. Schwartz, *A Monetary History of the United States, 1867–1960* (Princeton, N.J.: Princeton University Press, 1963).

[7] Friedman and Schwartz, *Monetary History*, 91–92.

[8] Friedman and Schwartz, *Monetary History*, 774.

so, after that date, the United States was on a de facto gold standard. But attaining prewar gold standard convertibility and maintaining it thereafter were neither without cost nor free of conflict. Chapter 8 describes the institution and operation of the international gold standard. At the $20.67 per ounce gold price, the dollar was equivalent to about five French francs, four German marks, and slightly more than one-fifth of a British pound. International gold flows and the consequent effects on bank reserves and domestic money supplies were the mechanism preserving the stability of these exchange rates.

Results of the International Gold Standard

Notice that the gold standard does not assure an absence of inflation or deflation; it merely assures that all nations whose monetary systems operate under gold standard rules will be similarly affected by changes in the supply of gold. After 1895, the world's supply of gold began to increase rapidly because of new mining discoveries in the Yukon, Alaska, and South Africa, and because of more efficient mining and smelting methods. These additions to the gold stock were a major cause of worldwide inflation after 1896.

The operation of the gold standard was complicated by international investment flows. During most years of the nineteenth century, Europeans loaned funds to the United States because interest rates were higher in this country. This allowed a somewhat higher American price level than would otherwise have been possible. The United States was able to accumulate a gold stock to cover temporary outflows because after 1874 it consistently sold more to foreigners than it purchased abroad and because of foreign (largely British) investment in the United States.

Internally, the fact that bank money was convertible into gold constituted a limit on banks' ability to expand the money supply. Banks had to keep a certain fraction of their

assets in gold to meet demands for conversion. Consequently, the degree to which the banking system could expand its loans was limited by the amount of gold it held. There was a demand for gold to finance import purchases that, under normal circumstances, was offset by gold inflows resulting from exports and foreign investment. If people's confidence in banks diminished, they were free to demand conversion of bank money into specie. Banks tried to maintain a safety margin above expected demands for gold by keeping their loans proportional to their reserves. But if confidence in the banks fell, depositors might demand more gold than the banks held.

The 1890s Gold Standard Crisis

In the early 1890s, the gold standard was threatened in the United States. Government policy since 1879 had been to redeem all paper money, including that issued as a result of silver purchases, in gold if the presenter requested it. Such demands increased as a result of the concern generated by the free silver movement (the political demand for unlimited coinage of all silver brought to the mint). The Bland-Allison Act (1878) and the Sherman Silver Purchase Act (1890) required the government to purchase growing amounts of silver, paid for in Silver Certificates and Treasury Notes of 1890, which could be redeemed in gold. Confidence in the government's ability to maintain convertibility fell, and the Treasury's gold stock dwindled. Worse, silver was overpriced at the mint, and it was more profitable to sell silver to the government than in the metals market. A combination of lower tariff revenues and increased government expenditures forced the reissue of silver certificates as fast as they were redeemed. This meant that the certificates would shortly be presented for payment in gold again. Widespread loss of confidence in banks and bank money, especially in the West, added further to the demand for gold.

The more likely the suspension of free convertibility or a political victory for the free

WE STAND FOR

The Gold Standard,

Protection and Prosperity,

Just Pension Laws,

And To Redeem All

REPUBLICAN PLEDGES

To The People.

FOR PRESIDENT — WILLIAM McKINLEY

FOR VICE PRESIDENT — THEODORE ROOSEVELT

■ The Republicans passed the Gold Standard Act in 1900 over the objections of silver supporters.
Source: Library of Congress.

silver forces, the worse the situation became. The depression of the early 1890s made matters even worse. Finally, with the help of J. P. Morgan, the government was able to sell bonds for gold and build up its reserves.[9] Some of the legislation that had generated the increased supplies of government-issued paper currency (the Sherman Silver Purchase Act of 1890) was repealed, and with the end of the depression, the threat to the gold standard was no more.

In 1900, Congress passed the Gold Standard Act, placing the United States on a full monometallic gold standard in law as well as in fact. The dollar was defined solely in terms of gold, and silver's monetary role was ended. But in the two previous decades, the issue of silver's monetary role had been one of America's greatest political controversies.

Silver and the Money Supply

Even before the Civil War, the legal definition of the dollar in terms of both silver and gold

had caused difficulties. Whenever the official "mint" ratio at which the government offered to exchange the two metals differed from the bullion market rates, the mint was deluged with sellers of the metal it overvalued, while that which it undervalued disappeared from circulation (see Chapter 8). In the 1850s, the market ratio of silver to gold had been less than the official 16 to 1 rate, and, consequently, silver coins had almost completely disappeared from circulation. As expensive money, silver was hoarded or used for nonmonetary purposes in which its value was greater than it was as coin.

Civil War inflation drove the price of silver in even subsidiary (less than $1 denomination) coins above their face values, and the few silver coins still in circulation disappeared, to be replaced by fractional paper currency or special ungummed postage stamps. In 1873, when Congress voted to resume coinage of silver, the mint was instructed to buy only the amounts required for the coinage of dimes, quarters, and half-dollars. Silver dollars had not been in circulation since 1836, and they were not included in the new coinage. At the time the new law went almost unnoticed, because silver was still slightly undervalued at the mint. Yet in a few years the coinage act was being denounced as the "Crime of '73."

The Silver Glut

This sudden reversal of attitudes resulted from events in both Europe and the American West. Many European countries abandoned bimetallic or silver standards after 1870 and released large stocks of silver from their bullion reserves. At the same time, silver production in the United States began to soar. The famous Comstock Lode in Nevada contained huge amounts of silver but relatively little gold, and the Comstock Lode was only one of a number of such "strikes." Additional silver discoveries were made in Idaho, Montana, and Colorado. Prior to 1870, the United States had mined at

---

[9] R. Robertson, *History of the American Economy*, 3d. ed. (New York: Harcourt Brace Jovanovich, 1973), 422.

most ten million ounces of silver in any single year. But by 1878, that figure had been tripled, and it doubled again by 1892. Over the same period, gold production declined.[10] Silver prices began to fall after 1875 and plummeted in the early 1890s. By 1875, silver's market value relative to gold was equal to the mint ratio of 16 to 1. It continued to decline, reaching 33 to 1 in 1894.[11]

Silver producers responded to the decline in their product's price by attempting to sell to the one buyer whose offer price had not fallen, the United States Mint. But the mint's response to the flood of silver infuriated would-be sellers; it bought only the amounts of silver actually needed for coinage, which was far short of the quantity silver producers wished to sell. The official price remained at 16 to 1 relative to gold, but at that price, the Treasury was not buying.[12]

The Free Silver Movement

As silver prices in the metals markets declined after 1876, a growing number of bills providing for increased silver purchases were introduced in Congress. These were clear examples of "rent seeking"; the silver producers were requesting that the government, and, through it, the taxpayers, increase their incomes above those obtainable through the sale of their output in the marketplace. The western miners' greatest strength was in the Senate, where their states' sparse populations did not determine representation. When farmers, greenbackers, and labor began to view additional silver coinage as a device to satisfy their demands for an expanded money supply and higher prices, the silver forces gained strength in the House as well. Their ranks included articulate spokes-

men such as Congressman Richard "Silver Dick" Bland of Missouri.

All these groups recognized that if the government purchased unlimited quantities of silver at 16 to 1 relative to gold, large quantities of silver would be brought to the mint. The results would be an end to deflation as the money supply increased and an increase in silver prices. The results desired by free silver's advocates might not have occurred even had their policies been followed. Inflation lowers debt burdens only if it is unanticipated, so that the interest rates on borrowed money do not include an allowance for its decline in purchasing power. If an individual borrows $100 for one year at 5 percent interest and prices are stable, the $105 that must be repaid at the end of the year gives creditors $5 in compensation for borrowers' use of their money over that period, plus a return of the same purchasing power loaned. If prices rise by 10 percent over this year and lenders do not anticipate this inflation, the $105 that borrowers return in 12 months will buy about 5 percent less than the $100 original loan principal. Under such circumstances, debtors gain, because they return less purchasing power than they borrowed. If the inflation is correctly anticipated, however, interest rates will rise to compensate lenders for the deterioration in money's value as well as loss of the use of their funds while they are loaned out.

Since the history of nineteenth-century America provides abundant evidence that, if anything, lenders overestimated the inflationary potential of free silver, it appears doubtful that borrowers would have gained from loans made after the passage of a free silver bill. Only those obligated to repay loans taken out before the passage (or anticipation) of such a bill would benefit. In sum, any gains to debtors from free silver were likely to be temporary.

Inflation raises the prices of all goods and services, not merely those of farm products and labor. To allow farmers and laborers to gain from inflation, the prices of their products

[10] *Historical Statistics*, 1:606.
[11] *Historical Statistics*, 1:606.
[12] M. Friedman, "Bimetallism Revisited," *Journal of Economic Perspectives* (Fall 1990), feels that the difficulties of bimetallism were overstated. However, the article does not appear to take the huge silver supply increases of the era into account.

would have had to rise more than the general rate of increase. Whether this would have occurred depends on relative supply elasticities, which were generally high for farm products before 1900. Moreover, an increase in U.S. farm products' prices would reduce their markets abroad. The large-scale immigration of the period also indicates substantial response to price changes in the labor market. Nevertheless, it is true that industrial output was rising faster than either labor inputs or prices; inflation might have had at least some of the desired effects.

The Silver Purchase Acts

The silver advocates never achieved the "free and unlimited coinage of silver at 16 to 1" that they sought, but they had some partial successes. In 1878, the Bland-Allison Act required the Treasury to purchase between $2 and $4 million worth of silver per month. Though the Treasury accumulated $380 million of silver under this legislation, silver prices continued to fall. Most secretaries of the Treasury limited their purchases to the minimum required by law. It proved difficult to circulate silver dollars; outside the West, people disliked their bulk and weight. After 1886, the Treasury was allowed to issue silver certificates—paper currency backed 100 percent by silver—instead of the coins that were popular only in the West.

As the 1880s ended, deflation had not ceased. (See Table 13.3.) When western senators found themselves holding the balance of power in a key vote on the new McKinley Tariff, legislation that was very important to Senate Republicans, they seized their opportunity. In return for their support on the tariff, the silver forces exacted approval of the Sherman Silver Purchase Act of 1890, which provided for the monthly purchase of 4.5 million ounces of silver by the Treasury at the going price. These purchases were to be made with yet another form of currency, Treasury notes of 1890, which were to be redeemable in either gold or silver.[13]

The new legislation disappointed both its boosters and its opponents. No sooner had it been passed than silver prices began another sharp decline, which reduced the value of Treasury purchases to only about one-third more than those under the Bland-Allison Act. The overall decline in prices continued. Proponents of "sound money" noted the increasing doubts about the United States' ability to maintain the gold standard, and the sudden gold outflows that seemed directly related to political developments. They argued that these declines in monetary reserves produced severe economic distress. The mid-1890s were indeed a period of severe depression.

The two silver-purchase acts combined resulted in the addition of over $500 million to the U.S. money supply. But the goal of free silver was never achieved. In 1892, the Senate passed a bill mandating unlimited silver coinage at 16 to 1, but the House refused to approve it.

The Triumph of the Gold Standard

The election of 1896 marked the high tide of free silver sentiment. The Democrats formed an alliance with the People's Party, or Populists, and the party platform advocated the free coinage of silver at 16 to 1.[14] The campaign can be viewed as a contest between the whole spectrum of values held by the small towns and rural areas against those of the large cities and industry, but these issues tended to be swamped by that of free silver. William Jennings Bryan, the Democratic nominee, made his famous "Cross of Gold" speech, denouncing the deflation caused by the gold standard in accepting the party's standard. Even the Republicans felt compelled to include a proposal for a world conference on the adoption of bi-

---

[13] Robertson, *History of the American Economy*, 422.
[14] Friedman and Schwartz, *Monetary History*, 110.

Table 13.3   Price Indices, 1860–1920 (All Items)

Year	Wholesale Price Index* (1910–1914 = 100)	Consumer Price Index (1967 = 100)
1860	93	27
1865	185	46
1870	135	38
1875	118	33
1880	100	29
1885	85	27
1890	82	27
1890	56.2 (1926 = 100)	—
1895	48.8	25
1896	46.5	25
1900	56.1	25
1905	60.1	27
1910	70.4	28
1915	69.5	30.4
1920	154.4	60.0

*Warren-Pearson Index to 1890, B.L.S. 1890–1920.
Source: U.S. Department of Commerce, Bureau of the Census, *Historical Statistics of the United States: Colonial Times to 1970,* 2 vols. (Washington, D.C.: Government Printing Office, 1975), 1:200, 201, 211.

metallic money in their platform. The election produced all the political fervor—and excesses—of a crusade. Some eastern workers had been told that if Bryan won the election, they need not appear for work because their jobs would no longer exist. William McKinley, the champion of "sound money" and the gold standard, defeated Bryan. The "Boy Orator of the Platte" lost the midwestern agricultural states as well as the East; he carried no state outside the traditionally Democratic South, the Great Plains, and the mining states.

Ironically, the cause for which Bryan campaigned was already becoming a reality, but through the mechanism of cheap gold, rather than silver. Rich gold discoveries in South Africa and the Klondike and the new cyanide process, which greatly increased the amount of metal that could be recovered from a given quantity of ore, poured a stream of gold into the world's coffers. The long deflation ended in 1896. As gold stocks and financial institutions for expanding the money supply based on such reserves grew, the rate of growth of the money supply increased. Moderate inflation, a little over 2 percent annually, replaced deflation.

PRICES AND ECONOMIC STABILITY

From 1860 to 1910, the American economy experienced deflation, inflation, and a boom-and-bust business cycle. (See Table 13.4.) The growth of real output, unemployment rates, and price changes all show considerable variation. Prices, for example, fell sharply just after the Civil War, in the later 1870s, and again from 1890 to 1896 (see Table 13.3). They rose

Table 13.4   Prices, Velocity, and Real Gross National Product, 1860–1920

Year	Consumer Price Level (1967 = 100)	Velocity	Real GNP (1929 Prices, in Millions)
1860	27	—	$7,300
1865	46	—	8,822
1870	38	4.12	11,028
1875	33	3.99	13,568
1880	29	4.97	16,832
1885	27	3.43	20,366
1890	27	2.93	26,196
1895	25	2.71	31,082
1900	25	2.53	38,197
1905	27	2.18	47,870
1910	28	2.20	56,499
1915	30	1.90	60,424
1920	60	2.20	73,313

Sources: Price data from U.S. Department of Commerce, Bureau of the Census, *Bicentennial Statistics* (Washington, D.C.: 1976), 390; Velocity from M. Friedman and A. Schwartz, *A Monetary History of the United States, 1867–1960* (Princeton, N.J.: Princeton University Press, 1963); and GNP from T. Berry, *Revised Annual Estimates of American Gross National Product* (Bostwick Press, 1976), 46.

in 1879–1882 and again after 1896, but the latter inflation, though prolonged, was modest by modern standards. Similar price trends were found throughout the developed world at this time.

In periods of recession or depression, unemployment among manufacturing workers and other urban employees could be high—as much as 8 to 13 percent in the mid-1880s and up to 18 percent in 1894.[15] The 1890s in particular were an era of great distress and substantial labor unrest. The impact of unemployment on those out of work was far worse in the nineteenth century than it is today. Not only were there virtually no programs of public assistance for the unemployed, but the labor force was also comprised of adult heads of families to a far greater extent than is the case presently, when many families contain more than one wage earner and the proportion of single individuals is also much higher. Even though the long-term trends in output, employment, incomes, and well-being were strongly upward, the path was anything but smooth, and increases in welfare were interrupted by periods of great hardship for some workers.

The Real Effects of Money-Supply Changes

In their monumental study, Milton Friedman and Anna J. Schwartz found a close relationship between aggregate economic activity and changes in the money supply.[16] More partic-

---

[15] R. Fogel and S. Engerman, eds., *The Reinterpretation of American Economic History* (New York: Harper & Row, 1971), 79–80.

[16] Friedman and Schwartz, *Monetary History*, 774.

ularly, they tracked changes in the supply of "high-powered" money in relation to the changes in economic activity. When there were gold exports or Treasury retirements of currency or of the bonds that backed national bank notes, the money supply either fell or grew more slowly. Expansion in these items raised the money supply. To some extent, changes in velocity tended to offset the effects of monetary expansion, because the long-run trend in velocity was down; each dollar did less work (was spent less often) as time passed. At least over time, flexible prices offset declines in the money supply, allowing increases in real output even in periods of substantial deflation, such as during the late 1870s. Nevertheless, sharp declines in high-powered money were associated with decreases in real output or its rate of growth. Only after 1896 were the trends in the growth of high-powered money, the ratio of bank reserves to bank money, and velocity sufficient to produce a sustained increase in price levels. Prior to that time, declines in velocity were more than enough to offset monetary growth, which was slightly higher than that of real output.[17] After 1896, a larger portion of the money supply was bank money, which turns over more slowly than hand-to-hand currency. The decline in velocity was also influenced by rising income levels. Income elasticity of money demand was high; people increased their money holdings more than in proportion to increases in income.

INSTITUTIONS AND THEIR EFFECTS ON STABILITY

Although the United States lacked a central bank until the very end of this period, the country was not entirely bereft of institutions with some stabilizing effects on monetary af-

fairs. If existing laws had been interpreted literally, the actions of the U.S. Treasury would have made matters worse. The law required payment of customs duties, the government's chief source of revenue, in gold. At least initially, the government was forbidden to deposit these proceeds in commercial banks. Under such rules, a substantial portion of the country's potential bank reserves might be beyond the banks' reach and would become available again only as the government made expenditures. Even before the Civil War, secretaries of the Treasury had circumvented this requirement by depositing government funds received from other sources with the banks and by prepaying interest and principal on government bonds in times of financial stringency. These techniques were developed and expanded later in the period. In 1911, Congress finally allowed the payment of customs duties by certified checks rather than gold.

Commercial banks themselves also developed some devices to reduce the risk of bank failures inherent in any fractional-reserve banking system. When depositors' demands for currency were high, many banks, particularly in the South, employed clearinghouse certificates, which normally served as evidence of interbank debts, as emergency currency as well as in settlement of their accounts with each other. Banks also made growing use of certified checks drawn on themselves under such circumstances, and a growing variety of other money substitutes— scrip, factory paychecks, and so forth—were devised and utilized by nonbank institutions.[18] Such measures, however, were stopgaps. They could ease banks' difficulties when the demand for currency exceeded their ability to meet it and might prevent bank failures, but they were also an indication that the basic situation had not changed. Further, while such expedients were in circulation, the United

---

[17] Friedman and Schwartz, *Monetary History*, 774.

[18] Friedman and Schwartz, *Monetary History*, 774.

■ This portrait merely hints at the sheer force of intellect and personality that allowed J. P. Morgan to function as a one-man central bank in 1907. *Source:* Library of Congress.

States would have two or more types of "currency" in circulation, with varying exchange rates between them, until the bank emergency was ended. This, of course, resembled the conditions prevailing in the days of state bank notes.

J. P. Morgan: The Banker as Central Bank

Bank failures were still common. In 1907, a particularly disastrous collapse of the New York banks and the stock market appeared imminent. The debacle's origins centered in trust companies, which were linked to the commercial banks through investment banking.[19] The panic threatened a complete collapse of the U.S. monetary system. Catastrophe was averted not by institutions, but by an individual. J. P. Morgan, by sheer force of will and the respect engendered by his vast knowledge of financial matters, was able to pool the resources of the New York banks and the major trust companies to meet runs on the banks and prevent a collapse of stock prices. Morgan assembled the bankers, informed them on successive days how much money was required (on one occasion he demanded $23 million in cash within 20 minutes), and how much each was to contribute. The bankers took their orders, and Morgan distributed the funds to banks in desperate need of cash to satisfy long lines of depositors eager to withdraw their funds. Other institutions he judged beyond saving were allowed to fail.[20] Morgan had done the same thing on a lesser scale several times previously, but he was 70 years old in 1907. No other individual could hope to function as Morgan had in 1907—that is, as a one-man central bank.

The Instability of the Private Banking System

Morgan was a titan, but he was also mortal. Without him the basic weaknesses of American commercial banks remained. Although the banks themselves, and particularly their local and regional clearinghouse associations might devise means of using existing reserves more effectively, bankers had no means of increasing the aggregate volume of reserves in an emergency. The clearinghouse associations developed rules for their members that were designed to reduce the likelihood of trouble.

---

[19] J. Moen and E. Tallman, "Lessons From the Panic of 1907," *Economic Review* (Federal Reserve Bank of Atlanta, May/June 1990).
[20] J. Hughes, *The Vital Few: American Economic Progress and Its Protagonists* (New York: Oxford University Press, 1973), 439–453.

They set capital and reserve requirements, rules for the admission, disciplining, expulsion of members, and regular reports and audits. In times of crisis, loan certificates based on the assets of all banks in any clearinghouse, rather than a single institution, were issued. But such measures merely reduced the risks and were only as sound as the clearinghouses, most of whose members were likely to be affected by any downturn in economic activity in their regions.[21]

The structure of the American banking system contributed to its weakness in emergencies. Far too many American banks were small and tied to a limited range of economic activities in a small region. In part, this was the result of their own efforts to avoid competition; state laws forbade the banks to open branches outside the states in which they were chartered, and many prohibited all branches or sharply restricted them. Often such laws had the enthusiastic support of bankers eager for local monopolies.[22] But such small banks were vulnerable to slumps in the business of their specialized clienteles, and there were no local institutions with more diversified businesses from whom to request emergency aid. Both bankers and their depositors knew that the system was vulnerable to a sudden change in depositors' demand for cash. The system of pyramiding reserves (see Chapter 8) sometimes added to the system's difficulties. News of either a stock market crash or an increase in the bad debts of New York banks was likely to make banks holding their reserves as deposits in New York banks attempt to withdraw them while it was still possible.

Even outflows of funds due to no more than normal seasonal demands of farmers for currency might cause major fluctuations in the securities markets. When withdrawals exceeded normal or expected levels, so-called panics resulted, with stock and bond prices plummeting and call-loan rates reaching extremely high levels. Even though some state governments were beginning to insure bank deposits within their borders, the only sensible reaction to news of a bank run for most people was to attempt to withdraw their own deposits before the bank failed or suspended payments.

The Federal Reserve System

The Panic of 1907 had two major effects: First, it was the last straw for many Americans who had endured a series of bank collapses, suspensions, and the accompanying economic distress; second, J. P. Morgan's rescue operation indicated both that successful responses to such situations were possible, and that the system was under the control of a few individuals or banks. Although there was widespread agreement that a new institution was necessary to prevent further financial collapses, there was equally widespread disagreement over the form it should take and the source of its management. As a stopgap measure, the Aldrich-Vreeland Act of 1909 formally permitted banks to use emergency currencies backed by commercial paper (loans made to businesses), rather than gold, in times of crisis. This legislation also provided minimum requirements for the size of bank associations permitted to form clearinghouse arrangements in panics. It also set standards for the redemption of clearinghouse certificates after the return of normal conditions.[23] More importantly, the act established a National Monetary Commission of 18 congressmen and senators to make recommendations

[21] G. Gorton, "Clearinghouses and the Origins of Central Banking in the United States," *Journal of Economic History* (June 1985).

[22] At least one study concluded that banks failed to obtain monopoly profits. See J. Binder and D. Brown, "Bank Rates of Return and Entry Restrictions, 1869–1914," *Journal of Economic History* (March 1991).

[23] L. Davis, R. Easterlin, W. Parker et al., *American Economic Growth: An Economist's History of the United States* (New York: Harper & Row, 1972), 361.

for a more permanent solution. After prolonged study and debate, the Commission's report formed the basis of the Federal Reserve Act passed in 1913.

Debate over the form that the new institution would take was long and bitter. Both sides wanted a central bank, but agreement ended there. The Democrats and farm interests thought that such an institution should be free of Wall Street control. They wanted a system of regional central banks with control centered in the federal government rather than in the banking community, and a favorable attitude toward expansion of the money supply, if necessary through the issue of fiat money. The bankers and their eastern Republican allies wanted a single central bank largely independent of government control and a gold-based currency.[24] As might be expected, the result was a series of compromises.

The New Institution

The Federal Reserve Act gave the United States a central bank, or, rather, a group of 12 regional central banks. The act provided a new currency—federal reserve notes—that was to be issued by the new banks and backed by gold and commercial paper. This currency was less subject to limits on its total amount than were greenbacks or national bank notes, and it could be increased at the request of commercial banks. Federal reserve notes could be used as reserves by commercial banks, which obtained them by "discounting" their loans, that is, selling them to the Federal Reserve or by borrowing with the loans as security. At long last, the commercial banks had a lender of last resort. Member banks were required to keep their reserves in the Federal Reserve banks. All national banks were required to join the

Federal Reserve System, and state banks were eligible to do so if they could meet the systems's requirements. In practice, nearly all large banks did join. Ownership of the system lay with the member banks, which bought Federal Reserve stock in proportion to their own capital. Banks' returns on their stock were limited to 6 percent, with any additional profits accruing to the Treasury. The system imposed new and stricter standards of conduct, regulation, and inspection upon its members. In addition to its primary duties, the Federal Reserve became the federal government's bank of deposit, and it served as a far more efficient national clearinghouse for checks than anything the country had ever possessed before.

Defining the Fed's Role

The country now had a central bank, but the Federal Reserve's role, the lines of authority within the system, and even its personnel were yet to be determined. If the Federal Reserve Act were to be taken literally, the new central banks's mission was to expand the money supply in response to the "needs of trade." If this were done, the new bank would do little to ensure greater economic stability, because it would fuel the commercial banks' ability to make additional loans even in periods of inflation and do little or nothing to offset depression. In addition, it was not clear which Federal Reserve officials were to make which decisions and where the ultimate source of authority within the system lay. The authorizing legislation went to considerable lengths to minimize the representation of bankers on the boards of the district banks, but it was much less clear about their relations with any central authority. Nominally, the systems's control was vested in the Federal Reserve Board, a seven-member body composed of the Secretary of the Treasury, the Comptroller of the Currency, and five presidential appointees. In practice, the 12 District Federal Reserve Banks had a good deal of autonomy, far more than they do today.

---

[24] R. Johnson, *Historical Beginnings: The Federal Reserve* (Boston: Federal Reserve Bank of Boston, 1977), gives a detailed view of the politics and personalities which figured in the initial establishment of the Federal Reserve Banks.

On-the-Job Training for Central Banks Equally serious was the question of personnel. The Federal Reserve Act and practical politics were both oriented toward reducing the influence of the commercial banking community over the new institution, but the absence of one type of qualification or experience is hardly proof of another. The real problem, however, was that the Federal Reserve System was a new type of institution for the United States, and there were no people with practical experience in the role it was to perform. The tasks and objectives of central banking are quite different from those of commercial banking, but the only people in the United States with banking experience had gained it in commercial and investment banking. Thus, the personnel of an institution whose operations were crucial to the entire economy would have to learn on the job.

Defining the Mission A further difficulty lay in the implementation of monetary control. The purpose of a central bank is to control the money supply, rather than to make profits as commercial banks strive to do. Today, the Federal Reserve has three instruments with which to carry out monetary policy: changes in the reserve requirement (the ratio of reserves to deposits that member banks are required to maintain); open-market operations (the purchase or sale of government bonds to change member banks' reserves); and, finally, rediscount policy (variations in the interest rates charged on loans to member banks). In 1914, only the last was thoroughly understood. Open-market operations were legally possible, but difficult and one-sided until the Fed built up its own portfolio of bonds. Whether the aggregate effects of open-market operations were fully understood even in the 1920s is still a matter of debate among economists.[25] The

Federal Reserve had no authority to vary reserve requirements until 1935. Of the three control instruments, rediscount policy is the least effective.

In summary, the new central bank of the United States had all the powers of such an institution, but it was not staffed by people who understood central banking. There were no clear policy directives for the Fed's officers to follow, and the methods by which the banks' goals were to be accomplished were as unclear as the lines of authority among those responsible for making them.

CHANGES IN FINANCIAL INSTITUTIONS

In 1865, the financial markets of the United States were mainly local. Few lenders would extend credit where they could not literally "keep an eye on it." When capital was transferred between regions, it generally moved with its owners, and much the same was true of transfers between uses. Local businesses, no matter how bright their prospects might be, had to depend on local lenders and their own retained earnings to finance expansion. Rates of interest for similar investments showed large regional variations. Farm mortgage rates might be three times as high on the frontier as they were in the East, where capital markets were better organized. Institutions to marshal savings and make them available to investors were almost entirely geared toward short-term loans.

Such a situation made investment less productive than it might have been. The weakness of American financial markets hardly prevented investment; Americans had accumulated well over a billion dollars' worth of capital prior to 1860, and investment rose as a portion of gross national product. The problem was that allocation of investment funds

---

[25] E. Wicker, *Federal Reserve Monetary Policy, 1917–1933* (New York: Random House, 1969), argues that the Federal Reserve's officials did not understand monetary policy in the 1920s. Friedman and Schwartz, *Monetary History*, do not agree.

was inefficient. Despite high rates of return, projects in new areas where savings were scanty and loan rates high might be starved for funds, while those in the East, even though they might yield far less per dollar invested, had no difficulty obtaining financing because the supply of loanable funds was larger and markets for their allocation within the region better organized.

Gradually, however, these problems diminished. Interest rates in all sections of the country began to fall, becoming similar to those in New York City, the financial center of the nation.[26] Institutions were devised to ease the transfer of financial capital from one region to another. In addition, new areas became sources of interregional capital transfers. The Midwest was supplementing the traditional capital-surplus areas of the Middle Atlantic states and New England as a lender to the West by 1900. Even before that time, it had furnished a substantial market for eastern securities.[27]

Building a Financial System

These developments were aided by better and more current information. This sprang from a variety of sources; accounting and communication standardized the data and facilitated its transfer, and institutions like commercial paper houses specialized in buying short-term loans from bankers in capital-short regions and selling them to banks unable to find local uses for all their funds. The first credit-rating agencies appeared in the 1840s, and by the 1870s they had set up extensive networks that allowed lenders to assess risks in distant markets without travelling to them.[28] Telegraphic and later telephone com-

munication made information more current. These developments made information about investment opportunities cheaper and more accurate than ever before. Their effects were concentrated on short-term credit markets at first; long-term interest rate differentials fell too, but not to the same extent as short-term lending rates.

The interest rate convergence was least apparent in the South, an indication that the region's credit markets were less well developed and integrated into the national market than those of other sections of the country. Since the South was also a capital-deficient area, this is another indication of the sources of its poverty. Not only did the South have more difficulty generating capital internally because of its low incomes, its poorly developed capital markets did a relatively inferior job of attracting capital from other regions.[29] It may have been deficient in allocating the available investment funds as well. At least one study indicates that the South was handicapped by its investors' reluctance to finance anything but long-established types of industry, such as textiles. Thus, not only were the costs of accumulating capital in the South high, but allocation within the region was flawed.[30] Another local study discovered that Knoxville banks found limited opportunities for profitable investment in the local economy, although they were willing to lend there.[31]

Companies specializing in western farm mortgages reduced the risks of such lending for the individual eastern creditor (too much, given the unhappy history of most such firms). Through competition with each other and a

---

[26] L. Davis, "The Investment Market, 1870–1914," *Journal of Economic History* (September 1965).
[27] Davis, "Investment Market."
[28] A. Chandler, Jr., *The Visible Hand: The Managerial Revolution in American Business* (Cambridge, Mass.: Harvard University Press, 1977), 221–222.

[29] Chandler, *Visible Hand*. See also Davis, Easterlin, and Parker, *American Economic Growth*, 328–330.
[30] D. Carlton and P. Coclanis, "Capital Mobilization and Southern Industry, 1880–1905: The Case of the Carolina Piedmont," *Journal of Economic History* (March 1989).
[31] J. Campen and A. Mayhew, "The National Banking System and Southern Economic Growth: Evidence from One Southern City, 1870–1900," *Journal of Economic History* (March 1988).

growing list of other lenders, these firms brought down the rates paid by frontier agriculture. Easier incorporation, as general incorporation laws were enacted in more states, made it less difficult to raise the initial investment required for large-scale firms. Urban mortgage allocation was hindered by eastern investors' reluctance to make loans in rapidly developing western cities before 1900, even though rates there were not subject to the usury laws of some eastern states.[32]

Life insurance companies furnished a new and important source of investment funds. The assets of such firms grew from only $64 million in 1865 to over $5 billion by 1915. Because they sought long-term investments, an area in which American capital markets' deficiencies had previously been greatest, life insurance investments filled a most important gap. They were far better suited to finance investments in transportation or heavy industry, where the sums required might be large and the payoff period very long, than were commercial banks, which were better suited to short-term and highly liquid investments. Savings banks and other similar institutions were also beginning to make an appearance. These and the life insurance companies reflect the income gains experienced by a great many Americans. Members of the middle class were now able to set aside funds for long-term savings. With the exception of rural landholding, where saving was largely due to capital gains, savings had previously been largely restricted to the rich.

The Stock Market

The stock market was greatly extended in terms of the quantity and variety of securities that it handled, even as it became more concentrated in New York City. Even before the Civil War, most large cities had possessed

"stock exchanges"—something of a misnomer because typically these markets dealt almost exclusively in bonds. Stocks of industrial companies were rarely sold, and only the Boston exchange quoted their prices on a regular basis. Even the steel industry's initial capital came largely from individuals who dealt directly with the promoters of firms, such as Andrew Carnegie. Really new industries, such as automobiles, had great difficulty in obtaining financing from established institutional lenders even after 1900. If the auto industry is viewed as it appeared to investors then rather than now—as a new product of highly uncertain prospects requiring both huge amounts of capital for development and production and a long period before returns could be expected—lenders' timidity is easier to understand. The auto industry is said to have centered around Detroit because only there would the banks lend at least some automakers money.

With the extensive marketing of bonds during the Civil War, many Americans had gained familiarity with investments in which the lender had no direct management interest. In the postwar period, this made it easier to sell railroad stocks and bonds, and after 1897, those of industrial corporations as well. Gradually, banks ceased discriminating against industrial securities in making brokers' loans and assessing collateral. By 1914, industrial stocks were fully accepted as high-grade investments.

Investment Banks

Another late-nineteenth-century innovation in American finance was the investment bank. These institutions do not accept deposits and make loans as commercial banks do; their business is the marketing of securities. They buy securities or accept them on consignment from the firms issuing them and sell them to final customers. The investment bank extends the advantages of its knowledge to both the issuing firm and the securities buyers. For the

---

[32] K. Snowden, "Mortgage Lending and American Urbanization, 1880–1890," *Journal of Economic History* (June 1988).

■ Even in 1870, trading on the New York Stock Exchange was frequently heavy.
Source: Brown Brothers.

issuing firm, it sells stock at higher prices or obtains lower interest rates on bond issues than the firm could achieve on its own. It gives customers the benefits of its knowledge of the investment and its prospects, thus reducing their risks. Investment banks played a larger role in America, where commercial banks were small and oriented to local markets, than in Europe, where commercial banks tended to be multibranched national organizations. They may have biased investment toward large industrial firms as well.

In this period, the firm of J. P. Morgan & Co. had no peer among investment banks. Often Morgan provided firms that sought to sell stocks or bonds more than just access to the money market. In return for its services in selling securities, Morgan's firm might assume an active role in the management of the firm. The company's debt structure might be changed, with stock replacing bonds. Ineffective officers might be fired, and high-cost operations discontinued. Especially when the firm was experiencing difficulties, the money might come with one of Mr. Morgan's bright young men, who received a seat on the firm's board of directors to make sure that the money was profitably employed. The new man would report directly to J. P. Morgan, and no firm defied the wishes of the "Napoleon of Wall Street" lightly.

Such practices did more than safeguard investors' funds; they made securities much easier to sell. Once it was known that an ailing firm was being "Morganized," its securities assumed a new value. Not at all incidentally, this also raised the fees J. P. Morgan & Co. could charge for its services. Especially in the railroad industry, with its heavy burdens of debt and seemingly intractable competitive problems, smaller firms might be consolidated into large systems by investment bankers.

The Morgan influence may have led to cooperation among firms that had accepted his direction. There was far less prospect of individual firms' cheating on collusive agreements under circumstances where Morgan and his men were privy to the decisions of all firms. By 1910, Morgan or his associates held seats on over 100 corporate boards.

The "Money Trust" Although the Pujo Committee, a congressional body set up to investigate the "Money Trust" in 1912, did find that there were "common interests" among the members of the financial community, it was not able to establish that competition either among financial intermediaries or the firms they served had been eliminated. This probably reflected the facts. First, by no means did all industrial firms or railroads require the services of investment bankers. Nor were all who did controlled by them. Second, in many cases the bankers' remedies worked; firms regained profitability and with it lost the need for outside financing or direction. Third, J. P. Morgan & Co. was not the only investment banking concern. There were many others, not all in New York. Fourth, in some cases successful industrial firms used their profits to diversify into investment banking: The most prominent example is the Standard Oil Company. On balance, it appears that investment banks did more to mobilize capital and improve operating efficiency for the firms they served than they did to reduce competition among them. As Chapter 12 has shown, if there was a decline in competition during this period, it was slight, and the probability that competition actually increased is at least as great; nor did real interest rates rise.

The Increase in Savings and Investment

The levels of aggregate saving and investment in the American economy increased substantially after the Civil War. The proportion of investment to GNP was the highest ever recorded, between 25 and 30 percent. The reasons why, however, are not completely clear.

Undoubtedly, the improvement and extension of financial intermediaries that channelled savings into productive uses was one factor. Individuals now found that lending their funds was safer and more lucrative on an aggregate basis than it had been, because capital was now allocated more efficiently. At one time, the distribution of income in this period was thought to be so heavily weighted in favor of the rich that savings had to rise. The rich, it was claimed, made so much money that they simply were unable to spend it all. But there is little evidence of a massive shift in income distribution toward greater inequality during this era. If there was an increase in the share of income received by the upper income groups, it was far too small to account for the increase in aggregate savings.

The unprecedented rate of technological change may have been a significant cause of the upsurge in investment. Producers found that they had to continue investing in new equipment or lose their market positions. Since large-scale capital accumulation was a recent phenomenon for the United States, a very large portion of this investment represented net additions to the country's capital stock, rather than the mere replacement of depreciation. Furthermore, the investment was increasingly from domestic sources, and within these, represented firms' use of retained earnings and depreciation reserves, not new securities issues or other external sources. There is no question but that the increase in investment was an important factor in aggregate economic growth; the nation's capital stock rose twice as fast as the labor force, and the new capital was a vehicle for the introduction of technological change. These developments cast further doubt on the claims that the business leaders of the period played no positive role. They made the decisions to reduce the proportion of their own incomes devoted to consumption while raising labor's incomes to levels at which saving was a practical possibility for their employees.

SELECTED REFERENCES

Allen, F. *The Great Pierpont Morgan.* New York: Harper, 1949.

Davis, L., R. Easterlin, W. Parker et al. *American Economic Growth: An Economist's History of the United States.* New York: Harper & Row, 1972.

Friedman, M., and A. Schwartz. *A Monetary History of the United States, 1867–1960.* Princeton, N.J.: Princeton University Press, 1963.

Hughes, J. *The Vital Few: American Economic Progress and Its Protagonists.* New York: Oxford University Press, 1973.

James, J. *Money and Capital Markets in Postbellum America.* Princeton, N.J.: Princeton University Press, 1978.

Johnson, R. *Historical Beginnings: The Federal Reserve.* Boston: Federal Reserve Bank of Boston, 1977.

Kroos, H., and M. Blyn. *A History of Financial Intermediaries.* New York: Philadelphia Bank Company, 1971.

Kuznets, S. *Capital in the American Economy: Its Formation and Financing.* Princeton, N.J.: Princeton University Press, 1961.

Myers, M. *The New York Money Market.* New York: Columbia University Press, 1931.

Sylla, R. *The American Capital Market, 1846–1914: A Study of the Effects of Public Policy on Economic Development.* New York: Arno Press, 1975.

Timberlake, R. *The Origins of Central Banking in the United States.* Cambridge, Mass.: Harvard University Press, 1978.

U.S. Department of Commerce, Bureau of the Census. *Historical Statistics of the United States: Colonial Times to 1970.* 2 vols. Washington, D.C.: Government Printing Office, 1975.

West, R. *Banking Reform and the Federal Reserve, 1863–1923.* Ithaca: Cornell University Press, 1977.

Williamson, J. *Financial Intermediation, Capital Immobilities and Economic Growth in Late Nineteenth Century American Development: A General Equilibrium History.* Cambridge, U.K.: Cambridge University Press, 1974.

LABOR, UNIONS, AND THE STANDARD OF LIVING, 1865–1920

*N*early all dimensions of the American economy increased in this era of growth, and the labor force was no exception. The adult work force more than tripled, rising from 12,506,000 people in 1870 to 41,614,000 in 1920. These figures give a slightly overstated view of labor force growth. They include only those workers over 15 years old; the proportion of child labor was higher in 1870 than it was in 1920.[1]

CHANGING WORK FORCE DEMOGRAPHICS

Despite the decline in child labor, the proportion of the population available for work outside the home rose. Falling birth rates, longer lives, and heavy immigration raised the ratio of adults to the total population. Labor force participation rate for women rose by about 25 percent, from 18.9 to 25.4 percent of adult women over the 1890–1910 period.[2] By 1920, about one adult woman in five was employed outside the home, although the proportion was much higher for single women than for those already married.[3]

Other characteristics of the work force also changed. There was a substantial accumulation of labor skills. This is difficult to quantify, but workers gained useful expertise in the increasing variety of new jobs that appeared in this era, even after allowance is made for the obsolescence of skills made redundant by new methods and products. The amount of formal education possessed by the average American worker increased, but on-the-job training contributed at least as much to the growth in skills, and that quality change has yet to be measured.

Evidence on the massive redistribution of the labor force is much clearer. The period began with most American workers engaged in agriculture, and it ended with an even greater preponderance of employment in manufacturing, trade, and other urban occupations (see Table 14.2). By 1920, agricultural employment had begun to fall in absolute as well as relative terms. Labor growth trends reflected those in industries; manufacturing and construction employment grew rapidly in the early decades after the Civil War, but as the growth rate of these sectors slowed, public utilities, transportation, trade, education, and government employment furnished a growing portion of new jobs.[4] Mobility between agricultural and industrial jobs was apparently little different from that in contemporary Europe, although the gap between industrial and rural standards of living may have been smaller in the United States.[5]

There were geographic shifts in the labor force as well. While New England and the Middle Atlantic states retained more than proportionate shares of manufacturing jobs, their traditional predominance was declining. The states bordering the Great Lakes and the Ohio River combined rapid urbanization and a large share of the newer, more rapidly expanding types of industry and consequently achieved a growing share of industrial employment. The Great Plains states were largely

---

[1] U.S. Department of Commerce, Bureau of the Census, *Historical Statistics of the United States: Colonial Times to 1970*, 2 vols. (Washington, D.C.: Government Printing Office, 1975), 1:129.

[2] *Historical Statistics*, 1:133.

[3] *Historical Statistics*, 1:133.

[4] *Historical Statistics*, 1:133.

[5] See T. Hatton and J. Williamson "Integrated and Segmented Labor Markets: Thinking in Two Sectors," and J. Rosenbloom, "Occupational Differences in Labor Market Integration: The United States in 1890," both *Journal of Economic History* (June 1991), and Rosenbloom, "One Market or Many? Labor Market Integration in the Late Nineteenth-Century United States," *Journal of Economic History* (March 1990).

unsettled in 1865, and their new populations concentrated on agriculture; they grew rapidly until the land was settled, then saw their growth rates slow. The South, with its high birth rates and limited opportunities outside a not very productive agricultural sector, experienced persistent outmigration after 1900.

Overall, these changes in labor allocation were along the lines predicted by economic theory. Labor moved from areas and occupations where wages and incomes were low to those where they were high.[6] Movement from areas where labor was relatively abundant to those where it was particularly scarce also occurred. Labor movements were slow, however, and affected by many factors in addition to wage disparities.[7]

The Black Labor Force

After 1900, southern blacks began to migrate from the farms where they had been employed since the war to northern cities. It may appear strange that black interregional migration required a generation or more after emancipation. The most coherent explanation is that for ex-slaves, both money incomes and amenities had improved very considerably within the South when freedom was attained. There

was migration from 1865 to 1900, but chiefly within the South. Large-scale movement to the North began only when a generation with no personal memories of slavery appeared, educational disparities had been reduced, and a pool of previous migrants became sizable enough to ease adjustment costs for their peers. Wages for low-skilled workers rose rapidly in northern cities after 1900, increasing the economic "pull" of northern cities.[8] This movement became especially pronounced after World War I raised the demand for labor while shutting off immigration. The greater freedom, civil rights, and personal dignity available through migration carried more weight for blacks than did noneconomic motives for other migrants. Despite this, the black migration was primarily a search for economic betterment; it was greatest from those southern regions where incomes were especially low.[9] In addition, it was directed toward the highest-wage jobs open to blacks. Blacks' restricted access to education hampered relocation to the North, just as it had been so within the South.[10]

Female and Child Labor

A growing proportion of women began to work outside the home. Both demand and supply changes were factors in this trend. The rapid expansion of job opportunities in trade, the mechanization of manufacturing, and changing social attitudes resulted in larger numbers of jobs in which women's performance was equal or superior to men's. Particularly after 1900, new jobs required

[6] For evidence from a primarily agricultural community, see J. Kearl and C. Pope, "Choices, Rents and Luck: Economic Mobility of Nineteenth-Century Utah Households," in R. Gallman and S. Engerman, eds., *Long-Term Factors in American Economic Growth* (Chicago: University of Chicago Press, 1986). Rosenbloom, "Labor Market Integration," stresses the importance of changes in demand for labor, which often appeared greater than the supply responses.

[7] L. Galloway and R. Vedder, "The Mobility of Native Americans," *Journal of Economic History* (September 1971). Labor mobility, especially that of blacks, may have been lower in the South. See G. Wright, *Old South, New South: Revolutions in the Southern Economy Since the Civil War* (New York: Basic Books, 1986), and J. Donohue, III and J. Heckman, "Continuous versus Episodic Change: The Impact of Civil Rights Policy on the Economic Status of Blacks," *Journal of Economic Perspectives* (December 1991).

[8] P. Graves, R. Sexton, and R. Vedder, "Slavery, Amenities, and Factor Price Equalization: A Note on Migration and Freedom," *Explorations in Economic History* (April 1983).

[9] L. Davis, R. Easterlin, W. Parker et. al., *American Economic Growth: An Economist's History of the United States* (New York: Harper & Row, 1972), 215.

[10] R. Margo, *Race and Schooling in the South, 1880–1950* (Chicago: University of Chicago Press, 1990), Chap. 7.

■ By 1900, women, particularly those in urban areas, were joining the work force, attracted by new clerical and sales jobs that required an education rather than physical strength.
Source: Records of the Public Buildings Service: National Archives.

education rather than muscle and thus gave women a comparative advantage. From 1890 to 1930, the dominant influence on female employment was the increase in labor supply. So great was the response that clerical employment expanded faster than demand, and its traditional wage premium decreased.[11]

Urbanization reinforced a shift toward smaller families and later marriages. Even so, as late as 1920, marriage spelled the end of outside employment for most women. In that year, about half of all single women were gainfully employed, in comparison to only one-tenth of their married sisters.[12] After 1900, women entering the labor market tended to be better educated than their predecessors, improving their access to clerical work.[13]

Labor force participation by women produced greater freedom and wider experience as well as income. Child labor was less ben-

[11] C. Goldin, *Understanding the Gender Gap: An Economic History of American Women* (New York: Oxford University Press, 1990), 106–107.

[12] *Historical Statistics,* 1:133.
[13] Goldin, *Understanding the Gender Gap,* 106–107.

■ Child laborers demanded more than wages, as this photo indicates.
Source: Picture Collection, The Branch Libraries, The New York Public Library.

eficial. This institution did not begin with industrialization. Farmers have long regarded their offspring as supplements to their own labor. Industrial work for children could have some different characteristics from that in agriculture. On the farm, children were working under their parents' supervision, but in factories they might be directed by people who had little or no personal interest in their welfare, and their conditions of work were seldom open to inspection by their parents. Nevertheless, it appears that child labor was by no means the norm, and most children who were in the labor force worked with their parents on farms or in small businesses. Even in these cases, the incidence of child labor in the United States was far less than it was in Europe.[14]

Where it existed, child labor could generate conditions intolerable by modern standards. The work forces of some industries in which skill requirements were low sometimes included children no older than six. The numbers of children in the work force increased to a peak of about two million employed youngsters between the ages of 10 and 15 in 1910. This was 18 percent of all children in this age group and about 5 percent of the total work force.[15] After this date, the incidence of child labor declined rapidly under the combined pressures of growing incomes (which rendered children's contributions less necessary), compulsory school attendance laws, and restrictions on child labor itself. The major force behind the new attitudes was the growth in

[14] S. Lebergott, *The Americans: An Economic Record* (New York: Norton, 1984), 369–370.

[15] G. Walton and R. Robertson, *Growth of the American Economy*, 4th ed. (New York: Harcourt Brace Jovanovich, 1979), 324.

incomes that occurred in this period. People began to believe that the economy could now afford to sacrifice the output achieved through such an offensive practice, especially if children's lifetime earnings were likely to be higher if their formative years were spent in school. Much of the opposition to legal restrictions on child labor came from parents who bore the direct burden of such changes. By 1920, many states had laws setting maximum hours and minimum wages for women. Wages and hours for adult men, however, were still determined in a marketplace where employers' bargaining positions were strong.

PRODUCTIVITY, WAGES, AND HOURS

Although productivity increases contributed more to economic growth in this period than they had at any time in the past, most of the increase in total production originated, as previously, in increases in the quantity of inputs. Still, for the period 1889–1913, real output per unit of input grew at 1.3 percent annually, about one-third of total growth over that time. Labor productivity increased three to four times as fast as capital productivity.[16] Caution should be used in drawing conclusions from this, however, because the productivity of any input is partially determined by the amounts of other resources with which it works. In the late nineteenth and early twentieth centuries, the supply of capital grew much faster than that of labor. This is another way of saying that the quantity of tools available to the average worker rose; their quality improved as

well, and the supply of high-quality raw materials also increased. Workers' output increased in part because they had more and better tools at their disposal. When productivity rises, resources become more valuable to employers, and their prices rise.

Real Wages

The evidence on real wage trends over the 1860–1920 period bears out this reasoning. For the period as a whole, real wages of nonfarm employees increased, even after allowance is made for the effects of unemployment. From 1865 to 1920, real wages slightly more than doubled.[17] The pace of real wage gains almost exactly matched that of productivity, which is no surprise. Barring some major shift in the compensation of nonhuman resources, workers' real incomes cannot increase faster than their output. If the base year of Table 14.1 is taken as 1860 rather than 1865, the growth in real wages is considerably less, about 47 percent. However, two factors cause this increase to be understated. First, the 1920 figures allow for the effects of unemployment, and those before 1900 do not, even though in some years of the nineteenth century there was substantial joblessness. Second, the higher 1920 wages were earned in a shorter work week, but the later income figures include no allowance for the increase in leisure time, although it represents an addition to workers' well-being. Finally, Table 14.1 includes only nonfarm incomes. These were considerably higher than farm incomes, at least in money terms, and over 1860–1920, the proportion of farm to nonfarm workers greatly diminished.

[16] J. Kendrick, *Productivity Trends in the United States* (Princeton, N.J.: Princeton University Press, 1961), 60. The higher figure is from R. Gallman, "The United States Capital Stock in the Nineteenth Century," in Gallman and Engerman, *Long-Term Factors*, 190.

[17] C. Long, *Wages and Earnings in the United States, 1860–1890* (Princeton, N.J.: Princeton University Press, 1960), 109–118. See also A. Rees, *Real Wages in Manufacturing, 1890–1914* (Princeton, N.J.: Princeton University Press, 1961), 3–5.

Table 14.1   Real and Money Wage Trends, 1860–1920

Year	Money Earnings per Year**	Real Earnings*	Loss from Unemployment**	Real Earnings after Loss from Unemployment*
1860	$363	$457	—	—
1865	512	328	—	—
1870	489	375	—	—
1875	423	403	—	—
1880	388	395	—	—
1885	446	492	—	—
1890	475	519	—	—
1895	438	520	—	—
1900	483	573	$42	$523
1905	550	621	35	582
1910	634	669	58	608
1915	692	684	93	591
1920	1,426	714	104	672

* 1914 dollars.
** Current dollars.
Source: S. Lebergott, *Manpower in Economic Growth: The American Record Since 1800* (New York: McGraw-Hill, 1964), 524–528.
Reprinted in Davis, Easterlin, and Parker et al., *American Economic Growth*, 212–213.

Another noteworthy feature of Table 14.1 is the great short-run variation in incomes. These reflect the violent gyrations of the American business cycle. Simple money income figures are an especially misleading gauge of welfare during this period. Although money incomes declined over 1865–1879, the price level fell even faster, and deflation continued until 1896. Thus, in some years real wages rose even though nominal wages fell. On the other side of the coin, although money wages more than doubled from 1915 through 1920, real wages increased by a scant 14 percent because World War I generated rapid inflation. Finally, the figures are averages for all workers and do not reflect changes in the relative earnings of skilled and unskilled workers. The data indicate that the gap between skilled and unskilled workers' incomes grew

for most of the period, then declined rapidly during World War I.[18] Wages may have been flexible over long periods, but a recent study found that Ohio manufacturing workers' money wages fell very little in the depressions of 1893 and 1908: Decreased demand for labor resulted in layoffs and reductions in hours worked.[19]

The overall picture, then, is one of substantial increases in the purchasing power of the average worker's wages over 1860–1920. But the dimensions of the increase are quite

[18] P. Lindert and J. Williamson, "Three Centuries of American Inequality," in P. Uselding, ed., *Research in Economic History* (Greenwich, Conn.: JAI Press, 1976), 64.
[19] W. Sundstrom, "Was There a Golden Age of Flexible Wages? Evidence From Ohio Manufacturing, 1892–1910," *Journal of Economic History* (June 1990).

sensitive to the choice of base and terminal years. Prices in 1914 dollars were about one-fifteenth their 1990 level, so the average non-farm wage around the start of World War I would be equivalent to about $10,300 in modern real income. These trends are averages, and there were wide variations in wages between occupations and regions of the country, and sometimes even between similar jobs in the same town. Although these disparities had diminished by the end of the period, that process apparently began only after 1900.[20] Wage variations in 1920 were still much greater than is the case today.

Shorter Work Hours

Workers also gained from a reduction in the number of hours worked per day or per week over the 1865–1920 period. These gains may appear greater than they really were because of the shift from farm to nonfarm labor. Although farm labor worked extremely long hours at planting and harvest seasons, it enjoyed substantial decreases in hours at other times, particularly winter. Factory and other urban jobs offered a more regular pace of work and more hours of employment per year. In 1860, the average manufacturing work week was about 65 hours over 6 days. By 1880, the work day averaged 10 hours, and by 1920 it was 9, with a half-day on Saturday, and the weekend began to mean something more than Saturday night and Sunday.

Some skilled or privileged workers had shorter hours than these. Construction craftsmen generally worked about an hour less per day than was customary in manufacturing, and miners were more successful in obtaining shorter hours than were most other workers. Federal government employees had a 48-hour work week throughout the period. There were also less fortunate workers. Because continu-

ous operations were more fuel-efficient, steelworkers put in 12 hours a day, 7 days a week, which meant a 24-hour shift at the end of each week or whenever the shifts changed—a pace that required continual recruitment of new unskilled, mainly immigrant, labor.[21] In some "sweated" industries, the hours of labor were limited mainly by workers' physical endurance. In general, the greatest gains in workweek reductions came after 1890.

Unemployment

American workers had made considerable progress in terms of wages and hours, but the transition from farm to urban occupations imposed new costs. For the farmer, bad times meant poor crops, low prices, or both, which caused income reductions. But unless there were additional circumstances, such as a mortgage falling due simultaneously, there was no loss of livelihood. For the industrial worker, bad times could mean lower pay or shorter hours—or the loss of a job. In the conditions of this period, unemployment meant a total loss of income. As employment patterns changed (see Table 14.2), a growing portion of American workers became vulnerable to layoffs. Unemployment was more than a remote threat: Depressions were tragically frequent over the years from 1865 to 1900. There was a substantial amount of unemployment from 1873 to 1879, and from 1893 to 1898 the nation endured continuous unemployment rates of 11 percent or more, with a peak of 18.4 percent in 1894.[22]

These figures understate the impact of unemployment on industrial workers; they indicate the portion of the entire labor force

---

[20] Rosenbloom, "Labor Market Integration."

[21] M. Shiells, "Collective Choice of Working Conditions: Hours in British and U.S. Iron and Steel, 1890–1923," *Journal of Economic History* (June 1990).

[22] S. Lebergott, *Manpower in Economic Growth: The American Record Since 1800* (New York: McGraw-Hill, 1964), 164–190.

Table 14.2   Occupational Distribution of U.S. Labor, 1860–1920

Year	Agriculture, Forestry, and Fishing	Mining	Manufacturing and Construction	Trade, Transport, and Finance	Service	Total*
1860**	59.0%	1.6%	18.3%	7.4%	13.2%	99.5%
1870	50.4	1.5	23.2	11.4	13.6	100.1
1880	50.1	1.8	23.0	12.0	13.2	100.1
1890	42.8	2.0	26.1	14.8	14.2	99.9
1900	37.6	2.6	27.5	16.7	15.6	100.0
1910	31.6	2.9	28.7	19.3	17.6	100.1
1920	27.4	3.0	31.4	21.7	16.5	100.0

* Totals may not add to 100.0 percent because of rounding.
** Data not strictly comparable with later years.
Source: Calculated from U.S. Department of Commerce, Bureau of the Census, Historical Statistics of the United States: Colonial Times to 1970, 2 vols. (Washington, D.C.: Government Printing Office, 1975), 1:138.

without jobs. A large percentage of the work force was still employed in agriculture, where unemployment had little effect. Thus, rates of joblessness among urban workers were much higher than these figures indicate. In periods of high unemployment, many of those who retained their jobs had only part-time work and reduced wages. Labor turnover in some but not all manufacturing was very high by modern standards,[23] so the figures may not represent long-term suffering for all those affected. After 1900, unemployment became less severe, but even in the "good years" from 1900 to 1914, rates varied from 1.7 to 8 percent, and averaged over 4 percent for the period. The lower figure would indicate about the absolute minimum rate of unemployment achievable in a market economy under early twentieth-century conditions. These rates vary with social institutions (in our period, unemployment compensation and welfare assistance), demographics (work forces with high proportions of new jobseekers and second earners have higher rates), rates of technological change, and social attitudes, all of which seem to have raised the "normal" or "frictional" unemployment rate in the 1970s and 1980s. However, very high rates of unemployment are an indication that, at least temporarily, there are more unemployed workers than vacancies, and those out of work may experience great difficulty in finding any sort of job, particularly in the hardest-hit regions. Other factors affect the impact of unemployment as well. Few workers had substantial amounts of savings to tide them over a jobless spell in this era.

Work Conditions

Other problems facing labor were industrial accidents and diseases. In many industries, particularly commercial fishing, mining, railroading, and steel, accident rates were very high. Men who were new to industrial work labored long hours near machinery designed with little or no concern for safety; some of

[23] S. Carter and E. Savoca, "Labor Mobility and Lengthy Jobs in Nineteenth-Century America," *Journal of Economic History* (March 1990).

them worked under conditions that no modern worker, let alone private or governmental safety inspectors, would tolerate today. Noise, heat, and lighting deficiencies were the most obvious difficulties, but at least these were partially recognized as problems. Other sources of illness and premature death were not even known. Medical research was in its infancy and had not yet focused on the long-range effects of exposure to dust, soot, noise, and fumes from a variety of chemicals. We have little information about the incidence of job-related disease, but it must have been high. Where the causes of disease were unknown, there was little hope of instituting successful preventive measures.

The Legal Climate and Job Safety

Those suffering injury on the job could expect little or no compensation. A few employers might give small payments to accident victims or their families, but they were under no legal obligation to do so. Without accurate information on the incidence and causes of occupationally related diseases, insurance protection could not even be offered. The law offered job-related-accident victims little relief. If an injured worker hired a lawyer and sued, his employer had several lines of defense. If the employer could show that the worker had been aware of the hazards of the job when hired, or that his injuries were due to the actions of other workers, the plaintiff could not collect

■ The members of this rough-hewn, Massachusetts construction crew exhibited the hardiness required of typical wage-earning males around 1900.
Source: Courtesy of Edith LaFrancis and The Ashfield Historical Society.

damages. In cases of industrial illnesses, there seldom were methods of tracing the disease back to the job, and even if these existed, the employer could use the same defenses as in accident cases. Pensions were rare, so old age was feared as a time in which people who could no longer work would be dependent on others for support.

The Supreme Court repeatedly struck down statutes and reversed lower court decisions that attempted to ameliorate these problems. In particular, it voided state laws establishing employers' responsibilities for industrial accidents and took an extremely one-sided view of virtually all contracts of employment. Shortly before World War I, there were a few signs of change. After 1908, railroad workers were covered by a law that allowed them to collect payments for injuries suffered on the job, voiding the fellow-servant and contributory negligence defenses against such claims that employers had traditionally used. Full-fledged workmen's compensation laws were enacted two or three years later.[24] From 1914 on, a growing number of states passed such laws in forms the courts would accept. In addition, safety procedures began to be devised and enforced by both legal authorities and by employers themselves. Employers discovered that it might be cheaper to prevent accidents than to pay compensation to victims or, at least in the case of skilled workers, endure the loss in output that resulted from their absence.

Increases in safety that have costs are not unquestionable improvements in welfare. Only if the marginal benefits of improved safety exceed the costs of providing them does aggregate well-being increase. It is possible that the benefits from improved safety might be worth less than the costs imposed on employers, consumers, and the workers themselves. For example, a change in work rules that reduced paper cuts received by bank tellers while handling checks at the cost of doubling depositors' service charges might be a substantial cost for a trivial gain in safety. However, while such considerations may have validity today, they were much less germane in the high- (and serious-) accident work environment of the nineteenth and early twentieth centuries, particularly when the absence of accurate information about the risks involved in different occupations is taken into account. When moves for increased workplace safety began, the possibility of benefits that exceeded the costs of providing them was great. Even so, intentions did not always produce results. Initial federal and state efforts to improve coal mining safety were ineffective at best.[25]

IMMIGRATION

America has been a nation of immigrants (voluntary and involuntary)—or their children—from the first European settlements, but the latter half of the nineteenth century and the first decade and a half of the twentieth century saw an unprecedented volume of immigration to the United States. From 1865 to 1920, over 28 million people entered the United States, a number nearly equal to the nation's entire population just prior to the Civil War. Immigration had slowed during that conflict, but it soon increased again, reaching the levels of the peak years of the 1850s by 1873. Then it declined again as America endured the depression of the 1870s. From 1880 on, the volume of immigration rose to unprecedented levels, peaking in the decade from 1905 to 1914, when over a million persons per year entered the United States.

---

[24] My thanks to Professor Fishback for this information.

[25] P. Fishback, "Workplace Safety During the Progressive Era: Fatal Accidents in Bituminous Coal Mining, 1912–1923," *Explorations in Economic History* (July 1986).

The "New Immigrants"

As the volume of immigration rose, the origins of the immigrants began to change. The influx of northern Europeans—Scandinavians, British, Irish, and Germans—who made up the bulk of new arrivals before 1890 declined relative to that from southern and eastern Europe—Italians, Poles, Russians, and other Slavic groups, who came in still greater numbers. In addition, there were immigrants from Canada, the West Indies, and even from Asia: from China before 1882, and from Japan.[26] The new arrivals' religions, languages, and customs differed more dramatically from those of the United States than had those of earlier immigrants. A much smaller proportion spoke English, and the percentage of those literate in any language was lower than it had been among the "old immigrants," with the possible exception of the Irish. The portion of skilled and professional workers may also have been lower, though the official statistics may understate the human capital possessed by the immigrants. In religion, the "new immigrants" were heavily Roman Catholic, with substantial numbers of Jews and Orthodox Christians.

Motives for Migration

The data make it clear that the primary motive for voluntary immigration had not changed. The chief attraction of the United States was the hope for a better material standard of life than the immigrants had known in their native lands. Eastern and southern Europe furnished their inhabitants with abundant reasons to seek betterment or even survival elsewhere: poverty, tyrannical governments, social structures that restricted opportunity for the talented and ambitious, population pressures on the land, and ancient conflicts and hatreds were all common. For the Russian Jews, such pressures were particularly acute. Religious persecution and a government that made them scapegoats for all the real and imagined evils that flourished in Czarist Russia gave them little reason to stay in their ancestral lands.

Despite these "push" factors, the "pull" of the United States was more influential in the Atlantic migration. In this era of low steamship fares and minimal restrictions on travel between nations, emigrants from Europe could literally have gone anywhere on earth. Yet in overwhelming numbers they chose the United States. Even more significantly, immigration to America is strongly correlated with periods of high demand for labor in the United States economy, much more so than with events in the countries from which the immigrants came.[27] Immigrants came to America in periods of full employment and rising wages, rather than in response to wars, famines, or political repression in Europe. They were strongly attracted to cities where wages were high,[28] and they came in huge numbers. From 1890 to 1914, almost 15 percent of the American population had been born abroad, the highest such rate since the colonial era, though only a 10 percent increase over the percentage of foreign-born in 1860. Immigration and international capital flows are strongly correlated, although the direction of causation is now in some dispute.[29]

---

[26] *Historical Statistics,* 1:107–108.

[27] R. Easterlin, "Influences in European Overseas Migration Before World War One," *Economic Development and Cultural Change* (April 1961). See also B. Thomas, *Migration and Economic Growth* (Cambridge, U.K.: Cambridge University Press, 1953).

[28] Rosenbloom, "Occupational Differences."

[29] Thomas, *Migration,* found that European, especially English, capital followed migration to the United States S. Fenoaltea, "International Resource Flows and Construction Movements in the Atlantic Economy: The Kuznets Cycle in Italy, 1861–1913," *Journal of Economic History* (September 1988) concluded that at least in Italy, foreign investment and consequent construction activity attracted immigration.

■ Ellis Island, New York: the immigrants' gateway to the United States.
Source: Photograph by Burt G. Phillips, Museum of the City of New York.

Immigrants' Regional and Occupational Distribution in the United States

The new Americans may have come largely from rural backgrounds, but they settled mainly in the cities of the East and Midwest. Most immigrants found jobs in mining and manufacturing. They comprised more than half the work force in copper and iron mining, clothing factories, and steel, and held about one-fifth of all jobs in American industry by 1910. Immigrants comprised 34.5 percent of all mining employees, and 25.1 percent of those in manufacturing. In agriculture, the professions, and clerical work, they were less well represented. Even so, the picture of all immigrants as unskilled peasants or laborers is incorrect. A sizable portion obtained skilled jobs in industry or were craftsmen of every variety imaginable. Others became or were foremen. In the professions, such as chemistry, engineering, designing, and medicine, the immigrants' representation was roughly proportional to their share of the population.[30] One study has concluded that the value of the human capital that the immigrants brought may have exceeded European direct investment in the United States.[31] Since immigrants

[30] A. Niemi, *U.S. Economic History: A Survey of the Major Issues* (Skokie, Ill.: Rand McNally, 1975), 217–219.
[31] L. Neal and P. Uselding, "Immigration: A Neglected Source of U.S. Economic Growth, 1790–1913," *Oxford Economic Papers* (March 1972).

tended to be disproportionately male and in the prime of working life, their labor force participation rates were very high. As might be expected of an urban population with low incomes, so too were those for immigrants' children.

Immigrants had come to America seeking a better life and prepared to work to achieve it. However, most accounts of immigrant life at this time paint a grim picture of desperate poverty in fetid, disease-ridden slums, with entire families working long hours for wages that barely permitted survival. Writers like Jacob Riis found situations in the New York slums comparable to those in Calcutta.

Prejudice and Exploitation

The efforts and ambitions of immigrants were not admired by native Americans, and, in some cases, were even more fervently derided by those who themselves had once been immigrants. Their speech, dress, religions, customs, and poverty were objects of scorn and ridicule. Such views were not merely the unlovely if understandable reactions of those forced to compete with immigrants for jobs and housing; they extended to American intellectuals and business leaders, too.

There were blatant attempts to take advantage of immigrants' handicaps in obtaining information about jobs, wage levels, working conditions, and the means of redressing wrongs available to those who understood American political and legal systems. Immigrants might be met on the docks by agents of some manufacturer or mine owner, offering jobs that the new arrivals had no means of evaluating against American alternatives. Once hired, the immigrants might find themselves in some isolated company town where the employer controlled housing, stores, and the police in addition to jobs, and took advantage of all aspects of these monopolies. Even if they lived in large cities, language barriers and long hours of work might make it very difficult for immigrants to obtain infor-

mation about job markets or consumer alternatives. If any of them truly expected to find America's streets paved with gold, discovering that those in their slum were not paved at all must have been the least of the immigrants' disappointments.

All these things and more happened to some immigrants. In the case of illegal aliens, many of them still do. Even so, there is massive evidence that immigrants' conditions of life in America were very different from their point of view than they appeared to observers whose standards were those of middle- and upper-class America. The conditions under which immigrants lived, bad as some of them may have been, have to be compared to those left behind in Sicily or Russia. Immigrants continued to come in increasing numbers. Significantly, the flow increased as letters from friends and relatives in America told those in the "Old Country" that conditions were much better than those of Poland, Sicily, Russia, or Japan.[32] People who had found American life superior urged those left behind to join them. Often they were able to give more than advice: They financed the voyage, or assisted in obtaining jobs and housing in America. In 1909, 90 percent of the immigrants passing through Ellis Island had prepurchased railroad tickets to their ultimate destinations within this country.[33]

If recent immigrants used their money to bring their families and friends to America, it is clear that those already here could have returned to Europe had they chosen. But as in earlier waves of immigration, the flow was heavily toward the United States. About one-third of the immigrants did eventually return to their homelands. Some had failed to find

---

[32] Y. Muryama, "Information and Emigrants: Interprefectural Differences of Japanese Emigration to the Pacific Northwest, 1880–1915," *Journal of Economic History* (March 1991).

[33] R. Vedder, *The American Economy in Historical Perspective* (Belmont, Calif.: Wadsworth Publishing Co., 1976), 131.

opportunity here, and others found the cultural differences or separation from old acquaintances too much. Still others returned as rich men by the standards of Italy or the Balkans. In light of their decisions, then, the behavior of most immigrants indicates clearly that they had found what they sought in America.

Immigrants suffered social and religious discrimination. Upon arrival, each new group was labeled "dirty," "criminal," and "ignorant," and other even less complimentary terms. The Chinese, especially on the West Coast, were frequent victims of blatant racism. Not only were they subject to mob violence, but barriers to the ownership of property were imposed on them. In 1882, further Chinese immigration was forbidden, the first instance of such conduct in United States history. The Japanese were treated differently only in degree and time.

Economic Discrimination Economic discrimination, however, was considerably less. Wages of most immigrant groups were lower than those of native Americans, but so were the immigrants' skill levels and ability to speak and read English. When these factors are taken into account, virtually the entire differential between immigrants' wages and those of native Americans disappears. Ethnic groups containing high proportions of unskilled or illiterate workers or those unable to speak English received incomes well below those obtained by groups that did not have these disabilities.[34] The initial study indicating minimal economic discrimination provoked a good deal of controversy, but has since been confirmed for both sexes by additional research.[35] One study did conclude that the wage differential for southeastern European immigrants was approximately 10 percent greater than could be explained by performance-related characteristics. However, even in this case, the authors hypothesized that the lower wages for this group were likely to continue only as long as immigration from southeastern Europe continued to be very high. This is an indication that the American labor market had not been able to adjust fully over the 1890–1914 period, but not that it would not do so. Also, it presents ample evidence that economic discrimination, if it existed, was not a barrier to further immigration.[36]

Market conditions in America gave immigrants some protection against discrimination. In most years of heavy immigration, the demand for labor was high. No employer wants to pay very much for labor, but what must be paid depends on labor's alternatives. Within the limits imposed by what the worker can obtain elsewhere and the full value of workers' product, if the choice is between increasing wages or losing labor, employers will raise wages. They will not knowingly pay any worker more than the value of his or her product, but they may not be able to pay less and retain the worker's services if there are other jobs in which labor is equally productive. It will raise another employer's profits to offer a worker some additional fraction of the difference between current pay and the full value of output, and workers tend to be as alert to their own best interests as are employers.

---

[34] R. Higgs, *Transformation of the American Economy: An Essay in Interpretation* (New York: Wiley and Sons, 1971), 114–119.

[35] P. Hill, "Relative Skill and Income Levels of Native and Foreign-Born Workers in the United States," *Explorations in Economic History* (January 1975); M. Shergold, "Relative Skill and Income Levels of Native and Foreign-Born Workers: A Re-Examination," *Explorations in Economic History* (October 1976); and M. Fraundorf, "Relative Earnings of Native and Foreign-Born Women," *Explorations in Economic History* (April 1978).

[36] P. McGouldrick and M. Tannen, "Did American Manufacturers Discriminate against Immigrants before 1914?" *Journal of Economic History* (September 1977).

Immigrants' Standards of Living

Immigrants quickly discovered that it was to their advantage to obtain as much information about job markets as possible. There were many sources of such information: acquaintances (one reason why nonEnglish-speaking immigrants tended to cluster together; information costs were lower), employment brokers, and dealing with employers themselves. Clearly, it paid to increase one's capabilities in English. Since the newcomers tended to settle in large cities where there were many different employers, labor markets quickly became competitive for most immigrants. Not surprisingly, those who had been in the United States longest tended to have the highest wages, the most job skills, and the best information.

Whatever their native tongues, most immigrants learned English and sent their children to school. The children did well in their parents' adopted country; although the proportion of laborers, service workers, tailors, and other low-wage occupations among immigrants was above the American norm, the occupations of immigrants' children indicated substantial progress. The proportion of physicians, engineers, lawyers and judges, and scientists within this group was at least twice as great as that of their parents, and, in most cases, above that for native stock as well. (See Table 14.3.) The proportion of salespeople showed a similar rise, which is an indication that economic discrimination could not have been a major burden for this group. Over the same period, the percentage of people of foreign stock in low-wage, low-skill occupations fell, often by as much as one-half to two-thirds.[37] For the immigrants and their chil-

[37] Lebergott, *The Americans*, 342–343, 370–376. Data from E. Hutchinson, *Immigrants and Their Children, 1850–1950* (New York: Wiley and Sons, 1956).

Table 14.3   Occupational Concentration in 1910 (Overall Concentration = 100)

	Foreign Born	Foreign Stock
All occupations	100	100
Accountants	62	131
Engineers	47	104
Lawyers	25	102
Physicians and dentists	45	86
Teachers	39	75
Domestics	173	87
Charwomen, porters	208	104
Janitors	168	102
Construction laborers	169	84
Transport Laborers	224	58

Source: E. P. Hutchinson, *Immigrants and Their Children, 1850–1950* (New York: Wiley and Sons, 1956), Tab. 39. Reprinted in S. Lebergott, The Americans: An Economic Record (New York: Norton, 1984), Tab. 26.4, 344.

dren, the idea of America as the land of individual opportunity and progress was no myth.

The Economic Impact of Immigration

Immigrants were hated and feared by many Americans. It was claimed that immigration, by adding to the supply of labor, would drive wages down. Since real wages did not fall, the simplest form of that statement is false. Immigration did not actually depress wages because it was so strongly correlated with periods of full employment. Yet it is probable that immigration did prevent as rapid an increase in wages as might otherwise have occurred. Although there was a good deal of political action aimed at restricting entry into the United States, proponents of such policies had very limited success before World War I. They did succeed in barring the Chinese and sharply restricting Japanese immigration. In addition, entry into the United States was subjected to various restrictions and taxes. During World War I, a bill to restrict immigration through a literacy test was passed.

Throughout this period, the contribution of immigration to the United States economy was highly positive. On a macroeconomic basis, immigration added to the work force in an era when most economic growth stemmed from additional quantities of inputs, of which labor was by far the most important. As noted earlier, immigrant labor was a bargain for the United States, not so much in terms of the wages paid to it, but because other nations had borne the costs of rearing and educating a large, strongly motivated body of labor whose services aided the American economy. The population growth resulting from immigration made profitable the utilization of economies of scale in many industries. On the microeconomic side, the roll call of immigrants who made significant individual contributions to their new country is long and varied. Not only does it extend over every field of human endeavor, it includes activities in which native Americans had shown little or no aptitude.

One group that did suffer heavily from discrimination was not composed of immigrants. After all possible influences on job performance (skill, location, age, literacy, and experience) are taken into account, American blacks received from 15 to 20 percent less for equivalent work than did whites.[38] Black immigrants from the West Indies, however, did considerably better.[39] In the South, many of the new industrial jobs that appeared for the first time after 1900 were closed to blacks.[40]

---

[38] Higgs, *Transformation*, 120–123.
[39] T. Sowell, *The Economics and Politics of Race* (New York: Morrow, 1983).
[40] Wright, *Old South, New South*, 177–186.

PERMANENT LABOR UNIONS

As Chapter 10 has shown, labor unions were formed in the United States before the Civil War, but their organization and operations were beset with enormous difficulties. The prevailing legal and social climate was bitterly hostile. Unions faced two even more formidable economic obstacles in demonstrating to prospective members that it might be worth risking the community's wrath to join: First, employers found most workers easy to replace, whether with other people from the same labor market, workers imported from another city, or products made by nonunion labor. Second, labor unions were unable to survive depressions. Consequently, few labor unions had been able to achieve permanent wage levels above those resulting from competitive markets' operations.

It was less difficult to organize a union in periods of full employment, because labor markets were tight and employers might be willing to agree to higher wages. Under these conditions they could pass wage increases on through higher product prices. But when business conditions were bad, it was nearly impossible for unions to function. Then employers wanted to cut wages, reduce employment, or both, and the threat of a strike against an already unprofitable firm was empty. Before 1870, less than a dozen American labor unions had survived a severe depression, and, if anything, the severity of the business cycle increased after 1870.

Yet additional forces appeared that made American workers more willing to seek the benefits of cooperation. By 1914, unions had at least discovered the formula that permitted permanent organization, and had succeeded in raising their members' wages above the competitive-market level in a few industries.

Changing Labor-Management Relations

As the size of business firms increased, older forms of labor-management relations were lost. Formerly, most shops, craft establishments, and manufacturing firms were small, and their owners often knew their workers personally. Not infrequently, owners spent most of their time doing the same work as their employees. Supervision was a simple task, because there were at most only a few stages in each firm's operations, and many of the workers were familiar with all of them. But as plant size and specialization increased, this relationship was often lost. The owner delegated close supervision to foremen, and might have ceded even executive duties to a salaried manager. Relations with the labor force became impersonal and sometimes bureaucratic. Job security was threatened by both cyclical unemployment and rapid technological change, and the individual worker had little or no voice under such conditions.

These circumstances, together with the traditional concerns over wages, hours, and working conditions, encouraged the formation of organizations to represent workers. While today we think of labor unions as centered in the manufacturing sector of the economy, this was not the case before World War I. Most successful labor organizations occurred in trades more closely allied to traditional methods, such as printing and various craft skills, not the new manufacturing industries.

The combination of wage-eroding inflation and tight labor markets during the Civil War had sparked increased interest in unions. Many were formed, initially on a local basis. It was soon realized that it was necessary to confront all employers in an industry, or at least in the local market, simultaneously. Attempts were then made to form common fronts both between the employees of different local firms and between those performing similar work, regardless of location or industry.

These efforts bore some fruit; in the early 1870s there may have been several hundred thousand workers enrolled in unions. But 1873 marked the beginning of the slump that historians termed the "Great Depression" (until the 1930s brought new dimensions to that term). Its effects crushed all but a handful of unions. Labor had yet to find an effective counter to unions' most fundamental weakness: They were most successful in periods of full employment, when workers' bargaining position improved even without organization. When it deteriorated in slumps, they either had no effect or converted proposed wage cuts into unemployment.

Labor and Political Action

Some labor leaders began to believe that if U.S. social and political institutions could be made more sympathetic to labor, workers' goals might be achieved by changing the climate in which economic activity took place. It might be possible to obtain a larger voice in the distribution of income and the organization of production through political action than had so far been achieved through bargaining with employers.

The first such effort after 1865 grew out of dissatisfaction with the results of more narrow economic efforts. The National Labor Union (NLU) began as an organization that combined the local unions of several cities and a few national craft unions. Initially, its goals were largely economic—wages, working conditions, and especially the eight-hour day. But a union cannot expect much success unless it represents a large portion of the labor producing a particular item, and the NLU had organized only a minority of the workers in any single labor market. Since its efforts under such conditions were unsuccessful, the NLU expanded its vision. It began to ally itself with groups seeking an increase in the money supply and an end to private monopoly. In addition, it sought the replacement of private ownership with workers' cooperatives—an idea then much in vogue among British workers. After a crushing defeat at the polls in 1872, however, the NLU disappeared.

The Knights of Labor

The next effort to reform society—along what lines was never completely clear—bore the resounding title of the Noble and Holy Order of the Knights of Labor. The organization grew slowly for the first decade after its founding in 1869. One of its handicaps was an elaborate ritual and secrecy, which to many Catholic workers (or their priests) bore too close a resemblance to the Masons. The Knights advocated an eventual end to the wage system. They emphasized education and cooperation and sought to enlist the entire working class.

Membership in the Knights was open to everyone, including employers and people not even in the labor force. Only Pinkerton detectives, lawyers, and liquor sellers were excluded. In pursuit of their goal, the Knights tried to organize all the workers in a region into a single "mixed local" without regard to the nature of the work done by individuals. More importantly, no regard was paid to whether people had joined the Knights as individuals or as members of an existing (usually skilled) craft union. An organization such as the Knights is inherently unsuited to bargain with either individual employers or even with an entire industry. This did not bother the Knights' leadership, however, because they were opposed to attempts to shorten hours or raise wages by collective bargaining anyhow. They also opposed strikes in pursuit of such objectives.

A Rapid Rise—and Fall
Ironically, it was a strike against one of Jay Gould's railroads—a strike that the Knights' leadership opposed on principle—that gained the Knights a huge increase in membership in 1885 and 1886. If there ever were an authentic "robber baron," at least in public opinion, it was Jay Gould. The news that a labor organization had challenged such an ogre and won spread like wildfire among American workers. In fact, the Knights had done little more than survive the conflict; they did not regain the cut in pay that had triggered the strike. Nevertheless, the event attracted hordes of new members for the Knights, many of whom expected the organization to compensate for their lack of bargaining power. Within a year, the Knights had over 700,000 members. This was by far the largest labor organization yet seen in the United States. But many of those who joined the Knights in that 1886 surge had thoroughly unrealistic expectations of both the aims and the capabilities of the organization in which they had enrolled. While unskilled workers saw the Knights as an avenue to the achievement of labor's traditional goals, the leaders of the Knights were opposing a national movement for an eight-hour working day.

The organizational weaknesses of the Knights and the disparity between the goals of leaders and the rank and file caused a collapse as spectacularly swift as the rise had been. By 1900, the Knights of Labor existed mainly on paper. Their demise was due more to self-inflicted wounds and inept leadership than to employers' opposition. At no time did the Knights' leadership appear able to understand that few workers were willing to wait until the organization gained sufficient political power to restructure the entire economy before obtaining any material betterment. The leaders were willing to forfeit short-term opportunities to improve wages, hours, and working conditions in pursuit of this goal. To most members, this was incomprehensible.

Defections of the Craft Unions
Craft unions, whose skilled members had some bargaining power versus employers because they were difficult to replace, were very reluctant to merge

■ The Chicago Haymarket Riot of 1886 put organized labor on the defensive for years to come.
Source: Library of Congress.

their proven organizations with much larger numbers of largely unskilled workers in the mixed locals that the Knights favored. As the craft unionists could see, such moves diluted whatever bargaining power they might have, while it did nothing to improve the lot of the unskilled. Yet the Knights were unable to resist the temptation to form mixed locals, and attempted to "raid" craft unions for members. Craft unions recognized this threat to their hard-earned gains and after repeated warnings to the Knights had no effect, they withdrew from that organization and formed the American Federation of Labor in 1886.[41]

By their very nature, the Knights of Labor could be no more than a debating society. Their membership was too small to exercise significant political power, and their leaders could neither appreciate workers' needs for immediate economic gains nor hold them to the policies they desired. In reality, workers found the Knights offered only a rapidly fading hope.

The defection of the craft unions was not the only blow the Knights suffered in 1886. The organization had promoted a rally in Chicago's Haymarket Square to generate enthusiasm for a general strike in belated support of the eight-hour-day movement—a move in which the Knights' leadership reluctantly followed the rank and file. Someone (it was never determined whom) threw a bomb into the ranks of the police. The police responded with gunfire that killed or wounded many of the demonstrators. Four men were hanged for murder and several others sentenced to long prison terms as much for their anarchist politics as for any clear association with the

---

[41] G. Grob, "The Knights of Labor and the Trade Unions, 1878–1886," *Journal of Economic History* (June 1958).

crime. All those convicted were probably in-nocent, but so high were the feelings engen-dered by the affair that Governor John P. Altgeld's pardon for those imprisoned cost him his political career. It now appears almost certain that the violence was not instigated by the Knights. Nonetheless, many people re-garded it as typical of the entire union move-ment. The repercussions made labor's relations with the legal system even worse than the bitter hostility existing prior to the events in Haymarket Square.

The Knights' basic problem was obvious: To achieve their goals, they had to organize a large portion of the American electorate. Prob-ably even the entire American work force would not have been sufficient to give their policies the necessary support. But many workers would not risk joining the Knights because, unless the organization achieved that unlikely goal, membership was dangerous. Worse, there was no material reward in the short term. To have any hope at all of success, the Knights required a huge membership (and, in all probability, a much clearer sense of di-rection). They never came close.

The American Federation of Labor

The American Federation of Labor (AFL) achieved one long-sought goal of American la-bor organizations: It was the first large-scale union to achieve permanent organization, sur-viving both depression and the worst employ-ers could offer. The Federation succeeded by being virtually everything the Knights were not.[42] The AFL was exclusive, limiting its at-tempts at organization to skilled workers with some bargaining power. The new union was not interested in people who hoped to draw

on its strength rather than increase it. Rather than welcoming additional members, the Fed-eration's unions restricted entry, recognizing that labor scarcity meant higher wages. It was resolutely nonideological. When Samuel Gompers, its long-term leader, was asked what the Federation's goals were, he is said to have replied, "More."

In contrast to the centralized leadership of the Knights, the AFL was locally organized and controlled, and the basic decisions were in the hands of men close to local conditions and the wishes of their members, because all worked at the same type of jobs. The Feder-ation would not indulge in symbolic gestures; it was reluctant to strike unless there was some prospect of gaining union objectives by doing so. Protests against wage cuts in periods of poor business were thought to be losing prop-ositions by AFL leaders—quite correctly. Al-most without exception, such strikes had ended in failure, and unions could not gain from them.

New Goals and Results

To employers, the Federation unions were antagonists, but no threat to their own sur-vival, as some other unions proclaimed themselves to be. The AFL accepted the basic institutions of capitalism, seeking only a larger share of its products for union mem-bers. An attempt by socialists, led by David DeLeon, to gain control of the AFL in 1893–1895 failed. Henceforth in their bargaining, the Federation unions would continue to seek agreements with employers, not class warfare. The railroad brotherhoods, like the AFL organizations of skilled workers, fol-lowed similar procedures.

The American Federation of Labor needed more than astute bargaining strategy and effective organization to succeed. Under Gompers' direction it was able to provide other benefits for its members. Because its members were skilled and well paid for the time (and able to extract further concessions

[42] For a different view of the formation and early opera-tions of the AFL, see G. Friedman, "Strike Success and Union Ideology: The United States and France, 1880–1914," *Journal of Economic History* (March 1988).

from some employers), the unions levied sizable membership dues. These were used to accumulate strike funds, which gave the union some staying power in disputes, and also to pay sickness and death benefits to members. Under such policies, membership benefits could be maintained, and the AFL was far more successful in keeping its members than earlier unions had been.

Even so, success was modest. Ten years after its formation, the AFL had perhaps 270,000 members, largely from existing unions. But the Federation had already survived the severe depression of the early 1890s, something few other unions had done. In the prosperous years after 1900, it achieved considerably more. There were 1.5 million Federation members by 1904 and 2 million on the eve of World War I.[43] In each of these years about one-third as many workers belonged to independent unions. The Federation had few, if any, members in mass-production industries. Most of its strength was in skilled crafts, such as printing, molding, and carpentry. The United Mine Workers were almost unique among Federation unions; they were an industrial rather than a craft union, with eligibility determined by the industry in which they worked rather than each worker's specific job. At no time before 1914 were all unions combined able to organize as much as 8 percent of all American labor.[44] Given this data, the wage and hours gains achieved by American labor over this period cannot be attributed to organized labor.

Labor's Left Wing

Ideological unionism was not dead, but it produced almost as many leaders as followers. Often left-wing unions showed as much vitality in fighting each other as they did in their relations with employers. Aside from generalized opposition to the private ownership of productive resources, the left wing of the American labor movement never succeeded in presenting a unified program, let alone instituting it. The small socialist, communist, and anarchist unions, a few of which were affiliated with the AFL, achieved no lasting successes. One group, the Industrial Workers of the World (IWW) gained some strength in western mining, lumbering, and farm labor. The IWW also waged a spectacular but ultimately losing struggle in a 1913 silk workers' strike in Patterson, New Jersey. It was an anarchist organization that advocated the overthrow of capitalism. The penchant of the Wobblies, as the IWW were nicknamed, for flaming rhetoric, strikes, and a readiness to at least associate themselves with violence made the organization a target for all the power of both employers and the law. The IWW had equally serious problems in its relations with workers; it was not particularly interested in day-to-day gains or permanent organization, both of which reduced its already limited appeal. IWW membership never exceeded 10,000 workers, and was usually far less. Its opposition to American participation in World War I intensified the public vendetta against the IWW, and the organization was all but wiped out in the early 1920s.

Labor in an Unfriendly World

Almost to the very end of this period, American labor unions had to face relentless and united hostility from most of the other institutions in the country. The legal status of unions was hazy. Although unions themselves had not been illegal since 1842, even their most basic objectives and policies, such as organizing in attempts to raise wages, might be. Labor unions by their very nature are concerted actions to raise members' welfare; as such, they resemble price-fixing agreements by

---

[43] *Historical Statistics*, 1:177.
[44] *Historical Statistics*, 1:126, 178.

■ Wobbly leader Big Bill Haywood is shown leading a parade in Lowell, Massachusetts, in support of a textile workers' strike.
Source: Library of Congress.

product sellers. Like these, unions are more effective if they control all labor in the pertinent market, that is, if they have monopoly power. The Sherman Act had declared "conspiracies in restraint of trade" illegal, and the earliest successful prosecutions under this legislation were of labor unions whose activities were held to fall under this definition. In the *Danbury Hatters* case (1901), a small union was held liable for the business losses suffered by employers during a strike.

Employers could be expected to be hostile, but in addition, management could usually count on support from the courts, police, the press, and often some intellectuals and the clergy as well. Popular opinion tended to regard unions as strange and somehow un-

American. Prevailing economic doctrine stressed the idea that competition, if unhindered, produced ideal economic results in all markets. From this, it followed that attempts to interfere with the competitive process, especially through joint action to raise prices, could not fail to be harmful.

Antiunion Activity

Friendly courts allowed employers to use weapons that made effective action by unions all but impossible. They might issue injunctions against union activity that forbade even the payment of union officers, or denied unions access to their own records. Employers might force workers to sign agreements not to join unions (yellow-dog contracts), under which the employees could be sued for violations of contract if they engaged in union activity. Names of union members might be circulated to all potential employers (blacklisting), and union membership lists were obtained through company informants. Government could be counted upon to limit or forbid picketing, to provide police or militia protection for strikebreakers, or even to send federal troops to break a strike by railroad workers that interrupted mail deliveries.

Where the courts failed to restrain unions, some employers went beyond the law. Attempting to organize a union was physically dangerous; many union organizers were beaten or even killed. Where the police or militia could not or would not suffice, Pinkertons or gangs of hired thugs might be hired to threaten striking workers, to protect strikebreakers hired to keep facilities operating, or to provoke an incident as an excuse to attack workers. Some workers were not averse to similar tactics, meeting guns and clubs with bullets, dynamite, and fire. Some labor disputes, particularly in mining, read like small-unit combat reports rather than labor-management disputes. In this area as in most others, however, the advantages generally lay with the employers.

Bargaining Disparities

Above all else, employers could often afford to wait, and unions, especially if strikes had been called to force employers to recognize the union, could not. In such cases, unions seldom had an opportunity to prepare their members for a long period without pay. Before 1900, only a few unions had strike funds, and they might be denied access to these by blanket injunctions. Fewer still could support their members, even at subsistence levels, for more than a few days or weeks, especially if large numbers of workers were involved. The plight of their families might soon force strikers to return to work on the employer's terms. Many of the new manufacturing firms were owned by self-made men to whom a union was an intolerable interference with management prerogatives. Such men believed that crushing unions was a matter of principle. A series of famous and often bloody disputes whose very names have become symbols of bitter conflict—Homestead, Pullman, and Ludlow—resulted in the destruction of most unions in manufacturing and many of those in mining as well. Recessions continued to plague unions, even if the principles of survival were now known. In such an atmosphere, the ability of some unions to survive and even expand was near-miraculous.

Labor in a Changing Environment

After 1900, the climate in which labor unions operated softened a little. Employers had organized the National Association of Manufacturers (NAM) in 1902, largely as a propaganda organization to sell the public on the advantages of the open shop (in which no worker could be required to join a union under any circumstances, including the employer's recognition of a union) and other antiunion views. The NAM was quite successful, but at least its approach was persuasive; it marked a transition from the days when employers felt no need to enlist public opinion as long as force was available.

The aims and effects of the National Civic Federation were less clear. This group's membership included some established leaders in the business, financial, and political fields, as well as union leaders, such as Samuel Gompers and John Mitchell. It gave a forum in which labor's point of view could be presented and solutions to labor conflicts developed. The Federation urged a more conciliatory approach, including collective bargaining and the mediation of disputes in which labor and management were unable to reach agreement.

In 1912, another goal of American labor was attained. The Clayton Act of that year, stating (incorrectly) that "the labor of a human being is not an article of commerce," exempted labor unions from the antitrust laws. At about this time, some groups' attitudes toward unions had begun to soften. Segments of the clergy and the press now took either favorable or neutral stances instead of their previous opposition. Some other goals, such as the abolition of debtors' prison, expanded free (meaning without tuition charges) public education, and shorter working hours, were gained through the concerted efforts of unions and a variety of other groups by 1914.

U.S. Labor Unions: A Breed Apart

The basic characteristics of American labor unions that persist to this day emerged during this period, especially in the AFL and the railroad brotherhoods. In this country, unions have been chiefly concerned with the pragmatic pursuit of economic goals. So-called "bread and butter unionism" is primarily interested in wages, hours, and working conditions. Such unions have shown little interest in the ideological concerns of many European labor unions, such as class struggle and the abolition of private capital. The roots of these differences are unclear, but it can be argued that they are a reflection of the greater mobility of workers in the United States, both between employers and through promotion on the job.[45] American workers, who believed that their current jobs were not necessarily lifetime commitments, designed their unions with a view toward short-term gains within the existing system. However, several recent studies have found that manufacturing workers in several areas stayed with one employer for long periods and enjoyed opportunities for promotion within the firm. This may help to explain why such firms were not often unionized.[46]

Class consciousness did not develop in the United States to any great extent. American society was far more open and mobile than Europe's, and both labor and management were new to their status. Those people most likely to be imbued with a sense of class differences were recent immigrants, for whom the American contrast with Europe must have been particularly great.

Such attitudes also encouraged labor to connect wages with performance on the job and made American labor more receptive to technological change than were European workers. These attitudes helped produce higher incomes, new opportunities, and still further flexibility.

Pragmatism also played an important role in the development of American unions. Bread and butter unionism worked; such unions proved capable of making progress toward many of their goals, even though for only a small portion of the work force. A union organized for other purposes, such as the long-term transformation of the existing economy, is unlikely to be either motivated toward or effective at the achievement of day-to-day improvements within the existing system.

American unions' failure to follow a more radical path does not appear to be linked to any systematic effort to exclude immigrants with such views from the United States. There is little evidence of attempts to develop such a policy, and in a world without fingerprints, passports, or social security numbers, even less indication that it could have been effectively carried out. Nor has the United States ever lacked the ability to produce its own radicals. The radicals' problem, for both the home-grown and imported varieties, lay in attracting a following, and neither group achieved much success in this regard.

---

[45] W. Sandstrom, "Internal Labor Markets Before World War I: On the Job Training and Employee Promotion," *Explorations in Economic History* (October 1988).

[46] Carter and Savoca, "Labor Mobility," and Sundstrom, "Internal Labor Markets."

In consequence, American labor unions have been far less politically oriented than have many European labor groups. Even the association between the Democratic Party and organized labor dates from the 1930s, not this period. Nor can even the modern connection really be compared to that between British unions and the Labor Party. The American Federation of Labor announced a policy of "rewarding labor's friends and punishing its enemies" at the polls. Given the small numbers of union members, this strategy was more effective than a close affiliation with any political party might have been.

INCOME DISTRIBUTION AND THE RESULTS OF ECONOMIC GROWTH

There is no question that working people in the United States had increased their material welfare from 1865 to 1920. Their wages provided greater purchasing power, and they worked shorter hours. Moreover, a larger portion of workers were now in high-wage occupations than in 1865, which meant that the gains of labor were more widely shared. But this does not tell us whether the gains in aggregate income were more or less equally distributed. How large were workers' income gains in relation to those of capital and its owners?

Did the Rich Grow Richer?

Enormous fortunes were accumulated by some business leaders, and in this period there was little hesitation about flaunting wealth. In his will, J. P. Morgan bequeathed to New York City the art collection that became the Metropolitan Museum of Art. The city was given only about one-quarter of Morgan's personal art portfolio. Yet John D. Rockefeller described Morgan as "not even rich." Standards varied. Such accumulations of wealth have been presumed to indicate growing inequality of both income and wealth. The distribution of wealth almost certainly did shift in favor of the rich in the two decades prior to 1914. However, the evidence on income distribution does not support a firm conclusion that substantial alterations occurred in that area.

Income distribution, as indicated in earlier chapters, had not been equal in America since the earliest colonial period, and may well have become less so in the first century after independence. But the changes in income distribution between 1875 and 1914 were not large.[47] Data from income tax returns (the United States levied income taxes during the Civil War and until 1872), while fragmentary, indicate no increase in income inequality.[48]

These trends should be placed in context. The American population was becoming increasingly urban and contained a growing portion of foreign-born persons after 1850. Both these factors tended to increase income inequality. Thus, the development of at most a weak trend toward greater inequality of income over this period is a remarkable phenomenon. The rich certainly became richer in an absolute sense between the Civil War and 1914. But there is little to indicate that the pace at which their incomes rose was faster than that achieved by the poor and the middle class. The period began with a huge transfer of income and wealth from the rich to the very poorest Americans. The Civil War conferred a huge increase in incomes on American blacks, and imposed a great capital loss on their former masters. Blacks made further rel-

---

[47] Lindert and Williamson, "Three Centuries of American Inequality," 92–95.
[48] L. Soltow, "Evidence on Income Inequality in the United States, 1865–1965," *Journal of Economic History* (June 1969).

■ By 1894, some Americans enjoyed much more than subsistence incomes.
Source: Photograph by Byron, The Byron Collection, Museum of the City of New York.

ative income gains in the postbellum period. Equality of relative income gains, of course, does imply that the absolute income gains of the rich were greater.

The Effects of Labor Mobility

Improved labor mobility would tend to reduce income inequality in comparison to that produced by a period in which people were more limited in their choices of jobs and locations. It made those owing their incomes to inherited wealth less secure, and it gave people whose talents and ambition were their only inheritance more scope to receive returns on that endowment. In an economic environment where there is a good deal of individual mobility, people can move up and down the income scale even if the scale itself does not change. That is, even if the proportion of income received by the poorest or richest 10 percent of income recipients does not change over time, each group may contain a substantial number of different persons as time passes. American workers tended to be mobile, both geographically and occupationally, and the result was a substantial reduction in differences between per-capita incomes in various regions of the country, as indicated in Table 14.4.

The Effects of Urbanization

The increase in urbanization would tend to overstate any increase in inequality. Although urban incomes were higher in money terms, they purchased a lower quality of life than that in rural areas in this period in such areas as food quality, the incidence of pollution, and living space per person. Since living costs were higher in the cities, the gap between urban and rural incomes was not as great as comparisons of money income would indicate.

At the same time, the growth of cities produced important gains in economic efficiency and hastened their dispersion through the economy. Cities made communications easier, so markets functioned better in urban

Table 14.4   Regional Personal Income per Capita Relative to the National Average (National Average = 100)

Regions	1880	1900	1920
Northeast	141	137	132
New England	141	134	124
Middle Atlantic	141	139	134
North Central	98	103	100
East North Central	102	106	108
West North Central	90	97	87
South	51	51	62
South Atlantic	45	45	59
East South Central	51	49	52
West South Central	60	61	72
West	190	154	122
Mountain	168	139	100
Pacific	204	163	135

Source: R. Easterlin, "Regional Economic Trends, 1840–1950" in S. Harris, ed., *American Economic History* (New York: McGraw-Hill, 1961), 528. Modified (data for the West in 1900 changed) and reprinted in R. Higgs, *The Transformation of the American Economy, 1865–1914* (New York: John Wiley and Sons, 1971), 108.

areas. Urban conditions encouraged specialization and the utilization of economies of scale, and even fostered invention.[49] Capital and labor were more readily available to innovators within cities, and highly specialized versions of both were only likely to be found in large cities. Selling costs were lower in urban markets. Just as they had with international migration, it appears that the attractions of city life (higher incomes and a more varied life-style) improved relative to the disadvantages, and this provoked a relocation of population toward the cities.

Changes in Urban Life

After 1900, city life had begun to lose some of its old terrors. A combination of new technology and new economic institutions had produced dramatic improvements in public health. Improvements in medical knowledge as well as the technical capacity to improve the purity of water supplies and provide adequate sanitation were not sufficient in themselves. To be effective, these innovations required total or near-total participation by the entire population. Laws had to be devised to force everyone to use sewers and observe public health regulations and to contribute to their cost through taxes. Much the same was true of police and fire protection, lighting, water supply, and even traffic control. Under urban conditions, there were far more externalities than was true of rural life; one person's activities influenced the quality of his neighbors' lives as well as his own. Once this was recognized, laws could be formulated that increased the costs of actions that reduced others' welfare, or prevented them.

The Results of Preventive Medicine

The new pipes, filters, pumps, and chemicals now available made possible the application of what doctors had learned about disease causes and transmission agents. In 1914,

---

[49] Higgs, *Transformation*, 72–76.

American cities were still noisy and polluted, and more crowded than ever, but the epidemic diseases that had been the scourge of urban life for as long as cities had existed were being conquered. The urban death rate had fallen by almost one-third in about 25 years, and the improvement in child and infant mortality was even greater. Infant mortality in Massachusetts, for example, declined 41 percent from 1870 to 1919.[50] Death rates from typhoid, scarlet fever, cholera, smallpox, and diphtheria had all fallen by 50 percent or more. Life expectancy at birth for all Americans increased from 47.3 to 54.1 years in the first two decades of the twentieth century.[51] The decline in height of adult Americans noted in Chapter 9 was halted and reversed after 1890, despite great increases in urbanization and immigration, two of its major sources.[52]

One estimate of the benefits from public health measures in this period concluded that they returned 25 cents annually for every dollar invested in them.[53] The payoffs came in longer working lives, fewer days lost to illness, and lower costs of treatment, all of which allowed the same work force to produce more goods and services. People suffered less, both in terms of their own pain and through the loss of loved ones, especially children.

Education

Another area in which investment yielded high returns to society was education. By the 1890s, all states had public school systems, and no other country educated so large a portion of its school-age population as the United States.[54] The quality of education also improved. Even after the Civil War, the school year had been no more than three months in many areas. Now it was extended, and education was required for more years. The number of high schools and colleges also increased. A growing number of American universities now had science programs worthy of the name. Land grant universities and the Department of Agriculture began to apply formal science to areas long approached only through folklore, tradition, and rule of thumb. The result was a growing awareness of why and how processes produced their results, making efforts to improve them more predictable.

There was a strong correlation between expenditures on education and per-capita incomes in each state. The extension of education, as noted earlier, was linked to the decline in child labor. The cost of providing additional education thus was not merely the expenditures on schools and teachers, but also the foregone output of children who were now in school rather than employed. The cost was well worth paying: Education was a high-yield investment.[55] As growth became increasingly centered in productivity increases rather than additions to the supply of resources, the policy made good use of the one resource whose potential productivity could be increased without limit: people. Education also fostered labor mobility.

The increase in labor mobility fostered the movement from low- to high-productivity jobs (see Tables 14.1 and 14.4), and thus increased overall economic output. The ability to respond to a greater range of employment opportunities also increased personal freedom and expression. The monopsony power of local employers was reduced, and people had a

---

[50] *Historical Statistics*, 1:57.

[51] *Historical Statistics*, 1:55.

[52] R. Fogel, "Nutrition and the Decline in Mortality Since 1700: Some Preliminary Findings," in Gallman and Engerman, *Long-Term Factors*, 465.

[53] E. Meeker, *The Economics of Improving Health, 1850–1915*, Unpublished dissertation, University of Washington, 1980. Cited in Higgs, *Transformation*, 72.

[54] A. Fishlow, "Levels of Nineteenth-Century American Investment in Education," *Journal of Economic History* (December 1966).

[55] Fishlow, "Levels."

better chance of employment that provided both high wages and personal fulfillment.

A BETTER LIFE?

Were Americans better off in 1914 or 1920 than they had been in 1865? In material terms, their incomes were higher, allowing them to spend more on nonessential items—the things that make life interesting, allow for personal expression, and so constitute a culture. For most Americans, the range of attainable choices had widened, and it is the choices open to the average citizen that distinguish rich from poor economies.

Choices had not widened in consumption alone. The enormous changes in location, occupation, education, and social structure that took place over this period indicated that large numbers of people had been able to change their contributions to economic life as well as the rewards they drew from it. By no means does this imply that in these conditions everyone could rise from poverty to millionaire status by hard work and clean living. A very few, like Andrew Carnegie, had actually done so. But the real test of social and economic mobility is whether people in any line of work may realistically aspire to something they consider better than their current situation, or know that their personal failings could cause them to lose things they value. By and large, most Americans lived in such circumstances. On average, they gained, but by no means equally or even in proportion to initial status, talent, or effort. Riches have never been a disadvantage as a base for the efforts of the talented and ambitious, especially not in an age such as this, where economic success was all but worshiped. Others, less selective in their choice of parents, might reap lesser rewards for equal or even superior effort. But some Americans were burdened with disadvantages

not of their own making. Blacks had barely shed the worst of slavery's heritage, and had not yet obtained society's recognition that they deserved equal opportunity. American Indians were still denied the right to try to improve their circumstances, both by law and in practice. Even so, the dividends on human capital were higher in the United States than anywhere else. The extent and the pattern of international migration are powerful evidence of this.

The Measurement of Well-Being

Incomes, leisure, health, and even ranges of choice are all measurable, and all had increased for the average American. Can we conclude from this that Americans enjoyed life more at the end of this period than at its beginning? We have no way of knowing. Economists have yet to devise measurements of the enjoyment derived by different individuals from consumption, especially over long periods of time, and the persons who reaped the benefits of the period's economic growth were often not those who had produced it. In material terms, life was more abundant. But it was also different, faster-paced, and not all the changes were unmitigated blessings.

Some of the gains resulting from improved economic capabilities—those in health and reduced infant mortality, for example—appear to be unarguable. In other cases, perhaps the best conclusion is to be drawn from an observation of people's response to the new opportunities. There was very little to prevent at least a substantial number of Americans from living as they had 50 years before. But as the opportunities for participation in the modern economy appeared, there were few indeed who failed to take advantage of them. In sum, the old ways were still available, but even those who complained most about the changes wrought by modern life did not appear to believe that conditions would be improved by turning back the clock.

SELECTED REFERENCES

Brody, D. *The American Labor Movement*. New York: Harper & Row, 1971.

Commons, J. et al. *History of Labor in the United States*. 4 vols. New York: Kelley, 1921–1935.

Davis, L., R. Easterlin, W. Parker et al. *American Economic Growth: An Economist's History of the United States*. New York; Harper & Row, 1972.

Dubovsky, M. *Industrialism and the American Worker, 1865–1920*. Arlington Heights, Ill.: Harlan Davidson, 1975.

Easterlin, R. *Population, Labor Force, and Long Swings in Economic Growth: The American Experience*. New York: Columbia University Press, 1968.

Erickson, C. *American Industry and the European Immigrant, 1860–1885*. New York: Russell and Russell, 1967.

Gallman, R., and S. Engerman, eds. *Long-Term Factors in American Economic Growth*. Chicago: University of Chicago Press, 1986.

Gutman, H. *Work, Culture, and Society in Industrializing America*. New York: Random House, 1977.

Higgs, R. *The Transformation of the American Economy: An Essay in Interpretation*. New York: John Wiley and Sons, 1971.

Kendrick, J. *Productivity Trends in the United States*. Princeton, N.J.: Arno Press, 1961.

Kuznets, S., and E. Rubin. *Immigration and the Foreign Born*. New York: National Bureau of Economic Research, 1954.

Lebergott, S. *Manpower in Economic Growth: The American Record Since 1800*. New York: McGraw-Hill, 1964.

———. *The Americans: An Economic Record*. New York: Norton, 1984.

Lindert, P., and J. Williamson. "Three Centuries of American Inequality," in P. Uselding, ed. *Research in Economic History*. Greenwich, Conn.: JAI Press, 1976.

Long, C. *Wages and Earnings in the United States, 1860–1890*. Princeton, N.J.: Arno Press, 1975.

Nelson, D. *Managers and Workers: Origins of the New Factory System in the United States, 1880–1920*. Madison, Wis.: University of Wisconsin Press, 1975.

Rees, A. *Real Wages in Manufacturing, 1890–1914*. Princeton, N.J.: Arno Press, 1961.

Thomas, B. *Migration and Economic Growth*. Cambridge, U.K.: Cambridge University Press, 1953.

U.S. Department of Commerce, Bureau of the Census. *Historical Statistics of the United States: Colonial Times to 1970*. 2 vols. Washington, D.C.: Government Printing Office, 1975.

Wright, G. *Old South, New South: Revolutions in the Southern Economy Since the Civil War*. New York: Basic Books, 1986.

DOMESTIC AND FOREIGN COMMERCE, 1865–1914

*T*he economic growth that occurred in the United States from 1865 to 1914 constituted an enormous increase in the volume of goods and services produced. Because this increase in production was considerably larger than the increases in either the labor force or total population, it could also be expected to produce an increase in specialization and exchange and in the variety of goods produced. Growing urbanization increased the need for exchanges of goods and information. The types of goods produced and portion of total output exchanged rose even faster than the aggregate volume of production. This development was facilitated by improvements in productivity and transportation, but changes in the institutions through which exchanges took place also played a vital role.

As productivity gains allowed relatively smaller numbers of specialists to turn out greater volumes and varieties of goods, interactions between regions, firms, and individuals also increased. Before the Civil War, American cities had been centers of commerce rather than industry. After 1865, cities whose economic base was manufacturing became common. These cities required a national distribution network to market their products, often at points and times distant from their origins. Such transactions would not have been possible without improved communication and information. Producers required new information; they had to know the demand characteristics, customers' creditworthiness, and the nature of competition within new markets. Urban markets had changed, as growing incomes and wider ranges of consumer choice allowed customers to substitute between purchases. Someone had to hold the goods between manufacture and sale, so financial services were necessary. In many cases, institutions had to be developed to perform entirely new functions.

Improved information resulted from the revolution in communications. First the telegraph and later the telephone allowed nearly instantaneous transmission of information. Forms of contracts were devised that shifted risks from producers, wholesalers, and retailers to speculators, and thus greatly eased the access to credit enjoyed by many market participants. The new institutions (credit-rating agencies, insurance, and grading systems) both reduced the cost of information and increased its accuracy.

NEW PATTERNS OF POSTWAR COMMERCE

Changing Consumption Patterns

Increases in per-capita incomes and increased urban populations resulted in substantial increases in the proportion of consumer income spent on durable goods. As peoples' incomes rose, they spent smaller portions of the total on food and other basic survival requirements, and thus had growing portions of any income increase available for discretionary purchases. At one time, it was believed that consumer spending on durable goods was closely tied to the appearance of the mass-marketed automobile and installment loans, which dated from the 1920s. Now, however, it is known that the proportion of consumer incomes spent on furniture and other factory-produced goods was almost at modern levels shortly after the Civil War. Eventually, lamps, furniture, and other household items became commonplace, so that demand for them reflected mainly replacement of worn-out items and the formation of new families rather than first-time acquisitions. As this occurred, new consumer durables, such as iceboxes, sewing machines, bicycles, and a growing range of lei-

■ An early version of the phone: Its invention spawned new approaches to business.
Source: The Bettmann Archive.

sure equipment, replaced the initial goods as mainstays of growth.[1]

In the case of basic furniture, the increase in purchases after the war may overstate the change in production. In earlier times, much furniture had been made by its ultimate users in their own homes. Although these furnishings were not purchased with money, they were obtained at a cost in alternative uses of time. In that sense, they still represented a use of income.

New Products and Marketing Innovations

However, purchases after 1865 included a number of items new to American households. Some were relatively complicated machines that frequently were employed in the purchaser's work, such as bicycles or sewing machines. These expensive items were difficult to sell unless there was some assurance that they could be repaired if they broke down. It is no accident that successful automobile manufacturers learned to employ interchangeable parts and to copy the sales methods of makers of farm machinery, sewing machines, and bicycles in establishing chains of dealers trained and equipped to provide service. Henry Ford was an early leader in the provision of credit to dealers and customers—yet another example of his grasp of the conditions under which his cars were sold.[2] Agricultural machinery makers had been selling their products on credit even before the Civil War, and makers of expensive consumer durables learned to emulate them. At the same time, urban sellers of nondurables (groceries and dry goods) began to operate on a cash-and-carry basis; they no longer offered credit or delivery services as they once had. Urban merchants realized that their customers were paid more frequently than farmers, made more shopping trips, and might be more difficult to evaluate as credit risks than were members of small rural communities.

The greater volume and variety of consumer goods also forced changes in merchandising. In earlier times, the occasional visits

---

[1] H. Vatter, "Has There Been a 20th-Century Consumer Durables Revolution?" *Journal of Economic History* (March 1967).

[2] A. Chandler, Jr., *Giant Enterprise: Ford, General Motors, and the Automobile Industry* (New York: Harcourt, Brace, and World, 1964), 34–35.

of a peddler whose entire stock was carried in a backpack or a small wagon, plus three or four visits to the nearest market town per year, had to satisfy most Americans' requirements for goods they could not make for themselves. Most antebellum stores served a rural market and carried a wide variety of goods. Such establishments might accept payment in goods, farm produce, or occasionally even in labor performed for the storeowner, although, of course, cash payment was always welcomed.

Pricing Changes

Determining the price of each item sold was a time-consuming process. Most of the store's inventory was at least partially handmade, few items were identical, and fewer still bore brands identifying their makers. Because of the nature of such merchandise, and also because bargaining was at once a social process and a source of possible gain for a shrewd haggler, goods' prices were neither posted nor fixed. Instead, they were determined by bargaining between the store owner or his clerks and the customer. Payment in kind, of course, required more haggling. Such methods were practical only where the volume of transactions was small, store personnel had wide discretion and experience, and the variety of goods was limited. These conditions gave sellers an opportunity to practice price discrimination; buyers found few bargains in such circumstances. As incomes, population, and especially urbanization increased, and new technology resulted in more uniform products, sales methods began to change. Gradually, stores began to post prices, as Quaker merchants had long been doing. This facilitated a larger volume of business, and reduced the skills required of store personnel. It also reduced the storeowners' problems of inventory valuation.

The Guarantee

Greater uniformity in manufactured goods also made possible another new practice. Items might now be guaranteed, with refunds if they were not satisfactory, even in cases where the seller was not the original maker of the good. Prior to this time, retailers' policy, at least for goods not of their own manufacture, had been strictly *caveat emptor* ("let the buyer beware"). A growing range of items were now packaged or labeled by the manufacturer. Labeling began with food manufactures in an attempt to gain competitive advantages. There had been no point in attempting to establish a reputation for quality when every maker's goods might be mixed together in the store's bins or barrels. But with labels or packaging, the product's origin was recognizable, and the maker might be able to profit from providing quality goods. Consumers also gained, both because food items were now likely to be fresher or cleaner, a consideration that had not ranked high when most sales were from bulk stores.[3] The new methods gave producers an incentive to protect their reputations for quality goods by holding to uniform standards over large volumes of output.

New Developments in Retailing

Two seemingly contradictory trends in retailing had appeared prior to the Civil War. As urban markets grew in size because both population density and incomes were rising, some stores began to specialize in narrower ranges of products. Another indication of growing discretionary income was the increasing prevalence of "stores" providing services rather than physical items—theaters, beer gardens, restaurants, and other places of amusement. Except in small towns, the general store was replaced by establishments specializing in ready-to-wear clothing, hardware, groceries, meat, books, and often even more narrow categories within such items. These stores were aided by the improvements in transportation, communication, advertising, finance, printing, and sometimes by such specialized sup-

---

[3] A. Chandler, Jr., *The Visible Hand: The Managerial Revolution in American Business* (Cambridge, Mass.: Harvard University Press, 1977), Chap. 7.

porting services as refrigeration. As cities and the number of stores grew, it became more necessary to proclaim each store's existence, function, and location.

Running directly counter to this development was the appearance of the department store. These French innovations had begun to appear in the largest American cities in the 1850s (Alexander Stewart opened the Marble Dry Goods Palace in New York City in 1846.) After the Civil War, they spread rapidly. Few towns of any size or pretense to sophistication were without a department store (or a general store masquerading as one) by 1914. New York had Lord & Taylor, Macy's, Bloomingdales', and B. Altman by 1890. Carson Pirie Scott and Marshall Field & Co. in Chicago, Jordan Marsh in Boston, Wannamaker's in Philadelphia, the Emporium in San Francisco, and others were founded before 1900. In the next decade, other well-known establishments, such as Hudson's, Rich's, I. Magnin, Nieman-Marcus, Bullocks', and Shillito's, appeared.[4]

Department stores were really a series of specialized stores under one roof, with each department being separately managed; sometimes departments rented space from the store's owner. The parallels with the new multiproduct manufacturing firms are clear (see Chapter 12). Department stores used such innovations as fixed prices, guaranteed merchandise, cash registers, and improved accounting methods. Possibly they could not have existed without them. The large size of some department stores allowed them to perform their own wholesaling functions (some began as offshoots of established wholesaling operations) and to deal directly with manufacturers, seeking quantity-purchase discounts that were invaluable competitive tools.[5] Department stores offered their customers sav-

ings in shopping time as well as money; the pace of urban life was quickening.

Chain Stores

Chain stores also appeared in this era. The Great Atlantic & Pacific Tea Company began operations as a retailer of tea and coffee in 1859. It soon found that its stores could easily sell other groceries as well. Employing the same principle of quantity purchases to reduce unit costs that had been the basis of its success in tea sales, the A&P chain had grown to 200 stores by 1900. By 1921, it had 4,500 outlets. Other tea stores developed into the Grand Union, Kroger, and Jewel grocery chains. In 1920, there were no less than 120 grocery chains, and 808 chains of all types.[6] As the chains grew, they too began to perform their own wholesaling functions. By World War I, chain store competition had provoked efforts among independent sellers to pool purchases to obtain the same discounts. Both department and chain stores stressed rapid inventory turnover and found that, once established, additional product lines were easily added. Such expansion, rather than increasing the sheer size of the establishment, resulted in substantial cost reductions.[7] In the early 1880s, F. W. Woolworth opened seven variety stores in southeastern Pennsylvania, selling nothing that cost more than a dime. The "five - and ten-cent stores" were really small department stores specializing in low-priced goods. Public response was enthusiastic, and soon they were a fixture in American cities.[8]

Mail-Order Retailing

Department, chain, and specialty stores all served an urban clientele, but the appearance of mail-order houses allowed farmers to gain some of the advantages they offered. Wider

---

[4] Chandler, *Visible Hand*, 225–227.
[5] Chandler, *Visible Hand*, 225–229.

---

[6] U.S. Department of Commerce, Bureau of the Census, *Historical Statistics of the United States: Colonial Times to 1970* (Washington, D.C.: Government Printing Office, 1975), 2:847.
[7] Chandler, *Visible Hand*, 236.
[8] Chandler, *Visible Hand*, 234.

■ Lively trade was conducted in early department stores, as this illustration of Bullocks' in New York City demonstrates.
Source: Culver Pictures.

selection and prices reflecting competition and economies of scale came to the countryside when Montgomery Ward began circulating his single-page "catalogue" among members of the Grange in 1872. Consumer response encouraged the new firm to expand both its offerings and its clientele. Sears, Roebuck & Company was founded in 1886, and several other mail-order houses followed.

It is difficult for modern readers to imagine how eagerly isolated farmers and their families awaited the arrival of the Wards or Sears catalogue. Only those whose horizons had been suddenly extended beyond the narrow range of choices offered by small country stores, no matter what the individual might have desired or dreamed of, could fully appreciate the worlds opened up by these catalogues. Mail-order houses were initially hampered by the deficiencies of the U.S. postal system. Rural mail delivery was not instituted until 1896, and the parcel post system began operations in 1913. Farmers' success in obtaining these services from government at considerably less than their full cost represented one of their earliest successes in rent seeking. Even prior to these innovations, the mail-order houses expanded significantly after 1900 by utilizing the services of various express delivery companies. By that time, Sears, Roebuck and Co. was the largest retailer in America.[9]

By 1900, these new types of retail stores had affected the markets in which they operated. Owners of more traditional outlets protested against the increased competition. The outcry was occasioned by a reduction in the rents (monopoly profits) that they had previously enjoyed.[10] But the protests at this time

---

[9] Chandler, *Visible Hand*, 230–233.
[10] Chandler, *Visible Hand*, 229, 232–233.

■ Workers at the Chicago headquarters of Sears, Roebuck and Co. filled mail-orders received from catalogue subscribers across the country.
Source: Courtesy of Sears, Roebuck and Co.

were largely in vain: Local, or perhaps even state, legislators might be sympathetic, but the Supreme Court struck down attempts to protect local sellers from interstate commerce.

WIDER CHOICES

The economic growth and integration of this period resulted in a greater range of choice for consumers. Not only was there a much wider range of items, but frequently the consumer also had a choice between similar items from a variety of producers. The increase in discretionary income meant that a larger percentage of all consumer purchases could be expressions of individual choice rather than acquisitions of basic necessities. This situation undoubtedly aided consumers, but it presented sellers with increasing difficulties. More and more of what they sold encountered competition, both in the conventional sense, and in the case of discretionary spending, from a widening list of alternatives. Firms selling luxury items of any type might now find their products competing for consumers' dollars against home furnishings, appliances, sporting goods, musical instruments, books, phonographs, and even such services as travel, resorts, and amusements. Under such conditions, adequate sales were no longer assured simply by meeting the prices of similar goods.

New Forms of Advertising

Both producers and retailers responded by trying to make their goods more appealing to consumers. Advertising was more widely used, in both its informative and persuasive forms. In the cases of bananas, cigarettes, appliances, and other new products, advertising was necessary to inform people of the product's very existence, to let them know what it was, and why they might find it desirable. As previously, much advertising simply provided consumers with useful information of the "where and how much" variety.

In earlier years, advertising had been largely restricted to simple announcements in newspapers and handbills, but after 1900, advertisements began to resemble those of the modern era. Improvements in printing and lithographing techniques and the great increase in the number of magazines and other periodicals facilitated this trend. Advertising could now be directed to specific groups rather than to the general public. Specialized advertising agencies appeared to advise retailers of the appropriate marketing strategies for their goods. As might be expected, some of the most extravagant claims were made for products whose real effects were difficult to ascertain. In that era, such approaches were frequently used to market patent medicines; today they are employed to sell sporting goods and cosmetics. Although some ads were deceptive or even fraudulent, most contained at least some information useful to consumers in making informed choices.

Persuading consumers that a product was better, or at least a "better buy," was easier if the product itself could be changed, or if its reputation had been firmly established in consumers' minds. The superior performance of some goods, such as Colt revolvers, Winchester rifles, Singer sewing machines, and McCormick reapers, had already gained these items favorable reputations. Efforts were made to build such views of other goods through advertising (including slogans and testimonials), and through changing the appearance, function, or quality of the product itself. Where the product itself could not be altered, packaging and brand names were used, as with Morton's salt. These methods, if successful, allowed sellers to capitalize on the real or fancied differences that made their products better than competitors'. This would encourage repeat sales and make demand less price elastic.

■ National advertising helped promote 1910 fashions.
Source: Warshaw Collection of Business Americana, Smithsonian Institution.

Brand Names and Consumer Welfare

Prepackaged and branded goods were easier for stores to handle and convenient for consumers because there was greater assurance of uniform quality between purchases. Consumers were now able to determine which makers' output to buy or avoid. The registration of trademarks and brand names also allowed sellers to protect their products' reputations against attempts by sellers of lower-quality goods to offer them in similar packages or as the same goods.

Product differentiation could take many forms, including improvements in the goods themselves or modifications to meet specialized needs, as in tools, furniture, or clothing. In some cases, particularly foods and patent medicines, it might entail lacing unpalatable, unwholesome, or useless contents with alcohol, chemicals, or narcotics to increase their appeal while function was, if anything, impaired. Growing consumer sophistication, sensational "muckraking" exposés, and the 1906 Pure Food and Drug Act discouraged the worst of such practices.

On the whole, the result of various efforts in product differentiation was a wider series of choices open to consumers, whose chances of finding products that exactly met needs, wants, or preferences were enhanced. If the new marketing practices per se added to firms' costs, as they generally did, they often allowed production economies by widening markets and giving access to economies of scale. They also tended to promote increased competition between sellers, and thus lower profit margins. In any case, consumers still had the choice of buying goods produced and distributed under the old methods. Since manufactured goods' real prices fell, the new methods were more efficient than those they replaced.

Wholesaling

Before most goods are presented to the final user, they pass through the hands of people who link the producer with the retailer. The wholesaling function becomes increasingly important in any economy with a high degree of specialization. The concentration of manufacturing in the East and Midwest and that of particular items in smaller regions, increased the tasks of the distribution system.

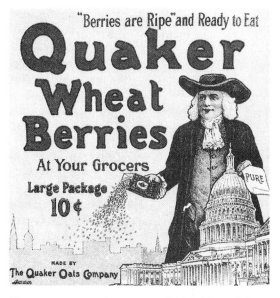

■ Quaker Oats made a commercial breakthrough by nationally advertising a product that was uniform in size, weight, and price.

So did the emergence of expanded and specialized retail outlets, which replaced direct sales by manufacturers to final consumers in local markets. Consequently, the proportion of the total work force engaged in various aspects of distribution increased by about one-half.

Wholesaling was affected by developments elsewhere in the economy. Improvements in credit markets allowed wholesalers to begin to supplant commission merchants as early as the 1840s. Commission merchants sold manufacturers' output on consignment, acting as selling agents for the maker. They did not take title to the products themselves. Unlike the commission merchants, who, in effect, used the manufacturers' credit, wholesalers financed themselves and purchased the goods they distributed. Frequently they extended credit to the retailers to whom they sold. Especially in the early years, wholesale and retail activities were intermingled. Some wholesalers maintained retail outlets, and some large-scale western retailers, for example, Marshall Field & Co., performed wholesaling functions for the smaller stores in their regions. Wholesale firms employed salesmen who visited retailers, saving them time and travel, and allowing more frequent changes in stocks. Formerly, many retailers had been forced to travel to the East to select each year's inventory.

As time passed, most mixed-function businesses tended to specialize in one level of activity. There was also increased specialization within the wholesaling function, much as had begun to appear at the retail level. Firms began to handle only groceries, dry goods, hardware, or other narrow product lines. After 1900, wholesale houses began to encounter increasing competition from large-scale retailers, such as chain and department stores and associations of independent retailers. The use of brand names encouraged direct sales from manufacturers to retailers. Although wholesalers' sales continued to increase in absolute terms, they suffered about a 13 percent drop in the proportion of all items sold at retail that had first passed through their hands in the 60 years after the peak of their power in 1869.[11]

The Role of the Middleman

Those who buy products only to sell them in the same physical form to someone else at a higher price have always had a public relations problem. To many people, it appears that since distributors do not physically change the items that they handle, they do nothing but raise their prices. Not infrequently the middleman apparently attempts to persuade customers to pay higher prices still.

There is no doubt that the income of distributors originates in the difference between the prices at which goods are purchased and those at which the same items are sold. But this does not make the distributor useless at best and an expensive parasite at worst, one whose only "function" is to raise prices; such views are accurate only to the extent that middlemen perform no function of value to ultimate consumers, or charge more than the opportunity cost of such services. All too often people forget that corn flakes at the factory in Battle Creek, Michigan, are not as convenient for consumption in Colorado as those in a Denver supermarket. In fact, they are not really even the same commodity. If consumers could buy directly from the original producers, they might not find them willing to sell in convenient quantities or to hold inventories to assure a constant supply. These are the functions of distribution, and clearly they both involve the expenditure of time and other scarce resources and are of value to consumers.

The growing volume and variety of goods that became standard items of consumption in this period and the more extensive geographic markets in which they were sold complicated the tasks of distribution. Not only did a much greater variety of goods and services, many in new forms and quantities, have to be distributed over a wider area, but many of them, and the means of producing and distributing them, required continuous servicing. If the proportion of final goods' prices representing distribution costs rose at all during the period, the increase was modest.[12] The task was not accomplished without waste nor to the satisfaction of all consumers. This hardly distinguished distribution from any other economic activity. Overall, there was substantial improvement. The quantity, quality, and variety of goods available to consumers all increased dramatically over this half-century,

[11] Chandler, *Visible Hand*, 224.

[12] S. Lebergott, *The Americans: An Economic Record* (New York: Norton, 1984), 318.

while their prices fell in relation to per-capita incomes.

INTERNATIONAL TRADE

Even though the U.S. share of all world trade nearly doubled from 1870 to 1900 and continued to increase thereafter, exchanges of goods and services with other nations became less important to the welfare of the American population. This paradox resulted from the growth of the American economy. Not only did aggregate American economic growth exceed that of nearly all the country's major trading partners, but it also resulted in great diversification. American exports grew at rates equalling or only slightly below that of the overall economy, but imports failed to keep pace. In 1870, imports were 7.9 percent of U.S. GNP and exports were 6.2 percent. By 1900, the figures were 4.3 and 7.4 percent, respectively, and in 1914 they were 4.9 and 6.1 percent.[13] Immediately after World War I, these figures, particularly exports, rose because the United States was the only undamaged industrial nation, and its food and manufactured goods helped Europe to recover from that catastrophe.

As might be expected, the massive internal changes that took place in the American economy affected international trade. Before the Civil War, the United States had exported agricultural products such as cotton, tobacco, wheat, and raw materials. Its imports were largely semifinished and finished manufactured goods. Since the early days of the nineteenth century, trade had been heavily concentrated on Europe. After the war, although agricultural products remained important, cotton and tobacco lost ground to beef, pork, and wheat. Exports of crude food-

stuffs (chiefly wheat and beef) peaked in 1880 and thenceforth fell as a portion of total exports. Processed foodstuffs (flour, packed meat, and other semiprocessed foods) increased in importance until 1890 and maintained a larger share of total exports than did crude foodstuffs.[14] American industrialization caused the proportion of manufactured imports to decline, while the export of finished goods from the United States increased. The proportion of semifinished and finished goods in American exports more than tripled by 1914 and continued to rise thereafter, reflecting U.S. primacy among the world's industrial powers. However, the growth of American manufacturing had little effect on the composition of exports until the turn of the century. Tables 15.1 and 15.2 detail these changes.

Internal and External Markets

There is little evidence that export markets were important to any large sector of the American economy except agriculture. For most producers, the growth of the domestic economy was overwhelmingly the largest component of the demand for their products, and domestic markets were the primary influence on the nature of product development and manufacture as well. With its large, rapidly growing population and high per-capita incomes, the U.S. economy constituted the largest single aggregation of purchasing power on earth, offering ample scope for the achievement of economies of scale in any manufacturing process. The design of consumer and capital goods reflected the conditions of the domestic market, rather than that for exports.

American agriculture, however, offered a major exception to this pattern. As much as one-quarter of U.S. wheat production was exported before 1900, and in periods of rapid agricultural expansion, the proportion of the

---

[13] *Historical Statistics*, 2:887.

[14] *Historical Statistics*, 2:898-899.

Table 15.1   Composition of U.S. Merchandise Exports and Imports

Exports

Year	Crude Materials	Crude Foodstuffs	Manufactured Food	Semimanufactured Goods	Finished Manufactures	Total*
1860	68.7%	3.8%	12.3%	4.1%	11.4%	100.3%
1870	56.8	11.1	13.5	3.7	14.9	100.0
1880	29.5	31.6	23.4	3.5	11.3	99.3
1890	36.6	15.6	26.6	5.4	15.7	99.9
1900	24.8	16.5	23.3	11.2	24.2	100.0
1910	33.6	6.4	15.1	15.7	29.2	100.0
1914	34.3	5.9	12.6	16.1	31.1	100.0
1920	23.3	11.4	13.8	11.9	39.7	100.1

Imports

Year	Crude Materials	Crude Foodstuffs	Manufactured Food	Semimanufactured Goods	Finished Manufactures	Total*
1860	11.3%	13.0%	16.9%	9.9%	48.6%	97.7%
1870	13.1	12.4	22.0	12.8	39.9	100.2
1880	21.3	15.0	17.7	16.6	29.5	100.1
1890	22.8	16.2	16.9	14.8	29.3	100.0
1900	33.2	11.5	15.6	15.8	23.9	100.0
1910	37.1	9.3	11.7	18.3	23.6	100.0
1914	34.3	13.1	12.0	16.8	23.7	99.9
1920	33.8	11.0	23.5	15.2	16.6	100.1

*Totals may not add to 100.0 percent because of rounding.
Source: U.S. Department of Commerce, Bureau of the Census, *Historical Statistics of the United States: Colonial Times to 1970*, 2 vols. (Washington, D.C.: Government Printing Office, 1975), 2:889–890.

increase in farm products shipped overseas was higher still. As much as one-half of the increase in wheat and pork production was exported.[15] This pattern reflected both increases in American agricultural productivity and changes in economies abroad. European populations and incomes were also rising at this time, and the attractions of these growing markets, when combined with decreasing barriers to international trade (particularly before 1880) drew a growing stream of food imports from many quarters of the world. Such developments put increasing pressure on the Continent's grain and meat producers, forcing many of them into the production of other crops or even out of agriculture. The range of American agricultural products was increased by lower ocean freight rates, improved handling and loading methods, and refrigerated ships.

---

[15] Davis, et al., *American Economic Growth: An Economist's History of the United States* (New York: Harper & Row, 1972), 558.

Table 15.2   The Balance of Trade, 1860–1920
(in Millions of Current Dollars)

Year	Total Exports	Total Imports	Trade Balance*
1860	$400	$362	$38
1870	451	462	−11
1880	853	761	92
1890	910	823	87
1900	1,491	930	570
1910	1,919	1,646	273
1914	2,532	1,991	541
1920	8,664	5,784	2,880

* A positive figure denotes an excess of exports over imports.
Source: U.S. Department of Commerce, Bureau of the Census, *Historical Statistics of the United States: Colonial Times to 1970*, 2 vols. (Washington, D.C.: Government Printing Office, 1975), 2:884–885.

Changing Import Patterns

The changes in imports were less dramatic, but they too reflected the growing wealth and industrialization of the United States and the increases in international specialization that took place at this time. (See Table 15.1.) Although imports of manufactured goods fell in relation to total imports, this decline had nearly ceased by 1900. American industrialization produced a growing demand for some inputs, such as copper and tin, that were either unobtainable within the borders of the United States or not present in sufficient quantities at current price levels. Growing American incomes spurred demand for coffee, sugar, silk, tropical fruits and oils, and other luxuries or their ingredients. With the exception of chemicals and a few resource-specific products that were cheaper to transport as finished or semi-finished goods than as raw materials, imports did not constitute a significant proportion of the needs of any American industry by 1910. The U.S. economy produced a wide variety of goods, and its overall productive efficiency was superior to that of any other nation.

New Trading Partners

In addition, some changes in the direction of trade occurred. A larger portion of American exports now went to Canada, Asia, and Latin America, and a lesser portion went to Europe. The traditional primacy of Europe, and especially Britain, as a destination for American exports declined as new overseas markets were developed, sometimes at European expense. Still, nearly two-thirds of American exports were sent to Europe after 1900, and only the Canadian market rivaled those of Britain and Germany. Americans might talk of the "limitless markets" of China, but the United States never succeeded in sending as much as 9 percent of its exports to the entire continent of Asia in any single year of this period.[16] As World War I would make tragically clear, the developed nations of the world were each others' best customers.

Europe furnished slightly more than half of all U.S. imports throughout this era, and its

---

[16] *Historical Statistics*, 2:903–904.

share fell only slightly before World War I, but American imports increasingly came from the Continent rather than the British Isles. Britain alone had provided a third or more of all American imports before 1860, but she was no longer the only industrial economy in Europe, and the United States had little need to import most British specialties. After 1900, France and Germany combined furnished a larger share of imports than did the United Kingdom, and the share of all other European countries approached that of Britain.[17]

Within the Americas, Cuba, with its sugar and tobacco, retained its position as the largest single Western Hemisphere source of American imports. After 1900, however, Cuba's primacy was increasingly challenged by Canada, Brazil, and Mexico. The Americas and Asia furnished the United States with imports, not markets. Exports to these regions were consistently less than imports from them.[18]

The Balance of Payments

For virtually its entire history before 1874, the United States had bought more merchandise from other nations than it had sold to them. The difference was made up through the earnings of its merchant marine and by borrowing abroad. Foreigners had purchased securities issued in the United States in lieu of goods. In the 1830s and 1840s, the foreign exchange brought in by immigrants could also be applied against the trade deficit. From these sources, plus gold exports after 1849, the United States earned enough to pay interest and dividends on its foreign debts, to finance remittances to the overseas relatives of immigrants, and to cover the travel expenses of Americans in Europe. For about a decade after the Civil War, these trends largely continued, although the war had all but ended the role of

the American merchant marine as a source of foreign exchange.

By 1914, however, the picture was very different from conditions prior to 1874. The United States exported more than it imported and did so every year but two after 1874. Until 1895, the United States had continued to increase its foreign debts, borrowing more from foreigners than it repaid or invested overseas. Interest and dividend payments made to foreigners had increased as America's foreign debts grew. After the mid-1890s, American citizens began to make significant foreign investments, and in the twentieth century, the net foreign debt of the United States began to fall.

Another growing source of foreign claims against the United States was immigrant remittances to relatives abroad, a flow that more than offset the foreign exchange brought into this country by new arrivals. The numbers of those already here and their increasing ability to aid their families in the "Old Country" were more than enough to offset the effects of even the heavy immigration of the last quarter-century of this period. As the American merchant marine lost its competitive edge, foreign ships carried a larger proportion of American imports and exports, and shipping charges added to the volume of foreign claims. Still, the balance of payments, unlike the balance of merchandise trade, must always balance; foreign claims against the United States must equal American claims against the rest of the world. America's earnings from the export surplus and the continued flow of European investment were sufficient to meet foreign claims arising from the needs of debt service, shipping payments, and remittances, and even left a small surplus that was used for gold imports to add to U.S. monetary reserves or, later, to finance American overseas investment.

The Role of Industrialization
The sources of these developments lay in American domestic growth and monetary policies. Industrialization proceeded faster in the United States than it did in Europe, so that

---

[17] *Historical Statistics,* 2:906–907.
[18] *Historical Statistics,* 2:906–907.

American price levels declined relative to those of other nations. As American goods became cheaper to foreigners, the price of foreign goods rose within the United States. This was the case both before 1879, while the American price level was being pushed down to allow resumption of the prewar gold standard (see Chapter 13), and after fixed exchange rates had been reestablished.[19] After 1879, the combination of fixed exchange rates and greater productivity increases in the United States than abroad made American goods increasingly attractive buys in foreign markets. Foreigners discovered that while a British pound sterling always bought $4.86 (give or take about three cents) after 1879, that $4.86 purchased a growing amount of American goods. Price levels in the United States were still falling in relation to those of the country's major trading partners on the eve of World War I. The terms of trade continued to move in America's favor in all decades except the 1880s, although the trend was slower than it had been in the first half of the century.[20]

Industrialization increased the variety of items that the United States produced. Many were goods that had formerly been imported. Both trends became especially marked after the mid-1890s, and the trade surplus grew with particular rapidity after they took hold.

World War I greatly increased the American trade surplus. It also changed the country from a net debtor on foreign account to the world's largest net creditor. During the war, both private citizens and the U.S. government made huge loans to the Allies. Foreign investments in the United States were sold as a means of financing American exports to the combatants, who could not pay with goods while their economies were devoted to war

production. The war hastened America's rise as a creditor nation, but did not begin it. American overseas investment and debt repayment had been increasing faster than European investment for over a decade prior to the war. In 1914, American investments in other countries, all privately owned, were about $3.5 billion, while foreign investments in the United States were valued at $7.2 billion.[21] The impact of World War I on international trade and finance will be further discussed in Chapter 16.

Tariffs

Trade between nations had become easier after 1870. Both physical and political barriers were reduced: Communications improved as transatlantic telegraph cables were successfully laid and shipping rates continued to fall. Barriers imposed by government action were also reduced. More and more European nations reduced their tariff rates and relaxed other trade restrictions, allowing foreign goods to enter their markets in more nearly equal competition with domestic producers than ever before. This trend was reversed in the 1880s, but while it endured, international trade was as free from political interference as it has ever been, and international specialization increased. There were only two major exceptions to this trend: Czarist Russia and the United States of America.

The U.S. government had gradually reduced tariff rates in the 1850s but sharply increased them to cover the costs of the Civil War, raising them again in 1864. By 1860, the average tariff rate on items subject to duties had been just under 20 percent and about one-fifth of all imports entered the United States duty-free. By 1865, the average rate of tariff was almost 48 percent, and by 1870, virtually

[19] J. Kindahl, "Economic Factors in Specie Resumption: The United States, 1867–1879," *The Journal of Political Economy* (February 1961).
[20] Davis, et al., *American Economic Growth*, 566.

[21] *Historical Statistics*, 2:869.

NO SAUCE FOR THE GANDER

■ Tariffs benefited the special interests of U.S. producers, not the general public, both in 1914 and today.
Source: Culver Pictures.

all imports were subject to tariffs, as the duty-free list was drastically reduced. By and large, tariff rates were held at from 40 to 50 percent of the value of the goods upon which they were levied until 1914, when the introduction of the federal income tax and popular opposition to the tariff provided both an impetus to reduce rates and an alternative source of revenue (customs duties provided nearly half of all federal government revenues between 1865 and 1913).[22] The proportion of duty-free imports was increased after 1872, and by the time rates were finally cut, nearly half of all American imports were not subject to duties.[23]

The Rationale for Tariffs

High tariffs were a cornerstone of Republican party policy, and the Republicans controlled both Congress and the Presidency for most of the time between the Civil War and 1912. Even when the Democrats were in power, there was little effective tariff reduction. A few manufacturing interests (and their employees) were fervent advocates of high tariffs and exerted disproportionate influence on policy-making.[24] Although farmers generally supported tariffs, they received few benefits from this stance. The United States had a huge surplus of agricultural exports at this time and even had rates on agricultural imports been raised to prohibitive levels, they could have had only a minor effect on the fortunes of American farmers. Although one purpose of tariffs was to furnish revenues for the federal government, there was no real effort to determine whether lower rates might not have produced more revenue by increasing the amount of imports more than in proportion to the rate reductions.

It may well be, however, that the reason high tariff rates were maintained for so long was that they were not very important to most Americans. Tariffs did raise the price of imports and distorted resource allocation into less productive patterns, but the aggregate effects on the American economy were small. Imports were not a large portion of domestic consumption for most items, and there was considerable internal competition even in most of the American industries receiving protection that compensated for the lack of that from abroad. Since foreign trade was unimportant to most Americans, neither argument that high American tariffs limited foreigners' ability to earn dollars and thus restricted their purchases of American exports, nor that they increased rents to protected industries at con-

---

[22] *Historical Statistics*, 2:1106.
[23] *Historical Statistics*, 2:888.

[24] See B. Baack and J. Ray, "The Political Economy of Tariff Policy: A Case Study of the United States," *Explorations in Economic History* (January 1983).

sumers' expense would have much impact. With the exception of a few small industries, such as tin-plated steel and sugar refining, U.S. producers generally did not need tariff protection to survive or even flourish. Many of them proved it by successfully exporting their products to the very countries against which they sought tariff protection.

Even so, there was a gradual increase in the opposition to high protective tariffs. Much of it was based on the general antipathy toward anything that smacked of monopoly, a primary feature of Progressive thought at this time. Charges that the tariff was the "mother of trusts," even if not particularly valid, had widespread political appeal. Such opposition was influential in forcing the rate reductions and expansions of the duty-free list that occurred after 1900. Nevertheless, even the total abolition of all protective tariffs would have resulted in only slight reallocations of American resources, with little effect on the overall cost of living. The tariff survived as long as it did because it conferred substantial benefits on a few owners and employees in protected industries, at the cost of almost unnoticeable reductions in the welfare of all other Americans. Such a situation produces a political equation of formidable strength today; we should not be surprised to find that it was equally effective a century ago.

IMPERIALISM

From 1870 to 1914, the developed nations of the world extended their political dominion over virtually the entire globe. By the eve of World War I, there were few nations that were not either exercising control over other regions or subject to those that were. Africa was almost entirely divided among half a dozen or so European powers; only Liberia (in which blacks of American ancestry practiced their own brand of local imperialism) and Ethiopia retained their independence. Imperial Russia had expanded into central Asia and was attempting to extend its control into Manchuria, Korea, and China. Britain and France took over all of southern Asia except a few buffer states (Persia, Afghanistan, and Siam) and the crumbling remnants of the Ottoman empire. China escaped outright partition only because the European powers that nibbled at her borders and extracted a series of humiliating concessions were unable to agree on the division of so rich a prize. Japan and Russia fought a war on Chinese soil in 1895 to determine which nation would extend its control over the northeastern provinces of the Celestial Kingdom. The Chinese were unable to make an effective protest. The islands of the world became part of the empires of one developed nation or another. Only Latin America escaped outright loss of sovereignty, and many Central and South American nations were able to preserve no more than nominal independence. The new extension of European control was unlike most previous colonial empires; most of the recently acquired areas did not attract European settlers in any numbers, as had most of the earlier colonies.

There was one notable exception. Japan escaped the fate of other underdeveloped nations by a rapid transformation from potential victim to aggressor in 40 years. Only half a century from its "opening" by Commodore Perry's squadron, Japan itself had joined the ranks of the Great Powers. By 1914, the European empires had nothing to teach the Japanese about forcible extension of national power.

The Rise of American Imperialism

The United States began its imperialist career, at least on the new model, rather late. There had, of course, been continuous expansion into territory held by the Indians since the early seventeenth century, but this had been through extension of settlement. Even the Mexican War had resulted in the acquisition of lands that Mexico had claimed, but settled very thinly or not at all (California might be a partial exception). Although our attitudes might differ today,[25] the idea from the time of the first settlements was that land left in its natural state by the Indians could be taken at will for more productive uses—and it was, with little regard for prior commitments. The U.S. purchase of Alaska in 1867, largely to keep it from British control, had been in this vein.

The United States was hardly a great military power in the late nineteenth century. In no year from 1870 to 1897 did it have as many as 50,000 men in all its military services combined,[26] and American forces were clearly designed for employment within North America or the United States itself. There was little capacity for overseas adventures; the U.S. Navy was hardly worthy of the name. Indeed, it was fortunate that its capacity to even defend the American coast was never tested in this period.

After 1890, the American stance changed with startling speed. The United States began to construct a modern navy and took a far more active political and military role outside its own borders than it had for decades past. Before this time, there had been no consistent support for interference in the internal affairs of other countries, even in cases where U.S. citizens' lives were in jeopardy. In one instance, the United States refused to intervene to prevent Nicaragua's execution of William Walker, who had attempted to gain political control of that country once too often. But this attitude changed, both in regard to local governments and toward other nations' efforts to extend their control into areas where the United States had or was attempting to obtain interests.

The Perils of Imperialism

The United States and Imperial Germany came close to violent clashes in Samoa and the Philippine Islands (1898) and exchanged very strong language over German attempts at intervention in South America. After some qualms by the Cleveland administration, in 1898 the United States annexed a short-lived Hawaiian republic set up by American citizens who had overthrown the native monarchy. American ambivalence over Latin American adventures ended; at the very least, the United States made no effort to avoid war with Spain, and the Spanish-American War (1898) resulted in U.S. control over Puerto Rico and Cuba, as well as Guam and the Philippines in the Pacific. When Colombia balked at American efforts to obtain permission to build a canal across the Isthmus of Panama, the United States gave active support to a revolt in that area and prevented its suppression by Colombia (1903). Not surprisingly, the new Republic of Panama granted the United States permission to build its canal. From about 1900 on, anyone meeting the ultimate source of authority in Central American or Caribbean nations was almost as likely to confront a colonel in the U.S. Marines as he was a native of the area. Under the Roosevelt Corollary to the Monroe Doctrine, the United States assumed the right to intervene in Latin America at any time it appeared necessary—to the United States—to restore order or assure the payment of debts to foreigners. This policy was to some extent a response to British and German attempts to collect debts with battleships when diplomatic efforts were unsuccessful.

Even more startling departures from traditional American policy occurred in the Far

---

[25] It is by no means certain that attitudes would be different. South American governments have made little serious effort to preserve Indian lands against encroachment, and the record of indigenous governments in Southeast Asia is worse. For a discussion of the historical patterns, see Lebergott, *The Americans*, Chapters. 1–2.

[26] *Historical Statistics*, 2:1141–1142.

■ Construction of the Panama Canal in 1912 was a major undertaking.
Source: Panama Canal Company.

East. The Philippine Islands and Guam were acquired from Spain when the Spanish-American War ended, just before the turn of the century. In the case of the Philippines, American sovereignty was extended over a nation that had previously been told to regard the United States as its liberator from Spanish rule. The Filipinos were a civilized people who had been Christian for centuries. It required a brutal war (1899–1901) unpleasantly prescient of a later Southeast Asian expedition to force the Philippines to accept American rule. The United States may have made no territorial demands on China, but it was anxious to avoid exclusion from those made by other powers.

The Motives for Imperialism

Imperialism has been defined as "the formal or informal extension of sovereignty beyond the borders within which it was previously exercised."[27] The actions of the United States just described fit the definition, as did those

---

[27] R. Zevin, "An Interpretation of American Imperialism," *Journal of Economic History* (March 1972).

■ Were the Philippine Islands (and the rest of the U.S. overseas empire) a white elephant? The cartoon indicates that some Americans thought so.
Source: New York *Herald,* 1898.

of Europeans and the Japanese. If there were any difference at all between American imperialistic activities and those of other nations, it lay in the scale of such activity, not its nature. In comparison with that of other nations, the imperialism of the United States was modest, particularly in view of the country's size and capabilities. But the motives that inspired imperialism appear similar among all its perpetrators at this time.

What were these motives? Two rather contradictory explanations for imperialism commonly offered are the need for overseas markets to stave off the results of overproduction in advanced capitalistic societies and the need for raw materials not obtainable within the borders of such nations. A further motive often proposed is the lure of profitable overseas investments, sometimes thought to be made necessary by a tendency toward a falling rate of profit as capitalism develops.

Such motives do not appear to explain American imperialism or any other nation's

at this time. Even had the markets among 100 million Americans possessing the world's highest incomes been inadequate to absorb all that the U.S. economy was capable of producing, it seems a little strained to envision anyone seeking rescue by adding the demand represented by Guam to this domestic market. Even if all the areas of formal and informal American control are combined, the picture is only slightly less ridiculous. Furthermore, far from representing an addition to American markets, the regions of overseas imperialism exported more to this country than they imported from it.[28] It remains to be explained how markets are expanded by increasing the cost of reaching them. The extension of political control over regions that did not welcome it required the expenditure of money and lives, and it is anything but certain that such activity made the people who bore it more inclined to buy American products.

The need-for-raw-materials argument appears even less well justified by the facts. First, the areas acquired or controlled were by and large neither known nor even suspected sources of raw materials that the United States lacked. As Finley Peter Dunne's "Mr. Dooley" remarked, most Americans did not know whether the Philippines were islands or canned goods before their acquisition.[29] Second, there was virtually no thought that U.S. natural resources were inadequate, or ever might be. The United States then produced an export surplus of most important industrial raw materials, and those it imported did not originate within its new empire. Had raw materials been a primary motive for imperialism, the United States would have directed its at-

---

[28] *Historical Statistics,* 2:903–907.
[29] For a fascinating and humorous commentary on political and social events in the United States at the turn of the century, see Finley P. Dunne, *Mr. Dooley on Ivrything and Ivrybody* (New York: Dover, 1983).

tentions toward Canada. (Mexico may be a partial exception to this conclusion.) Third, it is not necessary to control an area politically to trade with it. In this era, even the regions controlled by other imperialist powers were open to U.S. trade and investment, often on more favorable terms than those of the controlling state itself.

Imperialism did not provide investment outlets, and investors both in the United States and elsewhere were under no illusions that it did. The areas where imperialistic activity was centered over 1870–1914 offered neither markets nor resources on better terms than those already available elsewhere. In the absence of political control, the risks of investment in such regions had proven to be unacceptably high, which was why only minor fractions of the international investment were directed to them.[30] Although the return on American overseas investment was higher than the domestic rate, the difference was slight, no more than would be accounted for by greater risks. Moreover, most American investment abroad was in areas outside U.S. political control. It amounted to no more than 1 percent of total investment by this country before 1897, and 6 percent of that from 1900 to 1929.[31] Prominent businessmen in the United States were strongly opposed to imperialistic ventures, and their ranks included J. P. Morgan and Mark Hanna, the voices of financial and industrial capital.

Neither the American empire nor those newly acquired by other nations attracted large proportions of these nations' foreign investment, and much of what little did occur was undertaken for political or military pur-

poses rather than the prospect of economic gains.[32] No clear-cut evidence of a decline in the rate of profit has ever been demonstrated for this period. Foreign investment by both Europeans and Americans was overwhelmingly in countries well able to maintain their political independence under stable governments. In fact, the United States was itself the recipient of more foreign investment than any other single country over this period. Other regions of large-scale foreign investment were the self-governing dominions (not the colonies) of Great Britain.[33] Contrary to imperialists' slogans, then, trade did not follow the flag in any meaningful sense of that expression. In a recent and extensive study, Professors Davis and Huttenback concluded that the British Empire, by far the most extensive and populous of all the imperial acquisitions, resulted in an overall reduction in the income of British citizens.[34] The less promising ventures of other nations can hardly have generated better results.

If the need for markets, raw materials, or profits from overseas investments—indeed, any rational economic motive—does not explain American imperialism, then what is the answer? If it somehow developed out of the nature of capitalism, we must then explain why imperialism is at least as old as civilization (paleontologists would suggest it is older) and has occurred under regimes that by no stretch of the imagination could be termed capitalistic: Cro-Magnons, Assyrians, Imperial Chinese, Aztecs, and Incas were all

---

[30] See H. Feis, *Europe, the World's Banker, 1870–1914* (New York: Norton Reprint, 1965), for a discussion of the prospects and motives for overseas investment at this time.

[31] S. Lebergott, "The Returns to U. S. Imperialism, 1890–1929," *Journal of Economic History* (June 1980).

---

[32] Zevin, "Interpretation." See also Hughes, *Industrialization and Economic History*, Chap. 8; W. Woodruff, *The Impact of Western Man* (New York: St. Martin's Press, 1967), Chap. 2; L. Davis and R. Huttenback, *Mammon and the Pursuit of Empire: The Economics of British Imperialism* (New York: Cambridge University Press, 1988); Feis, *Europe, the World's Banker*; and Lebergott, "The Returns to U.S. Imperialism."

[33] Feis, *World's Banker*.

[34] Davis and Huttenback, *Mammon and the Pursuit*.

■ Other Americans gloried in the new overseas possessions.
Source: Denver *Rocky Mountain News,* 1900.

enthusiastic practitioners of imperialism. The roots of imperialism appear to lie in disparities of political and military power, not the natures of the highly diverse economic systems involved. As befits an activity whose costs have consistently exceeded its gains, most of the motives for imperialism are noneconomic.

If we examine the causes of imperialism, we find cultural and racial chauvinism play large roles. Americans and Europeans of this period were inclined to believe that their political and economic systems were superior to those of any other country, and at the time, they had some basis for this opinion. These nations had achieved representative governments, predictable legal systems, and high standards of living, health, and technological progress. Many had done so within the memories of men still active. When these achievements were contrasted with the political chaos then plaguing much of Latin America or the inept brutality that passed for government in many other regions, it is easy to see why outsiders reached the conclusion that conditions could be improved by the introduction of institutions that had produced such good results in their homelands. It seldom occurred to the proponents of such improvements to inquire whether the changes were welcomed. All too

often the less-developed areas furnished "proof" that outside control was needed. The murdered missionary, continuous tribal warfare, slavery, broken contracts with the outside world, or the barbarous mistreatment of their own nationals all appeared adequate rationales to the advocates of intervention.[35]

Today, the very notions of "Manifest Destiny," the "White Man's Burden," or the "Civilizing Mission" and other justifications for assuming control over distant nations may appear transparently racist and/or chauvinistic nonsense. At the time, however, they were regarded very differently. Nor were these the views held by tiny political or economic elites within the imperialistic nations; they were the opinions of large numbers of ordinary people. President Theodore Roosevelt was cordially detested by much of the American business community; but "Teddy" was the most genuinely popular president since Andrew Jackson. His ardent and outspoken imperialistic opinions apparently enhanced the esteem in which he was held by the electorate. The fortunes of those British politicians who opposed the Boer War (from 1899 to 1902 Britain conquered the previously independent Boer republics of southern Africa) would reinforce this view.

The Costs of Empire

Imperialism's costs may have exceeded the gains achieved by the nations that practiced it, but those costs were very low. Industrialization conferred an enormous military advantage on the Europeans, Americans, and Japanese over nations that had not achieved it. Ridiculously small forces with modern equipment, organization, and training could and did overcome large armies using tradi-

---

[35] J. Hughes, *Industrialization and Economic History* (McGraw-Hill, 1972).

tional military methods and weapons. Often the imperialistic forces found local allies eager to even old scores, just as they had among American Indians. Nor were imperialist adventures likely to carry great domestic political costs. To oppose the imposition of stable governments and western ideas of justice merely because the prospective beneficiaries did not want them was to seem to favor the continuation of practices that the West found abhorrent. If there were military casualties, the troops involved were long-term professionals, not draftees. Those carrying out the imperialist mission presumably had a clear idea of the risks they incurred by military service, and these were generally minimal.

Great Power politics was another factor contributing to imperialism. The United States acquired several areas (Alaska in 1867 and Hawaii in 1898) to forestall their control by other powers, generally Britain. This, of course, could be a self-sustaining process. Nations aspiring to Great Power status required large military forces, and the military tended to seek employment that justified its existence. The U.S. Navy was powerfully influenced by the seapower theories of Albert T. Mahan. Mahan regarded a strong blue-water navy as absolutely essential for the maintenance of U.S. security. Such a navy required bases, both in the United States itself and in outposts from which American foreign trade and critical arteries such as the Panama Canal could be defended. If military aspirations were sufficiently grandiose, acquisition of new outposts might only cease when they reached those of another Great Power.

Finally, even though imperialism was not profitable to the nations that practiced it, the lack of positive returns for the country as a whole did not mean that some individuals or firms might not find it a means to extract rents from both their own governments and the areas where it occurred. They might be able to shift most of the costs of their actions to taxpayers and the military.[36] If the United Fruit Company could count on the support of the Marines without charge, it might be easier to extract concessions from Central American governments that could resist pressure from firms, but not military force. Once again, a situation in which a small group might reap concentrated gains that were considerably lower than the aggregate cost borne by a much larger, less organized population generated rent-seeking activity. If "glory" could be added to unimpressive empirical returns, so much the better.

Further support for these views is indicated through the manner in which most imperialistic ventures were proposed. Theodore Roosevelt urged the American people to "Forget their pocketbooks for once," and support the Spanish-American War. Only when the costs of their proposals were questioned did the imperialists begin to talk of markets, fields for investment, or sources of raw materials. There were links between economic development and imperialism, but it was the former that reduced the costs of imperialism. Imperialism may have been cheap, but that did not make it profitable on an aggregate basis.

American imperialism and that of other developed nations during this period was real enough, but its links to economics were weak. The real causes lay in cultural, political, and technological developments, and only secondarily in any rational calculations of potential costs and gains. Whatever the record of the United States may have been within the areas in which it was active, the political harvest was almost certainly negative. Latin Americans have shown a lasting distrust of the United States ever since this period. They had legitimate cause to resent both the tactics of the United States and the premises on which they were based.

---

[36] Zevin, *Interpretation.* See also Davis and Huttenback, *Mammon and the Pursuit.*

SELECTED REFERENCES

Chandler, A., Jr. *The Visible Hand: The Managerial Revolution in American Business.* Cambridge, Mass.: Harvard University Press, 1977.

Cohen, B. *The Question of Imperialism: The Political Economy of Dominance and Independence.* New York: Basic Books, 1973.

Davis, L., R. Easterlin, W. Parker et al. *American Economic Growth: An Economist's History of the United States.* New York: Harper & Row, 1972.

Davis, L., and R. Huttenback. *Mammon and the Pursuit of Empire: The Economics of British Imperialism.* New York: Cambridge University Press, 1988.

Feis, H. *Europe, The World's Banker, 1870–1914.* New York: Norton Reprint, 1965.

Hilgert, F. *Industrialization and Foreign Trade.* Geneva, Switzerland: League of Nations, 1945.

Hughes, J. *Industrialization and Economic History: Theses and Conjectures.* New York: McGraw-Hill, 1970.

Livesay, H., and G. Porter. *Merchants and Manufacturers.* Baltimore: Johns Hopkins University Press, 1971.

Maizels, A. *Growth and Trade.* Cambridge, U.K.: Cambridge University Press, 1970.

Ratner, S. *The Tariff in American History.* New York: Van Nostrand, 1972.

Taussig, F. *The Tariff History of the United States.* 7th ed. New York: G. P. Putnam's Sons, 1923.

U.S. Department of Commerce, Bureau of the Census. *Historical Statistics of the United States: Colonial Times to 1970.* 2 vols. Washington, D.C.: Government Printing Office, 1975.

Wilkins, M. *The Emergence of Multinational Enterprise: American Business Abroad from the Colonial Era to 1914.* Cambridge, Mass.: Harvard University Press, 1970.

Williamson, J. *American Growth and the Balance of Payments, 1820–1913.* Chapel Hill, N.C.: University of North Carolina Press, 1964.

Woodruff, W. *The Impact of Western Man.* New York: St. Martin's Press, 1967.

GOVERNMENT IN
AN EXPANDING
ECONOMY

*T*he 1870–1914 period has long been regarded as the high tide of laissez-faire, the philosophy of minimal government intervention in the economy. By modern standards, government's economic role in this period was indeed small, both in terms of aggregate fiscal impact (the proportion of GNP accounted for by government is indicated in Tables 16.1 and 16.2) and in the scope and nature of regulation. Still, government's impact on the U.S. economy increased, particularly after 1900.

THE LAISSEZ-FAIRE ERA

Real per-capita tax revenues increased after the Civil War to more than twice their level in 1850 or 1860.[1] Until 1870, the rate of tax increase for all levels of government combined probably exceeded that of per-capita income, but the pace then slowed, only to rise again after 1890. By contemporary standards, government purchased only a very small share of the economy's total output. Even so, it is clear that all three levels of government—federal, state, and local—were at no time restricted to the roles prescribed by laissez-faire. The laissez-faire philosophy does *not* imply no economic role for government. Private property cannot exist without guarantees of ownership rights that only government can make. Still, the governmental role in a laissez-faire economy is limited to maintenance of internal law and order, provision of security from foreign attack, settlement of disputes between citizens through the courts, and little else. Since these

activities all require resources, some form of taxation is also implicit.

Market Economies and the Role of Government

The laissez-faire philosophy rests on the belief that a market economy will produce optimum economic results through its operations, without interference by government. The market system is a device for expression of the interactions between human wants and scarce means of production. The interaction of supply and demand in competitive markets allows market economies to provide automatic (this does not imply either perfect or instantaneous) responses to changes in tastes, resources, or technology as these occur. It also generates continual pressure to use resources to produce the most highly valued mix of goods and services that available factors of production and techniques will allow.

The market system operates to provide the population with as much as possible of what it wants most through a most unlikely driving force—individual self-interest. (A less elegant term is greed.) Individuals' efforts to obtain as much as possible for themselves in a system of informed and voluntary exchange result in concern for others' wants and needs: Producers' incomes are greatest when they employ their talents and the services of any nonhuman resources they own in response to the priorities of others. Sellers take their customers' desires into account out of love for themselves, not their fellows. Their incomes will be higher if they produce what buyers want rather than what someone else has decided they should have. By responding to buyers, sellers increase their own ability to obtain desired goods. As tastes or productive capabilities change, the system generates pressures on producers and consumers alike to adjust to the new circumstances.

The market automatically incorporates and adjusts to information that other types of

---

[1] J. Legler, R. Sylla, and J. Wallis, "U.S. City Finances and the Growth of Government, 1850–1902," *Journal of Economic History* (June 1988).

economic systems might be slow to recognize or find difficult to accommodate. It provides a system of feedback that allows rapid and conclusive evaluation of alternatives through prices. Relative prices provide the essential communication, coordination, and incentives for efficient responses to economic stimuli.

Efficiency

Self-interested responses to scarcity generate economic efficiency. Consumers seek to maximize satisfaction from incomes insufficient to buy all of everything they might like to have. Consequently, they become bargain hunters.

Producers, especially in competitive markets, find that their profits can be increased by reducing costs as well as by raising prices. Since resources generally have multiple uses, inputs cannot be obtained at less than their opportunity costs. The market system exerts continual pressure to employ more efficient (input-minimizing) methods, because this allows producers either to produce a greater value of the same goods, or to use the resources saved in the production of other goods: Both raise incomes.

Once the economy has made a complete response to all available opportunities to

■ Wash day in a New York City tenement: Notice how space was at a premium.
Source: Underwood Photo Archives.

increase income (the economist's long-run equilibrium), a competitive market system will turn out the largest possible output of the items most highly valued by consumers permitted by the available means of production. Moreover, it will generate a system of prices for these goods that reflects their value in terms of alternatives foregone, that is, the real cost of any scarce good. In addition, the system produces a maximum degree of human freedom; each person may produce or consume as he or she wishes, subject only to the costs imposed by alternatives foregone. The market economy is the most efficient response yet developed to the fundamental economic problem of scarcity.

The market system developed long before any comprehensive analysis of such an institution had been worked out, but by the end of the nineteenth century, economists had formulated a complete theoretical description of the operations of market economies. In part, the theory of the market system developed as an alternative to the extensive mercantilist intervention practiced by most governments in the seventeenth and eighteenth centuries. As is true of most ideas, the concept of minimal government intervention was selectively applied. Total allegiance to free markets was and is rare; few persons really welcome competition in their own jobs or for the items they wish to buy or sell.

Social Darwinism

One nineteenth-century doctrine carried the cause of economic nonintervention a great deal further than mere laissez-faire. Social Darwinism was an attempt to apply Charles Darwin's views on the role of biological selection of animal survival characteristics to economic affairs. The theory of markets views income distribution as a reflection of individual productivity. Those resources or their owners that contribute a great deal to others'

satisfaction, as indicated by consumers' willingness to pay for the product, receive high incomes; those making smaller contributions receive less. The resulting income differences (a market system's operations guarantee income differentials unless people themselves are uniform in all productivity-influencing attributes) provide incentives to self-interested individuals to become more productive, that is, to produce, within the limits of their capabilities, what others want to buy, or to do so more efficiently.

Social Darwinism not only stressed these roles of income differences, it viewed the attributes that generated them as hereditary, like the characteristics that promoted or hindered the survival of animal species. To Social Darwinists, interferences with market-determined income differences would not only reduce the incentives for both high-income "donors" and low-income beneficiaries in the short run, over time they would enhance the survival chances of the less productive and discourage further development of high productivity. The proportion of those less able to produce would increase as the incapable passed on their characteristics to their offspring. The theories of Social Darwinism went a great deal farther than either free-market economists or biologists had pushed their ideas; few if, any of them believed that productivity was genetically determined.

Even though Social Darwinism was widely publicized by intellectuals, the press, and (surprise!) those with high incomes, it is not clear to what extent nineteenth-century Americans ever really accepted these ideas. There were too many examples of income mobility in both directions and of government actions that curtailed markets yet produced unquestionable improvements in general welfare (for example, the restrictions in individual freedom imposed by public health regulations) to make belief in the most extreme versions of this theory tenable. It was obvious that some of the poor were talented and ambitious and some children of the rich had inherited material possessions, but not personal attributes, from their parents. Social Darwinism was a very convenient prop for those opposed to joint efforts by workers or voters to raise incomes through unions or government measures because it viewed these as morally wrong and economically ruinous, stressing the economic virtues of individual rather than joint action. At least in direct form, little redistribution occurred until the very end of the period.

Market Failure

The sweeping changes that occurred with industrialization, the rise of giant corporations, and urbanization required changes in existing economic institutions and the development of some entirely new ones. When institutions change or are newly developed, individuals will try to shape them to their own advantage, or will devote resources to protecting themselves from losses that might otherwise result from others' attempts to gain. The very increase in incomes and wealth produced by these changes may have convinced some that it was now worth trying to achieve some form of redistribution.

The view of the completely self-regulating market system was honored in the breach as time passed. Both in the provision of government services, which sometimes had redistributive aspects, and in the regulations imposed on economic activity, there had always been an element of governmental intervention, however slight. In some cases, measures had favored one group over others or over the general public, as in tariff policy or legal attitudes toward workers' or producers' combinations. Even when the operation of a competitive economy is fully understood, some of the results it produces may clash with individuals' ethics as well as self-interest. The idea that under a market system people receive the

value of what they contribute to others' welfare also implies that those with high incomes have a disproportionate voice in deciding what is to be produced; they have a great many money "votes" for their own desires. There may be people whose productivity is very low or negative for reasons beyond their own control (the critically ill, for example). Such persons will have little or no voice in a pure market system, while the rich can influence what constitutes productivity in others by their purchases.

At the end of the nineteenth century, it was clear that not all markets provided either buyers or sellers with a wide range of choice. The impact of monopoly may well have been overstated at this time, but it was obvious that the economy was not perfectly competitive, and there were widespread fears that monopoly was increasing. Nor was the economy completely stable; even though a market system contains automatic adjustment mechanisms that reallocate resources as circumstances change, it cannot prevent such changes and probably makes them more likely than do many other economic systems. Reallocative adjustments cannot always be made quickly enough to prevent individual hardship. If jobs are lost in one town or industry because of a change in tastes or techniques, the unemployed resources will be pressured to take their best alternative occupations, but the process may require a prolonged period of search for those alternatives. For individuals, these alternatives are often inferior to their previous employment.

THE ECONOMIC FUNCTIONS OF GOVERNMENT

Even the idealized model of a market economy, in which all markets are perfectly competitive and information is freely available to all parties, contains a very definite role for

■ Among the famous cartoons drawn by satirist Thomas Nast is this one, which ridiculed Tammany Hall, the New York City political machine. *Source:* Library of Congress.

economy is not neutral: It carries an implicit acceptance of the consequences of unregulated private action through markets.

The views of most Americans favoring a limited economic role for government were more than a mere self-serving justification of the status quo on the part of those favored by current conditions. As the preceding pages have emphasized, there is ample evidence that most U.S. citizens had prospered under the limited government involvement of this era. Furthermore, American pragmatism had allowed departures from laissez-faire in cases where the gains from such actions were obvious. But the changing economy produced conditions that demonstrated the inadequacy of institutions designed for a period in which most people were small-scale farmers with limited ties to the rest of the economy.

Rent Seeking

Government can also be used by individuals to achieve gains for themselves regardless of the cost to others. In transactions carried out through markets, each party pays directly for the items obtained, and sellers will not continue to provide goods whose costs of production exceed their sale prices. But government breaks this direct connection between costs and benefits. Goods provided through government still impose costs on the economy in terms of alternatives foregone. But those costs may be borne by people other than those who receive the government-produced or funded goods. For the aggregate economy, there is no such thing as a free good made from scarce resources. Nevertheless, it is quite possible that individuals may succeed in shifting the opportunity cost of the items or services they obtain through government action to others. Government can be used to create rents for individuals, through income transfers, protection from competition, or other forms of favoritism. Since the recipients

government. Certain economic activities can only be performed effectively by government: security, the settlement of disputes, and the provision of public goods (which provide benefits to the economy exceeding their cost, but once produced, have zero marginal costs). In addition, the very process of defining rules, or refusing to do so, influences the climate in which economic activity occurs, and hence the activity itself. When the extent to which individuals are responsible to others for the consequences of their actions is defined, the scope for economic activity is changed. It must also be recognized that the refusal to use government action to influence some element of the

of these rents pay less than the full cost of providing them, they are likely to demand more than is economically efficient from the viewpoint of the entire economy. Further waste may occur because those who would be required to pay for such transfers (taxpayers or consumers) are likely to devote resources to the prevention of such losses. Resources devoted to rent-seeking or its prevention can only redistribute or retain existing real income through these uses; the economy sacrifices the alternative output it might otherwise have achieved. In a world of scarcity, this means that total welfare is reduced.

Professors Lance Davis and Douglas North have observed that both the private and governmental institutions of a market system tend to be stable unless some individuals or groups perceive an opportunity for gains from changing them that exceeds the costs of institutional change.[2] Perceived gains may originate in access to economies of scale, externalities, the correction of market failures, attitudinal changes concerning risk, or income redistribution (not necessarily toward greater equality), through the employment of the government's coercive powers.

The first four types of change add to total incomes and need not (although they frequently do) involve income redistribution. Because no one will lose in absolute terms, they may be achieved by purely voluntary means and are unlikely to generate opposition. For example, legal provision for corporate structures might allow a firm to mobilize sufficient capital to allow full utilization of econ-

omies of scale in manufacturing. Government aid to railroad construction (at least in the form of grants of otherwise useless land) might be another example if the railroads were expected to make a much greater contribution to aggregate income than indicated by their receipts alone, and private capital was not available because railroads were regarded as a high-risk investment.

Market failure can result from high information costs. Especially in new markets, information may be difficult and costly to obtain, but once mechanisms to generate it are established, they are often subject to increasing returns: The same mechanisms can provide additional information without a proportional increase in costs. When mortgage companies established their agent networks in the capital-starved West and sold eastern investors their own securities rather than individual mortgages, they allowed funds to flow from areas of low interest rates but accurate information to regions where high interest rates had not previously sufficed to compensate for investors' inability to evaluate the risks involved.[3]

Redistribution and Economic Efficiency

Income redistribution might be direct, through government's tax and spending policies, or through grants or withdrawal of monopoly power to some private group. Income redistribution can only award to recipients what is taken from donors, so opposition to such programs is inevitable. If such policies are to be instituted and maintained, the resistance must be overcome. Actions taken through the government are less reversible than those done through market transactions. If benefits fall or costs rise, the volume of market transactions will be reduced if not

[2] L. Davis and D. North, "Institutional Change and American Economic Growth: A First Step Toward a Theory of Institutional Innovation," *Journal of Economic History* (March 1970). See also L. Davis, R. Easterlin, and W. Parker, *American Economic Growth: An Economist's History of the U.S.* (New York: Harper & Row, 1972), Chap. 17; D. North and L. Davis, *Institutional Change and American Economic Growth* (Cambridge, U.K.: Cambridge University Press, 1971); and D. North, *Structure and Change in Economic History* (New York: Norton, 1981).

[3] Davis and North, "Institutional Change."

eliminated; but government programs that produce results less desirable than expected may not be so easy to discontinue. Examples are tax policy, tariffs, the control of monopoly through public utility regulation and antitrust, and the grant of monopoly power to professional groups through laws that allow them to limit their own membership.[4] All these, and more, were areas of government activity from 1870 to 1914.

North and Davis found that government actions had both positive and negative economic effects in this period. Governments' fiscal powers might be used because private financial markets were poorly developed, for example, in canal financing. As capital markets grew and corporations became more common, government aid became less necessary. It was not used to the same extent for railroads as it had been for canals, nor was it employed for manufacturing. On the other hand, urbanization, with its numerous positive and negative externalities and growing need for public goods, favored the growth and extension of government services, as did the rise of a national market, which placed a premium on the accurate compilation and distribution of information.[5] Government's aggregate size and goals are not determined solely by dispassionate assessments of costs and benefits. Ideology also plays an important role; people develop institutions to further their views on what the economic environment should provide (equity or ideology).[6] Through this period, the prevailing attitudes were very much in favor of individual responsibility for each person's welfare and of action through the market.

Thus, there are two possible roles for government in a market economy. Government is an absolute necessity for the efficient functioning of private markets. But it is also a mechanism for introducing inefficiency into the system through the encouragement of rent-seeking behavior that may be very difficult to excise. It has been observed that stable and long-established political systems encourage the formation of rent-seeking groups because the gains, if achieved, are likely to be long lasting and the results of change more predictable. But the same author concluded that the U.S. economy in this period was not stable; technology and resource supplies were changing rapidly, and effective rent-seeking coalitions were difficult to form while entry into most markets remained open and the federal structure made it difficult to achieve governmental aid that extended over the entire economy.[7] Others view this period as a watershed in which government became increasingly receptive to efforts to promote rent-seeking, rather than devoted largely to the promotion of aggregate economic growth.[8]

THE SIZE OF GOVERNMENT

In 1902, the aggregate impact of local government expenditures was larger than either federal or state government spending, a status achieved about 1890. As yet, we still lack specific data on state and local government expenditures before 1902, but they undoubtedly conformed closely to tax revenues.[9] By modern standards, the aggregate fiscal impact of government was very small throughout the period, but there was a rising trend after the Civil

---

[4] Davis and North, "Institutional Change."
[5] Davis and North, "Institutional Change." See also Legler, Sylla, and Wallis, "U.S. City Finances."
[6] North, *Structure and Change*, Chap. 5.

[7] M. Olson, *The Rise and Decline of Nations: Economic Growth, Stagflation, and Social Rigidities* (New Haven, Conn.: Yale University Press, 1982), 94–117.
[8] T. Anderson and P. Hill, *The Birth of a Transfer Society* (Stanford, Calif.: Hoover Institute Press, 1980). See also J. Hughes, *The Governmental Habit: Economic Controls From Colonial Times to the Present* (Charlottesville, Va.: University of Virginia Press, 1977).
[9] Legler, Sylla, and Wallis, "U.S. City Finances."

Table 16.1 Government Spending, 1860–1920
(Millions of Current Dollars)

Year	Federal Spending	Percent of GNP	State Spending	Percent of GNP	Local Spending	Percent of GNP	Aggregate Percent of GNP
1860	$63.1	1.6%	—	—	—	—	—
1870	309.7	3.7	—	—	—	—	—
1880	267.6	2.7	—	—	—	—	—
1890	318.0	2.4	—	—	—	—	—
1902	572.0	2.6	$188	0.9%	$959	4.4%	7.9%
1913	970.0	2.4	398	1.0	1,960	4.9	8.3
1920	3,763.0	5.1	1,397	1.9	4,567	6.2	13.2

Source: U.S. Department of Commerce, Bureau of the Census, *Historical Statistics of the United States: Colonial Times to 1970*, 2 vols. (Washington, D.C.: Government Printing Office, 1975), 1:224; 2:1123–1132.

War.[10] This increase was concentrated in areas with large urban populations. Spending apparently rose more rapidly than did population, although perhaps it no more than kept pace with per-capita income, which rose strongly after 1870.[11] As Table 16.1 indicates, the data show no clear trend in federal spending relative to GNP between 1880 and 1913.

Both state and local spending show greater rates of increase after 1902. As the nation urbanized, city spending replaced county as the chief source of local spending. This was a primary cause of the increase after the Civil War: Cities spent more per capita than county government, and large cities more still.[12]

Even by 1900, however, total spending by all levels of government was just under $20 per U.S. citizen. Local governments accounted for 45.9 percent of this amount, the states for 16.6 percent, and the federal government for the remaining 37.5 percent. By these measures, government expenditures were 8.3 percent of GNP. Clearly, if the criterion was aggregate fiscal impact, the role of government in the United States was slight. Public spending on goods and services shows no rise in relation to GNP before 1900, remaining at about 5 percent, and it rises only to 6 percent in the first decades of the twentieth century.[13] Transfer payments had become more important, particularly for the federal government, after the Civil War.

The taxes to support this spending were levied on property (almost entirely real estate) at the local level, while the federal government relied largely on tariff income, with lesser amounts from excise taxes on liquor and tobacco. The states also relied heavily on property taxes.[14] (See Table 16.2.)

[10] L. Davis and J. Legler, "The Government in the American Economy, 1815–1902: A Quantitative Study," *Journal of Economic History* (December 1966). This finding was confirmed by Legler, Sylla, and Wallis, "U.S. City Finances."
[11] Davis and Legler, "Government in the Economy."
[12] Legler, Sylla, and Wallis, "U.S. City Finances."

[13] Data are from Thomas Berry, *Revised Annual Estimates of American Gross National Product*, Bostwick Paper #3 (Richmond, Va.: Bostwick Press, 1978). These estimates appear to imply lower per-capita income levels than are generally accepted.
[14] U.S. Department of Commerce, Bureau of the Census, *Historical Statistics of the United States: Colonial Times to 1970*, 2 vols. (Washington, D.C.: Government Printing Office, 1975), 2:1106–1120.

Table 16.2   Federal, State, and Local Tax Revenues per Capita, 1850–1902
(Constant 1914 Dollars)

Year	Federal	State and Local	State	Local
1850	$2.05	$2.20	$.74	$1.46
1860	2.05	3.22	.89	2.33
1870	8.64	5.36	1.30	4.06
1880	6.82	6.02	1.04	4.98
1890	7.24	9.01	1.74	7.27
1902	7.54	12.64	2.29	10.35

Source: J. Legler, R. Sylla, and J. Wallis, "U.S. City Finances and the Growth of Government, 1850–1902," *Journal of Economic History* (June 1988).

The largest single item of federal government spending was defense. Consequences of the Civil War, such as veterans' pensions and interest and principal repayments on the national debt, ranked second. State government spending was distributed over many functions, with only hospitals, education, and general administrative costs receiving sizable portions. Local governments spent most of their funds on education and highways, with public utilities receiving a growing, but still small, share after 1900.[15]

The Redistributive Aspects of Government Spending

Federal taxes and expenditures had some redistributive effects, at least in a geographic sense. Since revenues were largely derived from tariffs and excise taxes, their impact was generally concentrated on eastern seaports and urban areas. Military spending, the largest single federal expenditure, was heavily directed toward the frontier. It was so far out of proportion to the damage that Indians might have inflicted that two students of the period's fiscal policies suggested, only half in jest, that it would have benefited most states to import a few moderately hostile Indians, if they were not already present, because their presence did so much to raise federal spending. This policy, and that of establishing post offices in sparsely settled regions where the volume of mail was insufficient to finance them from local revenues, helped transfer income to the new regions of the country. The regions enjoying an excess of federal spending in relation to revenues collected were the Old South, which contained the District of Columbia and only one major seaport, Baltimore; the Rocky Mountain States, with their army outposts; and New England, which received large sums through repayment of government debt to its bondholders and through veterans' pensions.[16]

There is some evidence that federal expenditures rose in recessions and offered countercyclical effects, but in view of the overall magnitude of government spending and its variations (and the virulence of the business cycle), the results could not have been very significant. In general, the inclination at all levels of government was to spend whatever

[15] *Historical Statistics*, 2:1119–1120.

[16] Davis and Legler, "Government in the Economy."

amount was raised by current taxation and to tax whatever seemed a likely source of revenue incapable of effective protest. Little attention was paid to the macroeconomic effects of such programs, and even less was understood about them. The federal government did not even have a formal budget until 1921, and few areas of expenditure were sensitive to the business cycle except as they related to the banking system. Thus, the aggregate tax and expenditure policies of all levels of government were neither oriented toward the prevention of major economic fluctuations nor large enough to accomplish this before 1914. Tables 16.1 and 16.2 indicate that taxation and spending levels for all governments had a tendency to increase permanently after major wars.

GOVERNMENT PROGRAMS AS A SOURCE OF GROWTH

Chapter 9 pointed out that aggregate government spending is only one measure of public expenditures' impact on the economy. The effects that these expenditures produce in other sectors of the economy may be more significant. If government expenditures are concentrated on activities that are uncommonly productive (or the reverse), the amount of spending or its relation to GNP may not indicate its effects on economic growth. In this period, there were at least four "uncommonly productive" types of government expenditures.

Railroads Government aid to western railroads directed capital toward a use in which the social rate of return was at least twice that obtained on private capital. Thus, government assistance to at least some western railroads yielded a rate of return to the aggregate economy twice that obtained by the railroads themselves from such funds. However, it is

not at all clear that those railroads' own (private) returns were insufficient to attract construction funds.[17] Much the same is true for government expenditures on education and agricultural research, but public health measures probably required government, rather than private, spending to be effective.

Public Education There appear to have been very high social rates of return on education, particularly at the primary and secondary levels, where efforts were concentrated at this time.[18] Although high school enrollment began to increase rapidly after 1900, even in 1914 only one person in nine among those of high-school age or older was a graduate.[19] Colleges in that period enrolled about 1 in every 35 persons in the 18- to 24-year-old age group.

Despite the large numbers of former slaves and immigrants, whose literacy rates were low in relation to that of native whites, no nation in the world had higher literacy rates than the United States by 1914.[20] American educators stressed the fact that enrollment in publicly supported high schools and colleges was open to all, but only a small portion of low-income groups' children attended. In those days of child labor and ready employment for unskilled workers, the cost of education in terms of foregone income rose steeply with age. For all but the most determined of the poor, the cost of advanced schooling was too high. Nevertheless, the ability to use education was a significant factor in improving economic efficiency.

[17] L. Mercer, "Building Ahead of Demand: Some Evidence for the Land Grant Railroads," *Journal of Economic History* (June 1974).
[18] A. Fishlow, "Levels of Nineteenth-Century American Investment in Education," *Journal of Economic History* (December 1966).
[19] Davis and Legler, "Government in the Economy."
[20] Fishlow, "Levels of Investment." See also "The American Common School Revival: Fact or Fancy?" in H. Rosovsky, ed., *Industrialization in Two Systems: Essays in Honor of Alexander Gerschenkron* (Huntingdon, N. Y.: Robert E. Krieger Publishing Company, Inc., 1966).

■ Students at Tuskegee Institute at the turn of the century were among those given the rare opportunity of getting an advanced education.
Source: Library of Congress.

The achievement of American blacks in attaining literacy is especially noteworthy. In 1865, of course, virtually all of the newly liberated blacks were illiterate. By 1900, 55.5 percent of all nonwhites were literate, and by 1920, the figure had climbed to 77 percent.[21] When it is remembered that this education came at high costs in foregone earnings for people (especially adults) whose incomes were pathetically small, it indicates the determination of blacks to gain full participation in the American economy.

Public Health Public health measures, and the regulations that made them effective, created a more productive work force and reduced the incidence of premature deaths, particularly among children and infants (see Chapter 14).

Agricultural Research Although the Morrill Act provided federal funds and land grants to support state colleges in 1862, it was not until the turn of the century that the agricultural

schools and experimental farms established through this legislation began to produce significant results. Even the principles of basic research procedures were unknown when this effort began. The contribution that such sciences as chemistry, geology, and statistics could make to agricultural research was not realized; it took time to develop effective programs. After 1920, however, the application of science to agriculture began to produce large increases in productivity.

Other Programs Federal land policy was really a transfer of wealth from public to private hands. The land produced far more income for farmers and cattlemen than it had as part of the public domain. The high tariffs of the period cost more in resource misallocation than they produced in revenue, but the overall impact was slight. Veterans' pensions owed far more to the efforts of pressure groups such as the Grand Army of the Republic than they did to any degree of economic rationality. They were one of the earliest examples of successful

---

[21] *Historical Statistics*, 1:382.

rent-seeking. Most defense spending contributed neither enhanced security nor technological spinoffs during this period, but military spending was far below its present dimensions. Expenditures on roads may have had high social returns, but I am unaware of studies on this point. Since the "uncommonly productive" aspects of government expenditures accounted for a large portion of the total, it seems safe to conclude that government expenditures were about as productive as those of the private sector, although the range of variation between the results of various programs was probably wider.

THE INCREASING SCOPE OF GOVERNMENT

If the fiscal impact of government, even when its areas of primary concentration are considered, was modest, another factor was the impact of government regulatory activity. New laws modified private economic activity by providing and changing the rules under which it occurred. The details of bank regulation, monetary policy, international monetary considerations, immigration, and the Federal Reserve have already been discussed, as has most of the important labor legislation. In this period, government at all levels began a concern with the conduct of many other aspects of economic life. Conditions of life in the cities were the occasion of much concern, and government activities aimed at humanitarian goals, such as regulation of the conditions under which women and children worked, had an impact on labor force productivity and even on the size of the work force.

Public Utilities Regulation

Some urban developments posed a dilemma. The provision of services such as water, gas, electricity, and sometimes intraurban transportation was subject to great economies of scale. A single source of such utilities, once established, might well be able to provide service to additional customers at only a slight addition to its costs. Thus, if the costs of such services were to be minimized (and in some cases, such as telephones, if convenient service was to be provided at all), the total cost of doing so for any number of patrons would be least if a single firm handled the entire operation. But such a supplier would be a monopolist, and worse, a monopolist controlling a product that had no acceptable substitutes. There was no guarantee that such a monopolist would charge prices reflecting only his low costs of production. Indeed, there were sound reasons to believe that such a market position would be turned to the seller's advantage. A more competitive market structure might involve higher prices than the monopolist's if economies of scale were large.

Two solutions were available. Cities might provide the benefits of economies of scale to their citizens by operating such services themselves (a direct expansion of local government), or they might persuade private sellers to accept regulation of their prices, output, and production methods in return for a grant of exclusive rights to the entire urban market. The relative advantages of public ownership and regulated monopolies were topics of continuous debate throughout this period, as they are today. In addition, there was the problem of ensuring efficient operation under either system, that is, making sure that prices not only reflected costs of operation, but that those costs were as low as input prices and modern technology allowed.

The legal case for regulation received a powerful boost in 1877. In that year, the Supreme Court ruled that firms whose activities affected large numbers of people (that operated "in the public interest") were subject to government regulation for the common good. The decision in *Munn v. Illinois* clearly allowed scope for the expansion of economic regulation, but did not spell out the forms it might take or the range of activities subject to such considerations. It was not even clear whether the decision made any firm subject to regulation or restricted the government to those in designated fields of operation. In the opinion of some economists, this decision marked a major change in policy: *Munn v. Illinois* indicated a change in government's role from the promotion of private economic activity toward redistribution of the fruits of current activity.[22]

Regulation of Interstate Commerce

The concern over the procedures of large, privately owned firms had spurred efforts to control them. The first attempts to do so were at the state level. The operating practices of grain elevators and railroads were of great interest to farm groups. The so-called Granger Laws were upheld for intrastate commerce by the United States Supreme Court, but that body took an extremely restrictive view of what constituted intrastate commerce. In effect, the states' reach extended only to those firms doing business entirely within their borders. As reflected in the *Wabash v. Illinois* case (1886), the High Court in effect removed the railroads from state control and left the regulation of interstate commerce to Congress. As Chapter 12 indicated, railroad procedures, especially pricing policies, were a subject of growing popular concern. Even more, the railroads were beginning to consolidate into regional systems, which reduced or eliminated competition between them in large areas.

In 1887, Congress passed the Interstate Commerce Act, bringing under federal control those railroad procedures beyond the states' reach. The act stipulated that railroad rates were to be "reasonable," forbade discriminatory rates, rebates, and other forms of favoritism, and prohibited the formation of price-fixing agreements between railroads. To enforce the act, the Interstate Commerce Commission (ICC) was established and given powers to collect information and issue cease-and-desist orders to the roads. However, by 1891 the Supreme Court had effectively denied the commission power to control rates, allowing it only to rule on the reasonableness of charges, and allowing the railroads to appeal such decisions in the courts.

Economic historians are anything but unanimous about the effect of the new legislation and its implementation. One study concluded that the ICC soon became the captive of the railroads, responsible to nobody but those it supposedly regulated. In this view, the commission became a convenient device for rate-fixing, and its "maximum" rates in fact became the minimum rates the roads had never been able to agree upon or maintain among themselves.[23] Another view is that the commission was captured by the railroads' customers, particularly farm interests, and their pressure for rate reductions eventually left the railroads insufficient income to maintain their equipment properly or attract new investment. The short-term gains for farmers and other shippers resulted in a near-collapse of the roads during World War I.[24]

The Interstate Commerce Act was revised and strengthened in 1904, 1905, and 1910. The commission received more authority and greater ability to resist challenges to its decisions through the courts. But the first attempt at federal regulation was at best a mixed success. Railroad rates might be more stable (after 1900 they rose less than did other prices) but the railroads' problems persisted. The rate of return on capital invested in them was less than its opportunity cost, yet the railroads'

---

[22] Anderson and Hill, *Birth of a Transfer Society.*

[23] G. Kolko, *Railroads and Regulation, 1871–1916* (New York: Norton, 1970). Prices of railroad stocks rose with the passage of the Interstate Commerce Act, indicating that investors expected the railroads to control the Commission in their own interests.

[24] A. Martin, *Enterprise Denied: Origins of the Decline of American Railroads, 1897–1917* (New York: Columbia University Press, 1971).

high fixed costs made exit from the industry very difficult. Whether railroads' difficulties stemmed entirely from regulation or had other causes, their ability to maintain existing service became increasingly doubtful.

Antitrust

In another response to public pressure, Congress passed the Sherman Antitrust Act in 1890. Both the Republicans and the Democrats had campaigned for some type of anti-monopoly legislation, and the bill sailed through both houses of Congress, gaining approval by a combined vote of 393 to 1. The Sherman Act forbade "contracts, combinations in the form of trusts or otherwise, or conspiracies in restraint of trade" and "monopolization or attempts to monopolize, or combinations or conspiracies to monopolize" in interstate commerce. It was a bill everyone could vote for, and it was left to the courts to determine what these phrases meant in practice, as had been the case in transportation regulation.

Initial Interpretation of the Sherman Act
For the first few years after the act was passed, the courts' decisions indicated that the Sherman Act meant very little. President Cleveland's attorney general had publicly declared that he would not enforce such legislation. The act was used successfully only against labor unions. The Supreme Court gave it an extremely narrow interpretation in 1895, ruling that although the American Sugar Refining Company controlled 98 percent of the U.S. supply of refined sugar as a result of a series of mergers, the company was engaged in manufacturing, not interstate commerce. Hence, it was beyond the reach of the act.[25] In all, the

government lost six of the first seven cases it brought under the Sherman Act. However, in 1899 the *Addystone Pipe* case established the principle that price-fixing agreements between firms were illegal under the act, regardless of the form they took. This decision effectively reversed that in the case against the American Sugar Refining Company. The consistent application of this view of collusive agreements has been the most important contribution of antitrust enforcement to this day. Now price-fixing agreements were no longer merely unenforceable under the law, they were criminal offenses.

The government also used the Sherman Act to change the structure, rather than just the collusive conduct, of large firms, although in this instance with less profound effects. In 1904, the *Northern Securities* case established that the act could be used to preserve at least some elements of a competitive market structure through the prevention of a merger between two large railroads.[26] The high point in the use of the Sherman Act to promote a more competitive industrial structure was 1911, when the Court ordered the dissolution of the Standard Oil company and the American Tobacco company into a number of smaller firms. Both of these large firms had actively sought monopoly power and taken maximum advantage of it once attained. Even so, these decisions marked no attempt to establish a purely competitive structure of many small firms in each market. In both decisions, the Court stressed that the dissolutions were ordered because of the firms' conduct, which made it clear that their market power was the result of long-continued and deliberate attempts to gain monopoly positions. Other firms achieving equally dominant positions through less aggressive methods, the Court hinted, might be exempt from dissolution

[25] V. Mund, *Government and Business*, 3d ed. (New York: Advocate, 1960), 161. N. Lamoreaux takes a different view. In her opinion, the Court was trying to preserve states' rights to regulate firms through imposing conditions in their corporate charters. See *The Great Merger Movement in American Business, 1895–1904* (Cambridge U.K.: Cambridge University Press, 1985), 162–169.

[26] The *Northern Securities* case reflected a change in the Court's attitude toward federal versus state authority. Lamoreaux, *Great Merger*, 166–169.

■ Even before World War I, powerful presidents had difficulty getting their economic programs enacted.

proceedings. Consistency was not a dominant feature of the Court's decisions: In 1920, the *United States Steel* case established that mere size—at least at that time—was no offense. The giant corporation was held not to have monopolized the steel industry (as it had been established to do) on the curious grounds that it had been able to control steel prices only through agreements with other steelmakers. Since U.S. Steel had discontinued such practices, the Court said it was not in violation of the Sherman Act.

Once eliminated, competition sometimes proved more difficult to reestablish than had been anticipated. Although the American Tobacco and Standard Oil companies were split up into a number of smaller firms, the new firms in both cases were large enough in relation to their markets to preclude textbook-style perfect competition. The courts had to divide existing assets so as to produce viable firms in dissolution procedures, and the economies of scale in both cases were considerable. The difficulties were compounded by the fact

that the new firms were managed and staffed by the same people who had served their predecessors.

The Clayton and Federal Trade Commission Acts

The Clayton and Federal Trade Commission Acts, enacted in 1912, were attempts to clarify the government's antitrust position in the area of application and the definition of offenses. As such, they probably produced still greater confusion. Labor unions were specifically exempted from the provisions of the antitrust acts for their normal organizing and collective bargaining activities: The nature of unions had previously made them vulnerable to prosecution under these laws. Unfortunately, although the list of prohibited business activities under these laws was clear enough—price discrimination, tying agreements, interlocking directorates, and the acquisition of competing firms' stock were all barred—these were forbidden only if they would substantially reduce competition. The Federal Trade Commission was established to enforce these acts. The FTC added little to the overall impact of the antitrust laws other than another means of prosecuting firms for activities that were already illegal under other statutes, such as fraud or the Sherman Act. The requirement of substantial reductions in competition for offenses under the Clayton Act made its provisions even more subject to court interpretation than were those of the Sherman Act, which it had been intended to clarify.

If antitrust legislation was intended to establish a more nearly competitive structure within most American industries (through increasing the number of sellers in each market), it failed to do so. Except for the two major dissolutions, the Sherman Act and subsequent laws left the existing market structure substantially untouched. However, this is an inadequate measure of the total effect of antitrust legislation.

The Sherman Act had clearly established the principle that competition was to be favored over monopoly. If the courts were not willing to make the existing market structure more competitive, they were equally unwilling to allow less competition than the current industry structure would produce if firms acted independently. The prohibition of price-fixing, which later decisions extended to nearly all attempts to restrict or exclude competition, did not end such practices. But it reduced them and limited their impact. It was now considerably more difficult for firms to collude and all but impossible for them to prevent or punish cheating. As a result, price-fixing combinations became more difficult to form and less effective in operation.

New Government Services

The data on tax burdens indicate that the American taxpayer did not have to part with a large portion of income for government services. Nevertheless, government began to provide a number of new or expanded services during this period. As federal spending grew with the economy, some of the increase was channeled into the provision of useful information (the Weather Bureau, Bureau of Standards, and Geological Survey were all established in this half-century). Growing concern with public safety in its various aspects resulted in the foundation of the Bureau of Mines and the Food and Drug Administration. Both agencies were designed to improve standards where the average individual might not be competent to evaluate the problems involved. As noted earlier, a Bureau of Roads was established, and, in 1916, the federal government committed itself to the construction of a national highway system in partnership with the states. All of these could in various ways be seen as improving the performance of the market economy by providing better information or an improved environment in which to conduct private business.

Concerns with economic affairs resulted in the formation of a Department of Com-

merce and Labor (later divided into separate agencies), the elevation of the Agriculture Department to full cabinet status, the Forest Service, and a variety of others. Even the conservation movement could be regarded as an attempt to control the use, or misuse, of natural resources through government control and action. The State Department became more concerned with economic affairs. It provided more information on foreign markets, products, and regulations to Americans interested in foreign trade than it previously had. Occasionally it even tried to develop overseas interests where none had previously existed.[27] These expansions of the scope of governmental action, while modest, were a substantial increase from those of 1860.

State and local governments had also expanded in the areas of traditional activity, such as schools, public health, and even (very hesitantly) expanded welfare. The small proportion of total output devoted to governmental purposes may support the conclusion that the United States was still committed to laissez-faire in 1914. But the trends were away from this position, as evidenced by the expansion of government activities in general and the passage of child labor and compulsory schooling laws, which were expressly designed to restrict the field of private decision making.

The Income Tax

The United States had taken another momentous step away from tradition when the Sixteenth Amendment to the Constitution was ratified in 1913. This amendment overcame previous legal barriers to the institution of an income tax (the Constitution had previously, though not consistently, been interpreted as prohibiting the imposition of direct taxes on any basis other than population). The new tax was enacted the same year. While its initial

---

[27] R. Zevin, "An Interpretation of American Imperialism," *Journal of Economic History* (March 1972).

TO BE FILLED IN BY COLLECTOR.

Form 1040.

INCOME TAX.

TO BE FILLED IN BY INTERNAL REVENUE BUREAU.

List No. ....

.... District of ....

Date received ....

THE PENALTY
FOR FAILURE TO HAVE THIS RETURN IN
THE HANDS OF THE COLLECTOR OF
INTERNAL REVENUE ON OR BEFORE
MARCH 1 IS $20 TO $1,000.
(SEE INSTRUCTIONS ON PAGE 4.)

File No. ....

Assessment List ....

Page ....   Line ....

UNITED STATES INTERNAL REVENUE.

RETURN OF ANNUAL NET INCOME OF INDIVIDUALS.
(As provided by Act of Congress, approved October 3, 1913.)

RETURN OF NET INCOME RECEIVED OR ACCRUED DURING THE YEAR ENDED DECEMBER 31, 191....
(FOR THE YEAR 1913, FROM MARCH 1, TO DECEMBER 31.)

Filed by (or for) .... of ....

(Full name of individual.)   (Street and No.)

in the City, Town, or Post Office of .... State of ....

(Fill in pages 2 and 3 before making entries below.)

1. GROSS INCOME (see page 2, line 12) .... $

2. GENERAL DEDUCTIONS (see page 3, line 7) .... $

3. NET INCOME .... $

Deductions and exemptions allowed in computing income subject to the normal tax of 1 per cent.

4. Dividends and net earnings received or accrued, of corporations, etc., subject to like tax. (See page 2, line 11) .... $

5. Amount of income on which the normal tax has been deducted and withheld at the source. (See page 2, line 9, column A) ....

6. Specific exemption of $3,000 or $4,000, as the case may be. (See Instructions 3 and 19) ....

Total deductions and exemptions. (Items 4, 5, and 6) .... $

7. TAXABLE INCOME on which the normal tax of 1 per cent is to be calculated. (See Instruction 3). $

8. When the net income shown above on line 3 exceeds $20,000, the additional tax thereon must be calculated as per schedule below

	INCOME.	TAX.
1 per cent on amount over $20,000 and not exceeding $50,000.... $		$
2 " " 50,000 " " 75,000....		
3 " " 75,000 " " 100,000....		
4 " " 100,000 " " 250,000....		
5 " " 250,000 " " 500,000....		
6 " " 500,000		
Total additional or super tax		$
Total normal tax (1 per cent of amount entered on line 7)....		$
Total tax liability		$

■ By 1914, income taxes were here to stay, but rates were very low by modern standards.

■ Crowds gathered to protest possible U.S. involvement in World War I, as this 1914 photo shows.
Source: Library of Congress.

fiscal impact was slight, the long-term consequences were not. In the first year, only 350,000 returns were filed because tax became effective only at very high income levels.[28] But the precedent that had been set would become much more influential later than even the most pessimistic opponents had claimed.

The tax was progressive; it applied only to incomes above a certain level, and as incomes rose beyond the minimum taxable point, the tax rates increased faster. At incomes over $5,000 (equal to $70,000 in today's purchasing power), the rate increased from 1 percent to a "confiscatory" 6 percent on the portion of income over $500,000 per year.[29] Since few Americans had taxable incomes of as much as $3,000 per year in 1913, the income tax was borne by the rich. It was one of the first explicit measures aimed at reducing the inequality of income distribution. Since the income tax replaced tariffs as a major source of government revenue, its effects were doubly progressive: The burden of tariffs had fallen largely on low- and middle-income consumers. As had the Sherman Act and the Federal Reserve Act, the income tax law indicated that American voters were no longer willing to accept all the results generated by the unhindered operation of the market system. But in less than a year, events would produce a far larger economic role for government than most Americans had ever thought possible.

WORLD WAR I

When war broke out in Europe in August 1914, it came as a distinct shock to the nations involved. A conflict between the developed nations of Europe had been thought to be impossible. At worst, if the unthinkable happened, a war would be very short because its costs would be too great for even those wealthy nations. To strengthen these assumptions,

---

[28] *Historical Statistics*, 2:1110.
[29] *Historical Statistics*, 2:1111–1112.

some noted that the workers' movements in many European nations that had recently gained considerable political strength often felt more sympathy for each other than for their own governments, and would never fight in a "capitalists' war." Others pointed to the network of alliances ensuring that each nation, if attacked, could count on help. But workers' representatives rose to sing the "Marseillaise" after the declaration of war was passed in the French Parliament. In the Reichstag, the song was "Deutschland Uber Alles," but there was no lack of labor support in that body either, and workers of both nations marched off to slaughter each other. In the late summer of 1914, Europeans watched as those alliances, like tumblers clicking into place in a lock, dragged almost the entire continent into war.[30]

It soon became apparent that even the most pessimistic scenarios had drastically underestimated the cost of conflict. But the war dragged on for four terrible years. Not only did it consume incredible quantities of men and supplies, it produced an unforeseen casualty. Trade between the belligerents was, of course, discontinued. Only then did Europeans discover that they had been each others' best customers. The war shattered the network of international trade and monetary agreements that had been so important in Europe's material progress. It would not be reestablished until the 1960s.

The Course of the War in Europe

The Germans had planned to crush the French before aid from France's Russian and British allies could become effective. However, that effort failed because Russia mobilized much faster than anyone had expected. Consequently, the war in western Europe became a bloody stalemate. Neither side could advance

even a few miles save at a cost that could not be sustained long enough to force a decision of the entire war. The war became a conflict of endurance. The nation that could sustain its military efforts longest would win. Once this was recognized, the belligerents tried to turn their full productive capacities toward furthering their own military efforts while destroying those of their enemies.

The British established a naval blockade of Germany that could not be broken by Germany's smaller and not very adventurous fleet. But the Germans knew that Britain was more dependent on overseas trade than they: Britain imported most of her food, as well as large quantities of industrial raw materials. The Germans attacked British trade with the only weapon they possessed that could reach it—submarines. Submarines had difficulty identifying ships and sank vessels belonging to neutral nations: There was no means of determining a ship's cargo—or passengers—through a periscope. The British blockade of the Central Powers had little effect before 1916. But as German stockpiles of imported materials dwindled and the substitutes developed by scientific research failed to keep pace with ever-growing lists of shortages, the impact on German living standards grew. In 1917 it became acute.

In Britain and France, the diversion of shipping to military purposes, combined with losses to submarines, also reduced living standards. Even more serious reductions had already been imposed by the diversion of resources, particularly labor, to the war. All the combatants found their productive capacity inadequate in the face of the war's enormous demands. The Germans were almost totally isolated from overseas trade, especially after the British began to control the trade of European neutrals (1916) to shut off that avenue of access to the outside world. As the war's costs rose, the Allies began looking to the United States, the only major industrial nation not already involved. They sought ad-

---

[30] B. Tuchman, *The Guns of August* (New York: MacMillan, 1962).

Table 16.3 United States Foreign Trade, 1914–1920
(Millions of Current Dollars)

Year	Total Exports	Total Imports	Exports to Europe	Imports from Europe
1914	$2,365	$1,894	$1,486	$896
1915	2,769	1,674	1,971	614
1916	5,483	2,392	3,813	633
1917	6,234	2,952	4,062	551
1918	6,149	3,031	3,859	318
1919	7,920	3,904	5,188	751
1920	8,228	5,278	4,466	1,228

Source: U.S. Department of Commerce, Bureau of the Census, *Historical Statistics of the United States: Colonial Times to 1970,* 2 vols. (Washington, D.C.: Government Printing Office, 1975), 2:903, 906.

ditional supplies of both munitions and food from the United States as their own productive capacity was overwhelmed. By 1916, the initial trickle of orders from the Allies had become a flood. American producers were eager to deal with buyers in no position to argue about price. After some hesitation, the Wilson administration allowed them to respond to the demand. U.S. exports began to increase rapidly, both to meet European demand and to supply traditional European export markets, such as Latin America, with the goods formerly obtained from Britain and Germany. The dimensions are indicated in Table 16.3. In the Far East, Japan began to supply markets accustomed to purchasing their manufactured goods from Britain, and to carry the cargos that had previously travelled in British ships.

The additional source of supply in the United States eased one of the Allies' problems, but paying for the increased imports was difficult. Because they had diverted so much of their productive capacity to war demands, the Allies had little to sell to the United States, which, in any case, had no increased need for imports. European exports to the United States fell off sharply even as the flow of American goods rose. From 1914 to 1917, U.S. ex-

ports doubled, while imports rose only 55 percent. Exports to Europe more than tripled, but imports from that continent fell by almost 40 percent.[31] Some form of payment had to be devised to cover the widening trade gap.

Europe had traditionally made up its deficit in direct trade with the United States by running surpluses with other regions from which the United States was a net importer. Now, however, that avenue was no longer available. Europe had few goods to export to any region. Since they could no longer finance imports from America with their own exports, Europeans employed other means. The Allies shipped gold to the United States and sold their portfolios of American securities. As these resources neared exhaustion, they began to borrow from America.

Private Loans to the Allies

British and French bonds were sold, not to the U.S. government, but to private citizens in this country. The firm of J. P. Morgan & Co. was active in purchasing war material on behalf of the French and British governments

---

[31] *Historical Statistics*, 2:903, 906.

and in marketing their bonds in the United States. The desperate Allies used this arrangement to its fullest. Any group whose members might be able to buy bonds or influence someone else to do so could attract a dashing young British or French officer to tell of German "atrocities" and detail how American purchases of his government's bonds would help to preserve civilization and freedom from the "Huns." Inadvertently, the Germans aided these propaganda efforts through their own ill-considered and worse-timed submarine warfare and efforts to obtain help from the Mexican government to keep the United States fully occupied in the Western Hemisphere.[32] The propaganda of both sides appears crude and unbelievable today, but the United States was new to the world of total war. Few of its citizens, not even recent immigrants, knew much about Europe as a whole.

In all, the Allies sold U.S. securities worth $4 billion, shipped over $1 billion in gold, and borrowed some $5 billion from private sources in the United States. After American entry into the war, the U.S. government loaned the Allies another $9.5 billion. From a large-scale debtor, the United States had been transformed into the world's greatest international creditor in only six years.

The Economic Impact of U.S. Entry into the War

The initial effect of the war on the U.S. economy, however, was a financial panic. As Europeans scrambled to sell their portfolios of American securities, stock and bond prices fell so low that the New York Stock Exchange had to be closed. The U.S. unemployment rate began to rise in 1914; it averaged over 8 percent for all of 1915 and reached nearly 11 percent at the depth of the recession (see Table 16.4).

At the time European orders for American goods really began to increase, then, the economy had very substantial unused productive capacity. By the fall of 1915, the amount of slack was beginning to be reduced, and in 1916 it disappeared in some industries. During the years of active American participation in the war, unemployment continued to fall. At the war's end, it was less than 2 percent. The war all but ended immigration, and after 1916, the American armed forces began to increase rapidly. Under such conditions, the bargaining position of workers improved greatly, and wages rose as a portion of GNP.

These circumstances reduced employers' resistance to union organization, and government and legal attitudes also favored unions. By 1920, perhaps 12 percent of the labor force was unionized. Blacks began a large-scale migration from southern agricultural employment to urban occupations, chiefly in the North. This was their first significant occupational shift since Emancipation.

American farmers gained as European demands for meat and grain skyrocketed, reflecting that continent's disrupted trade patterns and wartime resource diversions. High demand was supplemented by government-guaranteed prices after the U.S. declaration of war in April 1917. These circumstances encouraged farmers to expand production by tilling more land, most of it less fertile than the acreage already under the plow. Farmers also increased the amount of machinery employed, enabling them to spread a diminished labor supply over more land. Much of this attempt at agricultural expansion was financed by borrowing, a course that appeared safe enough while prices for farm products were high and rising. In general, despite the moves to increase output, agricultural production had shown only slight increases before 1918, even though the prices of most farm products had at least doubled.[33] The effects of farmers' in-

---

[32] B. Tuchman, *The Zimmermann Telegram* (New York: Viking Press, 1958).

[33] *Historical Statistics*, 1:511.

Table 16.4   The Statistical Impact of World War I

Year	Money GNP (Billions of Dollars)	Real GNP* (Billions of Dollars)	Defense Expenditures** (Billions of Dollars)	Wholesale Prices***	Military Personnel	Unemployment Rate
1914	$38.6	$125.6	$.348	68.1	165,919	7.9%
1915	40.0	124.5	.344	69.5	174,112	8.5
1916	48.3	134.3	.337	85.5	179,376	5.1
1917	60.4	135.2	.618	117.5	643,833	4.6
1918	76.4	151.8	6.149	131.3	2,897,167	1.4
1919	84.0	146.4	11.011	138.6	1,172,602	1.4
1920	91.5	140.0	2.358	154.4	343,302	5.2

*In 1958 dollars.
**War and Navy departments.
***Bureau of Labor Statistics data, 1926 = 100.
Sources: U.S. Department of Commerce, Bureau of the Census, *Historical Statistics of the United States: Colonial Times to 1970*, 2 vols. (Washington, D.C.: Government Printing Office, 1975), 1:135, 200, 224; 2:1114, 1141.

creased efforts became visible only as the war ended. Farm prices had risen considerably faster than the overall price level. Under such encouraging stimuli, the total debts of American farmers had more than doubled from 1912 to 1920.[34]

The Arsenal of Democracy?

The United States declared war on Germany on April 6, 1917. From the Allies' point of view, the American role was clear. As the world's greatest industrial power, with a population of over 100 million people, the United States would supply materials and manpower to supplement their own until American mobilization was completed. The economic might of the United States would support a military effort much larger than either the Allies or Germany, weakened as both were by years of war, could produce from their own resources. In fact, despite distinguished rec-

ords by a few units and individuals, the direct military contribution of the United States to the war was quite modest. At the war's end, only a small part of the American army had seen action. Nevertheless, by fall of 1918, over one million U.S. troops had reached France, and Germany recognized the situation for what it was. After a last-gasp offensive in the spring of 1918 had almost, but not quite, brought a German victory, the Kaiser's forces were nearly spent. With few reserves, and its civilian population facing growing shortages of food and nearly all other goods, Germany was faced with the prospect of an eventual assault by American forces in overwhelming strength. Accordingly, the German generals told the Kaiser that the war was lost. The speed with which the German collapse occurred after the U.S. entry into the war made it easy for Americans to overrate their contribution to the Allied victory.

On the civilian front, harnessing America's economic potential to the needs of war proved far more difficult than anyone had expected. The United States had not fought

[34] *Historical Statistics*, 1:491.

a major war since 1865, and the Civil War had been a very different type of conflict. The most recent American combat experience, in 1898, had been a series of blunders in which American failures in supply, medical care, and even elementary sanitation killed five men for every one who died in battle.[35] Troops had been sent to Cuba and Puerto Rico in woolen winter uniforms, inadequately supplied, and with no knowledge of the tropical diseases that proved more deadly than Spanish bullets. Efforts to support the American expeditions in the Caribbean had resulted in a huge traffic jam on the railroads, backing up traffic from the invasion ports in Florida all the way to the Carolinas.

Only in 1915 had the U.S. Army exceeded 100,000 men. As a result, there was scarcely enough experienced personnel to train the forces that would be needed for a major military effort in Europe. Supplies of almost all types were even scarcer. In some cases, not even the American military realized what was needed. For all its industrial might, the United States had little capacity to produce some of the tools of modern war, and the American forces fought with French cannon and British combat aircraft.

The U.S. Military Buildup

After 1916, little unused productive capacity remained in the American economy; increased output of military goods could only be achieved by expanding overall capacity or diverting resources from the production of civilian goods toward the demands of the American military and the Allies. The task was complicated by the diversion of labor into the armed forces. The prewar military strength of the United States had been about 165,000 men in all services combined, but in 1918 the army and navy expanded to nearly 3 million.[36] This

military expansion required about 7 percent of the U.S. labor force. Even so, the total number of people employed rose slightly during the war, as unemployment all but vanished.[37] A military draft was instituted, but it was no sooner implemented than it became apparent that some types of skilled workers would contribute far more to the war effort in the factories than they could in the trenches, so a system of deferments was developed. Although 24,234,000 men registered for the draft, the overcrowded training facilities and the general chaos of forced-draft mobilization resulted in actual induction of only 2,820,000.[38] To the extent that draftees were paid less (in money and kind) than the wages that would have generated voluntary enlistments, conscription disguised some of the war's costs.

Economic Mobilization

Economic mobilization had slightly more success. By reducing the production of some items for civilian use, diverting others to the military, and discouraging consumption by a variety of devices, including "wheatless" and "meatless" days and price controls, more than 20 percent of GNP was made available for military uses. Even though this was a huge increase in military production over prewar levels, American conversion to a wartime economy was far from complete by November 1918. In that year, for example, the United States produced nearly one million passenger cars.[39] Conversion to war production had, however, built up enormous momentum. Despite widespread cancellation of contracts for military production, spending by the War Department was nearly twice as great in 1919 as it had been in 1918. Through the war years, despite efforts to increase output from existing resources, output rose only slightly. Real in-

---

[35] *Historical Statistics*, 2:1140.
[36] *Historical Statistics*, 2:1141.

[37] *Historical Statistics*, 1:126.
[38] *Historical Statistics*, 2:1140.
[39] *Historical Statistics*, 2:716.

vestment rose very little (it doubled in money terms, as did prices), and what did occur apparently had not been brought into production by the war's end. In sum, the full capacity of the American economy was not yet at the disposal of the U.S. and Allied armed forces when German resistance ended.

The problems of effective conversion did not stem from a lack of effort. If anything, there were far too many plans for mobilization, and far too little coordination between them. This should not be surprising: Almost nothing was known about the capacity of individual industries, and less about the inputs various sectors required from each other even in peacetime. The types and quantities of materials necessary for modern war were total mysteries. Physical requirements and capacities available depended on the war policies; an expanded fleet required more steel, but the steel industry's capacity depended partially on the labor supply, which was influenced by draft policy, and also on other needs for steel. Only the most abstract models of sectoral interactions had been devised by economists, and these were useless without empirical data.

The Diversion of Production to the Military

Since the demands of the American and Allied military and those of the civilian population far exceeded available capacity, a system of priorities was necessary. A series of government boards was established to increase the production of vitally needed goods, limit that of nonessentials, simplify designs, and limit varieties of many commodities. Unfortunately, there was little coordination among these efforts. Some critical problems, such as the relative priority of American and Allied military needs, were never fully resolved. Attempts might be made to prohibit the production of some "nonessential" item, for example, only to discover that just a portion

of total output met that definition. With consumer incomes soaring as a result of full employment and inadequate taxes, many producers had strong motivation to continue supplying the civilian market. Producers found themselves facing demand from the military, the Allies, and American consumers, all of whom had seemingly unlimited purchasing power, at a period in which they found it more and more difficult to obtain labor and other resources.

Government intervention in the economy reached levels that exceeded the fondest hopes of all but the most optimistic prewar Socialists. In the most extreme case, the federal government took over the management and operation of all U.S. railroads. Under the strain of a huge increase in traffic heavily oriented toward the East Coast, the railroads had proved unable to handle the volume. The government operated the railroads as a single unit, compensating the owners on the basis of the profits generated in the three previous years. This arrangement achieved considerable progress toward a solution of the transportation crisis, but it was a startling departure from peacetime economic policies. Food purchases for the Allies were consolidated under the Food Administration, ably led by Herbert Hoover. The Shipping Board and Emergency Fleet Corporation built merchant ships and coordinated maritime traffic. Efforts to increase shipbuilding capacity were designed to overcome expected losses to Central Powers, submarines, and resulted in a large increase in both production and capacity, far exceeding peacetime requirements.

The job of tying together the work of several thousand government agencies was given to the War Industries Board, under the direction of Bernard Baruch. The mission and methods of the War Industries Board were not well defined, and it lacked authority over the military's purchases. Some progress was made in standardizing designs of tools and persuading users to accept these modifications. On the whole, it was impossible to overcome the two great barriers to effective planning: the lack of information on both war needs and the capacity available to meet them. Priorities were difficult to establish; even the military was fighting a new type of war and might not know how urgently it needed various goods. Even where priorities were established, they were difficult to maintain, because the War Industries Board had no authority over prices, and many customers were far more concerned over output than prices, a situation that did not encourage producers' voluntary compliance with the Board unless they received the priority ratings they desired.[40] In the general euphoria after the war, it appears probable that the effects of all these planning efforts were highly overrated. However, their success in achieving cooperation between the firms in some industries would be a factor in the trade association movement of the 1920s. Many of the people active in the substitution of federal compulsion for markets would reappear in similar activities under the New Deal. Many of the expanded powers assumed by the federal government were retained after the war because they were convenient devices for concealing the true cost of government action. They had a far greater postwar impact than the increase in federal spending as a portion of GNP, which tripled.[41]

War Finances

A large part of the government expenditures incurred for the war were met by borrowing. Such a method need not be inflationary if the government borrows funds that would otherwise have been spent for civilian consumption or investment. But government borrowing during World War I far exceeded this limit, and most of it was financed by substantial increases in the money supply. Not only did the Federal Reserve Board urge commercial banks to loan money to individuals for bond purchases, the banks were assured that if they lacked the necessary reserves to support this extension of credit, the Federal Reserve would lend them the necessary funds, accepting either bonds or commercial paper as security. Individuals were also told it was their patriotic duty to buy bonds, and were urged to borrow to do so.

The federal government found that its new central bank was a very convenient mechanism for the support of its borrowing. Some of the restrictions on the Federal Reserve's ability to expand the money supply were relaxed to aid the process: It reduced the gold reserve required for demand deposits from 100 to 40 percent, and, in 1917, member bank reserve requirements were cut.[42]

The Federal Reserve System had only begun operations in 1914, and in its first few years could only expand the money supply as gold flowed into the United States to finance European purchases. The Federal Reserve lacked a bond portfolio that it could sell, and with the gold inflow, its rediscount policy was ineffective. Even after it acquired bonds that might have been sold to reduce the money supply, the Federal Reserve remained subservient to the wishes of the Treasury, which wanted to keep interest charges on the growing volume of federal debt as low as possible.[43] The U.S. money supply doubled over the war years, and real output increased only modestly, as Table 16.4 shows.

About one-quarter of the war's financial costs were tax-financed, a proportion only

[40] R. Higgs, *Crisis and Leviathan: Critical Episodes in the Growth of American Government* (New York: Oxford University Press, 1987), 139–141. Higgs believes the WIB had great coercive power.

[41] Higgs, *Crisis and Leviathan*, Chap. 7.

[42] P. Studenski and H. Kroos, *Financial History of the United States* (New York: McGraw-Hill, 1952), 294.

[43] M. Friedman and A. Schwartz, *A Monetary History of the United States, 1867–1960* (Princeton, N. J.: Princeton University Press, 1963), 212–213.

■ Movie star Douglas Fairbanks urged Americans to buy war bonds in 1918.
   Source: U.S. War Department General Staff photo in the National Archives.

slightly greater than that of the Civil War. Income tax rates were raised to as much as 70 percent in the top bracket, and the number of persons liable to the tax increased more than twelvefold. However, the rates were not increased to these levels until 1918, well after federal spending had begun to rise.[44] An excess profits tax was levied on corporate income. Despite the tax increases, the national debt rose by almost $24 billion from 1914 to 1919.

Much of the increase in production was beyond the reach of civilian consumers. Efficiency of production probably declined, which further increased the extent to which demand growth outstripped that of supply for nearly all goods. The result was rapid inflation. (See Table 16.4.) Prices more than doubled over the 1916–1920 period. Inflation began in earnest in late 1915, and in 1916 wholesale prices rose 23 percent. The next year saw a 37 percent rise. After that, the rate of inflation moderated, but massive government deficits continued

[44] *Historical Statistics*, 2:1110, 1112.

well into 1919, and prices did not stop rising until the middle of 1920.[45] After the war, as government spending fell, high wages, full employment, and the pent-up earnings of the war years fueled a rapid expansion of consumer demand.

The war's end saw an abrupt cessation of the mobilization effort, and the conversion to a peacetime economy was as chaotic as the mobilization effort had been. The armed forces were quickly demobilized and their personnel returned to civilian life. Many government contracts for war material were cancelled on the first business day after the Armistice. Despite this, there was only a slight increase in unemployment. The demand for exports continued, construction increased within the United States, and federal deficits were continued for almost a year after the end of the war. Business attempted to rebuild depleted inventories, further bolstering civilian demand.

The Aftermath

The United States, at least in contrast with the European combatants, appeared to have emerged from the war almost unscathed. Some 116,000 U.S. servicemen had lost their lives, over half of them to disease and accident rather than military action. This loss was about one-fifth that of the Civil War, from a population three times as large. In contrast, Europe's losses were appalling. One estimate is that the Continent suffered 13.5 million military and civilian deaths.[46] Since these deaths were so heavily concentrated among the most productive members of the work force, the long-run portents of these losses were even worse than the numbers might indicate.

The American economy was fully employed and prosperous, and its productive potential was greater than it had been in 1914. In one view, however, the scope of private economic activity had been permanently reduced, largely for ideological reasons.[47] Europe, however, had suffered enormous material losses in addition to half a generation of her young men. The network of international trade that had been a cornerstone of European growth and welfare before 1914 was shattered; it would be further damaged by the peace treaties that formally ended the war. All countries had suffered from wartime inflation, but the extent of price increases was highly variable among nations, further complicating the resumption of international trade. Many of Europe's overseas markets had been lost to the United States and Japan. The question of unprecedented amounts of international debts incurred not for investment, but for destruction, had not even been recognized for what it was.

The United States was now the financial as well as the industrial leader of the world—a role for which it was totally unprepared. It had accumulated some unpleasant wartime legacies of its own, that is, inflation, considerable overcapacity in agriculture, shipbuilding, and coal (industries that had no prospect of adequate peacetime markets for their current productive potential), and a mass of war-induced private debt. Yet in 1919, neither the internal nor the external problems appeared serious to most Americans. In comparison to their own circumstances in 1914, and particularly in regard to those of Europe, Americans were better-off than they had ever been. Yet there were signs that the United States was almost as unprepared for the type of peacetime activity that took place in the 1920s as it had been for war in 1914.

[45] *Historical Statistics*, 1:199.
[46] J. Hughes, *Industrialization and Economic History: Theses and Conjectures* (New York: McGraw-Hill, 1970), 240–241.

[47] Higgs, *Crisis and Leviathan*, Chap. 7.

SELECTED REFERENCES

Anderson, T., and P. Hill, *The Birth of a Transfer Society*. Stanford, Cal.: Hoover Institute Press, 1980.

Davis, L., R. Easterlin, W. Parker et al. *American Economic Growth: An Economist's History of the United States*. New York: Harper & Row, 1972.

Faulkner, H. *The Decline of Laissez-Faire*. New York: M. E. Sharpe, 1977.

Fogel, R., and S. Engerman. *The Reinterpretation of American Economic History*. New York: Harper & Row, 1971.

Friedman, M., and A. Schwartz. *A Monetary History of the United States, 1867–1960*. Princeton, N.J.: Princeton University Press, 1963.

Higgs, R. *The Transformation of the American Economy, 1865–1914: An Essay in Interpretation*. New York: John Wiley and Sons, 1971.

———. *Crisis and Leviathan: Critical Episodes in the Growth of American Government*. New York: Oxford University Press, 1987.

Hughes, J. *The Governmental Habit: Economic Controls from Colonial Times to the Present*. New York: Basic Books, 1977.

Kennedy, D. *Over Here: The First World War and American Society*. Oxford, U.K.: Oxford University Press, 1980.

Kolko, G. *Railroads and Regulations, 1877–1916*. New York: Norton, 1965.

Lamoreaux, N. *The Great Merger Movement in American Business, 1895–1904*. Cambridge, U.K.: Cambridge University Press, 1985.

MacAvoy, P. *Economic Effects of Regulation: The Trunk-Line Railroads and the Interstate Commerce Commission Before 1900*. Cambridge, Mass.: MIT Press, 1965.

Martin, A. *Enterprise Denied: Origins of the Decline of American Railroads*. New York: Columbia University Press, 1971.

North, D. *Structure and Change in Economic History*. New York: Norton, 1981.

North, D., and L. Davis. *Institutional Change and American Economic Growth*. Cambridge, U.K.: Cambridge University Press, 1971.

Olson, M. *The Rise and Decline of Nations: Economic Growth, Stagflation, and Social Rigidities*. New Haven, Conn.: Yale University Press, 1982.

Rockoff, H. *Drastic Measures: A History of Wage and Price Controls in the United States*. New York: Cambridge University Press, 1984.

Stein, A. *The Nation at War*. Baltimore: Johns Hopkins University Press, 1980.

Studenski, P., and H. Kroos. *Financial History of the United States*. New York: McGraw-Hill, 1952.

U.S. Department of Commerce, Bureau of the Census. *Historical Statistics of the United States: Colonial Times to 1970*. 2 vols. Washington, D.C.: Government Printing Office, 1975.

The Age of Turmoil, 1920–1945

10.

Los Angeles
(population 576,673)

Census figures refer to the year 1920.

P A R T IV

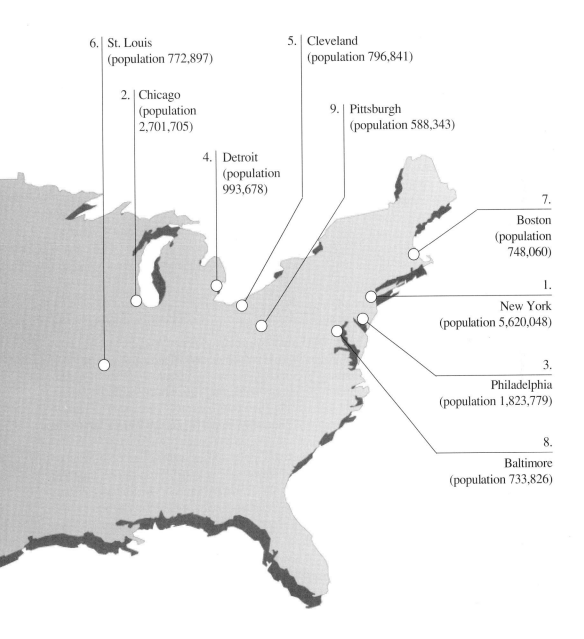

6. | St. Louis
(population 772,897)

2. | Chicago
(population
2,701,705)

5. | Cleveland
(population 796,841)

9. | Pittsburgh
(population 588,343)

4. | Detroit
(population
993,678)

7.
Boston
(population
748,060)

1.
New York
(population 5,620,048)

3.
Philadelphia
(population 1,823,779)

8.
Baltimore
(population 733,826)

*T*he two decades between World War I and World War II were marked by dramatic changes in the economy. Even more sweeping changes occurred during World War II. After a decade of "normalcy" following World War I, America endured the greatest depression in its history, the most rapid and far-reaching conversion from peacetime to war production, and the most profound institutional changes in its entire history. The era is even more remarkable when it is realized that nearly all these changes took place in about 15 years. The 1920s were a decade of economic growth, stable prices, full employment, and general, if not universal, prosperity. The beginning of this period, then, gave little indication of what lay ahead. It appeared as though the United States had returned to an improved version of the "Good Years" of 1900–1914, with the added assurance that new government and especially central bank action was available to offset any unfavorable developments in the market economy, in the unlikely event that these might occur. It was widely accepted that the U.S. economy would continue to generate improved living standards for nearly all citizens for the indefinite future. But the future proved more indefinite than anyone could imagine.

THE DIMENSIONS OF INSTABILITY

The period from 1920 to 1945 was one of extremes. In nearly every dimension of performance, there were changes whose magnitude and impact surpassed anything occurring previously or since. Moreover, these appeared in nearly every aspect of economic activity; the very nature of work began to change, along with its location, the type of effort involved, and the results it produced. The extremes of macroeconomic performance were even more startling.

The United States had been the only major industrial economy to emerge from World War I with all dimensions of its productive capacity not only unscathed, but enhanced. The country's new position as a center of international finance gave American attitudes greater influence in the postwar world than ever before. Through the 1920s, those attitudes retained or exceeded the optimism that had characterized previous decades. Initially, conditions resembling those of the prewar era—economic growth and full employment—were the result. But the very nature of U.S. economic growth was changing.

Productivity advances accounted for a much larger portion of increases in aggregate output during the 1920s than in previous decades. Consequently, resources were reallocated between regions, types of production, and types of labor to a greater extent than ever before. Urbanization increased, and services grew faster than manufacturing output. The changes reflected an economy in which income could increasingly be devoted to discretionary purchases rather than basic survival needs. They certainly also indicated an accelerating pace of technological change, with improvements in communications and transportation that may have provoked an increase in competition, particularly within local and regional markets.

But it was the changes in output, both positive and negative, that dominate the economic history of the period. These, which are outlined in Table IV.1, also produced changes in the other macroeconomic indices that were without precedent over such a short length of time. The expansion of the 1920s gave way to a decline after 1929, which abruptly became the economic cataclysm of the Great Depression. A halting, incomplete recovery in the later 1930s was transformed into an almost frenzied increase in output and activity during World War II, with unemployment rates as improbably low and growth rates as high as they had been the reverse in the 1930s. Measures of economic performance during these 25 years can only hint at the impact these abrupt and enormous reversals had on those who lived through them. As the data in Table IV.1 indicate, this was truly an age of turmoil.

Growth, Price, and Income Shifts

Real growth rates ranged from a decline of 14.8 percent in 1932, as the economy slid toward the trough of the Great Depression, to a peak of 16.1 percent positive growth in 1941. Consumer prices fell 10.7 percent in 1921, and wholesale prices declined more than three times as much. In 1941, the inflation rate was 12.3 percent, but even the further price increases generated by World War II had not brought consumer prices up to their 1920 levels by 1945. Unemployment rates show equally extreme variation, from 24.9 percent in 1933 (which may substantially understate the real dimensions of joblessness) to 1.2 percent in 1944.[1] Few economists familiar with what economic data existed in the 1920s would have believed any of these figures possible. Fewer still would welcome a repetition of the conditions generating them.

Except in the case of inflation, such rates of change have never been equalled in twentieth-century America, and, in most cases, not even approached. Small wonder that as the period progressed, the American people developed strong desires for economic security and stability! Largely as a result of the upheavals of this period, there was widespread popular support

---

[1] Data from U.S. Department of Commerce, Bureau of the Census, *Historical Statistics of the United States: Colonial Times to 1970*, 2 vols. (Washington, D.C.: Government Printing Office, 1975), 1:135, 200, 210–211, 226–227.

Table IV.1   The Dimensions of Turmoil, 1920–1945

Year	GNP (in Billions of Current Dollars)	GNP per Capita (in Current Dollars)	Real GNP (in Billions of 1958 Dollars)	Real GNP per Capita (in 1958 Dollars)
1920	$91.5	$860	$140.0	$1,315
1921	69.6	641	127.8	1,177
1922	74.1	673	148.0	1,345
1923	85.1	760	165.9	1,482
1924	84.7	742	165.5	1,450
1925	93.1	804	179.4	1,549
1926	97.0	826	190.0	1,619
1927	94.9	797	189.8	1,594
1928	97.0	805	190.9	1,584
1929	103.1	847	203.6	1,671
1930	90.4	734	183.5	1,490
1931	75.8	611	169.3	1,364
1932	58.0	465	144.2	1,154
1933	55.6	442	141.5	1,126
1934	65.1	514	154.3	1,220
1935	72.2	567	169.5	1,331
1936	82.5	643	193.0	1,506
1937	90.4	701	203.2	1,576
1938	84.7	651	192.9	1,484
1939	90.1	691	209.4	1,598
1940	99.7	754	227.2	1,720
1941	124.5	934	263.7	1,977
1942	157.9	1,171	297.8	2,208
1943	191.6	1,401	337.1	2,465
1944	210.1	1,518	361.3	2,611
1945	211.9	1,515	355.2	2,538

Source: U.S. Department of Commerce, Bureau of the Census, *Historical Statistics of the United States: Colonial Times to 1970*, 2 vols. (Washington, D.C.: Government Printing Office, 1975), 1:135, 199, 224, 226–227, 229.

for changes in the institutions that influenced economic activity, and the goals toward which they were directed. Most of these changes occurred within government, particularly at the federal level. Others were the result of new regulations on the private sector.

Per-capita income exhibited almost equally dramatic shifts. Population growth had slowed in the 1920s. This permitted a 4 percent annual rate of aggregate economic growth (not especially rapid by prewar standards) to produce an increase of about 27 percent in per-capita incomes from 1920

Wholesale Prices (1967 = 100)	Gross Investment (Billions of Dollars)	Unemployment Rate (Percent of Work Force)	Growth in GNP (Percent from Previous Year)
79.6	—	5.2%	−4.3%
50.3	—	11.7	−8.6
49.9	—	6.7	15.8
51.9	—	2.4	12.1
50.5	—	5.0	−.2
53.3	—	3.2	8.4
51.6	—	1.8	5.9
49.3	—	3.3	.0
50.0	—	4.2	.6
49.1	$16.2	3.2	6.7
44.6	10.1	8.7	−9.8
37.6	6.8	15.9	−7.6
33.6	3.4	23.6	−14.7
34.0	3.0	24.9	−1.8
38.6	4.1	21.7	9.1
41.3	5.3	20.1	9.9
41.7	7.2	16.9	13.9
44.5	9.2	14.3	5.3
40.5	7.4	19.0	−5.0
39.8	8.9	17.2	8.6
40.5	11.0	14.6	8.5
45.1	13.4	9.9	16.1
50.9	8.1	4.7	12.9
53.3	6.4	1.9	13.2
53.6	8.1	1.2	7.2
54.6	11.6	1.9	−1.7

to 1929. The increase would be greater still if 1921 were used as a starting date, because in that year there was a severe, though short-lived, recession.

The course of income distribution during the 1920s is unclear (in part because the data for earlier periods are even less conclusive). One study found that income distribution became considerably less even during the 1920s, with most of the population receiving very small gains or even suffering income reductions, while the rich garnered the vast majority of the aggregate rise in income. Wealth holdings (which are not income) also became more concentrated.[2] However, the statistics on which these conclusions rely had not been adjusted for tax avoidance in response to the high marginal rates of taxation during the war and early 1920s, and greater compliance induced by lower rates thereafter. Nor do they reflect the fact that the rich took a substantial portion of their incomes in the form of undistributed corporate profits in the initial portion of the decade, and less in the latter half. The data may therefore seriously overstate any increase in inequality.[3] Data on consumption trends in the 1920s indicate that income gains were widely shared.

During the terrible 1929–1933 period, per-capita income fell by about one-third and barely regained its previous level by 1940. The 1930s, then, were an era of zero economic growth. The entire economy forfeited the additional output that normal increases in capacity and technological improvement would have produced. Had the economy grown at only 3 percent per year during the 1930s (a 25 percent reduction from the growth rate of the 1920s), 1940 GNP in 1929 dollars would have been $144 billion. In fact, it was only $121 billion, 19 percent less than what would have occurred with even this modest rate of growth. Per-capita incomes rose sharply from 1940 through 1945, but much of this represented military production rather than goods contributing directly to an increase in living standards.

Income distribution became more equal during the 1930s, largely because property incomes, which accrue to the wealthy, fell proportionally more than wages. Most of the shift occurred before 1933, and was not due to New Deal redistribution of incomes.

Before the 1930s ended, there had been a substantial recourse to government to prevent further recurrence of such extreme instability and to protect citizens from the consequences of what had already occurred. By 1945 there was no doubt that the age of laissez-faire was over in terms both of fact and popular attitudes. Indeed, for a time, the pendulum appeared to have swung very far in the opposite direction; many people seemed to think that all sources of real economic security lay in government. Nongovernmental institutions that promoted individual security through joint action, from labor unions to life insurance, also flourished.

DEMOGRAPHIC CHANGE

Population increased, but for much of the period the rate of increase was declining, especially in the 1930s. In the 1920s, a prolonged decline in the death rate was not fully offset by the spectacular increases in life expectancy that occurred in the previous two decades. (See Chapter 14 and Table IV.2.)

---

[2] C. Holt, "Who Benefitted from the Prosperity of the Twenties?" *Explorations in Economic History* (July 1977); and R. Lampman, *The Share of Top Wealth-holders in National Wealth, 1922–1956* (Princeton, N.J.: Princeton University Press, 1962). See also *Historical Statistics*, 1:302.

[3] G. Smiley, "Did Incomes for Most of the Population Fall from 1923 to 1929?" *Journal of Economic History* (June 1983).

Table IV.2   Population Statistics, 1920–1945

Year	Total Population (in Thousands)	Life Expectancy at Birth (Years)	Infant Mortality per 1,000 Live Births
1920	106,461	54.1	85.8
1925	115,829	59.0	71.7
1930	123,077	59.7	64.6
1935	127,250	61.7	55.7
1940	132,122	62.9	47.0
1945	139,928	65.9	38.3

Source: U.S. Department of Commerce, Bureau of the Census, *Historical Statistics of the United States: Colonial Times to 1970*, 2 vols. (Washington, D.C.: Government Printing Office, 1975), 1:10, 55, 57.

Despite the economic chaos, there were some very considerable and un-arguable gains in the well-being of Americans: longer life expectancy and a major decline in the infant mortality rate.

There appears to have been a close association between the falling birth rate and urbanization. Growth in the urban population accounted for 85 percent of the total increase in the 1920s, but this implied a slower rate of aggregate increase than had occurred when America's population was largely rural. Children were more expensive in the cities; food and housing expenses were greater, and they were not productive assets as they were on the farm.

Immigration, which had gone far to offset a declining domestic birth rate prior to 1914, was sharply curtailed after 1921, falling to less than one-third its 1900–1914 average by the late 1920s. In the 1930s, it declined still more. In that decade, marriages and childbearing were deferred because of the depressed economic conditions. With the return of prosperity in the 1940s, the birth rate began to rise again, an increase that culminated in the postwar "baby boom."

NEW PATTERNS OF GROWTH

Population growth was not the only indication of a slowdown in the pace at which the United States was accumulating productive assets. In the Depression, and again during World War II, investment was insufficient to replace the deterioration of the existing capital stock.

Even before the Depression, growth in aggregate output was not main-tained from its traditional sources. Increases in output became more de-pendent on increases in productivity, rather than "more of the same" methods.[4] Periods of technological advancement improved job opportunites

---

[4] *Historical Statistics*, 1:225.

■ The price of growth: Note the air pollution in this photo of nineteenth-century Pittsburgh.
Source: Library of Congress.

for women, and, this period was no exception.[5] The absolute contribution of increases in output per unit of input doubled in the first three decades of the twentieth century (most of the increase occurred after 1920). Since rates of increase in physical inputs declined, the relative contribution of productivity increased still more. Productivity gains had accounted for about one-sixth of all growth in 1900, but in the 1920s the figure had grown to over two-fifths. In the twentieth century, as much as 80 percent of the gains in real per-capita income were attributable to gains in factor productivity.[6]

If growth is to be based on productivity increases, the efficient allocation of resources to their most productive uses is vital, and that of the largest single input—human resources—especially so. The period showed rapid and

[5] C. Goldin, *Understanding the Gender Gap: An Economic History of American Women* (New York: Oxford University Press, 1990), 94.
[6] L. Davis, R. Easterlin, and W. Parker et al., *American Economic Growth: An Economist's History of the United States* (New York: Harper & Row, 1972), 39.

substantial changes in trends in this aspect of economic performance, as in so many others.

The combination of a market economy, geographic, occupational, and social mobility, and an effective system of formal and vocational education had served the United States well in the pursuit of economic efficiency. By no means was America an economy in which all talent was instantly recognized, developed, and rewarded. Nevertheless, the barriers to rational uses of human skills along the lines dictated by productivity were lower in the United States than anywhere else. In the 1920s, there were several important developments that reduced them even further. By the end of the decade, women and blacks had been able to demonstrate that they could perform the jobs previously reserved for white males. The impact of mass-produced automobiles and trucks had greatly increased the range of choices open to both buyers and sellers in local and regional markets. This increase in alternatives forced, through competition, a more rational evaluation of human talent. The gains were tenuous, but they were much greater than the groups affected had experienced previously. It was now easier to move from one type of job to another than it had been.

The 1930s were a massive setback: An excess of job seekers allowed full rein for the exercise of prejudice by employers (and fellow employees). In addition, many of the government responses to the Depression reduced mobility, by attempting to restore the status quo, providing aid only to those

■ Pittsburgh during the Great Depression is shown. Limiting production was an expensive method of cleaning up the air.
Source: Archives of Industrial Society, University of Pittsburgh.

who remained in or waited to resume their previous occupations. The lost ground was more than regained in the extremely tight labor markets of World War II. By 1945, even though there were still instances in which talented people were denied a chance to improve or practice their skills, discrimination was less common than ever before. Further, the momentum for its continued decline was well established.

Increased labor productivity also stemmed from movements between regions and occupations. These, of course, had occurred from colonial days, but now the pace accelerated. The farm population, which traditionally had lower incomes than other occupations, fell in absolute as well as relative terms in the 1920s and 1940s. States in which average incomes were high and job opportunities plentiful gained population at the expense of those less favored. Manufacturing employment rose very little during the 1920s, but service employment and "white-collar" jobs showed substantial increases.[7] The Pacific Coast, the area around Washington, D.C., and Florida attracted the largest share of migrants. Appalachia, the Great Plains, and southern rural black populations showed declines. As had the immigrants before them, the internal migrants were responding to economic opportunity.[8] Relocation from low- to high-wage occupations benefited both the migrants and the economy.

As always, new industries appeared, old ones declined, and the growth rates of various sectors of the economy showed wide variation. The 1920s saw rapid growth in services, heavy industry, and public utilities, while coal, railroads, and agriculture declined. Despite depression and war, the changes in occupational patterns continued. In much of the period, however, there was more growth in government (largely by default) than in the private sector.

CHANGING INSTITUTIONS AND ATTITUDES

During the 1920s, it may well have seemed to most Americans that the country had, in President Harding's phrase, "returned to normalcy." While the 1920s were by no means a static era, persons accustomed to the economy of previous decades must have found these years a comfortable time of growth upon familiar foundations.

But existing institutions appeared to be utterly incapable of dealing effectively with the Depression. The effects of that catastrophe were not yet over when the military challenge of the Axis threatened the autonomy of the United States, both politically and economically. The last 15 years of this era, then, were a time of profound questioning and readjustment of

---

[7] *Historical Statistics*, 1:139.

[8] L. Galloway and R. Vedder, "The Mobility of Native Americans," *Journal of Economic History* (September 1971).

American political and economic attitudes and the institutions designed to reflect them.

In the prolonged unemployment of the Depression, the American faith in each individual's responsibility for his or her own welfare was badly shaken. There obviously were large numbers of people who could not find any sort of work at any wage, and the economy's response to the excess supply of labor was too slow to avoid widespread human suffering. Many of the unemployed ultimately had no alternative but to turn to government for immediate relief. They and many others questioned the nature of an economic system that had come so close to total collapse. One result of this change in attitudes was the institution of government programs, such as Social Security and unemployment compensation, both of which were unprecedented departures from the traditional economic role of the federal government. Another change was the widespread view that in times of economic emergency the federal government should "do something"—an attitude that may have begun in the mobilization for World War I. Never again would a president of the United States gain public approval for statements such as Warren G. Harding made in 1921: "There has been vast unemployment before and there will be again. There will be depression and inflation just as surely as the tides ebb and flow. I would have little enthusiasm for any proposed remedy which seeks either palliation or tonic from the public treasury."[9]

For the first years of World War II, the United States paid a terrible price for its recent attitudes on international affairs (isolationism and attempts to substitute treaties, such as the Kellog-Briand Pact outlawing war for defense spending, despite growing evidence of Axis aggression), and it watched other nations pay still more. The war enormously increased the role of government in the economy, both directly in the military sphere and through the redirection of economic activity toward the support of the armed forces. In World War I, American popular opinion had overrated the degree to which American economics might have contributed to the Allied victory. But the role played by the U.S. productive capacity in the second conflict was genuine, and direct military participation of American armed forces was on an enormously greater scale than it had been two decades earlier. The actions taken by government to redirect the economy were generally effective this time. (Their economic efficiency was another matter.) This success probably bolstered the belief that government could accomplish almost any task, given a little time and unlimited spending authority.

The appearance of such attitudes, however, is understandable. So too is the fact that actions taken under conditions in which the political or economic survival of the United States was thought to be at stake were often neither well coordinated nor the best of all possible responses to the

---

[9] R. Gordon, *Economic Instability and Growth: The American Record* (New York: Norton, 1974), 21–22.

circumstances occasioning them. Both the New Deal and the expansion of production in the early years of the war show no consistent pattern of procedure. In each case, the goals were clear enough, but there seemed to be no time in which to closely analyze the nature of programs, compare them with alternatives, or assess their full costs. Some now-obvious mistakes were made in the pressure-cooker atmosphere in which actions to fight the Depression or the Axis had to be made. But the results achieved in the latter case made many Americans sure there were wider, if not universal, additional applications to be made.

SELECTED REFERENCES

Bernstein, M. *The Great Depression: Delayed Recovery and Economic Change in America.* New York: Cambridge University Press, 1988.

Brunner, K. *The Great Depression Revisited.* Boston: Martinus Nijhoff, 1981.

Chandler, L. *America's Greatest Depression, 1929–1941.* New York: Harper & Row, 1970.

Davis, L., R. Easterlin, W. Parker et al. *American Economic Growth: An Economist's History of the United States.* New York: Harper & Row, 1972.

Denison, E. *The Sources of Growth in the United States and the Alternatives Before Us.* New York: Committee for Economic Development, Washington, D.C., Supplementary Paper #13, 1962.

Friedman, M., and A. Schwartz. *The Great Contraction, 1929–1933.* Princeton, N.J.: Princeton University Press, 1965.

Goldin, C. *Understanding the Gender Gap: An Economic History of American Women.* New York: Oxford University Press, 1990.

Gordon, R. *Economic Instability and Growth: The American Record.* New York: Norton, 1974.

Haberler, G. *The World Economy, Money, and the Great Depression, 1919–39.* Washington, D.C.: Brookings Institute, 1976.

Higgs, R. *Crisis and Leviathan: Critical Episodes in the Growth of American Government.* New York: Oxford University Press, 1987.

Kindleberger, C. *The World in Depression, 1929–1939.* 2d ed. Berkeley Calif.: University of California Press, 1986.

Schwartz, A. "Understanding 1929–33," in *Money in Historical Perspective.* Chicago: University of Chicago Press, 1987.

Temin, P. *Did Monetary Factors Cause the Great Depression?* New York: Norton, 1976.

U.S. Department of Commerce, Bureau of the Census. *Historical Statistics of the United States: Colonial Times to 1970.* 2 vols. Washington, D.C.: Government Printing Office, 1975.

Walton, G. *Regulatory Change in an Atmosphere of Crisis: Current Implications of the Roosevelt Years.* New York: Academic Press, 1979.

THE TWENTIES— GROWTH AND COLLAPSE

*T*here is a tendency to view the decade from 1920 through 1929 as a mere prelude to economic disaster. With hindsight, it seems certain that portents of the Great Depression must have been obvious. The 1920s have been scrutinized by many authors seeking causes of the Depression. After their proposals have been analyzed, about all that can be said is that some of the phenomena they cited either contributed to the decline or worsened it once begun. But even six decades later, there is no single, universally accepted sequence of events occurring in the 1920s that was the major source of the economic disaster that began in 1929.

Some of the explanations are pretty clearly based on the *post hoc, ergo propter hoc* fallacy in reasoning, that is, the idea that chronological sequence necessarily implies causation. They have nothing to recommend them but temporal sequence. The lack of respect for law engendered by Prohibition, greater freedom for women, the values (or lack thereof) of the "Lost Generation," greater concentration on material welfare at the expense of higher ideals have been proposed as causes of the Great Depression. None has causal relationships to later events based on much more than proponents' determination to find a source in previous events.

TWENTIES PROSPERITY

Contemporary observers saw few indications indeed that the 1920s would be the last decade in which economic events bore any semblance to those of the "Good Years" of 1900–1914. During the decade, not only had the United States returned to "normalcy" by dismantling the government control apparatus built up during World War I, but it had achieved some substantial gains over prewar conditions. Real income, productivity, and employment all increased in conjunction with a price level that, if anything, fell slightly over the era. The 1920s were *not* a period of inflation in which all economic activity was concentrated on speculation or the New York Stock Exchange. The prosperity of the "New Era" was real and widespread.

The economic data for the period indicate that real output grew at from 3 to 4 percent per year, depending on the base year chosen. This rate was well above that of population growth, so it was possible for the welfare of all Americans to increase simultaneously, although, it is claimed, either at widely differing rates or even under circumstances where the gains of high-income individuals exceeded other groups' losses.[1] Productivity rose, particularly in manufacturing, and real wages increased, although in industry they failed to keep pace with the increase in output. Real production in manufacturing increased 50 percent from 1921 to 1929. Unemployment, after the short but severe recession of 1920–1921, remained very low by modern standards, averaging only 4.6 percent for the entire decade, and only 3.3 percent after 1922.[2] Prices fell over the decade: The 1920–1921 recession caused sharp deflation in retail and particularly wholesale prices, but after 1922 the price level was essentially stable until the end of the decade.[3] The 1920s, then, were a decade of full employment, stable prices, and economic growth. The major macroeconomic

[1] C. Holt, "Who Profited From the Prosperity of the Twenties?" *Explorations in Economic History* (July 1977). See also J. Williamson, "American Prices and Urban Inequality Since 1800," *Journal of Economic History* (June 1976).
[2] U.S. Department of Commerce, Bureau of the Census, *Historical Statistics of the United States: Colonial Times to 1970*, 2 vols. (Washington, D.C.: Government Printing Office, 1975), 1:135.
[3] *Historical Statistics*, 1:200, 210–211.

indicators hardly present clear-cut warnings of the economic cataclysm with which the decade ended.

Despite a good overall record, the 1920s began with an intense depression whose causes might have given the discerning some unease over the prospects for future stability. As Chapter 16 revealed, economic activity continued at high levels after the end of World War I, fueled in part by the federal government's continued deficit spending, European demand for American exports, and expansion in the money supply. There was also considerable pent-up domestic demand for capital and consumer goods whose supply had been curtailed by the war. In 1920, most of these spurs to aggregate demand were abruptly reduced. European recovery, particularly in agriculture, caused American exports to decline from $8.6 billion in 1919 to only $4.5 billion in 1921.[4] The federal government's budget had a $13.4 billion deficit in 1919, but in 1920 this was converted to a surplus of $291 million, largely through a sharp reduction in government expenditures.[5] This was a drastic change in the fiscal impact of the government on the economy, equivalent to about 15 percent of GNP. A comparable change today (1992) would mean a change of over $670 billion— sufficient not only to eliminate the current deficit, but to pay off a sizable fraction of the national debt as well. At the same time, and for related reasons, the Federal Reserve System sharply curtailed credit.[6] The result of these sharp, large-scale policy reversals was a severe recession in the United States, and similar policies gave the same results in much of Europe. The U.S. unemployment rate reached 11.7 percent, and wholesale prices fell by about one-third. Although the depression was

short-lived (by 1923 the unemployment rate was only 2.4 percent), it had clearly been caused by the government's fiscal policies and the monetary policies that supported them.[7]

That these macroeconomic influences could have been changed so drastically, with so little regard for their impact on unemployment and output, could have been viewed as an augury of things to come, or at least of government reaction to economic fluctuations if these were to occur. However, it was not, and for the next eight years it appeared there would be little reason for government intervention aimed at improving the macroeconomic situation. The government's actions indicated that public spending's effects on the economy could no longer be disregarded when the federal budget accounted for nearly 10 percent of GNP, over twice the level of prewar years. Nevertheless, with only minimal intervention by the Federal Reserve System and a steadily declining role (and taxes) from the federal government, the U.S. economic performance over the 1920s was good. Rates of per-capita income increase were comparable to those of earlier decades; slower aggregate growth was offset by a reduction in population growth. The record compared particularly well with that achieved by nearly all European countries over the same period.

SOURCES OF GROWTH

The introduction to this section indicated that economic growth increasingly stemmed from increases in output per unit of input (productivity advances), rather than on mere increases in the quantity of inputs. Investment rates were high; net investment averaged about 10 percent of GNP during the decade. Not only

---

[4] *Historical Statistics*, 2:884.
[5] *Historical Statistics*, 2:1104.
[6] M. Friedman and A. Schwartz, *The Great Contraction* (Princeton, N.J.: Princeton University Press, 1965), 226–230.

[7] R. Gordon, *Economic Instability and Growth: The American Record* (New York: Harper & Row, 1974), 15–23.

did the nation's stock of productive equipment grow rapidly, but the capital-output ratio began to fall. A dollar invested in new capital equipment produced a greater amount of additional output than had formerly been the case. This reversed the prewar trend, when the supply of capital had increased so rapidly relative to that of labor and raw materials that the effects of increased relative supply swamped those of technological change. The decrease in population growth, and particularly in the growth of the labor force during and after World War I, was an important influence on investment. Scarcer labor meant rising wage rates, and firms increased the rate at which they substituted capital for labor. The new technology, with electrical and gasoline motors replacing steam and waterpower in factories, tended to produce fewer jobs for unskilled labor.[8]

Manufacturing and Construction

The increase in capital productivity was especially pronounced in manufacturing. A large proportion of all equipment was brought up to the highest feasible levels of performance. The substitution of electricity for steam power grew rapidly, as did the changes in plant layout that made the most of its advantages. Older, less efficient plants were rebuilt or abandoned, and new factories were located more advantageously in relation to markets, inputs, or both. As a result, manufacturing production rose nearly two-thirds from 1919 to 1929, although there was virtually no change in manufacturing employment.[9] The increase in manufacturing productivity made nearly the entire increase in the work force available to

aid the growth of other sectors; employment gains were concentrated in trade, services, and construction. These sectors, together with public utilities, grew faster than the aggregate economy.

Significant changes began to occur within some industries. Over 1923–1925, General Motors began the now-familiar practice of annual model changes in its cars. This practice was an important factor in its rise to the number one position in the auto industry. Many small-scale carmakers found it increasingly difficult to compete with the large integrated auto producers who could take advantage of all available economies of scale, often by turning out several lines of cars that shared common components.[10] Construction was another leading industry. The boom in residential building, both in single-family houses and in urban apartments, was a reflection of higher incomes, greater availability of credit and longer mortgage periods, and more widespread automobile ownership. Even so, although many studies of this period have focused attention on the automobile, construction, and electrical appliance industries, the growth in consumer durables production only slightly exceeded that of the aggregate economy.

The mass-produced, privately owned automobile and the network of roads built in response to it made the growth of the suburbs possible. For the first time in at least six decades, Americans were becoming a nation of homeowners. During most of the previous period of urbanization, they had lived primarily in rented housing—apartments and residential hotels for the middle class, and tenements and boardinghouses for the poor. The housing boom peaked in 1926, and thereafter construc-

[8] H. Oshima, "The Growth of U.S. Factor Productivity: The Significance of New Technologies in the Early Decades of the Twentieth Century," *Journal of Economic History* (March 1984). See also W. Devine, "From Shafts to Wires: Historical Perspective on Electrification," *Journal of Economic History* (June 1983).
[9] *Historical Statistics*, 2:666, 668.

[10] A. Chandler, Jr., *Giant Industry: Ford, General Motors, and the Automobile Industry* (New York: Harcourt, Brace, and World, 1964), 148–152.

tion activity centered on business structures, public-utility equipment, and roads.

Declining Sectors

There were, as always, sectors that grew less rapidly than the entire economy or even declined. Some of these, particularly coal and shipbuilding, suffered from excess capacity that had been installed to meet wartime demands. Both shipbuilding and the merchant marine had been greatly expanded during the war, but many of the merchant ships constructed under war emergency programs were not launched until after the end of hostilities. In the 1920s, these ships had to compete with the results of similar programs in other nations. World trade did not regain its prewar volume until 1924, and even after that date was hampered by a web of currency restrictions and trade barriers. The consequence was a worldwide glut of shipping, and the U.S. merchant marine was ill-equipped for the competition that it engendered.

Coal production stagnated in the 1920s, and prices fell as oil and natural gas production more than doubled. The coal industry had internal problems as well. The United Mine Workers pressed for wage increases in excess of productivity gains, raising unit labor costs, and mineowners' investment in cost-reducing technology was limited. In the face of increased competition from cleaner, more convenient fuels, such policies contributed to chronic unemployment in coal-producing regions.

Cotton and woolen textile production, particularly in New England, also failed to keep pace with aggregate economic growth. Rayon, the first widely used synthetic fiber, began to compete with natural materials. A greater difficulty for the textile industry was that consumer spending on clothing grew no faster than the growth of income, or even at a slower pace.

The railroads lost passenger traffic to automobiles moving along the new network of all-weather highways and were hard-pressed to maintain their freight business against growing competition from trucks. Commercial aviation had appeared, but it would not have a significant impact on other forms of transportation for several decades. Although the railroads had been returned to private ownership after World War I, the industry had not yet overcome its prewar difficulties. In a misguided effort to aid financially troubled roads, the Transportation Act of 1920 required profitable railroads to contribute some of their earnings to the support of lines unable to generate adequate rates of return. There were two major faults in this policy: First, the railway industry as a whole failed to generate profits equal to opportunity costs, so the funds to be reallocated between its components were insufficient; and second, the policy penalized efficient carriers to subsidize those whose performance was below par.

Agriculture

Most studies of lagging sectors in the American economy of the 1920s devote a good deal of space to the problems of the nation's farmers. Even before the war, agricultural employment had begun to decline, and the sector's problems continued in this decade. During the war, American farmers had been urged to increase their production of basic commodities by government guarantees of high grain and meat prices. These efforts, often financed with borrowed money, had only become effective after the war ended. The new production efforts were largely based on an expansion of cultivation onto lands of lower fertility than those already in use. They made economic sense, if at all, only if farm goods' prices remained high. Farm debts to commercial banks alone had more than doubled from 1915 to

1922, and farmers also borrowed heavily from insurance companies and other financial institutions, particularly after 1920.[11] The wholesale prices of farm products fell by more than 43 percent from 1919 to 1922, a drop considerably greater than the drop in nonfarm goods.

At the same time, taxes on farm property also increased. Faced with heavy burdens of fixed costs, farmers had little choice but to maintain production. If any individual among the millions of American farmers reduced output, his action would have no noticeable impact on prices, but that farmer's income would decline because he had less produce to sell. A concerted reduction in output by many farmers might raise the price of their crops, but was impossible to coordinate. Individual farmers knew that they could benefit doubly from others' output reductions by increasing their own output and selling more at the higher price, "free-riding" on others' actions. No voluntary organization could overcome this problem.

Farm Incomes

Real incomes per farm in the 1920s averaged almost exactly what they had been in the "Golden Years" of 1910–1915. Farm populations declined through the era, and, consequently, farmers' per-capita incomes rose slightly.[12] Still, farmers' complaints were based on real grievances. First, farm incomes had been much higher over the 1916–1920 period, and farmers naturally compared the current situation to their most favorable recent experience. Second, the postwar income levels had only been attained by working a larger acreage and selling a higher proportion of what the land produced. The tractor was rapidly replacing draft animals on American farms, and, consequently, less land was required to pro-

duce "fuel" in the form of oats and hay. Approximately 24 million acres of land were released for cash-crop production by this agency.[13] Though farmers increased the amount of goods they marketed, their incomes failed to rise relative to those of the prewar period, and their costs of production were higher. While farm incomes were static, or nearly so, others' were not; farm incomes declined substantially relative to nonfarm. Farmers had difficulty carrying their debt and tax burdens, and foreclosures on farm property increased.

The disparity between farm and nonfarm incomes was not equally shared. Farmers on marginal land, or those unable to afford the new, cost-reducing machinery and techniques were more seriously affected than those in a position to adopt new methods or diversify their crops. The Northern Great Lakes States, the Ozarks, and the Appalachians were all areas of considerable farm distress. Farm incomes in California, and, to a lesser extent, Florida, which produced citrus fruit and out-of-season vegetables for urban markets, were higher than the average.

The Farmer's Dilemma

The source of most farmers' problems was obvious. The demand for agricultural products was both price- and income-inelastic. Consumers would not increase their purchases of farm products in proportion to either reductions in their prices or increases in their own incomes. Foreign markets for U.S. agricultural exports did not offer the relief from this dilemma that they had before the war; they declined through the 1920s. The changing nature of much nonfarm work, with fewer jobs requiring great physical exertion, even resulted in a per-capita decline in the consumption of some foods, such as grains.

To raise their incomes under such circumstances, farmers had three choices. First, they

---

[11] *Historical Statistics*, 1:491.
[12] *Historical Statistics*, 1:232.

[13] *Historical Statistics*, 1:510.

■ A reaper around 1910: Note that two people were still needed to operate it.
Source: H. Armstrong Roberts.

could change occupations, moving to higher-income jobs. Some farmers did. Despite a rural birth rate substantially above the national average, the farm population fell 1.5 percent in the decade.[14] Second, those remaining in agriculture could raise their incomes by reducing aggregate production, because with an inelastic demand for most farm products, prices would rise more than in proportion to the decrease in quantity supplied. This, however, required concerted action, and there was no agency to coordinate the production plans of all farmers. In its absence, output-reduction measures were bound to fail, as indicated above. Most of the new techniques reduced

costs only at high volumes of output, which compounded the difficulties of output reduction. Third, demand for agricultural products might somehow be increased.

Government Aid

Since consumers in domestic markets would not buy more agricultural products, especially at higher prices, farmers requested help from the government. A variety of proposals was made, culminating in the two McNary-Haugen Bills, which were twice passed by Congress, in 1924 and 1928, only to be vetoed by President Coolidge. Under this legislation, the federal government would have purchased enough of each year's major crops to raise prices to their 1909–1914 levels in relation to those of all other goods (the parity ratio).

---

[14] *Historical Statistics*, 1:497.

These government purchases could not be sold within the United States without reducing prices again, so the government was to sell them on the world market for whatever they might bring. To prevent goods acquired abroad at bargain prices from being resold in the United States, high tariffs were to be levied on all agricultural imports. The government would lose on its overseas sales, but taxes were to be levied on participating farmers (actually, processors of agricultural products) to make up the losses. The McNary-Haugen Bills contained no limits on aggregate farm production; a weak point, because such programs, once enacted, would have generated large increases in farm production, and world demand for farm products was also price-inelastic.

Farmers did receive some government assistance in the form of loan guarantees and permission to form output-restricting marketing associations. In cases where the crops affected were produced by small numbers of farmers in restricted areas, enabling the associations to enforce their output limits, they had some success. For the major farm crops, however, they were unworkable. In 1929, the Agricultural Marketing Act encouraged the formation of such marketing associations, but it also went a good deal further. For the first time, the government established a fund with which to buy agricultural products in an effort to stabilize their prices. The purchase fund was swamped by the effects of the Depression. With nonfarm incomes declining and pushing agricultural prices even lower, farmers had no alternative but to increase production. The increased output overwhelmed the funds. Farmers' attempts at rent-seeking remained, on the whole, unsuccessful, but they had achieved a more favorable response from government than ever before.

The preceding discussion of declining sectors should not be construed as an indication that the aggregate performance of the American economy was unsatisfactory during the

1920s. The usual macroeconomic indicators (growth, prices, and employment) give an accurate picture of the overall situation. Declining sectors are normal features of a market economy: They do not indicate worsening performance by their very existence. The aggregate data indicate that the growth sectors were more than sufficient to offset those that declined. Although the representatives of slow-growing or declining industries were more prone to request government assistance than they had been earlier (perhaps because, in so many cases, their current difficulties were linked to government policies), they seldom received it.

The Trade Association Movement

One aspect of the government's response to requests for assistance was significant. In urging agricultural producers to form trade associations, the federal government was expanding a policy that it had already established in its relations with manufacturing. Considerable latitude was extended to trade-association operations, and government efforts to enforce more traditional antitrust laws were not noted for either vigor or originality of approach in this decade. In particular, after the *U.S. Steel* case (1920), the government made no effort to change the existing structure of industries. Its view of several forthright attempts to restrict competition was also decidedly benevolent.

Trade associations developed from wartime cooperation among firms. At that time they had been encouraged to exchange information on production levels and costs. From this it was a short step to discussing prices, and using this information to restrict competition required even less imagination. Some trade associations compelled their members to furnish other producers with prior notices of all price changes. Others insisted on the use of pricing formulas that made it easy to detect any sales at prices below those "recommended" by the association.

The courts allowed virtually every trade association activity that was not clearly labelled price-fixing. At the same time, there was a wave of mergers. In some cases, there were efforts to achieve economies of scale. Although mergers are a dubious mechanism for reducing production costs within any single production unit, Chrysler and General Motors apparently achieved some success through such methods, by adding volume "downstream" from facilities that possessed underutilized economies of scale. Other mergers were vertical or conglomerate, attempts to diversify into new areas of activity. In the public-utilities field, there were some mergers designed to produce monopoly. The performance of the stock market in the late 1920s made it easy to obtain funds to finance mergers. In spite of this activity, however, it is unclear whether industrial concentration increased. The shares of total industry output controlled by the largest firms did not change significantly in most industries.

INCOME DISTRIBUTION

World War I had caused a leveling of incomes within the United States. The war increased the demand for unskilled labor much more than it did that for skilled workers, and wage differentials narrowed substantially. Low-income groups, who bear the brunt of joblessness, benefit more from full employment than do those with higher incomes. After the war, however, there may have been a trend favoring upper-income groups. One study has found that by 1929 the distribution of income

■ The automobile was one of the most conspicuous indicators of prosperity in the 1920s.
Source: Museum of Science and Industry, Chicago.

was similar to the patterns observed just before the war.[15] That prewar distribution of income had been substantially less equal than is the case today. The functional distribution of income was also little changed from earlier decades; the share of income accruing to property in the late 1920s was about the same as it had been two decades earlier—an implication that labor's share was also unchanged.[16] In manufacturing, real wages rose less rapidly than productivity, so that the portion of income accruing to property in that sector increased. But this does not appear to have occurred in other sectors of the economy, nor was manufacturing employment an increasing share of all jobs during the 1920s.

The share of income accruing to unincorporated enterprises declined, an indication of the decline of the farm sector rather than of any change in small business. But the proportion of aggregate income going to employees rose almost exactly as much as proprietors' incomes fell. One study claims to have discovered a decided increase in inequality during the 1920s, with the rich, or even just the very rich, receiving all or slightly more than the total gains in income generated in the entire economy, while the incomes of middle- and low-income groups either remained unchanged or even fell slightly.[17] However, it now appears that this paper relied on faulty data and failed to allow for tax avoidance that may have negated much of the trend toward greater income equality during and immediately after the war. The distribution of income may have become slightly less equal during the 1920s, but the view that the rich obtained all or nearly all the income gains of this decade no longer appears tenable.[18] The evidence that income gains were widely, if not necessarily equally, distributed is very strong.

The 1920s exodus from low-income jobs and regions would tend to produce greater income equality. The very low unemployment rates that have previously been discussed would be another; these tend to aid the poor far more than those whose incomes already reflect skills or property ownership. There is ample evidence that the middle class and many others shared in the prosperity of this decade. Increases in single-family housing, in homes with central heating, plumbing, gas, and electricity, and in the ownership of consumer durables, such as automobiles, electrical appliances, and more elaborate furniture, all represent broad-based income gains: The rich already possessed these items. In this decade, the labor force participation rates of married women rose, and female wages grew in relation to those of men in similar jobs.[19] Shorter hours of work, higher real wages, and longer life expectancy all indicate improvements in the lot of the vast majority of Americans. A larger proportion of all children now attended high school, and child labor continued to decline. New amusements (radio, the movies, professional sports, and the Sunday afternoon automobile ride) made life more interesting. Whether the income gains of the 1920s were equally distributed or not, there were obvious gains by large numbers of people who could by no means be considered rich. The proportion of all families owning houses wired for electricity, indoor flush toilets, and automobiles all doubled or more in this dec-

[15] P. Lindert and J. Williamson, "Three Centuries of American Inequality," in P. Uselding, ed., *Research in Economic History* (Greenwich, Conn.: JAI Press, 1976).
[16] *Historical Statistics*, 1:236.
[17] C. Holt, "Who Profited from the Prosperity of the Twenties?" The rich could obtain more than the total increase in incomes if the share of the non-rich fell.

[18] G. Smiley, "Did Incomes for Most of the Population Fall from 1923 through 1929?" *Journal of Economic History* (March 1983).
[19] C. Goldin, "The Female Labor Force and American Economic Growth, 1890–1950," in R. Gallman and S. Engerman, *Long-Term Factors in American Economic Growth* (Chicago: University of Chicago Press, 1986).

■ Automobile showrooms, like the one shown in this 1929 photo, allowed buyers to examine automakers' wares. *Source:* H. Armstrong Roberts.

ade, and in each case the gains accrued to more than half the total population.[20]

LABOR UNIONS

For labor unions, however, the 1920s were a period of falling membership. Union organization had burgeoned during the war, and by 1920 about 5 million workers were members of labor unions. This was about one-eighth of the work force, by far the largest portion yet organized. After 1923, however, labor union membership did not exceed 3.7 million for the rest of the decade, despite substantial growth in both employment and the labor force. Only one American worker in twelve belonged to a labor union in 1930. Nearly half the decrease in union membership was concentrated in the metals, machinery, and mining industries.[21]

On the surface, it seem strange that unions should fail to increase their membership in

---

[20] S. Lebergott, *The Americans: An Economic Record* (New York: Norton, 1984), 433.

[21] *Historical Statistics*, 1:177–178.

this period. Tight labor markets should have made it easier to organize and bargain. However, the rapid introduction of labor-saving technology in manufacturing weakened unions' strength in that sector. Much of the growth in employment was concentrated in the service industries, an area of chronic union weakness. Employers' attitudes toward unions had not become more positive in the 1920s, and there was a vigorous anti-union movement that received a good deal of support from the courts. The use of injunctions and yellow-dog contracts was widespread. With the courts inclined to favor employers, such devices could be used to cripple unions' organizing efforts, and even allowed the employers to sue unions that had been able to organize firms' employees. There was also an extensive development of company unions. These "tame" unions' major purpose was to shield the firms whose workers they enrolled from organizational efforts by unions more likely to bargain vigorously on their members' behalf.

Despite the legal and institutional opposition that American unions encountered at this time, some labor historians have concluded that the unions' decline owes a good deal to their own lack of effort. Employers' opposition to unionization was scarcely a new phenomenon, and American unions had recorded their previous gains under far more difficult conditions than those prevailing in the 1920s. The contemporary union movement, largely restricted to skilled craftsmen as it was, may not really have had much interest in extending its activities into manufacturing, or even in keeping its toehold there. This would be especially true if organizing manufacturing workers necessitated changes in union structure. Workers in mass-production industries could not easily be organized along craft lines, and new institutions would be required to meet their needs. The leaders of American unions at this time were not dy-namic or visionary. High wages and steady full employment may ironically have been obstacles to unions' organizing efforts, particularly in manufacturing, the scene of unions' greatest failure in this decade. It has been alleged that American unions consciously traded high wages for current members against expansion during this period.[22]

FOREIGN ECONOMIC RELATIONS

World War I had abruptly transformed economic relations between the United States and the rest of the world. Unfortunately, there was little recognition of this fact in America, and consequently only slight modification of American policies and practices occurred. The United States continued the practices of earlier decades, when its role in international finance had been that of a large-scale debtor with only minor interests in overseas investments. During the war, the U.S. government had loaned nearly $10 billion to the Allies, an unprecedented act for this country. The bulk of the loans had been to Britain and France, but smaller sums had been advanced to Russia, Belgium, Italy, and other countries. The British and French had made larger loans to the other Allies.

Loans to support military expenditures are unlike normal business transactions in that even if they achieve their purpose, they do not produce additional income from which they can be repaid. At best, they are a purchase of political advantage—a consumer expenditure, not an investment. Nonetheless, successive American administrations insisted that the

[22] P. Temin, *Lessons from the Great Depression* (Cambridge, Mass.: MIT Press, 1989), 120.

loans be repaid by the Allies. The only concessions made were reductions in the principal due, and these only after it became apparent that the loans could not be repaid.

Problems of War Debt Repayment

If foreign countries were to repay American loans, they could only do so by providing this country with more goods and services than they purchased from it, using the dollars so obtained to discharge their obligations. They could also ship gold (the international money), but the Allies' debts were far beyond the amount that could be repaid from gold reserves already depleted by the war. Thus, Europeans had no alternative but to run a trade surplus with the United States (or at least with other countries). America, however, had traditionally run an export surplus. Prior to the war, this surplus had financed interest and principal payments on American debts to foreigners, with something left over for U.S. investment abroad.

After the war, the structure of international debts was reversed. The United States was now a large-scale international creditor, not a debtor. Nevertheless, the United States export surplus continued, as its productivity gains outstripped those abroad. Duties on U.S. imports were sharply raised in 1921 and again in 1922, making it more difficult for foreign producers to sell in American markets. They remained at about their pre-1914 rates until 1930, when they were raised yet again in a disastrously misguided attempt to export unemployment (the Smoot-Hawley tariff). The Europeans made their own mistakes; the British attempted to return to the gold standard at the prewar pound sterling-dollar exchange rate, at which the pound was seriously overvalued. British exports became more expensive to foreign buyers, but imported goods' prices within Britain fell.

Even so, foreigners were able to make some payments on their debts and finance purchases of American exports. The source of this ability lay in foreign loans made by private citizens and institutions in the United States. Ironically, many of these loans were extended to Germany. American private investment abroad rose by about $10 billion from 1919 to 1930. The Treaty of Versailles required Germany to make reparations payments to the Allies for the damage done by German forces during the war. Since the German people were not eager to reduce their own living standards to make these enforced "gifts" to their erstwhile foes, they found loans from the United States to be very useful. Some of the funds were used within Germany, often for civic purposes with little direct economic payoff, and the remainder financed reparations payments and German investments in eastern Europe. To the extent that any repayment of war debts was received, the United States provided the funds itself. Loans to Germany may have avoided some European conflict at this time (the French, in particular, were determined to make Germany pay for the war). At the same time, the loans also delayed recognition that the reparations payments imposed on Germany were utterly unrealistic, probably uncollectible, at least from German domestic resources, and clearly worsened international relations.

The United States had little experience in foreign investment, and almost none at all in lending to governments. A high proportion of the loans extended, both to Germany and in Latin America, were for extremely dubious projects that might never generate sufficient income to finance repayment. A large portion of American and other international lending at this time was in short-term, highly liquid forms. Such funds were likely to be quickly withdrawn from the borrowing countries if conditions there became unfavorable. This, of course, would probably worsen the difficulties of the nation from which the funds were withdrawn.[23]

In one instance, the U.S. contribution to international finance was positive, although, to an extent, after American policies had helped to create the problem. The United States was active in persuading the Allies to scale down the reparations demanded from Germany in 1925 and 1928, and it also reduced the principal of loans to the Allies.

FALSE PROSPERITY?

Given the events of the 1930s, it is tempting to see in the economic conditions of the 1920s the seeds of disaster. In such a view, even the most firmly established evidence of real economic gains is somehow unreal, and those who spoke of the achievement of "permanent prosperity" at the time appear victims of delusion—or worse. But even though the 1920s were followed by a period of economic disaster and a long, halting, incomplete recovery, temporal sequence alone does not establish the conclusion that there was something in the course of economic affairs then that made the Great Depression inevitable.

As the early pages of this chapter have stressed, by the usual macroeconomic criteria, the performance of the American economy in the 1920s was at least as good as that of recent decades. Who would not exchange the recent record of growth, price stability, and unemployment rates for that achieved 70 years ago? Americans enjoyed a better material standard of life at the end of the decade than they did at its beginning. People were obtaining more

education, their health was better, the hours of work shorter and less arduous, and their ranges of choice wider. Personal freedom, especially for women, had increased for the average American (Prohibition would have to be excepted from this generalization). When the American achievements are contrasted with the lack of similar progress in Europe, they appear even more remarkable.

If the performance of the private economy was good, government's economic policies were another source of satisfaction to most Americans. The federal government consistently ran surpluses, taking in more through taxes than was expended on current public operations. The excess funds were used to reduce the national debt, which fell by about one-third. By modern standards, the tax burden was very light, and over the decade it grew lighter still. About three-quarters of all federal revenues came from income taxes, and these bore more heavily on upper-income groups than had previous federal taxes. The tax structure was made even more progressive over the decade, with rates reduced for all but the very wealthy after 1921.[24] The federal government's share of total income was about 5 percent, a very low figure by modern standards. There had been minor recessions in 1924 and 1927, but these had caused only slight reductions in income and employment, and had responded well to open-market operations by the Federal Reserve System. There was considerable confidence in the efficacy of government action: The enforcement of Prohibition, it was thought, would present few problems to the nation that had recently won the war.

Truly, it must have appeared to most Americans that if they worked hard and saved part of their incomes, they could look forward, if not to riches, at least to growing and substantial prosperity. But in 1929 these rosy prospects disappeared in a 12-year nightmare. Many Americans still bear the psychic scars

---

[23] C. Kindleberger, *The World in Depression, 1929–39*, 2d ed. (Berkeley, Calif.: University of California Press, 1986). See also H. Feis, *The Diplomacy of the Dollar, 1919–1932* (New York: Norton, 1950) (1966 reprint).

[24] *Historical Statistics*, 2:1110–1112, 1120–1124.

of a period in which there seemed to be no work, no income, and little reason to hope that things would improve.

THE GREAT DEPRESSION

The downturn that began in the summer of 1929 initially appeared similar to the recessions of 1924 and 1927. Despite the trend that began in that year, 1929 itself was not a year of high unemployment. The jobless rate for the year was less than 4 percent, and the rate of real economic growth was the highest in four years, 6.7 percent. A slump had been re-garded as overdue by most business forecasters; but if recent history were any guide, it was expected to be no cause for great concern. But the downturn grew steadily worse for four terrible years, until in 1933, fully one-quarter of the American labor force was unable to find jobs of any kind and at least as many more were working shorter hours or less intensively than they wished. Even after the low point had at last passed, recovery was agonizingly slow. A severe recession-within-a-depression during 1937 raised unemployment rates to levels surpassed only at the very worst of the Depression. In 1941, after eight years of New Deal policies, and a year after defense spending had begun to rise in anticipation of active American participation in World War II, the

■ The hardships endured by migrant workers during the Great Depression provided the inspiration for such novels as John Steinbeck's *The Grapes of Wrath.*
Source: F.S.A. photo by Dorothea Lange.

unemployment rate was still 9.9 percent. It had not been even that low for 10 years.

Mere figures, such as those in Table 17.1, are inadequate to express the human suffering caused by such massive joblessness. There was very little support for the unemployed outside their own resources. Few of the middle class and almost none of the poor possessed savings capable of tiding them over more than a few months without work. Even these meager savings might be reduced or lost entirely in the general collapse of financial institutions. Public programs to aid the indigent were inadequate even under normal circumstances, and, in any case, were designed to provide only temporary help. They were not intended to provide the sole support of millions of families over years in which there simply were no jobs available. In many cases, the state and local governments that provided such assistance proved unable to finance it because their tax revenues dwindled as property values declined and rents fell.[25] Private charities were overwhelmed, and they too suffered from reduced incomes. Some state and local governments were unable to pay the salaries of even their regular employees. They skipped paydays or paid in scrip, which might be accepted for less than half its face value.

Nor can aggregate figures depict the highly uneven incidence of unemployment among industries and regions. In 1932, the American steel industry was producing at one-quarter of its capacity. For such cities as Pittsburgh and Gary, Indiana, this meant unemployment rates of 50 percent and more. Unemployment in any single sector has multiplier effects: Lost incomes mean fewer customers for other products and hence less jobs and lower incomes in other sectors as well.

For those recently hired or the objects of prejudice, conditions were still worse. Blacks had only recently gained access to urban and industrial jobs. They bore the burden of limited seniority as well as racism. A 1935 survey of living conditions for American blacks established two yardsticks against which to measure actual incomes. One was a budget sufficient to provide adequate nutrition, but almost nothing else except the most basic clothing and shelter. The other was an "emergency budget," which was deemed adequate only for the short-term maintenance of life: It jeopardized health if continued over long periods. The income of the average black family was sufficient to purchase even the emergency budget in only 5 of the 59 cities surveyed.[26] Discrimination against women, especially against married women and those in clerical

Table 17.1 Unemployment and Unemployment Rates, 1929–1942

Year	Unemployment (Thousands)	Rate (Percentage of Labor Force)
1929	1,550	3.2%
1930	4,340	8.7
1931	8,020	15.9
1932	12,060	23.6
1933	12,830	24.9
1934	11,340	21.7
1935	10,610	20.1
1936	9,030	16.9
1937	7,700	14.3
1938	10,390	19.0
1939	9,480	17.2
1940	8,120	14.6
1941	5,560	9.9
1942	2,660	4.7

Source: U.S. Department of Commerce, Bureau of the Census, *Historical Statistics of the United States: Colonial Times to 1970*, 2 vols. (Washington, D.C.: Government Printing Office, 1975), 1:135.

[25] L. Chandler, *America's Greatest Depression, 1929–1941* (New York: Harper & Row, 1970), 47–51, 189.
[26] R. Sterner, *The Negro's Share: A Study of Income, Housing, and Public Assistance* (New York: Negro University Press, 1940), 85–87.

occupations, increased sharply.[27] Incomes were considerably higher in the cities than in small towns or rural areas. Under such conditions, bare survival was a noteworthy achievement.

The Psychological Costs

Nor could all the costs of unemployment be measured in terms of lost income or even physical deprivation. To a much greater extent than today, Americans believed that all worthwhile individuals could find and hold jobs adequate to support themselves and their families. Failure to do so meant that there was something wrong with the individual, rather than the economy. People had been taught that those unable to find and hold jobs were bums or worse, not really deserving of help. For people holding these values, the effects of years in which constant search for work produced only short-term jobs with pay and conditions far below those previously obtained, or even no work at all, can barely be imagined. The transition to such conditions was swift; most of the Depression's victims had no warning.

The Depression had consequences not merely for fast-buck artists, who knew they were taking risks, but also for millions of people who had followed the traditional prescriptions of hard work and frugal living. Not only might such people have to endure being told that, in effect, nobody wanted their efforts, but the savings they had painfully accumulated might be lost in bank failures or declining asset values. The experiences of the Depression left indelible scars on those who lived through them. They go far to explain why the grandparents of today's college students take so much interest in the material possessions,

steady employment, and economic security that now are assumed to be the birthrights of most, if not all, Americans.

How could the unemployed survive under such conditions? They used up savings if they possessed any, sold or borrowed against the cherished accumulations of a lifetime, lost mortgaged homes, took whatever help they could obtain from relatives, friends, or charitable agencies, stole—and endured. In 1932, *Fortune* magazine commissioned a sympathetic study of the plight of the unemployed titled "No One Has Starved."[28] The title's premise was almost certainly wrong at the time it was written, and the Depression was to grow worse for two more years. In the first few years, newspapers were full of accounts of those found in really desperate circumstances, but as the Depression dragged on, such stories were too commonplace to merit further attention.

Lost Opportunities

In addition to the direct effects of unemployment, the Depression imposed other costs. The economy produced far less than its potential: Citizens went without goods that could have been produced. So great was the lost output in the 1930s that if we assume a continuation of the 1920s' rate of economic growth, the additional output would have sufficed to provide first-class housing and medical care for every American who lacked them. Foregone production was greater than that devoted to World War II in the next decade. A whole decade of growth had been lost; real output in 1939 had barely regained the levels initially reached in 1929. Even after recovery had reached that point, the economy was still capable of producing far more. The unemployment rate attests to that. Real GNP in 1958 dollars was $203.6 billion in 1929. At the

[27] C. Goldin, *Understanding the Gender Gap: An Economic History of American Women* (New York: Oxford University Press, 1990), 110–112.

[28] "No One Has Starved," *Fortune*, September 1932.

trough of the Depression in 1932–1933, it had fallen to only $141.5 billion. By the same measures, gross private domestic investment fell from $40.4 to $4.7 billion.

The rate of investment was far below normal; in some years, it was not even sufficient to replace depreciation. At least until the New Deal launched its soil-conservation and Civilian Conservation Corps programs, even farm land and natural resources suffered from inadequate maintenance. Family formation and birth rates fell.

Few, if any, areas of economic activity were unaffected by the Depression. Labor's aggregate situation worsened with unemployment and underemployment. Surprisingly, however, real wages actually rose in most Depression years, for those who retained full-time jobs.[29] Rent and interest income fell. Landlords and mortgage holders often allowed tenants to stay on even though they could not pay rent or amortization payments. If they were evicted or foreclosed, there were no alternative customers with better prospects, and foreclosure might force recognition of the property's true value, possibly revealing the owners to be as bankrupt as their tenants. At the very bottom of the Depression, in 1931 and 1932, corporate profits were negative; incorporated firms as a whole lost money. It would be a long time before property income recovered; profits did not regain 1929 levels until 1940 or 1941, and rent and interest income reached its previous peak only in the mid-1940s or even later.

Causes of the Depression

How could such an enormous disaster occur? As with any such calamity, there is no lack of after-the-fact explanations. Some are clearly wrong. A depression, particularly one of this magnitude, is not an inevitable consequence of the prosperity that preceded it. History reveals no other economic collapse of equal severity, and no trend at all for especially severe downturns after periods of high prosperity.

Moreover, it is difficult to link the Depression's sources with World War I. Although the war did precede the Depression, it was more than a decade past in 1929. The two events were separated by so long and prosperous an era that it is very difficult to see the nature of any causation.[30] The Depression was most severe in Germany and the United States, the two industrialized economies probably most and least affected by the war. Although the foreign economic relations of the United States had been drastically altered by the war, these were only a minor part of aggregate economic activity in America.

Both income inequality and monopoly had been at least as pronounced for decades before 1914 as they were in the 1920s, and the previous era had not produced a comparable depression. Indeed, that period is regarded as one of high and growing prosperity. Economic growth in the 1920s was concentrated on a few sectors of the economy, but that too is a normal pattern, and, if anything, the range of growth sectors was unusually broad. Heretofore, new sectors had appeared as old mainstays of expansion waned.

As Table 17.2 indicates, "overcapacity" does not appear to explain many of the events leading up to the 1929 debacle. A few industries (especially automobiles and residential construction) had apparently been expanded beyond the existing demand for their products at current prices, but the number of those who had not yet obtained modern conveniences in their homes, such as appliances, radios, or other mainstays of 1920s growth, was large. Even more, the variety of products available

---

[29] *Historical Statistics*, 1:164.

[30] Peter Temin disagrees. He finds that the war's effects on international finance (and monetary authorities' failure to recognize them) were a causal factor. See *Lessons*, Chap. 1.

Table 17.2   Changes in Consumption, 1902–1931

Years	GNP (Billions of Dollars)*	Flow of Goods to Consumers (Billions of Dollars)*	Flow of Goods Divided by GNP
1902–1906	$23.6	$18.2	77.1%
1907–1911	30.1	24.1	80.0
1912–1916	38.9	30.8	79.2
1917–1921	71.6	54.9	76.7
1922–1926	84.8	66.8	78.8
1927–1931	89.9	73.0	81.2

*Figures in current dollars.
Sources: U.S. Department of Commerce, Bureau of the Census, *Historical Statistics of the United States: Colonial Times to 1970*, 2 vols. (Washington, D.C.: Government Printing Office, 1975), 1:231. See also S. Lebergott, *The Americans: An Economic Record* (New York: Norton, 1984), Chap. 33.

to consumers was expanding rapidly. The apparent rise in consumption in the 1927–1931 period, however, is more indicative of the collapse of investment late in those years than of any increased tendency to consume.

In addition, many business firms still did not have the latest, most productive capital goods. Although farm incomes had failed to grow, the agricultural sector was a smaller portion of the economy than it had been before the war. At best, it appears that such structural explanations can account for only a trifling portion of the Depression. While they may have worsened its impact, structural factors were not the cause of the Great Depression.

The Stock Market Crash

In many studies of the beginning of the Depression, the spectacular rise and even more spectacular collapse in prices on the New York Stock Exchange play a major causative role.[31] Although the stock exchange was an important instrument of investment and the

great crash did occur at the beginning of the Depression, the nature of its effect on the rest of the economy is unclear.

The rise in stock prices had begun in the mid-1920s. It was solidly based: Corporate profits were high, and for some years stock prices did no more than reflect the good earnings and excellent prospects of many corporations. Those who had owned stocks at the start of the period or purchased them soon after it began had made good investments. Not only did they receive increasing dividends on their shares, but they also profited from the rising value of the stocks themselves. For some years, yields on stocks remained about the same.

Gradually, however, as the experiences of the early investors became known, there was more interest in purchasing stocks for quick resale as their prices rose, that is, for capital gains rather than dividend income. As long as the speculative demand for stocks continued to increase, so did stock prices. By late 1928, stock prices were increasing considerably faster than dividends, and it had become much less profitable to buy stocks to hold for income at the new prices. This development made little difference to purchasers who

---

[31] The best of these is J. Galbraith, *The Great Crash* (Boston: Houghton Mifflin, 1954).

■ Among today's collector's items are newspapers recording the stock market crash of 1929. The crash was only the beginning of the economic woes that were to plague the United States during the Great Depression. *Source:* Brown Brothers.

expected to sell their stocks at enhanced prices in a short time. However, they could do so only as long as even more optimistic speculators were attracted to the market.

Margin Purchases The profits to be made from stock speculation were increased by the use of margin purchases, among other devices. A margin purchaser might borrow up to 90 percent (in rare cases) of the value of the stocks purchased. In that case, on resale, he received the entire increase in stock prices as a return on an investment of as little as 10 percent of the shares' initial price. Investment trusts, sometimes in several layers, were set up to magnify this process. In these trusts, the majority of the capital gains accrued to the venturesome minority who held the trusts'

common stock. Margin loans appeared safe and highly liquid to lenders; the loans were against highly liquid assets whose prices were rising. Stockbrokers had no difficulty obtaining financing from banks or large industrial firms, some of which began to consider stock-market profits easier and far more quickly obtained than those from the production and sale of goods.

In the euphoria of the moment, many investors forgot or repressed the idea that such leverage arrangements were equally effective in magnifying losses as well as gains. Further, in a world of scarcity, even the supply of optimists is limited, and once stock prices stopped rising, there was no longer any reason to buy them. This was particularly true for stocks purchased on margin. The high interest rates on brokers' loans, which had appeared no burden when large capital gains were expected in a few weeks or months, now imposed higher costs than the stocks' dividend returns. Once it was clear that there was little prospect of any further increase in stock prices, speculators began to sell their shares, and as stock prices began to decline, even those not inclined to sell began to receive demands from their brokers to put up a larger share of the securities' prices in their own funds. If they could not, the brokers would sell the stock to protect themselves and recover the funds they had lent to margin buyers. Thus, once stock prices began to fall, the likelihood was that they would not decline gently, but would fall at an accelerating pace. And so it was.

As stock prices began their initial decline, pessimistic forecasts and unmet margin calls increased the volume offered for sale, driving prices down still further. Stock prices peaked in September 1929. After that date the price decline quickened, and by late October it had become a collapse. Stock prices declined precipitously, and after one brief rally late in 1929, continued a downward trend for the next several years. Standard & Poor's index of corporate stock values fell from 26.02 in 1929 (1941–43 = 10) to 21.02 in 1930. By 1932, the index was at 6.93.[32]

Did the Crash Cause the Depression?

The great stock market crash wiped out billions in securities values. It was sudden and (incredibly) almost completely unanticipated, and it affected many of the people who made America's investment decisions. In concert with a falling general price level, the crash sharply raised the price of investment funds. Nevertheless, it is difficult to assign a major causative role in the Depression to the stock market crash. Stock prices had under-

gone violent fluctuations before without major repercussions on the rest of the economy. Moreover, it is now clear that declines in real economic variables had begun even before stock prices peaked, let alone began to fall. There may have been some indirect effects because of the reduction in investors' wealth, but for at least a year, investor confidence was not a casualty.[33]

The Federal Reserve System had been disturbed by the massive increase in stock speculation after 1926 and had attempted to reduce the flow of funds to the stock market by raising discount rates in 1928, the use of "moral suasion" (attempts to persuade member banks not to lend for stock speculation), and a final sharp discount-rate increase in the late summer of 1929. As long as optimism prevailed in the stock market, these efforts had little effect. To the extent that they had any impact at all, they merely forced those seeking funds for stock purchases to borrow from other sources.[34] The increased interest rates may have discouraged real investment, but with opinions about stock prices at the current pitch of feverish optimism, no conceivable increase in interest rates would have had much of an effect on speculators.

Once stock prices had fallen, the reduced wealth of securities owners may have made them less willing to consume and invest. But only a small portion of the American population actually owned stocks; stocks represented only a minor portion of the nation's total wealth, and business optimism did not collapse for about a year after the stock market crash.[35]

Most economists grant the crash a minor (and, of course, negative) role in the

---

[32] *Historical Statistics*, 2:1004.

[33] P. Temin, *Did Monetary Forces Cause the Great Depression?* (New York: Norton, 1976), Chap. 4.

[34] E. White, "The Stock Market Boom and Crash of 1929 Revisited," *Journal of Economic Perspectives* (Spring 1990).

[35] Temin, *Monetary Forces*, 69–74.

Depression. In one study, however, the crash is seen as a major factor in both the initiation of the Depression and, because stock prices continued to decline for several years, in the worsening economic conditions of the next four years.[36]

Causes of the Depression: The Monetarist View

Monetarists have concluded that changes in the money supply are the chief determinant of short-run changes in real economic parameters. The leading monetary history of this period found that the U.S. money supply declined by over one-third from 1929 to 1933. Further, the money supply had failed to rise in the previous few years. This, the authors concluded, was the real source of the Depression. A series of bank failures caused over one-third of all U.S. banks to fail outright, liquidate, or merge with other banks for survival.[37]

Collapse of the banking system has an effect on market economies similar to that of the failure of the circulatory system on the human body. Money is as essential to exchanges as blood is to the function of all cells in the body. If money is no longer available, or if its supply is suddenly reduced, the impact on all forms of economic activity will be severe, since there are almost no good short-run substitutes for money. The greater the degree of specialization (which, in turn, indicates the degree of economic development), the more severe are the effects of monetary contraction.

The Role of the Federal Reserve System

Professors Friedman and Schwartz found the cause of the monetary collapse (that, in turn, underlay the general economic system's downfall) in the actions, or lack thereof, of the Federal Reserve System. The impact of the system's mistakes was made worse by changes in bank regulations that had been instituted in the Federal Reserve Act of 1913. No longer could banks unable to meet depositors' demands for cash suspend payment, so that their own obligations (bank notes, or, more recently, demand deposits) would continue to circulate and be accepted for payments at a discount from face value. Under the Federal Reserve System's regulations, banks unable to redeem their obligations in full had to suspend all operations, which meant that checks drawn on them would not be accepted, no matter how heavily discounted.

It had been assumed that competently managed banks under Federal Reserve System regulation would always have a source of emergency reserves: They could borrow from the Federal Reserve Banks. Moreover, the central banks could always make loans to member banks against good collateral (commercial paper), and, thus, the member banks could not fail. Even in the 1920s, the evidence was very much to the contrary: 5,882 banks, nearly 1,000 of them members of the Federal Reserve System, had failed in the decade.[38] If the United States had gained a central bank in the "Fed," its commercial banks had changed little. Many were small and had confined most of their loans to their immediate locales, so that if local business was hard-hit, many of the banks' assets would decline in value. What efforts there had been toward bank consolidation or the formation of multibank chains were largely among similar institutions in the same regions. Not only did these measures do little to promote diversification, they often tended to be the work of incompetent or unscrupulous promoters. Consequently, they served only to spread trouble within the banking community.

Also, it had been assumed that what the Federal Reserve Banks could do, they would.

---

[36] F. Mishkin, "The Household Balance Sheet and the Great Depression," *Journal of Economic History* (December 1978).

[37] Friedman and Schwartz, *The Great Contraction*, 299.

[38] *Historical Statistics*, 2:1038.

But there was no statute that clearly defined their obligations to member banks, and there were few persons in authority within the system with the imagination to see the proper course of action during a bank crisis, or the consequences if it were not followed. Had the Federal Reserve System operated as a central bank was expected to, monetarist analysis would expect only a small reinforcement of the downturn from the monetary system. But the help for member banks that the Federal Reserve System had been established to provide was not forthcoming. During successive banking crises, the system either did nothing to aid commercial banks, or actually made the situation worse. The New York Federal Reserve Bank had lowered its discount rate immediately after the stock market crash. But to do more than this, the New York Federal Reserve Bank required support from the rest of the Federal Reserve System. It was not to be had.[39]

Too Little, Too Late No significant action was taken to expand the U.S. money supply until the spring of 1932, when the Federal Reserve System finally began to buy bonds on the open market. By this time, the commercial banks had undergone two waves of runs, each resulting in more bank failures than its predecessor and guaranteeing even greater panic in any recurrences.[40] Under these circumstances, the Fed's purchase of $1 billion in bonds that might have forestalled the banking collapse in 1929 or 1930 was far too little and much too late. This was the only significant expansionary action in almost four years before the trough of the Depression was reached. In this period, the Federal Reserve Banks essentially refused to operate as a central bank. They acted to protect themselves rather than the

■ Scenes like this one, showing a run on a Chicago bank in 1932, would become rare in the 58 years to follow.
Source: Franklin D. Roosevelt Library.

commercial banks, evaluating loan requests on criteria appropriate only under normal business circumstances. At no time were the Federal Reserve Banks themselves in any discernible danger of failure, but over one-quarter of all the commercial banks in the United States failed.

There were three waves of bank failures: in late 1930 and early 1931, in late 1931, and again in late 1932. Each was of increasing severity, and the last culminated in the "bank holiday" of the spring of 1933, when all the surviving banks in the United States were closed by order of the federal government (many had already been closed by state governors). The bank holiday gave banks time to sell assets for cash with which to meet depositors' demands for currency, and to undergo examination and recertification by

---

[39] Friedman and Schwartz, *The Great Contraction*, 363.
[40] Temin disputes the influence of the late 1930 bank failures, which he feels were not primarily induced by the Depression. See Temin, *Lessons*, 46–52.

government examiners. As the banks re-opened with government approval, deposits began to flow back into them. The crisis was over for the banking system, but in four years its effects on the rest of the economy had been disastrous. Worse still, monetarists believe, the banking crisis was almost entirely avoidable.

In the monetarist view, over the crucial 1929–1933 period, the Federal Reserve Banks, the so-called lenders of last resort for the commercial banks, not only imposed stringent terms for loans to banks facing massive "runs," but in some cases actually took actions that increased the pressure on the banks they were set up to aid.

Misguided Policies In the clearest case, when Britain abandoned the gold standard in 1931 (the Bank of England no longer offered to buy or sell gold at a fixed price in pounds sterling), gold began to flow out of the United States. Foreigners who held dollars were afraid that the United States might abandon the gold standard or devalue the dollar, and they converted their dollars into gold, which was then exported from the United States. Although at this time the American gold reserves were at almost the highest level yet recorded, and the outflow of gold was obviously not based on changes in the international value of the dollar or the U.S. trade balance, the Federal Reserve authorities reacted to the gold outflow by raising rediscount rates within the United States—the traditional remedy for gold movements brought about by inflation relative to price levels in foreign countries. Further, Federal Reserve policy was evenhanded only in its potential for disaster: When gold later began to flow back into the United States, the Federal Reserve Banks "sterilized" it. They paid commercial banks for the gold with bonds, not checks on themselves, which did not allow an expansion of the money supply.[41] (By this time, however, commercial banks may well have preferred bonds to the opportunity to make loans.)

The "Banker's Bank" and Its Contribution to Collapse Throughout the period, the U.S. central bank failed to use all of its available resources for aiding the commercial banks. If it was restricted by its own regulations, it never asked Congress to relax or change them, particularly not to allow a vigorous program of open-market bond purchases. Not only did the Federal Reserve System treat its own member banks as bad credit risks (which, given its policies, many were), it allowed its officials to make repeated public statements about the shaky position of the banks, further reducing public confidence in them. Incredibly, even after it was apparent that unemployment was at catastrophic levels and commercial banks were faced with unprecedented demands for cash, there were officials of the Open Market Committee who not only opposed monetary expansion, but actually advocated measures to reduce the money supply.[42]

Whether the Federal Reserve System was responsible for the inception of the Depression (through its increasing restrictions on monetary growth in 1928 and 1929) or not, it seems indisputable that the central bank did little to reduce the slump's impact and that the sum of its actions had a strongly negative effect that extended well beyond 1933. Long after the banking crises ended, the surviving banks did not trust the Federal Reserve System: They maintained reserves far in excess of legal requirements through most of the 1930s. This policy by the commercial banks reduced the effects of expansionary monetary policies caused by the inflow of gold in the period following 1933.

---

[41] Temin, *Lessons,* 380–384.

[42] Temin, *Lessons,* 384–389.

The Monetarists' Scenario: A Summary The monetarists' scenario for the Great Depression, then, runs as follows. Slow monetary growth over the years 1928 to 1929 brought on a recession. In 1930, a wave of bank failures in the Midwest caused the public to try to convert bank deposits into cash. Because the Federal Reserve System refused to increase the money supply in compensation, it fell sharply. As the money supply declined, either prices or the level of economic activity had to fall, and this trend was intensified by an increase in the demand for money to hold (falling velocity). While prices did fall, the primary result of the decline in the money supply was the catastrophic slowdown in real economic activity that we know as the Great Depression. Under the existing circumstances, the Federal Reserve System was the only institution capable of really effective countercyclical action. Not only did the System fail to provide such action, except for the 1932 open-market purchases, it worsened the situation, particularly in the critical period late in 1931 during which a bad recession became a near-total economic collapse. Had the Federal Reserve taken vigorous action to expand the money supply in the early part of the slump, there would still have been a recession, but it would have been mild, probably no worse than those of the mid-1920s. Instead, the Federal Reserve even abandoned policies that would have produced some offsets to declines in member bank borrowing and the gold stock, and thus mitigated the aggregate monetary contraction.[43]

Behind the Fed's Policies The reasons for the inept policies of the Federal Reserve System seem to have been based partially on lack of recognition of both the severity of the Depression and the role of a central bank in internal (rather than international) economic affairs,

and the absence of clear-cut leadership within the system. Prior to 1929, the New York Federal Reserve Bank, under its governor, Benjamin Strong, had exercised a disproportionate influence on the system's monetary policies. Strong had a better understanding of the proper role of a central bank than did most of his contemporaries, both in regard to internal and international policy. He also possessed the force of character and persuasive powers to bring others to his point of view. But Strong died in October 1928, and his successor lacked the vision, ability, and personality required to turn the entire System toward monetary expansion.[44] The gold outflow in 1931 represented a situation that the existing authorities "understood," and their reaction was precisely that prescribed by orthodox central banking procedures under normal circumstances. But circumstances in 1931 were anything but normal.

It may be, as Professor Wicker has claimed, that the Federal Reserve authorities' only criteria were those for international monetary stability and that internal economic considerations had little or no influence on its decisions.[45] Another study claims that many small, locally oriented banks were already in shaky financial condition in 1929, often because their assets were heavily concentrated on agricultural loans. For such banks, almost any downturn, whether in agricultural prices, American farm exports, the weather, or general business conditions would impose severe difficulties. Most of these took place in the early years of the Depression, and tight

---

[43] P. Trescott, "Federal Reserve Policy in the Great Contraction: A Counterfactual Assessment," *Explorations in Economic History* (July 1982).

[44] Again, Temin disputes this view, citing correspondence in which Strong expressed the same views toward the gold standard as his successors. *Lessons*, 14, 34–35.

[45] E. Wicker, "Federal Reserve Policy, 1922–33: A Reinterpretation," *Journal of Political Economy* (August 1965). See also Wicker, "A Reconsideration of Federal Reserve Monetary Policy During the 1920–21 Depression," *Journal of Economic History* (June 1966).

monetary policy merely hastened the inevitable.[46] Had banks been allowed to have branches, their loans might have been more diversified and their overall position stronger, as was true in Canada, but only a few states allowed even limited branch banking in 1929. Falling bond prices, which reduced the value of another component of bank assets, also impaired bank solvency, but these were consequences, not causes, of the Depression.[47]

Federal Reserve policies may also have been based on incorrect evidence or interpretation thereof. What appeared to be low rates of interest (an indication that monetary policy was "easy") might actually indicate severe monetary stringency if prices were falling, as they were. For example, a 2 percent nominal interest charge, when combined with 8 percent deflation, becomes a real interest rate of 10 percent, at least if borrowers anticipate deflation correctly. In recent work, a leading monetarist claims Federal Reserve authorities believed monetary policy was easy over the years 1929 to 1931 because short-term rates were falling.[48]

About all that can be said in defense of Federal Reserve authorities' policies is that they had plenty of company. Fiscal policy at the time was equally misguided. Very few people recognized the Depression for what it was—a massive reduction in aggregate demand. There were even fewer people who realized that once unemployment had reached the levels that prevailed after 1931, recovery through the normal operation of the market system was unlikely to be rapid.

An Alternative Explanation

The monetarists' explanation of the Depression has been challenged by Peter Temin.[49] In the extended discussions that followed the appearance of Temin's book, a somewhat clearer picture of the relation between monetary and nonmonetary causes has begun to emerge. In Temin's view, the stock of money fell through 1930, just as the monetarists claim, but it declined because the demand for money fell, rather than the supply. The stock of money at any instant is the result of interactions between the supply of money and the demand for money. To Temin, the demand for money declined because of reductions in income—a scenario in which changes in the stock of money are a result of income changes rather than their cause. The fall in income in turn stemmed from a reduction in consumption spending, partially due to the decline in farm incomes and exports of American goods. Changes in wealth caused by the stock market crash and the general fall in securities values also contributed to the decline in consumption. However, the reduction in consumption was too large to be explained by these factors alone, and it was not concentrated on spending for durable consumer goods. This fall in consumption was unique to the 1929–1930 downturn. In similar periods (1920–1921 and 1937–1938), consumption either declined less than the other components of aggregate demand or even increased. The decline in consumption remains controversial: Subsequent research has both supported and refuted Temin's initial study.[50]

In contrast to the monetarists' explanations, Temin argues that bank failures did not

[46] E. White "A Reinterpretation of the Banking Crisis of 1930," *Journal of Economic History* (March 1984), and "The Stock Market Boom and Crash of 1929 Revisited," *Journal of Economic Perspectives* (Spring 1990).
[47] White, "Reinterpretation."
[48] A. Schwartz, "Understanding 1929–33," in Schwartz, *Money in Historical Perspective* (Chicago: University of Chicago Press, 1987).

[49] Temin, *Monetary Forces.*
[50] A. Schwartz, "Understanding 1929–33," cites work by Mayer and Gandolfi and Lothian indicating no unusual decline in consumption. Temin, *Lessons*, 43, notes confirmation of his findings by Hall.

have a significant effect on either the supply of money or on aggregate demand. Evidence from short-term interest rates, he concluded, fails to support the monetarists' contention that the supply of money fell while demand remained stable or increased. Investment spending and the business expectations that influenced it fell no more than they did in other, less serious downturns. However, the decline in investment spending over 1928–1930 was far more heavily concentrated in expenditures on construction and equipment than was the case in 1920–1921 or 1937–1938, during both of which the major reductions were in inventory spending. Since plant and equipment expenditures were likely to recover more slowly than other forms of investment, this fact had major implications for the duration of the Depression as well as its severity. Business expectations, according to Temin's findings, remained optimistic until late in 1930.

Moreover, Temin found that the real money stock (the nominal stock of money adjusted for changes in its purchasing power) grew until 1932, long after the Depression was firmly established. While the nominal money stock did fall, it did not do so rapidly enough to offset deflation. Temin further argues that it would have been a year or so after deflation began before price declines became "built into" people's expectations and hence into the expected real interest rate. Given this line of thought, anticipated real interest rates fell until late in 1930, then rose. Temin concluded that banking panics resulted from public reaction to declines in the value of securities held by the banks. The declines in bank asset values, however, in turn stemmed from the previous fall in incomes. Thus, the chain of causation, in Temin's view, runs from income to money, rather than in the opposite direction. Monetary forces in this explanation may have contributed to the severity of the Depression, but they did not cause it.

Temin's work remains the center of controversy.[51] Even if it is fully accepted, it does more to refute the monetarists' contentions than to present a complete alternative explanation. Temin does not explain much of the drop in consumption, which in his view was the ultimate cause of the Depression, and as noted, some other researchers' work does not support his findings. Still, his work, and that of later analysts, has made the monetarist model tenable only under much more restrictive assumptions than those initially employed and casts grave doubt on the importance of bank failures. It must also be noted, however, that even if Temin's views are fully accepted, the Federal Reserve is not absolved. Temin's analysis does not extend to the Federal Reserve reaction to the gold outflow of late 1931 or to its belated open-market purchases in 1932.

Recent work has not resolved the quandary. Professor Schwartz' recent work states that monetary changes were significant, but not the sole cause of macroeconomic changes over 1929–1933. Causality tests indicate at least some support for monetary changes' impact on the economy over 1929–1939, but they indicate at least some support for the role of income changes as well.[52] One passage in Professor Temin's latest book indicates that the Depression was caused by efforts to retain the gold standard at unrealistic exchange rates; so the proximate cause was central bank policy, especially in the United States, France, Great Britain, and Germany.[53]

[51] For a good summary of the early years of the debate, see P. Passell and S. Lee, *A New Economic View of American History* (New York: Norton, 1979), 372–383. See also White, "Reinterpretation," and Trescott, "Federal Reserve Policy." Current presentation of the monetarist position is Schwartz, "Understanding 1929–33." Temin's most recent study is *Lessons*.
[52] Schwartz, "Understanding 1929–33."
[53] Temin, *Lessons*, 12–23.

Other Factors Contributing to the Depression

Although the ultimate causes of the Depression remain unclear, some of the reasons why it persisted so long are easier to understand. A number of economists have developed theories of investment cycles that place much of the impetus for economic growth on construction and other highly capital-intensive industries. When the long-term trend in construction is up, recessions tend to be brief and mild, especially if there are other sectors that are large-scale users of investment funds. If the construction cycle is in a downswing, however, depressions tend to be severe and prolonged, and the construction cycle peaked in 1926. Public utilities and automobiles, two other major foci of investment during the 1920s, also had more capacity than could be profitably utilized by the end of the decade.

Whether the "long-swing" investment cycle contributed to the onset of the Depression or not, once income and investment had declined as they had by 1931, the incentives to invest were severely reduced. With only 20 percent of existing durable goods capacity in use, there was little incentive to build more factories or re-equip existing plants. Until existing capacity was fully utilized, new investment would depend on the appearance of technical advances or new products. Unfortunately, the 1930s were not a decade of great technical progress. Increases in income would have to originate in rising consumption or government spending rather than investment. International trade was not large enough in relation to the American economy even under normal circumstances to generate a major increase in aggregate demand, and during the Depression, foreign commerce had declined even more than internal economic activity. In the view of some supply-side economists, the increase in U.S. tariff rates negotiated in the 1930s Smoot-Hawley Tariff was an important causal factor in the decline.[54] However, neither the magnitude nor the timing of the trade restrictions support this contention. U.S. exports declined by only 2 percent of GNP over 1929–1931; clearly not all of the fall was due to increased trade barriers. Further, the bulk of the decline occurs after domestic economic activity had fallen sharply.[55] Others place considerable emphasis on international trade's collapse as a cause of the Depression.[56]

To the extent that growth had been centered on durable goods production in the 1920s, there was a further difficulty. The demand for durable consumer goods is in large part a function of how long the owners of such commodities want cars and major appliances to last; they can substitute maintenance and reduced use for new purchases. Spending on capital goods is largely dependent on the aggregate rate of economic growth and on the utilization of existing productive capacity. Thus, demand for the products of these sectors would decline, and under Depression conditions, it would not be easy to transfer productive resources to new sectors.

International Trade and Fiscal Policy

Government macroeconomic policies were no better than those of the Federal Reserve during the initial years of the Depression. The framework of international trade collapsed as nation after nation sought to export unemployment by raising barriers to the entrance of foreign goods. The idea behind these actions was either to protect existing domestic producers from overseas competition or to generate new import-replacing industries. But when all nations employed similar methods, the result was to reduce business and employment in each country's export industries.

---

[54] J. Wanniski, *The Way the World Works* (New York: Basic Books, 1978).
[55] *Historical Statistics*, 2:887, 888.
[56] C. Kindleberger, *The World in Depression*, revised. (Berkeley, Calif.: University of California Press, 1986).

Moreover, the jobs lost were in areas of greater relative productivity and hence higher incomes than those gained. The United States, through the Smoot-Hawley Tariff of 1930, raised its tariff rates and extended the range of dutiable imports to levels comparable to the high-tariff era before 1900. As nations left the gold standard, they tried to gain advantages for their exports through competitive devaluations of their currencies.

The Hoover Administration's Role After a brief flirtation with expansionary measures, American fiscal policy was also geared to making the Depression worse instead of better. President Hoover has been vilified as a man unmoved by the suffering of the unemployed, but this was unfair. Personally, Herbert Hoover was a humanitarian, with a distinguished record in famine relief activities in Europe during and immediately after World War I. But his efforts to end the crisis were severely handicapped, not least by his inability to grasp the dimensions of the problem. Government statistics on economic activity in general, and particularly on unemployment, were quite sketchy before the mid-1930s. Many contemporary economists viewed the possibility of prolonged unemployment on any significant scale as extremely unlikely.

President Hoover believed that the federal government was obligated to maintain a balanced budget and that to allow revenues to fall short of expenditures for any prolonged period was to invite national bankruptcy. He also believed, apparently quite sincerely, that relief payments to the unemployed without some form of quid pro quo would ruin the moral fiber of the recipients and bankrupt the country to boot. A few of his advisors, such as Treasury Secretary Mellon, wanted to allow the Depression to "liquidate" the economy, as a sort of traumatic process of competition, from which a sounder, more efficient national economy would emerge. There is no evidence,

however, that such draconian views ever formed the basis of any Hoover administration policies. In fact, much of what was done required a compromise of the president's publicly stated principles. No previous administration had ever pursued countercyclical policies as actively as did President Hoover.[57]

In 1929, the federal budget had been in surplus. Revenues exceeded current expenditures by over $700 million. The immediate reaction of the government to the Depression was a cut in taxes and an increase in spending, particularly on public works projects. This program would meet with the approval of most modern economists as an appropriate response to the downturn.[58] However, the federal budget was so small in relation to the aggregate economy, and the effects of the Depression so great, that these policies had no visible effect.

Government revenues declined. They were heavily dependent on progressive income taxes and thus fell even faster than income as the tax base declined. The budget surplus became a deficit, and the deficit grew. But a deficit large enough to reverse the decline in private economic activity was politically and possibly physically impossible. The Hoover administration's response to this situation was to reduce spending. The deficits continued, and in 1932 a large tax increase was enacted. Since higher taxes could only reduce an already inadequate volume of private spending (and in this case would not finance a compensating increase by the government), this was the wrong policy. Nevertheless, it was supported by both Houses of Congress. The Democratic Party's presidential candidate,

---

[57] R. Higgs, *Crisis and Leviathan: Critical Episodes in the Growth of American Government* (New York: Oxford University Press, 1987), 162–163.
[58] Temin finds that these measures were undertaken to balance the federal budget per se with no intention of expanding the economy. *Lessons*, 27.

Franklin D. Roosevelt, attacked it as inadequate rather than wrong.

Higher taxes on shrinking incomes did not balance the federal budget, but they further reduced aggregate demand. At the time, there were few politicians (or economists) who viewed the Depression as a massive shortfall in aggregate demand whose cure lay in additional spending, whether directly through the government, or through tax cuts or monetary expansion by the public. Since there was no recognition that these measures might raise the tax base, the tax increase appeared to offer the only means of achieving a balanced budget. The view that a balanced budget might not be the most appropriate measure under Depression conditions was never considered.

Positive Steps Some programs that were enacted had positive aspects. The Federal Farm Board's purchases of agricultural products in the attempt to maintain or increase farm incomes at least added to aggregate demand, although they also required that recipients remain in farming, where long-term prospects were not good. The Reconstruction Finance Corporation was established by the Hoover administration to extend loans to businesses, including the desperate commercial banks, that were unable to obtain financing from conventional lenders. While this program indicated that there was little recognition of the effects of Federal Reserve policies on money markets, it also shows that the Hoover administration was not a total prisoner of conservative ideology. Most RFC loans went to large firms. Once again, however, the effort was too small. Although President Hoover could not bring himself to support direct federal payments to the unemployed, federal loans to the states to support relief programs were authorized in the last months of his administration.

Herbert Hoover was a political victim of the Depression. He lacked the understanding of macroeconomics and monetary theory necessary for an effective response to the economic decline. But he was hardly alone in that. It may have been necessary that the nation experience a massive failure of the traditional remedies for depression before more imaginative measures became politically acceptable. (Some New Deal measures contained considerably more imagination than coherent reasoning.) The timid moves toward economic expansion made by the Hoover administration were hopelessly inadequate, but their failure probably made government measures on a more adequate scale even more difficult. By late 1932, it was becoming clear that even if the economy did contain forces that would automatically restore full employment, the widespread suffering produced by the Depression required that something be done to speed their operation.

SELECTED REFERENCES

Brunner, K., ed. *The Great Depression Revisited.* Boston: Martinus Nijhoff, 1981.

Chandler, L. *America's Greatest Depression, 1929–1941.* New York: Harper & Row, 1970.

Friedman, M., and A. Schwartz. *A Monetary History of the United States, 1867–1960.* Princeton, N.J.: Princeton University Press, 1963. (Chapter 7 of this work has been published separately as *The Great Contraction*, 1965.)

Galbraith, J. *The Great Crash, 1929.* Boston: Houghton Mifflin, 1954.

Goldin, C. *Understanding the Gender Gap: An Economic History of American Women.* New York: Oxford University Press, 1990.

Gordon, R. *Economic Instability and Growth: The American Record.* New York: Norton, 1974.

Kindleberger, C. *The World in Depression, 1929–39.* Revised ed. Berkeley, Calif.: University of California Press, 1986.

Schwartz, A., ed. *Money in Historical Perspective.* Chicago: University of Chicago Press, 1987.

Stein, H. *The Fiscal Revolution in America.* Chicago: University of Chicago Press, 1969.

Temin, P. *Did Monetary Forces Cause the Great Depression?* New York: Norton, 1976.

———. *Lessons from the Great Depression.* Cambridge, Mass.: MIT Press, 1989.

U.S. Department of Commerce, Bureau of the Census. *Historical Statistics of the United States: Colonial Times to 1970.* 2 vols. Washington, D.C.: Government Printing Office, 1975.

Wicker, E. *Federal Reserve Monetary Policy, 1917–33.* New York: Random House, 1966.

18

INCOMPLETE
RECOVERY AND
THE NEW DEAL

*I*n the spring of 1933, the U.S. economy was in desperate straits, with the unemployment rate at nearly 25 percent. Even that figure understated the severity of the Depression: Many of those who did have jobs were working either part time or at work that did not fully utilize their productive potential. It has been estimated that nearly half of all American workers had been unemployed at some time during the preceding year.

Real GNP was only 70 percent of the 1929 figure, approximately what it had been in 1922. The results of a decade of growth had been lost, as well as the potential growth that might have occurred after 1929. Wage and salary income was three-fifths of its 1929 levels, proprietors' income and rents had fallen by two-thirds, and corporate profits had become losses. Farm incomes had fallen more than those for other proprietors, and delinquencies on farm mortgages had become epidemic. Real wages of the fully employed had fallen

surprisingly little, only from $834 to $811 in 1914 dollars. The Depression's real impact on labor incomes, of course, was through unemployment. When adjusted for joblessness, real earnings of the average employee had declined by 30 percent.[1] Prices had fallen; by 1933, the consumer price index was at 75 percent of its 1929 level.

Nor was the worst necessarily over. The collapse of commercial banking threatened to become total. By March 1933, more than half the states had ordered all banks within their borders to close temporarily. This was a tacit admission that under existing circumstances banks were incapable of meeting depositors' demands for cash. Banks' efforts to convert assets into cash through the sale of their securities portfolios drove already depressed bond prices down still further, sometimes impairing the solvency of even those few institutions that had no initial need to sell. Mortgages were unsalable for more than a fraction of previous values, if at all, and prime commercial paper (high-quality, short-term business loans) did not exist. The Federal Reserve still provided no significant help. Discount rates were increased again in the spring of 1933, and no sizable open-market purchases were made after that of 1932.[2]

Population growth fell as marriages were deferred and couples put off having children. The birth rate fell far below that for the 1920s, which in itself had been well below nineteenth-century rates. Demographers predicted that the U.S. population would age and even decline absolutely if such trends continued. Declines in population growth and family formation affected the economy. Increases in the supply of labor were the primary source

■ Unemployment figures for the Great Depression do not include those driven to selling apples. These people were considered gainfully employed.
Source: AP/Wide World Photos, Inc.

[1] U. S. Department of Commerce, Bureau of the Census, *Historical Statistics of the United States: Colonial Times to 1970,* 2 vols. (Washington, D. C., Government Printing Office, 1975), 1:164.
[2] M. Friedman and A. Schwartz, *A Monetary History of the United States, 1867–1960* (Princeton, N. J., Princeton University Press, 1962), 324–328.

of economic growth (although under prevailing conditions the existing labor supply was only too obviously more than adequate), and the demand for housing was strongly linked to population growth. Social infrastructure (roads, schools, water, and sewer systems) were only slightly less directly connected. All of these had been important factors in the economic growth of the previous decade.[3]

Trends in wages and population growth gave little hope that consumption spending would soon increase. Even if individuals' incomes somehow rose, the prospects for future unemployment were so great that most of any increase would be set aside for a rainy day whose imminence was only too apparent. Prospects for increased investment spending were even worse. Investment had fallen from $40.4 billion in 1929 to only $5.3 billion in 1933 (figures in 1958 dollars).[4] At this level, capital was not being replaced as fast as it depreciated. Even so, inventories of goods were excessive and were being reduced through holding production at less than sales. There was a huge amount of unused capital that would inhibit new investment spending until back in use. That could occur only if aggregate demand somehow increased. New inventions were another source of additional investment spending, but this avenue offered little promise. In contrast to the leading sectors of the 1920s (autos, public utilities, appliances, chemicals, and construction), the 1930s developed few new, rapidly growing industries requiring heavy investment. Foreign trade had declined precipitously: Not only was the Depression worldwide, but many countries tried to restrict their imports. American imports and exports were now little more than one-third their 1929 levels.[5]

---

[3] A. Hansen, "Economic Progress and Declining Population Growth," *American Economic Review,* (March 1939).
[4] *Historical Statistics* 1:229.
[5] *Historical Statistics* 2:889.

The final component of aggregate demand was government spending. Increases here were far too small to compensate for the massive declines in other areas of expenditure. The federal government had reluctantly begun to provide loans to railroads, banks, and state governments through the Reconstruction Finance Corporation. A few public works projects, such as Hoover Dam on the Colorado River, had been started. A program to support the mortgage market had just commenced. But these efforts were very small in relation to the shortfall in aggregate demand, and the administration was at least as concerned with their impact on the federal deficit as it was with their potential for increasing employment. In any case, federal government spending was only 3 percent of GNP. State and local governments, lacking the federal government's ability to finance deficits, were grimly attempting to cut spending and to increase taxes to finance what could not be avoided.

The Response to Catastrophe

After President Hoover had been defeated for reelection in November 1932, there was virtually no cooperation between the outgoing and incoming administrations. The new president would not be inaugurated until March 1933. The policies of Franklin D. Roosevelt were anything but clear to the electorate, adding uncertainty to the general climate of fear.

An economy that could reach such disastrously low levels of activity was bad enough, but the lack of clear indications of recovery were even more discouraging. Some contemporary economists added to the gloom: According to their analyses, declining population growth and the end of the geographic frontier had curtailed two of the major traditional uses for investment funds. In an economy where people did not consume their entire incomes, new uses for these continually rising savings were required to avoid

■ The building of Boulder (now Hoover) Dam was one of the larger projects implemented by the government during the Depression.
Source: UPI/Bettmann Newsphotos.

cumulative decline. Some massive increase in investment spending (on new products or processes) or a large increase in government spending would be necessary to bridge the increasing gap between incomes and consumption expenditures. If a remedy was not developed, the outlook was for continued, even increasing, unemployment with only sporadic growth at best. The "stagnationists" believed that neither of the two potential off-

sets to this prospect was likely to occur.[6] Four years after the onset of the Depression, it was by no means clear that the economic climate would not continue to deteriorate.

In spite of the desperate circumstances and outlook of the early 1930s, the people who had already endured so much and been given

---

[6] Hansen, "Economic Progress."

so little reason to expect improvement made no move to rebel. Conservatives feared that the Depression would produce a left-wing revolution that would sweep away the basic institutions of capitalism or at least change the form of government, but no credible movement directed to such changes ever appeared. Farmers prevented a few foreclosure proceedings against their neighbors by force or threats; there were some urban protests against evictions and the meager levels of government assistance; and unemployed war veterans marched to Washington, D.C., in 1932. Under the desperate conditions, labor disputes may have had more than the usual quota of violence, and a few new developments, such as sitdown strikes, did occur. But there was nothing that could be termed a real challenge to established authority. The record supports the views of historians such as Crane Brinton, who concluded that revolutions occur when people become dissatisfied with the pace of progress, rather than in protest against deteriorating conditions.[7] Despite the rhetoric of right- and left-wing demagogues (Huey Long, Father Coughlin, and Francis Townshend, among others), some of them skilled in the use of a new communications medium (radio), the prevailing attitude was one of numbed resignation. The deficiencies of the traditional system spurred interest in alternatives ranging from Technocracy to Communism. But it is difficult to find the influence of any of these on subsequent events or institutions.

THE NEW DEAL

Franklin Delano Roosevelt assumed the duties of the presidency in March 1933. The new administration had an obvious mandate to take action against the Depression, but the

---

[7] C. Brinton, *The Anatomy of Revolution* (New York: Vintage Books, 1965).

■ President Franklin D. Roosevelt effectively used radio to generate support for his many reforms. *Source:* Brown Brothers.

form that action would take was by no means clear. During his campaign, Roosevelt had promised the voters a "new deal," but he had not been very specific about proposals designed to end the Depression.

There was no reason to believe that these proposals would include any fundamental changes in fiscal policy. Before his election, the new President had criticized the Hoover administration's budget deficits, and Roosevelt himself apparently believed strongly in a balanced federal budget. As governor of New York, Roosevelt had raised state taxes to balance the budget. Initially, the new administration reduced several types of federal spending, particularly salaries. The only tax changes ever proposed during the New Deal were increases in existing levies or new forms of taxation. Only after 1938 was there any explicit recognition that government might increase aggregate demand when private spending had fallen.

Roosevelt was far more pragmatic than Hoover had been, however, and when it became apparent that the goal of a balanced budget conflicted with other administration programs, he "temporarily" abandoned the balanced budget. Overall, particularly during the first term, the macroeconomic views and implementation policies instituted by the new administration were merely different from those held previously. By modern standards, the measures devised were certainly not more efficacious. The New Deal saw the causes of the Depression in a conjunction of problems within individual sectors (banking, finance, labor, agriculture, and others), rather than as a massive shortfall in aggregate demand.[8]

The "Hundred Days" Legislation

The new administration quickly proposed, and Congress enacted, a series of measures designed to end the Depression and prevent its recurrence. In the first hundred days after President Roosevelt's inauguration, a wide range of legislation was passed, often after only cursory examination and debate. The sense of urgency limited analysis, with Congress literally equating the situation to war.[9] Some of the new laws enacted relief programs that were intended to assist unemployed or particularly hard-hit sectors and institutions. Other programs were designed to produce economic recovery. A third set of policies was oriented toward reform. Expanded scope for government regulation of economic activity was one facet of the reform measures. Another, very sensibly, was the provision of agencies that generated far more information about the economy than had ever been available before.

Initial New Deal Remedies

New Deal policies were developed to deal with the perceived shortcomings of the economy on a case-by-case basis. As such, the programs were often uncoordinated; they frequently conflicted. If there was any unifying principle in the New Deal's view of the Depression, it was that prices of various items (labor, farm products, and industrial products) were too low. It was expected that conditions would improve if these prices could be raised, generally through policies unique to each sector concerned.[10] This view, however, suffered from two deficiencies. First, it confused symptoms with causes: Prices had fallen because there had been a massive decline in aggregate demand, rather than because of conditions in specific markets. Second, attempts to raise prices in the face of prevailing low consumer incomes ignored the fact that someone had to buy goods at the higher prices sought by New Deal policy. Unless they somehow increased aggregate demand before or at least simultaneously with prices, policies stemming from this line of thought could not produce the economic expansion desired.

At best, the piecemeal approach was an inefficient recovery policy. The lack of overall coordination increased duplication and waste; many New Deal programs were established in total independence of any others. Unless these programs were instituted on a broad front, they were unlikely to succeed, regardless of cost. If the prices of individual goods rose while most consumers' incomes remained depressed, the result would be a decline rather than an increase in the quantities demanded. As production of the now-more-expensive

[8] R. Gordon, *Economic Instability and Growth: The American Record* (New York: Harper & Row, 1974), 62–64.
[9] R. Higgs, *Crisis and Leviathan: Critical Episodes in the Growth of American Government* (New York: Oxford University Press, 1987), 172–173.

[10] Gordon, *Economic Instability,* 63. See also Chandler, *America's Greatest Depression,* Chap. 13.

items fell, so would employment in the sectors producing them. Programs based on this policy of "reflation," such as the National Recovery Act, to be treated in greater detail later, were counterproductive.

Some New Deal policies were experimental, and were either abruptly dropped, supplemented, or even reversed as alternative programs were developed. These methods had some unfortunate results. Some highly questionable programs, such as the National Recovery Administration, were introduced. In addition, there was no recognition that these programs were germane only under Depression conditions. Some were continued long after the only circumstances in which they might have had any justification had disappeared. As such, they became pure rent-seeking devices that reduced overall economic welfare. Government programs, once instituted, develop lives of their own. By 1939, in one view, the programs and court decisions regarding them had eroded property rights to the point where there remained no ultimate limits to government control of the economy.[11] These comments are not a criticism of the New Deal's goals. The Roosevelt Administration was sincerely committed to ending the suffering caused by the Depression and improving the lot of average- and particularly low-income Americans. But intentions should not excuse efforts from evaluations based on results, cost, and rationality.

Long-Term Consequences of the New Deal
Some programs had very high long-term costs, not least for the very people they had been established to help. Agricultural policy is a case in point: There was no question but that farmers suffered severe income reductions during the Depression, and that these occurred through declines in the prices of farm products. However, this did not mean that pro-

grams that raised the prices of farm products through imposing restrictions on the amounts produced were an efficient answer. These did little for farmers with the lowest incomes, whose need was greatest, and increases in food prices had adverse effects on hard-pressed consumers and taxpayers. Support for labor unions and higher wages may have benefited the majority of those working when such policies became effective. But they also made finding jobs more difficult for the unemployed.

In a few cases, what appeared at the time to be outright waste might have been the most effective policies available under the circumstances. If it was necessary to require "make-work" employment, such as leaf raking, of the unemployed as the political price of rendering them assistance, the compromise was well worth making. It might have been impossible to support the unemployed in any other manner, and such programs were only slightly less efficient than straightforward cash grants.

Banking and Monetary Policy

One of the first acts of the new president was to order the closing of all commercial banks in the United States. The governors of most states had already ordered banks within their jurisdictions to close by this time (March 1933). The "bank holiday" proclaimed on March 6, 1933, prohibited the usual business operations of commercial banks. In particular, they were forbidden to pay out cash.

To the banks themselves, the next few weeks were anything but a holiday. While they were legally closed, the banks sold securities for cash. The Federal Reserve Banks were ordered to ease the conditions under which they would loan to member banks, and to issue more Federal Reserve notes against government-bond collateral. The banks were audited by government inspectors instructed to take an optimistic view of the current values of bank assets. If the bonds (and even more, the

---

[11] Higgs, *Crisis and Leviathan*, 182–185.

loans and mortgages) in most bank portfolios had been assessed at their actual market value in 1933, nearly all American banks would have been at least technically insolvent.[12]

As banks were found to be in satisfactory condition, they were issued licenses by the Treasury and allowed to reopen. About a month after the bank holiday was proclaimed, Federal Reserve System member banks controlling about 90 percent of the assets of all system members had reopened, and state banking authorities had allowed about 71 percent of the institutions under their control to resume operations also.[13] Banks found to be in really serious difficulties were not allowed to reopen or had to operate under restrictions imposed by the authorities. About 2,000 banks remained permanently closed after the holiday, but this was the result of prior circumstances, not that occasion itself.[14] The bank holiday program was a success. Public confidence in the banks was restored, and the outflow of currency that had placed so many banks in jeopardy was not only halted, but reversed. Cash flowed into the banks, and the waves of bank failures were over.

Shortly afterward, the government began attempts to rehabilitate the debt structure. For those who could not repay their obligations on schedule, loan periods might be extended. In some cases, government guaranteed repayment. Large volumes of existing business, agricultural, and residential debts were sold by private financial institutions to government agencies such as the Reconstruction Finance Corporation, the Home Owners' Loan Corporation, and the Federal Farm Mortgage Corporation. These agencies also made loans to financial intermediaries and purchased some of their debt and equity issues. Perhaps the

most important single measure in the changes instituted in the financial sector during this period was the insurance of bank and savings and loan association deposits, which will be discussed under reform measures. Ironically, however, this does not appear to have been part of the New Deal program, although it is widely credited to that source.[15]

Devaluation of the Dollar

The president had been authorized to reduce the gold content of the dollar by raising the price the Treasury would pay for gold. In a series of steps, the price of gold was increased from $20.67 per ounce to $35 by February 1934. This measure reduced the value of the dollar in relation to that of foreign currencies whose gold content was unchanged, and thereby reduced the price of American exports and raised the domestic price of imports. The primary reason behind the increase in gold prices, however, appears to have been the view that this would somehow increase the general level of prices within the United States and thus stimulate the economy. It was an article of faith within the New Deal that at higher prices business firms would increase output, which would in turn increase employment.[16] To prevent windfall gains and losses, the increase in gold prices necessitated the surrender of all gold coin and bullion to the Treasury at its previous dollar value, and the abrogation of contract clauses requiring payment in gold dollars or their pre-1934 equivalents.

How the increase in gold prices would raise all other prices, or why inflation would increase the level of real economic activity and employment, was never explained. But the de-

---

[12] Chandler, *America's Greatest Depression,* 79–84, 128.
[13] Chandler, *America's Greatest Depression,* 146.
[14] Friedman and Schwartz are inclined to be less charitable. See *A Monetary History,* 420–428.

[15] C. Kindleberger, *The World in Depression, 1929–39,* Revised. (Berkeley, Calif.: University of California Press, 1986), 199. See also S. Lebergott, *The Americans: An Economic Record* (New York: Norton, 1984), 447–448, 481; and Chandler, *America's Greatest Depression,* 150.
[16] Friedman and Schwartz, *A Monetary History,* 465.

valuation of the dollar did have some expansionary effects. Since its price was now higher in this country, gold flowed into the United States from abroad. When, as the law now required, the gold was sold to the Treasury, that agency paid with checks drawn on its account with the Federal Reserve or in gold certificates. These, when deposited in commercial banks, increased the banks' reserves and thus their ability to expand the money supply. The stock of monetary gold rose by more than $14 billion between 1935 and 1941, and this increase in "high-powered money" was supplemented by a further $1.7 billion in silver purchases.[17] The latter was intended as a relief measure for western silver producers, as in earlier decades. In the later 1930s, gold also flowed to the United States because of the worsening political situation in Europe. World production of gold and silver increased during the 1930s: They were among the few commodities whose prices had increased.

The United States refused to cooperate with other countries in devaluation policies, and thus added to the barriers springing up against international trade all over the world. From this time on, the United States was on a gold-exchange standard. Although there was an official price of gold, the Treasury would only buy gold from American citizens, who were required to sell any gold they acquired through mining or foreign trade; it would sell to foreigners or for export only under special circumstances.

Monetary Policy and Reforms

The Federal Reserve began a modest program of monetary expansion in 1933, buying some $600 million in bonds and reducing the discount rate. For most of the decade, the impact of such expansionary measures was blunted by the commercial banks' tendency to hold much larger reserves than were required by

law. Banks also concentrated their investment policies on the purchase of government securities rather than loans to private borrowers. This did not make monetary policy totally ineffective; there were avenues by which the Federal Reserve could deal directly with the public and thus increase the money supply. But it did make monetary expansion less effective. The money supply rose by about 50 percent from 1933 to 1937. The total reserve base ("high-powered money") rose by $6.8 billion from 1933 to 1936. Of this sum, nearly $3 billion was held as excess reserves by Federal Reserve System member banks.[18] Real output grew rapidly from the 1933 trough, but was still far from full-employment levels when monetary expansion ceased in 1937.

The Federal Reserve was reorganized in 1935. Responsibility for monetary policy was centered in a new body, the Board of Governors, rather than in the Reserve Banks. The Board controlled the Open-Market Committee, had responsibilities for setting required reserve ratios for member banks (a new tool of monetary policy), and approved Reserve Bank discount policy. Finally, all the reins of monetary policy were in the same hands. The Board's membership was almost entirely new, with only two members from the previous controlling body.[19] Nevertheless, monetary policy was scarcely more inspired than that from 1929 to 1933.

Commercial banks had accumulated large excess reserves by 1936. Under existing regulations, they were free to make more loans and thus expand the money supply. The Federal Reserve Board became convinced that if the banks did so, the volume of spending would increase faster than the supply of goods, and thus inflation would occur. The Board ignored two points. First, the unemployment

---

[17] Friedman and Schwartz, *A Monetary History,* 483–489.

[18] Chandler, *America's Greatest Depression,* 174–175.
[19] Friedman and Schwartz, *A Monetary History,* 445–449.

rate in 1936 was almost 17 percent; with large numbers of unemployed workers there are also many idle machines. There was much unused capacity in the economy, and supply would be highly elastic. Second, to the commercial banks those excess reserves spelled safety, not opportunity to expand loans. Bankers viewed those reserves as a first line of defense against a recurrence of depositors' mass demands for cash that many of them had narrowly survived.

The commercial banks' distrust of the Federal Reserve proved only too well-founded. In three steps over late 1936 and early 1937, the Federal Reserve effectively doubled the required reserves of member banks. The change wiped out about two-thirds of the banks' "insurance policy." Gold inflows were purchased with bonds, not Federal Reserve deposits, so they did not add to the supply of money. The money supply declined only a bit more than 1 percent, but the consequences were much greater.[20] The Federal Reserve's policy was implemented while an equally ill-advised fiscal program was instituted by the Treasury.

The "anti-inflation" policy was quite effective, even though it had been totally unnecessary. It caused a rapid decrease in economic activity. By 1938, the unemployment rate was 19 percent, as high as it had been in 1935. This was especially disheartening because in 1937 there had been signs that the economy might finally be on the road to complete recovery. Unemployment had been dropping, and investment spending had begun to spread into inventory accumulation. Once again the Federal Reserve System had acted as though economic conditions were completely normal, despite overwhelming evidence that they were not.

At least this time the contractionary policy was short-lived. Part of the gold-sterilization

and reserve-requirement changes that had caused the downturn were rescinded in 1938, and federal government spending was increased as well. Banks again began to accumulate excess reserves.

Expansionary monetary policy might have been effective in stemming the slide that began in 1929 if promptly instituted, but now it was much less so. With a strong assist from the Federal Reserve, the surviving banks' preferences had been altered in favor of excess reserves and government bonds rather than loans to private borrowers whose potential returns no longer outweighed risks.

From 1933 to 1937, the Federal Reserve authorities did little to promote recovery from the slump they had helped to cause. The increase in the money supply was due more to Treasury policy toward gold than to conscious actions taken by the Federal Reserve. The ineptitude of the Fed and the fiscal authorities in 1937 may have stemmed from the view that the mission of public agencies in countercyclical policy was limited to starting a recovery which, once initiated, would be self-sustaining. How the Fed's leaders could have reached this conclusion in 1937, when recovery still had so very far to go, remains unanswered. Even if it was thought that any recovery inevitably proceeded to full employment, that view hardly sanctioned contractionary policies rather than a mere cessation of stimuli.

Fiscal Policy

In its last two years, the Hoover administration had run budgetary deficits. The Roosevelt administration did the same in every year before 1941, after which the demands of war finance changed the situation out of all recognition. The deficit in 1937, however, was very small. Most modern economists agree that if fiscal policy is to be used to counteract the business cycle, the government should attempt to counter the source of the problem. If

---

[20] Friedman and Schwartz, *A Monetary History,* 516–534.

the economy is suffering from inflation, which is normally caused by too much purchasing power chasing too few goods, the government should reduce the amount of purchasing power available. It does this by running a surplus, withdrawing more money through taxes than it injects through its expenditures. The result will be a reduction in excess purchasing power and lower inflation. In a depression, the situation is the opposite; the problem is too little spending. In such circumstances, the proper fiscal policy is to increase net injections of purchasing power into the economy through deficits; government's expenditures should exceed its tax revenues. The shortfall is financed either through the creation of new money by the central bank or by borrowing funds that would otherwise have remained idle; it should not employ funds that would have been spent in some other way.

Given these criteria, the actions of the federal government throughout the Depression appear appropriate, yet recovery was incomplete. Professor E. Cary Brown investigated this seeming paradox and came to the conclusion that countercyclical fiscal policy had not worked because it had not been tried. After an examination of the fiscal record of the 1933–1940 period, Brown found that in only two years (1931 and 1936) were aggregate government budgets (federal, state, and local government combined) significantly expansive.[21] In addition, even with a generous allowance for multiplier effects, federal government deficits that never exceeded $5 billion were insufficient to offset declines in GNP that exceeded $40 billion.

Government's Aggregate Fiscal Impact

The federal deficits alone give a misleading picture of government's fiscal impact. State and local governments, which in aggregate had been running deficits when the Depression began, generally had balanced their budgets or even achieved surpluses by 1933, and continued this policy through 1940. They did so largely through increased taxation. Subsidiary governmental units were facing heavy welfare and relief demands, but given the minimal government of the time, there were few areas in which spending could be reduced in order to channel more funds to anti-Depression policies.

State sales taxes became common during the 1930s, and these have a restraining effect on consumer spending.[22] State, and even more, local governments cannot be expected to attempt countercyclical fiscal policy; most of whatever benefits might result from their actions would occur outside their borders. State and local government surpluses offset a considerable portion of the federal government's deficits. The expansionary effects of fiscal policy in 1931 and 1936 were the result of large veterans' bonuses. Both bonus bills were passed by Congress over presidential vetoes; President Roosevelt was almost as vehement in his opposition to the 1936 measure as President Hoover had been to that of 1931.[23]

Federal tax structure imposed barriers to the achievement of full employment that became considerably greater as incomes began to rise and New Deal policies developed. The 1932 tax increase much more than wiped out the temporary tax reduction of 1929. It raised income tax rates at all levels and extended the tax's incidence further into the middle class, which had previously been exempt. The poor were almost entirely below the income tax threshold, but they did not escape. Both state sales taxes and federal social security taxes bore disproportionately on low incomes. The social security tax, in particular, was strongly regressive at this time. Modifications in 1934

[21] E. C. Brown, "Fiscal Policy in the Thirties: A Reappraisal," *American Economic Review* (December 1966).

[22] Brown, "Fiscal Policy."
[23] Gordon, *Economic Instability,* 63.

and 1935 did not change the federal tax schedules significantly.

The result of the various tax changes was that for the first years of the New Deal, the federal tax structure imposed a great deal of "fiscal drag." As recovery proceeded and incomes grew, tax revenues would grow much faster. Given constant levels of federal spending, the budget would be in balance long before full employment was achieved. As incomes rose beyond the level at which the budget was balanced, further growth would be restricted by a growing federal surplus: Taxes would remove more income than federal spending plowed back into the economy (even in the unlikely event that welfare expenditures were not decreased). This was the fiscal program of the first four years of the New Deal; recovery never proceeded far enough to show its full effects.

Subsequent changes in fiscal policy only gradually became more beneficial. In 1937, the unemployment rate was declining, although it was still over 14 percent. In nominal terms, GNP was 88 percent of 1929, although since prices were now much lower, the two figures were about equal in real terms. Investment spending was increasing, and businesses had just commenced adding to their inventories—a most hopeful sign. In view of this evidence of "recovery," the federal deficit was reduced to only $400 million through cuts in relief programs, the end of the "one shot" veterans' bonus of 1936, and tax increases, in particular the new social security payroll tax.[24] During late 1937, the federal budget was, for practical purposes, in balance, even though the economy remained far below full-employment production levels. The monetary contraction engineered by the Federal Reserve must share the blame for the ensuing recession-within-a-depression of 1937–1938; but it is obvious that

there was little or no thought of the federal budget as a tool that in itself could have been used to expand the economy during the crucial years before 1938.

Throughout this period, the New Deal continued to regard deficits as unfortunate side effects of the costs of specific programs; general economic expansion was not a specific policy goal. New Deal expenditures programs were to promote recovery by direct effects on specified sectors of the economy, rather than through increasing aggregate demand. Deficits were to be eliminated as soon as falling unemployment allowed spending reductions. There was no consideration whatever of tax reduction as a device for economic expansion.[25] Recent revisions of Brown's work employing more modern theory have reached even stronger conclusions. Even the federal budget had a net expansionary effect only in 1931 (under the much-maligned Hoover administration), and then by less than 1 percent of GNP.[26]

After the 1937 debacle, there was more New Deal interest in the use of budgetary deficits to fill the gap between current and full-employment levels of spending. Marriner Eccles, the new chairman of the Federal Reserve Board, was an advocate of this policy.[27] Even so, the concept was never seriously pursued. The largest federal deficit before World War II was $4.5 billion—far too little, even when its multiplier effects were considered, to offset the shortfall in private demand. For the entire Depression, federal deficits totalled about $30 billion. This sum was barely enough to offset two or three years' income decline under the

---

[24] Chandler, *America's Greatest Depression*, 140.

[25] Gordon, *Economic Instability*, 62–64.
[26] L. Peppers, "Full Employment Surplus Analysis and Structural Change: The 1930s," *Explorations in Economic History* (Winter 1973).
[27] Eccles' ideas have recently been outlined by Professor Jonathan Hughes. See *The Vital Few: American Economic Progress and its Protagonists*, 2d ed. (Cambridge, U.K.: Cambridge University Press, 1986), 504–558.

most favorable assumptions. From 1934 to 1940, federal spending rose from $6.6 billion to $10.6 billion (the latter figure includes a half-billion dollars for additional defense spending). Total tax revenues over the same period rose faster, from $3 billion to $6.8 billion.[28]

The policies and record of the New Deal have been termed Keynesian. Supposedly they were derived from the theories of the British economist John Maynard Keynes, who believed that under certain conditions a market economy might produce substantial unemployment and at best only slowly regain full employment. Should such circumstances occur, Keynes advocated increased government spending and tax cuts to spur the growth of income. Keynes met President Roosevelt, but neither party appeared sufficiently appreciative of the other's genius, and nothing came of the meeting. Keynes' ideas, at least as they originated with him, had little or no effect on American fiscal policy before World War II.

The Failure of Countercyclical Policy

Aggregate monetary and fiscal policies did not end the Depression. They were seldom used as such, and were as often perversely employed as properly directed. In fiscal policy, some excuses can be made. Macroeconomics was still in its infancy. Even had American politicians gained a proper understanding of appropriate macroeconomic programs, they would have had great difficulty in persuading the electorate to accept them. The relatively modest deficits of the New Deal were widely attacked as "bankrupting the country" and "destroying the credit of the federal government." The balanced peacetime budget had been a cornerstone of American fiscal policy for so long that it might well have been impossible to gain political acceptance of expansionary policies of sufficient scope to deal with the Depression. It might not even have been physically possible after 1932, given the magnitude of the Depression and the modest size of the budget. American and British academic economists might conclude that serious depressions required unbalanced budgets, but they had little influence.

In the case of monetary policy, no adequate defenses appear possible. Some monetary authorities, at least, were aware of methods by which the money supply could be expanded, and the idea that monetary expansion was an appropriate device for economic stimulus was well established. It was impossible to conclude that empirical conditions did not warrant expansion if real-world evidence was taken into account. Monetary policy for most of this period lacks even the figleaf of ignorance to hide its errors of omission and commission.

Relief for the Unemployed

The Roosevelt administration, unlike its predecessor, accepted responsibility for easing the plight of the unemployed. It quickly launched programs to provide government-funded jobs and relief payments. However, there was still great opposition to direct money payments to the jobless without some sort of quid pro quo. President Roosevelt and Harry Hopkins, the director of the Federal Emergency Relief Administration (FERA), both desired measures that would preserve the self-respect and utilize the talents of the unemployed. It was decided that federal efforts to aid the unemployed would be concentrated on the direct provision of jobs.[29] Hopkins' agency began operations in May 1933. It was empowered to make grants to the states to supplement their efforts to provide money and work relief.

---

[28] *Historical Statistics*, 2:1105–1106, 1114.

[29] Chandler, *America's Greatest Depression*, 191–192.

If necessary, it could make additional grants without state partnership. Such FERA programs as the Civil Works Administration, Works Progress Administration, and Civilian Conservation Corps—all soon known by their initials—provided several million people with jobs each year.

The Conflicting Goals of Federal Employment Programs

Projects undertaken by these agencies included the construction of social overhead capital (parks, airports, roads, public buildings, water and sewer projects, erosion control, the reforestation and other environmental work of the Civilian Conservation Corps, and a wide variety of similar undertakings). Special programs sought to use the skills of unemployed artists, writers, teachers, dramatists, and other professionals. These programs constructed both physical and intellectual capital; some generated a good deal of useful information, both from direct investigation and from on-the-job experience, that aided later governmental decisions. While some of these programs were derided as "make-work," mere excuses to pay the unemployed (sometimes a valid charge), the basic idea was a humane response to the psychic effects of the Depression. The measures were frankly designed pri-

■ President Franklin Roosevelt visits a Civilian Conservation Corps (CCC) camp in the 1930s in this photo. The CCC helped ease the burdens of the Depression by putting men and boys to work on conservation projects.
Source: The Bettmann Archive.

marily to provide employment and income; the resulting products were a secondary consideration.

Harold Ickes, the Secretary of the Interior, led a different approach. Under Ickes' direction, the Public Works Administration also constructed social overhead capital, generally large-scale projects such as roads and dams. But the primary emphasis of the PWA was on the projects themselves. Every effort was made to complete them as efficiently as possible, using least-cost methods, regardless of the employment effects. Many PWA projects were highly capital- and material-intensive. They increased employment far less per dollar spent than did programs of the FERA. Nor were the jobs provided or their locations particularly well suited to the capabilities of the unemployed. PWA projects often required a good deal of time to plan before actual construction began. Although the PWA provided a peak of 714,000 jobs in 1936, this was far below the nearly 5 million employed under FERA programs at their maximum in 1934.[30] Table 18.1 indicates the aggregate impact of these programs.

Federally funded employment programs provided a cumulative total of more than 8 million jobs. Most of the projects were designed to minimize competition for labor with private employers. In view of the prevailing unemployment rates, such a precaution was unnecessary. Although the programs were a step in the right direction (at least given the ineptitude of efforts to increase private employment), they were too small, and at best provided more or less thinly veiled charity. There was no question that they were a "second-best" response to unemployment, necessitated largely by the New Deal's failure to end the Depression. A recent study has tentatively concluded that New Deal employment projects reduced job search by those working in

them because their long-term effects hindered labor mobility.[31]

However, if New Dealers insisted on treating the symptoms of the Depression rather than its causes, the programs were a response to the economic and human costs it imposed. While these programs did have a significant effect on the numbers of people totally without work after 1932, it must be remembered that those working under them were nevertheless not doing the type of work they would have chosen under normal conditions. In many ways, their situation was similar to a present-day individual collecting unemployment compensation—not without income, but clearly not working at a job of his or her choice either, and presumably willing to do so.[32]

Farm Relief

Farming was affected as adversely as any occupation by the Depression. The prices of most agricultural products fell below the none-too-remunerative levels of the 1920s, but farm production costs did not decline proportionately, and fixed costs, such as debt service and property taxes, scarcely fell at all. In 1929, wheat had sold for $1.04 per bushel and corn for 88 cents. Cotton brought farmers 17 cents per pound. By 1932, these prices had declined to 39, 32, and 5 cents, respectively.[33] Price declines for other crops and animal products had been equally large. Even at these prices, unsold stocks of all farm commodities were rising in the face of widespread hunger. The net income that American farm operators derived from

---

[30] Chandler, *America's Greatest Depression,* 196.

[31] R. Margo, "The Microeconomics of Depression Unemployment," *Journal of Economic History* (June 1991).
[32] M. Darby, "Three and a Half Million U.S. Employees Have Been Mislaid: Or, an Explanation of Unemployment, 1934–1941," *Journal of Political Economy* (February 1976). See also J. Kesselman and N. Savin, "Three and a Half Million Workers Were Never Lost," *Economic Inquiry* (April 1978), and S. Lebergott, *The Americans,* 464–465.
[33] *Historical Statistics,* 1:511.

Table 18.1   The Economy During the New Deal

Year	Nominal GNP*	Real GNP**	Unemployment (in Millions)	Rate of Unemployment	Rate of Growth
1929	$103.1	$203.6	1.55	3.2%	6.7%
1930	90.4	183.5	4.34	8.7	−9.8
1931	75.8	169.3	8.02	15.9	−7.6
1932	58.0	144.2	12.06	23.6	−14.7
1933	55.6	141.5	12.83	24.9	−1.8
1934	65.1	154.3	11.34	21.7	9.1
1935	72.2	169.5	10.61	20.1	9.9
1936	82.5	193.0	9.03	16.9	13.9
1937	90.4	203.2	7.70	14.3	5.3
1938	84.7	192.9	10.39	19.0	−5.0
1939	90.5	209.4	9.48	17.2	8.6
1940	99.7	227.2	8.12	14.6	8.5
1941	124.5	263.7	5.56	9.9	16.1

*Current dollars.
**1958 dollars.
†For unemployment.
‡1967 = 100.
Source: U.S. Department of Commerce, Bureau of the Census, *Historical Statistics of the United Sates: Colonial Times to 1970,* 2 vols. (Washington, D.C.: Government Printing Office, 1975), 1:135, 164, 210, 224, 266–267; 2:667.

---

farming fell to only one-third its 1929 level. Debt and other fixed-cost burdens were becoming unbearable. Slightly less than half of all farm mortgages and over half the total value of all farm mortgage debt were delinquent as 1933 began.[34] Nor were farmers spared the economic problems of the cities. Bank failures were even more frequent among small-town and rural institutions than they were in urban areas. When the local bank failed, farmers seldom had easy access to alternative sources of credit. Even agricultural unemployment was not unknown. Mortgage foreclosures, crop failures, and simple eco-

nomic defeat drove some farmers off the land. Increasing farm mechanization cost some agricultural laborers their jobs, particularly in the South. The government would not make direct loans to farmers, and there were no better jobs to which they could migrate in the early 1930s.

As in so many other cases, the New Deal response to farmers' plight was unique to that sector. The primary goal of government agricultural-assistance programs was an increase in the prices of agricultural commodities. While this, if achieved, would increase farmers' incomes, price-support programs had both short- and long-term drawbacks. Although the Depression had greatly intensified farmers' problems, the primary cause of low agricultural incomes had not changed in decades:

---

[34] Chandler, *America's Greatest Depression,* 64.

Real Annual Wages (1958 Dollars)		Consumer Price Index (1967 = 100)	Index of Manufacturing Production‡
Nominal	Adjusted†		
$2,911	$2,768	51.3	23
2,911	2,531	50.0	19
2,992	2,294	45.6	15
2,925	1,934	40.9	12
2,831	1,836	38.8	14
2,793	1,986	40.1	15
2,898	2,039	41.1	18
2,898	2,210	41.5	22
3,072	2,458	43.0	23
3,030	2,238	42.2	18
3,194	2,440	41.6	22
3,292	2,632	42.0	25
3,554	3,006	44.1	32

There were too many farmers, even in normal times. Their combined output was too large to be absorbed by markets at prices that allowed farmers to earn incomes comparable to other occupations. This was only relatively less valid for the 1910–1915 period than for the 1920s. The basic analysis is presented in Chapter 17.

The individual farmer had little choice but to produce as much as he could, regardless of the expected price. Most farmers had substantial fixed costs, which had to be met regardless of the volume of production. There were many farms that were too small or badly located, infertile, unsuited to large-scale, cost-reducing methods, or otherwise physically incapable of producing an amount of output that would yield a decent living at any realistically pos-sible price. In such cases, higher farm-product prices might reduce the poverty of those trying to wrest a living from agriculture, but they could not cure it.

The Parity Concept

If farm prices were to rise, some combination of increased demand, reduced output, or both was necessary. In addition, the problem of current farm debts and future agricultural credit supplies required attention. The New Deal's first response was the Agricultural Adjustment Act, a product of the hundred days in which the New Deal's basic legislation was enacted. In this law, the federal government accepted the principle of parity as a goal for agricultural prices. Parity meant that farm commodities' prices were to be increased relative to nonfarm

■ Farm auctions were common as farmers became the targets of foreclosures.
Source: The Depression Years as photographed by Arthur Rothstein (New York: Dover Publications, Inc., 1978), 22.

goods' until they bore the same relationship they had in some base period, usually 1910–1914, when farm goods' prices were exceptionally high. The parity concept ignored relative trends in demand and supply for farm and nonfarm goods. But it allowed farmers to mask rent-seeking as an appeal for "fair" treatment rather than a handout. A parity ratio of 100 would indicate that farm and nonfarm prices had the same relationship as had been the case in the 1910–1914 base period. A unit of farm goods, say, a bushel of wheat, would exchange for the same number of nonfarm goods, for example, sixpenny nails, as in the earlier period. In 1933, the actual parity ratio was 64.[35]

---

[35] *Historical Statistics,* 1:489.

Farm Production Quotas

To increase farm goods' prices to or nearer the parity ratio, supply would have to be reduced sufficiently to cause prices to rise to desired levels, or government could fix a minimum price and buy any quantity that remained unsold at that price. Because surpluses already existed for many farm products in 1933, some method had to be found to reduce both existing and future supplies, or the government would be forced to buy ever-increasing quantities of agricultural products that could not be sold in U.S. markets. The Agricultural Adjustment Act therefore provided a mixture of production controls, benefit payments, and government purchases of surplus agricultural products. Under the act, the government fixed national quotas for the production of virtually all major crops, beef, pork, and dairy products. The list of crops included in the program was extremely liberal, extending to sugar cane, flax, and grain sorghums.

The Department of Agriculture was empowered to establish quotas in an attempt to reduce quantities produced and thus push prices toward the parity targets. National quotas were then divided among regions on the basis of past production (another example of New Deal attempts to freeze the status quo ante), and within regions by the vote of the farmers themselves. The process favored the large producers, who had the most at stake. Those participating in the scheme received benefit payments from the government: All farmers gained to the extent that the agreements raised prices. To finance the program, a tax was levied on the processors of all agricultural products within the United States.

The whole program was price-fixing on a grand scale, and the act included a provision exempting participants from the antitrust laws. When it went into effect in 1933, some farm production was already in progress. Meeting the production quotas for that year required the destruction of several million young pigs and plowing under a large portion of that year's cotton crop. With an assist from nature in the form of a severe drought in the Great Plains (the beginning of the "Dust Bowl"), and other crop failures, the program was successful in raising the prices of most farm products.

Net agricultural incomes doubled by 1934 and continued to rise until 1939. Even so, farm incomes never regained 1929 levels in nominal terms until 1941. Because both price levels and the number of farms (though not the farm population) were substantially lower at the later date, this indicates that real income per farm was considerably higher in 1941 than in 1929. Real agricultural income per member of the farm population increased about 15 percent. By that time the demands of World War II were a greater influence on prices than were

crop-limitation schemes. At no time, however, was the goal of 100 percent parity ever achieved.[36] Output restriction became more difficult as farmers adjusted to the new regulations. The production quotas were imposed through acreage limitations, and farmers withdrew their least fertile land from production while cultivating their most productive acres more intensively. Yields per acre rose for all major crops during this period.[37]

The Agricultural Adjustment Act was declared unconstitutional by the Supreme Court in 1936, but similar programs were continued in a new guise under the Soil Conservation and Domestic Allotment Act. This legislation's ostensible purpose was the withdrawal of land particularly subject to erosion or depletion from cultivation or its conversion to crops less destructive of soil productivity. Farmers received government payments for withholding such land from the production of basic crops. A new provision was added: Under this law, farmers could borrow against the value of crops they had stored with the government's Commodity Credit Corporation. If the crops' market value rose to more than the value of the loan, farmers could sell their produce, repay the loan and interest, and pocket the difference. If crop values remained below the loan extended on them, the loan obligation could be discharged by allowing the Corporation to assume full title to the crops.

Help for Farm Debt

Farm finances were improved by several programs aimed at reducing debt burdens and improving farmers' access to credit. Since farms were virtually unsalable, even at a fraction of their pre-Depression values, many private mortgage holders, such as the life insurance companies, refrained from foreclosing on delinquent loans, asking merely that the farmers

---

[36] *Historical Statistics,* 1:484, 489.
[37] *Historical Statistics,* 1:500–501.

■ Tough economic conditions forced farmers to abandon marginal agricultural areas during the 1930s.
Source: The Depression Years as photographed by Arthur Rothstein (New York: Dover Publications, Inc., 1978), 24.

maintain the property and make whatever payments they could until better times. Alternatively, they might allow mortgagees to remain as tenants. Such decisions were not entirely motivated by concern for the farmers' plight, as indicated in Chapter 17. Financial institutions holding mortgages as assets against their liabilities to others were not willing to risk their own solvency by procedures that revealed the extent of the fall in asset values. Nevertheless, a combination of unpayable debts, low commodity prices, and unfavorable weather drove many small-scale or marginal-area farmers from the land, a process portrayed in such books as John Steinbeck's *The Grapes of Wrath.* The western Great Plains, the upper Midwest, and Appalachia were particularly affected by this process.

The Farm Credit Corporation was organized in 1933 to restructure existing farm debts and channel federal credit to agriculture. The Federal Land Banks, which had been established during the Wilson administration, refinanced farm mortgages or purchased them from private creditors. Funds were advanced for taxes or other pressing obligations, and, in some cases, for the purchase of additional land. By 1940, nearly 40 percent of all farm mortgages were held by the Farm Credit Administration or its subsidiaries, reflecting both the extent of federal aid to agriculture and the market's evaluation of farming's prospects.

New Deal Agricultural Policies: An Assessment

The agricultural programs of the New Deal were flawed. Above all, they were palliatives rather than solutions, attempts to raise the incomes of farmers by increasing the price of agricultural products. Unfortunately, most cases of real poverty among farmers—and they were numerous—stemmed from inability to respond to production incentives. Increasing the prices of commodities that wornout hill or jackpine farms could never produce in large amounts merely encouraged farmers to continue a struggle that in the long run was hopeless. As long as there were no alternative jobs available for the surplus agricultural population, such measures served as an inefficient form of welfare. After full employment was regained, they tempted people to remain in occupations offering little or no chance of income parity with other jobs. Most of the aid

went to the most efficient farmers who had least need of help; the really poor got little under such programs. In the case of cotton production, the new measures encouraged mechanization, and actually reduced the labor force required to harvest it.[38]

Another drawback to the agricultural assistance programs was that they offered aid only to those who agreed to remain in farming. While there were few, if any, alternative jobs open to those leaving agriculture in the 1930s, the basic provisions of these programs have remained essentially unchanged to this day. As farm productivity grew, the position of the small-scale farmers became worse, since they were, in most cases, unable to reduce their production costs to the extent that large-scale farms could. The programs imposed unnecessarily high costs per dollar of aid actually received by farmers, because of the expenses involved in holding surpluses and administrating production quotas. At the same time they gave farmers incentives to increase production, the programs pushed up the price of food and other farm products. Since the New Deal's farm programs clearly involved higher costs to the economy (food price increases, taxes, foregone alternatives) than the aid received by farmers, and thereby reduced overall economic welfare, they are a clear example of rent-seeking.

Other Relief Programs

Home mortgages prior to the Depression were typically "balloon mortgages," in which only interest charges were payable until the last few years of the mortgage. Then the entire principal of the mortgage fell due in a few large payments, or even only one. No wonder so

---

[38] W. Whatley, "Labor for the Picking: The New Deal in the South," *Journal of Economic History* (December 1983). See also G. Wright, *Old South, New South: Revolutions in the Southern Economy Since the Civil War* (New York: Basic Books, 1986), Chap. 7.

many melodramas were built around a single all-or-nothing mortgage payment! Such arrangements were extremely vulnerable to depression conditions.

Relief was complicated. Often housing values had fallen so low that foreclosed property could not be resold for even half its value when the mortgage was taken out. Either reducing the loan principal or foreclosing for resale inflicted a capital loss on the mortgageholder, sometimes threatening the survival of lending institutions. Even extending the repayment period for delinquent mortgages might produce severe cash-flow problems for creditors.

Government programs in this area were similar to those set up in agriculture. The Home Owners' Loan Corporation extended its own credit, purchased mortgages, and refinanced existing debts. Loans were guaranteed by the Federal Housing Administration established in 1934. The government began making loans to finance municipally owned public housing in 1937. Finally, institutions also changed: Most mortgages issued after this time provided for the now-familiar monthly payments amortizing both principal and interest, reducing risks to buyer and seller alike.

RECOVERY POLICIES

In its efforts to end the Depression, the New Deal achieved less than it did in either relief or reform efforts. Even the successes that were recorded were likely to be fortuitous.

The National Industrial Recovery Act

No program more clearly reveals the deficiencies of New Deal recovery policies than the National Industrial Recovery Act (NIRA), yet another product of the hundred days period in 1933.[39] No other New Deal legislation was more firmly rooted in the belief that business firms required the incentives of higher prices and protection from price competition to induce greater production. Higher production, ran the rationale for the NIRA, would require more workers, and thus reduce unemployment.

To achieve these goals, the act authorized the formulation of "codes of fair competition." So-called blanket codes were established as models, but each industry was urged to produce its own. The codes pledged each firm to "fair" methods of competition and employment, covering such matters as prices, wages, hours, output, trade practices, working conditions, and collective bargaining. They were to be formulated by representatives of business, labor, and consumers. Once a code was accepted by the National Recovery Administration, its provisions became binding on all firms in the industry, whether they had cooperated in shaping it or not.

In practice, the codes were largely designed by business. Labor generally had only a minor role in setting up the codes, and consumers none at all. Not surprisingly, the codes became price-fixing arrangements that the basic NIRA legislation exempted from the antitrust laws. A provision that was to have profound long-term consequences guaranteed employees the right to form their own organizations, choose their own representatives, and bargain collectively with employers. The blanket codes and most industry codes established minimum wages and maximum hours of work; the latter provision was designed primarily to increase the number of workers hired rather than improve their working conditions. By 1935, more than 500 codes had been drawn up, covering the vast majority of all industry.

---

[39] Chandler, *America's Greatest Depression,* Chap. 13.

Under the codes, the basic structure of each industry became a cartel for all practical purposes. Firms lost individual control over their own price and output decisions; they were required to furnish information to the code authorities that made evasion of the agreement's provisions difficult. The codes became the instrument by which prices were increased, free from the threat of competition. Wholesale prices rose nearly 23 percent from 1933 to 1935, although consumer prices and the GNP deflator exhibit much smaller increases.[40] Some of this increase probably indicated that wholesale prices had temporarily fallen below levels equating demand and supply at the trough of the Depression.

Flawed Policies

From the viewpoint of economic theory, the National Industrial Recovery Act appears to have been exactly the wrong medicine for the Depression. To be sure, as markets shrank, prices had fallen and competition for the remaining business had become intense, but this reflected the overall decline in income. Raising prices in the face of reduced demand could be accomplished only by reducing output, perhaps substantially.

To the extent that it had any effect, the NIRA could only worsen the Depression's impact. The immediate effect of price increases would be a reduction in the already shrunken purchasing power of consumers, and consequently an additional decline in output and employment. The existence of so much unused capacity made it unlikely that such programs could ever be put into effective operation (in the existing circumstances, producers' incentives to cheat, code or no code, would be overwhelming). Even if an increase in aggregate demand could somehow be achieved independent of the NIRA programs,

they would reduce its impact. The Supreme Court's decision that the act was an unconstitutional delegation of Congressional powers provided the Roosevelt administration with a graceful way out of a thoroughly ill-conceived program.

The next year, policy was completely reversed. Instead of support for legally sanctioned price-fixing, the administration began a vigorous program of antitrust-law enforcement under Thurman Arnold, the new head of the Department of Justice's Antitrust Division. While this policy had greater implications for reform than for recovery, it certainly would not inhibit the latter. But the abrupt policy reversal did nothing to strengthen the confidence of business leaders, few of whom placed great trust in the New Deal or its leader in any circumstances.

The Fair Labor Standards Act

After the demise of the NIRA, the provisions affecting labor were quickly incorporated into the National Labor Relations Act (called the Wagner Act after its sponsor), which was destined to play a prominent role in the labor history of the following decades. This act (1938) had elements of both recovery (or the New Deal version thereof) and reform.

The Fair Labor Standards Act set minimum wage levels and maximum hours of work: initially 25 cents per hour and not more than 44 hours per week. Any additional hours were to be compensated at overtime rates, in the hope that employers would hire additional workers rather than pay more per hour. This legislation, as well as the Social Security Act, attempted to reduce the supply of labor by tightening restrictions on child labor and on the employment of those over age 65.

Imposing a legal minimum wage under Depression conditions was a very dubious policy. Employees might be able to increase both wage rates and total employment if they were

---

[40] *Historical Statistics*, 1:198–199, 210–211.

assisted by minimum wage legislation or a labor union in dealing with a monopsonistic employer, but most labor markets were not monopsonistic. Under more competitive conditions, raising the cost of labor to employers, particularly when there was a huge surplus of labor at existing wage rates, was far more likely to reduce than to raise aggregate employment. Such laws may be consistent with other New Deal legislation, but implicit in them is a view that the demand for labor is fixed and cannot be increased, and that buyers' reactions to price changes do not matter.

REFORM MEASURES

The reforms instituted by the New Deal probably represent its most positive contribution to economic improvement. Curiously, the one institutional change of this period that was applauded by liberals and conservatives alike was not supported by the administration, although it was enacted at this time.[41] The Federal Deposit Insurance Corporation and its twin, the Federal Savings and Loan Insurance Corporation, provided insurance for deposits in commercial banks and savings and loan associations. All member banks of the Federal Reserve System were required to join the FDIC, and nonmember banks were allowed to do so. In practice, nearly all banks joined. The result was a major improvement in the stability of the commercial banking system. Bank runs all but disappeared completely because depositors were now assured of access to their cash from an insured bank in a few days, no matter how many of their fellows had cashed in their own deposits in the meantime.

---

[41] Kindleberger, *The World in Depression*, 199. See also Lebergott, *The Americans*, 447–448.

The Social Security Act

The first steps to provide public assistance to individual security were initiated—several decades after most of the countries of western Europe had instituted similar measures. The Social Security Act of 1935 provided a much wider range of benefits than the old-age pensions that normally come to mind when social security is mentioned. Direct aid to those unable to work—the aged, the handicapped, and dependent children—was provided, as was unemployment insurance.

The portion of the social security program that provided direct money payments to the needy was the forerunner of our current welfare system. For all its conceptual faults, the Social Security Act was the first explicit recognition that in a market economy there may be persons unable to provide for themselves. All facets of the program have been revised and expanded many times since 1935. Despite widespread criticism, the act's basic premise that individuals who cannot generate a decent standard of living through their own efforts have a claim on society's resources continues to receive popular support. The reconciliation of views on eligibility and support levels is another matter, and appears no nearer solution today than it was 57 years ago. As with other redistributional programs, the act became a useful instrument for rent-seeking in the hands of various pressure groups.

Social security also provided pensions for the retired. The program was to be financed by taxes on both individual incomes and employers' payrolls. Since both taxes increased employers' labor costs, both were borne primarily by employees. Inflation, changing demographics, and rent-seeking politics have made maintenance of the commitments of the Social Security Act problematical. Other developed nations have had similar experiences. Originally, the Old Age and Survivors' Insurance portion of the social security program was intended to form a base below which no covered individual's income need fall, but neither the contributions nor the benefits initially provided were envisioned as adequate sole income sources for the retired.

As did so many other New Deal programs, the Social Security Act contained provisions intended to reduce the labor supply. These included retirement at age 65 and the loss of accrued benefits if insured individuals received more than minimal income from labor after achieving eligibility for benefits. The purpose of these features of the act was to spread an (implicitly insufficient) demand for labor over as many individuals as possible.

Social security did remove some of the terrors of old age. No longer did people have to fear literally working until they died, possibly at jobs unsuited to the elderly, if they wished to avoid a loss of independence. Prior to the advent of social security, the elderly who lacked adequate savings faced bitter choices. They could depend on their children or turn to the public authorities for support that was both niggardly and subject to conditions designed to discourage and demean applicants. The legislation probably also encouraged greater interest in private pension plans. Higher income levels have nevertheless contributed more to the potential security of the elderly than social security by providing increased ability to accumulate private savings, either directly or in fringe benefits rather than wages.

Unemployment Insurance

Another result of the American experience during the Depression was a system designed to provide income to the unemployed. The program set up at this time was to be self-funding: A tax was levied on employers' payrolls and used to establish a fund from which payments could be made to those out of work. The length of time over which support would be given was limited, in order to provide in-

■ Publicity promoting the Social Security Act of 1935 attempted to reassure individuals who feared such a "radical" new notion.
Source: Social Security Administration.

centives for the unemployed to seek work. The plan was designed to encourage each state to set up its own program and to ensure conformity among the state plans. Once in operation, unemployment compensation not only provided relief to the jobless but proved to be a valuable device for increasing economic stability; it cushioned the decline in incomes resulting from unemployment and reduced the impact of multiplier effects that spread the impact of unemployment throughout the economy.

The Tennessee Valley Authority

The TVA is not easily classified. Originally conceived as a massive public works project designed to raise incomes in one of the poorest areas of the United States, it also represented a significant change in the economic role of government. The federal government built a series of huge dams in the Tennessee and Cumberland River valleys. The dams were primarily designed to generate hydroelectric power, but the project also improved navigation and provided flood control and recreational facilities. To improve the projects' effectiveness in flood control, the TVA began efforts to control erosion through reforestation projects and by teaching farmers soil-conservation methods.

The TVA assumed the character of a regional development project. The great dams' cheap electric power enticed industry to an area that in prior times had few attractions for manufacturing firms. The new jobs that resulted offered much better income prospects than had ever been available to the valleys' residents. Competition from TVA power drove some privately owned electric companies out of business, and TVA generating costs were used (unfairly, some claimed) as a yardstick in determining the rates to be allowed regulated utilities.

Other New Deal programs were extensions, sometimes much enlarged, of activities traditionally performed by government, although sometimes not at the federal level. The Tennessee Valley Authority, however, fit the classic definition of socialism: Here, government owned the means of production. Although plans were made for similar projects in other regions, little more than dam construction was accomplished elsewhere before World War II, except in the Pacific Northwest.

Private capital had been developing hydroelectric facilities for decades before the TVA appeared. However, it seems most unlikely that private projects would have financed the range of social benefits provided by this vast public enterprise. Some of these were costly public goods (flood control). In other cases it was difficult to assess benefits or assign them to specific individuals or even locations (erosion control). Such circumstances are often used to justify the provision of public goods. The costs and benefits to the national economy from the TVA have never been fully assessed. However, there was little doubt that the benefits in the immediate area were far greater than the costs, and that there was no prospect that such an undertaking would have been financed by private enterprise in the 1930s.

The Growth of Organized Labor

The 1920s had not been a good decade for labor unions in the United States. Earlier depressions had always caused substantial declines in union membership, so it could be expected that the Great Depression would be devastating for organized labor, and union ranks would dwindle.

For the first few years of the Depression, this prediction was confirmed, although the unions lost fewer members than might have been expected. Their membership fell from 3.6 to 3 million—a serious but not fatal decline. Shortly after the trough of the Depression, however, union membership began to increase, even though unemployment remained very high. Not only did the unions make up lost ground, they grew larger than ever before. By 1937, there were 5.8 million workers in union ranks, and three years later almost 9 million. The work force had also grown since the unions' previous peak of strength in 1920, so the gains as a portion of the work force were smaller. Still, the 1940 figure represented about 16 percent of the U.S. labor force—an all-time high. Much of the increase was in industries that had previously defied unions' efforts to organize them: the large mass-production manufacturing firms, most of whose workers were semiskilled or unskilled, not craftsmen.[42]

Labor in a New Climate

These developments were not quite as startling as the previous history of American labor might indicate. The climate in which labor now operated had changed. The Depression had greatly reduced the public's esteem for business and business leaders; the social, political, and legal situations had all swung far in unions' favor. The legal basis for organized labor's new position was the reenactment of Section 7 of the National Industrial Recovery Act as the National Labor Relations Act. Together with the Norris-LaGuardia Act (1932), the law now gave labor the legal right to organize.

Employers' legal positions were now much weaker. Not only were they obliged to recognize unions that had won representation elections and bargain with them in good faith, but labor relations were now enforced by the National Labor Relations Board and, if necessary, the courts. The Norris-LaGuardia Act had stripped employers of some of their favorite antiunion weapons. Yellow-dog contracts could no longer be enforced in the federal courts. Employers' access to the injunctions that had previously all but paralyzed unions attempting to organize their firms became only a memory. Instead, not only were labor representatives allowed to organize unions if they could persuade workers to join, but unions could also boycott and picket recalcitrant firms, even in cases where they did not represent the firms' employees (secondary boycotts). Employers were forbidden to interfere with unions' attempts to organize their

workers, to interfere in union organization or internal affairs, to discriminate against their members, or to refuse to bargain with a union that had won the support of a majority of their employees. The laws were broadly drawn, and the courts' interpretation of them tended to be as liberal as it had once been narrow.

New Union Structures

Changes in the nature of union organization were as important to the growth of organized labor as the new laws. Heretofore, nearly all American unions had been organized along craft lines; they were composed of workers who performed the same type of job, such as carpenters or printers. This type of organization was unsuited to large manufacturing plants that employed many different types of skilled workers, and even more, workers with no particular skill. The latter group, for example, assembly-line workers, often made up a majority of the work force in mass-production establishments. Even if unions representing all the craft skills utilized by such an employer cooperated, a very difficult proposition in itself, there remained the problem of the laborers whose jobs did not clearly link them with any specific union.

Such firms had been organized in some European countries, but not by craft unions. A new type of organization, the industrial union, had been developed. Workers qualified for membership in such unions on the basis of the firm for which they worked and the product it made, not the tasks that they performed. A lathe operator in a small Detroit machine shop might be a member of the machinists, together with all the shop's other employees, whose jobs were similar. The machinist's cousin performing exactly the same job in Ford's great River Rouge plant might now become a member of the United Auto Workers—together with assembly-line workers, carpenters, and even janitors. The industrial unions avoided the jurisdictional disputes that pitted union against union, often

---

[42] *Historical Statistics,* 1:178.

over issues that had little to do with normal labor-management concerns.

The older craft unions were not inclined to favor the formation of industrial unions, viewing them as a threat to their position within the labor movement. But industrial unions offered many previously unorganized workers an opportunity they had never before possessed. Industrial unions grew rapidly. In 1935, the Committee for Industrial Organization was organized, representing the industrial unions within the American Federation of Labor. After bitter disputes with craft unions over jurisdiction and "raiding" (attempts to persuade each other's members to change unions), the industrial unions formed their own organization, the Congress of Industrial Organizations. The CIO's strength was centered in the industrial unions that had just been organized in the steel, rubber, glass, and automobile industries.

Firms' responses to attempts to organize their employees varied. Some recognized the union as soon as it was obvious that it had the support of most of their workers. Others, such as Republic Steel and Ford, met efforts at unionization with company police and hired "goon squads" (sometimes provoking responses in kind). There were many injuries and some deaths before the recalcitrants understood that the days of such tactics and the attitudes they represented were over.

New Leaders, New Tactics

New union leadership also played an important role. One reason for the mass-production industries' lack of organization as this era began was the absence of any serious union efforts to do so in prior years. The new industrial union leadership was intensely interested in expansion of aggregate membership. Not only were they starting "from scratch" in most cases, but large gains in membership would improve their own positions within the labor movement. Significantly, John L. Lewis, the head of the only large industrial union within the old AF of L (the United Mine Workers), played a major role in supporting the new efforts.

Industrial unions' members were more dependent on political support than were the older craft unions; employers could often replace such workers easily. Consequently, they were far more politically active and partisan than the AFL had been, generally supporting candidates of the Democratic Party. New organizing tactics also were developed. Because employers could readily find other workers to replace them if they left work, the industrial unions made use of the sit-down strike, in which they stopped working but remained in the plant so that they could not be replaced by strikebreakers.

The Depression's Role in Union Growth

Public opinion toward unions in general had become more favorable, but the change in individuals' attitudes toward actually joining unions was even more beneficial to unions. During the Depression, the old attitudes about the individual bearing sole responsibility for his own welfare had been profoundly challenged.

Even for those who retained their jobs, the idea of inevitable progress, that is, that each job was at least potentially a stepping-stone to another, better position, appeared far less valid than in earlier decades. Such changes in thought provoked interest in organizations promising improvement of current conditions. Fear of arbitrary dismissal was one incentive to unionize. Often, nonunion jobs provided no effective appeal against the foreman, who could hire and fire on whatever basis he chose. Unions might be able to offer some benefits in case of layoffs, sickness, or injury, and they were obviously far better situated to insist on including such considerations in bargaining agreements. Unions, especially under Depression conditions, appeared much better equipped to bargain with employers over traditional concerns, such as

■ During the Great Depression, unions began using a new tactic, the sit-down strike, shown in this photo taken in Detroit in 1937. By remaining in the plant, union members prevented strikebreakers from working.
Source: UPI/Bettmann Newsphotos.

wages, hours, and working conditions, than were individual employees. From 1935 on, the annual number of work stoppages resulting from unions' attempts to organize workers and force management recognition was three to five times the number that occurred during any year of the 1920s.[43]

Union growth in the twentieth century was to be expected. The portion of the U.S. labor force organized was far below that of most industrialized European nations, and even the gains of the late 1930s only partially closed the gap. Even had the laws not been altered so much in unions' favor, the change in attitudes caused by the traumatic insecurity of the Depression (workers are far more interested in improving conditions in their current jobs when they cannot leave for

---

[43] *Historical Statistics,* 1:179.

alternative employment) would have led to increased interest in unions.

But the unions' growth probably hindered economic recovery. To the extent that organized labor gained higher wages for its members, unionization added desperately needed purchasing power to the recovery. But while wages are income to employees, they are costs to employers, and higher labor costs and greater employer uncertainty were unlikely to aid business expansion. Even the increase in purchasing power accrued to a small minority of workers, so it could not have greatly increased aggregate demand. Indeed, if the demand for labor was elastic, unions' net effect on aggregate wages was a reduction: They lost more in reductions in the number of people hired than they gained in higher wages for those retaining their jobs. Since real earnings per employee rose substantially more than did output per worker[44] (not, of course, entirely as a result of union activity), the increase in unit labor costs under circumstances where cost increases were especially difficult to pass on to consumers probably retarded the growth of employment in the 1930s.[45]

Reforms in Financial Institutions

Federal Reserve System reforms have already been discussed. The stock market crash caused the formation of the Securities and Exchange Commission in 1934. This agency was charged with improving the information available to participants in securities markets, and the prohibition of some activities that allowed "insiders" with early or unique access to information to capitalize on their superior knowledge. The scope of holding companies (firms whose assets were the stock of other companies) was greatly reduced. Public utility regulation was tightened.

THE NEW DEAL: AN ASSESSMENT

Any analysis of the effects of the New Deal must conclude that in one of its major endeavors, if not *the* major endeavor of the Roosevelt administration, it was a failure. It did not end the Depression: The unemployment rate in 1940 was still 14.6 percent. Although this was 10 percentage points better than the rate prevailing in 1933, it was still intolerably high, and many other nations had done far better even before rearmament spending for World War II became significant. Even its job programs were clearly "second-best" alternatives to unemployment, better than no work at all, but not the jobs individuals preferred. It may be disheartening to realize that the military malevolence of Adolf Hitler and his allies produced a greater decline in civilian unemployment in the United States in three years than all the good intentions and efforts of the New Deal in seven, but it is so.

Pluses and Minuses

There were positive accomplishments. Certainly, by 1940 the American citizen was better shielded from the effects of the Depression than had been the case in 1933. Due to such New Deal programs as unemployment insurance and public employment programs, there was now some assurance that the loss of a job need not mean a loss of all income. Nevertheless, it is hard to argue that an early return to full employment might not have done more for economic well-being than such measures.

---

[44] *Historical Statistics,* 1:164, 2:950.

[45] Several studies concluded that rising wages in general and union activity in particular impeded employment growth in the 1930s. See P. Temin, *Lessons from the Great Depression,* (Cambridge, Mass.: MIT Press, 1989), 120–124; and B. Bernanke, "Employment, Hours, and Earnings in the Depression: An Analysis of Eight Manufacturing Industries," *American Economic Review* (March 1986).

Had the primary goal been achieved, the secondary defenses would have been less important, and less used.

Some New Deal policies retarded recovery either directly or indirectly. At least one investigation has failed to support the oft-repeated charge that New Deal policies reduced private investment spending and thus slowed recovery,[46] but investment never regained pre-Depression levels during the 1930s. Attempts to cure the Depression by "reflating" prices were ineffective at best. Macroeconomic policy was hardly ever recognized as such, and at its best it was never more than mildly expansionary; usually it exacerbated the situation. The very serious macroeconomic errors of 1937 undoubtedly prolonged the Depression, and this occurred after four years' experience. If the promotion of monopoly power (admittedly, not for its own sake) was eventually abandoned in industry, it was continued in agriculture and labor, where, as usual, it restricted resource mobility and reduced aggregate incomes. The long-run effects of such programs were increasingly negative.[47] Redistributive efforts discouraged change by aiding sectors of limited potential and discouraging reallocation and change, the crucial elements in long-term growth. They also built up rent-seeking constituencies.

The efforts at "planning" were almost without exception disasters and could hardly have been otherwise. In nearly every instance, the New Deal ignored demand in efforts to promote supply, or vice versa. The attempts to promote recovery within individual sectors of the economy without attention to the impact elsewhere were in the same vein. Government spending nominally devoted solely to the promotion of recovery was apparently strongly influenced by political considerations. It was concentrated on "swing states" where it might influence the outcome of elections, and left states whose Democratic loyalties or irredeemable Republicanism were well established much more to their own devices.[48]

Income distribution apparently became somewhat more equal during the 1930s. However, the change was largely a transfer of income (and perhaps wealth) from the very rich—the top 1 or 5 percent of all income recipients in the country—to the middle class, rather than to the poor.[49] The change was largely due to the decline in property income, such as corporate profits and rents, which were highly concentrated among the rich. This resulted more from the Depression itself than from the New Deal's social programs or taxes. One study has concluded that most income shifts occurred before the advent of the New Deal.[50] Direct transfers either in money, as with welfare payments or unemployment compensation, or through government-subsidized housing, schooling, or jobs, contributed to greater income equality; pro-union legislation and minimum-wage laws did not.

Aggregate economic security was also increased. Even in the areas of the New Deal's greatest failings, countercyclical monetary and fiscal policy, some lessons had (finally) been learned. In the future there would be no gross errors comparable to those of 1929–1933 or 1937. The various provisions of the Social Security Act have thus far lived up to their title. At the same time, however, they have

---

[46] T. Mayer and M. Chatterji, "Political Shocks and Investment: Some Evidence from the 1930s," *Journal of Economic History* (December 1983).

[47] For discussions of this concept, see M. Olson, *The Rise and Decline of Nations: Economic Growth, Stagflation, and Social Rigidities* (New Haven, Conn.: Yale University Press, 1982), and D. North, *Structure and Change in Economic History* (New York: Norton, 1982).

[48] D. Reading, "New Deal Activity and the States, 1933–1939," *Journal of Economic History* (December 1973).

[49] P. Lindert and J. Williamson, "Three Centuries of American Inequality," in P. Uselding, ed., *Research in Economic History* (Greenwich, Conn.: JAI Press, 1976).

[50] D. North, T. Anderson, and P. Hill, *Growth and Welfare in the American Past: A New Economic History* (Englewood Cliffs, N.J.: Prentice-Hall, 1983), 160–161.

Table 18.2   Government Spending and Its Relationship to GNP, 1927–1940*

Year	GNP (in Billions)	Federal Spending (in Billions)	Percentage of GNP	State and Local Government Spending (in Billions)	Percentage of GNP
1927	$94.9	$2.8	3.9%	$7.9	8.2%
1928	97.0	3.0	3.1	—	—
1929	103.1	3.1	3.0	—	—
1930	90.4	3.3	3.7	—	—
1931	75.8	3.6	4.7	—	—
1932	58.0	4.7	8.1	8.4	14.5
1933	55.6	4.6	8.3	—	—
1934	65.1	6.6	10.1	7.8	12.0
1935	72.2	6.5	9.0	—	—
1936	82.5	8.4	10.2	8.5	10.3
1937	90.4	7.7	8.5	—	—
1938	84.7	6.8	8.0	10.0	11.8
1939	90.5	8.8	9.7	—	—
1940	99.7	9.1	9.1	11.2	11.2

*Figures in current dollars.
Source: U.S. Department of Commerce, Bureau of the Census, *Historical Statistics of the United States: Colonial Times to 1970*, 2 vols. (Washington, D.C.: Government Printing Office, 1975), 2:1114, 1132.

provided an entry for an ever-expanding cycle of rent-seeking activity.

Survival of the Market Economy

The New Deal left the United States economy a largely market-directed system. The TVA is a clear exception. Government control of prices, output levels, wages, and hours of work in agriculture and labor markets imposed new restrictions on private economic activity.[51] Other firms, especially in financial markets, were required to furnish more information to government agencies than in earlier times. Whether any of these developments (save the TVA) is "socialism" is a matter of definition.[52] In many areas of the economy, the constraints on private economic activity were increased. For the most part, however, economic activity continued to take place through the interplay of supply and demand in the marketplace. The role, and, consequently, the control of the federal government expanded considerably, both through direct spending and through programs funding activities by local and state governments. Recently it has been found that the New Deal tended to expand federal and state government activities at the expense of local government.[53]

Table 18.2 indicates that although the federal government's expenditures did grow in both absolute and relative terms, the increase was probably less than most impressions

---

[51] Higgs, *Crisis and Leviathan*, Chap. 8.
[52] Temin uses this definition. See Temin, *Lessons From the Great Depression*, Lecture 3.

[53] J. Wallis, "The Birth of the Old Federalism: Financing the New Deal, 1932–1940," *Journal of Economic History* (March 1984).

would lead us to expect. Much of the government's relative growth occurred through the collapse of the private economy, not from its own absolute increases. Indeed, the greatest proportional increase took place under Herbert Hoover, not Franklin Roosevelt. Had economic growth continued after 1929 at the modest annual rate of 3 percent, the federal government's share of total spending in 1940 would have been 6.4 percent. Even this figure assumes that federal expenditures would not have declined had economic circumstances been better. The rate of increase in total government expenditures was no greater in the 1930s than it had been for the three preceding decades.[54]

The changes made by the New Deal in the basic institutions of the American economy were surprisingly modest. In 1933, it would not have been difficult for the government to nationalize the commercial banks and probably the railroads (however well- or ill-advisedly), but no attempt was made to do so. The efforts to control the details of operations within various industries may have diverted efforts away from attempts to direct the aggregate economy. This is fortunate in light of the skills, information, and sense of direction available for such a task in the 1930s. The emphasis was largely on saving the market system, rather than replacing it, despite some rhetoric to the contrary.[55] The United States has always taken its social reforms the way the frontier took religion and castor oil—in large, infrequent doses, and only long after the need had become overwhelming.

---

[54] Wallis, "Birth."
[55] For a less benign view, see Higgs, *Crisis and Leviathan,* Chap. 8.

SELECTED REFERENCES

Chandler, L. *America's Greatest Depression, 1929–1941.* New York: Harper & Row, 1970.

Friedman, M., and A. Schwartz. *A Monetary History of the United States, 1867–1960.* Princeton, N.J.: Princeton University Press, 1962.

Gordon, R. *Economic Instability and Growth: The American Record.* New York: Harper & Row, 1974.

Hansen, A. *Business Cycles and National Income.* New York: Norton, 1951.

Higgs, R. *Crisis and Leviathan: Critical Episodes in the Growth of American Government.* New York: Oxford University Press, 1987.

Kindleberger, C. *The World in Depression, 1929–1939.* Revised. Berkeley, Calif.: University of California Press, 1986.

Leuchtenburg, W. *Franklin Roosevelt and the New Deal, 1932–1940.* New York: Harper & Row, 1963.

Mitchell, B. *Depression Decade: From New Era Through New Deal, 1932–1940.* New York: Holt, Rinehart, and Winston, 1947.

North, D. *Structure and Change in Economic History.* New York: Norton, 1981.

North, D., T. Anderson, and P. Hill. *Growth and Welfare in the American Past: A New Economic History.* 3d ed. Englewood Cliffs, N.J.: Prentice-Hall, 1983.

Olson, M. *The Rise and Decline of Nations: Economic Growth, Stagflation, and Social Rigidities.* New Haven, Conn.: Yale University Press, 1982.

Stein, H. *The Fiscal Revolution in America.* Chicago: University of Chicago Press, 1969.

Temin, P. *Lessons From the Great Depression.* Cambridge, Mass.: MIT Press, 1989.

U.S. Department of Commerce, Bureau of the Census. *Historical Statistics of the United States: Colonial Times to 1970.* 2 vols. Washington, D.C.: Government Printing Office, 1975.

Walton, G. *Regulatory Change in an Atmosphere of Crisis: Current Implications of the Roosevelt Years.* New York: Academic Press, 1979.

THE ECONOMICS
OF (ALMOST)
TOTAL WAR

W orld War II's European beginnings in the fall of 1939 had little immediate impact on the U.S. economy. American exports increased by about $1 billion from 1939 to 1940, but only about half that amount represented increased purchases by the combatants, chiefly Great Britain. Nor, through this period, was there much domestic military spending. Although the United States had 458,000 men and women on active duty in the armed forces (an increase of about one-third over 1930s levels),[1] the American military was far from prepared for war. An arms buildup had begun, but the U.S. Army (which at this time included the Air Force) was smaller than that of Bulgaria. There were deficiencies in the quality and amount of military equipment available, and these deficiencies restricted American military capabilities even more than the raw figures indicate.

After the fall of France in June 1940, it became apparent to many Americans that the war might not be just another European squabble that could be safely ignored, regardless of its outcome. In late 1940, only Great Britain remained in active opposition to Hitler's forces, and the consequences of Nazi supremacy in Europe were not pleasant to contemplate. Japanese-American relations in the Pacific and the Orient were deteriorating, and now the United States could no longer rely on substantial aid from friendly European powers in the event of a Pacific conflict. Rearmament assumed a new urgency.

By early 1941, the economic impact of the war on the United States was increasing. The hard-pressed British began to increase their orders for food and war material from America; they had already taken over French contracts made before that nation's defeat. The U.S. rearmament program was gaining momentum as well: Table 19.2 indicates that defense spending more than tripled between 1940 and 1941.

As Britain's military situation grew more desperate and its ability to pay for imports from the United States declined, the ties between the two countries increased. In March 1941, the Lend-Lease Program was instituted by the United States. In return for services rendered by the British (and a much smaller amount of British war material furnished to American forces), the U.S. government financed British purchases of war material in this country. Some of the goods sent to the British supposedly were loaned for the duration of the war. British services were only vaguely specified in the program, but, in fact, continued British resistance to Nazi Germany was invaluable to the United States. It was increasingly obvious that the United States would not be able to avoid becoming directly involved in the war, and the Lend-Lease Program helped to keep the terms on which America would have to fight from becoming worse than they eventually were. Had Great Britain been forced to surrender, and her industrial plants and possibly her fleet been added to Nazi strength, the war would have become enormously more costly for the United States. A transatlantic invasion of Europe without the use of British bases would have raised the war's costs in American lives as well as material. During the 1940–1945 period, a total of about $50 billion in Lend-Lease aid was provided to Britain and the other Allies. In return, the United States obtained foreign goods valued at about $8 billion.

---

[1] U.S. Department of Commerce, Bureau of the Census, *Historical Statistics of the United States: Colonial Times to 1970*, 2 vols. (Washington, D.C.: Government Printing Office, 1975), 2:1141.

■ After the fall of France during World War II, neutrality became difficult. By 1940, Britain sought U.S. assistance. *Source:* Cassel in the Brooklyn *Eagle;* Trustees of the Imperial War Museum, London.

U.S. ENTRY INTO THE WAR

With the Japanese attack on Pearl Harbor (December 7, 1941), the United States became an active participant in the war. As in World War I, the conflict absorbed incredible amounts of manpower and materials, and the productive capacity of the American economy was one of the Allies' key assets. Prospects for an Allied victory hinged on the speed and extent of American mobilization. Unlike World War I, however, this time the American contribution was actual rather than potential. The American war effort was based on the ability of the United States to produce enormous quantities of material, and no less important, transport them to the battlefields. The United States produced few really outstanding military leaders (Admiral Raymond Spruance was a conspicuous exception); its victories were largely the result of material superiority.

After the dark days of Allied defeat and retreat through the first half of 1942, the Axis forces were first checked and then forced into a defensive posture from which they never recovered. In the Pacific, an inferior American fleet dealt the Japanese Navy a stunning defeat at the Battle of Midway (June 1942). Japan was never able to replace the skilled pilots it lost there and at Guadalcanal six months later. In the European theater, the offensive power of Nazi Germany was broken in North Africa (1943) and at the Battles of Stalingrad and

■ After the Japanese attacked Pearl Harbor, all questions about U.S. involvement in World War II were silenced.
Source: General records of the Department of the Navy: National Archives.

Kursk (1942–1943). The Allies had received wholly unintentional help from Adolf Hitler, whose decision to attack the Soviet Union in 1941 was one of the war's great blunders.

The Production War

With the time so dearly purchased by the armed forces, the productive capacity of the American economy was converted to military output. The British, Canadian, and Soviet economies were even more totally mobilized. As a result, the Axis forces were drowned in a flood of machines. The United States produced huge volumes of material to equip its own forces and also augmented the supplies of British Commonwealth and Soviet forces. Table 19.1 gives a partial indication of the disparities in aircraft production during the crucial years of the war. British aircraft output increased the Allied total by somewhat more than the German total, and U.S. figures include a higher proportion of large multiengine planes than those of other nations. Patterns in most other types of war material were similar.

Once the war became a struggle between the adversaries' productive potentials, the Axis powers were doomed. Only Germany among them was then an industrial power of the first rank; and ironically, the German war

Table 19.1   *Comparative Aircraft Production, 1941–1944 (Total Aircraft)*

Country	1941	1942	1943	1944	Total
Japan	5,088	8,861	16,693	28,180	58,822
Germany	11,766	15,556	25,527	39,807	92,656
United States	19,433	49,445	92,196	100,752	261,826
USSR	15,735	25,430	34,900	40,300	116,365

Source: United States Strategic Bombing Survey (Washington, D.C.: Government Printing Office, 1948).

effort was hampered by the Nazis' own propaganda. The German leaders were convinced (in late 1940, apparently with good reason) that the war would be short. The German economy was not fully mobilized for war until early 1943.[2] By then it was far too late. Although Germany achieved some remarkable feats of production after that date, the Nazi war effort was fatally handicapped. In addition to leadership whose dictatorial powers and instability made responses weighing costs against benefits difficult, the Germans lacked a basic understanding of the interactions of various sectors of their own economy. The Allies, particularly the Americans, had developed national income accounting, a tool that proved invaluable in determining the demands that war production programs would place upon the available resources. Production bottlenecks could be foreseen and cleared up before they hindered production. Fewer unanticipated crises developed in the American, British, and Canadian economies as a result, while the Germans were continually required to meet unexpected shortcomings on an emergency basis. By 1944, Allied intelligence experts had a better grasp of the capabilities of the German economy than did Hitler and his followers.

In a long war, neither Italy nor Japan proved capable of equipping their forces sufficiently to offset the Allies' growing numerical superiority. The Japanese admiral who planned the attack on Pearl Harbor had warned his government of precisely that before the war began. Admiral Yamamoto, who had studied at Harvard University and was quite familiar with American industrial capacity, told his superiors that Japan's only hope was to win a position of such dominance that the United States might be unwilling to pay the price to break it. Moreover, he said, this would have to be attained in less than a year. The attack on Pearl Harbor, the Japanese thought, would begin the process by demoralizing and dividing the United States.[3] This may have been a bigger miscalculation than Japan's underestimation of American economic potential and the speed with which it could be mobilized. Whether the willingness to fight a war through existed in America before Pearl Harbor or not, it certainly did thereafter, and the Japanese military expansion lasted only six months.

---

[2] D. Landes, *The Unbound Prometheus: Technological Change From 1750 to the Present* (Cambridge, U.K.: Cambridge University Press, 1969), 413–415.

[3] G. Prange, *At Dawn We Slept: The Untold Story of Pearl Harbor* (New York: McGraw-Hill, 1981), 84.

Table 19.2   The Economic Dimensions of Mobilization, 1939–1945

Year	GNP (in Billions of Current Dollars)	Real GNP (in Billions of 1958 Dollars)	Military Spending (in Billions of Dollars)	Federal Deficit (in Billions of Dollars)	Civilian Labor Force (in Millions)
1939	$90.5	$209.4	$1.4	$2.9	55.6
1940	99.7	227.2	1.8	2.7	56.1
1941	124.5	263.7	6.3	4.8	57.7
1942	157.9	297.8	22.9	19.4	60.3
1943	191.6	337.1	63.4	53.8	64.9
1944	201.1	361.3	76.0	46.1	66.3
1945	211.9	355.2	80.5	45.0	66.2

* GNP deflator.
Source: U.S. Department of Commerce, Bureau of the Census, *Historical Statistics of the United States: Colonial Times to 1970,* 2 vols. (Washington, D.C.: Government Printing Office, 1975), 1:132, 135, 198, 224; 2:1105, 1114, 1141.

CONVERSION TO A WAR ECONOMY

The basic task confronting the United States was that of increasing military production. At least initially, there were several avenues by which this might be accomplished. First, the economy's total output could be increased, with the bulk of the added production going to war needs. Alternatively, the composition of existing output could be shifted to favor the war effort. Either method would produce other problems: Increased military-goods output would raise the money incomes of the workers and firms making it, without a proportionate increase in civilian goods and services on which the added wages and profits could be spent. This generated inflationary pressures and would also reduce incentives; if additional income would buy few if any more goods, it would not motivate people to produce. A means of countering inflation and maintaining incentives became increasingly important as the economy neared capacity output levels.

It was soon apparent that this was more than a theoretical problem; the war's demands far exceeded the available productive capacity. Systems of priorities and allocative mechanisms to meet them had to be developed to determine which war goods had first call on available means of production, and which alternative uses of those resources had to be sacrificed first.[4] In addition, the means by which military goods were produced might also have to be determined.

Initially, the wartime buildup caused few difficulties. Unemployment was still widespread in the United States when the war began in Europe, and this situation continued for almost two years. Under such conditions, additional production was readily obtained by putting unemployed resources back to work. This involved little reduction in current production for the civilian economy. But by the time of Pearl Harbor, the unemployment rate

---

[4] R. Higgs, *Crisis and Leviathan: Critical Episodes in the Growth of American Government* (New York: Oxford University Press, 1987), 203–204.

Military on Active Duty (in Millions)	Unemployment Rate (%)	Price Index* (1958 = 100)	Industrial Production (1967 = 100)
.3	17.2%	43.2	22
.5	14.6	43.9	25
1.8	9.9	47.2	32
3.9	4.7	53.0	38
9.0	1.9	56.8	47
11.5	1.2	58.1	51
12.1	1.9	59.7	43

was at 7 percent and falling rapidly. Shortages of some types of labor and services had already appeared and were rapidly becoming more serious. Prices, which had remained almost stable in 1940, were now beginning to rise, despite the government's institution of informal inflation-control programs. By mid-1942, increases in war production could no longer be obtained by utilizing previously idle capacity; almost none remained. Henceforth, sacrifices in current or potential civilian output would be necessary, or production methods would have to be changed.

Nevertheless, there was a huge increase in total production. As Table 19.2 illustrates, real output grew by 59 percent from 1940 to 1945, and industrial production approximately doubled. Defense spending, which had been 1.5 percent of GNP in 1939 and 1.8 percent in 1940, reached 37.8 percent in 1944. The overall impact of government demand on the economy's capacity rose even more than these figures indicate. Not only did federal nondefense spending rise slightly more than enough to offset a reduction in expenditures by state and local governments, but there was a quantum jump in the range and depth of government regulation of all types of economic activity. The draft, which substituted government coercion for monetary inducements to enter military service, was the outstanding example, but there were many others.[5] By 1944, government spending of all types and levels accounted for 58.2 percent of GNP.

Far-Reaching Changes in the Labor Force

Such a massive increase in government expenditures, when combined with expansionary monetary policies, soon accomplished what the New Deal had not: It ended the Great Depression. Unemployment fell to levels that many economists had considered impossible. It had been thought that 2 to 4 percent of the work force would always be unemployed as the normal consequence of entry into the labor force, movements between jobs, seasonal and

---

[5] See Higgs, *Crisis and Leviathan,* 203–204, 226.

■ World War II's economic demands opened up many jobs not traditionally held by women.
   Source: Library of Congress.

accidental layoffs, and similar causes. Such levels were the cost of individual freedom and mobility. But over 1943–1945, the jobless rate was less than 2 percent of the work force. These extremely low rates were *not* merely the consequence of the great increase in military manpower, which removed men from the unemployment rolls.[6] The civilian labor force grew substantially during the war. In part, this reflected normal population growth, but a new and more important factor was the entry of large numbers of people who had not worked outside the home in more normal times. Women and those younger, older, or less qualified than the normal range of employees responded to the incentives of high wages, steady work, and large amounts of overtime at even higher pay rates, as well as patriotism. Labor input grew even more than employment figures indicate: The average work week in manufacturing, for example, increased from 38 hours in 1940 to 45 in 1944.[7] The low unemployment rates are even more remarkable

---

[6] Higgs disagrees. Higgs, *Crisis and Leviathan*, 226.

[7] *Historical Statistics,* 1:169.

because the groups contributing most to the labor force increase normally have above-average rates of joblessness.

The male labor force did not shrink during the war, although its composition changed. The war, as did other periods in which labor markets were extremely tight, gave women and minority groups a chance to show that they could handle a much wider range of jobs than those previously open to them. About five million women joined the labor force during the war, and the skills they acquired became a vital force in the postwar assault on the barriers to female entry into those jobs under normal conditions. Labor force participation rates and relative wages for married women increased sharply during the war, and never fell to pre-1940 levels thereafter.[8] In addition, resource mobility was spurred by the war. Many firms began making products for the military that were quite different from anything they had manufactured in peacetime, and this encouraged postwar entry into new industries, and greater competition throughout the economy.

Bigotry, American Style

Minority groups' experience was similar to that of women, with one exception. The Nisei, Americans of Japanese ancestry, or at least those living on the U.S. mainland, were interned in thinly disguised concentration camps because they were considered to be security risks.[9] They were often forced to sell their property for a fraction of its value. The treatment of the Nisei was a national disgrace, inexcusable even in the climate of wartime hysteria in which the ornamental cherry trees given to the District of Columbia by the Japanese government were cut down as a "patriotic" act. No Nisei committed a disloyal act during the war. The 442nd Regimental Combat Team, all of whose enlisted men were Japanese-Americans, won more citations for valor and suffered higher casualties than any other U.S. military unit.

The Opportunity Costs of War

Diversion of productive capacity proved more difficult than simple expansion of aggregate output. Once the economy was operating at or beyond full-employment levels, further increases in military production could only be obtained by the diversion of resources from their current uses, or by new methods. Production of certain goods that competed strongly with military needs, such as automobiles, major appliances, and housing, was forbidden, and a variety of other items was restricted, at least for civilian use. Nevertheless, the United States was the only major combatant able to maintain or even increase aggregate civilian consumption during the war. In real terms, consumption fell slightly in 1942, but by 1944 it was about 10 percent above the 1940 level.[10] These figures, however, are not as reliable indicators of civilian welfare during the war as they would be in peacetime. They contain no allowance for the changes forced by adjustments to shortages or total absences of some goods, or for the deterioration in quality of others. Coerced labor reallocation, inconveniences, and longer hours, (with consequent higher accident rates) reduce the improvement in well-being. Nor do official statistics reflect the impact of government-controlled prices reflecting far less than the

---

[8] C. Goldin, "The Female Labor Force and American Economic Growth," in R. Gallman and S. Engerman, *Long-Term Factors in American Economic Growth* (Chicago: University of Chicago Press, 1986).

[9] Ironically, Hawaiian Nisei were not interred because they were too large a portion of the total population.

[10] *Historical Statistics,* 1:318. See also R. Gordon, *Economic Instability and Growth: The American Record* (New York: Harper & Row, 1974), 84.

true costs of some goods. By these criteria, real consumption per capita fell by almost 7 percent from 1941 through 1943.[11]

The major diversions of capacity, however, came at the expense of the labor force (through conscription), and of investment, which fell to less than half its prewar levels (it should be recalled that these had been below the long-term norm). State and local government activities were also curtailed.[12] Under wartime conditions, resources could not be devoted to increasing future productive capacity if the cost of doing so was current military production. In a few cases where shortages of capital imposed especially severe restrictions on war production, the government built factories and leased them to private operators for the duration of the war. The major increase in military goods, however, came from the increase in overall output. (See Table 19.2.) The expansion was sufficient to overwhelm the Axis powers.

The Controlled Economy

The increasingly complex reallocation process was directed by a series of government agencies. Particularly scarce inputs were rationed and in some cases directly allocated to high-priority uses. The extent of government regulation was unprecedented; not even the emergency measures employed during World War I approached the scope of those employed to increase and direct production during the second conflict.[13] The War Production Board, established in 1942, was responsible for the overall direction of industry. A system of

priorities was established, under which users of materials critically important to the war effort, such as steel, copper, and aluminum, were ranked in order of their estimated contribution to military production. The most vital received first consideration, and were guaranteed all the scarce inputs they needed. Lower priority users received less. In general, civilian production, which had the lowest priorities, had to make do with whatever materials were left.[14]

Although this method of allocation ensured that high-priority users received ample supplies of materials and labor, it was not very efficient. It gave first-line users only limited incentives (particularly since prices for these inputs were controlled by government) to conserve scarce inputs. Wasted material, or perhaps even some of that used in war production, might have been used elsewhere at no sacrifice in military goods (methods of production might have been altered to conserve scarce materials).

Other agencies allocated manpower, both between military and civilian occupations and within each of these uses. As it had been in earlier wars, conscription was used to fill the military ranks. All men of military-service ages who were neither unfit for service nor deemed to be contributing more to the war effort in their civilian occupations were liable to induction. (Definition of the latter category proved a fertile ground for pressure-group politics.)

Transportation was controlled by yet another government agency. Through these mechanisms, the primary goal of American economic activity was changed from civilian consumption to support of the war effort. The various agencies' activities were coordinated

[11] R. Higgs, "Wartime Prosperity? A Reassessment of the U.S. Economy in the 1940s," *Journal of Economic History* (March 1992).
[12] Gordon, *Instability and Growth*, 85.
[13] Higgs, "Wartime Prosperity," and *Crisis and Leviathan*, 203–204.
[14] Gordon, *Instability and Growth*, 88. See also R. Robertson, *History of the American Economy*, 3d ed. (New York: Harcourt Brace Jovanovich, 1973), 711.

by the Office of War Mobilization, which was set up in 1943.

The control agencies were set up in great haste. For at least the first two years, their operations were conducted with almost frantic urgency. Neither the speed with which they were established nor the need for immediate action on their part allowed for reasoned consideration of the available alternatives or the full ramifications of each decision that they made. Inevitably, mistakes, often of duplicated effort, were made. But in the aggregate, it is much easier to point to problems in efficiency than it is to dispute the overall effect. The essential tools of war were produced quickly and in huge amounts. By the end of 1942, the Allies had gained at least quantitative parity with the Axis. Soon thereafter, they achieved numerical superiority, and, in many cases, a qualitative edge as well.

Lessons from the Wartime Economy

The mobilization process was essentially a substitution of government planning for the normal direction of the economy by market forces. Productive resources remained privately owned, as before, but their owners lost much of their peacetime freedom to decide the volume, price, and manufacturing techniques of the items they made, subject only to market forces. Government controls were pervasive; they extended even to regulation of the type, quantity, and price of inputs, and the nature and hours of production, as well as the price and amount of output. There is no doubt that government planning achieved most of its major objectives during World War II, including, of course, the single overriding concern that the armed forces received the tools required for victory.

However, whether many of the lessons learned at this time can be applied to the conduct of a peacetime economy is questionable.

Virtually all production affected by the planning system was directed to the requirements of a single customer—the government. The government was more than just a customer; it exercised a great deal of control over the aggregate amounts of inputs, the conditions under which they were employed, and the ultimate "consumers'" use of the results. (Any history of the war will reveal the military's dissatisfaction with some of the weapons it was issued: The lives of servicemen might be substituted for input costs.) The public authorities had, and used, the power to resolve most disputes in their own favor, and to make all decisions on the basis of short-term objectives.

Even though the demands of modern war were complex, the task of meeting them was simple in comparison to those of a peacetime economy. Under normal conditions, the desires of millions of individuals (most of whom prize variety and the right to change their minds) provide the impetus for production. Under such conditions, the priorities to which resource allocation must respond are far less obvious or unidirectional, and their direction and speed of change are less under control. Thus, the success of wartime planning in meeting its objectives over 1941–1945 may not be an accurate indicator of the results that would be obtained if the same planning mechanisms were applied to the needs of a peacetime economy in which individual needs were highly individualistic and variable. In war, the costs of foregone civilian choice are simply ignored.

It must also be remembered that wartime planning enjoyed the overwhelming support of the American population. Given the circumstances of World War II and the obvious objectives of a powerful enemy, there was a consensus that the war's needs must be met—at least at the level of sacrifice actually involved. Ideology, in the sense of popular

■ U.S. industrial production was crucial to Allied military strength during World War II. Without it, well-equipped units such as these shown at Omaha Beach, France, in June 1944, could not have been maintained. *Source:* U.S. Coast Guard Photo/Underwood Photo Archives.

opinion about what is acceptable or "fair," regardless of the goals of official policy, is an important determinant of the actual, as opposed to the physically possible, potential of any economic system.[15] It is difficult to imagine such a national consensus under normal peacetime conditions.

---

[15] D. North, *Structure and Change in Economic History* (New York: Norton, 1981), Chap. 5.

MACROECONOMIC PROBLEMS

World War II and its demands on the American economy ended the Great Depression, but the war created its own macroeconomic problems. The rising level of aggregate demand decreased unemployment, eliminated unused productive capacity, and raised incomes. However, when military spending rose, there were no offsetting reductions in other components of demand. The result was increasing pressure on productive capacity and growing inflationary potential. Some indication of the increase in demand can be garnered from Table 19.2. The labor force grew by over 22 million persons between 1939 and 1945, an increase of about 40 percent. Moreover, as opposed to prewar conditions, virtually the entire wartime labor force was employed, and wages were much higher (military wages were less than those of civilians, but the armed forces were paid in kind as well as money, and the equipment with which they were furnished also added to aggregate demand).

At any instant, an economy's ability to produce additional output is limited by the available amounts of labor, capital, and raw materials, and by the technology with which these are employed. Once all resources are in use and production employs the most efficient techniques available, output cannot be increased without increases in resource supplies, the employment of new technology, or a relaxation of social constraints on the production process; there is a "lid" on output. Once this point is reached, more of any single product can be obtained only by reducing the amount of something else.

During the 1941–1945 period, there were few changes in technology, and supplies of some if not all inputs were fixed or even declined. To some extent, however, social regulations on production were relaxed, and these allowed output to rise. The increasing employment of women outside the home and the opportunities for individuals who had previously been excluded from the jobs that they now performed, or even the labor force itself, are all examples of relaxed social constraints. So too were the extension of the work week and a general increase in the pace of effort. Even so, in an economy as materialistic as that of the United States, and given the short time

available for adjustment, such changes could not keep pace with the increase in demand.

The Impact of Defense Spending

By late 1941, it was clear that the demands of the war would outstrip any conceivable increases in output that were readily attainable. Efforts to raise capacity through conventional methods, such as investment and human training, also used resources, and hence would interfere with production for current use once all resources were employed. The demands of the military placed restrictions on labor force expansion. In addition, there was the problem arising from the additional incomes earned in production of military goods. There was no corresponding increase in civilian production on which those vastly increased incomes could be spent. The multiplier process made the rise in demand greater than just the initial increase in incomes. In total, then, the potential volume of spending was rising beyond the ability of the economy to satisfy demand at current prices. Inflation is an inevitable companion of the extreme levels of demand in times of total war.

Spending could rise without limit, but as the previous paragraphs indicate, there were steadily increasing restrictions on the potential increase in physical output. Nor was it possible to restrain spending. Government expenditures, particularly in the early years of the war, could not be decreased. Indeed, there was painful evidence that current military spending was inadequate. As resources had to be bid away from other employment, military spending was likely to accelerate still further. Simultaneously, if consumers found that their higher incomes actually bought fewer goods and services as the output of civilian products fell to allow greater military output, incentives might suffer. They might also suffer if taxes were raised sufficiently to finance the entire volume of military spending: Even though inflationary pressures might be muted, aftertax incomes would be no greater or even smaller than they had been before the war, despite a much greater work effort. Thus, government faced a delicate task. There seemed to be no method of financing the war that avoided the problem of balancing a diversion of output with the maintenance of incentives.

Wartime Finance

Increases in government spending could be financed through increased taxes, borrowing, or the creation of new money. In the end, a combination of all three methods was employed. About half the war's costs were tax-financed, a considerably higher portion than in either the Civil War or World War I. As incomes rose, the tax revenues of the federal government increased even faster because of the progressive nature of the income tax. This did not yield sufficient revenues, however, and the tax structure was revised. Rates were increased, and the range of incomes liable to taxation was extended downward in each year from 1940 through 1944. By the latter year, the effective rate on taxable income in excess of $1 million per year was 90 percent, and all incomes of $600 or more were subject to tax. Prior to 1940, all incomes under $5,000 had been exempt. Since prices in 1940 were roughly one-tenth their 1992 level, and real incomes were much lower, income tax burdens now were borne by middle-income groups and to some extent even the poor, as well as the rich who had traditionally been subject to income levies. These changes raised the number of persons filing income tax returns from 7.5 million in 1940 to 49.9 million in 1944.[16]

The government also began withholding taxes from wages and salaries as they were paid, rather than allowing individuals to settle their tax obligations with a single annual payment. The corporate income tax was increased, an excess profits tax levied, and excise taxes raised and extended. The changes raised the internal revenues of the federal government from $5.3 to $40.1 billion over the 1940–1944 period, but at the same time expenditures rose from $9.1 to $95 billion. The result was (then) unprecedented levels of federal deficits: over $45 billion in each of the war's last three years.[17] These were financed largely by borrowing from nonbank institutions and from the public.

Had the government only borrowed funds that would otherwise have been spent by the lenders, this borrowing would not have been inflationary. However, the scope of bond financing was far greater than this spending diversions alone could support. On the day after Pearl Harbor, the Federal Reserve had assured the Treasury that the central bank would buy at par (face value) all government bonds that could not be sold elsewhere on these terms. This pledge made government bonds far more liquid than they had been before it was extended; bond owners could convert them into cash at their face value at any time. The federal government's debt rose by about $215 billion during the war. Of this amount, the Federal Reserve Banks purchased $21 billion. Commercial banks, responding to Federal Reserve encouragement, bought another $60 billion.[18] Currency in circulation increased by $17 billion.

The result was a sharp increase in the money supply, which more than doubled over the war years, and continued to rise, although at a slower rate, for some years thereafter. As long as the Federal Reserve was committed to

---

[16] Tax data are from *Historical Statistics,* 2:1110.

[17] *Historical Statistics,* 2:1105, 1107, 1114.
[18] Gordon, *Economic Instability and Growth,* 85–87.

■ Bond sale rallies were major events during World War II.
Source: Reprinted with special permission of North America Syndicate.

■ World War II curtailed civilian economic activity. Scenes like these were prevalent during the conflict. *Source:* H. Armstrong Roberts.

supporting government bonds prices, the central bank was essentially powerless to control, or at any rate to reduce, the money supply. Open-market operations could not be employed, because bond sales might require price reductions. The discount rate was no longer a control mechanism, because commercial banks could sell bonds to the Federal Reserve at guaranteed prices in lieu of borrowing. In any case, commercial banks had large excess reserves when the war began. Reserve requirements had been raised to their legal maximum in 1941, and no further restraint through this avenue was possible without a change in the law.[19]

---

[19] M. Friedman and A. Schwartz, *A Monetary History of the United States, 1867–1960* (Princeton, N.J.: Princeton University Press, 1962), 556.

Inflation

The increase in the money supply, coupled with highly expansionary fiscal policy, made rapid inflation inevitable. The federal deficit was now about ten times its peak in the 1930s, and there was no question but that the economy had regained full employment levels. The increase in the aggregate price level was surprisingly small: only about one-third from 1940 through 1945. Most of the increase occurred before the United States was fully mobilized. As Table 19.2 indicates, the general price deflator increased about 21 percent from 1940 through 1942, and then a further 13 percent to the end of the war. Inflation appears less than might have been expected for a number of reasons. First, and perhaps most importantly, consumer spending rose much less than did incomes. Income can only be either consumed or saved, and the portion of income saved during the war was four to five times the normal rate. It appears that many people expected a return to depression conditions after the war, and they also expected prices to fall. In anticipation of these conditions, they accumulated money and financial assets.[20]

Furthermore, although high wages, abundant overtime, and increased labor force participation rates increased incomes during the war, many of the normal avenues by which people spent increases in income were closed or restricted. New cars, housing, and major appliances were unobtainable at any price; they simply were not being manufactured. Many minor luxuries, such as meat, were strictly rationed. Travel possibilities were very limited. All forms of public transportation were crowded, and military needs had priority. Travel by private automobile was still possible: One could drive anywhere within the limits imposed by the basic gasoline ration of three gallons per week and the virtual unobtainability of replacement tires. Many vacation resorts were closed, and overtime work reduced the opportunity for shopping and leisure activities. There were drawbacks to some of the consumer goods that remained obtainable. Price controls and end-of-the-line materials priorities reduced quality and restricted choice. Finally, appeals to support the war effort by restricted consumption and war-bonds purchases had some effect. Through the combined influence of all these effects on saving and consumption, the velocity of circulation of money declined after 1942, despite high levels of aggregate economic activity.[21]

Rationing and Price Controls

Other more direct efforts were made to reduce the wartime impact of inflation. If money incomes rise and the supply of goods and services fails to keep pace, prices will rise under normal market conditions. But inflation does not affect all people equally; those whose incomes rise faster than the average of all prices will gain an increasing share of all output at the expense of those whose incomes have failed to rise as fast as inflation. In the absence of any other influences on allocation, shortages will be resolved in favor of those with increased ability to pay, and at the expense of those whose real incomes have fallen. During World War II, this tendency was reduced through the use of rationing and of price controls.

To ensure that all consumers received at least some of such items as sugar, coffee, meat, shoes, gasoline, and certain types of clothing, these goods were rationed; they had to be purchased with ration stamps as well as money. The total supply of ration "points" that could

---

[20] Friedman and Schwartz, *Monetary History*, 558–561.

[21] Friedman and Schwartz, *Monetary History*, 558.

be applied to each item was restricted to approximate equality with the supplies available. Stamps were issued to individuals by local boards. The basic allocation was an equal amount per person, with some adjustments for special needs. Thus, the rationing process, by requiring two types of money for the purchase of essential items of consumption, kept them within the reach of most consumers, albeit in smaller amounts than people were willing to buy at the prevailing prices. The system was not perfect: Ration stamps could not be legally exchanged between the individuals to whom they were originally allocated, which limited the expression of individual preferences. Also, there were complaints about the decisions of local ration boards.

Another form of inflation control was a nationwide system of wage and price controls. The Office of Price Administration "froze" prices at their March 1942 levels. After this action, sellers were forbidden to charge more than the ceiling prices established thereby. Some difficulty was encountered almost at once. Food prices and wages could not be controlled for some time, in part due to the political efforts of labor unions and the farm bloc. Price controls, in conjunction with rationing and the lower propensity to consume, reduced the rate of inflation during the war and lessened its impact on those whose incomes lagged behind the rate of price increase. Prices became an imperfect indicator of consumer satisfaction because many markets did not clear at the regulated exchange rates. On the whole, however, the system was reasonably successful for the duration of the war. Where production cost increases threatened to make production of some goods unprofitable at controlled prices, thus threatening their withdrawal from the market, government preferred to subsidize producers rather than allow price increases.

Understandably, under such conditions producers concentrated on those items for which profit margins were greatest and reduced or discontinued output of others. They also attempted to maintain profits by reductions in quality. Some items became virtually unobtainable or disappeared completely, and others bore little resemblance to their prewar counterparts—two factors not reflected in the official price indices.[22]

Since the war raised the aggregate demand for farm products and disrupted the normal channels of world trade, American agriculture benefited from swiftly rising prices. America was the only nation with agricultural exports available to fill the worldwide gap, and farmers were encouraged to increase output by draft deferments, the elimination of all government restrictions on acreage under cultivation (see Chapter 18), and prices guaranteed at not less than 110 percent of parity levels.[23]

Wage Controls

Wage controls proved much more difficult to implement effectively. In 1943, under the "Little Steel" formula, wage increases were to be limited to not more than a 15 percent rise over their 1941 levels. The rationale was that this would compensate workers for inflation, but not add to its pressures. However, the need to remedy both real and imagined inequities, to meet special needs, and to attract labor to crucial programs made it very difficult to hold to this ceiling.[24] Firms resorted to "promotions" and to payment of a growing portion of total compensation in the form of fringe benefits in order to attract and hold labor in the face of growing shortages of qualified workers. Overtime work also allowed labor incomes to rise even in cases where limits on hourly wages were observed. The wage control program thus had only limited success, and

---

[22] Friedman and Schwartz, *Monetary History*, 559.
[23] Robertson, *History of the American Economy*, 525–526.
[24] Gordon, *Economic Instability and Growth*, 89.

■ Consumers were obliged to count ration stamps as well as money when buying many goods during World War II. *Source:* Franklin D. Roosevelt Library.

official statistics on wage levels overrate its achievements. The growth of fringe benefits, such as pensions, medical insurance and programs, and (largely after the war) paid vacations, proved very popular with labor. Particularly in unionized industries, where there was a single organization to assemble and present workers' claims in a unified form, fringe benefits became an increasing portion of employee compensation. Union growth was both legally sanctioned and encouraged by labor-market conditions, and the strength of American unions increased.

The Mixed Success of Economic Controls

The control packages had considerable apparent success in limiting price increases during the war. However, it has been suggested that their impact is overrated. Some observers argue that the controls merely repressed inflation rather than preventing it. This view is supported by the rampant inflation that occurred after controls were abolished in the postwar period.[25] Another consideration not included in the official statistics is the deterioration in quality of many wartime consumer goods.[26]

As always occurs when prices are prevented from equating quantities supplied and demanded, there was evidence of extralegal forms of allocation. Charges that some suppliers were far kinder to favored buyers than they were to the general public were endemic. Black markets, with sales at prices far above the controlled levels, appeared for many products. As economic theory would suggest, black markets were especially common in markets where the spread between legal maximum prices and those customers were willing to pay was greatest, and where the origins of illegally sold commodities could not be traced. There is also some evidence that the controls were more effective earlier in the war. Again, this is hardly surprising; patriotic fervor and support for the war effort was then at its peak, and means of circumventing controls had not yet been devised. This was also the time in which controlled prices were closest to market-determined rates, and so gains from evasion were smaller than they became later.

On the whole, controls were reasonably successful in their primary purpose: They achieved a more widespread distribution of articles that would have been restricted to those with high incomes under free market allocation. They also probably served to maintain general incentives (it can hardly be said that they did so for items whose prices were forced down, however). Over time, price controls in periods of substantial inflationary pressure prevent the market from allocating resources to their highest-value uses, but the process was not continued long enough in World War II to produce major misallocations.

Obviously, the system was not "fair"; it would be impossible to provide solutions regarded as equitable by all parties under circumstances where supplies were far below normal levels. For that matter, unregulated market economies do not produce "fair" distribution of scarce goods either; nor does any other type of economic system. Mistakes were made, both in allocation and in setting up the mechanics of distribution. The controls worked as well as they did because they received a great deal of popular support. Many Americans were willing to put up with shortages and inconvenience if they were convinced that everyone else shared their situation and that the overall purpose of the program causing these irritations was worthwhile. The maintenance of controls imposed some costs on the war effort. At its peak, the Office of Price Administration employed over 300,000 part-time and full-time workers, and there were 5,400 local price and rationing boards.[27]

THE COST OF THE WAR

No economist would advocate war as the proper means of ending a depression. In addition to moral considerations, on which economists are (at best) no better qualified to

---

[25] Friedman and Schwartz, *A Monetary History*, 557–558. See also H. Rockoff, "Price and Wage Controls in Four Wartime Periods," *Journal of Economic History* (June 1981), and "The Response of the Giant Corporation to Wage and Price Controls in World War II," *Journal of Economic History* (March 1981).

[26] H. Rockoff, "Indirect Price Increases and Real Wages During World War II," *Explorations in Economic History* (October 1978).

[27] Robertson, *History of the American Economy*, 712.

comment than anyone else, war is a costly human activity. In a world where all economists agree that the available means of production are already insufficient for the demands placed on them, war destroys some resources and increases the scarcity of many others. It substitutes the consumption of humans for human consumption as the primary goal of economic activity. Had the United States been able to spend $1.476 trillion (the estimated total cost of World War II as of 1990) on sending people to the movies rather than into combat, the expansive effects on the economy would have been equal to those of the same amount of military spending, and those on human welfare very much superior. *Any* massive spending program would have stimulated economic recovery in 1941—or 1933.[28]

However, World War II, or the U.S. role therein, can hardly be viewed exclusively as a

program for economic recovery. In view of the nature of the political opponents that the nation faced in this conflict, the war was a necessary price for the maintenance of our political freedoms. It is easy to imagine scenarios in which the war's cost to the United States would have been far greater.

The war may have been a political necessity, but it cannot be regarded as an unmitigated economic boon. A great portion of wartime economic activity was directed toward ends that had no immediate payoff in enhanced human welfare. The statistical record indicates that World War II levels of real per-capita income in the United States were not regained until the mid-1950s. However, these figures treat the military goods that at times accounted for nearly two-fifths of total output during the war as equivalent to the consumer goods of the later period in their contribution to human well-being. While the benefits of life in a world free of the threats that bulked so large in 1941 must not be

---

[28] *Historical Statistics*, 2:1140.

■ Following the surrender of the Japanese in 1945, Americans did, at last, celebrate peace.
Source: Underwood Photo Archives.

underestimated, surely the income figures understate the increase in welfare that occurred in the decade after 1945. In sum, while we cannot simply subtract the war years' military expenditures from total income to arrive at an accurate measure of welfare, neither can we include them in full.

The Net Result

There were a few economic gains from the war. It can at least be argued that only a political emergency of the war's magnitude could have prompted the increased spending necessary to end the Great Depression. In this case, the gain is the increased understanding of macroeconomics that resulted from the war. There were some results of wartime research that have proved valuable in peacetime: radar, the jet engine, computers, some medical advances, and, for good or ill, nuclear energy.

Probably a better case can be made for the loosening of restrictions on geographic and occupational mobility that wartime changes produced for individuals. Women and minorities gained access to a much wider range of jobs as a result of wartime labor shortages. More importantly, they kept these advances, at least in the form of easier entrance, permanently.[29] Few modern students can imagine how blatant and smotheringly restrictive racial and sexual discrimination was just five decades ago. Such practices cost the United States dearly in wasted human talent. Individual geographic mobility was also greatly enhanced in the war's aftermath. A similar process occurred as firms took wartime contracts for production

of goods they had never considered making in peacetime, and learned the technology of industries other than those in which they had previously operated. Shocks to the established order and continuity of social institutions are an important factor in maintaining economic vitality and competition.[30] So was the rapid introduction and dissemination of new technology that occurred in the postwar period, in part as a consequence of the war's effect on the economy.

The costs of the war were borne largely by those who experienced it. Obviously, a very high portion of the war's costs was paid by the 405,000 Americans who died in service, and the thousands more who were wounded. Enforced military service cost millions of other Americans the higher incomes they could have earned in alternative occupations. The economy lost the foregone potential of all this misallocated or prematurely ended human potential. Loss of investment, perhaps tempered by war-induced technological progress and institutional change, was another cost of the war. The loss of civilian choice of consumption and occupational choice must also be included.

After the euphoria of military victory had faded, Americans had a new concern. The high levels of income and economic activity during the war had clearly stemmed from massive government spending. But military spending had been reduced as soon as victory was achieved in Europe, and with Japan's surrender, it had plummeted. As government spending fell and 12 million military personnel returned to civilian life, what would prevent a recurrence of the Great Depression?

---

[29] Gavin Wright has suggested that these effects were especially pronounced in the South. See *Old South, New South: Revolutions in the Southern Economy Since the Civil War* (New York: Basic Books, 1986), Chaps. 7, 8.

[30] This is a central theme for Mancur Olson. See *The Rise and Decline of Nations: Economic Growth, Stagflation, and Social Rigidities* (New Haven, Conn.: Yale University Press, 1982), Chaps. 2, 3.

SELECTED REFERENCES

Friedman, M., and A. Schwartz. *A Monetary History of the United States, 1867–1960.* Princeton, N.J.: Princeton University Press, 1962.

Gordon, R. *Economic Instability and Growth: The American Record.* New York: Harper & Row, 1974.

Higgs, R. *Crisis and Leviathan: Critical Issues in the Emergence of the Mixed Economy.* New York: Oxford University Press, 1986.

Milward, A. *War, Economy, and Society.* Berkeley, Calif.: University of California Press, 1977.

North, D. *Structure and Change in Economic History.* New York: Norton, 1981.

North, D., T. Anderson, and P. Hill. *Growth and Welfare in the American Past: A New Economic History.* 3d ed. Englewood Cliffs, N.J.: Prentice-Hall, 1983.

Olson, M. *The Rise and Decline of Nations: Economic Growth, Stagflation, and Social Rigidities.* New Haven, Conn.: Yale University Press, 1982.

Rockoff, H. *Drastic Measures: A History of Wage and Price Controls in the United States.* New York: Cambridge University Press, 1984.

U.S. Department of Commerce, Bureau of the Census. *Historical Statistics of the United States: Colonial Times to 1970.* 2 vols. Washington, D.C.: Government Printing Office, 1975.

Vatter, H. *The U.S. Economy in World War II.* New York: Columbia University Press, 1985.

Wright, G. *Old South, New South: Revolutions in the Southern Economy Since the Civil War.* New York: Basic Books, 1986.

The Modern American Economy and Its Prospects

4.

Los Angeles
(population 1,970,358)

1945 to Present

Census figures refer to the year 1950.

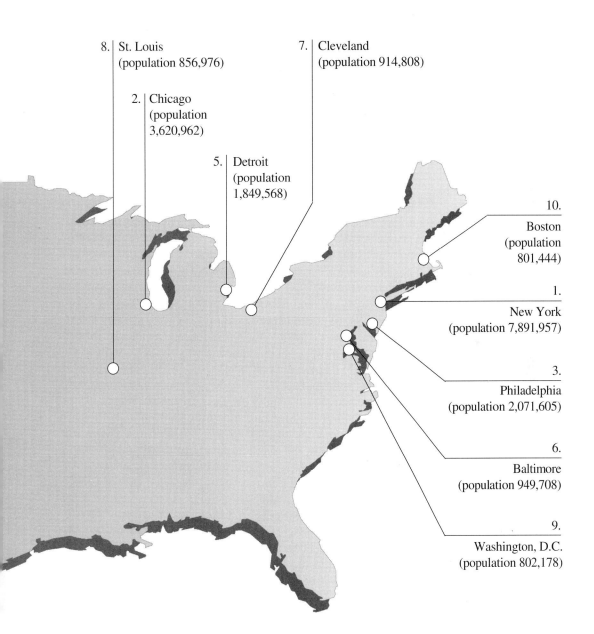

8. | St. Louis
(population 856,976)

2. | Chicago
(population
3,620,962)

7. | Cleveland
(population 914,808)

5. | Detroit
(population
1,849,568)

10.
Boston
(population
801,444)

1.
New York
(population 7,891,957)

3.
Philadelphia
(population 2,071,605)

6.
Baltimore
(population 949,708)

9.
Washington, D.C.
(population 802,178)

*T*he four-and-one-half decades after World War II have, in general, been characterized by "good times." Most indicators of economic welfare have shown substantial improvement; the health of the economy and the welfare of U.S. citizens have improved greatly since the 1930s. Real gross national product has tripled; per-capita real income was 2.37 times its 1947 level by 1990. Postwar recessions have been far less severe than the Great Depression, or even the lesser slumps of other periods, and their impact on the individual has been muted by a growing range of social welfare programs. Life expectancy and other indicators of health have increased. Levels of education have shown significant improvement. The gains in income have been widely shared: Although the distribution and even the definition of income remain areas of controversy in economic discussion, today the arguments center around the extent to which long-run income distribution has become more equal.

As were all previous eras of economic growth, this was a period of significant change. Population rose and shifted toward the West and South. Employment growth centered on services and government. New industries appeared as older sectors, in some cases synonymous with U.S. industrial strength, declined. Above all, the economic impact of government increased.

Recently it has been stated that the postwar period can be viewed as two rather disparate eras. The first, from 1945 to the late 1960s, was a time of unprecedented prosperity and progress, with few serious problems. Productivity and incomes rose at rates well above long-term trends, income distribution became more equal, and poverty and social and economic discrimination declined. Most indicators of health and well-being improved. Government economic policies, both micro- and macroeconomic, appeared successful. Countercyclical policy could be used to offset recessions; resources could be marshalled for any purpose important enough to merit attention. Americans could view the rest of the world from a detached viewpoint because foreign trade was a small portion of GNP and American industrial supremacy could be taken as a matter of course. American goods found ready markets overseas, while most nations struggled to find exports with which to finance them. The United States could use its persistent trade surpluses to provide aid and investment to nations less fortunate.

Around 1970 the picture changed. Incomes continued to grow, but the pace became more irregular. The reduction in poverty achieved previously not only ceased, but was reversed in the late 1970s and early 1980s. The productivity gains that had underlain the earlier gains also slowed; for a time incomes rose only because a growing portion of the population was in the labor force, offsetting stagnant or even declining wages. Effortless success in foreign trade was replaced by a struggle in which other nations appeared to enjoy as many advantages as the United States once had. Trade deficits replaced surpluses, and were sustainable only because foreigners purchased American securities, firms, and other assets with the proceeds of their exchanges with this country. Government policies were increasingly difficult to formulate and often ineffective. Macroeconomic stabilization policy, once so promising, seemed unable to deliver either price stability or full employment, let alone both. A growing sense of apprehension replaced the optimism of the initial postwar years.

The futile war in Vietnam seemed to exemplify the nation's problems: Massive expenditures resulted in (at best) a military draw and a clear-cut political defeat. The United States spent a larger portion of GNP on education and health than did either Germany or Japan, but achieved less by most measures. Research and development spending was greater than any other nation's, but productivity growth fell. Massive transfer payments after 1970 did little to reduce the poverty rate, except among the elderly. Efforts to respond to weaknesses sometimes revealed little consensus even on the nature, dimensions, and causes of problems: unemployment, income distribution, discrimination, labor productivity, and the relation of the environment to economic change are examples. Under these circumstances, formulation of coherent policies, let alone those integrated into some overall framework, was impossible. To some, it appeared that the United States could no longer support the full range of its political and economic ambitions. Others stressed the choices imposed on the United States by a changing world. Many implied unpleasant consequences for at least some Americans. Even so, it appeared to foreign observers that the U.S. reaction to these developments was to see each as a permanent cataclysm rather than a competitive challenge.[1]

No previous 45 years of U.S. economic history have been entirely free of problems. If there is one source of concern over the performance of the American economy that is common to both parts of this period, it is inflation. Consumer prices in 1990 were nearly seven times their 1946 levels. Since 1945 there have been no substantial periods of deflation, and few of even approximate price stability. Inflation has increasingly become divorced from other economic indicators. Once inflation seemed a phenomenon associated with high levels of economic activity, such as the very peak of peacetime booms or major wars. More recently, however, even though there is still a loose association between increased rates of inflation and levels of real economic activity, some positive rate of general price increase seems to occur at virtually any tolerable level of employment and output.

Once expectations of inflation become embedded in the economy, economic activity is adversely affected. The present value of long-term gains is reduced, and business decisions are skewed toward short-run profits. Buying existing goods (real estate, artwork, precious metals, and such) and

---

[1] See "Sam, Sam, the Paranoid Man," *Economist* (January 18–24, 1992).

holding them for appreciation appears to produce higher profits than increasing output. Saving and investment are reduced in favor of current consumption. Tax rates based on nominal rather than real values of assets, profits, and incomes further discourage additions to capacity. These attitudes can be very difficult to dispel; the severe recession of 1981–1982 was one price paid to break them. Inflation was a nearly universal condition, but the rates of price increase during 1974 and the 1979–1981 period equalled or exceeded those of every year since 1929 except the 1946–1947 reconversion boom.[2] Even though inflation subsided in the 1980s, it did not disappear.

Unemployment and attempts to reduce it suffered from problems of measurement and lack of understanding of long-term changes in its rates, causes, and impact. Currently, it appears that the "natural rate" of unemployment is perhaps 6 percent of the work-force. This rate is higher than that of earlier decades, due to changes in labor force participation rates, demographic factors, and social institutions, such as welfare, unemployment compensation, and tax policy. These determinants had changed long before their impact was noted, and policy adjustment is still incomplete.

It seemed that even a growing economy could not simultaneously provide environmental protection, increased occupational health and safety, economic support for the needy, greater levels of defense spending, and continued improvements in the aftertax real incomes of most Americans. (Whether it had done so before 1970 depended on aspirations then as much as cloudy memories today.) The economic situation of postwar America was still what it had always been: Nothing was free, and efforts to achieve one goal involved opportunity costs in slower progress or even lost ground in the struggle to attain other objectives simultaneously. But were the trade-offs worsening?

Concern grew that all new ends might have to be achieved through reallocation of existing output from other sectors. In the modern era, economic growth had become increasingly dependent on increases in productivity (increases in output per unit of input). In the 1970s, the rate of productivity improvement apparently declined and in some years even became negative.[3] Although increases in income from higher labor force participation rates were welcomed, their source was an obvious long-run dead end. In consequence, there was growing interest in the sources and trends in productivity within the U.S. economy.

---

[2] Council of Economic Advisors, *Economic Report of the President* (Washington, D.C.: Government Printing Office, 1985), 296.

[3] E. Denison, "Explanations of Declining Productivity Growth," Brookings General Series #354 (Washington, D.C.: 1979). W. Baumol, S. Blackman, and E. Wolff, *Productivity and American Leadership* (Cambridge, Mass.: MIT Press, 1989), see little evidence of a long-term decline in U.S. productivity growth. They view rates achieved over 1947–1965 as abnormally high. An alternative but also optimistic view is that of M. Darby. See his "The U.S. Productivity Showdown: A Case of Statistical Myopia," *American Economic Review* (June 1984).

THE DIMENSIONS OF GROWTH

In 1945, the U.S. gross national product in dollars of constant (1982) purchasing power was $1.355 trillion. That figure may have substantially overstated the level of economic welfare, because it was heavily influenced by war production; perhaps a more realistic base for the era would be 1947's $1.067 trillion. By 1990, real GNP had risen to $4.148 trillion in the same terms. Since the overall price level was nearly six times its 1947 level, the increase in current dollars is much greater, from $235.2 billion to $5.519

Table V.1   United States Economic Performance, 1946–1990

Year	Real GNP (Billions of 1982 Dollars)	Population (Millions)	Per-Capita Disposable Income (1982 Dollars)	Price Index* (1982–1984 = 100)	Civilian Unemployment (Percentage)
1946	$1,096.9	141.4	$5,115	19.5	3.9%
1948	1,108.7	146.6	5,000	24.1	3.8**
1950	1,203.7	152.3	5,220	24.1	5.3
1952	1,380.0	157.6	5,379	26.5	3.0
1954	1,416.2	163.0	5,505	26.9	5.5
1956	1,525.6	168.9	5,881	27.2	4.1
1958	1,539.2	174.9	5,908	28.9	6.8
1960	1,665.3	180.7	6,036	29.6	5.5
1962	1,799.4	186.5	6,271	30.2	5.5
1964	1,973.3	191.9	6,727	31.0	5.2
1966	2,208.3	196.6	7,280	32.4	3.8
1968	2,365.6	200.7	7,728	34.8	3.6
1970	2,416.2	205.1	8,143	38.8	4.9
1972	2,608.5	209.9	8,562	41.8	5.6
1974	2,729.3	213.9	8,867	49.3	5.6
1976	2,826.7	218.0	9,175	56.9	7.7
1978	3,115.2	222.6	9,735	65.2	6.1
1980	3,187.1	227.8	9,722	82.4	7.1
1982	3,166.0	232.5	9,725	96.5	9.7
1984	3,501.4	237.0	10,419	103.9	7.5
1986	3,717.9	241.6	10,905	109.6	7.0
1988	4,016.9	246.3	11,368	118.3	5.5
1990***	4,155.8	251.4	11,508	130.7	5.5

* Consumer price index.
** Basis of computation changed to include only those over 16 years old; formerly those 14–16 included.
*** Preliminary data.
Source: Council of Economic Advisors, *Economic Report of the President, 1991* (Washington, D.C.: Government Printing Office, 1991).

trillion. Population increased as well as income, so the rise in per-capita income figures was more modest. Real disposable income per person was $11,374 in 1990 and only $4,780 in 1947.[4]

The median income of American families in 1989 dollars rose from $16,700 in 1947 to $34,213 in 1990.[5] These figures reflect only one of two important influences: Incomes were growing, but family size was shrinking, so the family income figures slightly understate the rise in per-capita income. In addition to this increase in their purchasing power, Americans had access to a much wider range of government services and fringe benefits than ever before. By at least some measures (discussed in detail in later chapters), income distribution in the United States became substantially more equal (particularly to 1970) as well.

Unemployment rates were lower than they had been in the 1930s. Although there were recessions in 1949, 1954, 1958, 1961, 1970, 1974–1975, 1980–1982, and 1990 to the present (see Table V.1), the jobless rate reached 10 percent of the work force only for portions of 1982 and 1983. For those years and for 1975, the yearly unemployment rate exceeded 8 percent. The average unemployment rate for the 1945–1984 period was somewhat higher than those recorded for earlier periods of similar length[6] and average duration of unemployment rose—a development that may reflect the "cushioning" effects of unemployment compensation, favorable tax treatment of the unemployed, and changes in the demography of the work force more than difficulty in finding new jobs. Similar developments took place in the advanced industrial economies of western Europe, in particular those with generous welfare systems. Certainly there was no failure to produce additional jobs: The number of people employed in civilian occupations within the United States increased from 60 million in 1950 to 117.9 million in 1990, and the pace of job creation increased after 1970.[7]

The Changing Labor Force

Changes in the composition of the labor force assumed a new importance. In at least one major study, they were found to be the primary determinant of the unemployment rate, the distribution of income, and even the birthrate. Richard Easterlin concluded that the proportion of workers of various ages in the labor force, especially the portion of young males, has now replaced aggregate growth in the labor force as the single most important influence on not only aggregate unemployment rates, but also the distri-

---

[4] Figures from *Economic Report, 1991*, 286, 288, 317, 351.
[5] *Economic Report*, 320.
[6] S. Lebergott, "Changes in Unemployment, 1800–1960," in R. Fogel and S. Engerman, eds., *The Reinterpretation of American Economic History* (New York: Harper & Row, 1971), 82–83.
[7] *Economic Report, 1991*, 324.

bution of income between age cohorts, female labor force participation rates, and the birthrate.[8]

In Easterlin's view, before 1960 young males were in relatively short supply because of declining birthrates in the preceding decades and the reduction in immigration. Under these circumstances, young men found jobs easy to obtain. Salaries were generous by their parents' standards and promotions readily obtainable. Because of the scarcity of young males and long-run social trends, female labor force participation rates increased from 1940 to 1960. (In Easterlin's view, women of all ages have tended to compete for jobs more directly with young males than they do with older men, whose jobs have required greater training and skills than those possessed by most first-time female job-force entrants.) Since young men enjoyed such favorable income and employment prospects before 1960, labor force participation by younger women was restricted. Family formation and the birthrate increased sharply because families could afford more children. Women entering the labor force in this period tended to be from the older-age cohorts.

After 1960, as the children of the "baby boom" of the 1940s and 1950s entered the labor market, young men faced much less favorable prospects. The large numbers in their age cohort made competition for jobs much more intense. Labor force participation by older women declined, but that of younger women increased, producing even more severe job competition for young men. The high proportion of young women seeking and holding jobs after 1960 and the less promising long-run job outlook for the generation entering the labor force in the subsequent two decades resulted in lower birthrates. Other consequences of the labor market situation were higher rates of unemployment, divorce, and other indicators of social stress. Easterlin concluded that the relative position of each generation, that is, the effort required to match or better parents' living standards at comparable ages, is fixed for the cohort's entire working life.

If the Easterlin model is correct, the lower 1960–1980 birthrates will result in reduced unemployment in the 1980s (see Table V.1) and 1990s, an increase in the birthrate, and improved income prospects for younger workers as they enter the labor force. In this model, "long swings" of approximately two generations recur. In the swings, the experience of workers just entering the labor force generates major influences on economic growth, unemployment, the birthrate, and other indicators of social well-being. If this analysis is correct (to date the evidence is mixed), the traditional methods of reducing long-term unemployment by stimulating aggregate demand (the "Keynesian" prescription) will not work, since unemployment stems from demographic rather than economic factors. The relative improvement in new workers' employment prospects will occur whether expansionary macroeconomic policies are followed or not.

---

[8] R. Easterlin, "What Will 1984 Be Like? Socioeconomic Implications of Recent Trends in Age Structure," *Demography* (November 1978).

Claudia Goldin's recent work on female labor force participation rates and job success strongly complements Easterlin's work.[9] Goldin discovered that each female-age cohort's work experience differed, and that the cohort's relative success tended to be fixed by the circumstances under which it entered the labor force. Social factors such as discrimination, relative levels of education, birthrates, and attitudes toward nonhousehold work were also significant.

After 1940 the influence of these social factors declined, supporting greater female labor force participation. After 1950, fewer young, unmarried women entered the work force, improving job prospects for all women. The availability of new part-time jobs in a generally prosperous economy also improved their prospects. Older women who gained experience during World War II found themselves more employable when they became middle-aged.[10] Increasingly, women's work experience and job tenure now are similar to men's, even for married women with small children. The result is an increase in women's relative productivity and incomes as contrasted with men's.[11]

The relatively rapid growth in the U.S. population and especially the labor force may also help to explain the decline in labor productivity growth relative to other nations. Labor supplies (particularly those of less-skilled new workers and married women) increased rapidly in the United States, while investment rates had been low. Thus, capital per worker, especially new capital embodying the latest technical improvements, rose more slowly than in foreign countries. Since this deficiency was not offset by increased human capital, productivity growth suffered the double handicaps of lower capital-labor ratios and decreased input quality.

Despite its possible effects on the individuals involved, the rapid growth of the U.S. labor force in the 1960s and 1970s was a major contributor to the economic growth of those decades. Widespread impressions to the contrary, U.S. real economic growth in the 1970s was almost exactly equal to that of earlier, more fondly remembered decades, and, if anything, it slightly surpassed the gains recorded over 1900–1929 and 1946–1970. The record for the 1980s is marginally better, at least to 1989.[12]

In terms of international comparisons, the growth record of the United States since World War II is modest. Italy, France, West Germany, and especially Japan grew faster than the United States over these four decades. In recent years, U.S. performance is somewhat better. (See Table V.2.)

---

[9] C. Goldin, *Understanding the Gender Gap: An Economic History of American Women* (New York: Oxford University Press, 1990).

[10] Goldin, *Understanding the Gap*, 126–142, 159, 180, 214.

[11] Goldin, *Understanding the Gap*, 216.

[12] Bureau of Economic Analysis, *Long Term Economic Growth, 1860–1970*, Part V. Cited in S. Lebergott, *The Americans: An Economic Record* (New York: Norton, 1984), 494. Later data from *Statistical Abstract of the U.S.* (Washington, D.C.: Government Printing Office, 1991), 433.

SOURCES OF GROWTH

Since there was prolonged economic growth in this era, we would expect that changes in the American economy over the period facilitated the rise in output. Perhaps the most obvious growth-producing change was a major increase in the mobility of resources. Overwhelmingly, resources were transferred from areas and occupations in which the incomes they generated were low to those in which their earnings were greater. Agriculture, a sector of chronically low incomes, continued to lose workers to other types of employment. The agricultural work force declined from 10 million workers in 1945 to less than 3.2 million by 1990, and the exodus from farm employment was by no means over.[13]

Manufacturing employment increased very slightly from the immediate postwar period to the mid-1960s, then declined until 1970. The figure for 1990 is about 3 percent less.[14] If construction and mining employment figures are added ("goods-producing industries"), employment in this sector has risen by about 2.5 million since 1970, to 25 million, and the all-time peak was 26.5 million in 1979.[15] Despite claims that the United States is "deindustrializing," it is the only major market economy (not excepting Japan) to experience a gain in industrial jobs over 1960–1990. Manufacturing jobs did decline sharply as a portion of total employment. The bulk of the increase in the labor force found jobs in services, finance, wholesale and retail trade, and, particularly after 1960, with state and local government.[16]

Mobility increased between regions as well. People moved to the Pacific Coast, to Florida, and later to the entire "Sun Belt" along the Gulf Coast and the Mexican border. In more recent years, areas of "high-tech" employment have gained, and those centered on high-cost energy production, such as most oil-producing regions, have lost jobs and population. Urbanization increased, even though the populations of many large central cities stabilized or even declined after 1960. By that date, fully 87 percent of the entire American population lived, worked, or both in broadly defined metropolitan areas.[17] A short-lived movement of population back to the countryside and to small towns in the early 1970s was soon overwhelmed by rising energy costs and the continuing decline of agriculture.

Over the initial portion of the era, income disparities between regions declined. Some traditionally low-income regions, such as the South, achieved above-average rates of income gains. Improved communications also bettered the circumstances of even those who stayed put. Firms located

---

[13] *Economic Report, 1991*, 322.
[14] *Economic Report, 1991*, 334.
[15] *Economic Report, 1991*, 334.
[16] *Economic Report, 1991*, 335.
[17] L. Davis, R. Easterlin, and W. Parker et al. *American Economic Growth: An Economist's History of the United States* (New York: Harper & Row, 1972), 603.

Table V.2 Growth Rates in Real GNP, 1961–1990

Country	1961–1965 Annual Average	1965–1970 Annual Average	1971–1975 Annual Average	1976–1983 Annual Average	1984
United States	4.6%	3.0%	2.2%	2.5%	6.8%
Canada	5.3	4.6	5.2	2.7	6.3
Japan	12.4	11.0	4.3	4.4	5.1
France	5.9	5.4	4.0	2.5	1.3
West Germany	4.7	4.2	2.1	2.4	3.3
Italy	4.8	6.5	2.4	3.3	3.0
Great Britain	3.2	2.5	2.1	1.7	2.1

Source: Council of Economic Advisors, *Economic Report of the President, 1991* (Washington, D.C.: Government Printing Office, 1991), 411.

new plants in regions where returns on investment were higher, either because capital was scarce in relation to other inputs (chiefly labor) or to become better situated in regard to new and growing market areas. Labor mobility aids the formation of new industries, which are crucial to long-term economic growth.

The Critical Importance of Productivity Growth

To a greater extent than ever before, economic growth was now derived from productivity improvements rather than increases in the amount of inputs. Growth of the labor force was not rapid by nineteenth-century standards (although few other industrial nations approached U.S. rates), nor was the aggregate rate of investment high. The contribution of raw materials to output decreased substantially over this period. Consequently, maintaining the rate of increase in real GNP at the historical trend level depended on increasing the amount of output per unit of input. By one estimate, over 80 percent of the increase in output per worker in the postwar period can be attributed to productivity increases.[18] Increasing or even maintaining labor productivity growth with the low rates of investment prevalent in the United States became increasingly difficult.

In agriculture, where productivity gains were especially rapid (aggregate output rose despite a two-thirds reduction in the work force and a slight decline in acreage), farmers literally worked themselves out of their traditional jobs as the demand for agricultural products continued to lag behind

---

[18] Denison, "Explanations of Declining Productivity Growth."

1985	1986	1987	1988	1989	1990
3.4%	2.7%	3.4%	4.5%	2.5%	.9%
4.7	3.3	4.0	4.4	3.0	1.1
4.9	2.5	4.6	5.7	4.9	6.1
1.9	2.5	2.2	3.8	3.6	2.5
1.9	2.3	1.6	3.7	3.9	4.2
2.6	2.5	3.0	4.2	3.2	2.6
3.6	3.9	4.7	4.6	2.2	1.6

income growth. In manufacturing, output per worker rose rapidly, but demand for manufactured products rose at about the same rate as aggregate income, and manufacturing's share of GNP showed little change. Consequently, the sector enrolled a declining portion of all workers.

The Marriage of Science and Technology

New technology has often been successful in developing substitutes for particularly scarce or hard-to-work inputs, in addition to new products and methods. As with any other aspect of economic life, however, the gains are not free. Increased productivity achieved through these means requires interaction between researchers and those who use the methods and tools they develop. The ultimate human controllers of an automated assembly line must be familiar with a range of techniques and equipment far beyond the intellectual grasp of even the best engineers of a generation ago. On a more homely level, the use of a word processor may greatly enhance literary productivity, but it also demands an investment in logic from its operator. Broadening the market for such tools requires their producers to make them more "user-friendly." New methods and equipment can be acquired only through investment, which implies foregone consumption, that is, better tomorrows have a cost today.

Increases in productivity, stemming as they do largely from human ingenuity, allow far more optimistic assessments of humanity's long-run material prospects than ever before. They are based on the one resource that can fairly be termed inexhaustible: human imagination. Moreover, they offer an escape from many of the constraints imposed by other resource trends. Prospects for sizable growth in the American labor force over the next few decades are slim without a revolution in social attitudes, but the new methods allow increase in output per person to substitute quite effectively for the products of a larger number of hands. Productivity increases must be the dominant source of American economic growth over the next 20 years, and probably far beyond.

Improved productive capabilities have allowed Americans a greater range of choice in several senses. First, the same amounts of product may be turned out in fewer working hours, allowing for increased leisure time at no sacrifice in conventionally measured living standards. Alternatively, they can be used to raise those material standards or provide newer, more varied, or qualitatively superior goods.

New Choices and Adjustments in a Complex World

With increased productivity, humanity gains some welcome additions to the attainable range of social and personal choices as well. Growing output reduces the opportunity cost of devoting resources to environmental preservation. (This is an area in which intelligent choices are impossible except through utilization of the new scientific methods of analysis.) They also reduce the cost of aiding the less fortunate, promoting further growth, or in general that of pursuing whatever ends individuals or society may deem worthwhile.

The new capabilities have also produced new sources of both market and governmental failure. The modern economy is more crowded, both in terms of physical proximity in urban areas and in the sense that there are more activities that can affect the welfare of others without their consent. Producers' or consumers' use of the air and water as dumps for annoying or dangerous refuse, traffic congestion, or loud music that annoys neighbors are examples. Growing international trade and investment necessarily involve political relationships with other countries. In many cases, new circumstances and knowledge generate need for new forms of regulation. Technology may produce new forms of property (for example, air rights over an urban building site) that require new forms of law to secure them. However, the expansion of government to further worthy social objectives is a two-edged sword. Government action may be used to secure individuals' property rights, but it can also be used to limit them or transfer some of the proceeds they generate to others.

Two facets of recent economic development in the United States have encouraged rent-seeking. First, a wider role for government regulatory activity has been accepted, often on rather flimsy justification. Second, the gains from rent-seeking are likely to be much greater in a society where average incomes and wealth are high. The very pace of change threatens some types of jobs, life-styles, and consumption patterns. One result is efforts to prevent such change or to reduce its effects on those who feel adversely affected.

The Continuing Necessity of Choice

Widespread rent-seeking is not economically neutral; its effects extend far beyond the redistribution of existing wealth or incomes. Resources must be used to promote such transfers, and those who stand to lose will devote resources to the defense of their property or incomes. The services of lobbyists, tax consultants, lawyers, environmental and consumer advocates, and the host of others familiar to modern society cannot be simultaneously devoted to promoting or resisting the transfer of income and to generating more. As a result of their activities, aggregate output is reduced below the levels potentially possible: Rent-seekers' gains are less than the cost of their activities to society as a whole. However, as long as the direct gains to rent-seekers exceed the costs they incur to achieve them, such activities will continue.[19] Rent-seeking may not be directed toward direct transfers of income; its goal may be government protection from competition, so that costs are imposed on customers or would-be competitors rather than on taxpayers.

In addition—and this may well be the source of much of our current dissatisfaction—despite all the technological marvels that have enhanced our economic capabilities, choices between the ends to which these means may be devoted are still necessary. Human wants are the ultimate growth industry; they seem to increase slightly faster than the ability to meet them, no matter how rapidly productive capacities rise. At any instant, greater effort in pursuit of a single economic goal means that fewer resources are available to meet some other want. The growth of government may contribute to the continuation of economic scarcity. Often even successful responses to problems through government—those resulting in permanent resolution of the problem—produce an agency in search of a mission. Either there will be insistence that even vestiges of the original difficulty must be eliminated, regardless of cost (a phrase whose implications for economic efficiency are only too clear), or the agency looks for new dragons to slay to justify its continued existence. In other cases, the aims and methods of various agencies may conflict (the U.S. government subsidizes both lung-cancer research and tobacco production).

SELECTED REFERENCES

Anderson, T., and P. Hill. *The Birth of a Transfer Society.* Stanford, Calif.: Hoover Institution Press, 1980.

Baumol, W., and K. McLennan. *Productivity Growth and U.S. Competitiveness.* New York: Oxford University Press, 1989.

---

[19] M. Olson, *The Growth and Decline of Nations: Economic Growth, Stagflation, and Social Rigidities* (New Haven, Conn.: Yale University Press, 1982), provides an excellent discussion of this problem.

Baumol, W., S. Blackman, and E. Wolff. *Productivity and American Leadership.* Cambridge, Mass.: MIT Press, 1989.

Council of Economic Advisors. *Economic Report of the President.* Washington, D.C.: Government Printing Office, annual eds.

Davis, L., R. Easterlin, W. Parker et al. *American Economic Growth: An Economist's History of the United States.* New York: Harper & Row, 1972.

Denison, E. *Accounting for United States Economic Growth, 1929–1969.* Washington, D.C.: Brookings Institute, 1974.

Goldin, C. *Understanding the Gender Gap: An Economic History of American Women.* New York: Oxford University Press, 1990.

Gordon, R. *Economic Instability and Growth: The American Record.* New York: Harper & Row, 1974.

North, D. *Structure and Change in Economic History.* New York: Norton, 1981.

North, D., T. Anderson, and P. Hill. *Growth and Welfare in the American Past: A New Economic History.* 3d ed. Englewood Cliffs, N.J.; Prentice-Hall, 1983.

Olson, M. *The Rise and Decline of Nations: Economic Growth, Stagflation, and Social Mobility.* New Haven, Conn.: Yale University Press, 1982.

Porter, M. *The Competitive Advantage of Nations.* New York: Free Press, 1990.

Rosenberg, N. *Technology and American Economic Growth.* New York: M.E. Sharpe, 1972.

Rosenberg, N., and L. Birdzell. *How the West Grew Rich: The Economic Transformation of the Western World.* New York: Basic Books, 1986.

Simon, J. *The Ultimate Resource.* Princeton, N.J.: Princeton University Press, 1981.

Vatter, H. *The U.S. Economy in the 1950s.* New York: Norton, 1963.

THE PRIVATE
SECTOR, 1945–1984

At times it appears that the course of economic affairs in the postwar United States has been largely determined by government. Nearly all sectors of the economy are now affected by government to a greater extent than was the case even under the New Deal, and the influence of government is vastly greater and more pervasive than it was prior to the 1930s. The share of income that originates in the expenditures of all levels of government within the U.S. economy has risen from 19.5 percent in 1948 (when normal postwar conditions were established) to 32 percent by 1970 and 34.9 percent in 1990.[1] Government purchases of goods and services, however, were 8.3 percent of GNP; the balance was transfer payments, which changed the distribution of activity within the private economy.[2] Despite growth in government activity, the performance of the private sector continued to be the dominant force affecting economic welfare in the postwar United States.

THE CONTINUED DOMINANCE OF MARKET TRANSACTIONS

The market influenced employment patterns, regional growth, and income levels. Although some industries (for example, aerospace and defense-related production) were almost completely dependent on government demand, the gains and losses of most regions, occupations, and industries stemmed from changes produced by the interaction of supply and demand within the market sector. Industries whose products were in unusually great demand achieved above-average growth. Transfers of resources into more efficient uses and, even more, improvements within the same occupation were even more important for aggregate economic growth than had been the case in earlier periods.

As social restrictions on the occupations of women and minority groups decreased, these changes made possible the more efficient allocation of economic resources as well as the correction of longstanding social injustice. The reduction in employment discrimination benefited the aggregate economy as well as the individuals directly affected; it allowed the same work force to produce more output. The gains to the American economy from this source were potentially of an even greater magnitude than those already achieved through allocation of jobs by merit among the rest of the labor force.

Geographic Mobility

Social change combined with geographic mobility to give the United States a work force whose response to new opportunities was nothing short of extraordinary. The legacy of individual mobility that had always characterized American labor was even further developed after 1945. The U.S. population is highly mobile in geographic terms, and the impetus for mobility remains economic. U.S. citizens move to areas of higher wages, better climate, and improved prospects, and they do so as cheaply as possible.[3] High labor mobility in response to economic incentives can be a major advantage of the United States in a world where markets, resource patterns, and

[1] Council of Economic Advisors, *Economic Report of the President, 1991* (Washington, D.C.: Government Printing Office, 1991), 296.

[2] *Economic Report, 1991*, 288–289.

[3] C. Galloway and R. Vedder, "The Mobility of Native Americans," *Journal of Economic History* (September 1971). See also M. Greenwood, "An Analysis of the Determinants of Labor Mobility in the United States," *Review of Economics and Statistics* (May 1969).

especially technology change at ever-increasing rates. In another view, however, the high rate of job switching among American workers limits the acquisition and upgrading of job skills that are critical for the maintenance of long-run international competitiveness.[4]

The dimensions of geographic mobility are staggering. Although slightly more than one U.S. family in six has moved in each year since 1980, as opposed to one in five two decades ago, the decline appears largely due to the increase in home ownership. Crucial mobility indicators, such as the portion of families moving outside the original county of residence and that of renters who moved, have not decreased.[5] Nearly one-half (46.4 percent) of the U.S. population changed residence between 1985 and 1990.[6] The contrast with Europe's current difficulties in reallocating workers between regions and jobs could hardly be stronger.

Reallocation in search of better incomes and jobs is one thing: Achievement of these goals may be quite another. But the data on income mobility for individuals in the United States (see Chapter 22) indicate a high incidence of change. Moreover, conditions that foster ease of relocation, such as education and a reduction in regional differences, appear to be increasing.

Regional Gains and Losses

The latter form of mobility also made a greater contribution to increased income levels after World War II. For nearly the entire postwar period, the Pacific Coast, which combined a favorable climate with rapidly growing electronics, communications, and aerospace industries, attracted massive population flows from the rest of the country. In consequence, although aggregate West Coast incomes grew rapidly, the pace of increase in individual incomes there was modest by national standards. Later in the era, the Sun Belt (Arizona, New Mexico, and the Gulf states) also grew rapidly. Texas rode its combination of natural resources (petroleum, salt, and sulfur) and petrochemical, electronics, aerospace, and defense industries to spectacular growth. Its decline as oil prices fell was no less impressive. At one time, prospects for continued high energy costs appeared to point to rapid growth in the Rocky Mountain region, but the rebirth of competition in international oil markets makes this dubious. "High-tech" industries, such as those linked to the seemingly unlimited applications of computers, also contributed to regional growth; the classic example is California's "Silicon Valley."

As economic activity became increasingly centered on service and information rather than manufacturing, resource mobility increased. Many new activities have few requirements, such as natural resources or access to transportation, to tie them to specific localities. This development was as cogent in the international sphere as it was within the U.S. economy, and it has greatly increased competition in world markets.

Areas whose principal industries served slowly growing or declining markets or those whose chief products encountered increasing competition experienced chronic high unemployment, slow income growth, and at least relative outmigration. These dismal processes continued until the low-growth regions developed new occupations, improved efficiency, or lost sufficient population to allow their remaining workers' prospects to improve. The coal mining regions of Appalachia and the shoe and textile districts of New England have made their adjustments; regions heavily dependent on agriculture or some types of industry may be forced to do so.

---

[4] M. Porter, *The Competitive Advantage of Nations* (New York: Free Press, 1990), 116.

[5] U.S. Bureau of the Census, *Current Population Reports: Geographic Mobility Series* (Washington, D.C.: Government Printing Office, 1984), 80.

[6] U.S. Bureau of the Census, *Statistical Abstract of the United States* (Washington, D.C.: Government Printing Office, 1991), 19.

Regions where incomes were far above or below national norms tended to exhibit convergence toward the average, a development that some economists see in the world economy as well.[7] The South, traditionally a low-wage area, gradually began to gain income parity with other regions.[8] New investment avoided those states where labor costs were already high, resulting in lower income growth there than in regions with abundant low-wage labor and consequent high returns on investment. Where work forces grew rapidly, wages generally failed to keep pace with national rates of increase, and in regions where labor force growth was slow, wage rates grew at better-than-average rates.[9] This was also apparent internationally: The U.S. labor force grew much faster than that of its major competitors. When combined with lower rates of investment in America, the result was relative decline in wages.

AGRICULTURE

If there was any sector of the American economy in which the influence of productivity changes was paramount, it was agriculture. The total output of American farms rose substantially, but changes in the relative weight of various farm products reflected the influence of demand changes. Production of beef (until very recently) and poultry increased rapidly, an indication of the high income elasticity of demand for those foods. Cotton, hog, and tobacco output fell substantially. A few crops assumed new importance in the postwar

era, of which soybeans were the primary example. The nature of some farm products was altered in response to changing dietary preferences. Examples are consumers' growing preference for lean beef and a wider range of vegetables.

Only minor changes in the centers of agricultural production occurred from 1945 to 1990. Some additional land became available for crop production as a result of irrigation programs or new strains of traditional crops, but in most areas the pattern was one of increased production from lands already in use. Had government agricultural programs not intervened in efforts to raise market prices for farm products through reduced output (as in the 1983 Payment in Kind measure), output might have risen even more. Congress gradually became more willing to support farmers through high crop prices than through purchases of surplus output. (This point will be addressed in detail in Chapter 22.)

The Productivity Revolution

Trends toward greater output per farm worker had appeared long before 1945, but they greatly accelerated after that date. Production of farm products per labor-hour increased eightfold between 1946 and 1989.[10] The rate of increase in farm labor productivity was twice that achieved by industrial workers. Farmers increased the per-unit productivity of land as well. Output per acre began to rise after 1950, with the per-acre gains in yields of wheat, potatoes, corn, and tobacco (all of which doubled or more by 1970) exceeding those of hay and cotton.[11] These output gains enabled each American farm worker to pro-

[7] W. Baumol, S. Blackman, and E. Wolff, *Productivity and American Leadership* (Cambridge, Mass.: MIT Press, 1989).

[8] G. Wright, *Old South, New South: Revolutions in the Southern Economy Since the Civil War* (New York: Basic Books, 1986), Chap. 8.

[9] *Economic Report*, 1977, 243–245.

[10] *Economic Report, 1991*, 396.

[11] These trends have continued for some but not all crops in the 1980s. Tobacco yields, for example, have shown no gains, while those of wheat and cotton continue to rise. *Statistical Abstract, 1986*, and *Economic Report, 1991*, 396.

■ Farming methods today sharply contrast with those of the past. See page 519.
Source: Grant Heilman.

duce sufficient food and fiber for 47 people in 1970 whereas in 1946 the same worker's output provided for the needs of only 14 persons.[12] By 1990, output per farm worker was more than twice the 1970 figure.[13] Furthermore, this increased farm output came from a total acreage about 10 percent less than that of the earlier period. Although American agriculture was still a very long way from being able to supply the world's wheat requirements from a single flowerpot—or county—the postwar trend was in that direction in the United States and other developed regions. One consequence of these productivity advances was a reduction of over 71 percent in the farm labor force after 1950.

Economic analysis would indicate that if the amounts of land and labor required per unit of agricultural output fell, either some other input was increased, or technology improved (a shorthand term indicating an improvement in resource quality). Both these developments occurred. The average productivity of land rose; the small amounts

---

[12] U.S. Department of Commerce, Bureau of the Census, *Historical Statistics of the United States: Colonial Times to 1970,* 2 vols. (Washington, D.C.: Government Printing Office, 1975), 498.
[13] *Economic Report, 1991,* 396–397.

withdrawn from use tended to be the least productive acres. Land productivity increased as new knowledge allowed the production of greater yields from the remaining acreage. Such scientific advances led to more efficient machinery, more systematic choices and applications of fertilizers, a wider variety of plant and insect pesticides, and the development of new plant and animal strains. The latter is an area where genetic engineering promises much greater gains in the future.

The improvements in agricultural technology constituted a veritable revolution in farming methods. The modern farmers' market situation was, if anything, even more competitive than that of their Populist forebears. Consequently, obtaining and utilizing information on the most modern production methods—and buying the capital that made the most of them—was a matter of survival. In many cases, the new techniques could now be minutely tailored to take even minor variations in soil chemistry or growing conditions into account.

New Requirements in Human and Physical Capital

Farmers now found that a college education, preferably in both agricultural and business techniques, was a valuable tool in the new, rapidly changing environment. Since few of the ideas utilized by modern farmers originated on commercial farms, and of course the tools, chemicals, and seed employed there had not done so for decades, the last vestige of the American farmer's image as a self-sufficient producer disappeared. In addition to their purchases of fuel, machinery, chemical inputs, and knowledge, and a huge expansion in the use of financial credit, an increasing proportion of American farmers bought nearly all their food from stores.

At least for the basic crops and meat animals, efficient application of the new methods appeared to require larger production units.

Economies of scale were fully obtainable only on farms of considerably larger size than the typical American unit in the 1940s. And the increase in optimum size continued with startling speed. In 1950, American farms averaged 213 acres. In 1975, that average had increased to 387, and by 1990 it was 461.[14] When we combine the decline in aggregate farm acreage with the increase in average farm size, it becomes easier to understand why the number of farms decreased from 5.4 to 2.1 million over the same period.[15] Today the American countryside is dotted with homes that once were farm houses. The land their owners formerly tilled is now sold or leased to other farmers who have been able to expand. There may still be a place for the small farm in the production of specialty crops or dairying, but the day of the 100- or even 250-acre farm devoted to grain, cotton, or meat production is now over. Many small units are now farms in name only; their owners subsidize losses in farming from income gained in urban occupations. In recent years, farms with annual sales of less than $20,000 of agricultural goods generated net losses from farming. Even for larger farms, only at crop sales of $100,000 per year or more did farming generate a majority of the owners' incomes.[16] In most areas, a viable farm is now a small- to medium-sized business in which more than half a million dollars is invested.

Growing Competition in an Uncertain World

These developments have reduced the cost of food for consumers, but their impact on farmers has sometimes been traumatic. The necessity of making continual new investment and long-term commitments in a market

---

[14] *Statistical Abstract, 1991*, 644.

[15] Data from *Statistical Abstract, 1991*, 645, and U.S. Department of Commerce, Bureau of the Census, *Bicentennial Statistics* (Washington, D.C.: Government Printing Office, 1976), 405.

[16] *Statistical Abstract, 1986*, 646.

where prices may be drastically affected by developments even less predictable than those that have always made farming a high-risk occupation have inevitably meant that many farmers misjudged their ability to remain competitive. Export markets for major American grain crops are now subject to politically conditioned changes (the 1980 embargo on grain sales to the Soviet Union following that country's invasion of Afghanistan is only the most spectacular example) as well as steadily increasing foreign competition. Some nations have adopted new agricultural technology and often subsidize exports; in others, inefficient domestic producers are protected. The reduction in domestic inflation also imposed unforeseen burdens on many farmers (and their creditors). Those who borrowed heavily at the interest rates of the mid and late 1970s, in the expectation of long-term world food shortages and continued high farm-product prices, were particularly hard hit by drastic changes in both prospects.

Very large farms, particularly those managed as subsidiaries of large corporations, have shown no productive advantages save in a few specialty crops and have made little headway in the past few decades. Such farms should not be confused with individually or family-owned farms that have been reorganized as corporations for tax or other reasons by their owners. Such corporate farms constitute over 90 percent of all incorporated units,[17] and as such have no implications for competition in agriculture, because they alter neither the size nor number of farms. Any trend toward decreased competition in American agriculture is not obvious—least of all to farmers. Developments in transportation and even some import competition have worked to raise the intensity of agricultural competition.

---

[17] *Statistical Abstract, 1991,* 647.

Consequences of Technological Change in Agriculture

The introduction of new technology has not taken place costlessly. Debt burdens that some farmers incurred as they tried to utilize improved methods proved insupportable. Changes that increase output per unit of input while consumers' demand for farm produce is both price- and income-inelastic (and population is growing more slowly than farm productivity) mean that some producers will have to leave the industry. The transition to alternative occupations can be very difficult for people who had invested most of a working lifetime and a host of emotional commitments in farming.

The development of mechanical cotton pickers and new strains of vegetables that are suited to machine harvesting has reduced costs of production and raised consumers' living standards. At the same time, less backbreaking manual labor is required. The same developments, however, have eliminated the primary occupations of millions of low-income agricultural workers, many of whom lack the education and cultural flexibility to readily find and adapt to other occupations. This problem appeared even before World War II in the South, and it seems likely to become increasingly serious in California, Texas, and Florida. A small farmer forced from the land may at least be able to sell his land and obtain funds to tide him over the transition, but for an unskilled and barely literate migrant farm worker, displacement from the only job he and his family have ever known can mean the very bleakest of prospects. Still, the exodus will continue.

In addition, there have been environmental costs. Agricultural chemicals have been applied without proper appreciation of their full impact on wildlife, the crops themselves, or even the workers who distributed them. In some cases the danger was realized only after serious harm had been inflicted.

Farm incomes have not risen as rapidly as have all others in the United States, and in the 1980s they underwent substantial absolute reductions. To add to farmers' difficulties, there has been great variation in income trends. Net farm income more than doubled in two years (1973–1974), but it declined thereafter, and even after more than doubling since 1983, has never regained the levels achieved at the 1974 peak. Under such conditions, it is hardly surprising that most American farmers earn most of their incomes from nonfarm occupations. Nor does the future appear bright, at least if the farm population declines no faster than its present pace. Export markets are likely to become increasingly competitive as other nations' farmers adopt new technology. A growing number of nations that had experienced chronic deficiencies in domestic food production are now self-sufficient in major cereal, dairy, and meat products; some (including India) are now at least occasionally able to export as well. U.S. farmers can no longer take export markets for granted.

Government's influence on American agriculture grew to dimensions unimagined in the New Deal. Not only were there the subsidies and production controls introduced in that era, but American farmers were now affected by many of the same environmental, safety, and land-use policies that the rest of the population experienced, and often to a greater degree. Policies toward the distribution of government food surpluses had obvious implications. Political considerations became increasingly important, too: Was American food to be used as a political weapon, traded as nearly as possible along lines dictated by comparative advantage, or used for humanitarian purposes? Should American farmers receive additional assistance to maintain their export markets in the face of subsidized competition

from other nations? The strength and weakness of the dollar in international trade, the oil crisis, and a host of other phenomena made it clear that American farmers, to a greater extent than most other U.S. producers, were now operating in a world economy.

MANUFACTURING

Manufacturing was another sector of the economy in which productive capabilities grew faster than demand. Prices of manufactured goods, particularly those of consumer durables, fell in real terms after 1967.[18] Unlike agriculture, however, manufacturing retained or even increased its share of GNP, from 21.4 percent in 1950 to 23.0 percent in 1988. Manufacturing employment was more volatile. The number of workers employed in manufacturing rose from 15.5 million in 1947 to over 21 million in 1979. Although there have been claims that the United States is "deindustrializing," there were about 50,000 more workers employed in manufacturing in 1989 than there were in 1970, although this figure is less than the 1979 peak, and 1990 figures (reflecting the recession) showed an overall decline of about 300,000.[19] In comparison to other industrialized nations, the United States has a rising share of total industrial employment and of the world's exports of manufactured goods.[20]

Approximately one million new manufacturing jobs were created from 1982 to 1986. Nevertheless, total employment rose from 43.9 to 110.3 million over the 1947–1990 pe-

---

[18] *Economic Report, 1991*, 357.
[19] *Economic Report, 1991*, 334.
[20] Baumol, Blackman, and Wolff, *Productivity and American Leadership*, 105. See also "Can America Compete?" *The Economist* (January 18–24, 1992).

riod, so the portion of all nonagricultural workers employed in manufacturing declined from 35.3 to 17.3 percent.[21] By the end of the period, large numbers of those employed in manufacturing performed clerical, distributive, or administrative tasks within the manufacturing sector. Manufacturing's share of real GNP was 21.0 percent in 1970, 21.1 percent in 1980, and 23.0 percent in 1988.[22] As these figures indicate, labor productivity in manufacturing rose more than the national average and real prices of manufactured goods fell.

Science: A Growing Partner

The sources of growth in manufacturing, as in agriculture, have become increasingly tied to generalized scientific research and its application through technology. There has been an increase in research oriented toward the specific problems of individual firms or industries, based on the common ground of discoveries in pure research. Both the nature of twentieth-century patents (which are increasingly based on the results of formal scientific investigation rather than empirically developed ideas), and the rapid growth in the ranks of technically trained persons support this conclusion.[23] Once the basic principles of atomic and molecular structure were understood, improvements in the desirable properties of existing materials could be made, and entirely new synthetic materials that had no counterparts in nature, such as plastics, fibers, adhesives, insulation, and fiber optics, could be produced.[24]

The tasks of applied science in manufacturing have grown almost immeasurably more complex. Considerations of producer and product-user safety and the environmental impact of products and processes have generated an ever-expanding area of additional scientific inquiry and application. This concern with the social costs and benefits of new technology is a further indication of America's growing wealth and scientific capabilities, not merely its social values. It must be emphasized that these investigatory capabilities are still in a very early stage.

New technology, especially when coupled with an upsurge in investment after 1981, has given the United States a rate of increase in manufacturing output per labor-hour over 1979–1989 that compares very well with those of other industrial nations' and exceeds those of both Japan and Germany.[25]

The new developments have also reduced dependence on almost all natural resources, particularly the high-quality, high-content mineral deposits that constituted the only usable forms of such resources for most of human history. There are, however, some crucial exceptions to this greater access to alternatives. There are not, nor do there promise to be, substitutes for air and water. Thus, our stocks of these two essentials for human life must be maintained in usable form. For most uses, "usable" does not imply absolute freedom from pollution. It does, however, mean that the costs imposed on mankind by additional deterioration in the quality of air and water resources must not be allowed to exceed the benefits conferred by the activities that produced this deterioration.

The other exception, on which all our newfound and potential ability to generate substitutes for natural inputs depends, is energy. With sufficient supplies of energy, the

[21] Baumol, Blackman, and Wolff, *Productivity and American Leadership*, 105.
[22] Baumol, Blackman, and Wolff, *Productivity and American Leadership*, 299.
[23] N. Rosenberg, *Technology and American Economic Growth* (New York: M. E. Sharpe, 1972), 118.
[24] Rosenberg, *Technology*, 124–126. The following discussion is based on Professor Rosenberg's views.

[25] "Can America Compete?"

new techniques promise to compensate for limitations in the Earth's stock of conventional raw materials through more efficient use of available supplies, greater ability to locate and utilize lower-grade resources (stocks of which are enormous, relative to current rates of use, in most cases), and the ability to produce substitutes.[26]

By no means does the foregoing imply that natural resources will be free or even cheaper in the future. It simply means that natural resource supplies will not impose an insuperable barrier to further economic growth. Copper supplies, for example, may well not be able to support the demands placed on them by further growth employing the technology of the recent past. However, copper is being supplanted in its electrical applications by aluminum and fiber optics. The ultimate sources of these copper substitutes—clay and sand, respectively—appear ample for generations. As long as the range of substitutes for various applications of some raw material continues to increase, the absence of a single material that can replace it in all uses becomes less important. Fear that the limitations of the Earth's natural resources will impose catastrophic restrictions on human well-being is at least as old as the Reverend Malthus, who uttered such misgivings with regard to arable land in the early nineteenth century. It appears to be no better linked to reality than in his day.

The Role of New Industries

The overall growth performance of any economy is a composite of the rate of change in the output of all commodities that it produces. As more or fewer sectors exhibit especially rapid or slow growth, their performance influ-

ences that of the economy disproportionately. Within sectors, the same is true of individual industries. Typically, new products just beginning to be accepted by consumers tend to have particularly rapid growth. As customers become more familiar with a new product or service, its employment in the use for which it was originally intended increases. More, it is likely to find wider utilization, often in applications scarcely imagined by the original producers. This point is especially germane in the case of items purchased to express individual consumers' tastes, or those, like plastics or computers, that can be adapted to a wide range of applications. Supply may also increase; as production of a new good expands, producers may be able to exploit economies of scale or gain cost reductions through "learning by doing." The very success of such new products invites competition, either from additional producers of identical goods or close substitutes. Any or all of these developments reduce the item's price and further expand its market.

Eventually the impact of these factors will be largely complete, and the growth of the no-longer-so-new industry will slow. The same factors that aided the growth of one new item are likely to be more available to still newer goods as the public gains an appreciation for the benefits of innovation. As other new commodities appear, they partially or wholly replace those that preceded them into the market. Potentially, any item that attracts consumer or producer spending competes with every other one, since incomes are limited.

The period of time over which a new good enjoys rapid growth depends on the nature of the item. Once demand becomes largely based on replacement needs and aggregate economic growth, and the article has become familiar enough to invite competition from new substitutes, growth of the industry producing it will slow to that of the aggregate economy or less. If many good substitutes appear, produc-

---

[26] H. Goeller and A. Weinberg, "The Age of Substitutability," *American Economic Review* (December 1978).

tion may decline or even cease. Demand growth for a new producer input depends on the demand for the final products in which it is a component and the technology of the industries that employ it. The users may discover broader applications or develop substitutes for it.

New Products and Economic Growth

As the American economy diversified, the pace of technological change quickened and communication improved, the length of the potential growth phase for any single product has probably decreased. If substantial economic growth is to be maintained under such conditions, it is essential that the economy continually generate new products and the rapidly growing industries that produce them. To accomplish this, it is important that there be as few noneconomic barriers to new competition as possible. Competition from new products or methods is particularly important for the improvement of overall economic efficiency, both in the sense of reallocation of resources and the pressure that it exerts on established producers of older products to improve existing methods and goods. Because the established producers are likely to be more influential than new industries, they may attempt to impose barriers to the growth of new sectors, or limit the dispersion of new products or methods in an attempt to maintain their own incomes. Barriers to occupational mobility, restrictions on the use of new methods, discriminatory taxes, and a long list of other tactics have been employed by those opposed to the effects of change. Such tactics impose severe long-run burdens; even if innovations are made, these measures restrict their impact and range of application. In this area, the attitudes and political structure of the United States have conferred important advantages on the economy in comparison with countries where central government establishes all rules for economic activity, or social attitudes are slower to change.[27] A much stronger venture capital market than any other nation, plus high rates of new-firm formation, give the United States important advantages in this particular area.[28]

The Diversity of American Manufacturing

To the casual observer, the postwar American economy would appear to have developed few products whose growth was both rapid and, on an aggregative basis, large enough to have a significant impact on the national growth rate. But this impression is largely due to the enormous diversity of the economy and to the fact that so many once-new items quickly become taken for granted in the American environment. Few, if any, single industries have had the postwar economic impact of the railroads, cheap steel, or electricity in all its applications. Television would be frequently nominated as an exception, but in reality there are a host of others. Production of home freezers, plastics, air conditioning, industrial chemicals, frozen foods, synthetic fibers, and recreational equipment has expanded at rates that bolstered the aggregate growth performance. Computers, both in production and their contributions to other economic activity, may prove to be a greater accelerating factor than any other new postwar industry.

In addition, many individual products or types of products achieved rapid growth even within stable or declining industries. Textile production, for example, has not kept up with the aggregate pace of American economic growth in recent decades, but the output of

---

[27] See M. Olson, *The Growth and Decline of Nations: Economic Growth, Stagflation, and Social Rigidities* (New Haven, Conn.: Yale University Press, 1982), and D. North, *Structure and Change in Economic History* (New York: Norton, 1981), for illustrations of this point. Its applicability to non-Western economies is illustrated in E. Jones, *The European Miracle: Environments, Economics, and Geopolitics in the History of Europe and Asia* (Cambridge, U.K.; Cambridge University Press, 1981). A less optimistic assessment is M. Porter, *The Competitive Advantage of Nations* (New York: Free Press, 1990).

[28] Porter, *Competitive Advantage*, 530.

Table 20.1   Leading U.S. Industries, by Value Added, 1988

Rank and Identity	Value Added (in Millions of Dollars)	Total Employment (in Thousands)	Production Workers (in Thousands)
1. Transportation equipment (4)*	$143,500	1,816	1,196
2. Chemicals (5)	137,899	830	475
3. Industrial machinery and equipment (1)	129,342	1,898	1,196
4. Food (2)	128,766	1,465	1,046
5. Electronics (4) and other electrical goods	103,475	1,581	1,012
6. Printing and publishing (7)	94,109	1,498	799
7. Fabricated metals (6)	79,893	1,488	1,104
8. Instruments (8) and related products	76,094	986	507
9. Paper (9)	57,355	619	476
10. Primary metals (10)	56,487	726	582
Total U.S. manufacturing	$1,262,340	19,148	12,404

*Figures in parentheses indicate rank in 1982.
Source: U.S. Department of Commerce, Bureau of the Census, *Statistical Abstract of the United States, 1991*, (Washington, D.C.: Government Printing Office, 1991), 740–742.

synthetic fibers has grown far more rapidly than has the entire textile industry.[29] Dacron, orlon, nylon, and newer synthetic fabrics are supplanting wool, cotton, silk, and even rayon, the first synthetic fiber.

Some idea of the diversity of the American manufacturing sector may be gained from Table 20.1. Even under the very broad definitions that it employs, no single industry accounted for as much as 15 percent of all value added by manufacturing. It must also be kept in mind that manufacturing now accounts for between one-sixth and one-fourth (depending upon the measurements employed) of all economic activity. A comparison of these data with Table 12.1 is indicative of the changes

that have occurred in the American economy. Few of 1910's leading industries have retained their rank within American manufactures, and the leading industries have shown considerable change even over the 1982–1988 period. The greater importance of industries producing highly transformed products, where raw materials account for only a minor portion of the final product's value, is a feature of modern industry. In the postwar period, the growth of older industries, such as food, lumber, leather, textiles and apparel, and even metals (both fabricated and primary), lagged behind that of all manufacturing, while that of instruments, chemicals, rubber and plastic products, and transportation equipment exceeded it.[30]

[29] L. Davis, R. Easterlin, and W. Parker, *American Economic Growth: An Economist's History of the United States* (New York: Harper & Row, 1972), 456.

[30] *Historical Statistics*, 669–680, and *Statistical Abstract, 1991*, 1:750.

The Role of Computers and Automation

Changes in the control of production mechanisms profoundly altered manufacturing. Heretofore, machines had either provided the strength or speed that human muscles could not generate or had performed relatively simple, repetitious operations. Machines were often the simplest method of achieving high uniformity and accuracy over large volumes of production. Such tools generally required close human supervision: They had very limited ability to make changes or adjustments, for in that area there was no substitute for human judgment. But these restrictions began to diminish as computers and sophisticated control mechanisms capable of coordinating a great variety of processes simultaneously were developed and brought into use.

By programming instructions into a computer, it became possible to devise control mechanisms for whole groups of machines that could deal with variations in the material, move it from one machine in a coordinated group to the next, adjust for missing or defective components, and even switch to the production of different items. Human labor was now required mainly to set up and maintain the system, and to make adjustments that were beyond the computer's information or capabilities, such as major product changes.

Automation and Employment

Two points should be noted in regard to automation. First, it reduces the number of jobs

■ Automated assembly lines like this one at a NeXT Computer plant bear little resemblance to Henry Ford's first assembly lines.
Source: NeXT Computer, Inc.

in the areas in which it is used. Although it makes additional jobs available in other areas, they are unlikely to be suited to the capabilities of the displaced workers. The purchase and installation of automated equipment are enormously expensive, and such machinery is still best suited to the production of large quantities of fairly standardized products. Automation's chief impact on labor, then, is similar to that of previous advances in machinery. Either the displacement of labor from such occupations or their demeaning impact on the humans who perform them in the absence of automated machinery may be deplored, but not both simultaneously. The jobs that automation has not affected, as yet, are those requiring flexibility and the continual exercise of judgment.

Second, automation reduces the production costs of the goods it is employed in making, at least in comparison to other methods. Automation gives consumers better or cheaper products, or both, than are possible from alternative production methods. The reduction in product costs made possible by automation allows for an increase in real aggregate demand because consumers' incomes now purchase larger quantities of goods, which may increase employment in many sectors of the economy.

However, the beneficial effects of automation, large though they may be in aggregate, are widely diffused. The adverse effects, even though their total impact is less, are likely to be highly concentrated on those displaced. Consequently, there may be a potential for rent-seeking activity among persons trying to protect their current jobs.

Because of the nature of the jobs to which it is most readily applied, those people displaced by automation are likely to have difficulty in changing work; these occupations placed little emphasis on flexibility and imagination, as do the newer types of work. Often, age, lack of education, locational factors, or personal inclinations make the adjustment

process even more traumatic. The adaptability of the human race has always exceeded that of individuals on whom the impact of change is focused. Nevertheless, it now seems clear that even those persons who plan to spend their entire careers in the same job must expect to have to relearn it several times during their working lives. Many more persons will have to shift occupations completely.

The New Competition

A cursory statistical examination of the manufacturing sector of the American economy might lead some to conclude that economic power had become more concentrated and competition reduced during the postwar period. Ownership of manufacturing assets has gravitated toward fewer hands; the share of all of the manufacturing capacity and equipment owned by the largest 50, 100, or 200 corporations has increased substantially in the last three or four decades. In addition, the absolute size of large corporations, whether measured by dollars of sales revenue or amount of assets (but, particularly in recent years, not employees),[31] has also risen.

None of these developments really gives an indication of the trends in competition within the manufacturing sector. Absolute size of firms is all but useless when considered in isolation. One example should make the point: By any measure of absolute size, Sears Roebuck, and Co. is one of the largest firms in the United States. Clearly, however, Sears faces strong competitive pressure in every market within which it operates. Monopoly power is conferred, not by absolute size, but by size in relation to the market in which the seller operates. In the United States, most markets have undergone great expansion as a

---

[31] N. Rosenberg and L. Birdzell, *How the West Grew Rich: The Transformation of the Industrial World* (New York: Basic Books, 1986), 295–296.

■ Large and elaborate malls have nearly replaced storefront retailing of yore.
Source: © Jack Elness/Comstock.

result of the economy's postwar growth and the improvements in transportation and communication. We hardly think of increased competition in retail markets as one of the consequences of the interstate highway system, but that has been one of its effects. Unless the growth of sellers is assessed in relation to that of markets, no meaningful conclusions can be drawn about the extent of monopoly or its rate of change.

The absolute size of the largest manufacturing firms increased relative to the indus-

trial sector. In 1947, the 200 largest industrial firms produced 30 percent of all value added by manufacture, a figure that had risen to 43 percent by 1970.[32] Large firms grew more rapidly than did their smaller rivals. But the growth of such giant concerns was more the result of efforts at diversification than of increasing shares of individual markets. Large firms, aided by the revolution in production

---

[32] *Historical Statistics*, 686.

methods, have generated new divisions that turn out products quite different from those the firms originally produced. A much more important factor, however, has been the widespread incidence of conglomerate mergers. The large firms have acquired smaller firms that had no previous economic relationships with them, either as customers, suppliers, or competitors. Since 1970, however, large firms in many industries have failed to match the aggregate economy's growth.[33]

Conglomerates

Conglomerate mergers do increase the absolute size of the firms making them, but they do not necessarily—or even probably—increase the conglomerate's share of any individual market and thus its monopoly power, as normally measured. Opinions on the economic effects of conglomerates vary. Some economists feel that such large firms constitute a potentially dangerous concentration of economic power through their very size, and offer few or no advantages of increased efficiency in return. A conglomerate merger cannot directly result in enhanced economies of scale, because it has no effect on the size of actual production units, only on their ownership. Furthermore, critics of conglomerates charge that because production is so diversified, most decisions are made within the divisions of such a firm, or even at the plant level. As such, there might be little reason to expect conglomerate divisions' performance to differ from that of independent firms. Worse, there may be some reason to expect it to be less efficient. Some conglomerates were formed in the 1960s for no better reason than that securities-market conditions made it easy to finance them, or for the profits and tax advantages accruing from their formation rather than their long-term productive operations.[34] When economic

conditions changed later in the decade, firms that had grown by this route for no better reason than that it was easy to do so (Ling-Temco-Vought is an example), recorded very poor performances.

Other economists view conglomerates more favorably. They point out that the most tempting targets for acquisition are firms whose performance under current ownership and management is poor. This indicates that an acquiring firm might expect a higher rate of return from the assets of a badly managed firm than the owners are now obtaining. Thus, the present value of such a firm is greater for prospective new owners than it is for the current stockholders. In this scenario, the possibility of conglomerate mergers improves overall economic performance, both among firms actually acquired and among those forced to improve their operations to maintain their independence.[35]

Conglomerate firms, due to their larger size, may have better access to financial markets, advertising, and other inputs. However, for firms large enough to have any effect on national markets, these considerations are unlikely to have any significant effect on overall efficiency. About the only point on which there is widespread agreement is that conglomerates are not suited to analysis by the traditional methods developed for single-product firms.

Industry Structures

Economists have traditionally assessed the presence and extent of monopoly power within an industry using the concentration ratio, the share of total industry production controlled by the four or eight largest firms. For example, the concentration ratio in the do-

---

[33] Rosenberg and Birdzell, *How the West Grew Rich*, Chap. 9.
[34] See Porter, *Competitive Advantage*.

[35] D. Siegel and F. Lichenburg, "Productivity and Changes of Ownership of Manufacturing Plants," *Bookings Papers on Economic Activity* (Washington, D.C.: Bookings Institute), 1986. Porter feels that these are short-term advantages that do not affect the firm's rate of productivity growth over time. See *The Competitive Advantage of Nations*, Chap. 11.

mestic auto industry in 1986 was very high. The four largest firms (General Motors, Ford, Chrysler, and American Honda) had a combined share of total output that exceeds 95 percent. The concentration ratio in the domestic auto industry was therefore over 95 percent. Recently, another, more comprehensive measure of market structure, the Herfindahl index (the sum of the squared market shares of all firms in a given industry) has been developed. But an examination of the concentration ratios within American manufacturing industries reveals no pronounced overall trend, and few significant changes in recent years. Concentration ratios have increased in some industries (brewing is a notable example), but they have fallen in others (computers), and the overall situation appears little different from that of 1920, or even of 1900. To the extent that there has been an overall trend, Table 20.2 indicates that it has been toward reduced market power. But even such a view understates the degree to which competition has increased in the United States in the past few decades.

Technological change has greatly increased the extent and intensity of competition within most national markets. Today there are few products whose only rivals are goods made by other firms in the same industry. As consumer information and discretionary income have increased, competition from dissimilar goods that fulfill roughly the same needs has increased, in some cases enormously. At the turn of the century, there were no economic substitutes for steel; today many other metals, plastics, glass, carbon fiber, reinforced concrete, and even wood compete with steel use.

In an era where information is one of the most valuable commodities, a great many different types of firms may offer roughly the same computer services to customers. Virtually any firm, regardless of its primary orientation, that has unused mainframe computer capacity may compete for data-processing jobs. Moreover, this interindustry competition is highly resistant to anticompetitive methods. The costs, goals, and procedures of firms outside one industry may be very different from those within it, and all but impossible to assess. Moreover, information is almost uniquely portable: Competition is often nationwide or even international. Thus, price-fixing or market-sharing agreements are extremely difficult to form.

There is no question about the chief beneficiaries of these developments. The essence of wealth is an extended range of alternatives; these changes have given American consumers at every level a range of choice far beyond that available even a few decades ago.

The Growth of Foreign Competition In addition, the usual indicators of monopoly power assess only the relations between domestic producers and ignore the influence of imported goods. Imports furnish a smaller portion of total consumption in the United States than they do in most other nations; they were only 3 percent of U.S. GNP in 1948. In 1989 they were 9.1 percent.[36] The range of products in which imported goods compete with domestic products has widened as well. In the 1970s, the portion of the world's manufactured goods exported from their country of origin rose from 10 to 25 percent. Today, it seems obvious that the extent and intensity of competition are increasing within most, if not all, manufactured product markets.

In addition, "big business" is heavily concentrated within a shrinking sector of the economy. As a whole, large manufacturing firms have suffered reductions in shares of total industrial output and employment to smaller rivals. The rapidly growing service sector, at least on a national scale (which may not be an entirely appropriate measure), is highly competitive.

---

[36] *Economic Report, 1991*, 286, 404.

Table 20.2   Changes in Industry Structure

Sector	Total Net Sectoral Output (in Billions of Dollars)	Percentage of Each Effectively Competitive Sector		
		1939	1958	1980
Agriculture, forestry, fisheries	$54.7	91.6%	85.0%	86.4%
Mining	24.5	87.1	92.2	95.8
Construction	87.6	27.9	55.9	80.2
Manufacturing	459.5	51.5	55.9	69.0
Transportation and public utilities	162.3	8.7	26.1	39.1
Wholesale and retail trade	261.8	57.8	60.5	93.4
Finance, insurance, and real estate	210.7	61.5	63.8	94.1
Services	245.3	53.9	54.3	77.9
Total	$1,512.4	52.4	56.4	76.7

Share of Each Category in Total Output (in Billions of Dollars)		Percentage Shares		
		1939	1958	1980
1. Pure monopoly	$38.2	6.2%	3.1%	2.5%
2. Dominant firm	42.2	5.0	5.0	2.8
3. Tight oligopoly	272.1	36.4	35.6	18.0
4. Others: effectively competitive	1,157.9	52.4	56.3	76.7
Total	$1,512.4	100.0%	100.0%	100.0%

Source: G. Shepherd, "Causes of Increased Competition in the U.S., 1939–1980," *Review of Economics and Statistics* (November 1982). Reprinted in R. Ruffin and P. Gregory, *Principles of Microeconomics,* 2d ed. (Glenview, Ill.: Scott-Foresman & Co., 1986).

One partial offset to the trend toward increased competition is the impact of government. Laws have been enacted, and many more proposed, to protect established firms from competition, or even to rescue them from outright failure. As might be expected, this is particularly common when the competitors are foreign producers.

The Status of Industrial Competition in the 1980s In summary, the recurrent fears of consumer exploitation by "big business," at least in the sense of monopoly power, are now less justified than ever. Quite simply, when faced with a would-be monopolist's "pay my price or do without," there are few cases in which consumers—or other firms—cannot find alternative sources at little, if any, additional cost.

ENERGY

The provision of adequate energy supplies has profound implications for long-term economic growth. As was noted in the preceding section, the ability to find and exploit a growing range of substitutes for current inputs is dependent on adequate energy supplies. While at present American energy supplies seem adequate for the foreseeable future, developments in the past dozen years allow ample scope for concern. The problem is not physical supplies, the technology to employ them, or the market's ability to produce and allocate them efficiently, it is noneconomic interference with the process.

The actual number of energy sources is far more limited than the forms in which they are employed, as Table 20.3 indicates. Fossil fuels, the sun, falling water, geothermal, and nuclear energy, plus a few minor additions, comprise the entire list of sources at present. Energy can be applied through a variety of transmission media, such as electricity; but first it must be generated.

Energy use and economic growth are connected, but in recent years it has become apparent that the strength of the connection is dependent on trends in energy prices. During

much of the postwar period, real energy prices were falling, and energy consumption increased more rapidly than the rate of economic growth. After the oil price increases of 1973 and 1979, energy prices rose at one and one-half to three times the rate of inflation, and it became apparent that the relationship between energy prices and growth was far looser than had been supposed (or, after 1973, feared). The energy required to generate an additional dollar of GNP declined by about one-fourth from 1970 to 1984, and consumption by the average household fell in about the same proportion between 1979 and 1984. Despite substantial growth in incomes, energy consumption per capita was almost the same in 1990 as it had been in 1970.[37] As energy prices rose sharply and appeared likely to go on increasing, the classic market system responses appeared. Consumers learned to use substitutes (from sweaters and insulation to shorter commutes and changed architectural styles), and they re-equipped with more energy-efficient cars, machines, buildings, and (over a longer period) habits.

Changing Energy Sources

In recent decades, the sources from which energy is obtained in America have changed. Over the long run, the importance of coal has declined in most uses, as cleaner, less-polluting, more flexible fuels, such as oil and natural gas, became available. Such fuels are not only more easily transported and applied, they contain more energy per unit of bulk or weight and pose fewer waste-disposal problems. Coal has retained its importance only in electric power generation and steelmaking. Coal, oil, and natural gas provided 92.2 percent of all American energy in 1975, and still accounted for 86.3 percent of U.S. production and 88.5

Table 20.3   U.S. Energy Consumption, Total and Per-Capita

Year	All Energy* (in Trillions of BTUs)	Per-Capita (in Millions of BTUs)
1920	19,782	186
1930	22,288	181
1940	23,908	180
1945	31,541	236
1950	33,100**	218
1955	38,800	235
1960	43,800	243
1965	52,700	272
1970	66,400	326
1975	70,600	327
1980	76,000	334
1985	74,000	310
1990	81,500	325

* Includes natural gas, coal, crude petroleum, hydro, nuclear, and geothermal.
** To nearest 100,000,000,000 BTUs.
Source: U.S. Department of Commerce, Bureau of the Census, *Statistical Abstract of the United States, 1991* (Washington, D.C.: Government Printing Office, 1991), 566–567.

[37] *Statistical Abstract, 1986*, 556; *1991*, 567.

percent of consumption in 1990.[38] The remainder is provided by hydropower, nuclear energy, geothermal, solar, and fuel wood. Despite their comparative insignificance in aggregate terms, hydropower and nuclear energy are important in the generation of electrical power.

The change from coal to petroleum and natural gas stemmed in part from the physical properties of the various fuels as well as their relative prices. After the mid-1950s, however, petroleum prices were determined by government policy rather than market factors alone. The result was that the real prices of oil and natural gas fell, and consumers responded by using more of both and replacing coal-burning facilities with new equipment designed for oil or gas.

Natural Gas

The price of natural gas in interstate commerce was set by government regulators in the 1950s. Natural gas prices were maintained at this level, which became increasingly unrealistic, through the middle 1970s. Regulation led to growing shortages in states that did not produce gas; supplies within the producing states, not subject to price ceilings, were ample. Gas prices were raised in the late 1970s and price ceilings were finally eliminated, but the jump in prices that deregulation initially entailed was politically traumatic. After years of blaming Arabs, OPEC, greedy oil barons, and a host of other villains for high energy prices, Congress was forced to take measures that in the short run clearly increased natural gas prices, and there was no mistaking the immediate agent behind the rise. Restructuring the equipment and habits accumulated over decades of declining real prices required years of unwelcome adjustment for consumers, and resulted

---

[38] 1975 figures from *Bicentennial Statistics*, 631; 1990 data from *Statistical Abstract, 1991,* 566.

in sharp increases in profits for domestic producers, and greater efforts to find and exploit domestic gas reserves.

Oil

Nor was oil exempt from the influence of short-sighted policies. In an effort allegedly designed to increase domestic oil production and enhance the nation's defense capabilities, the Eisenhower administration imposed quotas on imported oil. The natural result of this decrease in competition was an increase in domestic oil prices above world levels. It became more profitable to search for and produce domestic oil than to do so abroad, resulting in a more rapid depletion of American reserves than might otherwise have occurred. One result was that the United States became increasingly dependent on foreign oil in the 1960s and 1970s. As it became more and more difficult to meet environmental restrictions in constructing new refineries, the United States also became increasingly dependent on foreign refining capacity.

The 1973 Energy "Crisis" When the Organization of Petroleum Exporting Countries (OPEC) restricted exports to the United States in 1973 and subsequently began a series of price increases, domestic reserves were lower than they would have been in the absence of the import quotas. To make matters worse, the price of domestic oil had been controlled at far less than world prices in an effort to combat inflation. Nevertheless, there were rapid increases in petroleum prices, especially for gasoline, whose price almost tripled, and the Nixon, Ford, and Carter administrations all attempted to restrict the rise in oil prices. American dependence on foreign oil increased as a result of the price ceilings and limited refining capacity, and attempts to restrain imports under these conditions only worsened matters.

■ The United States found itself in an unfavorable energy position following OPEC's 1973 restriction of exports; it was a position, ironically, largely of its own making.
Source: Lou Grant of the *Oakland Tribune,* © Los Angeles Times Syndicate.

Incredibly, the government decreed that the "windfall profits" gained by domestic oil producers should be largely taxed away and the tax proceeds used to subsidize imported oil. Had the program been expressly designed to increase American dependency on imported oil, it could hardly have been more effective: It reduced the profitability of domestic production while raising that obtainable from oil imports. Even worse, by holding down the prices actually paid by consumers, it reduced the incentives to conserve. The policies resulted in long lines at service stations in both the winter of 1973–1974 and in the spring of 1979. A series of highly unpopular nonprice rationing schemes only exacerbated general dissatisfaction. Significantly, when gasoline prices were first allowed to rise and then were entirely decontrolled, the lines disappeared. Some price restrictions on gasoline were continued through 1979 despite evidence from natural gas markets indicating that the removal of price ceilings gave consumers much greater incentives to conserve and resulted in expanded supplies because it was now more profitable to find and market gas. Eventually,

the lesson was absorbed, and in 1981 gasoline prices were decontrolled.

Conflicting Views on Energy Production

American policy on energy production, particularly after 1973, has often been confused and contradictory. Environmental regulations, such as limitations on strip mining of coal and the incredibly complicated (and dubiously effective) licensing regulations for new power plants, particularly nuclear units, both added to energy costs and made future supplies less certain. In some cases, it now requires so much time to comply with the legal restrictions on power-plant construction that no meaningful forecasts can be made of the demand for the power they will eventually produce. Perhaps the chief source of America's energy problems was a reluctance, particularly by government authorities, to admit that additional energy could not long be obtained for prices that did not cover its costs of production.[39] After 1981, more attention was paid to market forces, but government interference by no means disappeared.

Other aspects of energy production and use present additional difficulties. Thus far, efforts to control air pollution caused by coal have proved to be expensive and not very effective, and alternatives, such as in-site burning and coal gasification, owe considerably more to engineers' imaginations than to economic practicality. Even oil presents serious problems of pollution in production, transportation, refining, and consumption. With the passage of time and development of alternatives to oil-based fuels, petroleum may become too valuable in its nonfuel uses, particularly in petrochemicals, to allow its

---

[39] R. Hall and R. Pindyck, "The Conflicting Goals of National Energy Policy," *The Public Interest* (Spring 1977).

continued use as fuel. Natural gas is virtually nonpolluting, and the United States apparently has huge reserves of gas in previously unknown deep deposits and dissolved in brine. Both of these sources, however, will be very costly to utilize, and they may require further technological breakthroughs to become practical fuel sources. Other energy sources offer at best limited supplements to current sources. Use of refuse for fuel might ultimately be more valuable for its contribution to waste disposal than as an energy source. Wood fuels have a limited potential contribution, and have already increased air pollution problems.

Conventional fuels, then, will continue to be available, but there is no prospect that their real prices will ever return to pre-1973 levels. New sources of conventional fuels, such as oil shale, apparently will be even more costly than was OPEC oil at the peak of that organization's power.

Hydropower

Hydropower is clean, and it can be obtained from the same sources virtually forever (if the reservoirs are maintained), but there is little potential for large-scale additions to the nation's energy resources from waterpower. Virtually all the first-rate hydropower sites in the contiguous United States have already been harnessed. Some abandoned dams could be renovated and returned to operation, but most of these are small and on streams with irregular seasonal flows; they were abandoned for good reason. New hydropower stations are highly capital-intensive (a lower barrier than in the 1970s, as inflation and interest rates declined), both for generating and distribution facilities. But new dams tend to be ruinous to stream ecology. Hydropower, then, is like solar power; by no means a free good, at least in usable form. A few regions of the United States have potential for expanded geothermal power generation, but this is a wasting asset of uncertain duration. Harnessing wind flow

appears unlikely to become competitive with less exotic forms of generation, and this method suffers from localized and small-scale production potential.

Nuclear Power

Public opinion in the United States still appears strongly opposed to any significant expansion of nuclear power. This is unfortunate, because although there undoubtedly are risks associated with nuclear power, these, even after the incident at Three-Mile Island in 1979 (which caused no deaths at the time, and no significant long-term increase in morbidity or mortality), are actually less than those associated with some widely used fossil fuels, particularly coal. Thus, our choice of power generation sources apparently implies that certain, but widely diffused, deaths are preferable to a very low probability of mortality from new causes, which would cause fewer total casualties. Risks posed by nuclear power appear amenable to reduction by currently available technology. The vitrification of atomic wastes would reduce the dangers involved in their disposal below those of current storage methods. There is no reason why operating standards and equipment of nuclear power plants cannot be improved if necessary.

What does appear certain is that nuclear power will be part of the U.S. energy supply for at least the next few decades. Currently, it provides about 19 percent of all electric power in the United States. This amount is far too large to be replaced immediately by any reasonably priced alternative. Thus, the debate over nuclear power must actually be over the size of its role in energy production for the next generation, rather than whether it should play any role at all.

Alternative Energy Sources

The utilization of more exotic sources of energy, such as solar, fusion, or artificial fuels, remains far in the future, and costs per unit are still pure conjecture. Solar power, as opposed to heating, appears to be far from practical application, although there have been promising developments in photovoltaics recently. The expanded use of western coal or oil shale would draw heavily against that region's limited water supplies.

Coal and Its Costs

In summary, there are no currently available energy sources that have no drawbacks whatever, and in most cases these increase more than in proportion to additional energy obtained from them. The United States has enormous reserves of coal, perhaps enough for three to five centuries' consumption if some increase in prices is allowed. But aside from the direct effects of coal mining on the environment, the use of coal poses a serious threat to human safety. Contemporary coal use is estimated to cause from 10,000 to 20,000 deaths annually, chiefly through the effects of air pollution. This is at least the equivalent of a major nuclear disaster in an urban area every two or three years. Although no source of energy is completely free of threats to health and safety, few others pose the threats involved in expanded use of coal.

The Energy Outlook

Despite these cautions, there is no reason to regard the energy situation as potentially disastrous. Energy will probably be more expensive in the future, but additional supplies will be obtainable; total supplies will grow. It is hoped that an appreciation of the role of higher energy prices on the supply of and demand for that commodity has been gained from the debacles of the past dozen years. Increased prices induce both greater quantities supplied and reductions in amounts demanded, just as do increased prices for any commodity in a market economy. Producers are stimulated to develop substitutes for current energy sources, and consumers discover

a highly personal interest in energy conservation. Higher gasoline taxes would increase demand for energy-efficient automobiles. Price increases also make it feasible to tap reservoirs that under previous conditions would not have been economically exploitable, such as the North Sea, Alaska, and Mexico.

Current energy policy is still affected by the need to increase producers' incentives through higher prices, and the political benefits of maintaining low prices to consumers—at least until shortages reach the point of inconvenience.[40] American industry's response to higher energy prices has already been noteworthy; firms have reduced their energy consumption with no loss in output, and even achieved increases. As energy prices decline, industries will not discard the methods that produced these savings. Consumers' conservation responses were slower, but, generally, also permanent. The result is different patterns of economic consumption than those that evolved when energy was cheap, but "different" need not mean "worse."

LABOR FORCE TRENDS

Perhaps the most significant developments in the American labor force in these four decades were its massive growth and changes in composition. The civilian labor force grew from 59.4 million persons in 1947 to 124.8 million in 1990.[41] This rate of growth exceeded that of the population. Labor force growth stemmed not merely from demographic factors, such as birth and death rates and the growth in those age cohorts tending to have high rates of participation, but also from changes in social customs, especially in regard to women's participation in work outside the

---

[40] Hall and Pindyck, "Conflicting Goals."
[41] *Economic Report, 1991,* 322.

home. These developments more than offset a decline in participation rates among adult males, most of which appeared due to increased enrollment in institutions of higher learning and to early retirement. The change in female labor force participation was more significant: By the mid-1980s, the majority of American women could expect to work outside the home for most of their adult lives. Further, they would do so not merely before they had children or after their families had left home, but also even while their children were infants. So rapid was the increase in female labor force supply that women's incomes, which had been rising relative to male's before 1950, stagnated despite improved education and greater experience on the job, improving female productivity.[42] After 1980, the "gender gap" in wages began to decline.

Hours of work changed relatively little for most Americans: the average work week fell only from 40.3 hours in 1947 to 34.5 in 1990, and even that decline appears due to the growing importance of retail trade employment, with its large portion of part-time workers; manufacturing and construction work weeks showed almost no change.[43] Hours actually worked over the year did decline, as paid vacations and sick leave became standard and the number of holidays increased. By the 1970s, some experiments with new work-week arrangements, such as flexible hours and three-day weekends, had appeared, but there seemed to be no great preference for additional leisure. Many workers began to "moonlight" (take second jobs). Real gross wages for private nonagricultural workers rose from $196.47 per week in 1947 to $259.98 (both in 1982 dollars) in 1990. Even so, the 1990 figure was about 16 percent less than the 1972 peak and about the same as that for 1959. In manufacturing and construction the gains were larger, but the growing weight of retail trade in all employment, especially in the 1970s and 1980s, reduced the average for all workers.[44] Median family income rose slightly from 1971 to 1990; from $33,191 to $35,353 in 1990 dollars. This figure does not indicate the slight decline in family size over that period, but 1970–1989 was not an era of rapid income gains. Male workers fully employed in year-round jobs bore the decline; full-time year-round female workers gained about 12 percent over the period.[45] The gross wage figures quoted above do not include fringe benefits, which increased from 9 percent of total compensation in 1960 to 19 percent by 1988, or changes in working conditions, so they are not an exact measure of well-being. Until 1983, the Consumer Price Index overstated the increase in housing costs, which also served to understate wage gains. These figures also do not include the increased levels of government services that taxes on those wages provided, although there was increasing evidence in the late 1970s and 1980s that many people considered those services inadequate compensation for the taxes they paid. One attempt to adjust for these considerations found that real wages and fringe benefits rose 72 percent from 1960 to 1987; over 1973–1987 the increase was 13 percent. The most commonly cited real wage figures are those of the Bureau of Labor Statistics. Wage data compiled by the Social Security Administration and the Department of Labor Office of Employment and Unemployment Statistics both indicate larger (and comparable) wage gains in the 1980s than do

---

[42] C. Goldin, "The Female Labor Force and American Economic Growth, 1890–1980," in R. Gallman and S. Engerman, *Long-Term Factors in American Economic Growth* (Chicago: University of Chicago Press, 1986), and "The Gender Gap in Historical Perspective," in P. Kilby, ed., *Quantity and Quiddity: Essays in U.S. Economic History* (Middletown, Conn.: Wesleyan University Press, 1987).

[43] Goldin, "Female Labor Force," 336.

---

[44] Goldin, "Female Labor Force," 336.

[45] Goldin, "Female Labor Force," 320.

■ Modern employment offers wider opportunities for women and also the use of new capital equipment. *Source:* Comstock.

BLS figures.[46] Even these studies reveal slower gains than those of the 1960s and early 1970s.

As might be expected, aggregate wage trends masked substantial variations between industries, regions, occupations, and sectors. In manufacturing and construction, wage gains through the 1980s were larger as employment in those sectors remained stable or fell as a portion of the work force, many workers were represented by strong unions, and there were substantial gains in productivity. In retail trade and services, where the supply of labor expanded rapidly in both relative and absolute terms and productivity gains were modest, wage gains failed to keep pace with the average for the entire economy.[47]

Organized Labor

Because, for the most part, employment growth was strong from 1947 to 1984, it might be expected that labor unions would show substantial growth. In addition to the favorable job climate, the political situation was in general far more sympathetic to organized labor than it had been at any prior time save the late 1930s. Labor unions had grown rapidly during World War II, and for the first postwar decade they improved on those gains. In 1956, about 30 percent of the nonagricultural work

---

[46] R. Myers, "Real Wages Went Up in the 1980s," *Wall Street Journal* (August 21, 1990).

[47] *Economic Report, 1991,* 336.

force was enrolled in unions, an all-time high for the American labor movement. After that date, however, the union movement faltered; at best, its growth failed to keep pace with that of the labor force, and in some years, particularly in the 1980s, union membership declined. In 1945, labor union membership was just under 15 million. This figure increased to almost 18.5 million in 1956. Only in 1970 did union rolls list 20 million workers. The 17 million union members in 1990 constitute 13.7 percent of the U.S. labor force, and 16.4 percent of employed wage and salary workers.[48]

The very limited gains in union membership were in part a reflection of the fact that the economy changed faster than the unions. American unions are strong in manufacturing and construction, where a large majority of all production personnel, especially in large firms, are organized. But employment in these fields is now a smaller portion of the total; for practical purposes, the number of jobs in manufacturing has been stable for the past two decades. Unions have been less successful in organizing most of the rapidly growing sectors of the economy, such as retail trade, government employees (with some exceptions), finance, and services. They have only recently begun serious efforts to organize in most of these areas, and in general have found the task difficult.

The Decline of Union Strength

It appears unlikely that employment in the manufacturing sector will expand significantly. Even if the sector does not decline absolutely, productivity gains will have to rise at least in proportion to output if foreign competition is to be met. Since 1982, they have actually exceeded that pace. The maintenance of organized labor's current aggregate position requires an expansion into new fields. There are few remaining prospects in industry; vir-

tually all large firms' employees had been unionized by the mid-1950s. After this had been accomplished, the task of organizing the remaining industrial workers involved high costs per member gained, because the firms were small and often highly resistant to organization. In recent years, unions have lost most of the elections through which they sought recognition as workers' bargaining agents, and have even been repudiated by previously organized workers in a few cases.

Union Failures Some union efforts at new organization were misdirected. Two highly publicized attempts to unionize previously unorganized labor involved southern textile workers and farm labor in the West. The former group are employed in a highly competitive industry that is vulnerable to foreign competition as well as that of many unorganized American firms; in such circumstances, unions can achieve wage increases, if at all, only at a very high cost in reduced employment. The farm workers appear threatened by technological change. Thus, neither industry offers unions a chance to produce long-term wage gains in relation to competitive market levels.

In some cases, the lack of growth reflects little or no effort. Many unions appear to have become content with the status quo and are more interested in promoting the interests of their current membership than they are in expansion. The growing disparity between union and nonunion wages in comparable jobs, the resistance of some unions (especially old-line craft unions) to government efforts aimed at reducing race and sex discrimination in admitting new members, and various attempts to insulate themselves from nonunion competition are all classic symptoms of static monopoly power.

Unions in a More Competitive Economy More recently, even survival has become difficult for some American unions. As noted previously, competition has been increasing in the U.S.

---

[48] *Statistical Abstract, 1991*, 425.

■ This sign at a Chrysler plant in De Witt, New York, makes it painfully clear that not all Americans are happy with the results of international trade.
Source: © Michael Okoniewski/The Image Works.

economy due to technological change, improvements in transportation and communication, and the growth in foreign trade. The impact of most of these changes has been centered on manufacturing. Industries that had been accustomed to passing unions' wage increases on to customers in the form of higher prices now encountered growing resistance. As the elasticity of demand for manufactured products increased, unions found that wage increases could now be obtained only at the cost of large reductions in employment. In some cases, they were forced to accept wage reductions to retain existing jobs, as in the steel, airline, and auto industries. Collective bargaining agreements in the mid-1980s generally provided for smaller wage increases than those obtained by unorganized workers, often insufficient to match inflation.

The results of some unions' efforts may not even benefit all their own members. If wages are increased faster than the rate of labor productivity gains, that is, if they rise more than does real output per worker, over time the employer must either accept lower profits or pass on the higher labor costs to customers. As markets become more competitive, profit margins are likely to be small in

any case (corporate profits as a share of GNP fell in the 1980s). Customers will be highly sensitive to price increases by individual firms. Under such circumstances, wage increases will reduce the quantity of union labor demanded more than proportionately, thus displacing labor to nonunion employment, where the increase in supply forces wage levels down. Clearly, some unions have followed exactly these policies. The United Mine Workers, both under John L. Lewis' presidency and in the past decade, is one example. The steel and auto workers are others; in the 1970s, the steelworkers gained large wage increases even in the face of declining productivity and rapidly increasing foreign competition. Only when several large steel firms faced bankruptcy was it recognized that such policies could not be continued.

The Legal Climate The legal climate in which American labor unions operated became somewhat less favorable after the war. In the late 1930s, the Norris-LaGuardia and Wagner Acts had given unions wide latitude in their organizational and bargaining activities. The widespread labor unrest of the immediate postwar period resulted in the passage of the Taft-Hartley Act (1947). This amendment to the Wagner Act was an attempt to redress the problem of coercion of individual workers by the unions, both directly and through pressure on employers. Some of the assumptions embodied in the law, especially the idea that agreements negotiated with employers by unions' leaders might run against the desires of the membership, proved to be wrong.

Nevertheless, unions' freedom of action was restricted by the Taft-Hartley Act. The law provided for 80-day injunctions against strikes if the president of the United States felt the national interest was involved. Secondary boycotts (in which members of unions not directly involved might refuse to buy or even handle products of firms with whose labor policies they disagreed) and the closed shop (in which employers agreed to hire only union members) were forbidden. The act allowed individual states to pass "right-to-work" laws, which forbade even the union shop (an agreement that all workers in a firm that had recognized a union had to join it to retain their jobs). The latter provision may have had some effect on unions' ability to organize workers in the rapidly growing industries of the southern states, most of which had right-to-work laws. The chance to earn wages much higher than the previous alternatives open in that region was probably a greater barrier.

Evidence of serious corruption and misuses of union funds were unearthed in a few unions (notably the Teamsters). One result was the passage of the Landrum-Griffith Act in 1959. It provided tighter legal controls over union funds, the secret ballot in union elections, and made attempts to prevent persons with criminal records from gaining union office. In light of subsequent events, the Landrum-Griffith Act's success has been modest indeed. Despite the changing legislative climate, however, unions' current difficulties appear far more directly linked to economic developments than to changes in the labor laws.

The Future of Organized Labor

Neither popular opinion nor the direction of legislation is likely to turn in unions' favor in the near future. Strikes, particularly those by public employees that seriously inconvenience the general population, have cost the entire union movement goodwill. One example of this shift in attitudes occurred during the Air Traffic Controllers' strike in 1981, in which even other unions offered only token support to the strikers, and public opinion strongly favored the president, who fired the strikers. The problems of some unions in financial management, leadership, or both, while certainly not representative of all or even most organized labor, have added to the unfavorable publicity received.

Big labor is now regarded with no more esteem than big business. Some of this antagonism may be misdirected; strikes, although they may be highly publicized, are relatively uncommon. In only one year since the end of World War II (1947) have work stoppages due to labor disputes cost the American economy as much as 1 percent of total working hours. But the unions' situation may be indicated by the fact that a growing portion of all strikes now originate in established unions' wage and working-condition demands, rather than from organizational efforts.[49]

Most American labor unions now appear to be solidly middle-class organizations far more concerned with their current members' welfare than in improving either the lot of the working class (however that may be defined in America) or society as a whole. Unions have strongly supported minimum-wage laws, even though their members receive wages far above those mandated, and restrictions on imports. Such actions support the conclusion that union members' gains have come at the expense of consumers and unorganized workers, not employers. Unions have been instrumental in the growth of fringe benefits, such as pensions, insurance, medical care, and vacation provisions in employment contracts, which have become a prominent portion of most labor compensation.

Postwar Labor History

The structure of the American labor movement changed over the 1945–1984 period. The American Federation of Labor's membership had been approximately equal to that of the Congress of Industrial Organizations in 1939. By the early 1950s, the AFL was about twice as large as the CIO. In part, the growth of the AFL was due to changes in the affiliation of some member unions. The United Mine

---

[49] *Historical Statistics*, 1:179.

■ George Meany (left) and Walter Reuther (right) are pictured celebrating the 1955 merger of the AFL-CIO.
Source: AFL-CIO.

ade, the AFL-CIO has gained 1.16 million members if the Teamsters' readmission is considered, but lost about 700,000 from the original membership. Gains in government employees, teachers, and service workers have not offset losses in steel and auto workers, machinists, and other old-line unions.[51]

Two of the claims most frequently made for organized labor in America are not borne out by the facts. First, the union movement does not speak for all American labor; six of every seven workers are not organized. Second, despite spectacular successes gained by some unions in collective bargaining, unions are not the primary source of high wages in the American economy. Wage levels in both unionized and nonunionized industries appear more closely related to productivity than to the degree of organization, and as the economy becomes still more competitively structured, this trend is likely to continue.

Workers, under their mercurial president John L. Lewis, left the CIO, briefly rejoined the AFL, and then became an independent union. Other unions were expelled from CIO ranks in the late 1940s and early 1950s for Communist affiliations. In 1955, the two major organizations merged, becoming the present AFL-CIO. Even after this time, however, organized labor had difficulty in maintaining a solid front. The United Auto Workers disaffiliated from the AFL-CIO in 1968 in a dispute over political policy, and the Teamsters were expelled in the mid-1960s because of the corruption of their leadership (the Teamsters rejoined the AFL-CIO in 1987). Despite the merger, AFL-CIO membership in the 1960s remained between 15 and 16 million; the membership gains of that decade were recorded by independent unions, especially the Teamsters, whose membership swelled from three to nearly five million.[50] In the last dec-

BANKING AND FINANCE

Three trends dominated postwar developments in American financial institutions and markets. One was a culmination of the developments that had begun over a century previously. As communications became essentially instantaneous, financial markets became far more integrated and lending rates became uniform across the country. Second, the financial sector was strongly influenced by responses to what for a time appeared to be permanent inflation. As the rate of price increase has declined over the past decade, some of the changes made at that time have proved to be sources of trouble for financial institutions and their customers alike, as have changing conditions in energy markets. Bank and

[50] *Historical Statistics,* 1:176–177.

[51] *Statistical Abstract, 1991,* 424.

■ Foreclosure auctions, like this one in Boston's North End in 1990, were common as the real-estate boom of the 1980s collapsed.
Source: © Michael Dwyer/Stock Boston.

especially savings and loan association failures reached levels that existing government institutions were unable to counter without massive increases in general-revenue assistance.

Responses to accelerating inflation became apparent in the mid-1960s and grew more obvious as prices, and even more, expectations of future prices, continued to rise in the 1970s. Savers, borrowers, and the institutions that served them began to develop responses to what appeared a permanent problem. They became more sophisticated in their anticipation of price changes and their evaluation of nominal interest rates, which rose sharply. New types of financial assets were developed to meet the changed conditions; banks expanded their credit card and leasing operations.

An additional development grew out of the energy crisis. Large amounts of money were deposited in American banks by some of the OPEC nations. In a period when interest rates had been driven to record levels by inflation, the banks had to find ways to employ the funds deposited with them. When inflation rates declined in the 1980s, it was clear that they had not always done so with prudence. Savings and loan associations experienced even greater difficulty, with unprecedented rates of failure.

Commercial banks and other financial institutions adjusted their asset portfolios continuously over the era. Initially, they exchanged the large volumes of government securities that they had accumulated during the Great Depression and World War II for private securities and loans whose rates of return were higher. Later they made adjustments to these portfolios in response to changing conditions and prices in financial markets. In contrast to conditions during the Great Depression, the risks of lending to private borrowers declined in the postwar prosperity. In the last decade, however, it became apparent that some loans, particularly those to foreign governments, energy producers, commercial construction, and agriculture, were far shakier than they had initially appeared. So too were real estate loans in regions where mainstay industries were in difficulty. In 1988–1989, Texas alone accounted for over 80 percent of the assets of banks that had either failed or required assistance from the Federal Deposit Insurance Corporation, brought about by loans that ignored a combination of declining oil prices and increases in business office construction far in excess of demand.[52] Many banks in New Hampshire, heavy lenders during a construction and real estate boom that collapsed after 1989, were also forced to merge with stronger institutions.

Commercial Banks

The assets of commercial banks expanded enormously in the 1945–1980 period, but the number of banks declined. After 1980, the number of commercial banks in the United States stabilized or increased slightly. Banks were affected by new technology; data processing and improved communication, facilitated by computers, greatly increased individual banks' ability to handle a growing

and more varied amount of business. For most of the period, both state and local regulations made it difficult and, if existing banks were opposed, often impossible to found new banks. These rules had the enthusiastic support of most existing banks. Barriers to entry were relaxed after 1980, not always with beneficial results.

If the number of banks declined, the number of banking offices rose as branch banking expanded. Increasing numbers of states allowed banks to operate more than one office within their own borders or in a wider local area. In 1955, only 12 percent of all commercial banks had branch offices, but by 1970, nearly one-third of all banks had at least one branch.[53] From 1970 to 1989, the number of bank branches more than doubled.[54] Even so, the establishment of branches in other states remained illegal, and some U.S. banks expanded their operations overseas instead. Although the absolute size of banks expanded, concentration ratios did not; the largest American banks controlled a smaller portion of total bank assets in 1970 than in 1940, and their share was not expanding.[55] Since that time the growth of many large U.S. banks has been slowed by the necessity to provide increased reserves against losses on foreign loans, and mergers have been frequent. Large banks in the "money centers" are losing ground to regional and superregional banks, which appear to have taken better advantage of lending opportunities within the United States.[56] There has been a substantial expansion of foreign banking activity within the United States as well. The development of truly national or even international markets, at least for large loans, has increased competition within the American banking system.

---

[52] J. O'Keefe, "The Texas Banking Crisis: Causes and Consequences 1980–1989," *FDIC Banking Review* (Winter 1990).

[53] *Historical Statistics*, 2:1036–1037.
[54] *Statistical Abstract, 1991*, 500.
[55] R. Robertson, *History of the American Economy*, 3d ed. (New York: Harcourt Brace Jovanovich, 1973), 496.
[56] R. Feinberg and G. Hanson, "LDC Debt Will Restructure U.S. Banking," *Challenge* (March/April 1989).

Financial Regulation: Gains and Losses

One positive legacy of the New Deal era, if not the New Deal itself, was a much lower rate of bank failures in the early postwar era. As of 1970, there had not been as many as ten commercial bank failures in any single postwar year; a far cry from the first third of the century, when from 50 to several hundred failures or suspensions occurred even in normal years.[57] More effective regulation and better training for bankers, as well as a generally buoyant economy, deserve most of the credit, but the existence of the Federal Deposit Insurance Corporation virtually ended runs on banks rumored to be in financial difficulty.

In the 1980s, however, this record was marred. The number of bank failures had increased to as many as 200 per year. While most of the failing banks were small rural institutions, often heavily involved in local agriculture, large banks also were involved beginning with Continental Illinois National Bank in 1983, plus more in California, New England, and especially Texas. Sharply changing prospects for energy-related loans were particularly damaging for Texas banks. Loans to foreign governments, especially in Latin America and Eastern Europe, reduced the profits of large banks active in international lending, but generally did not threaten failure. In most cases where banks insured through the FDIC were involved, that agency arranged for banks' reorganization or absorption by larger institutions. By the late 1980s, however, the FDIC found its reserves inadequate to cover depositors' potential losses, and had to request additional funds from Congress.

Well over 90 percent of the funds placed with failed banks had been recovered and returned to depositors as of 1970.[58] But the ease with which this record was achieved in times of relative monetary stability led to commitments that proved difficult to keep in more turbulent times. Deposit insurance was gradually expanded; individual deposits are now protected up to $100,000, and insurance premiums charged to the banks were reduced, extending FDIC liabilities and reducing its income. When bank failures increased sharply in 1983, FDIC resources were strained. Even larger numbers of banks were in trouble over 1987–1990, and depletion of its lost reserves forced the FDIC to request federal Treasury help. At this time (1992), banks' operating records are improving, but the cost of regaining stability has been high.

Other Financial Institutions

Assets of commercial banks totalled more than $3 trillion by 1989, but as the data in Table 20.4 indicate, those of other financial institutions grew at a faster pace for much of the period. Still, they rivalled those of commercial banks only in aggregate. Increases in amounts of assets controlled by savings-oriented institutions reflected the concerns of an aging and affluent population concerned with retirement. Both because of legal restrictions and their own inclinations, institutions serving such needs place a high premium on the security of the funds deposited with them. As a growing portion of aggregate savings was channelled through risk-averse institutions, this may have reduced the supply of long-term investment funds available to new (and thus risky) investment prospects. In addition, these firms' responses to inflation reinforced this attitude. The rise of interest in venture-capital markets in recent times has gone far to offset such developments, however. Such markets deal almost entirely in investments in projects that would be unable to attract funds from more conventional lending sources.

The response to inflation also changed the roles played by various financial institutions.

---

[57] *Historical Statistics*, 2:1038–1039.
[58] *Historical Statistics*, 2:1039.

Table 20.4   Assets of Major U.S. Financial Institutions, 1945–1989
(in Millions of Current Dollars)

Year	Commerical Banks	Savings and Loan Associations	Mutual Savings Banks	Life Insurance Companies	Other Insurance Companies
1945	$146,245	$8,847	$16,962	$44,907	$7,851
1950	156,914	16,893	22,446	64,020	13,476
1955	199,244	37,656	31,346	90,432	20,305
1960	234,274	71,476	40,571	119,576	30,132
1965	356,110	129,580	58,232	158,884	41,843
1970	534,932	176,183	78,995	207,254	58,594
1975	1,095,400*	388,200	121,100	289,300	100,000
1980	1,855,700	629,800	171,500	479,300	222,500
1985	2,731,000	948,200	235,000	826,000	346,800
1989	3,299,000	755,700	280,000	1,300,000	513,600**

* To nearest $100,000,000.
** 1988.
Sources: (1945–1970) U.S. Department of Commerce, Bureau of the Census, *Historical Statistics of the United States: Colonial Times to 1970*, 2 vols. (Washington, D.C.: Government Printing Office, 1975), 2:968–1061, passim; (1975–1984) U.S. Department of Commerce, Bureau of the Census, *Statistical Abstract of the United States, 1991* (Washington, D.C.: Government Printing Office, 1991), 501–521, passim.

Some savings institutions devised new forms of deposits that were far more liquid than those they had previously offered. This increased their role as money substitutes. Certificates of deposit, money-market funds, NOW accounts, and other forms of deposit, as well as banks' credit cards, all tended to increase the volume of transactions that could be supported by a given money supply as conventionally defined. This development complicated the practice of aggregative monetary policy; it became difficult to even define the supply of money or its velocity.

As had been the case in many other areas, the influence of government regulation on financial institutions was not entirely positive. The regulatory impact on savings and loan associations, and many of the changes intended to assist them, proved especially damaging. Originally, savings and loan associations were under government restrictions on the interest rates they could pay to depositors. At the same time, their investments were limited to fixed-rate mortgages. While inflation and interest rates were moderate, these limitations had little impact. When inflation changed the prevailing structure of interest rates, but not the legal ceilings, such laws provoked massive shifts of funds. The consequences for institutions that could no longer attract deposits at capped rates could be serious: Rapid withdrawals of small deposits, soaring mortgage rates, and various types of credit rationing even at the unprecedented interest rates could result. In 1981, Congress deregulated the rates savings and loans could pay depositors, and reduced their capital requirements. In 1982, capital requirements were reduced still more, and the institutions were allowed to use less conservative accounting procedures. Perhaps more significantly, savings and loan associations were now allowed a much wider range of investments, most of which were totally outside their executives' experience. Meanwhile, regulation standards were relaxed. FSLIC inspections became less frequent, and inspectors became reluctant to classify institutions as insolvent, sometimes because of Congressional intervention on behalf of major campaign contributors.

The response to new circumstances proved disastrous. Savings and loan associations first raised interest rates offered to depositors to stem withdrawals. They soon found that returns on their investment portfolios, heavily weighted with long-term fixed-rate mortgages, were inadequate to pay the promised rates on deposits and their value fell as interest rates rose. To compensate, the associations began to seek new, high-return securities, an area in which they had no expertise. Many of their ventures into commercial real estate, high-risk bonds, and other ventures were involved investments that knowledgeable lenders would not touch. Others might have been profitable if the high oil prices or commercial construction booms of the early 1980s had continued, but oil prices collapsed in 1986, and office space expanded much faster than did potential tenants. Some associations offered ever-higher rates to depositors, trying to grow their way out of trouble. Since these deposits were insured by the FSLIC, the owners of the associations were encouraged to engage in risky ventures. Their desperate need for high returns, lack of knowledge of wider financial markets, and relaxation of regulatory standards made the savings and loans ripe for ill-considered or even criminal ventures. The Vernon Savings and Loan Association in Texas had some $2 billion in outstanding loans when it was closed by federal inspectors. An incredible 96 percent of these were in default, and many of the remainder were deferred-payment loans on which no payments were yet due.[59]

No parties to the savings and loan mess emerged unscathed. Federal government monetary and fiscal policies generated the inflation that required new responses from the associations. The basic regulations were flawed; savings and loans could not compete for funds without the ability to adjust either mortgage or depositor returns. The combination of short-term liabilities and long-term assets that they represented is extremely vulnerable, perhaps even unworkable under modern circumstances. The associations were denied permission to issue variable-rate mortgages. The regulators made no effort to warn Congress that allowing wider investments in a period of rapid financial change called for higher, not lower, capital requirements and adherence to strict accounting standards, or that regulatory efforts would have to be expanded under such conditions. Once it became apparent that many savings and loans were insolvent, the FSLIC delayed action, allowing the problem to grow beyond its ability to counter. Congress was reluctant to provide additional loss reserves to the FSLIC, and in consequence the bailout costs increased, standing at over $100 billion at this time. The Reagan Administration viewed the problem as an unfavorable verdict on deregulation. Neither Congress nor the Administration was eager to commit billions to a program that could not even restore the status quo. Some legislators exerted blatant pressure on regulators to allow insolvent associations to continue.

As a result, 489 savings and loan associations either failed outright or required FSLIC assistance in survival mergers or other help over 1980–1988. Another 1,226 merged voluntarily or were given new management without FSLIC aid.[60] The problems are heavily associated with a small portion of all associ-

---

[59] G. Benston and G. Kaufman, "Understanding the Saving-and-Loan Debacle," *The Public Interest* (Spring 1990).

[60] J. Barth and M. Bradley, "The Ailing S & Ls," *Challenge* (March/April 1990).

ations; the rate of return for all savings and loans was positive, though less than previous years, through the 1980s. As of July 1992, the worst appeared to be over. The Resolution Trust Corporation, established to liquidate the assets of failed savings and loans, had sold off about two-thirds of the assets it had acquired, generally at higher prices than anticipated. At the same time, surviving savings and loans reported record profits. But the record of the worst 5 percent was catastrophic.[61] For an industry under regulation designed to prevent failures, it is a sorry record.

SELECTED REFERENCES

Baumol, W., S. Blackman, and E. Wolff. *Productivity and American Leadership: The Long View*. Cambridge, Mass.: MIT Press, 1989.

Council of Economic Advisors. *Economic Report of the President*. Washington, D.C.: Government Printing Office, annual eds.

Davis, L., R. Easterlin, W. Parker et al. *American Economic Growth: An Economist's History of the United States*. New York: Harper & Row, 1972.

Feldstein, M., ed. *The American Economy in Transition*. Chicago: University of Chicago Press, 1980.

Gallman, R., and S. Engerman, eds. *Long-Term Factors in American Economic Growth*. Chicago: University of Chicago Press, 1986.

Goldin, C. *Understanding the Gender Gap: An Economic History of American Women*. New York: Oxford University Press, 1990.

Gordon, R. *Economic Instability and Growth: The American Record*. New York: Norton, 1975.

Nau, H. *The Myth of America's Decline: Leading the World Economy into the 1990s*. New York: Oxford University Press, 1990.

Olson, M. *The Rise and Decline of Nations: Economic Growth, Stagflation, and Social Mobility*. New Haven, Conn.: Yale University Press, 1982.

Porter, M. *The Competitive Advantage of Nations*. New York: Free Press, 1990.

Rosenberg, N., and L. Birdzell. *How the West Grew Rich: The Economic Transformation of the Industrial World*. New York: Basic Books, 1986.

U.S. Department of Commerce, Bureau of the Census. *Historical Statistics of the United States: Colonial Times to 1970*. 2 vols. Washington, D.C.: Government Printing Office, 1975.

———. *Bicentennial Statistics*. Washington, D.C.: Government Printing Office, 1976.

———. *Statistical Abstract of the United States, 1991*. Washington, D.C.: Government Printing Office, 1991.

[61] Barth and Bradley, "Ailing S & Ls."

THE UNITED STATES IN THE WORLD ECONOMY

The economic relations of the United States with the rest of the world from 1945 to 1990 may be divided into two distinct episodes. In the first, the rest of the world was unable to generate sufficient claims on the United States, at least through normal methods, to finance the desired level of imports from this country. The United States was a large-scale international creditor, with a massive surplus of exports over imports. The international value of the dollar was high. Foreign countries seeking to repair the widespread devastation of World War II needed huge amounts of goods from the United States—everything from food and consumer goods to tide their populations over through the recovery process to the capital goods with which to accomplish this feat. U.S. exporters faced little competition in foreign markets; their chief problem was in diverting goods from the booming domestic economy. One thesis holds that over 1945–1960, U.S. firms gained a distorted idea of what was necessary for international competition. When foreign producers began to compete their way back into world markets, the efforts necessary to regain position furnished valuable long-term experience for them. U.S. producers later had to learn to operate in a market shaped by hardened new rivals.[1] Another study concluded that 1945–1970 was an aberration even within the United States: Booming domestic demand, the backlog of innovation built up during the Depression and World War II, and growing supplies of major inputs combined to furnish unusually favorable conditions for growth. The era's growth rates in both output and productivity were far above the long-term average. Yet they are the standard of comparison to which subsequent decades are held.[2]

The Dollar Shortage

The war's physical damage and disruption of normal trade patterns had impaired other nations' abilities to produce and export sufficient goods or services to finance the imports they required. The slender gold reserves remaining after the war were inadequate to finance the massive import flows required, and most industrial nations were forced to devalue their currencies.

The worldwide "dollar shortage" was met, in part, by large-scale U.S. foreign aid programs. Aid was extended initially on a country-by-country basis. After 1948, aid to Europe was coordinated under the Marshall Plan. The Marshall Plan was an unprecedented peacetime step for the United States government. At least in Western Europe and Japan, it was highly successful. Even though factories, transportation systems, and other productive resources had been destroyed, the human knowledge and talent that made their effective use possible remained, as did most of the institutions through which they were applied. Indeed, the war, by sweeping away many of the old monopolistic and social restrictions on output expansion, had a favorable effect on institutions (which, of course, did not totally offset its cataclysmic impact on human and physical capital).[3] The Marshall Plan required coordinated efforts among all European recipients, and was one of the first steps toward the economic unification of the Continent.[4] When

---

[1] M. Porter, *The Competitive Advantage of Nations* (New York: Free Press, 1990), 306.

[2] W. Baumol, S. Blackman, and E. Wolff, *Productivity and American Leadership: The Long View* (Cambridge, Mass.: MIT Press, 1989), 65.

[3] M. Olson, *The Growth and Decline of Nations: Economic Growth, Stagflation, and Social Rigidities* (New Haven, Conn.: Yale University Press, 1982).

[4] See H. Nau, *The Myth of America's Decline: Leading the World Economy Into the 1990s* (New York: Oxford University Press, 1990), Chap. 4.

aid was provided to people who knew how to use it and had formulated effective recovery plans, the results were spectacular. By 1950, the major industrial countries had regained or surpassed prewar levels of real output. Recovery stemmed primarily from nations' domestic efforts, not foreign aid, but the Marshall Plan facilitated reconstruction of sectors that were the basis for much wider growth.

Both in this period and subsequently, restrictions on world trade were reduced and the world economy began to struggle back toward the relatively free exchange and specialization that had prevailed before World War I. Such institutions as the World Bank were established to aid recovery and further economic development. The financial institutions of the world were revised, and after the Bretton Woods Conference in 1946, the U.S. dollar increasingly began to supplement gold as an international reserve currency. The dollar was "as good as gold"; it could readily be converted into that metal at a constant rate of $35 per ounce. In the immediate postwar years, the United States held the bulk of the world's gold reserves, which were further protected by its massive trade surpluses and relatively low rates of inflation; there was no doubt that it could accommodate any request to exchange dollars for gold.

CHANGES IN THE U.S. TRADE BALANCE

In the mid-1950s, however, this situation began to change. The industrial nations of Europe, plus Japan, recovered from the war. But they achieved much more than this: Their economic growth, rather than slowing down, accelerated. As these economies grew, modernized, and diversified, they became less dependent on American exports. Their own exports increased, and they began to compete with the United States in third-party markets and then within America itself. Worldwide international trade doubled in the 1960s, increasing much faster than world production, particularly in manufactured goods. In the 1970s and 1980s, the per-capita income growth of middle-income nations was twice as rapid as that of the major industrial nations.[5] In the 1970s, productivity growth slowed noticeably in nearly all industrial nations.

The United States maintained an export surplus until the early 1970s, but it declined while other developments placed more and more dollars in the hands of foreigners. After 1965, inflation within the United States added to the nation's international problems.[6] Even so, the U.S. share of world industrial GNP in 1990 was identical to that in 1970.[7] Since that time it has continued to rise, despite the recent recession.[8]

Foreign aid programs were continued by the United States, although their focus shifted from Europe to the underdeveloped areas of the world. In these regions, aid was far less successful in promoting initial economic development than it had been in fostering recovery. The United States also spent large sums on overseas military bases, on the support of its allies' armed forces, and on the wars in Korea (1950–1953) and Vietnam (1963–1974).

As Europe recovered and began its economic integration under the Common Market after 1958, many American firms responded to the opportunity faster than did the Europeans themselves. Lured by the prospect of a large market in which incomes were growing more rapidly than in the United States, U.S. firms began to invest overseas. Canada, a traditional recipient of American foreign

---

[5] Nau, *The Myth*, 21.
[6] Nau, *The Myth*, Chap. 5.
[7] Nau, *The Myth*, 4.
[8] "Can America Compete?" *The Economist* (January 18–24, 1992).

investment, continued to attract massive flows of American dollars, and more recently Mexico has been a focal point of U.S. investment. Other nations pursued similar policies. By the 1980s, manufacture of many goods was truly international: The location of a firm's headquarters or the nationality of its owners might give little indication of the location of its activities. Assembly facilities in one country might rely on components made in a second, find markets for finished goods in a third, and rely on financial or transport services from yet other nations. These developments occurred in all the major manufacturing nations; capital became as internationally mobile as it was before World War I.

Prosperity in the United States meant growing demand for both foreign services, such as shipping and tourism support, and, even more, for imported goods. This meant growing competition for domestic industries, which in some cases were ill-prepared to meet it. Many U.S. firms had to learn how to compete for foreign markets and defend those at home because they had traditionally concentrated on domestic markets and their only rivals had been other domestic producers. Exports were often a tiny fraction of total production, and were generated largely by foreign buyers' requests, not American sales efforts. Rapid increases in energy costs, chaotic capital markets, volatile exchange rates, changes in government regulation, and growth in capital and labor supplies that differed between nations hampered adjustment.

For producers of goods in which foreign producers' comparative advantages were high, import competition meant failure and a forced reallocation of resources. American consumers benefited from wider choices, lower prices, and improved quality, and resources were shifted to higher-productivity (and higher-income) uses. But these gains, like any other economic developments, also involved costs. Resources seldom move to new uses smoothly. Skills, machinery, and locations specialized to one use may have no accessible alternative employment yielding comparable incomes. Moreover, the gains from international trade were widely dispersed and often not conspicuous; closed factories and unemployed workers are only too visible.

The Dollar Glut

The balance of payments deficits generated more dollars for foreign countries than were necessary to finance imports from the United States after the mid-1960s. At first, the excess over trade requirements was used to bolster foreign-exchange reserves, but this demand was soon satisfied. Foreigners then began to convert dollars into gold or required special incentives, such as high interest rates on dollar-denominated deposits or securities, to continue holding U.S. funds. The "dollar shortage" had become a "dollar glut." Although increased earnings on American foreign investments added to American claims on other nations, they were insufficient to offset the effects of additional overseas investment, foreign aid, military spending, and a declining export surplus. The usual process of adjustment would have been a revaluation of the dollar against gold and foreign currencies, but the United States was reluctant to take this step. Many nations held their international reserves in dollars rather than gold, and a U.S. devaluation would impose severe deflationary pressure on them.

In the early 1970s, the American export surplus vanished, and foreigners became unwilling either to hold more dollars individually or to allow their central banks to do so. In 1971, the United States devalued the dollar (the official dollar price of gold was increased). This reduced the amount of foreign currency that could be obtained for a dollar, that is, it made foreign goods more expensive in the United States and reduced the price of American exports in foreign currency. In 1973, there was a further devaluation, after which the dollar was allowed to "float." (Its value in terms of foreign currencies was determined by supply and demand, with some intervention by central banks.)

The Continuing Trade Deficit

The predicted effects of these measures, which should have reduced the American trade deficit, were only beginning to be felt in 1973. In the fall of that year, the Organization of Petroleum Exporting Countries (OPEC) began a series of sharp oil price increases. With U.S. oil production declining and inept policy responses that did little to reduce demand for petroleum products, the rapidly rising bill for imported oil swamped other developments through the 1970s. Since that time, the United States has continued to incur balance-of-payments deficits, although these decreased to less than half their 1987 peak by 1992. (The nearly balanced accounts for 1991 are due to foreign payments for the cost of the 1991 Persian Gulf War.) Table 21.1 gives details.

The claim that the United States has become the world's largest debtor seems overstated. Continued trade deficits of the magnitude of the late 1980s will eventually produce this result, but as of 1990, the United States received slightly more income from its overseas investments than it paid to foreign investors in this country.[9] Figures for U.S. foreign investments' value in relation to those of other nations in this country are generally given in acquisition-cost dollars. Since American investments overseas were made earlier than foreign asset purchases in this country, such figures do not allow for the appreciation of America's foreign assets and the effects of inflation. Consequently, the present value of U.S. investments abroad is understated.[10]

Developments in international trade were heavily influenced by inflation. The 1970s and early 1980s were a period of worldwide inflation, but rates of price increases varied between nations. Because inflation rates were lower in the United States than in some other nations, foreigners began to build up deposits in American banks and to buy American securities. Relative inflation rates were less favorable to the United States after 1968, however, particularly relative to Germany and Japan.[11] The possibility of government instability or restrictions on private economic activity in many countries further increased the flow of funds to the United States. American interest rates adjusted to inflation both more rapidly and more completely than did those of many other nations: Real returns on funds in America were high, while in many other countries they were negligible or even negative. Some OPEC nations accumulated massive trade surpluses that they literally could not spend as fast as they accrued. These too flowed to American banks. The result was an increase in the international value of the dollar to 1986, and a further widening of the trade deficit. The financial developments' impact was made greater by the deterioration of American productivity gains in the 1970s, particularly in relation to those of major trading partners such as Japan, West Germany, and the rapidly growing nations of the western Pacific. No longer did the United States have an export surplus to offset the financial flows. Growing trade deficits in the latter region were a major factor in these developments.

The evidence that traditional exports such as autos and steel were losing markets to other nations, some of whom appeared disconcertingly capable of competing in domestic markets as well, was a new experience for Americans. Growing foreign investment was even more disturbing. Some studies of these

[9] Council of Economic Advisors, *Economic Report of the President, 1991* (Washington, D.C.: Government Printing Office), 402.
[10] *Economic Report, 1991*, 258.

[11] *Economic Report, 1991*, 408.

Table 21.1   Foreign Trade Statistics, 1946–1990
(Millions of Current Dollars)

| Year | Merchandise | | | Net Services* |
	Exports	Imports	Net	
1946	$11,764	−$5,067	$6,697	$550
1948	13,265	−7,557	5,708	−250
1950	10,203	−9,081	1,122	−454
1952	13,449	−10,838	2,611	−1,662
1954	12,929	−10,353	2,576	−2,424
1956	17,556	−12,803	4,753	−2,702
1958	16,414	−12,952	3,462	−3,282
1960	19,650	−14,758	4,892	−1,382
1962	20,781	−16,260	4,521	−1,152
1964	25,501	−18,700	6,801	−779
1966	29,310	−25,493	3,817	−877
1968	33,626	−32,991	635	−385
1970	42,469	−39,866	2,603	−349
1972	49,381	−55,797	−6,416	974
1974	98,306	−103,811	−5,505	1,212
1976	114,745	−124,228	−9,483	3,400
1978	142,054	−176,001	−33,947	4,163
1980	224,269	−249,750	−25,481	6,093
1982	211,198	−247,642	−36,444	12,101
1984	219,900	−332,422	−112,522	2,742
1986	223,637	−338,083	−145,058	−1,687
1988	320,337	−447,323	−129,986	11,520
1990***	384,608	−489,860	−105,252	23,697

* Indicates separate services net from merchandise, exports, imports, and net.
** Includes foreign aid.
*** 1990 figures prorated from data for first three quarters.
Source: Council of Economic Advisors, *Economic Report of the President, 1991* (Washington, D.C.: Government Printing Office, 1991), 402.

trends concluded that they were irreversible because they were embedded in the structure of the American economy. Dire predictions were commonly made: The United States was becoming unable to compete in international trade, and was doomed to lose even domestic markets to foreign manufactured goods. Proponents of this view claimed that the U.S. economy was deindustrializing, and American workers faced a future of low-paying service jobs and stagnant or declining living standards. They called for increased protection for domestic industry, which otherwise would be competed out of existence. Others considered the deterioration in international competitiveness to stem from attempts to maintain political hegemony at ruinous cost to the economy upon which it was based, or to deterio-

Net Investment Income	Balance (Goods, Services, Income)	Unilateral Transfers**	Balance on Current Account
$560	$7,807	−$2,922	$4,885
1,484	6,942	−4,525	2,417
1,509	2,177	−4,077	−1,840
2,196	3,145	−2,531	614
2,347	2,499	−2,280	219
3,102	5,153	−2,423	2,730
2,965	3,145	−2,361	784
3,379	6,886	−4,062	2,824
4,294	7,664	−4,277	3,387
5,041	11,063	−4,240	6,823
5,047	7,987	−4,955	3,031
5,990	6,240	−5,629	611
6,233	8,486	−6,156	2,331
8,192	2,749	−8,544	−5,795
15,503	11,210	−9,249	1,962
15,975	9,894	−5,686	4,207
20,144	−9,639	−5,788	−15,427
28,856	9,467	−8,349	1,119
28,250	3,907	−9,775	−5,868
23,397	−86,385	−12,621	−99,006
10,969	−129,384	−16,009	−145,393
1,610	−113,857	−15,005	−128,862
4,601	−76,983	−15,678	−92,752

ration in performance that could be reversed, if at all, only through a painful major effort.[12]

[12] The classic statement of the former is P. Kennedy, *The Rise and Fall of the Great Powers: Economic Change and Military Conflict from 1500 to 2000* (New York: Random House, 1987). M. Porter, *The Competitive Advantage of Nations* (New York: Free Press, 1990), is a widely cited statement of the latter position.

Many such studies neglected the lesson that long-run economic growth requires continuous change in leading sectors. The United States could no more expect to continue exporting the same products to a changing world economy than it could to produce Model T Fords for domestic consumers in the 1980s. But in the 1970s and early 1980s, there seemed few offsets to a host of disturbing changes in

America's international position. Trade deficits grew, foreign products competed in a widening range of American markets, and the workers and producers most affected demanded protection.

Since 1986, the international situation of the United States supports a more optimistic view. The international value of the dollar has declined, and (more significantly for the long run) productivity growth in U.S. manufacturing has shown substantial and sustained improvement, both relative and absolute. Over 1979–1989, productivity growth in U.S. manufacturing was greater than that in either Germany or Japan, and today the United States has the largest share of manufactured exports of any nation in the world.[13] As Table 21.1 indicates, recent growth in U.S. exports is much more rapid than that in imports, and this trend has continued through early 1992. Contrary to widely held beliefs, the proportion of GNP generated by service activity is growing much more slowly (if at all) in the United States than in other developed nations.[14] American productivity in internationally traded services is very high[15] and in many domestic service sectors even higher. However, there may be an inherent tendency for service productivity to decline.[16] Most economists agree that relative productivity and its growth are the primary factors determining the level and growth rates of relative wages. The trends and implications of relative productivity

change will be discussed further later in this chapter.

THE NATURE AND DIRECTION OF FOREIGN TRADE

Early American foreign trade had been largely an exchange of American raw materials and agricultural products for European manufactures and tropical products, such as sugar and coffee. American shipping earnings supplemented the incomes gained from exports, and Europeans invested in the United States to offset chronic American trade deficits. Gradually, the American trade position changed. Agricultural exports continued, but were supplemented and then surpassed by shipments of manufactured goods to foreign customers as American industrial productivity achieved world primacy. The United States began to pay off its international debts after 1895. In the early twentieth century, overseas investments by the United States became significant.

In the 1945–1984 period, some of these trends were again reversed. Manufactured goods accounted for only two-fifths of American imports in 1947, reflecting the devastation of our industrial rivals; by 1989, they comprised 67 percent of the total. Manufactured goods were 73 percent of all American exports in 1989; they had comprised about three-fourths in the earlier period.[17] Table 21.2 shows postwar trends in import and export composition.

These changes mask still more violent short-term fluctuations, particularly in the 1970s. By 1975, U.S. manufactured imports had slumped to only 53 percent of the total: The current-dollar value of crude material and fuel imports increased fourteen-fold between 1970 and 1980, to 38 percent of the total at

---

[13] "Can America Compete?" Apparently the less optimistic conclusions in Porter, *Competitive Advantage of Nations,* are derived from international comparisons that end with 1985 data.

[14] Baumol, Blackman, and Wolff, *Productivity and American Leadership,* 115–116.

[15] Perhaps the most noteworthy accomplishment of American technology in the Persian Gulf was that of oil-fire firms, which extinguished the oil field fires in Kuwait, a job expected to require two to three years, if it could be done at all. Work commenced in March 1990; the last well was extinguished on November 6, 1990. Most of the work was done by U.S. and Canadian firms.

[16] Baumol, Blackman, and Wolff, *Productivity and American Leadership,* 124–135.

[17] *Economic Report, 1991,* 404.

Table 21.2   **Composition of U.S. Exports and Imports (Billions of Current Dollars)**

			Exports			
Year	Total	Agricultural Goods	Industrial Supplies and Materials	Capital Goods	Automotive	Other
1965	$26.5	$6.3	$7.6	$8.1	$1.9	$2.6
1966	29.3	6.9	8.2	8.9	2.4	2.9
1968	33.6	6.3	9.6	11.1	3.5	3.2
1970	42.5	7.4	12.3	14.7	3.9	4.3
1972	49.4	9.5	11.8	16.9	5.5	5.6
1974	98.3	22.4	26.2	30.9	8.8	10.0
1976	114.7	23.4	28.3	39.1	12.2	11.7
1978	142.1	29.9	34.0	47.3	15.7	15.2
1980	224.3	42.2	65.3	76.3	17.4	23.2
1982	211.2	37.2	58.0	76.0	17.4	22.5
1984	219.9	38.4	56.8	77.0	22.6	25.1
1986	223.4	27.4	59.4	82.9	25.3	28.3
1988	320.3	38.2	82.6	119.0	33.9	46.6
1990*	384.8	41.2	93.9	152.7	36.3	60.4

			Imports			
Year	Total	Petroleum	Industrial Supplies and Materials	Capital Goods	Automotive	Other
1965	$21.5	$2.0	$9.1	$1.5	$0.9	$8.0
1966	25.5	2.1	10.2	2.2	1.8	9.2
1968	33.0	2.4	12.0	2.8	4.0	11.8
1970	39.9	2.9	12.3	4.0	5.7	15.0
1972	55.8	4.7	16.0	5.9	9.0	20.2
1974	103.8	26.6	27.4	9.8	12.4	27.5
1976	124.2	34.6	29.1	12.3	16.8	31.4
1978	176.0	42.6	40.6	19.4	25.0	48.4
1980	249.8	79.4	52.9	31.4	28.1	58.0
1982	247.6	62.0	48.9	38.4	34.0	64.3
1984	332.4	58.0	66.0	60.5	56.6	91.4
1986	368.4	34.4	69.9	72.1	78.1	113.9
1988	447.3	39.6	83.1	102.2	87.9	134.5
1990*	489.8	57.9	81.8	115.7	86.2	148.4

* 1990 data prorated from first three quarters.
Source: Council of Economic Advisors, *Economic Report of the President, 1991* (Washington, D.C.: Government Printing Office, 1991), 404.

■ This Honda automobile plant in Marysville, Ohio, was the first auto plant built in the United States by a Japanese producer.
Source: Honda of America Mfg., Inc.

the latter date. Since 1981, the value of such imports has declined; they comprised 22 percent of all imports in 1984, and their share of the total was 11.8 percent in 1990.[18] The composition of exports showed more stability; manufactured goods continued to hold about a two-thirds share through 1984. U.S. exports of industrial goods increased more than three times as fast as those of other OECD nations in the 1980s, and were 89 percent of total exports by 1990. Exports of agricultural products, however, were 12 percent of all exports in 1970, 15.8 percent in 1975, 14 percent in 1980, and 10.7 percent in 1990, reflecting changing agricultural fortunes abroad, as modern farming methods spread through the world and government subsidies increased world food and fiber production.[19]

Old and New Trading Partners

The identity of the United States' major trading partners remained about the same through 1970, but more recently there have been some shifts, as Table 21.3 indicates. These figures

---

[18] *Economic Report, 1991,* 404.

[19] *Economic Report, 1991,* 404.

Table 21.3 Origins and Destinations of U.S. Foreign Trade

Area of Origin or Destination	1973	1975	1980	1985	1990*
			Imports		
Canada	23%	22%	19%	21%	19%
Western Europe	28	19	19	23	22
Japan	14	13	13	19	18
Australia, New Zealand, South Africa	3	2	3	2	1
OPEC	7	22	22	7	7
Other	22	22	25	28	32
Eastern Europe	1	1	1	0.5	0.4
			Exports		
Canada	23%	22%	19%	26%	22%
Western Europe	30	28	30	26	28
Japan	12	9	9	10	12
Australia, New Zealand, South Africa	3	4	3	3	3
OPEC	4	11	8	5	3
Other	24	25	29	28	30
Eastern Europe	1	1	1	2	1

* Preliminary data.
Totals may not add to 100 percent because of rounding.
Sources: U.S. Department of Commerce, Bureau of the Census, *Historical Statistics of the U.S.: Colonial Times to 1970*, 2 vols. (Washington, D.C.: Government Printing Office, 1975), 903; Council of Economic Advisors, *Economic Reports of the President, 1977, 1985, 1991* (Washington, D.C.: Government Printing Office, 1991).

understate trade with industrial nations because they do not include separate figures for Hong Kong, Singapore, Taiwan, and the Republic of Korea, which have become major exporters of manufactures. The proportion of our trade with these areas decreased during the oil shortage: 71 percent of American exports went to the world's developed nations in 1970, and 74 percent of all imports originated there. In 1975, the figures were 60 and 58 percent, respectively. By 1989, oil prices had fallen and 62 percent of U.S. imports and 65 percent of exports represented exchanges with the world's industrial nations.

With the exception of oil, whose influence can be expected to decline, it does not appear that the United States is dependent on the underdeveloped nations for either export markets or imports to any great extent. Because of their higher incomes and productivity, the developed nations of the world continue to be each others' best customers, and this is true even in world trade in raw materials.[20] Rapid growth of the nations on the western rim of the Pacific (Singapore, Taiwan, Hong Kong, and South Korea, as well as the continued expansion and diversification of Japan) has increased the importance of that region in U.S.

[20] E. Fried, "International Trade in Raw Materials: Myths and Realities," *Science* (February 20, 1976).

trade, while slower-growing regions have lost ground. The recent changes in Eastern Europe and the former Soviet Union, plus Western European economic unification in 1992 may have profound effects on U.S. direct trade with those regions as well as relations with those regions' suppliers and customers. Little more can be said than that both changes should increase the volume of international trade at the present (1992). Prospects of freer trade with Canada and Mexico seem likely to raise the volume of trade with our closest neighbors, which already rank first and third, respectively, among U.S. trade partners.

The aggregate importance of foreign trade to the U.S. economy has increased sharply in the past two decades. Imports, which had been about 4 percent of American GNP over most of the postwar period, rose to 6 percent in 1975 and 11.8 percent in 1990. For exports, which had slightly exceeded the relative importance of imports in the early years , the figures rose to 7.1 percent in 1975, declined to slightly less than 6 percent in 1984, and rose to 9.3 percent

in 1990.[21] The aggregate impact of foreign trade thus increased from about 8 or 9 percent of GNP over most of the postwar period to 20 percent in the 1980s. While this is a far smaller percentage of aggregate economic activity than foreign trade represents for most developed economies, it leaves little doubt that the U.S. economy is no longer operating in isolation.

FOREIGN INVESTMENT

The private overseas investments of the United States were only $14.7 billion in 1945. By 1970 they had risen to $120.2 billion, by 1984 to $795.1 billion, and in 1989 they were reported as $1.2535 trillion. U.S. international reserves and foreign assets of the U.S. government were an additional $1.594 trillion. At the latter date, foreign assets in the United

---

[21] *Economic Report, 1991,* 405.

■ U.S. producers also built factories in foreign countries. Pictured is one such plant, located in Mexico.
Source: © Steve Lunetta.

States (government and private) were $2.0763 trillion. These figures are not consistent, however. They mix assets valued at both current and historical (acquisition) values. The gold reserves of the United States, for example, are carried at the $35 per ounce historical value, but in 1992 the price of gold was over $350 per ounce. The investment income figures cited in Table 21.1 indicate that the current value of U.S. investments abroad still exceeds that of foreign assets in this country.

With the exception of petroleum, most American foreign investment has been and continues to be in developed countries. Profit-seeking investment will be placed where markets are large and property secure, not in areas where incomes are low and governments both unstable and hostile. About 60 percent of American foreign investments were in Canada and Western Europe in 1970. At that time, about 16 percent was in Latin America, and 24 percent in all other areas, some of which, such as Australia, were also developed countries.[22] Latin America's share of U.S. investment has increased in recent years, chiefly in Brazil, Mexico, and Argentina. Since 1970, overseas investment patterns have shown no major changes.

One result of the massive outflow of dollars in the later postwar period was an increase in foreign investment in the United States. Although this caused some popular resentment and concern, it was an inevitable outcome of the United States' continuing difficulties in achieving a balance in its international accounts by other means. As long as the United States continued to make dollars available to foreigners in amounts exceeding those they wished to spend for American products or hold in various short-term accounts, foreign-

ers could be expected to use their dollars in their own best interests. By 1988, net investment income flows indicated that foreign investment in this country was nearly equal to that of the United States abroad.

Another factor in foreign investment, both in the United States and in other nations, has been the effort to overcome trade barriers. Goods produced within the United States by factories owned by foreigners are not subject to tariffs, quotas, or other measures intended to restrict access to the domestic market. In some cases, particularly in the automobile industry, such plants produce cars sold under both U.S. and Japanese brand names. In return, virtually all automobiles now sold under U.S. nameplates contain parts made in other nations or are assembled abroad. The United States also invested in plants in Mexico (the *maquiladoras*) that were exempted from duty obligations on raw materials and parts used in products sent across the border. By 1988, 45 percent of U.S. merchandise imports from Mexico originated in the *maquiladoras*.[23]

Changes in the U.S. international economic relations were sometimes the consequences of domestic monetary, fiscal, and regulatory policies. In a world where transportation costs no longer were a barrier to long-distance shipment of even bulky goods, nations found that they could not pursue macroeconomic policies without considering their effects on international trade. In particular, policies that raised inflation rates or manufacturing costs above those of competitors quickly resulted in loss of international reserves or declines in relative currency values.[24] Nor could they pursue high-cost employment, development, or regulatory programs without regard to international consequences, because these affected the prices of

[22] U.S. Department of Congress, Bureau of the Census, *Historical Statistics of the U.S.: Colonial Times to 1970*, 2 vols. (Washington, D.C.: Government Printing Office, 1975), 870–871.

[23] *Economic Report, 1991*, 254.
[24] Nau, *The Myth*, is a strong proponent of this idea.

exports and imports. Since the sources of these changes had frequently been thought to be solely under the control of the nation instituting them, the new international repercussions were a shock. Frequently they led to attempts to shift pressures abroad, or to offset them through reductions in other foreign spending. Other nations seldom welcomed these efforts.[25] Disputes over these issues were often bitter, since participants were being asked (or pressured) to limit their own trade gains, hold unwanted international reserves, abandon internally popular programs, or restrict the actions of their own citizens for the benefit of foreigners. One example would be the United States' efforts to limit the agricultural subsidies furnished to European farmers under the European Economic Community's Common Agricultural Policy.

Trade Policy

Since 1945, industrial nations have generally reduced their tariff rates. This fostered the expansion of international trade and raised world incomes. However, it also restricted nations' freedom to pursue internal policies, or made their costs obvious, as noted above. Sometimes the result was attempts to restrict trade by quantitative restrictions (quotas), "anti-dumping" regulations forbidding foreign sales at less than domestic production costs, domestic-content requirements, and a host of other devices intended to impede foreign access to domestic markets. Political pressures often reinforced demands for such concessions. The United States was by no means the only nation to employ such measures, but it was much less than consistent in its pursuit of free trade. Protective devices were prominent in steel, automobiles, and textiles. Jobs "saved" by such policies were expensive: The cost to American consumers and

exporters was estimated at $120,000 per job preserved in the machine tool industry.[26]

More welcome developments were the free trade treaty signed with Canada in 1988 and the current (1992) negotiations for a similar agreement with Mexico, which had already reduced both tariffs and other import restrictions. Discussions were underway on a treaty between the United States, Canada, and Mexico to establish a North American Common Market. Preliminary negotiations began in 1991 on a free trade agreement for the entire Western Hemisphere.

Other alterations in America's trading positions stemmed from real factor shifts. Western Europe and Japan had achieved increases in productivity that considerably exceeded those recorded in the United States from 1947 through 1979, and consequently had grown much more rapidly. Both regions were now able to exploit technological advances that had been beyond their reach or neglected for years, sometimes from the era of World War I. Most were able to integrate the new technology into comprehensive modernization efforts in both capital and institutions, thus realizing its full potential. Consequently, productivity rose faster in these nations than in technological leaders, such as the United States. The Pacific "Gang of Four" (Singapore, Hong Kong, Taiwan, and South Korea) had made even greater gains after the mid-1970s. For some of America's international competitors, production techniques caught up to or surpassed those of the United States, resulting in increased competition for American goods in domestic as well as international markets, and lower prices, better quality goods, or both, for American consumers. Less obviously, rapidly growing nations' greater wealth and incomes also increased markets for goods in which the United States retained a comparative advantage.

---

[25] For a detailed discussion, see H. Nau, *The Myth.*

[26] *Economic Report, 1991,* 141.

CAN AMERICA COMPETE?

Relative productivity is the key to real income standing between nations over time. Labor whose output per hour or year rises faster than that of other countries can enjoy higher real wages without losing foreign markets. If productivity gains are less than other nations', markets can be retained only if relative real wages decline and production shifts to labor-intensive goods.[27] Declining exchange rates can preserve foreign sales, but these imply lower returns to workers in the exporting nation, and higher real import costs. Lagging productivity growth need not imply loss of foreign markets or absolute declines in real wages, but the standard of living will improve faster elsewhere. Productivity gains generate long-term benefits, but are not cures for trade deficits, differential inflation rates, or other short-term problems, particularly not those resulting from macroeconomic policies.

Discussions of recent developments in comparative productivity have two facets: Trends solely within the United States and comparisons with other nations. As noted earlier, American labor productivity gains (output per work-hour) from 1945 to 1960 were nearly twice the 1880–1984 average of 2.27 percent annually. This may be attributed largely to making good unutilized potential from the Great Depression.[28] The 1938–1950 increase in U.S. output per labor-hour was much faster than those recorded by other nations. This was an unusual situation; productivity had increased faster in about a third of the other industrial nations after 1890.[29]

After 1960, labor productivity growth across all sectors of the U.S. economy slowed because further gains stemmed from technology currently developed and innovated; the backlog of unused ideas was eliminated. Also, U.S. factor proportions varied from those of most other industrial nations. The American labor force grew much faster than most others due to natural increase, greater labor force participation by women, and immigration. Labor/capital ratios were higher in the United States, especially since investment rates were lower. Service employment increased faster than that in manufacturing to 1980, especially in sectors where productivity gains were low. The energy shortage of the later 1970s may have affected U.S. industry more adversely: An older industrial plant whose design reflected historically lower energy costs than those abroad had more difficulty adjusting to new factor costs. Even so, labor productivity growth during the 1970s slowed in nearly all developed nations. In many nations, the proportionate shift to service employment over 1965–1980 was three to four times greater than in the United States.[30]

The picture was not entirely gloomy, and some of its dimensions were exaggerated or misunderstood. Even during the 1960s and 1970s, U.S. manufacturing productivity growth continued, and since 1980 it has increased very sharply, both absolutely and in relation to foreign rivals. The increase in output per labor-hour in manufacturing may be slightly *above* the long-term level to 1984. The employment shift to those service industries in which gains in GNP stemmed from price increases rather than rises in real output adversely affected aggregate productivity trends.[31] U.S. manufacturing's share of real output did not fall, nor did that of services

[27] Baumol, Blackman, and Wolff, *Productivity and American Leadership,* 19.
[28] Baumol, Blackman, and Wolff, *Productivity and American Leadership,* 69–71.
[29] Baumol, Blackman, and Wolff, *Productivity and American Leadership,* 87–89. J. Williamson, "Productivity and American Leadership: A Review Article," *Journal of Economic Literature* (March 1991), sees the 1938–1950 period as less exceptional.

[30] Baumol, Blackman, and Wolff, *Productivity and American Leadership,* 120–121.
[31] Baumol, Blackman, and Wolff, *Productivity and American Leadership,* 131.

■ The United States is a strong competitor in some high-tech export markets. This airplane, manufactured by Boeing, based in Seattle, Washington, is used by airlines worldwide.
Source: Boeing Photo.

rise, but the relative prices of services recorded low productivity gains and the portion of such industries and their share of total employment grew. Overall service sector productivity in the United States, while lower than in manufacturing, is much higher than similar sectors in other nations, including Japan. Overall American productivity trends do not support pessimistic assessments of the nation's ability to compete in either manufactured goods or internationally traded services.

Long-term productivity growth has increased in most other developed nations since World War II. Nations with lower initial productivity have some growth advantages; if the technological gap is not too great, it is easier to copy efficiency-increasing practices than to discover them. This advantage decreases as the productivity gap diminishes, however. One major study of international productivity trends concluded that the gains recorded by other nations would slow as their levels of output per labor-hour neared those of the United States. However, most had productivity

growth rates from 1950 through 1979 nearly twice the U.S. long-term average. Even if productivity gains in Western Europe and Japan converge on those of the United States at rates reflecting both their performance in recent decades and the recent U.S. performance, 9 of the 15 nations surveyed would surpass American productivity by 2020 if growth rates here are maintained at their 2.27 percent long-term average. This by no means implies that the United States would be impoverished by that date. Indeed, that growth would raise American real per-capita gross domestic product from $19,800 to $43,164 in 1990 dollars.[32] But other nations would enjoy higher incomes.

Raising American labor productivity growth to slightly over 3 percent per year would give real income parity or superiority to all but Germany through 2020. An increase of less than one percentage point may not appear difficult to achieve, but this is a 45 percent

---

[32] Baumol, Blackman, and Wolff, *Productivity and American Leadership*, 253.

gain, hardly a minor achievement. What policies might be necessary to achieve this? The following list is compiled from the recommendations of several experts.[33]

1. Increased investment. The United States currently invests a smaller portion of income than most other developed nations. Higher investment would not only raise the capital/labor ratio, but would also decrease the average age of capital. Comparisons of U.S. and foreign investment levels overstate the gap because capital is relatively cheaper here, and also because the United States invests more in human capital (assessment of the quality and direct growth contribution of American education is extremely difficult), but some disparity remains.[34] Some propose doubling the investment rate to nearly 30 percent of GNP.
2. Reduce unproductive government spending. With the end of the Cold War, military spending (particularly overseas) can be reduced, and some of the technical resources now consumed redirected to more productive purposes. Other dubious government spending has proved difficult to cut. Federal deficit reduction would increase the proportion of current savings devoted to investment.
3. Raise research and development spending. Currently, American reseach and development spending is greater than that of either Germany or Japan in absolute amount, but a slightly smaller portion of income. The U.S. effort is reduced by the larger portion devoted to military research, though in recent years military research and development has declined and been partially replaced by corporate efforts.

4. Reduce rent-seeking activity. Although studies have thus far failed to indicate significant income costs, at a minimum, the trend toward redistributing existing income at the cost of growth should be reduced.
5. Improve education, particularly that of minority groups. Both for equity purposes and in view of the prospective labor shortage, the current waste of human potential must cease.
6. Minimize inflation. Rising price levels, especially when volatile, reduce the present value of future earnings, make long-term calculations difficult, and encourage asset acquisition and consumption rather than investment.

These developments imply neither that the United States has achieved permanent success nor that it might be unable to compete with foreign producers. Rather, it indicates that the maintenance of American exports requires a constant increase in factor productivity and also a constantly changing mix of economic activities. Above all, America must continue to compete internationally: Total reliance on domestic resources or begging or bullying trade partners for advantages we have not earned will lower our incomes, not raise them. The United States must generate new items for export that make use of its productive and innovative advantages; competition in virtually all long-established products can only be expected to increase. Considerable success has been recorded in this area; the United States and Japan have increased their shares of the world's "high-tech" exports at the expense of Britain, France, and Germany both over the 1960–1984 period and later in the 1980s.[35]

One measure of the success of a modern economy is now the rate at which jobs in long-established industries are eliminated as these

[33] Baumol, Blackman, and Wolff, *Productivity and American Leadership*; M. Porter, *The Competitive Advantage of Nations* (New York: Free Press, 1990); H. Nau, *The Myth*.
[34] Baumol, Blackman, and Wolff, *Productivity and American Leadership*, 188–190.

[35] Baumol, Blackman, and Wolff, *Productivity and American Leadership*, 104–105.

■ A container ship port in Tacoma, Washington, is shown. Facilities of this type owe their existence to the rising volume of international trade.
Source: Sea-Land Service, Inc.

are replaced by work in new sectors, that is, high "job death" rates imply even higher "job birth" rates.[36] Nor should foreign investment be restricted. If foreigners want to provide American workers with new and better tools, they should be encouraged to do so. Domestic savings rates are low in comparison to most industrial nations, and foreign investment adds to the stock of new capital that increases the productivity (and wages) of American workers. The fear of "foreign ownership of America" is vastly overstated. Foreign mul-

tinational firms account for about 4 percent of U.S. jobs and output—a low figure by international standards.[37]

American industries that have maintained their technological leads, such as computers and software, pharmaceuticals, chemicals, aircraft, and sophisticated construction engineering, have had little trouble in maintaining or even expanding their export markets. We may not think of American films, videos, and television programs as exportable goods, but they find markets all over the world. Other

---

[36] Rosenberg and Birdzell, *How the West Grew Rich*, 278.

[37] *Economic Report, 1991*, 261.

industries, including most capital goods, have had considerable success in responding to foreign competition through the introduction of new methods. American steel exports quadrupled from 1986 to 1991, indicating that some firms were competitive in world markets even though eulogies for the entire industry had been a growth industry in their own right. Overall, manufacturing now accounts for a slightly higher share of U.S. gross national product (23 percent *versus* 22 percent) than in the late 1960s, when the nation's technological supremacy was virtually unchallenged. Capital goods' share of total output has increased by about a third, and their share of exports has more than doubled.[38]

The automobile industry's position seems ambivalent; having made considerable strides in improving both productivity and product quality under the shield of "voluntary" import quotas on Japanese cars,[39] American producers appear unwilling to return to normal terms of competition. The quotas were little long-term help to American auto producers. Japanese firms responded by upgrading the quality of their exports, which now compete with the larger, more profitable types of American cars. They also constructed automobile plants in the United States. In some cases those plants exported cars to Japan.

Industries that have failed to match or exceed the technological gains made abroad, such as shoes, apparel, and textiles, have lost both foreign and domestic markets to imports. Since these sectors had been declining for years, the workers who finally lost jobs as plants cut back production or closed down were long-term employees with few alternatives.

Prospects for World Trade

World trade appears likely to increase if left to economic factors. Postwar trends in reduced transport costs appear likely to continue, and there is at least a possibility that political barriers to trade will continue to decline. Protectionist sentiment has not yet prevailed in the United States; it is obvious that some of its recent beneficiaries have profited at the expense of American consumers, while doing little or nothing to restore their long-term competitive ability.

If world trade continues to increase, the degree of specialization possible for each member of the world community—and the total incomes of the world's population—will rise. Despite the protests of industries and workers displaced by foreign competition, there is little doubt that the increase in foreign trade has been beneficial to the United States. It has increased competition and the range of choices open to U.S. consumers in many markets. It has given new opportunities to America's most efficient producers and forced others to change their operating methods. Like all economic changes, this has required adjustments, sizable and even traumatic ones for some individuals. But adjustments made along the lines indicated by comparative advantage will result in an increase in the incomes of American producers—and certainly of American consumers. Given the traditional sources of its economic growth, the United States should have little to fear from a process that places a premium on the ability to change.

---

[38] L. Lindsey, "America's Growing Economic Lead," *Wall Street Journal* (February 7, 1992).

[39] The only agreement that the Japanese made under less "voluntary" circumstances was signed on the deck of the U.S.S. *Missouri* in August 1945. At present (1992), they are again under pressure to further reduce exports.

SELECTED REFERENCES

Baumol, W., S. Blackman, and E. Wolff. *Productivity and American Leadership: The Long View.* Cambridge, Mass.: MIT Press, 1990.

Baumol, W., and K. McLennan, eds. *Productivity Growth and U.S. Competitiveness.* New York: Oxford University Press, 1989.

Council of Economic Advisors. *Economic Report of the President.* Washington, D.C.: Government Printing Office, annual eds.

Davis, L., R. Easterlin, W. Parker et al. *American Economic Growth: An Economist's History of the United States.* New York: Harper & Row, 1972.

Feldstein, M., ed. *The American Economy in Transition.* Chicago: University of Chicago Press, 1980.

Gordon, R. *Economic Instability and Growth: The American Record.* New York: Norton, 1975.

Kennedy, P. *The Rise and Fall of the Great Powers: Economic Change and Military Conflict From 1500 to 2000.* New York: Random House, 1987.

Nau, H. *The Myth of America's Decline: Leading the World Economy into the 1990s.* New York: Oxford University Press, 1990.

Olson, M. *The Rise and Decline of Nations: Economic Growth, Stagflation, and Social Mobility.* New Haven, Conn.: Yale University Press, 1982.

Porter, M. *The Competitive Advantage of Nations.* New York: Free Press, 1990.

Rosenberg, N., and L. Birdzell. *How the West Grew Rich: The Economic Transformation of the Industrial World.* New York: Basic Books, 1986.

U.S. Department of Commerce, Bureau of the Census. *Historical Statistics of the United States: Colonial Times to 1970.* 2 vols. Washington, D.C.: Government Printing Office, 1975.

———. *Bicentennial Statistics.* Washington, D.C.: Government Printing Office, 1976.

———. *Statistical Abstract of the United States, 1986, 1991.* Washington, D.C.: Government Printing Office, 1986, 1991.

GOVERNMENT IN THE POSTWAR ECONOMY

*T*he role of government has expanded greatly in the postwar U.S. economy, through both increases in the aggregate size of government and expansion of the range of functions performed by the public sector. Even more, the extent to which government influences private economic actions has increased. This growth of the public sector has been controversial; both its nature and extent have been questioned. Currently, however, there appears to be little consensus on the nature or focus of the critique. Some people question the aggregate dimensions of government; others point to its effects on specific sectors of the economy. Still others note its adverse impact on their own actions.[1] However, skepticism is evident whenever the claim is made that government action per se, no matter how well-intentioned, invariably produces gains in overall welfare. There is evidence that, on occasion, it fails to do so even in the areas directly impacted by government.

THE DIMENSIONS OF GOVERNMENT

The knowledge that government has expanded is commonplace, but some of the details of its growth are not well recognized. Table 22.1 indicates, as would be expected, that since 1929 government employment and spending have expanded faster than GNP and the labor force, and thus account for growing portions of both. This trend began well before the postwar period, as detailed in Chapter 19. What may be surprising is the degree to which both expenditures and employment growth have centered in state and local rather than the federal government. Federal spending rose in relation to that of other levels of government during the Great Depression. In the wartime period, it skyrocketed. After 1945, outlays decreased, but not to their prewar levels. Measures enacted in wartime or domestic emergency are seldom entirely reversed after the crisis has passed.[2] Since 1955, however, state and local government spending (aided by federal grants, especially after 1970) has increased about 24 percent faster than have federal expenditures.[3] Federal employment has declined as a portion of the civilian labor force and risen about 41 percent in absolute terms since 1955. Over the same period, however, the ranks of state and local government employees more than tripled. In 1990, about one U.S. worker in six was a government employee.[4]

The figures just quoted should be viewed in context. First, in recent years the federal government, and to some extent all others, has made increasing use of independent consultants and other experts on a temporary basis. These persons are not included in government employment data. Second, neither government expenditures nor employment figures indicate the growing influence of government on private economic activity. The true economic impact of government includes the private effort necessary to comply with expanded and intensified regulation. While the figures show that the aggregate dimensions of government are now much larger than they were in 1929, and there has been considerable expansion from the low postwar point in the late 1940s, they understate the actual expansion.

---

[1] A thoughtful discussion of the results of government interaction with economic activity is N. Rosenberg and L. Birdzell, *How the West Grew Rich* (New York: Basic Books, 1986), especially Chaps. 9 and 10.

[2] R. Higgs, *Crisis and Leviathan: Critical Episodes in the Growth of American Government* (New York: Oxford University Press, 1987), 227–230, Chap. 3.
[3] Council of Economic Advisors, *Economic Report of the President, 1991* (Washington, D.C.: Government Printing Office), 379.
[4] *Economic Report, 1991,* 334, 335.

Table 22.1   Government Expenditure and Civilian Employment, 1929–1984

Year	GNP (in Billions of Dollars)	Federal Expenditures (in Billions of Dollars)	State and Local Expenditures (in Billions of Dollars)	Total Government Spending as Percentage of GNP*	Civilian Employment (in Thousands)	
					Federal	State and Local
1929	$103.4	$2.7	$7.8	10.0%	533	2,532
1945	211.2	84.7	9.0	44.0	2,808	3,137
1948	261.6	35.5	17.6	19.5	1,863	3,787
1950	288.3	41.2	21.3	21.3	1,928	4,098
1955	405.9	68.6	31.7	24.3	2,187	4,727
1960	515.3	93.9	50.0	26.6	2,270	6,083
1965	705.1	125.3	75.5	26.9	2,378	7,696
1970	1,015.5	207.8	134.0	31.3	2,731	9,830
1975	1,598.4	364.2	235.2	34.1	2,748	12,025
1980	2,732.0	615.1	363.2	32.6	2,866	13,375
1985	4,014.9	985.6	516.7	34.9	2,875	13,519
1990	5,463.0	1,273.0	764.7	34.9	3,086	15,206

* Net of federal grants to state and local governments.
Source: Council of Economic Advisors, *Economic Report of the President, 1991* (Washington, D.C.: Government Printing Office, 1991), 335, 379.

Causes of Government Expansion

The causes of government expansion are political, social, demographic, and perhaps even historical. After World War II, the United States accepted its world power status. The implementation of this decision entailed large expenditures on American armed forces, aid to those of our allies, and foreign aid. But even larger sums were devoted to domestic purposes.

At the state and local government levels, the bulk of the additional spending financed education, streets and highways, and welfare programs. Growth in these governments' outlays reflected increases in population, enhanced interest in education, particularly higher education, the growth of the suburbs, and increasing attention to the needs of the less fortunate as average income levels rose. There was a general tendency to increase demand for government services at least in proportion to, and generally faster than, increases in income and wealth. Changes in private living standards also raised government spending. The larger portion of the population housed in single-family dwellings, often in entirely new communities, raised demand for social overhead capital of all kinds—roads, utilities, sewers, and police and fire protection. The increase in parents' aspirations for their children, as well as the increased numbers of children during the "baby boom," raised demands for education. Larger numbers of automobiles and the increased average annual mileage per auto produced demands for additional roads.

As Table 22.2 indicates, the growth in federal spending in the postwar period was not due entirely—or even largely—to increased military spending, at least since 1955. Military spending has risen more than eighteen-fold,

■ Suburban developments in the 1950s generated demand for additional government services.
Source: Photo Trends.

reflecting the enormous costs of new weapons systems, the higher wages needed to attract an all-volunteer force since 1973, and the inherent waste of military procurement. But over the same period, direct government expenditures on individuals, an area that is generally linked to efforts to make the distribution of income more nearly equal and to improve so-

cial welfare, rose nearly five times as rapidly. These figures incorporate a broad definition of military spending that includes all the expenses of the State Department, the National Aeronautics and Space Administration, and all support for scientific research as well as those of the Defense Department per se. They are contrasted with a narrow definition of social spending (one that excludes the areas of most rapid growth). Even so, the figures fail to support the contention that military spending has come at the expense of the needy. Transfer payments to individuals will continue to rise both absolutely and in relation to GNP for the foreseeable future. The collapse of the Soviet Union will undoubtedly allow sizable absolute reductions in military spending, further reducing its impact on the American economy.

The Role of Public Programs

In the 1980s, the increase in the portion of GNP allocated to government transfers (transfer payments do not involve performance of

Table 22.2   Military Spending and Transfer Payments to Individuals, 1950–1984 (Billions of Current Dollars)

Year	Defense Spending*	Percentage of GNP	Transfers to Individuals		Combined as Percentage of GNP
			Federal	State	
1950	$17.9	6.2%	$10.8	$3.6	5.7%
1955	40.4	10.0	12.4	4.0	4.1
1960	49.4	9.6	21.6	5.9	5.3
1965	59.0	8.4	30.3	8.8	5.5
1970	87.3	8.6	55.3**	20.1	7.4
1975	96.5	6.0	131.9	38.9	10.7
1980	152.5	5.6	235.4	65.7	11.0
1985	277.5	6.9	360.6	101.1	11.5
1990	327.5	6.0	488.2	162.9	11.9

* Includes all expenditures for space, science, technology, and international affairs.
** Transfer payments to U.S. citizens only.
Sources: U.S. Department of Commerce, Bureau of the Census, *Historical Statistics of the United States: Colonial Times to 1970*, 2 vols. (Washington, D.C.: Government Printing Office, 1975), and Council of Economic Advisors, *Economic Report of the President, 1991* (Washington, D.C.: Government Printing Office, 1991).

services or sale of goods in return for the receipt of public funds) to individuals slowed, but did not cease. Spending on transfer programs was reallocated within that sector, with the social security program gaining at the expense of others.

As Americans' incomes increased in the postwar period, a growing portion was devoted to public programs. In some cases, this reflected changes in living patterns; as a larger portion of the population chose an urban lifestyle, the externalities that are part of city life rose at least as fast as urban populations. Higher aspirations for children meant more schooling. The ability to analyze and, in some cases, compensate for unwelcome influences on human existence increased and resulted in greater government activity. Concern with the quality of life gained near-equal status with the acquisition of additional goods and services. In all these areas, there was at least some reason to view government as better suited to provide appropriate responses than was the private sector.[5]

New departments were established within the federal government: Health, Education, and Welfare (Education became a separate department in 1977); Housing and Urban Development; Transportation; and Energy. New agencies were established for environmental and consumer protection, occupational health and safety, and equal employment opportunity. Other levels of government were equally active in these areas. There was a noticeable expansion of government activity in traditional areas as well.

Most or all of these areas had been the scene of at least some governmental activity previously, but the new involvement went far beyond the scope and depth of anything attempted earlier, particularly at the federal level. In the late 1970s and 1980s, it was rec-

ognized that this expansion of governmental activity had economic dimensions, regardless of its primary focus. The savings and loan "crisis" of the late 1980s and early 1990s resulted in part from government regulators' errors of omission and commission. Most analysts view the increase of deposit insurance to $100,000 per account as a major cause of that debacle, and reduced financial oversight under traditional regulation as another. Whatever the intent of such policies, the cost was far beyond the resources of the Federal Savings and Loan Insurance Corporation. Congress' reluctance to acknowledge the insolvency of many savings and loans allowed them to accumulate further losses. Belated but overenthusiastic regulation that viewed assets as pessimistically as the savings and loans had overrated them, and forced sales at the bottom of the bond market, caused further losses. Making good the FSLIC's guarantees had cost taxpayers over $160 billion by early 1992, with a strong possibility of still further expenses. Few financial analysts believe the savings and loan debacle need have cost a major fraction of its current total, nor that government regulation and intervention did anything but exacerbate it.

New programs, regulations, and institutions employed scarce resources and affected the uses of those they regulated. Once it was recognized that programs had costs, it became appropriate to evaluate the results they produced in relation to those costs, and to scrutinize the costs in order to determine whether the same results might not be obtained at lower sacrifice in alternatives foregone.

Cost and Benefits of Government Intervention

Some government programs have been undertaken with little attention to either current or long-term costs. In others, secondary and tertiary effects of institutional changes had

[5] See T. Borcherding, ed., *Budgets and Bureaucrats: The Sources of Government Growth* (Durham, N.C.: Duke University Press, 1977).

been ignored. The government's provision of Medicare (1966) and Medicaid is an example. Both programs, however worthy their purposes, proved to be vastly more expensive than had been anticipated by their proponents. Incredibly, it appears that no consideration had been given to whether people might demand larger quantities of medical care when its costs to them were suddenly reduced to nearly zero. Indeed, this was not recognized even by those who championed the programs because some people were unable to buy adequate medical care from their own resources. The programs' costs were further increased by payment procedures that initially offered almost no resistance to price increases for medical services. Efforts to reduce the increase in government costs often raised the costs of physicians and hospitals through increased regulation and paperwork.

In other cases, government programs work at cross purposes. The Department of Agriculture sponsors research intended to increase crop output per acre and publicizes any useful results among farmers. It also imposes acreage restrictions on crops when farmers apply the knowledge it has provided too successfully. The list could be almost indefinitely expanded.

New goals pursued through public action often are extremely difficult to define clearly. The quality of life, in particular, appears to be a highly subjective concept. Programs aimed at enhancing it are subject to widely varying interpretations by a variety of pressure groups, few of whom appear compelled to extend their views beyond their own immediate concerns. In consequence, some programs probably cannot satisfy the very persons or groups supporting them, because proponents' goals are so different.

The Political Economy of Activist Government

In some cases, government appeared to be increasingly sensitive to short-run considerations, such as the state of the economy on the eve of the next election, almost regardless of the long-term consequences, such as possible inflation or the effects of resource misallocation. Such programs are generally designed to oppose changes induced by economic pressures and thus reduce long-term economic growth. To some economists, the business cycle in the postwar United States appeared to be influenced ever more heavily by political considerations.[6]

Unlike private economic activity, government programs do not disappear when their rationales disappear. The losses incurred by a private firm attempting to produce slide rules or button hooks will force it out of business. But no such forces exist in the case of government programs, particularly if these are a small portion of total public-sector activity. Agencies whose task has been completed seldom die: They may even grow.

Any economic decision involves weighing costs against benefits. If either one or the other is absent, the decision becomes trivial; if not, both must be specified as fully and accurately as possible. Overall welfare is enhanced only if the total benefits of an action exceed its costs. Aggregate welfare is maximized only when the difference between the benefits and costs of all actions is both positive and larger than those attainable through any alternative measures. Action through the government often allows proponents of some measure to forget or evade these simple analytical rules. Too often, attitudes and policies have been determined by an assessment of one side of the cost-benefit equation, a portion of the relevant considerations, or by ignoring inconvenient objections to preconceived decisions.

It is increasingly clear that government policies that transfer income or other benefits from large numbers of donors (taxpayers) to a much smaller number of recipients are attractive to politicians, as are programs that

---

[6] E. Tufte, *Political Control of the Economy* (Princeton, N.J.: Princeton University Press, 1978), Chaps. 1, 2.

deny large aggregate benefits to the general public in order to save a small group a concentrated loss smaller than the aggregate benefits. Donors or recipients faced with the prospect of small individual gains or losses are unlikely to respond politically, but the concentrated impact on the small group will ensure a response favorable to politicians protecting the group's interests. Such situations give pressure groups, whose members would gain or lose disproportionately from legislation, political clout far greater than that suggested by their numbers. It also gives such groups incentives to organize and increase their effectiveness.

Incumbent legislators are also likely to favor measures that produce immediately favorable effects, regardless of their long-term consequences. This is especially so in circumstances where elections are scheduled at a time when the favorable effects (tax cuts, spending increases, or jobs "saved" by government assistance) are evident, and the long-term costs (inflation, taxes, or resource misallocation) are not yet manifest. Such circumstances promote rent-seeking behavior (attempts to gain at others' expense), as well as efforts by prospective victims to defend themselves. Because both activities use scarce resources to determine the distribution of existing output rather than producing more, they reduce well-being below its potential.

Such considerations are particularly relevant when government aid to "sick industries" is under discussion. The sectors requesting aid are generally sizable; they find it easier to petition the government for help than to reduce costs or increase markets; and they are invariably representatives of older technologies. Aid to such industries can only come at the expense of more efficient, newer sectors, in the form of taxes, reduced markets, and higher input costs. Such measures hinder the long-term resource reallocation that keys economic growth. It can well be argued that government in the United States is not indif-ferent to the wishes of the citizenry: Rather, it is far too responsive, particularly to small but passionately concerned groups. [7]

THE ELUSIVE GOAL OF MACROECONOMIC STABILITY

As noted in Chapter 18, the federal government had not succeeded in regaining full employment during the 1930s. As the war drew to a close, concerns about postwar macro-economic conditions and confidence in the government's ability to influence them increased. As a result, Congress passed the Employment Act of 1946. This legislation committed the nation to the pursuit of "maximum employment, production, and purchasing power." Aside from establishing the Council of Economic Advisors and requiring the president to submit an annual economic report to Congress, the Employment Act did not specify the means by which these goals were to be achieved.

The overall economic performance of the United States in postwar decades was far better than it had been in the 1930s. No postwar recession even remotely approached the magnitude of the Great Depression. Economic growth averaged 3.5 percent annually between 1946 and 1970, better than that of the 1920s and more than thrice the rate of the 1929–1940 period.[8] Even the much-maligned 1970s saw

[7] See M. Olson, *The Logic of Collective Action* (New Haven, Conn.: Yale University Press, 1983); *The Growth and Decline of Nations: Economic Growth, Stagflation, and Social Rigidities* (New Haven, Conn.: Yale University Press, 1982); D. North, *Structure and Change in Economic History* (New York: Norton, 1981); N. Rosenberg and L. Birdzell, *How the West Grew Rich* ; and T. Anderson and P. Hill, *The Birth of a Transfer Society* (Stanford, Calif.: Hoover Institute Press, 1980).

[8] U.S. Department of Commerce, Bureau of the Census, *Historical Statistics of the United States: Colonial Times to 1970*, 2 vols. (Washington, D.C.: Government Printing Office, 1975), 1:226–227.

real economic growth of about 3 percent, and from 1980 to 1988 the United States was one of only two developed economies whose growth rates were higher than their 1960–1988 average.[9]

In most years, economic growth was rapid enough to accommodate both the increases in the labor force and the rise in productivity, so that unemployment did not increase. This trend faltered somewhat toward the end of the period, but under circumstances that made the unemployment rate an increasingly dubious indicator of aggregate economic performance. Even in the worst postwar years, unemployment rates never exceeded 10 percent for a full year, although they did so for some months in 1982 and 1983.[10] Unemployment was 5.5 percent or less from 1988 through 1990, the best three-year record since the late 1960s.[11] On two of the usual macroeconomic criteria the economy's performance was good. On the third, however (and, as indicated in Chapter 21, in the field of international trade from the 1970s to the late 1980s), the record was far less favorable.

The Problem of Postwar Inflation

Price stability became an elusive goal for most of the period. The return to low levels of inflation in the 1980s was achieved at such cost that its long-term continuation may be in doubt. It also became clear that at least one of the measures traditionally proposed as a means of controlling inflation (contractionary fiscal policy) was of little practical value. It was not that fiscal policy, properly applied, was ineffective; rather, there was no political will to take proper measures to combat infla-tion, such as reductions in government spending and tax increases. Such resolve was even rarer as a preventive measure than it was after inflation had begun to ravage the economy.

Unlike the American experience after other wars, prices did not decline after 1945. The Consumer Price Index rose by about one-third over the 1945–1948 period, and wholesale prices rose even more, over 50 percent.[12] In the immediate postwar era, most Americans enjoyed greater purchasing power than at any time for the previous 15 years. During the Depression, incomes were so low and uncertain as to discourage the purchase of anything not required for immediate consumption. During World War II, many goods were unobtainable, rationed, or of very low quality, and workers had little spare time in which to shop or enjoy new goods. Only after 1945 did consumers enjoy ability to buy and markets where their demand could be effective. The abrupt lifting of price controls in 1946 and the change in consumer attitudes (by that time it was evident that the Depression would not return), particularly in regard to price increases, also fed the inflationary pressures of the late 1940s.

Monetary policy from 1945 to 1951 was highly expansionary and only slightly offset by federal budget surpluses. High demand for investment goods and American exports further increased the pressures on the economy. Rapid inflation ended with the 1949 recession, but developments at that time set the pattern for the rest of the postwar era. Even in the slump, prices did not fall appreciably; they merely ceased to rise, or increased at a slower pace.

At the onset of the Korean War, there was another sharp burst of inflation, fueled by memories of World War II shortages. After 1952 price levels stabilized; consumer prices in 1964 were only 17 percent higher than those of a dozen years before.[13] Many economists

[9] *Economic Report, 1991,* 411. See also Department of Commerce, Bureau of the Census, *Statistical Abstract of the United States, 1991* (Washington, D.C.: Government Printing Office, 1991), 842.
[10] *Economic Report, 1991,* 322.
[11] *Economic Report, 1991,* 322.

[12] *Economic Report, 1977,* 241, 247.
[13] *Economic Report, 1977,* 241.

regard such rates of change as no more than indications of improvements in product quality, rather than a decline in money's value. But in the second half of the 1960s, this pleasant interlude ended. Price stability vanished; until the mid-1980s, inflation became an ever-worsening problem.

From 1967 through 1969, prices rose about 5 percent a year. In the 1970s inflation accelerated markedly. Prices rose 11 percent in 1974, and from 1979 through 1982, the Consumer Price Index rose 39.4 percent.[14] Inflation was then reduced to the 2 to 4 percent range for the rest of the decade, but only at the cost of the most severe recession in the postwar era. Even worse, by the standards of the earlier postwar period, the inflation of the 1970s was accompanied by disturbingly high rates of unemployment and erratic economic growth. In prior decades, inflation had been linked to very low unemployment rates (4 percent or less) and rapid economic growth, but now the inflation-unemployment trade-off, if one still existed, became far less favorable.

Government's Contribution to Economic Instability

How much did the government's macroeconomic policies contribute to this record? If the question is directed toward the influence of deliberate countercyclical fiscal policies, the answer appears to be "not much," at least before the mid-1960s. Little use was made of countercyclical fiscal policy during this period, and it was misused as often as it was correctly used (government spending was expanded to counteract the 1958 recession only in 1959, after recovery was already underway; a case of too much and too late). Most of the changes in tax or spending programs made prior to 1964 reflected the need to finance existing programs or those undertaken for purposes un-

related to stabilization policy, or to finance the institution of programs valued for their direct effects rather than macroeconomic impact. Nor was there any effective coordination of stabilization efforts between fiscal and monetary policy.

The Treasury–Federal Reserve Accord
The federal government ran sizable surpluses during the immediate postwar period—proper policy in a time of obvious demand-pull inflation. At the same time, however, the Treasury offset its own fiscal policy through its influence on monetary policy. To keep interest charges on the greatly increased volume of outstanding bonds as low as possible, the Treasury held the Federal Reserve System to its wartime promise to purchase at face value all government bonds that could not be sold elsewhere at par. Although the volume of federal debt did not increase in this period, some bonds were replaced by new issues as they matured, and private bondholders became eager to sell their government securities. The "accord" with the Fed kept the Treasury's interest costs down. But the central bank could take no effective measures to combat increases in the money supply at a time when it was obvious that the economy suffered from excess purchasing power.[15] American citizens were taxed through inflation rather than explicit taxes to offset higher interest rates on government debt. The impact on aggregate real incomes was much the same.

Since nominal interest rates on government securities were low (and real rates negative), commercial banks and other financial institutions were inclined to exchange them for higher-yielding private loans and securities. Had bond prices been free to vary, government bonds would have fallen to reflect their yields, and the prospect of capital losses

---

[14] *Economic Report, 1977,* 291.

[15] R. Gordon, *Economic Instability and Growth: The American Record* (New York: Norton, 1975), 107.

on bond sales might have inhibited some banks from selling their U.S. securities. As it was, there was nothing to prevent the sale of bond portfolios to the Fed. For commercial banks, such sales increased the excess reserves upon which they could extend additional loans and thus expand the money supply. Commercial banks were also willing to buy bonds from private individuals and firms, since resale to the Fed was free of any risk.

Under these conditions, the Fed could not use open-market sales to reduce the money supply: There were no buyers for low-interest government bonds at par. Thus, the Fed lost its most important instrument for regulating the money supply. Nor could it employ the others. Reserve rate requirements had been increased to their legal maximum by 1948.[16] With the banks' easy access to the huge volume of bonds still available in the private economy, rediscount policy could not be used. In 1951, the Fed was finally released from the "accord"; it allowed bond prices to fall and interest rates to rise. By 1953 the Fed had regained effective control over the U.S. money supply.[17]

Fiscal Policy
In the 1950s, monetary growth was slow and fiscal policy became increasingly contractionary. The Revenue Act of 1954 had established steeply progressive income tax rates, which reached a maximum of over 85 percent on taxable income of $1 million or more. As income grew and federal spending failed to keep pace, the unchanged tax rates began to generate a large-scale "fiscal drag." The tax program generated an increasing surplus at aggregate income levels well below those necessary to achieve full employment. Not only did the tax structure hinder the pursuit of full employment, its burden became greater the

closer the approach to full employment. If incomes continued to rise, the surplus would become even greater; the government would withdraw even more from the economy without replacing it through its expenditures.

There were recessions in 1958 and 1961, and recovery from both was sluggish and failed to bring unemployment rates back down to earlier levels. The failure to regain full prosperity gave the Democratic Party an issue on which to wage the 1960 election. Aggregate rates of economic growth were low, which gave rise to concerns on the international scene as well as domestically. The growth of the Soviet economy was rapid at this time, and it was feared that such growth might cause the uncommitted nations of the world to mark the disparity between Soviet and American economic performance or serve as the base for possible Soviet expansion.

Nevertheless, the macroeconomic record of this period is not completely dismal. Although countercyclical fiscal policies were little used or misused, the dimensions of government in the economy furnished some stabilizing effects during downturns. Government was now a large source of expenditures that did not decline in recessions, and thus the extent to which aggregate economic activity might fall was reduced. In addition, the so-called "built-in stabilizers," such as the progressive income tax, some government spending programs (particularly welfare, unemployment compensation, and farm price supports), actually tended to rise in slumps, even though their aggregate impact muted rather than eliminated recessions.[18]

The Brief Triumph of "New Economics"
When the Kennedy administration assumed office in 1961, attempts were made to stimulate the economy. The first efforts were through increased federal spending and efforts

---

[16] Gordon, *Economic Instability*, 107.
[17] Gordon, *Economic Instability*, 118.

[18] Gordon, *Economic Instability*, 124, 131.

to increase private investment through such measures as the investment tax credit and accelerated depreciation schedules. Although these programs did induce some expansion, the results were disappointing to an administration pledged to achieve rapid economic growth. Consequently, massive reductions in personal and corporate tax rates were proposed in 1962. The program was designed to increase economic growth and reduce unemployment; the first clear-cut use of countercyclical fiscal policy by any American government. The tax cut program was finally passed by Congress in 1964, after President Kennedy's death—a pace that should have caused the more ardent advocates of fiscal policy some serious reflection.

At about the same time, monetary policy became more stimulative as well, and although economists disagree over which of the two causes had the greater effect,[19] there is no doubt of the combined effects. The rate of economic growth increased, and unemployment, which had been 6.7 percent in 1961 and had not fallen below 5 percent since 1958, declined to 3.8 percent of the labor force in 1966.[20] The first effort at countercyclical fiscal policy was a success; these accomplishments were associated with only a slight increase in the rate of inflation. Many economists hoped to achieve further gains through "fine-tuning" the economy by using specific tax and spending programs to reduce the remaining pockets of high unemployment.

Political Economy Faces Reality—and Flinches

Both Congress and subsequent administrations appear to have absorbed only half the lessons of the 1964 tax cut. Expansionary fiscal measures, such as tax cuts and increased government spending, are generally politically popular, even if recent experience casts doubt on their effectiveness. Monetary expansion, although not the responsibility of Congress, lowers interest rates, at least temporarily, and makes credit more available. Both might be expected to accrue to the credit of political incumbents.

If the problem is excess demand rather than unemployment, however, the remedies are less palatable. Tax increases, reduced government spending, and monetary stringency may be effective, but they are no more welcomed than any other bitter pill. They have several characteristics that define a politician's nightmare. First, they are unpopular in themselves, but even more, they require time to become effective. Thus, if they are instituted to ward off inflation, they reduce incomes or slow their growth before rising prices become obvious. If they are withheld until the problem is evident to the electorate, for a time there will be income reductions, probably combined with increased unemployment, and inflation. Their impact is uneven, and those bearing the brunt, such as the residential construction industry, are unlikely to be forgiving at the next election. Finally, they represent the rectification of past errors, and Congress is no more willing to have its past sins exposed than any other body.

When the need for such policies arose, they proved far more difficult for Congress to accept and pass than expansionary measures; it should be remembered that Congress required two years to decide the distribution of tax-cut benefits after 1962. In 1965, the unemployment rate was low, and there was every indication that the U.S. economy was operating at or very close to its physical capacity. Federal spending was slated to increase through the institution of President Johnson's "Great Society" program of social expenditures. American military involvement in Vietnam had just begun, and its eventual costs were as yet unclear. In the end, the bills for domestic and foreign activity both proved far

---

[19] M. Friedman and W. Heller, *Monetary Versus Fiscal Policy: A Dialogue* (New York: Norton, 1969).
[20] *Historical Statistics,* 1:135.

greater than anticipated. In part, the cause was unduly optimistic military and economic forecasts. A greater share of the blame, however, must be laid to a reluctance to admit that the costs had been so badly underestimated that the tax cuts of a few years ago now had to be at least partially rescinded. No tax increase was enacted until 1968, when inflation was already well established. The form of the tax increase seemed better designed to reduce political damage than to combat inflation. The new taxes were to be temporary; they were presented as a surcharge rather than integrated into the permanent tax structure. Unsurprisingly, they were not very effective. Most taxpayers maintained their previous levels of consumption and paid the tax by reducing their savings.[21] Thus, long-run economic growth potential was reduced, because the pool of loanable funds diminished and investment fell. Monetary policy had become restrictive in 1966, but only temporarily. This policy was too limited in impact and duration to stem the pressures for inflation by itself.

Fiscal Policies of the Nixon Administration

The incoming Nixon administration, which had opposed the surcharge in the election campaign, found it necessary to retain the increased tax for a year after 1969, and then to reduce the surtax in stages rather than simply abolishing it. The Federal Reserve began a sharp reduction in money-supply growth. The result was an end to the long era of continuous expansion that had begun in 1962—the longest recession-free period in American history before the 1982–1991 expansion. The contractionary policies that brought on the recession of 1970 would probably have halted inflation had they been continued (by mid-1971 the rate of inflation had declined noticeably), but another consequence was an increase in the unemployment rate. Worse still, at least from a

political point of view, was the timing of these developments: Unemployment worsened before the rate of inflation moderated, and joblessness was not declining during the summer of 1971.

A combination of 6 percent unemployment and 5 percent inflation seemed to be a poor base from which to launch a reelection campaign. Accordingly, in August 1971 President Nixon announced his "New Economic Policy." The dollar was devalued and the Japanese and West Germans were pressed to raise the exchange rates of their currencies. A 10 percent tariff surcharge was imposed on merchandise imports into the United States. The intent was to rectify a growing balance-of-payments problem. Inflation in the United States, massive overseas spending by the government, and sharp increases in competition from foreign producers had resulted in a large outflow of dollars. Foreigners were unwilling to use such funds to purchase American goods or to hold them in short-term deposits in U.S. banks, and foreign central banks refused to accumulate further dollar balances. It was hoped that the new measures would raise American exports and reduce imports.

Wage and Price Controls

The most noteworthy aspects of the "New Economic Policy," however, affected the domestic economy. A freeze on all wages and prices was announced, effective immediately. This was the first time wage and price controls had ever been employed during peacetime in the United States. Phase One of the freeze was to be followed by a second period in which price increases were allowed within the limits imposed by the new Council on Wage and Price Stability. Although the price controls received widespread popular and political support when they were announced, they proved largely ineffective. In the varied economy of the United States, it proved all but impossible to determine the proper base prices for many items. Wage controls proved difficult to en-

---

[21] Gordon, *Economic Instability,* 166–169.

"Your Majesty, according to our study the shoe was lost for want of a nail, the horse was lost for want of a shoe, and the rider was lost for want of a horse, but the *kingdom* was lost because of overregulation."

■ *Source:* Drawing by Dana Fradon; © 1980 The New Yorker Magazine, Inc.

force against either mobile individuals or strong labor unions.

In cases where controls could be enforced, they soon began to produce distortions in the structure of relative prices. Price freezes in a market economy allow only price declines as a reallocative mechanism, and price declines are most unlikely under the circumstances prompting the imposition of such controls. Since underlying inflationary pressures remained strong, the controls distorted prices and output.

Employers and workers quickly developed responses that reduced the impact of the controls. Some goods that under normal circumstances would have been sold in the United States were exported. Others were simply not produced. Employees who appeared likely to quit unless they received wage increases above those sanctioned by the Pay Board received "promotions" consisting of higher salaries for the same work under different titles. Businesses changed the names of products or introduced "new" items for which no previous pricing standards existed. Where products and job status were clearly defined, the controls were effective. These developments made the actual impact of price and wage controls highly uneven and unfair. They also allowed a continuation of price increases.

Moreover, even though the controls had some impact on inflation when introduced (they were totally unexpected), they were an attempt to cure inflation by treating its symptoms while other government policies exacerbated its causes.[22] Monetary and fiscal policy both became stimulative in 1970, and even more strongly so in 1971. The federal government's 1971 deficit was $20.5 billion, by far the largest ever compiled to that time, and the money supply grew at an annual rate of 10 percent, much in excess of any sustainable rate of real expansion.[23] Most price controls were dropped in mid-1973, with the portentous exception of oil and gas (see Chapter 20). Since the factors that actually produced inflation had, if anything, been strengthened while price controls were in force, the result was an increase in inflation after the controls were lifted. By mid-1974, however, the current rate of inflation (nearly 12 percent) was recognized as more than a deferred reaction to the period of controls. Prices had not risen at this rate since the 1946–1948 period. In addition, unemployment rates were climbing toward a postwar high, which they attained in the following year. (The unemployment rate became even higher in 1982–1983.) Since that time, unemployment rates, even in boom times, have not regained the lows attained over 1945–1968.[24] Inflation was not brought down to reasonable levels until 1983.

1970s "Stagflation" and Growing Deficits

During 1970–1979, both monetary and fiscal policy appear to have been overly stimulative. Under any reasonable concept of full employment, given the current composition of the labor force, the federal budget showed a large full-employment deficit, and the rate of increase in the money supply, while erratic (in itself a cause for concern to many economists) has averaged out to considerably more than the long-run increase in physical capacity.

Even though it must be conceded that a variety of changes in the real economy have combined to increase the difficulties of stabilization policy in recent years, it seems fair to conclude that fiscal policy has, in general, contributed to the U.S. macroeconomic problems throughout this period, rather than to their solution. For the most part, monetary policy has achieved a better record, although it too has been anything but a consistent force for economic growth and stability.

The macroeconomic situation of the 1970s and early 1980s has been termed "stagflation," a combination of rising prices, slow economic growth, and uncomfortably high levels of unemployment by previous standards. In the United States, this situation was accompanied by growing federal deficits. The deficit rose faster than aggregate economic growth, reversing the trends of the early postwar decades.

The Fed Takes Charge

In 1979, President Carter appointed a new Chairman of the Federal Reserve, Paul Volcker. Under his leadership, the central bank began a determined anti-inflation policy. Money supply growth was cut or even halted; interest rates increased to unprecedented levels (for a time in 1980, the rate offered banks' most creditworthy customers was over 21 percent);[25] and credit was rationed even at these high rates. Unemployment rose; the recession of 1981–1982 was the worst in the postwar period. But inflation declined from 12 to less than 2 percent, and its corrosive influence on economic activity was reduced. High rates of inflation, especially when incorporated into interest rates and borrowers' expectations, make short-term projects more appealing than long-term investments; they provide incentives to buy existing assets rather than produce new ones; and they encourage consumption at the expense of investment. The Fed received

[22] E. Feige and D. Pearce, "The Wage-Price Control Experiment—Did it Work?" *Challenge* (July–August 1973).
[23] Gordon, *Economic Instability,* 175–178.
[24] *Economic Report, 1991,* 322.

[25] *Economic Report, 1986,* 310.

little help from fiscal policy in its endeavors, and federal budget deficits remained at (then) record levels throughout the period.

Real Tax Cuts and Promised Spending Reductions

In 1981, a new administration took office. President Reagan and his advisors were convinced that it was necessary to reduce the impact of government on the economy. They planned to cut taxes in order to raise economic incentives, reduce government spending (both for ideological reasons and to increase private production), and to reduce the regulatory activities of government. At the same time, they planned to increase defense spending even more than the Carter administration had intended after 1980. The expectation was that the private economy, when freed of excessive government restraints, would respond to these incentives and the rate of economic growth would increase, thereby increasing the tax base and partially offsetting the revenue losses from the tax cuts.

A large-scale tax cut was enacted in the summer of 1981: The original intent was to reduce personal income taxes by 10 percent for three successive years. The program was reduced to a 25 percent cut, and in 1982 some additional taxes were imposed, although not on incomes. In 1986, the federal tax structure was overhauled and simplified. Rates of personal taxation were reduced, and the number of tax brackets decreased to just three.

Far less progress was achieved in cutting domestic expenditures by government. The rate at which these had been rising relative to GNP was reduced or temporarily halted, but their relative impact did not decline. With a few exceptions, mostly continuations of programs begun under the Carter administration, little was accomplished toward reduction of regulatory burdens. It was discovered that regulations, whatever their aggregate impact, had vocal constituencies. Citizens deriving personal benefit, government employees who ad-

ministered the rules, and politicians deriving support from these groups made elimination of the most obvious forms of rent-seeking all but impossible. Even modifications were difficult to achieve.

Economic growth increased sharply in 1982, and reached 6.8 percent in 1984. Since that time, economic growth has been at or slightly above its 1960–1988 average. The Reagan tax cuts have generated huge federal deficits (up to $200 billion after 1983), because the anticipated spending reductions failed to materialize and economic growth did not match the optimistic projections incorporated in the tax cuts. These have proved sustainable without a catastrophic decline in domestic investment or a resumption of inflationary increases in the money supply largely because of a massive inflow of foreign investment. After declining from $206 billion in 1986 to $134 billion in 1989, deficits have expanded recently. For 1992, the combined effects of the structural deficit (reflecting revenue shortfalls in normal circumstances), the cost of the savings and loan bailout, and the recession have increased the deficit to a projected $340 billion. To date, the United States has failed to regain the combined levels of low unemployment, rapid growth, and stable prices recorded from 1947 to 1970. Perhaps, as one study has claimed, that period was an unusually favorable aberration.[26]

Can Stabilization Policy Succeed?

Since the late 1940s, economists have developed several views on the most effective processes for the pursuit of macroeconomic policy. No group's boundaries are sharply defined, particularly after its ideas have been widely discussed, but they may be divided into

---

[26] W. Baumol, S. Blackman, and E. Wolff, *Productivity and American Leadership: The Long View* (Cambridge, Mass.: MIT Press, 1989), 6, 65–71.

two groups. One, generally linked to John Maynard Keynes and subsequent developments of his ideas, believes that market economies are inherently unstable. They advocate policies designed to modify the levels of economic activity generated through markets. Others, in several subgroups, think that macroeconomic policy should provide a stable environment for market-oriented activity, which has strong tendencies toward full-employment growth. At least in the current state of economic knowledge, greater activity is likely to be destabilizing, whatever its intentions. Some would add that *any* macroeconomic policy undertaken through the political process is likely to be diverted (or perverted) to political goals.

The Intellectual Heirs of John Maynard Keynes

The first group regards changes in the government's tax and spending programs (fiscal policy) as the most effective stabilization tool. Members of this school advocate tax cuts and spending increases (raising the full-employment deficit) as appropriate counters to recessions. Their remedies for inflation would be measures that reduce the amount of aggregate demand, such as tax increases and reductions in government spending. Monetary policy is a secondary tool in this group's view; it can be used to encourage investment through reducing the cost of capital, or perhaps to counter inflation.

■ A view of U.S. monetary policy in the 1970s is presented in this cartoon.
Source: Reprinted by permission: Tribune Media Services.

Monetarism

Members of the nonactivist school take a skeptical view of aggressive stabilization policy. Many feel that fiscal policy is ineffective unless supported by money-supply changes, which can be used to greater effect without the complications of tax or spending changes. If monetary policy is to be effective, however, the income velocity of money (roughly, the rate at which money is spent) must be constant or at least predictable. In the mid-1980s, velocity fell sharply, and it is not yet clear whether this was a unique event, reflecting the sharp decline in inflation, or evidence of fundamental changes in institutions or attitudes toward holding money.

Others of this school emphasize the difficulties inherent in implementing activist policies. First, such policies will be more effective stabilization tools if they can be used to prevent major fluctuations in employment, growth, or prices rather than ameliorating them. But even the best-regarded forecasting models have compiled indifferent records in predicting recent economic phenomena. Both monetary and fiscal policies, once formulated, take time to produce their intended effects. Fiscal policy, in particular, requires prolonged legislative consideration. These factors require time beyond the coverage of current forecasts. Second, the widespread knowledge that activist policies will be undertaken may encourage consumers and investors to try to offset anticipated policy changes. Under these circumstances, macroeconomic policy can only be effective if the economic public is deceived. Third, activist and nonactivist economists may have the same goals (stable growth and prices, full employment), but activist fiscal policies are achieved through the political process. Politicians may have very different goals (their immediate constituents' wishes *versus* aggregate welfare) or time horizons, especially in regard to taxes and government spending programs. For these reasons, nonactivist econ-omists advocate measures encouraging private economic activity. In this view, market economies tend toward stable growth unless perturbed by monetary or fiscal policy changes.

Supply-Side Economists

At the time of the 1980 presidential election, yet another set of ideas received wide publicity: the supply-side view. Supply-side economists view efforts to achieve full employment and rapid growth through management of monetary aggregates or aggregate demand as inherently flawed. To them, the proper policy is the encouragement of increases in real output through increased incentives to producers (the term in this context emphatically includes employees). They would achieve these goals through reduced taxes, which allow producers to keep a greater portion of the income generated, and relaxation of most government regulation of private economic activity. Implicit in their ideas (and sometimes explicit as well) is the acceptance of wide ranges of income inequality. Supply-side economists do not advocate a cessation of all government domestic activity, but they wish to reduce its role to little more than the preservation of property rights, the settlement of disputes, and the preservation of order.

None of these schools of thought is happy with the recent history of stabilization policy. Monetarists believe that the long-term growth rate of the money supply has been excessive, and short-term fluctuations in the rate have been needlessly disruptive. They feel that the Fed's concentration on interest rates (save for a brief hiatus in the early 1980s), rather than on growth of the monetary aggregates, has been a primary cause of the poor performance of recent years. They also view federal deficits as competing for loanable funds that might otherwise go to productive investment. Advocates of fiscal policy would point to problems of timing and of magnitude in the implementation of their suggested remedies. No group would suggest that recent macroeconomic policy has reflected anything but political expediency. Supply-side economists argue that tax cuts have been insufficient to provide the increased incentives required for increased economic growth; they are particularly critical of the 1982 and 1989 tax increases, which they feel blunted much of the potential impact of the 1981 income tax cut. Both they and the monetarists see little progress in reducing the regulatory drag on the economy.

DOES AN EFFECTIVE MACROECONOMIC POLICY EXIST?

Fiscal Policy

A reasonably dispassionate analysis of all three schools indicates that each has serious shortcomings, at least in practical application. Nonactivists' reservations about fiscal policy appear well founded. Since it is conducted through the political process, it is nearly impossible to employ fiscal policy for anti-inflation programs. Further, changes in spending programs are subject to a "ratchet effect"; once a program is instituted, it quickly generates a constituency determined to preserve it, regardless of its purpose or current conditions. In practice, no changes in tax programs are made for their macroeconomic impact alone; they are one of the most fertile grounds for rent-seeking of all government activity. Consequently, tax changes are unlikely to be instituted quickly and all but certain to reflect concerns other than their impact on the aggregate economy. This, of course, applies to both fiscal policy and supply-side programs.

Monetary and Fiscal Policy

Monetarism also has its practical flaws. It is true that monetary policy, which is conducted by the central bank, at least under normal conditions, is relatively free of political influences. However, it is also true that recent institutional developments (wider ranges of money substitutes, such as certificates of deposit, credit cards, money-market funds, and the host of savings programs more or less open to checking), have made even definition of the money supply more difficult than it was when the monetarists' basic views were developed. Monetarism has other practical difficulties: Velocity, the link between the money supply and real economic activity, has recently become less stable, which means that there cannot be as much confidence in the real effects of money-supply changes. Monetarism provides a program for avoiding the catastrophic errors of the 1930s, but even monetarists admit that the lag between the institution of monetary policy and its effect is long and unpredictable in terms of the area of impact and timing. As yet, there is little empirical support for the rational expectations model in any markets other than those for financial assets.

Supply-Side Economics Supply-side economics has as yet offered little more than a series of truisms. It is obvious that a zero tax rate would yield no revenue, regardless of the tax base; and almost equally clear that total confiscation of all proceeds from economic activity (a 100 percent tax on all income) would yield no more, because the tax base would disappear. It follows that there is some tax rate between the two extremes that will yield the maximum total revenue from any given economy. The supply-siders have yet to indicate what this optimum rate is, develop any clear indication of whether current tax rates in the United States exceed, equal, or fall short of this level, or indeed explain why a tax rate that yields maximum revenues is necessarily the proper goal.

Stabilization Policy in a Changing Economy

Failures of the Indicators A final stabilization policy difficulty is that changes within the real sectors of the American economy may require a reassessment of the traditional numerical indicators of success or failure. Figures on industrial capacity and its rate of utilization are obviously in need of revision. Income distribution figures must be interpreted with caution, and those on international trade are known to contain substantial errors.

The New Labor Force The composition of the labor force has changed, and this, as well as macroeconomic conditions, influences unemployment rates.[27] The growing portion of female full-time workers has raised the average level of unemployment rates; such workers have higher unemployment rates than full-time male employees, even though not above the overall average. Other changes in the labor force have considerably greater impact. The increased proportion of the work force composed of young workers, minority groups, and those seeking only part-time employment has raised the portion of the labor force subject to above-average jobless rates under any conditions. It has been proposed that the unemployment rate among full-time workers who are also heads of families might be a better indicator of labor-market conditions, or that overall unemployment rates be adjusted to incorporate changes in labor-force composition. Certainly there are indications that 7 percent unemployment today is equivalent in its impact to much lower rates—perhaps less than 5 percent—in the 1960s or earlier.

Institutional Change Institutional changes have also contributed significantly to the changes in observed unemployment rates. For example, in 1972, those receiving public assistance under the Aid to Dependent Children and food stamp programs were required to register with the unemployment agencies. They were thus added to the unemployment rolls, although most persons so affected were probably unemployable at wages above the legal minimum.[28] More generous rates of unemployment compensation and welfare payments, as well as the nontaxability of such income combine to reduce the income disadvantages of unemployment. They encourage the unemployed to search for work until they locate a job that suits them, rather than accept the first employment offer. This phenomenon is particularly obvious in Western Europe. Nations with especially generous unemployment programs have high levels of unemployment regardless of the number of job vacancies. Minimum wage laws deter the employment of unskilled workers and their acquisition of training, which prolongs the period in which they are subject to above-average unemployment.[29]

Employment Growth The recent increase in unemployment rates does not stem from the American economy's inability to generate additional jobs. In the 1965–1990 period, the number of persons employed in the United States increased from 71 million to 117.9 million.[30] Unemployment rates increased because the labor force grew even more rapidly. If unemployment is concentrated among new labor-force entrants and those seeking only part-time work, its implications are different than

---

[27] R. Easterlin, "What Will 1984 Be Like? Socioeconomic Implications of Recent Changes in the Age Structure" *Demography* (November 1978).

[28] K. Clarkson and R. Meiners, "Government Statistics as a Guide to Economic Policy: Food Stamps and the Spurious Increase in Unemployment Rates," *Policy Review* (Summer 1977).
[29] M. Feldstein, "The Economics of the New Unemployment," *The Public Interest* (Fall 1973).
[30] *Economic Report, 1991,* 324.

if the same rates prevailed among full-time workers who were the sole support of their families. If, for example, full-time college students look for part-time work in order to attend more rock concerts than their parents are willing to finance, the increase in unemployment rates generated by this change hardly indicates any great rise in hardship—at least to the parents.

A growing number of economists now believe that these demographic and institutional factors, rather than stabilization policies, are the major long-term determinants of the unemployment rate.[31] If there is a trade-off between unemployment and inflation, they think it is a purely short-term phenomenon that depends largely on mistaken impressions about the course of future inflation. If this is correct, the long-term unemployment rate can be reduced only by changes in the characteristics of the labor force such as the skills, information, mobility, and attitudes of its members, and the institutions within which it is employed.[32] Only time can alter demographic conditions, but the U.S. labor force is no longer growing rapidly.[33] The proportion of workers subject to high unemployment rates is falling. This, together with changes in the nature of women's employment, can be expected to reduce unemployment.

Prospects for Stabilization Policy: Have We Learned Anything?

Some lessons about inflation and its control have been absorbed. Increases in the price of any individual good, for example, energy in the 1970s, represent the normal operation of the market system rather than inflation. While some goods' price increases were employed as a scapegoat for inflation, an analysis of their relation to price indices indicates that they were not the only source of price increases. This statement holds even in the case of oil in the 1970s. Further, it is much easier to prevent inflation than it is to cure it. Once inflationary expectations become widely accepted, they tend to become self-fulfilling. The reduction in savings rates and the shift from long- to short-term investment projects that results from this change in attitudes impose real costs on the economy, and require stringent monetary or fiscal contraction to overcome.

In summary, since the late 1970s, economists have more and better information about the macroeconomic aspects of the economy than ever before. They also have a great deal less confidence that they can generate exactly the conditions that their policies are designed to produce, even if their policies emerge from Congress or the monetary authorities in exactly the form in which they were submitted. There is little doubt that enough is now known to prevent either an economic collapse, such as the Great Depression, or hyperinflation of the sort experienced by some nations in war or its aftermath, but confidence in the degree to which anything more can be promised falls in proportion to the magnitude of the proposal.

Economists, if not politicians, now also realize that policy proposals must be scrutinized for their secondary or tertiary effects, as well as the likelihood that they will achieve their primary goals. Few now believe that inflation can be reduced to insignificant levels with no increase in unemployment rates. Also, we realize that some stabilization policy efforts have directly or indirectly reduced the economy's long-term growth rate by encouraging consumption at the expense of investment, reducing the level of employment, or slowing the productivity increases that over time offer the only hope of higher real in-

---

[31] Easterlin, "What Will 1984 Be Like?" See also Feldstein, "The Economics of the New Unemployment."

[32] This is a primary theme of Claudia Goldin's work. See *Understanding the Gender Gap: An Economic History of American Women* (New York: Oxford University Press, 1987), 214–216.

[33] Easterlin, "What Will 1984 Be Like?"

comes per person.[34] Government relief of economic distress must not be concentrated on efforts to preserve existing jobs; a rapid rate of "job death," in which old forms of employment disappear and are replaced by new, is essential to growth and the resource reallocation that inevitably accompanies it.[35] The aid that was provided to large firms, such as the Chrysler Corporation in 1979, even though temporarily successful, is a most dangerous precedent, because it interferes with resource allocation along the lines of highest return. Such measures do not preserve "good jobs"; they hinder movement to better ones. For obvious reasons, aid to entire industries has even more pernicious effects.

THE OLD REGULATION

The American economy has never been regulated by market forces alone.[36] The power of government has always been employed to define and enforce property rights, delineate the boundaries between legal and illegal conduct, settle disputes, define the monetary unit, and, in general, to provide a climate in which economic activity could take place under only those risks imposed by the market. Without these government services, markets could not function. As the economy became more urban and industrial, and the variety and complexity

of its products increased, the provision of useful information, protection against externalities, safety considerations, and the maintenance of a competitive environment assumed new importance. Government activity in all these areas dates from the nineteenth century or even earlier.

In recent years, a portion of government's regulatory activities have been extensions of those traditional roles. Most such efforts were designed to improve the operation of the market system, not substitute for it. There were exceptions; a few groups, such as farmers, had obtained favored treatment from government. Over time, the numbers of such groups increased. Support of the needy had always been a recognized function of government at some level, and it could be said that twentieth-century developments in this area represented no more than an expansion of traditional services. Until the second half of the twentieth century, however, the range of government programs explicitly designed to facilitate rent-seeking was quite limited.

Antitrust

The federal government (and some states) continued to enforce antitrust laws. Although the bulk of such activity still revolved around the Sherman Act's prohibition of various forms of anticompetitive behavior, as it always had, there were some attempts to break new legal ground. In particular, policies were developed to deal with some of the merger activity that appeared after the war. Such policies have had varying degrees of success, and their impact on the overall economy or even the industries in which they impacted can be questioned. It has been found, for example, that periods of intense merger activity see an increase in the number of firms, rather than a decrease. The number of new firms established

---

[34] E. Denison, "Explanations of Declining Productivity Growth," Brookings General Series Reprint #354 (Washington, D.C.: Government Printing Office, 1979). See also M. Porter, *The Competitive Advantage of Nations* (New York: Free Press, 1990), Chap. 12.

[35] Rosenberg and Birdzell, *How the West Grew Rich*, 278. The same study revealed that most jobs, even in the U.S. industrial sector, are not provided by giant firms, and very few additional jobs have been created by long-established firms in the past decade.

[36] J. Hughes, *The Governmental Habit* (New York: Basic Books, 1977), is a good statement of this proposition.

in these periods far exceeds those that disappear by merger.[37]

In general, the antitrust authorities were successful in persuading the courts that horizontal mergers (those between previously competing firms) virtually always had an adverse effect on competition. The courts refused to permit them in almost any circumstances where measurable increases in economic concentration could be demonstrated. They followed this policy through the 1970s, not only in national, but even in local markets. In recent years, this attitude has been relaxed; some large mergers between oil firms have been allowed, when evidence has been presented that competition will remain vigorous or even increase despite the mergers.

The courts were only slightly less hostile to vertical mergers (those between firms that buy from or sell to each other). Not only were a number of proposed mergers forbidden, but the dissolution of a number of existing vertical structures was ordered. Motion picture studios were ordered to sell the chains of theaters they once owned, and the du Pont Company was made to sell its large stock interest in General Motors in 1959. The Clayton Act was amended in 1950, making it more difficult for one firm to acquire the assets of another, and the courts and the Department of Justice made extensive use of the new law. In recent years, the Antitrust Division and the courts have been more permissive toward vertical mergers.

Conglomerate mergers' position before the law is not yet clear. The Antitrust authorities have not favored such mergers, but the existing laws were not designed to deal with them, nor is it easy to demonstrate that these have clear-cut effects on competition. Since 1973, the courts have been unwilling to accept any challenges to conglomerate mergers in which only a potential for reduced competition, rather than a current reduction, could be demonstrated. Clearly, conglomerate mergers cannot be evaluated by structural guidelines (concentration ratios or Herfindahl indices).

In the 1980s, merger activity increased, with a number of very large transactions. These culminated in the 1988 acquisition of RJR Nabisco Corporation by Kohlberg Kravis Roberts and Company, an investment banking concern. This was the largest merger in U.S. history; in real terms, the amounts involved (over $27 billion in current dollars) were larger than those required to form United States Steel in 1903. In this instance, the bankers hoped to sell the acquired firm's component divisions for more than the acquisition price. They were largely successful.

Many of these mergers were financed by the use of so-called "junk bonds," high-interest securities issued against future earnings. The KKR-Nabisco merger resulted in the issuance of some $18 billion in new bonds. "Junk bonds" have received a good deal of unfavorable comment, but most issues have paid interest and principal as specified. The stocks of merged firms have also done well in recent years, indicating that investors expected profits to increase.

IBM and AT&T

The IBM and AT&T cases (both decided in 1982) may reflect the last gasp of antitrust efforts based on narrowly defined market shares or industry structure. Recently, the courts have become more receptive to the idea that many, if not most, firms now face rivals whose primary operations lie in other industries, and that competition no longer is restricted to that between closely similar or identical goods.

Transportation

The preceding chapters indicate that government has never dealt with transportation at arm's length. Generally, it has either subsidized it or subjected it to discriminatory taxes.

---

[37] Rosenberg and Birdzell, *How the West Grew Rich*, 281–286.

■ The government provided additional roads to accommodate growing numbers of automobiles.
Source: © Georg Gerster/Comstock.

Currently transportation policy appears to be changing from tight regulation, including both prices and areas of activity, to a greater reliance on competition. But for at least three decades after 1945, the traditional policies of aid to various forms of transportation, often uncoordinated and occasionally at cross purposes, were continued.

Highways In the waning days of World War II, Congress authorized the construction of an interstate highways system. As initially proposed, it was to extend some 40,000 miles and be financed 90 percent by federal funds, with the balance coming from the states in which the roads were located. The system, with some expansions and alterations, is now all but complete. The interstate system, in conjunction with regulations that favored trucks at the expense of railroads and technical improvements in the trucks themselves, diverted a large volume of long-distance freight to the highways. For the railroads, the losses were more serious than volume figures alone would suggest, because trucks competed most effectively for the high-value shipments that contributed disproportionately to revenues.

Railroads Rail passenger service had been declining since the 1920s; Americans apparently preferred private automobile travel. After a brief revival during World War II, rail passenger service declined precipitously. In the early 1970s, the railroads turned over all passenger service except their commuter lines to a government corporation (Amtrak). Despite large subsidies, Amtrak has failed to cover its operating costs, and has been forced to discontinue service on some of the routes it took over. Railroads fared only relatively better in the freight business, largely because of competition from other forms of transportation that received favorable treatment from the government. Water transport, pipelines, and long-distance transmission lines reduced the volume of high-bulk, low-value cargo availa-

ble to the railroads, just as trucks wrested away a growing portion of the more lucrative small-lot shipments. Although air freight ton-miles flown rose rapidly after 1960, this form of transportation conveyed only 0.35 percent of domestic intercity freight in 1989.[38] Its importance is limited to a few instances of particularly valuable or perishable items.

For many years the federal government had provided a variety of subsidies for most forms of transportation and had substituted control by the Interstate Commerce Commission for that of supply and demand. Water transportation and later trucking were particular beneficiaries of federal largess; the government built and/or maintained their rights of way, charging them far less than the full cost of its services.

Airlines Air travel was even more heavily subsidized: government-financed airports, navigational and air traffic control facilities, and government research on aircraft and equipment are only the most obvious benefits provided the airlines. In addition, many air carriers received air mail contracts whose rates tended to be set more in accordance with the airlines' revenue requirements than cost of carriage. Beyond the explicit and implicit subsidies, government regulation of various forms of transportation protected many of them from competition. Rate structures might be set with a view to allowing several modes of transportation to "compete" for business in which one had large cost advantages over all others. Regulators were often reluctant to recognize that some forms of transport were not well fitted to move certain types of goods. Almost invariably, they opposed (with the enthusiastic support of their clients) the entry of new firms into regulated markets.[39] The results

---

[38] *Statistical Abstract, 1991,* 603.
[39] M. Cohen and G. Stigler, *Can Regulatory Agencies Protect the Consumer?* (Washington, D.C.: American Enterprise Institute for Public Policy Research, 1977).

were what might have been expected: Monopoly profits for the protected firms (and their employees), and high prices to consumers.

Deregulation

Recently such policies have come under increasingly hostile scrutiny, and many have been modified. In 1978, the first step was taken: Domestic airlines were given wide latitude in setting their own fares and were allowed to enter new routes. In addition, the regulation-imposed barriers to entry into the industry were abolished. The outcome followed the predictions of economic theory. Fares were reduced (the prevalence of discount fares is not captured by most statistics), service was increased, and airlines' share of intercity passenger service rose from 10 percent to 17 percent over 1970–1989.[40] Some old-line carriers found themselves unable to meet the new competition. Airline employees found the new competitive climate difficult; with the airlines less able to pass on wage increases to passengers, many were forced to accept reduced wages to retain their jobs. Although the number of airlines has not permanently increased, and the use of the "hub" concept restricts competition in some airports, real air fares today are about one-fifth lower than before deregulation. Much the same results were observed when regulation of the trucking industry (which, with its thousands of small firms, should never have been regulated) was relaxed: increased competition, new entry, and lower profits and wages for established firms and their employees, particularly the members of the Teamsters' union.

Farm Policy

Agriculture began to receive favored treatment from government 40 years after transportation did, but farmers more than made up for lost time. After 1945, farm incomes were at least as dependent on federal farm policy

as they were on the current state of agricultural markets. Government agricultural policy objectives have been conflicting. One primary goal was to raise the incomes of American farmers through increased product prices. However, this was to be accomplished without the accumulation of large agricultural surpluses (and without depressing overseas markets for America or her allies). The number of family-owned and operated farms was to be maintained as well.

Given the highly elastic long-run supplies of most farm goods (which stemmed in part from the government's agricultural research and publication efforts), and the low domestic price and income elasticities of demand for most major farm products, this combination of objectives proved impossible to attain. As noted in Chapter 20, there are wide variations in farmers' ability to utilize the cost-reducing improvements in technology that give some hope of survival under such conditions. Small farms, at least in the major crops, are increasingly unable to utilize the new methods effectively. As differences in the amount and cost of output between different types of farms became more pronounced, splits began to appear in the farm bloc. Owners of small farms typically favor very high price supports and strict controls on output, especially from large farms. The operators of larger, more efficient farms are less inclined to favor high support prices if these cannot be obtained without limits on output. The decreasing number of farmers in the total population has worsened the effects of this split. It now appears that small farms are no longer able to compete, even with government assistance, in most major farm crops. The income figures noted in Chapter 20 testify to that.

Payment in Kind and Price Supports

One novel effort to meet several problems of government involvement in agriculture took place in 1983. Surpluses of many agricultural products had been accumulating in government storage, imposing increasing costs. At the same time, the total output of American

[40] *Statistical Abstract,* 603.

farms could not be sold on domestic or international markets at the level of government-supported prices. The Reagan administration offered to provide the amount of crops that farmers might have grown out of its surplus stocks if they would withdraw their land from the production of any similar crops. Recipients of government surplus stocks were free to sell them. Agricultural output declined sharply for that year, and the outlays of the Department of Agriculture rose by about one-half. Market prices for farm products rose slightly. The "payment in kind" experiment reduced government surpluses, but at enormous cost, and it was not repeated. In recent years, real net farm income has never been more than half that in the glory year of 1974. Agricultural subsidies have accounted for one-quarter to one-third of net farm income, at a cost to taxpayers of from $12 to $17 billion annually.[41]

The farm program has failed. Government assistance to agriculture has not been able to shelter farmers from the economic pressures that have driven millions of them into other occupations on either a full- or part-time basis. From 1972 to 1989, the farm population fell by over one-half. Incomes in nonfarm occupations remain well above those of most American farmers, and far above those generated by farming alone. The distribution of agricultural income is less equal than that of the rest of the economy. Laws have been passed limiting total price-support payments to individual farmers to not more than $55,000 annually for each of three crops; it could be argued that attempts to reduce agricultural poverty are overdone in such cases. Price supports have increased the cost of food to American consumers, and surpluses have imposed burdens on taxpayers as well. At the same time, these price supports threaten to drive the products of American farms from international markets. Other nations, particularly the European Economic Community, subsidize their farmers at even greater cost.

Government signals to farmers have been wildly inconsistent. In the mid-1970s, farmers were urged to maximize output, increasing both acreage and the intensity of cultivation, to feed a hungry world. They were also encouraged to make long-term additions to capacity, and to borrow to finance them. A few years later, acreage restrictions were once again imposed. The farm program has failed because its objectives simply cannot be realized simultaneously. It is impossible to increase efficiency, maintain high-cost producers, and supply consumers with low-cost food (in terms of both prices and taxes) at the same time.

INCOME DISTRIBUTION

Only in the postwar era was government deeply involved in efforts to change the distribution of income generated by market forces. Although public assistance in one form or another dates back to colonial times, historically, aid to the needy was intended to provide little more than subsistence incomes for those clearly incapable of generating their own. No effort was made to provide more than what might suffice for bare-bones subsistence, at least by American standards, and applications for aid were not encouraged. There is no evidence to indicate that much more than these goals was ever met, and some that points to failure to achieve even these minimal objectives.

The new trends in aid took both general and personal forms. During the New Deal and particularly after 1960, various types of stabilization policies were developed and expanded. Aimed at ensuring high levels of current employment and economic growth, they were to provide greater security of private

---

[41] *Economic Report, 1991*, 377, 395.

incomes and enhanced opportunity to raise incomes through job mobility. Economic growth has done more to raise the incomes of the poor than any other policy. Rapid growth raises the demand for labor and reduces unemployment. It also promotes gains for those already employed, because it improves chances for promotions and facilitates transfers to better jobs.

Only in the postwar period was it realized that policies that assumed every American belonged to a family containing at least one full-time wage earner were of little help to those whose circumstances were different. For those unable to work or prevented by discrimination from obtaining jobs that fully utilized their capabilities, macroeconomic policies were not the answer. For the aged, the very young, the handicapped, and increasingly, single mothers with limited work skills, work incentives were a cruel joke. Others might find themselves trapped in depressed areas, unable to move to regions with better job prospects, but facing prolonged unemployment if they remained. Such groups are a minority in the United States, and do not constitute the entire low-income group, but they were more numerous than once believed, and some are increasing. The nature of poverty itself is changing. A growing number of today's poor are entirely without employment opportunities rather than confined to low-paying jobs.

Growth in Redistribution

The general increase in postwar income and wealth provided more job opportunities and better occupational choices for low income people. Higher average incomes allowed for the provision of aid to the less fortunate and for broadening the opportunities open to all individuals. Education was expanded. Overall, the United States spent about three times the portion of GNP on education in 1983 that it had in 1948. Real spending per public school pupil more than quadrupled from 1948 to 1970.[42] The average educational level of the population increased, with blacks recording the largest gains, particularly in terms of quality of schooling.[43] Civil rights legislation apparently helped American blacks to raise their incomes.[44] The proportions of high school and college graduates among the population and the availability of vocational and special education programs all increased. The government launched a large-scale effort to provide training for low-skilled workers and the hardcore unemployed through the Comprehensive Employment and Training Act, a program whose costs and results are highly controversial. From 1973 to 1982, 27 million persons were enrolled at a total cost of $58 billion. Only 15 percent of CETA participants found jobs through the program. The Job Corps program, however, has been much more successful.

Programs that provided aid for those unable to work were also expanded. Welfare programs, such as Aid to Dependent Children, unemployment compensation, and social security, grew in terms of both the portion of the population covered and the amount of benefits per individual. Programs that provided aid in kind, such as food stamps, Medicare and Medicaid, job training, and subsidized housing, expanded much faster than those providing cash payments. In combination, such programs accounted for a major portion of the growth in government expenditures. Transfers to individuals increased faster than total government spending from 1955 through 1975, and maintained their share thereafter (see Table 22.1). This was particularly true of measures providing income in kind and education. By the standards of any

---

[42] *Historical Statistics*, 1:373.

[43] R. Margo, "Race, Educational Attainment, and the 1940 Census," *Journal of Economic History* (March 1986).

[44] J. Donohue, III and J. Heckman, "Continuous versus Episodic Change: The Impact of Civil Rights Policy on the Economic Status of Blacks," *Journal of Economic Literature* (December 1991).

previous era, the United States became more generous toward the less fortunate, devoting a growing share of total income to programs designed to assist them.

Trends in Income Distribution

There is no question about the magnitude of the effort. What were its results? At first glance, these appear disappointing. Table 22.3 shows the distribution of pretax money incomes by quintiles of families. The table reveals that although there has been some income redistribution toward greater equality since 1929, most of it has occurred through a fall in the share received by the truly rich—the top 5 percent of all families. All other income groups have shared in the redistribution, and the poor, even proportionally, gained only slightly more than did the middle class. Moreover, the bulk of the redistribution occurred prior to or during World War II. After some further reductions in inequality to 1970, the distribution trends reversed, although not to 1929 levels. In absolute terms, the average incomes of each quintile have risen considerably.

However, the figures in Table 22.3 have some serious shortcomings. They reflect only money incomes and neglect income received in kind. Transfers in kind are heavily concentrated among the lower-income groups, but the data in Table 22.3 do not include such income. The value of education, medical care, food stamps, and subsidized housing provided to the poor may be difficult to calculate exactly, but it is surely positive; were it not, such goods would not be accepted, let alone sought. The data in Table 22.3 also ignore the impact of personal taxes, which make after-tax incomes slightly more equal than pretax incomes. More seriously, the data ignore the impact of demographic factors. Contrary to general opinion, the typical low-income family contains fewer people than a high-income unit. A large proportion of low-income families are composed of the elderly or young adults, and thus contain few children. Another group overrepresented in the low-income ranks is single-parent families. A high proportion of families with above-average incomes have two or more income earners; those in the top quintile average nearly two full-time workers each. In any case, the lowest

Table 22.3   Distribution of Pretax Money Incomes by Quintiles and Top 5 Percent of All Families, 1929–1982

Quintile	1929	1948	1955	1972	1981*	1989
Lowest 20 percent	3.5%	5.0%	4.8%	5.4%	4.4%	4.6%
Second 20 percent	9.0	12.1	12.2	11.9	10.2	10.6
Third 20 percent	13.8	17.2	17.7	17.5	16.3	16.5
Fourth 20 percent	19.3	23.2	23.4	23.9	23.8	23.7
Top 20 percent	54.4	42.5	41.8	41.4	45.3	44.6
Top 5 percent**	30.0	17.1	16.8	15.9	18.8	N.A.

Totals may not add to 100 percent because of rounding.
* Data for 1981 for families and unrelated individuals; income distribution in this group is less equal than that for families.
** Included in top 20 percent.
Sources: U.S. Department of Commerce, Bureau of the Census, *Current Population Reports,* Series P-60 (Washington, D.C.: Government Printing Office, 1990). S. Lebergott, *The Americans: An Economic Record* (New York: Norton, 1984), 498, 501.

Table 22.4   Adjusted Relative Income Distribution (Shares of Income Received by Quintiles of Equal Population)

Year	Lowest 20 Percent	Second 20 Percent	Third 20 Percent	Fourth 20 Percent	Top 20 Percent
1952	8.1%	14.2%	17.8%	23.2%	36.7%
1962	8.8	14.4	18.2	23.1	35.4
1972	11.7	15.0	18.2	22.3	32.8

Source: E. Browning, "How Much More Equality Can We Afford?" *The Public Interest* (Spring 1976).

two quintiles of American families as ranked by money incomes contain considerably less than 40 percent of all family members. These considerations mean that the gap between per-capita incomes for members of upper- and lower-income quintiles is less than that for families. (See Table 22.4.)[45]

When the income figures are modified by these considerations, a different picture emerges. The revised figures indicate a substantially greater degree of income equality at all periods than do measures that ignore these considerations. They also indicate a substantial movement toward greater income equality through the early 1970s.[46] These figures have not been updated recently, and are unlikely to offset all the trends noted in Table 22.3. Nevertheless, they indicate that income distribution data should be carefully scrutinized, as much for what it excludes as for its content.

---

[45] President's Council on Income Maintenance Programs, "The Meaning of Poverty," in *Poverty Amid Plenty: The American Paradox, Report of the President's Commission on Income Maintenance Programs* (Washington, D.C.: Government Printing Office, 1969). See also "The Change in Inequality of Family and Individual Income," *Report of the Council of Economic Advisors, 1974* (Washington, D.C.: 1974), and I. Sawhill, "Poverty in the U.S.: Why Is It So Persistent?" *Journal of Economic Literature* (September 1988).

[46] E. Browning, "How Much More Equality Can We Afford?" *The Public Interest* (Spring 1976).

The Search for a Definition of Income Distribution

Income is not equally distributed in the United States: The top quintile receives from three to nine times the total income of the lowest quintile, depending on the income distribution measurements employed. Furthermore, the results obtained by analysis are strongly influenced by our definitions of both income and the groups who receive it. Even apparently straightforward changes in data may not indicate what the numerical changes appear to show. For example, a growing influence on income-distribution figures in recent years is the "decoupling effect," which occurs as extended families become less prevalent. The elderly are now less likely to live with their children, and young adults are more prone to leave home and establish independent households as or before they complete their education, rather than waiting until marriage as they previously did. Both changes increase the number of families without changing the total income they generate, and thus tend to raise the portion of low-income families, but it is doubtful that they indicate reduced well-being. Divorce and other forms of marital breakup by definition divide the family's income (probably very unevenly) between two units, but do nothing per se to increase it. The increases in "marital instability" are now the largest single cause of poverty in the United States, accounting for between one-fifth and one-quarter of the total.[47] Another demographic factor increasing inequality in recent years is the increase in multiple-earner families. When both marriage partners have full-time, year-round jobs, incomes are generally well above the U.S. average, and such families have become increasingly common.

Earnings differentials have increased, especially after the mid-1970s. In 1974, male college graduates' median earnings were 27 percent greater than those of high school graduates; by 1988, the difference was 53 percent. For women, the income premium for a college education was 89 percent in 1988. Smaller gains accrued to high school graduates versus those with nine to eleven years' schooling.[48] It is possible that the lower tax rates of the 1980s both provided greater incentives to upper-income groups to raise their incomes and lower incentive to conceal or disguise it in tax shelters and the like. Taxable income for high-income groups expanded sharply after 1982.

If this list captures the major sources of recent income distribution changes, some conclusions can be made. First, with the possible exception of tax policies, the changes are not the result of government policy or readily amenable to public programs. Stricter enforcement of child-support payments may ease the impact of single-parent poverty. Improved or expanded education will have long-term results at best.

Income Mobility

One final point concerning income distribution has only recently begun to receive attention. To many persons, poverty (and perhaps wealth) are different conditions if they are temporary rather than a lifelong circumstance. Different policy conclusions may well arise from the discovery that most people at the income extremes are there only temporarily, and not consigned to permanent poverty or assured of permanent wealth. If most persons are able to change their relative incomes, income mobility over generations is even more prevalent and a different view of poverty emerges.

Two recent studies indicate that during their working lives, or even in as little as 8 to 15 years, most Americans experienced sizable changes (both increases and decreases) in their incomes relative to the national average. In short, they moved up or down the ladder of income distribution for some considerable portion of its length.[49] The changes were not trivial: The average movement was over one-fifth the entire income range in the 1957–1971 period, and twice that in 1969–1978.[50] These studies indicate that substantial income changes are not merely possible for individuals in the American economy, they are the norm. This is almost equally true at every income level, high or low. Children of wealthy or poor parents also changed income status as they formed their own families: Only 36 percent of the children of families in the top quintile retained that status, and 56 percent of those born into the lowest quintile moved into higher groups by the time they became adults.[51] Other studies, most unfortunately concentrating on movements between "high-status" and "low-status" jobs (it could be questioned whether a high school shop instructor who quits his $30,000 teaching job to earn $75,000 as a master plumber has lost status), and between the occupations of parents

[47] Sawhill, "Poverty in the U.S."
[48] U.S. Department of Commerce, Bureau of the Census, *Current Population Reports*, Series P-60 (Washington, D.C.: Government Printing Office, 1990).

[49] B. Schiller, "Equality, Opportunity, and the Good Job," *The Public Interest* (Spring 1976). See also G. Duncan, *Years of Poverty, Years of Plenty* (Ann Arbor, Mich.: University of Michigan Press, 1984).
[50] Schiller, "Equality, Opportunity."
[51] Duncan, *Years of Poverty, Years of Plenty.*

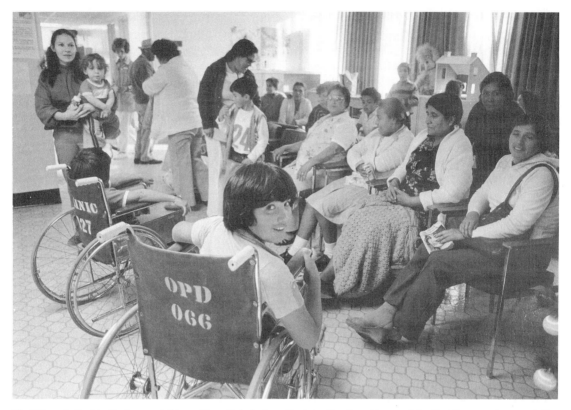

■ Although the medical care at this welfare clinic is free, the long line is evidence of the fact that care is essentially rationed at these facilities.
Source: Photo © Melanie Carr/Zephyr Pictures.

and children reveal high degrees of individual and intergenerational mobility within the United States.[52]

These findings do not support the claim that relative income levels are rigidly stratified for most Americans. They do, however, reveal that income mobility for blacks was less than that for most Americans.[53] There is also some evidence that the progress of different demographic groups and educational levels within the American black community has been very uneven, with young, well-educated blacks at or very near income parity with whites, and a widening disparity for less well-equipped groups.

While evidence of income discrimination against women and minority groups (lower pay for persons of the same productivity) is now diminishing, the embodiment of previous unequal treatment and preparation for employment in individual capabilities will linger for years.[54]

---

[52] S. Lebergott, *The Americans: An Economic Record* (New York: Norton, 1984), 508–511.
[53] Schiller, "Equality, Opportunity."

[54] An excellent discussion of this issue is T. Sowell, *Race and Economics* (New York: David McKay, 1975).

Clearly, the forms in which income transfers are made and financed influence the incentives to individual effort of both recipients and taxpayers. The aggregate effects on income may be quite large. If the evidence of the Browning, Schiller, and Duncan studies is accepted, however, two conclusions emerge. First, income distribution in the United States is more nearly equal than commonly accepted evidence indicates. Second, individual progress is eminently possible, even probable.

THE NEW REGULATION

In the past few decades, some analysts have claimed that the nature and objectives of much government regulation of the economy have changed significantly. They see a shift in emphasis from measures designed to improve the operation of a market economy, in which the resolution of the basic questions of what, how, and for whom was left to the interplay of supply and demand, to new objectives. The new regulation introduces governmental judgments (or those of private groups acting through the government) on both goals and the means and methods through which they are to be pursued.

The old regulation sometimes failed to fulfill the expectations of those who instituted it. On occasion it became the tool of the very interests it had been designed to control, and it was always more responsive to well-organized groups than to the public at large (implications for consumer welfare should be obvious). Even when it fulfilled the role for which it was designed, regulation did not invariably promote the general welfare.

Under the new regulation, however, government does not merely identify a problem, such as automobile-caused air pollution or global warming, provide information (perhaps based on government-sponsored research), or act as a mechanism by which injured parties can protect themselves, such as the right to sue for damages. Instead, it might specify both the extent to which the problem is to be addressed and the means by which this is to be done; for example, new cars must not emit more than specified amounts of pollution and they must achieve these levels through the use of catalytic converters in their exhaust systems. Greater safety must be achieved through air bags or automatic seat belts. Government may no longer merely inform consumers about hazards contained in goods; it may require specific modifications in the goods before they are allowed to be sold. In some cases, government may mandate treatment that clearly would not have resulted from the operation of even perfectly competitive market forces—or perhaps even from the desires of injured parties.

Behind the New Regulation

Expansion of government's regulatory activity was no doubt inevitable under modern circumstances. Most of the population lives in urban areas; technology both produces more serious pollution problems and offers means for their detection and amelioration; and with growing income levels, more concern is afforded to the quality of life. The assessment of these conditions often requires expertise beyond the capabilities of the average citizen, particularly when assessing the long-term consequences, and this probably also contributed to increased regulatory activities. Social attitudes for most of this period indicated a growing tendency to seek solutions through government rather than through the market.

Regulation's Successes
Some new government programs and agencies have made remarkable achievements. Water pollution, although still a serious problem, is on the decline in the United States. The At-

"Well, in my opinion, February could be greatly improved by a little global warming."

■ Environmental concerns, whether realistic or not, became more common after 1970.
Source: Copyright © Robert Mankoff and the Cartoon Bank.

lantic salmon has returned to New England's rivers; dams and pollution that destroyed its habitat a century ago have been removed. Lake Erie and the Detroit River, once regarded as dead, now support flourishing sport fisheries. A number of endangered species, notably the nation's symbol, the bald eagle, have increased their populations. Death rates in automobile accidents have been reduced through safety measures now required as standard equipment on new cars. (Curiously, the use of by far the most effective item of this required equipment—seat belts—is not mandatory in all states.) Some dangerous pesticides have been banned from use, and research for less environmentally disruptive methods of insect and plant pest control continues to produce useful results. Socially, advocates of overt discrimination no longer obtain widespread approval. Opportunities for women and minority groups are vastly wider than they were two decades ago, and there is abundant evidence that these incentives have promoted an increase in the acquisition of job skills that can now be practiced, particularly among women.

"Progress" at Any Price?
But there have also been costs, and in many cases these have been much greater than were necessary to achieve the results obtained. Any reallocation or modification in the employment of scarce resources involves costs; no

He says we're a dangerously overloaded, unsafe, small craft, and we have to turn back.

MAYFLOWER

■ The range and impact of regulation increased far beyond previous levels in the 1970s.
Source: Reprinted by permission: Tribune Media Services.

more fundamental proposition exists within economics. The existence of costs implies that economic well-being will be enhanced only if the benefits received through incurring them exceed the value of the alternatives foregone. Welfare is increased when resource productivity is increased, rather than merely changed. It is equally true that the mere existence of costs is no deterrent to economic action: Costs and benefits must be compared if rational actions are to be taken. Further, the mere indication that the costs of a given measure are less than the benefits it would produce is insufficient; we must be as certain as available knowledge permits that we could not generate an even greater surplus of benefits over costs by some other use of the same resources. Too often these simple rules have been forgotten.

In some cases, proponents of action in one field ignore the possibilities of far greater gains through action elsewhere. Millions of dollars are spent every year to reduce the already statistically infinitesimal risk of death from air crashes or nuclear-reactor breakdowns. Even total success in the former area could save at most a few hundred lives annually and best estimates in the latter are for even smaller gains.[55] Attention is lavished on efforts to eliminate food ingredients that pose even smaller risks of cancer. Yet little has been done to rid our highways of drunk drivers, who kill well over 10,000 people each year, generally under circumstances where the casualties had far less choice about exposure to their attentions than the areas of more intense regulatory concern.

The aggregate costs of regulation are not trivial, and they are far greater than the budgets of the government agencies that oversee the laws. Actual compliance with the new environmental, safety, and employment regulations alone was estimated to cost over $100 billion annually in the mid-1970s. The paperwork required to document it cost another $40 billion.[56] All this is added to costs of production, and hence to prices. A large portion of all new investment in the United States is devoted to meeting regulatory requirements, even though the economy desperately needs more modern facilities with which to meet foreign competition. Foregone services of key personnel diverted to responses to the new measures reduce growth and increase costs. Perhaps even more serious in the long run, mandated solutions deny the consideration of alternatives that has been a strong point of market-produced responses.

In a few cases, the only result of regulation has been higher costs. By the government's own estimate, the Department of Energy contributed to shortages of petroleum in the 1970s

[55] The Union of Concerned Scientists, an antinuclear group, estimates the total U.S. deaths from nuclear power at about 120 per year. B. Cohen, "The Hazards of Nuclear Power," in H. Kahn and J. Simon, *The Resourceful Earth: A Response to Global 2000* (New York: Basil Blackwell, 1984), 545.
[56] M. Weidenbaum, "The Economic Cost of Big Government," *Challenge* (November–December 1979).

rather than reducing them, at an annual cost of $9 billion. Despite the innumerable regulations it has issued, the fines it has levied, and the inspections it has conducted, the efforts of the Occupational Health and Safety Administration have produced no change in the long-term trend in industrial accident rates.[57]

None of the foregoing is intended to imply that all regulatory activity, or even all new activity, should be discontinued. Rather, it is a plea for recognition of the fact that if government regulation is to improve the aggregate human condition, the benefits it produces must exceed the costs of gaining them. Particularly where regulation, however well-intended, produces interferences with reallocation of economic resources to new uses, the long-run results are unlikely to be positive.

SELECTED REFERENCES

Anderson, T., and P. Hill. *The Growth of a Transfer Society.* Stanford, Calif.: Hoover Institution Press, 1980.

Baumol, W., S. Blackman, and E. Wolff. *Productivity and American Leadership: The Long View.* Cambridge, Mass.: MIT Press, 1989.

Baumol, W., and K. McLennan, eds. *Productivity Growth and U.S. Competitiveness.* New York: Oxford University Press, 1989.

Borcherding, T., ed. *Budgets and Bureaucrats: The Sources of Government Growth.* Durham, N.C.: Duke University Press, 1977.

Council of Economic Advisors. *Economic Report of the President.* Washington, D.C.: Government Printing Office, annual eds.

Duncan, G. *Years of Poverty, Years of Plenty.* Ann Arbor, Mich.: University of Michigan Press, 1984.

Friedman, M., and A. Schwartz. *A Monetary History of the United States, 1867–1960.* Princeton, N.J.: Princeton University Press, 1963.

Goldin, C. *Understanding the Gender Gap: An Economic History of American Women.* New York: Oxford University Press, 1990.

Gordon, R. *Economic Instability and Growth: The American Record.* New York: Norton, 1975.

Kahn, H., and J. Simon, eds. *The Resourceful Earth: A Response to Global 2000.* New York: Basil Blackwell, 1984.

Kennedy, P. *The Rise and Fall of the Great Powers: Economic Change and Military Conflict from 1550 to 2000.* New York: Random House, 1987.

Nau, H. *The Myth of America's Decline: Leading the World Economy into the 1990s.* New York: Oxford University Press, 1990.

Olson, M. *The Rise and Decline of Nations: Economic Growth, Stagflation, and Social Rigidities.* New Haven, Conn.: Yale University Press, 1982.

Porter, M. *The Competitive Advantage of Nations.* New York: Free Press, 1990.

Rosenberg, N., and L. Birdzell. *How the West Grew Rich: The Economic Transformation of the Industrial World.* New York: Basic Books, 1986.

Ross, M. *A Gale of Creative Destruction: The Coming Economic Boom, 1992–2020.* New York: Praeger, 1990.

Sowell, T. *Race and Economics.* New York: David McKay, 1975.

Stein, H. *The Fiscal Revolution in America.* Chicago: University of Chicago Press, 1969.

Tufte, E. *Political Control of the Economy.* Princeton, N.J.: Princeton University Press, 1978.

U.S. Department of Commerce, Bureau of the Census. *Statistical Abstract of the United States, 1991.* Washington, D.C.: Government Printing Office, 1991.

U.S. Department of Commerce, Bureau of the Census. *Historical Statistics of the United States: Colonial Times to 1970.* 2 vols. Washington, D.C.: Government Printing Office, 1975.

---

[57] Lebergott, *The Americans*, 520n.

THE AMERICAN
ACHIEVEMENT AND
PORTENTS FOR
THE FUTURE

A ssessment of the economic history of the United States of America does not encourage pessimism over the consequences of economic growth. As we have seen, the American economy's output has grown from levels that allowed only the most precarious grip on survival for the handful of early settlers. The rate of increase has consistently outpaced that of population. Today, with little more than 5 percent of the Earth's population, the United States produces between one-fifth and one-quarter of the planet's entire economic output. As Table 23.1 indicates, levels of output and consumption per capita in the contemporary United States compare very well with those of other industrialized nations. The data in Table 23.1 give indications of what income in various countries actually buys at local prices; that is, it approximates purchasing-power parity.[1] They confirm relative productivity studies: U.S. output per worker is high by international standards (and consumption a larger share of total production). In addition, U.S. labor force participation rates are high: A larger share of American population is in the work force. There has been little change in these relations since 1985.[2]

Income growth over time has also been impressive. To the extent that meaningful comparisons can be made between very different life-styles, the best guess is that the average contemporary American citizen enjoys

---

[1] A. Bergson, "The U.S.S.R. Before the Fall: How Poor and Why," *Journal of Economic Perspectives* (Fall 1991).
[2] Council of Economic Advisors, *Economic Report of the President, 1991* (Washington, D. C.: Government Printing Office), 411.

Table 23.1* *Output and Consumption per Worker and per Capita, United States and Selected OECD Countries, 1985 (United States = 100)

Nation	GDP per Worker	Consumption per Worker	Consumption per Capita
United States	100.0	100.0	100.0
Germany	80.6	75.7	69.3
France	81.4	80.0	68.1
Japan	67.9	62.4	65.7
Great Britain	69.8	69.3	65.6
Italy	81.0	79.8	64.6
Finland	63.5	56.4	61.7
Austria	70.5	63.0	59.0
Spain	73.7	73.9	46.1
Ireland	61.5	55.9	37.2
Greece	44.9	46.8	37.0
Portugal	37.9	36.3	32.3
USSR	36.7	25.0	28.6
Turkey	31.8	29.0	20.0

Source: A. Bergson, "The U.S.S.R. Before the Fall: How Poor and Why," *Journal of Economic Perspectives* (Fall 1991).

a real income about 12 times that of the typical eighteenth-century colonist, who even then enjoyed the world's highest income.

It is easy to forget how recent some of the gains were. Table 23.2 indicates that not only were real incomes far lower a generation or two ago, those incomes bought a much less varied life. Most expenditures had to be devoted to basic existence, and little remained for "quality of life" purchases.

Table 23.2   Consumption Expenditures of City Wage- and Clerical-Worker Families of Two and More Persons, 1888–1891 to 1960–1961

	1960–1961	1950	1934–1936	1917–1919	1901	1888–1891
Families covered	19,455*	5,994	14,469	12,096	11,156	2,562
Average family size (persons)	3.6	3.3	3.6	4.9	4.0	3.9
Average pretax money income (current dollars)	$6,763	$4,299	$1,518	$1,505	$651	$573
Post-tax money income (1950 dollars)	$4,877	$4,005	$2,659	$2,408	$1,914	$1,793

Average Current Outlays for Goods and Services (1950 Dollars)**

	1960–1961	1950	1934–1936	1917–1919	1901	1888–1891
Total	$4,604	$4,076	$2,564	$2,163	$1,817	$1,671
Food and drink	1,297	1,335	1,030	854	952	797
Clothing	541	473	309	343	—	—
Shelter***	539	448	356	252	—	—
Fuel, light, refrigerator, and water	207	153	158	126	—	—
House furnishings and equipment	297	281	119	109	—	—
Household operation	225	167	80	479****	—	—
Auto purchase and operation	635	457	150	—	—	—
Other transport	50	81	57	—	—	—
Medical care	243	213	88	—	—	—
Personal care	130	93	55	—	—	—
Recreation	194	191	67	—	—	—
Reading	34	36	37	—	—	—
Education	42	19	11	—	—	—
Tobacco	88	80	46	—	—	—
Miscellaneous	82	49	11			

* Thousands (estimated).
** Prices in 1950 were just over one-sixth (17.4 percent) 1990 levels.
*** Figures are not for owner-occupied residences.
**** Total for last 10 categories, 1917–1919.
Source: W. Baumol, S. Blackman, and E. Wolff, *Productivity and American Leadership: The Long View* (Cambridge, Mass.: Oxford University Press, 1989), Table 3.6, 37–38.

■ Modern-day supermarkets bear little resemblance to their predecessor, the general store.
Source: H. Armstrong Roberts.

Low as the figures for the late nineteenth and early twentieth centuries may seem, the standard of living and variety available to the average American had improved greatly by those decades. Today's supermarket offers over 8,000 items to shoppers;[3] but as late as 1850, the typical food of most American families at most if not all meals was a one-pot stew composed of whatever required the least preparation.[4] Yet nineteenth-century Americans ate more and better food than either their ancestors or the vast majority of the world's inhabitants. Housing 150 years ago was cramped, often without windows or interior partitions, poorly heated and lit, and generally

[3] S. Lebergott, *The Americans: An Economic Record* (New York: Norton, 1984), 68. The original source is *Progressive Grocer* (April 1981), 101. In the past decade, variety has increased.

[4] W. Baumol, S. Blackman, and E. Wolff, *Productivity and American Leadership: The Long View* (Cambridge, Mass.: MIT Press, 1989), 34–36.

Table 23.3 Living Conditions, U.S. Cities, 1855–1860

City	Population	Sinks	Baths	Water Closets
Boston	200,000	31,000	4,000	10,000
New York	630,000	n.a.	1,400	10,000
Albany	62,000	n.a.	19*	160*

* Private baths and water closets only.
Source: W. Baumol, S. Blackman, and E. Wolff, *Productivity and American Leadership: The Long View* (Cambridge, Mass.: Oxford University Press, 1989), 42.

as filthy as its inhabitants. The figures cited in Table 23.3 represent conditions in a relatively wealthy and long-developed area of the United States. Even those scarce baths were not overused: At this time, *Hall's Journal of Health* cautioned its readers not to bathe more than once a week.[5] Indications are that the warning was heeded.

Income and budget figures probably give a better indication of earlier twentieth-century Americans' well-being (particularly to persons who share the same attitudes) than they do for the colonial era. Income distribution, for example, is far less unequally apportioned today than it was when one-fifth of the population were slaves. Also, the differences in life-styles between income groups today are less than they were in earlier times. In previous centuries, the rich consumed many items that the poor could not obtain at all, rather than in lesser quantity or quality as is the case today. Other goods and services that we take for granted today simply did not exist. The increase in the quantity of material possessions of the average modern American is less significant than the growth in variety provided by modern living conditions.

THE FRUITS OF ECONOMIC GROWTH

In nearly every aspect, Americans in 1992 have far more available choices than those open to citizens of earlier periods. This greater variety of life is a direct consequence of the process of economic growth in the United States. As the preceding chapters have stressed, growth entailed far more than mere increases in total output. As output increased faster than population or the labor force, the result was something other than "more of the same." Increases in per-capita output sustained over three centuries and more, as in this country, involved changes in most aspects of economic activity.

Alterations in methods, occupations, institutions, and allocation criteria, together with the results they produced, reinforced the belief that change could improve the human condition. As we have seen, that attitude was central to American thought from the earliest days, and American conditions reinforced it powerfully. Receptivity toward the new and different, in methods, products, and people, in combination with the automatic evaluation of change provided by the market system produced America's wealth. Progress in recognizing the benefits of diversity, especially in people, was anything but smooth, but it has

[5] Baumol, Blackman, and Wolff, *Productivity and American Leadership,* 43–44.

■ Retailing around 1900: Notice the unwrapped bread.
Source: Brown Brothers.

been a consistent feature of American economic life. This resulted in a great deal more than a greater quantity and wider variety of material goods; it made possible a degree of individual freedom that would not have been possible under any other system.

Even in the United States, the lesson was not easily learned, and it may not be fully absorbed even today. Most Americans of the 1990s would find it difficult to comprehend the laws, and even more, the customs and attitudes, that limited individual expression until the very recent past. Even though people migrated to America because its society imposed fewer restraints on the individual than did other nations, the difference was very much one of degree, not kind. Only in the very recent past have restrictions limiting the economic roles of women, "outsiders," members

of minority races or religions, or other identifiably distinct people been seriously questioned. The iron grip of social custom was often little less confining for majority group members. Both sources of restrictions have proved difficult to eradicate even under circumstances where their incidence and fundamental acceptance were less than elsewhere, and evidence of the benefits conferred by their absence abundant.

American economic institutions were not developed solely through a continuous effort to increase measurable production, nor are they today. The American Civil War is only the most obvious example of evidence to the contrary. The adjustment to institutional changes that stemmed from noneconomic causes, as in Douglass North's concept of ide-

■ The way we lived "then" is illustrated by this photo of a pioneer homestead located in Cades Cove, Tennessee. *Source:* Grant Heilman.

ology, has also played an important role in the process of economic development.[6]

The Role of the Market

Nevertheless, the American setting, in which the basic social institutions encouraged a great diversity among agencies and individuals seeking change, plus a mechanism (the market) that provided an efficient and, above all, automatic evaluation of efforts to produce change, has been extremely effective in promoting economic growth.[7] Societies that promote diversity of effort are likely to be especially successful not only in discovering new ideas, but in selecting the most effective among them, and achieving their widespread innovation.[8] The market environment does more than reflect rapid changes in products and methods; it encourages rational evaluation and employment of the most valuable resource of any nation—its people. Assessment of each person's productive capabilities encouraged rational labor force allocation to jobs in the static sense, and this should not be underestimated. Asking job candidates "What can you do, and how well?" may only seem common sense to people accustomed to the American economic environment. In much of the world, however, the response to such a question, if it is asked at all, still is less important than those to "Who were your parents?" or, "To what tribe, region, or religion

[6] D. North, *Structure and Change in Economic History* (New York: Norton, 1981), Chap. 5.
[7] This, in the view of N. Rosenberg and R. Birdzell, distinguishes the West from virtually all other societies, and explains its economic success relative to that of the societies of Africa, most of Asia, and elsewhere. See *How the West Grew Rich: The Economic Transformation of the Industrial World* (New York: Basic Books, 1968).

[8] This is a central theme for Rosenberg and Birdzell. See *How the West Grew Rich*, especially Chap. 10.

■ The way we live now: Compare this home with the pioneer homestead on page 715.
Source: Dennis Barnes.

do you owe allegiance?" (In such societies, discrimination by race or sex is likely to be so common as to eliminate applications from the "wrong people"; these groups have learned there is no point in making the effort.)

On a more dynamic basis, the continuous introduction of new goods and techniques has provided a steadily widening scope for the utilization of individual talents as well as for increased specialization within jobs. Economic growth gives more range for individual expression both within work and in personal life. A rising margin over subsistence makes resources available for cultural expression, and also permits choices that forfeit some material income to more leisure time, more fulfilling work roles, and greater cultural expression even in utilitarian objects.

The Role of Rational Employment of Human Resources

Technological change might produce sudden breakthroughs in the range of jobs open to individuals, as did factory production or the rise of wholesale and retail trade in the nineteenth century. Changing social attitudes toward racial differences, women's employment, or even in the size of the average family

required longer periods to produce their effects. However, in the long run, the impact of such innovations may well be greater. Wherever rational assessments of human potential appeared, they became profoundly subversive of methods based on other values. Nor has this been only a force for the economic growth already achieved; it is a most useful heritage today. U.S. labor force growth is now declining relative to the recent past. Consequently, it is essential that each individual make his or her maximum contribution to aggregate production. Labor scarcity in the 1990s will undoubtedly encourage rational use of women and minority groups, as it has in the past.[9] In comparison to other nations, the United States has been a labor-scarce economy. Even so, especially rapid gains in incomes and access to particularly desirable jobs by those previously denied access have occurred in periods when labor markets were especially tight, such as World Wars I and II, and the prolonged boom of the 1960s (when demographic trends were also favorable). Given the relatively limited role of government in the United States and the more favorable cultural environment, market conditions have been more potent sources of employment equality here than abroad. The results produced by markets, however, are likely to be continuous increments rather than spectacular leaps.

Education

Recent declines in employment barriers have been closely linked with new attitudes toward education. The extent to which individuals could realistically aspire to various careers influenced their development of job skills. For many years, women and blacks were not likely to seek education that prepared them for business or professional employment. Such education was, of course, expensive, but that was

---

[9] See C. Goldin, *Understanding the Gender Gap: An Economic History of American Women* (New York: Oxford University Press, 1990), 215–217.

■ A new vice president at a New York bank: In recent decades, the number of female executives has risen sharply.
Source: © David M. Grossman/Photo Researchers, Inc.

not the major barrier to its acquisition by such groups. Even should they obtain the necessary skills, the incentives to do so were less than those for white males. If only a few employers were willing to hire outside stereotyped roles and fewer still did so on an equal basis, there was little point in incurring high costs to prepare for such work. As an investment, such education yielded a noticeably lower rate of return for blacks and women.[10] Since economic pressures strongly reinforced the social barriers, it is hardly surprising that few "outsiders" sought preparation for such occupations. Since 1960, however, the proportion of professional degrees obtained by women has more than doubled, and women now receive more than half of all Bachelor's degrees conferred by American universities.[11]

The greater tendency toward rational employment of human resources has done more for the American economy than merely increase the incomes of individuals benefiting from these circumstances or satisfy aspirations for social justice. From its earliest days, America has gained from the contributions of

---

[10] A. Niemi, Jr., *U.S. Economic History,* 2d ed. (Chicago: Rand McNally, 1980), 298–303.

[11] Goldin, *Understanding the Gender Gap,* 216.

persons who had not been permitted to use or develop their talents fully in their native lands. Migration patterns have indicated strongly that America provided what such persons sought.[12] The United States modified its labor market institutions to take advantage of the immigrants' contributions, a process that increased labor force participation rates and the dissemination of skills. Even more, the American economy was traditionally a borrower of imported techniques. The combination of new people with new ideas proved extraordinarily successful in deriving the best from each and producing further development.

DID ECONOMIC GROWTH INCREASE WELL-BEING?

The growth in incomes and, to some extent, the increased range of choices that the development process allowed can be measured. Nevertheless, quantitative increases in these areas are an uncertain indicator of corresponding increases in human well-being. In material terms, there is no doubt that the average American citizen today enjoys a quantity and range of possessions far greater than did his or her forebears, but there is no reliable manner in which to measure the satisfaction that people have derived from such goods at any one period, let alone over centuries. Comparisons of our current situation with the satisfaction our ancestors obtained from their standards of living can only be conjectural.

Some items that can reasonably be assumed to produce benefits (for example, increased leisure time) are not assigned values.

Others, such as expenses incurred in preventing or treating pollution, crime, and accidents, are treated as additions to welfare, although at best they represent the cost of maintaining the status quo. As such, they are really contained within the value of other output. Many government activities that are treated as final products in the national income accounts are also intermediate goods. In the modern economy, the incidence of such double counting has risen. Finally, per-capita income figures can also give only statistical averages; they may mask growing or decreasing deviations from the mean.

Another problem arises from the basis on which most people make conclusions about their own well-being. The available evidence indicates that most people compare their circumstances with those of the communities in which they live, and make conclusions about their own welfare largely from changes against that standard, rather than in an absolute sense.[13] If this is valid, today's greater income equality may ironically have reduced rather than increased the satisfaction provided by larger per-capita incomes. Not only are more persons' incomes growing at the same rates, but there are fewer exceptions. "Keeping up with the Joneses" is just as difficult as ever, and now the fortunes of the Smiths, Browns, Lees, and Lopezes must also be taken into account. Many people whose real incomes increased at the average rate achieved by the postwar United States consider themselves little better-off than they were in 1947, even though their real incomes have more than doubled. This hardly constitutes evidence that growth is not worth the effort; a person remaining at the 1947 average real-income level would consider it substantially reduced if his or her neighbors had shared in the income gains recorded since that time.

---

[12] J. Hughes, *Industrialization and Economic History: Theses and Conjectures* (New York: McGraw-Hill, 1970), 146–150. See also S. Kuznets, "The Contribution of Immigration to the Growth of the Labor Force," reprinted in Fogel and Engerman, *The Reinterpretation of American Economic History* (New York: Harper & Row, 1971).

---

[13] R. Easterlin, "Does Money Buy Happiness?" *The Public Interest* (Winter 1973). The discussion below reflects the themes of this article.

The Dimensions of Improved Welfare

Income

It is not easy to recognize the magnitude of the gains achieved within a generation or two, even after reference to such data as that in Table 23.2. By today's standards, nearly 60 percent of all American citizens in the 1947–1950 period had real incomes below the current poverty threshold—about $13,400 in current dollars for a family of four.[14] Yet the late 1940s were a period of full employment and rapid economic growth in the United States. Income levels were well above those of any preceding era, and the income gap between the United States and the rest of the world had never been wider. It remains an open question under these considerations whether the income gains enjoyed by most Americans in recent decades have added to their happiness.

Life Expectancy

However, there are certain aspects of life in the contemporary United States that are both strongly linked to economic growth and can only be regarded as improvements in human well-being. Life expectancy at birth was only 50 years in 1900. Even that figure represented a considerable advance over the conditions of most of the nineteenth century, to say nothing of the colonial era.[15] Currently, U.S. life expectancy is over 76 years, and it has increased by approximately five years over 1965–1989—a noteworthy achievement since much of the gain has come through improved longevity at advanced ages rather than reductions in infant or child mortality.[16] For black Americans, the increases in the expected span of life have been greater, from 33 years in 1900 to over 70 years today.[17]

Health and Disease

Many diseases that had taken a fearful toll of American lives throughout history are now almost or entirely unknown. Afflictions that imposed a heavy cost in suffering, such as polio, have been practically eliminated. The death rates from still others, such as heart disease, have been curtailed. Partially in consequence, the causes of death have changed. Cancer has become more frequent in the United States, but the two primary sources of that change are indicative of economic gains and the use (or misuse) made of them. More Americans now live to the advanced ages at which cancer is most prevalent. Further, the association between long-term use of tobacco and lung cancer is now obvious. There has been no age-adjusted increase in cancer deaths (aside from lung cancer) over the 1950–1980 period. Indeed, the death rates from several other common forms of cancer declined substantially over these decades.[18] The United States has reduced infant mortality in recent years, perhaps because the reduction in birth rates has allowed higher standards of infant and maternal care. Even so, the 60 percent reduction in infant mortality in the United States achieved between 1965 and 1989 still leaves the rate well above that of Japan and the Scandinavian countries. It is even inferior to that of far poorer nations such as Spain, Singapore, and Taiwan.[19]

Preventive medicine has made great strides, and has made a much larger contribution to the decline in death rates than curative medicine has. Nevertheless, modern

---

[14] Council of Economic Advisors, *Economic Report of the President, 1977* (Washington, D.C.: Government Printing Office, 1977), 216.

[15] Department of Commerce, Bureau of the Census, *Bicentennial Statistics* (Washington, D.C.: Government Printing Office, 1976), 379.

[16] World Bank, *World Development Report: The Challenge of Development* (Washington, D.C.: World Bank), 205

[17] Department of Commerce, Bureau of the Census, *Statistical Abstract of the United States, 1986* (Washington, D.C.: Government Printing Office, 1986).

[18] R. Peto, "Why Cancer?" in Kahn and Simon, *The Resourceful Earth: A Response to Global 2000* (New York: Basil Blackwell, 1984), 533.

[19] *World Development Report, 1991*, 258–259.

physicians now routinely repair damage or cure diseases for which the only response not so long ago was lifelong pain or disability for most patients, if they survived at all.

Wider Choices

Improved health standards are hard to regard as anything but evidence of increased well-being. But in other, less conclusive areas of evidence, there is also much to reinforce the conclusion that Americans are better-off than they were in previous eras. In comparison with their forebears, Americans today enjoy an almost incredible range of choice in jobs, location, diet, life-styles, and amusements. Today's individual has a greater chance of finding exactly the job, location, commodity, or the life-style that exactly meets his or her preferences.

The Work Environment

Work conditions have also improved. Jobs require less time, involve far less physical effort and discomfort, and provide much greater scope for self-expression than did those of earlier periods. Some economists have calculated that including the value of increased leisure time in per-capita incomes would add from 20 to 40 to the rate of growth of per-capita product.[20]

Assembly-line jobs, supposedly the epitome of mindless drudgery in the modern world, currently employ only a small minority—perhaps 3 percent—of all American workers. The majority of American workers have jobs that place varying degrees of emphasis on their judgment and ability to respond to changing conditions. In the nineteenth century, however, the range of jobs open to the average male worker was far more limited. For most women, choices were limited to whatever differences might result from marrying

one suitor rather than another: There were few alternatives to homemaking. In the colonial period, alternatives were even more restricted, and one-fifth of the population were slaves.

It is difficult to believe that most Americans were perfectly content with these limited opportunities, given the speed with which alternatives were accepted as they became available. Not all small farmers found their work satisfying in either economic or psychological terms; large numbers of them abandoned farming and rural life at the first opportunity. The idea that all urban workers were "craftsmen" who found their creative jobs both lucrative and emotionally satisfying, is, of course, utter nonsense. Such jobs did exist, but most urban work in the nineteenth and earlier centuries was dull, dirty, arduous, often dangerous, and precarious as well. Such jobs provided only the starkest form of subsistence incomes. In addition, the barriers to entry into more desirable jobs were far greater and less "fair" than they are today.

Education

Education is both a source and a product of economic growth. Greater knowledge, as well as the flexibility instilled by the learning process, increases overall productivity, especially over time. Only societies that have achieved some substantial margin above subsistence can afford to withdraw a large portion of their young adults from the work force and invest in increasing their long-term productivity. A properly structured education is both a capital and a consumer good: In addition to raising direct vocational skills or increasing aptitude for further training, it adds to the individual's enjoyment and variety of life. The U.S. achievement in this area is noteworthy. In 1988, 60 percent of the college-age cohort of this country was enrolled in some form of higher education. Only Canada, with 62 percent, provided more of its young adults with tertiary education. Even if it is conceded that quantity is not necessarily quality, the gap be-

---

[20] L. Davis, R. Easterlin, and W. Parker et al., *American Economic Growth: An Economist's History of the U.S.* (New York: Harper & Row, 1972), 45.

tween the United States and all other nations is very large. Uruguay, Argentina, and Finland sent from 40 to 48 percent of their young adults to higher education in 1988; no other nation managed more than 37 percent.[21] Such educational attainments are an important asset in a world in which the ability to respond to change is an absolute necessity for economic success. In America, the largest gains in access to education have been made by minority races and women.

Collective Security

Economic growth has meant a reduction in self-employment, but it has also produced gains in economic security. Individual incomes and wealth have increased, allowing a greater portion of income to be devoted to saving. The aggregate increases made possible public programs devoted to offsetting events that individuals' efforts could not. Higher incomes also funded the research that resulted in reduced threats to health. The consequences have been greater protection from catastrophic illness and unemployment.

It may appear that the largely self-sufficient frontier farmer had little to fear from variations in the business cycle or unemployment. This is largely correct. However, he and his family were still vulnerable to bad weather, accidents, disease, and other events. Adverse developments in any of these areas could throw the family on the uncertain charity of neighbors, who might be similarly affected and, in any case, had little to spare beyond their own needs. Old-age security at this time meant that one or more children would be required to stay with their aging parents, or that the parents not outlive their ability to support themselves. We may mourn the disappearance of the extended family in cases where several generations lived together voluntarily, but frequently the association was a matter of necessity rather than affection.

Quality of Life

The growth of knowledge that is so closely interwoven with intensive economic growth has allowed the development of effective concern for other aspects of life. Regard for the human and physical environment is far more likely to generate positive action in rich than in poor societies. Where levels of real income are desperately low, the only concern is for the next meal. Poor societies cannot afford concern for the unproductive or for the long-term consequences of actions that generate an immediate increase in incomes.[22] Often such societies cannot even develop the means to analyze such effects, let alone respond to them. It is now becoming clear that the destructive impacts that primitive races had upon the flora, fauna, and soil on which their incomes depended were restricted more by their limited capacity to inflict damage than by any ethic of conservation or foresight.

Economic growth provides both a margin over subsistence that reduces the temptations of environmentally ruinous practices and a wider choice of alternatives to such methods. Further, it increases these abilities over time, generally producing alternatives faster than it generates resource shortages.

Finally, economic growth allows the use of resources in areas other than for the mere satisfaction of basic survival needs. Attention to the highest expressions of human culture—not merely art, literature, and music, but also care of the less fortunate—requires resources beyond those necessary to sustain currently productive individuals. It is clearly easier to devote some of the fruits of growth to such purposes than it is to divert some portion of a fixed productive capacity from its existing employment. Growth also reduces social stress. Few persons in any society find their

---

[21] *World Development Report, 1991*, 260–261.

[22] E. Eckholm, *Losing Ground: Environmental Stress and World Food Prospects* (New York: Pergamon Press, 1976).

■ The welding of automobiles by robots illustrates the decrease in the number of American laborers involved in assembly-line manufacturing.
Source: Courtesy of Chrysler Motors Corporation.

current incomes so large, or their charitable motive so strong, that they are willing to donate significant portions of their wealth to others for unrestricted use. Even when transfers are accomplished through the political process, it is easier to divert portions of income gains, which are not already committed to the satisfaction of long felt wants.

■ In recent years, some people have found it more difficult and expensive to obtain mooring space than to buy the boats moored there.
Source: © Jerome Wexler/Photo Researchers, Inc.

The Scorecard on Economic Growth

Taking all the aspects of economic growth into account, perhaps the easiest way to determine whether economic growth has increased human welfare is to offer recipients of 1992 incomes the chance to live as did middle-class Americans a century or two ago. The chance to dine with Thomas Jefferson, talk politics with Benjamin Franklin, or even to see some of the great figures of our past might well be intriguing. It is difficult to imagine that most of us (with the exception of microbiologists) would respond with equal enthusiasm to the food available in the average household at the end of a long winter. The finest medical care available even 50 years ago (and the results it produced) would evoke incredulous horror.

Interestingly enough, a close approximation of the life-styles of earlier centuries is still readily available today, and might be considerably cheaper than the current version of the "good life." Few practice back-to-the-land life-styles for long, but such efforts provide a partial appreciation of why our ancestors tried so hard to change their lot, saving at high costs in foregone consumption, and routinely undergoing risks that would daunt a Hollywood stuntman. Life in earlier days was not only less varied, it was shorter, more arduous, and contained little in the way of amelioration of physical difficulties.

Undoubtedly, economic growth has had adverse consequences. In addition to the familiar list (pollution, crowding, the possibility of universally catastrophic war, and so forth), the modern era is not kind to people who could function only in a slower-paced society. If these were the sole results of growth, we might well be better-off living as our ancestors did. Fortunately, such is not the whole picture. Growth has provided humanity with a far greater capacity to make successful responses to constraints on income and life that could only be met with endurance, which often proved insufficient, not so very long ago. The problems of previous eras appear trivial in the light of modern capabilities, but they appeared very different to those who lacked effective counters to epidemic diseases, famine, or other scourges of the past. No doubt later generations will find our concerns no less puzzling in view of their enhanced capabilities. Although it is often difficult to admit, on close examination, all previous "Golden Ages" have large areas that exhibit a great deal of tarnish and often actual corrosion when compared to the life of today's average citizen.

THE SOURCES OF MODERN ECONOMIC GROWTH

From 1920 to 1990, real economic growth in the United States averaged over 3 percent annually.[23] Although this figure is subject to all the reservations pertaining to national income accounting as a measure of economic welfare, it nevertheless indicates that the output of goods and services, adjusted for price changes, increased at a faster pace than did population.

What have been the chief causes of twentieth-century economic growth, and what do current trends in these factors appear to indicate for the future growth of the American economy? This forecast must necessarily be restricted in extent; extending predictions for more than a decade or so is pure speculation. Meaningful economic forecasts for a generation are probably impossible; those for a century hence, whether for the United States or planet earth, cannot be taken seriously. About all that can be said with any assurance about the distant economic future is that it undoubtedly will be quite different from the present. Most long-range economic forecasts involve so many interrelated assumptions about population growth, the pace and direction of technological change, the influence of social and political factors on the economy, climate, and even the objectives of economic activity, that they are at best mere exercises in logic.

For the next decade or so, however, it may be possible to make statements in which we may place some confidence. We have fairly good information about current supplies of most productive resources, their probable trends in the near future, and their current contributions to the growth process. With somewhat less confidence, we may predict the course of technological change in the near future. Projections of productivity trends involve more guesswork, but it is fair to assume that relations between inputs and outputs will continue to change at rates close to those recently observed. Even so, readers should be cautioned that the first estimate of U.S. economic growth in 1962 proved to be about 25 percent too low.[24]

The common method of measuring the contributions of productive inputs—labor, capital, and raw materials (land)—to total output assumes that the total payments to each factor approximate its current contribution to total output. If so, the share of each factor in national income is an approximate measure of its elasticity of output. If labor receives 75

[23] For 1920–1970, *Historical Statistics of the U.S.: Colonial Times to 1970*, 2 vols. (Washington, D.C.: Government Printing Office, 1975), 1:226–227. For 1970–1990, *Economic Report, 1991*, 411.

[24] E. Denison, *Sources of Economic Growth in the United States* (New York: Committee for Economic Development, Supplemental Paper #13, 1962).

percent of all factor payments (in wages, salaries, and fringe benefits), we assume that a 1 percent increase in total labor inputs, holding the quantities of all other factors constant, would result in a 0.75 percent increase in total output.

Productivity Growth

In modern economies, growth rates can be expected to exceed the sum of all factor contributions. The difference between the actual growth rate and that attributable to increases in factor supplies is ascribed to productivity increases. Strictly speaking, this method is appropriate only in a fully adjusted, perfectly competitive economy, but most economists agree that it yields useful predictions in the American economy.[25] Over time, increases in productivity have assumed greater relative importance in U.S. economic growth. Their absolute contribution in the 1900–1960 period was twice as great as it was in the last six decades of the nineteenth century.[26]

Productivity gains, particularly in labor, have a special importance: They are the one growth source that by definition means gains in per-capita output. They compensate for declines in the rate of growth of other inputs. In recent times, productivity gains have become the largest single source of American economic growth. Over the 1840–1900 period, a time of very rapid growth in the labor force, stock of capital, and usable natural resources, they generated about one-sixth of the total increase in output. In the next six decades, as the growth rates of most productive inputs declined and technical progress speeded up, they were the source of 44 percent of all economic growth.[27]

Labor

Growth in the labor force has always had a greater impact on the aggregate growth rate of the United States than changes in the quantity of any other input. In the twentieth century, it accounted for slightly more than one-third of the total increase. In recent years, as the "Baby Boom" generation entered the work force and social attitudes toward married women's employment outside the home changed, the labor force growth rate increased. In the 1960s and 1970s, the American work force increased about half again more rapidly than in either of the two preceding decades. In the 1980s, growth rates fell by about 60 percent, to approximately the long-term average. They are expected to decline even more in the 1990s.

Labor force changes depend on more than just changes in the size of the population.[28] In recent years, labor force participation rates have increased (a larger portion of the total population was available for work outside the home). The chief cause of this development was an increase in the proportions of married women and teenagers seeking work. Other factors that influence labor's contribution to the growth rate are the number of hours worked per year (determined by social conventions on working hours, holidays, and the extent of unemployment) and the ages at which people enter and leave the work force. Changes in the education of the labor force are better regarded as productivity increases than as quantitative changes in labor inputs. In the 1960s, these factors remained constant or rose slightly due to the low rates of unemployment prevailing through that decade.[29] In the 1970s, a rising

[25] Denison, *Sources for Economic Growth*. See also Davis, Easterlin, Parker et. al., *American Economic Growth*, 35.
[26] Davis, Easterlin, Parker et. al., *American Economic Growth*, 39.
[27] Davis, Easterlin, Parker et al., *American Economic Growth*, 39.

[28] R. Easterlin, "What Will 1984 Be Like? Socioeconomic Implications of Recent Trends in the Age Structure," *Demography* (November 1978).
[29] Easterlin, "What Will 1984 Be Like?" See also E. Denison, "Explanations of Declining Productivity Growth" (Washington, D.C.: Brookings General Series Reprint #354), 1979.

portion of part-time workers and women (who tend to take less productive jobs than full-time male workers) reduced or even eliminated the positive contribution of labor force growth. From 1965 through 1990, labor force growth in the United States has been much more rapid than in other developed nations.

The Future Role of Labor

It appears that several influences on the labor force contribution to growth will become more influential in the 1990s and beyond. First, aggregate growth rates in the work force will decline: The number of potential new entrants is no longer rising rapidly. Second, as the labor force ages, a larger portion of all workers will gain additional skills, and women will gain access to the entire job spectrum. These developments will increase labor productivity. Finally, the 1960–1985 period was one in which the educational achievements of new workers rose markedly. It is unlikely that a similar increase can be achieved in the near future. One study claims that when changes in the composition of the work force are considered, the much-discussed decline in productivity of the 1970s never took place; there was no departure from age-adjusted, long-term trends in productivity growth. This may account for the above-average increases in productivity recorded since 1981.[30] Changes in attitudes toward work might occur, but their direction is uncertain and the effect likely to be small.

Institutional and Legal Changes

Institutional changes may also be influential. Recently, some economists have claimed that changes in labor regulations (as well as failures to change union work rules) and other aspects of the legal climate have affected unemployment rates, labor mobility, and other important factors germane to productivity. Whatever the intent of these developments, the results have not been wholly beneficial. More generous rates of unemployment compensation, favorable tax treatment of such compensation, as well as welfare benefits and private sector innovations, such as supplemental unemployment benefits and the increase in multiple-earner families, have increased the average duration of job search even among persons whose work motivation is high.[31] Minimum wage laws reduce the employment options of the least skilled members of the work force, while at the same time increasing employers' training costs. Government retraining programs may encourage the movement of labor from low- to high-productivity employment, but aid to "sick" industries and efforts to prevent movement of firms to regions offering lower operating costs hinder it. Steeply progressive tax rates may discourage additional effort by the most productive workers, whose skills are difficult to replace on short notice. Taxing interest income at rates that make real returns negligible or even negative discourages saving, especially in periods of high inflation.

One study found that the combined effect of efforts to reduce environmental damage, employee accidents and occupational diseases, and losses due to criminal activity caused a combined drop of about 0.5 percentage points in the aggregate growth rate. It should be kept in mind that this apparently insignificant reduction is in fact one-sixth or more of the total recent growth rate, and that such influences have, if anything, grown in the decade since the study was completed.[32] Regulatory

---

[30] M. Darby, "The U.S. Productivity Slowdown: A Case of Statistical Myopia," *American Economic Review* (June 1984). H. Nau, *The Myth of America's Decline: Leading the World Economy Into the 1990s* (New York: Oxford University Press, 1990), claims recent productivity increases stem from increases in investment after 1982.

[31] M. Feldstein, "The Economics of the New Unemployment," *The Public Interest* (Fall 1973).
[32] E. Denison, "Effects of Selected Changes in the Institutional and Human Environment upon Output per Unit of Input" (Washington, D.C.: Brookings General Series Reprint # 355), 1978.

changes may produce compensating improvements in the quality of life, but these are not measured by national income statistics, mainly because they are difficult to assess quantitatively.

Innovation versus Government Regulation As this volume has stressed, one strength of the American economy has been the ability to develop a continuous series of new occupations and industries, through allowing or encouraging innovations within the context of a market economy, where they compete with the results of more established producers. This was fostered by receptive attitudes in consumer goods and investment markets. The institutions of a market economy allowed innovators, successful or otherwise, to reap a large portion of the results of their activities. In the long run, economic growth is critically dependent on innovation and change, and the long run now appears to be a smaller number of calendar time units than it was a few decades ago.

Some recent developments in institutions and their behavior, particularly in government, hamper response to new opportunities because of excessive concern with the inevitable by-products of innovation: reduced incomes for individuals and firms that are slow to respond, and changes in the impact of economic activity upon the quality of life.[33] Debate over proper income distribution cannot be resolved to the satisfaction of all interested parties, and that over the appropriate trade-off between environmental impact and safety versus conventional economic activity appears no closer to solution. Therefore, any response to these problems must be a compromise.

In seeking a workable solution, the costs of gains in environmental purity, reduced ac-cident and disease rates, and a closer approach to "ideal" income distribution must be assessed realistically. These costs are not zero, nor are the benefits the protective measures confer infinite; were either true, there could be no rational opposition to maximizing them. Nor are the benefits conferred by increased material welfare a trivial concern for most Americans. These considerations are particularly important if they involve attempts to avoid the effects of change. Attempts to preserve obsolete industries generally result in increased long-term costs, both to those directly involved and in terms of potential income lost in other sectors. "Job Death" is not an indication of economic disaster; it is most prominent in periods of rapid "Job Birth" in new sectors and industries.[34]

But the political dice are loaded against new industries and new products. Although they produced the vast majority of new jobs in the American economy in recent decades, while large firms lost more jobs than they generated,[35] new firms tend to be small, diversified, and fully occupied with market activity. The rivals whose positions they threaten tend to be larger, more concentrated, and convinced that the route to survival is distinctly smoother if it leads through government aid rather than increased efficiency—let alone a complete reallocation of productive resources. Humankind must have ethical standards if it is to have any goals whatever, but efforts to keep low-productivity jobs aid no one in the long run.

Investment and New Capital

Increases in the quantity (not quality) of capital have accounted for slightly more than 20 percent of recent American economic growth. This is an area over which many students of

---

[33] M. Porter, *The Competitive Advantage of Nations* (New York: Free Press, 1990), Chap. 12.

[34] Rosenberg and Birdzell, *How the West Grew Rich*, 265–269. See also Porter, *Competitive Advantage of Nations*, 530, 723–733, and Chap. 10.
[35] Rosenberg and Birdzell, *How the West Grew Rich*, 297–298, 6 *n.*

the growth process have become increasingly concerned. The rate of capital formation in the United States, at least as it is conventionally measured, is among the lowest of all industrial nations. In the 1970s, declines in capital formation are alleged to account for more than 20 percent of the overall growth decline in the private sector, with low research and development spending, increased energy prices, and the costs of government regulation each accounting for from 10 to 15 percent of the total.[36]

Capital formation is not only a matter of increasing the amount of capital (tools) per American worker; the replacement of depreciated capital and rapid growth in the capital stock relative to the labor force are the chief mechanisms for the introduction of technological change into the production process. Historically (1813–1987), these two factors may have accounted for as much as 60 percent of U.S. labor productivity growth.[37] Thus, low rates of investment may have a dual impact on long-term growth.[38]

It is possible that the deficiency in U.S. capital formation rates is overstated. Capital costs are lower here than in other industrial nations; thus, spending figures may understate relative capital formation. Also, modern capital formation has assumed a different guise in the United States. The education and on-the-job training of the work force may be increasingly important supplements to growth in the stock of plant and equipment. Together, these factors substantially reduce and may even eliminate the U.S. capital formation de-

ficiency.[39] As previously noted, the economic impact of education is very difficult to assess.

Inflation and Investment
Inflation has played a large role in the observed decline in personal savings (one source of investment funds). It may also have caused corporate management to concentrate on short-term goals at the expense of those attainable only over longer periods. Changes in investors' attitudes toward expected profit levels may have reinforced these changes in investment policy.[40] Some analysts also point to the impact of government in such varied areas as tax structure, environmental and safety regulations, and direct redistribution of income, all of which have increased consumption or otherwise reallocated resources away from investment.[41] However, these points appeared more cogent in the late 1980s than today.

Even policies that reduce inflation have an adverse short-term effect on investment. Such policies must reduce monetary growth or even the money stock, and hence impact heavily on sectors that are sensitive to interest-rate changes, such as residential construction. Over longer periods, however, investment should benefit from the greater security afforded by lower rates of price change. Inflation currently (1992) is near its low point for the past two decades, with few prospects for increases in the near future. In sum, there appear to be no insuperable barriers to increased rates of aggregate investment in the United States. Like any other proposition in economics, increased investment has a cost in foregone consumption, but that is merely the cost of higher future living standards. If current figures understate U.S. capital formation, the productivity gains from given increases in investment rates could be larger than anticipated.

[36] W. Baumol and K. McLennan, eds., *Productivity Growth and U.S. Competitiveness* (New York: Oxford University Press, 1989), 9.

[37] Baumol, Blackman, and Wolff, *Productivity and American Leadership,* 175.

[38] Denison, "Explanations of Declining Productivity Growth." See also Porter, *Competitive Advantage of Nations;* Baumol and McLennan, eds., *Productivity Growth and U. S. Competitiveness;* Baumol, Blackman, and Wolff, *Productivity and American Leadership;* and many others.

[39] Baumol, Blackman, and Wolff, *Productivity and American Leadership,* 188–189.

[40] Porter, *The Competitive Advantage of Nations,* 528–529.

[41] Denison, "Some Explanations of Declining Productivity Growth."

Natural Resources

The contribution of increases in the amounts of usable natural resources to the overall rate of increase in output has been quite small (less than 3 percent of the total) in this century, and declining. This is due less to reduced absolute rates of increase in such inputs than to the high capital and labor content of most modern products. For example, few of us would imagine that the price of copper, silicon, or other raw materials employed in computers constitutes a major influence on their costs. The growing importance of services in the American economy reinforces this trend. Most goods today are far more than processed lumps of raw materials; growing portions of output have little or no raw material content whatever. Although additional amounts of most raw materials appear likely to be available only at increased costs per additional unit, barring some technological breakthrough, developments in raw materials supply appear unlikely to exert major influences on the U.S. growth rate. As technology increases the range of substitutes for most natural resource inputs, supplies of natural resources exert even smaller constraints on growth.[42]

Aggregate Resource Supply

Prospects for greater amounts of productive resources are not especially promising for the next decade. For all practical purposes, the persons who will join the labor force over the next 18 years are already with us, and their numbers will not increase at the pace of the two previous decades. Indeed, this may be a much longer-term trend: Despite discussion of changing attitudes toward childbearing on the part of American women, particularly those in their thirties, the birth rate has not risen significantly in recent years. It may have ceased the decline that began about 1960, but that is all.[43] Labor force participation rate increases offer little more promise; higher rates than those currently observed would require major social changes, which generally take long periods of time to become effective. Changes in the rate of investment are within the economy's grasp, but will have only about half the direct impact of an equal increase in the rate of labor force growth. Moreover, the investment increases that it was hoped would result from the tax reductions of the early 1980s have not been maintained, at least by conventional measures. Enormous changes in the growth rates of natural resources would be required to make a significant impact on the aggregate growth rate of the economy. A 100 percent increase in the rate of growth of all natural resources combined would raise that of total output by less than 5 percent, or from 3 percent annually to less than 3.15 percent.[44]

The Importance of Increasing Productivity

Given these prospects, the best opportunity for increased rates of economic growth lies in productivity, that is, increasing output by raising the efficiency of production rather than the quantity of inputs. In this area, the outlook is encouraging. Not only has the rate of productivity increase accelerated in the last decade (and possibly even in the 1970s, if allowances are made for labor force demographics),[45] increased productivity has some very desirable effects in addition to those on aggregate output. Productivity increases can offset declines

---

[42] Goeller and Weinberg, "The Age of Substitutability," *American Economic Review* (December 1978). See also Rosenberg, *Technology and American Economic Growth* (New York: Harper & Row, 1972), 198–201. A contrary view is implied in G. Wright, "The Origins of American Industrial Success," *American Economic Review* (September 1990).

[43] *Statistical Abstract of the United States, 1991.*
[44] Rosenberg, *Technology and American Economic Growth*, Chap. 6.
[45] Darby, "The U.S. Productivity Slowdown."

in quantities of inputs. They encourage more rational use of resources and work against discrimination on any basis other than ability. At the same time, they force the consideration of alternative uses of nonhuman inputs as well. Finally, productivity increases are based on the one productive resource that is truly inexhaustible—the human ability to reason, learn, and apply knowledge. It would take a brave prophet indeed to predict a decline in the pace of technological change in the current world; the opposite appears more likely.

Increased attention to raising the rate of productivity increase will necessitate a reduction in its opposite—rent-seeking. Raising output per unit of input is generally accompanied by large-scale movements of resources from one use to another, rather than by efforts to prevent such changes. Much the same is true of the removal of social or political barriers to the rational employment of resources. Ultimately, it is the development of new knowledge and its introduction into economic activity that make possible continuous productivity increases, and this cannot occur without changes in the structure of the economy. Better utilization of currently available knowledge can yield gains, but without the infusion of really new ideas, it is a long-run dead end.

The Importance of New Research

The function of pure research is the generation of new knowledge where answers are sought for their own sake, rather than because of their immediate applicability to current problems. As the predominance of Americans among recent Nobel Prize winners in science indicates, pure research has been a strong point for the United States in the twentieth century. The diversity of research efforts, which means that a larger portion of all possible avenues of inquiry are covered and the evaluation of new ideas is done by a large community with few or no vested interests in anything other than the development of knowledge, has long been a source of economic growth for western economies, and particularly for the United States.[46]

The nature of pure research does not make it well fitted to production through the market. The knowledge gained may have no immediate applicability; may not be suited to the productive abilities of the generators; or may be evidence that some line of inquiry is a dead end. Especially in cases where the costs of inquiry may be enormous, these characteristics make pure research ill-suited to the support of private, profit-seeking firms. Furthermore, the end product of research is information, and there is no more mobile commodity. Research efforts in one nation may well find their major economic applications elsewhere.[47] Nevertheless, nations at the technological forefront have limited opportunity to borrow from others.

Even though the private returns to such activity may be low and highly uncertain, the social returns tend to be very high, although often in unexpected forms.[48] For this reason, it is often proposed that pure research be largely supported by government, possibly with a few large firms also contributing within their own areas of interest. Most private activity, in this view, should concentrate on the application of ideas developed elsewhere, or the use of existing information to improve current products. This procedure yields quicker and more certain returns, and appears to be an area in which the response of market economies is swift and effective in comparison to those of other systems of economic organization.

Research Spending Trends There have been several trends in spending on all aspects of research and development in the past four decades. Expenditures increased from 0.6 percent

---

[46] Rosenberg and Birdzell, *How The West Grew Rich*, Chaps. 8, 9.

[47] I am indebted to Professor Gavin Wright for this insight.

[48] E. Mansfield, "Technology," in Feldstein, *The American Economy in Transition*, 591.

of GNP (largely private spending on development) in 1940 to over 3 percent in 1970 (still mostly on development, but with a significant increase in funds for pure research).[49] In recent years, the aggregate portion of GNP spent on research and development has declined somewhat, but this appears to be more than accounted for by a decline in military research, a most welcome development that should be further increased by the ending of the Cold War.[50] Private and university research efforts generally yield more immediately productive results than those concentrated, as the federal government's are, on space technology and national defense.[51] Research in oceanography, climatology, and other similar areas might well be more economically beneficial than the areas of government concentration at present; certainly its payoffs would be more quickly obtained.

Problems with Government-Funded Research
If private research is narrowly focused and heavily slanted toward development (largely changes in existing products) rather than true research, government research support has weaknesses beyond the concentration on defense. Diversity is essential for efficient generation of new knowledge, and centralization of research funding in one organization does not promote simultaneous funding of a variety of investigations in the same field.[52] In this area, the United States, with its federal government structure and considerable degree of autonomy for a variety of research organizations, has some important advantages over more centralized nations.

Government may promote something other than pure research. It may devote funds toward a response to some problem area, but at the same time specify that they are to be used to develop one specific means of mitigating it, with no consideration of alternatives. Unless bureaucrats who apportion research monies possess technical expertise superior to those who actually perform the investigations, it can be doubted that the results, even if they reduce the impact of the problem, will always be optimum. Further, this process may result in slower application of superior methods when they appear; government is far more resistant to change than is the market. A higher return could be obtained on government research dollars, even within specified areas, if only performance changes were specified, leaving their achievement open to the full range of alternatives. This point is particularly evident in recent efforts to improve occupational and consumer safety.

The Need for New Knowledge For all these problems, efforts to generate and apply new knowledge hold great promise as sources of new economic growth. Most of the obstacles in this avenue of approach are institutional: If people created these barriers, they can also remove them. The inevitability of diminishing returns to all other growth sources makes some continued effort along these lines absolutely necessary, even if only to preserve current living standards, rather than attempting to raise them. Undesirable consequences of technological change can best be countered by encouraging the broadest possible range of investigation. Nor is it possible to deny the importance of continued economic growth. Barring some revolution in human nature, responses to mankind's problems will require more capabilities than those we already possess; our current productive capacity does not satisfy all our wants. The form that economic growth assumes, and the ends to which it is directed, are more within our control today than at any previous time.

[49] Rosenberg and Birdzell, *How the West Grew Rich*, 177.
[50] Baumol and McLennan, *Productivity Growth and U.S. Competitiveness*, 9–10.
[51] Denison, "Explanations of Declining Productivity Growth."
[52] For a cogent presentation of this point, see Rosenberg and Birdzell, *How the West Grew Rich*, Chap. 10.

SELECTED REFERENCES

Baumol, W., S. Blackman, and E. Wolff. *Productivity and American Leadership: The Long View*. Cambridge, Mass.: MIT Press, 1989.

Baumol W., and K. McLennan, eds. *Productivity Growth and U.S. Competitiveness*. New York: Oxford University Press, 1989.

Berger, P. *The Capitalist Revolution*. New York: Basic Books, 1986.

Council of Economic Advisors.*Economic Report of the President*. Washington, D.C.: Government Printing Office, annual eds.

Davis, L., R. Easterlin, W. Parker et al. *American Economic Growth: An Economist's History of the United States*. New York: Harper & Row, 1972.

Denison, E. "Some Explanations of Declining Productivity Growth." Washington, D.C.: Brookings General Series Reprint #354, 1979.

———. *The Sources of Economic Growth in the United States and the Alternatives Before Us*. Washington, D.C.: Committee for Economic Development, Supplementary Paper #13, 1962.

———. *Trends in American Economic Growth, 1962–1982*. Washington, D.C.: Brookings Institute, 1985.

Goldin, C. *Understanding the Gender Gap: An Economic History of American Women*. New York: Oxford University Press, 1990.

Kahn, H., and J. Simon. *The Resourceful Earth: A Response to Global 2000*. New York: Basil Blackwell, 1984.

Kennedy, P. *The Rise and Fall of the Great Powers: Economic Change and Military Conflict From 1500 to 2000*. New York: Random House, 1987.

Kuznets, S. "Innovations and Adjustments in Economic Growth," in R. Puth, ed. *Poverty, Ecology, and Technological Change: World Problems of Development*. Durham, N.H.: University of New Hampshire Press, 1972.

Nau, H. *The Myth of America's Decline: Leading the World Economy Into the 1990s*. New York: Oxford University Press, 1990.

Olson, M. *The Rise and Decline of Nations: Economic Growth, Stagflation, and Social Rigidities*. New Haven, Conn.: Yale University Press, 1982.

Porter, M. *The Competitive Advantage of Nations*. New York: Free Press, 1990.

Rosenberg, N. *Technology and American Economic Growth*. New York: Harper & Row, 1972.

Rosenberg, N., and L. Birdzell. *How the West Grew Rich: The Economic Transformation of the Industrial World*. New York: Basic Books, 1986.

U.S. Department of Commerce, Bureau of the Census. *Statistical Abstract of the United States, 1986, 1991*. Washington, D.C.: Government Printing Office, 1986, 1991.

———. *Historical Statistics of the United States: Colonial Times to 1970*. 2 vols. Washington, D.C.: Government Printing Office, 1975.

AUTHOR INDEX

SUBJECT INDEX